David Hartley
on
Human Nature

SUNY series in the
Philosophy of Psychology

Michael Washburn, editor

David Hartley on Human Nature

Richard C. Allen

STATE UNIVERSITY OF NEW YORK PRESS

Production by Ruth Fisher
Marketing by Fran Keneston

Published by
State University of New York Press, Albany

© 1999 State University of New York

All rights reserved

Printed in the United States of America

No part of this book may be used or reproduced in any manner whatsoever without written permission. No part of this book may be stored in a retrieval system or transmitted in any form or by any means including electronic, electrostatic, magnetic tape, mechanical, photocopying, recording, or otherwise without the prior permission in writing of the publisher.

For information, address State University of New York Press, State University Plaza, Albany, NY 12246

Library of Congress Cataloging-in-Publication Data

Allen, Richard C., 1948–
    David Hartley on human nature / Richard C. Allen.
        p. cm. — (SUNY series in the philosophy of psychology)
    Includes bibliographical references and index.
        ISBN 0-7914-4233-0 (alk. paper). — ISBN 0-7914-4234-9 (pbk. : alk. paper)
    1. Hartley, David, 1705–1757. Observations on man.
    2. Philosophical anthropology. 3. Physiology. 4. Psychology.
    5. Apologetics. I. Title. II. Series.
    B1376.O253A55 1999
    128—dc21   99-17961
                                                                                              CIP

10 9 8 7 6 5 4 3 2 1

To
Catherine Ann Shoupe

Those who are not fond of much close thinking . . . will not thank me for endeavouring to introduce into more public notice such a theory of the human mind as that of Dr. Hartley. His is not a book that a man can read over in a few evenings, so as to be ready to give a satisfactory account of it to any of his friends who happen to ask him what there is in it, and expect an answer in a few sentences. In fact, it contains a new and most extensive *science*, and requires a vast fund of preparatory knowledge to enter upon the study of it with any prospect of success.

But, in return, I will promise any person who shall apply to this work, with proper furniture, that the study of it will abundantly reward his labour. It will be like entering upon *a new world,* afford inexhaustible matter for curious and useful speculation, and be of unspeakable advantage in almost every pursuit, and even in things to which it seems, at first sight, to bear no sort of relation. For my own part, I can almost say, that I think myself more indebted to this one treatise, than to all the books I ever read beside; the scriptures excepted.

— Joseph Priestley, 1774

Contents

Preface xi
Abbreviations xv
Chronology xvii

1. Remembering David Hartley 1

2. Portrait of a Benevolent Man 27

3. The Theory of Vibrations 83

4. Perception and Action 131

5. Mindful Bodies, Embodied Minds 177

6. Languages 205

7. The Emergence of the Self through the Transference of Emotion 265

8. Transformations of the Self 297

9. Annihilation of Self 331

10. The Whole Body Fitly Joined Together 357

11. Revolutionary Science 375

12. Recalling David Hartley 397

Notes 407
Bibliography 437
Index 459

*P*reface

> But when the New Age is at leisure to Pronounce, all will be set right: & those Grand Works of the more ancient & consciously & professedly Inspired Men will hold their proper rank, & the Daughters of Memory shall become the Daughters of Inspiration.
>
> —William Blake, "Preface" to *Milton*, 1804

Milton's daughters read to him in his blindness. When they spoke the familiar words from the "Grand Works" their father knew and loved, they served as bearers of memory. In reading Hartley for you, I hope to be faithful to these "daughters of memory": I aim to discover and present what Hartley wrote in a way that accurately depicts the content and contours of his thinking.

In this regard, it is important to remain sensitive to the senses of words as Hartley used them, especially the meanings he gave to his terms of art and technical vocabulary. His use of "idea," for example, differs somewhat from Locke's; and some key words, such as "annihilation," bear a distinctive meaning.

Words are but markers of places and boundaries in the geography of knowledge and imagination; it is the geography itself that situates them and reveals their patterns and interconnections. And here it is essential to remember that the boundaries between realms, their clustered settlements, and their routes of trade and exchange were not then as they are today. This book is one in a series in the philosophy of psychology. In Hartley's day, "philosophy" commonly meant "natural philosophy"—of which Newton's *Principia Mathematica* was the paradigm—and "psychology" scarcely existed as a "science," although Hartley does use the word to describe his own work. The following account of Hartley's psychology contains discussions of topics whose relevance may not at first sight be apparent. These include the mathematical "doctrines" of "fluxions" (i.e., calculus) and of "chances" (probability), and the issue of the relationship of algebra to geometry; the chemical theory of "the powers of attraction and repulsion" by which material bodies cohere and decompose; the search for a "lithontriptic"—a medicine that would dissolve kidney and bladder stones; and, in religion, the "everlasting gospel" of universal salvation. That Hartley compounded these elements into his psychology is in part owing to the fact that these were the realms of knowledge that interested and inspired him. But, in addition, that Hartley was able to synthesize a psychology out of these elements was also owing to the fact that he *could* do so; in an age in which natural philosophers were, like the rest of the educated population, expected to be theologically literate, the ways between chemistry and religion were not, as they are in the contemporary landscape, impassable.

The Scots tongue today retains a meaning that was once available in English: a "gate" is a road rather than a barrier. The name of the town of Windygates in Fife means "the windy road." Hartley and his contemporaries saw gates where we see—gates. They saw roads rather than barriers, ways to connect farms and fields rather than prohibitions on access. Recovering a sense of the geography of knowledge present to Hartley requires that we follow him through—or better, along—the gates.

A number of works have helped me gain a familiarity with this geography: these include D. P. Walker, *The Decline of Hell* (1964); John Yolton, *Thinking Matter* (1983) and *Perceptual Acquaintance from Descartes to Reid* (1984); Daniel N. Robinson, *An Intellectual History of Psychology* (3d ed., 1995) and *The Philosophy of Psychology* (1985); and D. G. C. Allan and Robert E. Schofield, *Stephen Hales* (1980). I have also benefited greatly from reading Robert E. Schofield, *Mechanism and Materialism* (1970); Arnold Thackray, *Atoms and Powers* (1970); and I. Bernard Cohen, *Franklin and Newton* (1956). Despite the many contributions to scholarship on Newton and the Newtonians during the past forty years, I would still warmly recommend Cohen's grand work to anyone interested in the world of Newtonian thought. To mix metaphors, these works are part of the "furniture" Joseph

Priestley speaks of in the passage I have chosen for an epigraph. They have aided and guided my attempt to apply myself to Hartley's *Observations*, and I recommend them to readers of this book.

Understanding the geography of knowledge of a past age also requires that we trace the correlations between the named places of the past and those of the present: we must connect Hartley's sense of intellectual geography with our own. To further this task of correlation, it is useful for both author and reader to make comparisons with later philosophers and psychologists. I find, for example, a similarity between Hartley's concept of the verbal transference of emotion and Jung's use of word association in developing his theory of the complex (§7.2). I also, in §4.4, compare Hartley's theory of perception with Gerald M. Edelman's account of the biology of consciousness, and particularly with his concepts of reentrant and global mapping. More importantly, I discern a much more general and profound affinity, indeed a resonance, between the *Observations* and one of the works I esteem most highly—William James's *Principles of Psychology* (1890). I studied James before I read Hartley, and the *Principles* was on the shelf before me as I wrote the paragraphs and pages of this book. Although I could be charged with providing a Jamesian interpretation of Hartley, I do not think this is the case. Rather, my study of Hartley has led me to the conviction that there is a deep connection between Hartley and James, that James's *Principles* is in many respects a restatement, in a new idiom, of the psychology of Hartley's *Observations*. And that conviction can be situated within a still more general one: that the "way of ideas" of Locke and Hartley and the "pragmatist" psychologies of James, Dewey, and, more recently, James J. Gibson bear a relationship of continuity and complementarity rather than of opposition—despite the fact the latter often see themselves in opposition to the former. To gain a sense of this issue, the reader may wish to read, along with *David Hartley on Human Nature*, John Yolton's *Perceptual Acquaintance* and Edward S. Reed's *Encountering the World* (1996a). If you do so, please keep in mind that I started reading Gibson and Reed only after I had completed the first six chapters of this book.

In pointing out such affinities, I do not suggest that Hartley only provided a first attempt to articulate what twentieth-century writers have said so much better; rather, I hope that the connections will help us deepen our appreciation and understanding of all the thinkers, and provide a richer resource for our own observations of humanity and understanding of ourselves.

In contemplating the image of Milton's daughters, Blake attained an insight: that partial and distorted reading of the "Grand Works" of the past places a barrier before future understanding; but that memory, when it "sets right" a work, is also inspiration, revealing beneath the barrier the course of an ancient and still serviceable gate. By seeking to set right Hartley's "Grand Work," this book aims to help us find that gate—and to recognize our companions, the daughters of memory, to be the daughters of inspiration.

Thanks to: Michael Washburn, for seeing the relevance of Hartley to our age, and for consistently supporting the writing and publication of this book; Graham Berry, at Dundee University, for our many conversations concerning Hartley's chemistry and physics; W. Hartley Russell, for his hospitality during my stay at Donnington Hospital, and for kindly granting me access to the Hartley family papers; Cecilia Millson, Sheila and David Flower, and Chris Byng, for their hospitality, and for helping me better appreciate the history of Donnington and of the Hartley family; Christine Gascoigne, Keeper of Rare Books, Norman Reid, and Cilla Jackson, at the St. Andrew's University Library, for their expert help during the many hours I spent in the rare book room—back in the eighteenth century; the librarians and archivists at the Calderdale Central Library, Halifax, for their help with the Hartley–Lister correspondence and for permission to quote from Hartley's letters; Paul and Judy Brett, for their hospitality while I was at the British Library; Peter Turvey, at Offton, Suffolk, for his genealogical research; Gail Mandell and Tom Parisi, at Saint Mary's College, for reading chapters of the work; Bob Webb, for helping me understand Hartley's influence on the Unitarians; Alan W. Hewat, for his thorough and intelligent editing; Jane Bunker, Ruth Fisher, and Fran Keneston, at SUNY Press, for their contributions to making this book a reality; and John Yolton and Daniel N. Robinson, the readers for SUNY Press, whose insightful comments and recommendations pointed out those areas in which the work required revision. And my special thanks to my dear wife, Catherine Ann Shoupe, for listening to me on many a rainy night in Fife, as I worked through what I intended to say next, and particularly for her careful and perceptive reading of the work.

Abbreviations

B   John Byrom. 1854–57. *The Private Journal and Literary Remains of John Byrom.* Edited by Richard Parkinson. Publications of the Chetham Society, vols. 32, 34, 40, and 44. Manchester: The Chetham Society. Citation is to volume, part, and page: *B* 2.1.126 is to volume 2, pt. 1, page 126.

C   Samuel Taylor Coleridge. *Collected Works.* Princeton: Princeton University Press. Citation is to volume and page.

HU   John Locke. [1690] 1975. *An Essay Concerning Human Understanding.* Edited by Peter H. Nidditch. Oxford: Clarendon Press. Citation is to book, chapter, and section.

L   The Correspondence of David Hartley and John Lister. Calderdale Archives, Calderdale Central Library, Halifax. Each letter bears the reference SH:7/HL plus a number; Hartley's letter of 15 November 1735 is SH:7/HL/1. Citation is to the number only: *L* 1.

OM   David Hartley. *Observations on Man, his Frame, his Duty, and his Expectations.* Because the text is unchanged throughout the editions, and because readers may wish to consult the edition that is most readily available to them, citation is to part, chapter, section, and proposition: *OM* 1.3.3.89 is to part 1, chapter 3, section 3, proposition 89. The 1791 folio edition numbers all

xv

the propositions consecutively, so that proposition 1 of part 2 is given as proposition 100, proposition 2 as 101, etc.

T   W. B. Trigg. 1938. "The Correspondence of Dr. David Hartley and Rev. John Lister." *Transactions of the Halifax Antiquarian Society* 10:230–78. Trigg quotes a number of the letters and provides some contextualization for them. Citation is to page.

Chronology

21 June 1705	D.H. baptized at Halifax Saint John. His father was David Hartley, B.A. 1695, Lincoln College, Oxford; a clergyman, he served at Luddenden, 1698–1705, at Illingworth, 1705–17, both villages near Halifax, and at Armley, Leeds. His mother was Evereld (Everilda) Wadsworth, christened 2 February 1676, at Elland, Yorks.; married David Hartley Sr., 12 May 1702. Their daughter Elizabeth was christened 22 Feb 1704. The date of 30 August 1705, given by D.H.'s son David in the biographical note in the 1791 folio edition of the *Observations,* is incorrect.
14 Sept 1705	Evereld Wadsworth Hartley, D.H.'s mother, buried.
25 May 1707	David Hartley Sr., marries Sarah Wilkinson. They have three children: John (m. Mary Holker, Elland), Bernard, Mary (m. Thomas Bradley, Halifax).
1720	David Hartley Sr., dies at Armley.
21 Apr 1722	D.H. admitted sizar, Jesus College, Cambridge, as son of David Hartley, Clerk, deceased, Ovenden, Halifax. — "Title: Dr. Dorson" (Gray 1855).
Michalmas term 1722	D.H. matriculates. His tutor is John Warham.
3 Jan 1723	D.H. awarded Rustat Scholarship.
27 May 1723	John Byrom at Cambridge, promoting proposals for "printing and publishing a new method of shorthand."

1726	D.H. receives B.A.
1727	Isaac Newton dies at age eighty-four (b. 1642).
13 Nov 1727	D.H. is fellow "in the room of Mr. Lucas."
8 Oct 1729	D.H. "received College testimonials" (Gray 1855).
1729	D.H. receives M.A.
Early 1730?	D.H. appointed Master of Magnus Grammar School, Newark. "He was apparently offered, and accepted, the mastership of the grammar school, for, although there is no record of his appointment in the Corporation Minutes, he appears in the Call Book of the Archdeacon of Nottingham as 'ludi magister' at Easter, 1730. He was not in Holy Orders, and is therefore the first master of whom we can definitely say that he was a layman" (Jackson 1964, 92–93).
Feb 1730	Practicing medicine in Newark. "Dr. *Nettleton* . . . in a Letter to Me, dated *February* 27, 1730, when the *Small Pox* was much at *Newark,* he says, where due Care is taken of the Choice of the infectious Matter, Inoculation will very rarely fail of Success."
1730?	According to Arthur Gray (1855), D.H. "published anonymous medical works which attracted the attention of a London physician and removed to a larger practice at Bury St. Edmund's."
21 May 1730	D.H. marries Alice Rowley, at Saffron Walden, Essex.
22 July 1731	Alice Rowley Hartley buried at Bury St. Edmunds St. Mary; died giving birth to David Hartley. "I have heard she was very handsome, and very engaging. He was extremely in love with her, but he did not enjoy his union with her for more than a year, . . . He was extremely afflicted, and remained attached to her memory all his life; notwithstanding that, he had the strongest and most rational friendship for my mother [Elizabeth Packer]. . . . He respected, esteemed, and loved her; but his first wife had had his youthful heart" (Mary Hartley, in Warner 1817, 106).
23 July 1731	David Hartley, son of D.H. and Alice Rowley, baptized in private ceremony. Later an M.P. and Rockingham Whig. As Minister Peniplotentiary for the British government, he signed, along with John Adams, Benjamin Franklin, and John Jay, the articles ending the American Revolutionary War. Dies 19 Dec 1813.

Chronology

April 1732	D.H. corresponds with James Jurin regarding smallpox inoculation, from Bury St. Edmunds.
12 Jan 1733	Date given at end of D.H.'s first known publication, *Some Reasons why the Practice of Inoculation ought to be Introduced into the Town of Bury at Present.*
2 Mar 1735	D.H. writes letter from Bury to sister, Elizabeth Booth: "I have lately gained the knowledge of some things in physic, which have been of great use to me; but the chief of my studies are upon religious subjects, and especially upon the true meaning of the Bible. I cannot express to you what inward satisfaction these contemplations afford me. You remember how much I was overcome by superstitious fears, when I was very young. I thank GOD, that He has at last brought me to a lively sense of his infinite goodness and mercy to all his creatures."
13 June 1735	John Byrom writes: "went with Mr. Lloyd to Queen's, saw Mr. Davis, at Mr. D's. chamber, came out and walked into the fields and talked about Dr. Hartley's book" (*B* 1.2.622).
26 June 1735	Byrom: "Mr. Davis sent me his gown and Dr. Hartley's paper on benevolence, never to sacrifice a greater pleasure for a less" (*B* 1.2.634).
1 Aug 1735	Date of marriage settlement between D.H. and Elizabeth Packer.
25 Aug 1735	D.H. marries Elizabeth Packer, at Nowton, Suffolk. Elizabeth Packer (1713–19 Feb 1778) is the fifth child and only daughter of Robert Packer and Mary Winchcombe, of Donnington Castle, and Bucklebury, near Newbury, Berkshire. Elizabeth is living in Bury at time of marriage. According to D.H. and Elizabeth's daughter, Mary Hartley, "Her family were much against the match, and did for some time retard it."
late 1735	D.H. and Elizabeth move to Princes Street, Leicester Fields, London.
15 Nov 1735	D.H. to John Lister: "The chief result of both Reason and Scripture as appears to me is Universal Happiness in the most absolute sense ultimately" (*T* 234).
1736	At "beginning of the year" D.H. experiences the first symptoms of the stone, while drinking the waters at Bath.
9 Mar 1736	D.H. reintroduces himself to John Byrom at Richard's Coffeehouse, London. Byrom comments: "I did not know him; he was so much thinner" (*B* 2.1.10).

13 Mar 1736	D.H. writes to Lister on universal salvation: "And undoubtedly nothing is so irreconcilable [to] Reason as eternal Punishment, nothing so contrary to all the Intimations God has given us of himself in his Works. Have you read Sir Is. Newtons Commentary upon Daniel & the Apocalypse? It affords great Light to many Passages both of the old and new Testaments."
1 April 1736	D.H. elected Fellow of the Royal Society; sponsors are Benjamin Hoadley and George Edward Wilmot.
26 July 1736	Mary Hartley, daughter of D.H. and Elizabeth Packer, christened at Westminster St. Anne; dies 7 July 1803 in Bath.
2 Dec 1736	D.H. to Lister: "I have wrote two small Treatises abt. a year & half ago, but without any Design of publishing them in their present Form. I call them, The Progress to Happiness deduced from Reason—& from Scripture."
7 May 1737	D.H. begins taking Mrs. Stephens's medicine.
18 July 1737	D.H. begins diary of taking Stephens's medicine.
28 Nov 1737	D.H. writes: "I walk'd abroad as far as the Custom-house, having confined myself for Twenty Weeks, taking the Medicines regularly, without stirring out of Doors."
20 Nov 1737	Queen Caroline dies.
1738	Publication of *Ten Cases of Persons who have taken Mrs. Stephens's Medicines for the Stone.*
27 April 1738	"*Mrs. Stephens* has proposed to make her Medicines for the stone Publick, on Consideration of the Sum of 5000 *l.* to be raised by Contribution, and lodg'd with Mr *Drummond, Banker.* He has receiv'd since the 11th of this Month, about 500 *l.* on that Account" (*Gentleman's Magazine* 8 [April 1738]: 218).
22 June 1738	Byrom notes "I should have gone to Hammersmith once more to Dr. Hartley's, . . . Mrs. Hartley has been very ill, is better, but very weakly" (*B* 2.1.208).
15 July 1738	Anonymous letter attacking D.H., "To the Author of the History of the Works of the Learned," printed in *History of the Works of the Learned.*
19 Aug 1738	D.H. responds to criticisms in the *History of the Works of the Learned*: "To the Author of the History of the Works of

Chronology xxi

the Learned" and "An Abstract of some Experiments, serving to illustrate the ten foregoing Cases," reprinted from *Ten Cases of Persons who have taken Mrs. Stephens's Medicines for the Stone*.

Oct 1738 D.H. publishes "Account of Persons who have taken Mrs Stephens's Medicines for the Stone" in *Gentleman's Magazine*, 548–50. A continuation appears in the issues for November, p. 606, and December, p. 661.

23 Nov 1738 D.H. sends John Lister part of his "History of Man," described as "An Introduction to the History of Man in Four Parts, ... considering him in his corporeal, mental, moral, and religious capacities," of which D.H. states he has the third and fourth parts written.

1738 Hermann Boerhaave dies.

29 Jan 1739 John Lister comments upon the two papers Hartley sent him: "I cannot say how proper it would be to trust the public with your 'Observations': I doubt not they would be very entertaining and satisfactory to many thinking persons.... Yet the public methinks should rather be taught to have all their hopes and fears engaged in their present conduct, as if an eternity of future happiness or misery depended upon it."

6 Feb 1739 Byrom notes: "and went to Dr. Hartley's, where I dined; the Dr. full of Mrs. Stephens, had five letters about her, four good, one unsuccessful; said that the Duchess of Newcastle had learned shorthand" (B 2.1.212–13).

20 Feb 1739 Date given in *A View of the Present Evidence for and against Mrs. Stephens's Medicines, as a Solvent for the Stone. Containing a Hundred and Fifty-five Cases. With Some Experiments and Observations*. The work includes an account of D.H.'s case.

19 Apr 1739 Nicholas Saunderson dies.

13 May 1739 D.H. writes to Lister concerning resentment and necessity, claiming that resentment is never justifiable: "I wish I cd. bring my own Practice nearer my Theory."

14 June 1739 Parliament passes act conditionally granting Joanna Stephens £5,000 for the formula for her medicine. She presents the Archbishop of Canterbury with the recipe on June 16.

2 Sept 1739	D.H. composes a prayer, "For a Blessing on the Composition, Publication, and Success of his 'Observations on Man'" in which he writes: "I . . . humbly implore thy blessing upon my studies, and particularly upon the design which I have now undertaken."
26 Oct 1739	Proposal for Byrom's shorthand published.
5 Mar 1740	The trustees appointed to verify the effectiveness of Stephen's medicine do so. Trustees include Stephen Hales, Peter Shaw, William Cheselden, and D.H.
17 Mar 1740	Joanna Stephens receives the £5,000 awarded by Parliament.
7 June 1740	Winchcombe Henry Hartley, son of D.H. and Elizabeth Packer, baptized. D.H. writes this day to Lister: "My Wife was brought to bed of a Boy abt. a fortnight ago. She is very well, but the Child is in great Danger from a Thrush & Gripes." Winchcombe Henry Hartley dies in 1794.
9 Dec 1740	Stephen Hales writes to S.P.C.K., recommending D.H. as a subscribing member.
1741	*De Lithontriptico* published in Basel and Leiden.
6 Jan 1741	D.H. becomes member of S.P.C.K. and keeps his membership until his death.
26 Sept 1741	D.H. to Lister: "I have voided a great many solid Bits of Stone lately & am become much more easy I thank God under Motion, than ever since my Illness. I shd be glad of your Remarks upon any faulty Passages in my Latin Letter. There will be a 2d. Edit. soon perhaps. My Wife desires her humble Service."
May 1742	D.H., Elizabeth, and children move to Bath. On May 26 D.H. writes to John Lister: "I am come [to Bath] with my family to settle on account of the many illnesses, and particularly some affecting the lungs, which my wife has had in town. We have got a very pleasant house in the new Square, where we breathe good country air, and I hope it will please God to give my wife a confirmed state of health."
15 Oct 1745	John Lister writes to D.H.: "I am glad you have finished your book, [for your own ease and satisfaction]. Intense thought is prejudicial to health. Perhaps it is better not to publish you wd thereby draw a shower of paper arrows upon you, and tho you might be shield against such soft mettle, yet it is

Chronology xxiii

troublesome to be always upon the self defense and to be engaged in war of any kind."

1746 — Second edition of *De Lithontriptico* published in Bath. Appended to it is D.H.'s *Conjecturæ quædam de Sensu, Motu, & Idearum Generatione.*

22 May 1746 — D.H. writes to John Lister: "I teach my little girl Latin partly because it helps her brother, who is four years younger to learn and partly on her own account. I propose she shall go into Greek and even Hebrew if she likes it. And I never intend that she shall meddle with the prophane authors."

21 Aug 1746 — Winchcombe Howard Packer, brother of Elizabeth Hartley, dies without issue.

21 Oct 1746 — Henry John Packer, last surviving brother of Elizabeth Hartley, dies without issue. Elizabeth Hartley and her son, Winchcombe Henry Hartley, inherit the Packer and Winchcombe estates. "Though my father was the kindest of brothers to them," Mary Hartley wrote, "they treated him always with *hauteur*." She adds: "My uncles were men of the world, and men of pleasure. They knew not my father's value; and were even offended with him for the true kindness he shewed them, in giving them good advice. They drank hard, . . . that compelled him, both as a physician and a moralist, to endeavour to dissuade them from. At such interference they would sometimes be angry; but when they were in their best humour with him, they would say, 'You foolish dog, can'st you see, that the sooner we kill ourselves, the better it will be for you and your family.'" The brothers got their wish.

23 Jan 1749 — D.H. writes to Lister from Donnington Castle, concerning his *Observations*: "My book is all printed, but I do not know how soon it will be out."

Oct 1752 — D.H. publishes his own formula for a "lithontriptic mass and electuary" in the *Gentleman's Magazine*.

Sept 1754 — Joseph Priestley initiates correspondence with D.H.

1755–57 — D.H. corresponding with Stephen Hales.

18 Apr 1757 — D.H. receives letter from Hales: "I am sorry to find that your calculous complaints continue."

28 Aug 1757 — D.H. dies at Bath. He was actively practicing medicine up to the time of his death.

2 Sep 1757　　D.H. buried at St. John the Baptist Church, Old Sodbury, Glos. Burial record states: "August 28th died David Hartley Esq. who had long practiced Christianity & Physick with the greatest reputation in the City of Bath & was buried Sept 2 at Old Sodbury."

1

Remembering David Hartley

> Have you found leisure to look into Dr. Hartley's *Observations upon the Frame, Duties, and Expectations of Man* since your retirement to Monticello? I envy the age in which that book will be relished and believed, for it has unfortunately appeared a century or two before the world is prepared for it.... Its illustrious author has established an indissoluble union between physiology, metaphysics, and Christianity. He has so disposed them that they mutually afford not only support but beauty and splendor to each other.
>
> —Benjamin Rush to Thomas Jefferson,
> 2 January 1811 (Rush 1951, 1074–75)

1. A Daughter of Memory

David Hartley wrote a book with a curious title, *Observations on Man, his Frame, his Duties, and his Expectations*. It was published in 1749 by Samuel Richardson, the author of the novels *Pamela* and *Clarissa*. Who remembers Hartley and his work? Historians of psychology know about Hartley, and some speak of the *Observations* appreciatively. Peter

Gay calls Hartley "perhaps the most inventive and certainly . . . the most influential psychologist of the eighteenth century" (1969, 181). Daniel N. Robinson writes that the *Observations* is "one of the great syntheses of the eighteenth century," and he adds that "perhaps more than any single work previously published, [it] is a treatise in *modern* psychology" (1995, 271). Hartley is also acknowledged by historians of social and political philosophy. Isaac Kramnick identifies Hartley as "the towering intellectual influence that informed and shaped the optimism of Priestley and his circle" (1986, 15); Kramnick writes that "Priestley's popularization of Hartley, whom he ranked with Newton, would make Hartley's ideas available after 1775 to dominate British social and psychological thought" (24). In addition, Hartley receives attention from students of British Romanticism, who have long debated his influence on Coleridge and Wordsworth—Coleridge named his first child after him. But even among those who credit its importance, Hartley's work is a somnolent daughter of memory. Benjamin Rush would not envy our age.

The comments of Gay, Robinson, and Kramnick indicate that it was not always thus. Writing of the *Observations* in 1774, Joseph Priestley stated: "I think myself more indebted to this one treatise, than to all the books I ever read beside; the scriptures excepted" (1774a, xix). Equally indebted was Benjamin Rush. When appointed Professor of the Institutes of Medicine (i.e., theoretical physiology) at the University of Pennsylvania in 1792, Rush relied heavily upon "Dr. Hartley's treatise" for the content of his course of lectures (Rush 1948, 94). He later described himself as a "disciple" of Hartley in the matter of universal salvation (Rush 1951, 780).[1] In 1794, two years after Rush began giving his lectures, Coleridge called Hartley "he of mortal kind / Wisest" in his poem "Religious Musings" (ll. 368–69)—and envisioned him, along with Milton, Newton, and Priestley, at the forefront of "the mighty Dead" who will "Rise to new life" (ll. 361–62) at the Second Coming of Jesus. When Benjamin Rush wrote to Jefferson in 1811, he was hardly alone in thinking that Hartley had established an "indissoluble union" between Christianity, physiology, and metaphysics—the common term then for psychology.[2]

The sense of indebtedness, indeed of discipleship, that Priestley, Rush, and Coleridge express continued to be felt well into the nineteenth century, especially among Unitarians who revered Hartley as a moral exemplar (see R. K. Webb 1998). On the recommendation of the Rev. Lant Carpenter, who called Hartley his "spiritual father" (1842,

89), Harriet Martineau at age 19 studied Priestley's 1775 abridgment of the *Observations* "with a fervour and perseverance which made it perhaps the most important book in the world to me, except the bible." Over thirty years later, Martineau remained captivated by Hartley's image: "I cannot at this hour look at the portrait of Hartley prefixed to his work... without a strong revival of the old mood of earnest desire of self-discipline, and devotion to duty which I derived from them in my youth.... I am bound to avow (and enjoy the avowal) that I owe to Hartley the strongest and best stimulus and discipline of the highest affections and most important habits that it is perhaps possible... to derive from any book" (1877, 1:104, 105).

Hartley's influence was not limited to Britain and America. Translations of the *Observations* into German (1772), French (1802), and Italian (1809) made Hartley's ideas available in Europe. The French translator was the abbé Roch-Ambroise Sicard, director of the National Institution for Deaf-Mutes in Paris and a hero in the history of the education of the deaf (see Lane 1984a, 1984b; Sacks 1989). Later in the century, in the context of a discussion of aphasia in his Tuesday lessons, Jean-Martin Charcot stated that Hartley "a parfaitement reconnu la véritable constitution de ce qu'on appelle le mot" (1887, 1:468, see Brett 1921, 2:284).

Also greatly indebted to Hartley were the nineteenth-century psychologists who built their systems upon the concept of association—most notably James Mill, John Stuart Mill, Alexander Bain, and William B. Carpenter. In his review of Bain's *The Senses and the Intellect* and *The Emotions and the Will* in the *Edinburgh Review* of October 1859, John Stuart Mill credited Hartley with making the crucial discovery that association can produce "chemically" compound ideas that appear to be as simple, say, as water:

> It was reserved for Hartley to show that mental phenomena, joined together by association, may form a still more intimate, and as it were chemical union—may merge into a compound, in which the separate elements are no more distinguishable as such, than hydrogen and oxygen in water, the compound having all the appearance of a phenomenon *sui generis,* as simple and elementary as the ingredients, and with properties different from any of them: a truth which, once ascertained, evidently opens a new and wider range of possibilities for the generation of mental phenomena by means of association. (1859, 294)

Hartley, as he himself acknowledged (*OM* 1.1.2.10), was hardly the first to observe that ideas regularly call up other ideas—and that their patterns of association are creations of experience and habit. Aristotle, in *De memoria et reminiscentia* (451b), observed that when one idea or image calls up another, the gate from the one to the other will be the relationship either of similarity, of conflict, or of temporal or spatial contiguity. Though such gates occur naturally and haphazardly, people had long understood that they may be artificially improved. Throughout the centuries between Aristotle and Hartley, scholars sought to cultivate ordered gardens, or build "theaters," in the wild wood of association; the results of their efforts were the various Arts of Memory (Yates 1966, 1969; Bolzoni 1991). For Ramon Lull (ca. 1235–1316) and later adherents to Lullism such as Giordano Bruno (1548–1600), the Art promised to be the *clavis universalis*—the key to the deep structure of reality. To John Locke, naturally occurring associations provided no such key. In his *Essay concerning Human Understanding* (*HU* 2.33), he dwelt upon the irrational wildness of association. Nonetheless, a general process of association is the basis for Locke's notion that "simple" ideas of color, shape, smell, and texture together form the "complex" idea of, for example, an orange. Against this background, Hartley's key innovation, according to Mill, lies in his proposal for a psychological chemistry: he is the first to suggest that even *experientially* "simple" ideas are constructs that are generated through the compounding of the psychological equivalents of hydrogen and oxygen—that is, out of other, dissimilar sensory or ideational elements. It is this insight that opens the way for psychologists to theorize that *association* names the fundamental activity that produces *all* mental phenomena. In this chemistry of ideas, the edifice of the mind is generated through the continuous and interactive repetitions of this single process.

Although he granted Hartley the credit for the initial insight, John Stuart Mill also thought that later thinkers far surpassed Hartley. In his Preface to the 1869 edition of James Mill's *Analysis of the Phenomena of the Human Mind,* John Stuart Mill states that his father's work "is not only an immense advance on Hartley's in the qualities which facilitate the access of recondite thoughts to minds to which they are new, but attains an elevation far beyond Hartley's in the thoughts themselves. Compared to it, Hartley's is little more than a sketch, though an eminently suggestive one" (Mill [1829] 1869, 1:xvii–xviii). Moreover, Mill writes that Hartley "carried his doctrines so long in his mind without communicating them, that he has become accustomed to leap over many of the intermediate links necessary for enabling other persons to reach his conclusions, and who, when at last he sits down to write, is unable to recover them" (xi). As a result, his *Observations* is a book made up of "hints rather than of proofs" (xi)—hints concerning "the phenomena of the human mind" that are entangled with useless and irrelevant matter. According to Mill, it was the task of later psychologists to develop a coherent and complete system on the basis of these oracular fragments.

Twenty years after John Stuart Mill wrote his Preface to his father's work, and during the years Charcot was delivering his Tuesday lessons at the Saltpêtrière Hospital, William James labored on his *Principles of Psychology* (1890). Although James was critical of "the assumption that our mental states are composite in structure, made up of smaller states conjoined" (1890, 1:145; see §4.1), he acknowledges Hartley's lead in answering the questions, "How does a man come, after having the thought of A, to have the thought of B the next moment? or how does he come to think A and B always together?" He adds that "these were the phenomena which Hartley undertook to explain by cerebral physiology. I believe he was . . . on the right track, and I propose simply to revise his conclusions by the aid of distinctions which he did not make" (1890, 1:553). In a manner analogous to the way John Stuart Mill described Bain and his father, William James presents himself as improving the track, or gate, originally surveyed by Hartley.

James completed his *Principles of Psychology* a little less than one hundred years after Rush delivered his first lectures on the institutes of medicine in Philadelphia, after Coleridge praised Hartley as the "wisest" of mortals, after Sicard translated the *Observations* into French — and after Priestley fled from England to the United States. (In July 1791, a mob, directed by government agents, destroyed Priestley's home, laboratory, and library in Birmingham; among the manuscripts burnt was a compilation of illustrations of Hartley's psychology he had worked on for years.) Throughout that century, Hartley remained a living presence: although his language could be improved upon, the direction of thought he had indicated was one that could be taken. People could and did read the *Observations* for its content—for its insights and observations, and for its theoretical position—and not only because it was a work of historical significance.

It is now a little more than one hundred years since William James wrote his *Principles of Psychology*. And no psychologist in our century has thought that Hartley has something to say to us. I think he does.

Moreover, I think that we are in a better position to understand Hartley's work than were James Mill, Alexander Bain, John Stuart Mill, or even William James. What one takes away from a text depends upon what one brings to it. Priestley had cautioned that the *Observations* "contains a new and most extensive *science*, and requires a vast fund of preparatory knowledge to enter upon the study of it with any prospect of success"—and then promised to "any person who shall apply to this work, with proper furniture, that the study of it will abundantly reward his labour" (1774a, xix). John Stuart Mill's comment that Hartley offered hints rather than proofs contains an element of truth: for example, here and there in the *Observations* Hartley does hint, circumspectly, at a heterodox cosmology—a cosmos in which "infinite material worlds have existed from all eternity" (*OM* 2.1.6, Cor.). Yet, more generally, Mill's image of an isolated and inarticulate writer says more about the furniture of Mill's mind than it does about the content and structure of the *Observations*. Thanks to our mental furniture, we may be able to perceive and appreciate the depth, richness, originality, and coherence of Hartley's *Observations on Man*. And to the degree that we live in an age that Rush could envy, an age that welcomes attempts to unify physiology, "metaphysics," and religion, we may find in Hartley's work something to relish.

2. The Proper Furniture

Hartley is the author of a "great synthesis"—a synthesis that presents a comprehensive account of human nature. In this regard, Rush's comment to Jefferson is exactly right: Hartley seeks to establish a union between "physiology, metaphysics, and Christianity" in which they "afford not only support but beauty and splendor to each other." Hartley, in other words, is the creator of what some today call a "full spectrum" psychology (Engler 1986, 49).

What, then, are the colors in the spectrum? I suggest the following five: In the *Observations on Man,* Hartley proposes a theory of neurophysiology, "the doctrine of vibrations"; he offers an account of perception and action; he emphasizes the primacy of language for thought; he offers a model of psychological development; and he shows how the development of the ego leads to its transcendence, to the "annihilation" of the self. Let us preview each of these.

First, Hartley proposes a theory, the "doctrine of vibrations," that explains the transmission of signals along a nerve in terms of "the subtle influences of the small parts of matter on each other" (*OM* 1.1.2.11). As we shall see in chapters 2 and 3, the theory is based upon a speculative Newtonian theory of matter and upon the chemical theory that Hartley's colleague Stephen Hales derived from it. According to the theory, the fundamental properties of matter are forces of attraction and repulsion. When at rest, particles exist in states of temporary stasis; when disturbed by the "subtle influences," the attractions and repulsions, of other particles, they "vibrate" and further attract or repel still other particles. Hartley turns to the theory to explain how the nervous system transmits signals, learns to recognize specific stimuli, and experiences pleasure and pain.

Second, Hartley offers an account of perception and action. This account assumes that "the powers of generating ideas, and raising them by association" are also explicable in terms of "the subtle influences of the small parts of matter." For the purpose of explaining how a person makes sense of sensations, the fundamental "subtle influences" are the "joint impressions" that correlate sight, hearing, touch, movement, etc. It is the associative connections between the parts of the brain responsible for the various sensory modalities, including those involved in motor activity, that *generate* the "ideas" that enable a person to perceive a world—and to act within it.

Third, Hartley emphasizes the primacy of language for thought: "We think in words," he writes, "and invent chiefly by means of their analogies" (*OM* 1.3.1.83; see chapter 6). According to Locke, we form ideas, which we then name: because words are "voluntary signs, they cannot be . . . imposed by [the speaker] on things he knows not. . . . Till he has some *ideas* of his own, he cannot suppose them to correspond with the conceptions of another man; nor can he use any signs for them" (*HU* 3.2.2). Hartley reverses the process. Speaking a language is, first of all, a complex motor skill that relies upon a process of forming associations between sounds heard and sounds spoken, and then possibly between visible marks that are seen and made. We speak before we know fully what we are saying: when we as children learn a language, we babble words before knowing fully what the words mean. In Hartley's psychology, language is an "algebra," a system of indeterminate symbols whose values are derived through the inventiveness of our largely analogical applications of them.

Fourth, Hartley offers a model of psychological development. He does this in his description of the "six classes of intellectual pleasures and pains": imagination, ambition, self-interest, sympathy, theopathy, and the moral sense. I propose that we think of these six classes as forming the two ends of a triangular prism, with each end consisting of two basic orientations and a means of regulating them (see chapters 7 and 8). In this interpretation, the prism models the structure of the psyche. The prism's nearer end is that of imagination, the orientation toward objects as sources of pleasure or displeasure, and of ambition, whereby pleasure or pain derive from one's awareness of oneself as an object of the attention of others. In this first triangle self-interest is the ego, which attempts to manage and satisfy the requirements of imagination and ambition. The prism's farther end combines sympathy, the orientation of personal intersubjectivity, and theopathy, the person's relationship with the divine. (The word *theopathy* appears to be Hartley's invention.) Hartley calls the moral sense the "monitor" of sympathy and theopathy; it is a higher ego, or self, beyond the ego. The prism represents, moreover, a structure that is epigenetic, dynamic, and transformative. Hartley states that the earlier orientations "model" the orientations that follow them, and in turn the later orientations "new-model" the earlier. Just as there are imaginative and ambitious forms of sympathy, there are also sympathetic forms of imagination and ambition. Which forms predominate depends upon the person's "primary pursuit"—the orientation that functions as the person's fundamental mode of experience and interaction. And in the course of a life, the person's primary pursuit may shift from one orientation to another and to yet another. With each shift, the person's sense of self undergoes a transformation.

Fifth, Hartley identifies theopathy as one of the basic orientations that constitute the structure of the psyche. This is not to say that every person necessarily has religious commitments. Although theopathy names a mode of being, not everyone loves God. Similarly, although sympathy names a basic mode of being, not everyone is kind. In some people, the theopathic mode becomes pathological, while in others it remains undeveloped.

The point, simply, is that theopathy names a fundamental mode of being. The cogency of Hartley's inclusion of theopathy in the structure of the psyche would be obvious to anyone who has taken to heart the tenth book of Augustine's *Confessions* or Rabbi Moses ben Jacob Cordovero's *Palm Tree of Deborah,* to name just two of the many works that could be cited. But the point is not simply warranted by the contributions of theologians and philosophers; theopathic experiences and activities, by their widespread presence, are facts that a properly scientific psychology should take into account. Countless people in all cultures say that their relationship to the divine, however conceived, is the central element in their lives and the core of their identities. This itself is a fact so evident and important that, to it, a psychology that aims at completeness should find it impossible to turn a blind eye.[3]

3. "Only the Former Concerns Us Here"

A full-spectrum psychology that combines physiology, development, and spirituality; an account of the generation of perceptual categories and of capacities for action; an emphasis upon the primacy of language; a detailed developmental model of the psyche; a model that affirms theopathy as one of the six fundamental modes of human experience—these are not the features to which summaries of Hartley's thought have commonly called attention.[4]

Consider, for example, a typical treatment of Hartley: that in Howard C. Warren's *A History of Association Psychology* (1921). Warren's work is admirable for its serious treatment of Hartley as the founder of the associationist movement in psychology. Warren also deserves credit for noting that, in Hartley's work, the "law of association" applies equally to sensations, ideas, and muscular motions (1921, 160); Hartley, in other words, is concerned to show how gaining the skill to play the piano is as much a matter of "association" as is learning to read. Nonetheless, Warren's discussion of Hartley is severely limiting. He declares that, of the two parts of the *Observations*—"the first part comprising Hartley's psychology... the second his ethics and theology"—"only the former concerns us here" (51). Then, having jettisoned half of Hartley's text, he further narrows the focus: Hartley's desire "to furnish a history and analysis of the different classes of pleasure and pain," he tells us, "does not concern us" (52). That analysis, after all, is "over-minute" (63). Warren has ruled that more than three-fourths of the *Observations* is of no relevance to psychology. But the parts Warren decides to ignore are the parts that pertain to three of the main features described above: it is in Hartley's "over-minute" analysis of the six classes that one finds the core of his theory of development; it is in his "ethics and theology" that the higher orientations of sympathy and theopathy are most fully explored; and, with these ignored, there is little to synthesize. By saying that we need not bother to read three-fourths of the *Observations,* Warren presents a truncated and one-dimensional version of Hartley's thought.

Still, in ruling most of the *Observations* irrelevant to psychology, Warren followed the lead of certain of the "associationists" whose history it was his aim to write. There was a long-standing precedent for his practice of fragmentary reading. In 1775, Joseph Priestley published an abridged edition of the *Observations,* entitled *Hartley's Theory of the Human Mind, on the Principle of the Association of Ideas.* The edition contains "so much of the *Observations on Man* as relate to the doctrine of association" (1774a, xi). Although Priestley intended to bring out a companion volume that would contain the ethical and religious sections of the *Observations,* the very presence of *Hartley's Theory of the Human Mind* suggested that the "doctrine of association" could stand alone. It was copies of this edition that, in the late 1820s, the reading group made up of John Stuart Mill and his friends "raised ... to an extravagant price" ([1873] 1924, 104) in the secondhand bookshops, when they decided to study the work.

John Stuart Mill had already studied the *Observations* in the early 1820s, under his father's direction. While the son read Hartley, the father began composition of his *Analysis of the Phenomena of the Human Mind,* which was published in 1829 (see J. S. Mill 1924, 57–58). Although deeply indebted to Hartley for the "law of association," in his *Analysis* James Mill scrupulously sought to describe "mind" without reference to "body" or "God." He limited himself to what Hartley said about the association of *ideas* (as distinct quanta of consciousness) and declined to discuss what Hartley had to say about physiology, about the structures of the psyche, or about a person's experience of the presence of the divine.

James Mill's avoidance of physiology could appear to be prudent, given how very little was known about the brain and nervous system. Beginning his *Analysis* with a discussion of the sense of smell, he acknowledges that "the object of the sense of smelling then are odorous particles, which only operate, or produce the sensation, when they reach the organ of smell" (1869, 1:11). But Mill immediately declines the challenge of physiology: "But what is meant by odorous particles we are still in ignorance.... Still farther, When we say that the odorous particles, of which we are thus ignorant, reach the nerves which constitute the organ of smell, we attach hardly any meaning to the word reach." He then concludes: "These observations... show us how imperfect our knowledge still is of all that is merely corporeal in sensation, and enable us to fix our attention more exclusively upon that which alone is material to our subsequent inquiries—that point of consciousness which we denominate the sensation of smell, the mere feeling, detached from every thing else." In Mill's view, such points of consciousness are the fundamental phenomena of the human mind; it is goal of analysis to discover laws that describe their forms of association. One can know both the points and the laws without attending to particles of matter, whether emanating from the rose or comprising the organ that registers its scent. In the language of the times, metaphysics is independent of physiology.

Hartley, in contrast to Mill, had proposed a physiological theory, the "doctrine of vibrations," to account for the "indissoluble union" between physiology and metaphysics. Benjamin Rush saw, in this union, beauty and splendor, but to many it was Hartley's chief failing. In his *Dissertation on the Progress of Ethical Philosophy*, for example, Sir James Mackintosh criticizes "the work of Dr. Hartley" for being "encumbered and deformed by a mass of physiological speculations, groundless, or at best uncertain, wholly foreign to its former purpose, which repel the inquirer into mental philosophy from its perusal" (1836, 245).[5] Mackintosh goes on to reveal that the problem with Hartley's "physiological speculations" is not that they are groundless or uncertain; rather, it is that they are present at all. The "greater confusion" to which "metaphysicians" of Hartley's stamp fall is that of attempting "to derive the intellectual operations from bodily causes." Mackintosh emphasizes that the "error" of doing so "is deeper and more fundamental than any other; since it overlooks the primordial and perpetual distinction between *the being which thinks* and the *thing which is thought of;*—not to be lost sight of even for a twinkling, without involving all nature in darkness and confusion" (245).

But what exactly is the problem with deriving "the intellectual operations from bodily causes"? Why does Hartley's "mass of physiological speculations" encumber and deform his work? The answer lies in the actions of, and responses to, Hartley's bulldog, Joseph Priestley.

4. Hartley's Bulldog

Priestley first read the *Observations* sometime between 1752 and 1755, while a student at the dissenting academy at Daventry. He wrote in his memoirs that Hartley's work "immediately engaged my closest attention, and produced the greatest, and in my opinion, the most favorable effect on my general turn of thinking through life" (Priestley [1806] 1970, 76).[6] Priestley publicly affirmed his debt to Hartley in 1774, in his *Examination of Dr. Reid's "Inquiry into the Human Mind on the Principles of Common Sense," Dr. Beattie's "Essay on the Nature and Immutability of Truth," and Dr. Oswald's "Appeal to Common Sense in Behalf of Religion"* (1774a). This work—in which Priestley states that the *Observations* "contains a new and most extensive *science*," so that studying it is "like entering upon *a new world*"—provides the epigraph for the book before you now.

Priestley's exaltation of Hartley occurs within the context of his disparagement of Reid, Beattie, and Oswald. "Such a theory of the human mind as that of Dr. Reid," Priestley writes, "adopted by Dr. Beattie and Dr. Oswald (if that can be called a *theory* which in fact *explains* nothing) does not, indeed, require much study; but when you have given all possible attention to it, you find yourself no wiser than before. Dr. Reid meets with a particular sentiment, or persuasion, and not being able to explain the origin of it, without more ado he ascribes it to *a particular original instinct*, provided for that very purpose. He finds another difficulty, which he also solves in the same concise and easy manner. And thus he goes on accounting for every thing, by telling you, not only that he cannot explain it himself, but that it will be in vain for you, or any other person, to endeavour to investigate it further than he has done" (1774a, xx). Priestley also suggests that one reason why Reid, Beattie, and Oswald produced such a "theory" explaining nothing is their ignorance of Hartley's work: he writes of his "surprise that none of the authors on whom I have been animadverting should seem to have heard of *Dr. Hartley's Observations on man,* except Dr. Beattie, who appears not to have understood him" (319). Priestley is in effect claiming that Reid, Beattie, and Oswald simply do not understand what a good scientific theory is; to draw a contemporary analogy, their "theory" is to Hartley's what the "theory" of creationism is to natural selection as an explanation of evolution—a pseudo-science that itself explains nothing and that also denies that further investigation is possible.

To put a check to this dissemination of nonsense, Priestley recommends that readers become familiar with the paradigm of a genuine science of human nature, Hartley's *Observations*. Unfortunately, the apparent popularity of the pseudo-science of Reid and his allies suggests that the public does not fully understand and appreciate Hartley's achievement; and to remedy this, Priestley announces his intention to go beyond simply recommending that people read Hartley. "It occurred to me," he writes, "that the most effectual method to divert the attention of the more sensible part of the public from such an incoherent scheme as that of Dr. Reid, and to establish the true science of human nature, would be to facilitate the study of *Dr. Hartley's Theory*. I therefore communicated my design to the son of that extraordinary man, who was pleased to approve of my undertaking. Accordingly I have now in press an edition of so much of the *Observations on Man* as relate to the doctrine of association" (1774a, xi).[7] Priestley's abridged edition of the *Observations* appeared the following year. Priestley thought that the comprehensiveness of the whole was itself a bushel that hid the many individual lights that shined in it. He writes, at the beginning of the new edition: "For many excellent articles (I may say *all* the articles) in this great work, have been, in great measure, lost to the world, in consequence of being published as parts of so very extensive a system" (Hartley 1775, v). All too many readers, in Priestley's view, would not stay with a book that demanded more than "a few evenings" to "read over" and "a few sentences" to summarize (Priestley 1774a, xix). A partial solution would be to publish the "articles" separately: the material concerning association in one volume, and the discussion of religion in another.

Priestley thus forcefully brought Hartley's *Observations* to the attention of "the more sensible part of the public," but he did so by placing it into a polemical context: Hartley's theory is the paradigm of "the true science of human nature," and as such it is the antithesis of "such an incoherent scheme as that of Dr. Reid." The true science illuminates the vacuity of the false.

Or so it does to those who think with Priestley. Some did. Many did not. And among the latter was Thomas Reid. In his discussion of Hartley in his *Essays on the Intellectual Powers of Man*, Reid writes that "the tendency of his system of vibrations is to make all the operations of the mind mere mechanism, dependent on the laws of matter and motion" (1785, 84–85). Note the presence of the qualifier *mere*. Reid insists that a "mere mechanism" could never possess qualities of consciousness: "If one should tell of a telescope so exactly made as to have the power of feeling; of a whispering gallery that had the power of hearing; of a cabinet so nicely framed as to have the power of memory; or of a machine so delicate as to feel pain when it was touched; such absurdities are so shocking to common sense that they would not find belief even among savages; yet it is the same absurdity to think that the impressions of external objects upon the machines of our bodies, can be the real efficient cause of thought and perception" (1785, 95). Reid's key objection to Hartley's theory lies in the last clause of this sentence: Reid acknowledges that external objects do make impressions on our bodies; he denies that such impressions are the "real efficient causes" of our sensations and perceptions. According to Edward Read, "Reid's claim was that *explanation* of the causal interrelationships among these three kinds of events [stimulus, sensation, and perception] is not possible" (1997, 26; see §11.1, Read 1997, 24–30, and Yolton 1984). Hartley's error, in other words, was his failure to distinguish between the conditions necessary for perception and the "efficient causes" of perception. From the fact that something is a necessary condition for a phenomenon, it does not follow that it is the phenomenon's cause. Consequently, as Mackintosh put it, the attempt "to derive the intellectual operations from bodily causes" is an "error" that is "deeper and more fundamental than any other."

Isaac Kramnick calls Priestley "the preeminent scientist in the Anglo-American world in the era of the American and French Revolutions"—and "the central figure in political, educational, and religious radicalism in his native Britain" (1986, 3). He also writes that "Hartley, thanks to Priestley, was everywhere" (29). Be this true, the statement requires its complement: So was Reid. And if we take the names as synecdoches, we may add this observation: after 1785, an inquirer into mental philosophy was faced with a choice: Priestley or Reid.

Those who sided with Priestley thought a union of physiology and metaphysics to be necessary, the foundation of "the true science of human nature"—the "new and most extensive *science*" the study of which is "like entering upon *a new world*." Those who aligned with Reid thought such a union to be impossible, and the attempt to create it an error that involves "all nature in darkness and confusion." And Priestley was Hartley's bulldog, his champion. Those who revered Priestley exalted Hartley—and for reasons articulated by Priestley. Those who despised Priestley had little affection for the "one treatise" to which Priestley acknowledged himself more "indebted... than to all the books I ever read beside; the scriptures excepted."

5. "The Sparkle of Divine Glory"

To most readers today, that neurophysiology and psychology afford each other support and illumination may appear self-evident. Hartley and Priestley thus meet with our approval; they anticipated the true science of human nature. Still, I do not think Benjamin Rush would envy us. In his letter to Jefferson, he praised Hartley for establishing "an indissoluble union between physiology, metaphysics, and Christianity." Similarly, Priestley rated Hartley's *Observations* the second most important book in his life. Priestley was a man, according to one attentive observer, whose "glory" was "celestial," who "seemed present with God by recollection, and with man by cheerfulness" (Schimmelpenninck 1860, 32).[8] To Rush and Priestley, Hartley had demonstrated that metaphysics is as indissolubly bound to theology as it is to physiology: his greatness, or glory, lies in his awareness that the true science of human nature unites all three. Today, however, that the science of psychology emerges out of their union is something many would scarcely find plausible. Neurophysiology and psychology—yes; but what does either have to do with theology, or religion, or spirituality? How many today would be prepared to say that these can be disposed so as to "afford not only support but beauty and splendor to each other"?

The separation of psychology from religion is not a new development. To the admirers of James Mill's *Analysis,* Hartley's extensive treatment of religious topics—of the genesis of a child's idea of God, of the place of the theopathic affections in the development of the self, of the eventual "annihilation" of that self in a mystical union with God—would have appeared as foreign to the purpose of laying out a science of mental phenomena as was his physiological theory. Perhaps worse still, what Hartley says about theopathy and self-annihilation may have appeared declassé, for it hinted at an affiliation with the world of radical religion. Viewed in the context of this world, Hartley has much more in common with William Blake than with James Mill.

Howard C. Warren and many others tell a story of association psychology in which Hartley appears near the beginning, the provider of hints that others will go on to develop. But Hartley himself told a quite different story—a story of the salvation of all people that is also a story of the person's union with God. And we can frame a history of those who told this story, about those who proclaimed the "everlasting gospel" of universal salvation and who sought "self-annihilation"; in this history, Hartley appears in the middle, after Peter Sterry and Jeremiah White, chaplains to Cromwell, after Fénelon and Madame Guyon, after Jane Lead and Richard Roach, and in the company of John Byrom and George Cheyne. Or it may be truer to say that he appears late in the story, if you begin it with Plotinus and Origen and then turn to John Scotus Erigena and Rabbi Moses de Leon. Hartley, in other words, keeps company with mystics, kabbalists, millennarians, and visionaries—with, that is, the sorts of people likely to repel the sober inquirer into mental philosophy.

Of the fire for which heavens and earth are "reserved . . . against the day of judgment" (2 Peter 3.7), Jeremiah White writes in his *Restoration of all Things* that "this Fire was kindled when Christ was born, and burnt first upon the green Tree, the Cross which bears the goodliest Fruit that ever the World brought forth" ([1712] 1779, 172). He calls this fire "a Sparkle of divine Glory which sends forth its Objects in the Bosom of Jesus Christ, flying through the World, feeding itself upon all worldly things till it appear a clear and universal Flame." This fire is the fire of divine love, "the Root, the Original, the Measure, the Flower, the Sum and Substance of all Perfections whatever" (185). When considering Hartley, bear in mind that he was interested in understanding how the "odorous particles," which James Mill stated are "the object of the sense of smelling," are able to "produce the sensation, when they reach the organ of smell." But bear equally in mind that he was also interested in the "Objects" that the fiery "Sparkle of divine Glory" sends forth to renew the world. He tried to explain how particles reach the organs of sense, and also to explain how God's love reaches "all worldly things."

To the inquirers into mental philosophy, it is as if Hartley simultaneously made too little of religion and too much of theopathy, thus giving offense for being simultaneously atheistical and enthusiastic. A person siding with Reid, Mill, or Mackintosh could conclude that to speak, as Hartley does, as if both physiology and spirituality are integral to psychology would hinder the development of the science; to further the science, it would be better to discount his "premature" or "groundless" hypothesis concerning the one and simply to ignore what he said about the other. While psychology respected the primordial distinction between the thinking being and thing thought, theopathy was a topic about which it had best, in its own discourses, enforce a silence.

It is this silence, I believe, that accounts for later writers' failure to recognize the developmental aspect of Hartley's psychology. Surveys of the emotions are common in works dealing with human nature; one finds them in Hume's *Treatise of Human Nature*, in Mill's *Analysis*, and in Bain's *The Emotions and the Will*. But what is noteworthy about the surveys in these three works is that they are inventories of the emotions people have. Commenting on "classic works" in "the 'scientific psychology' of the emotions," William James wrote: "I should as lief read verbal descriptions of the shapes of rocks on a New Hampshire farm as toil through them again. They gave one nowhere a central point of view, or a deductive or generative principle. They distinguish and refine and specify *ad infinitum* without ever getting on to another logical level" (1890, 2:448–49; see ch. 7). A psychology that focuses exclusively upon "points of consciousness" will find it impossible ever to get to a central point of view, generative principle, or higher logical level. Hartley must do so—if he is to explain how odorous particles reach the nerves in the nose, how the love of God reaches all humanity, and also how these two senses of *reach* are equally applicable to a human being. For Hartley, psychological development bridges the space between physiology and transcendence. But take away the two termini and the span collapses; the rubble that is left simply appears to be an "over-minute" inventory of the emotions. Those who then happen upon the scene will be unaware that there was ever a structure here at all. And why should they pause? An over-minute inventory of the shapes of emotional concretions would not concern them.

In their analyses of the "phenomena of the human mind," the "association psychologists" assumed that the minds whose phenomena it was their task to investigate were the minds of their peers and readers—that is, of individual and independent adult men, uninfluenced by social, political, or religious forces. They avoided saying anything about the body, childhood, growth, social life, politics, religion, pathologies of the soul, and the yearning for transcendence. But these are the topics to which Hartley's observations gravitate. His entire project can be understood to address the question, *How does a child learn to love?* And that is a question that the associationist psychologists, like both the empiricist and common sense philosophers, did not ask. Like Hume's *Treatise* or Reid's *Inquiry* and *Essays*, the works of Mill and other associationists are largely empty of the voices of children.

6. "The Frown of Hate"

How does a child learn to love? All children will in time grow into beings who overflow with love: this is the radiant optimism of the doctrine of universal salvation. To appreciate Hartley's answer to the question, and his affirmation of the doctrine, requires a careful reading of the *Observations*. But just as Blake wrote that "there is a Smile of Love," so also he added that "there is a Frown of Hate": in fact many people do not love at all, or at best in a crippled manner. As well as showing how we all will learn to love, Hartley's psychology must also account for how the frown of hate comes to writhe the faces of some. To give a full account of health, it must also describe sickness. Because his account of the genesis of anger and cruelty is highly focused, it may serve as an epitome of his "over-minute" method of analysis.

Hartley discusses the genesis of feelings of anger and of the habits of cruelty in a section concerning "The Affections by which we rejoice at the Misery of Others" (*OM* 1.4.4.97). He describes the "nascent state of the passion of anger" as one that "is nearly allied to fear, being a continuance of the same feelings." In the early stages of life, a child experiences situations in which he is threatened with harm or is actually harmed. Then, subsequent to the threat or injury, "the appearance, idea, approach, actual attack, &c. of any thing from which a child has received harm, must raise in his mind, by the law of association, a miniature trace of that harm." The child has become sensitized to the source of the harm, and when confronted either with it or with its various representations and concomitants, he flinches inwardly from the memory, the "miniature trace," of it. Now, as a general physiological rule, Hartley notes that it is "the tendency of all pain to prevent the recurrency of the circumstances by which it is introduced" (*OM* 1.4.4.98); in the particular instance of a response to actual or imagined threats of harm, the child "by degrees ... learns, from observation and imitation, to use various muscular exertions, words, gestures, &c. in order to ward off or remove the causes of uneasiness or pain, so as to strike, talk loud, threaten, &c." (*OM* 1.4.4.97). The child learns to strike out either physically or verbally at that which he fears in an attempt to defend himself against it. Striking out, intended to ward off a blow, is virtually a reflex response to a perceived or anticipated threat.

Next, Hartley notes a many-to-many relationship between the potential causes of harm and the feelings of "uneasiness" these causes elicit: "The same harm often arises from different causes, and different harms from the same cause." Moreover, "these harms and causes have an affinity with each other: and thus they are variously mixed and connected together, so as that a general confused idea of harm, with the uneasy state of the nervous system, and the consequent activity of the parts, are raised up in young children upon certain appearances and circumstances." A tendency of association is to link together initially disconnected elements of experience and to generalize them into a more or less "confused" idea, whenever there is sufficient "affinity" among them for association to operate; such affinities may be either spatiotemporal or symbolic. In this instance, causes of harm and feelings of unease mix, connect, and progressively coalesce into, on the one hand, a "general confused idea of harm," and, on the other, an attendant "uneasy state of the nervous system, and the consequent activity of the parts." A child who has been repeatedly harmed or threatened with harm, at home or at school, enters into a generalized state of fear, anxiety, and suspicion, and manifests the "activity of the parts" through a variety of symptoms.

Accompanying the emergence of this state, where various specific threats and the responses to them have coalesced into a "general confused idea" and an equally general sense of unease, is a shift from the stimulus of perceived external threats to the response, the feeling of uneasiness, so that the feeling itself becomes a stimulus that prompts further responses, including continued feelings of unease. The child who comes to experience his world as a threatening and hostile environment is filled with continuous uneasiness; this uneasiness, which persists even when no immediate threat of harm is present, is the child's lived reality; and, given its presence, the child will be primed to "defend" himself at the first and slightest sign of a threat; moreover, he will be ready to strike out at *anything* that appears to be a cause of unease. But the causes of unease are various and confused. In addition to actual threats of harm, they also include denials of gratification: "By degrees the denial of gratifications, and many intellectual aggregates, with all the signs and tokens of these, raise up a like uneasiness.... And thus it happens, that when any harm has been received, or other mental uneasiness occasioned, a long train of associated remainders of painful impressions enhance the displeasure, and continue it much beyond its natural period. This is the nascent state of the passion of anger."

In a contemporary example, the child leaves off the warfare of the playground, where he defends himself against the bullying and taunts of his persecutors, and lashes out at some inanimate object that "denies" his gratification. A computer in the schoolroom, which frustrates his attempt to make it work, becomes the object of his fury. When his teacher intervenes, her attempt to control his banging at the keys, whether through rebuke or appeal, creates another occasion of mental uneasiness that elicits "a long train of associated remainders of painful impressions": the bullying by classmates, the occasional pleasure of getting the better of some of them, the erratic mixture of threats and pleading, of blows and caresses, at home, the long history of occasions of failure and frustration. And as part of the cluster are the "signs and tokens of these"—the words that define and confirm the inadequacies of his self: *We don't want to play with YOU—He's no good at school, not like his sister; I just don't know what's to become of him —You're so clumsy. Can't you do anything right?* The resulting blow is aimed at the confused constellation of these "associated remainders"; the child strikes at the keyboard or the teacher, but the blow is disproportionate to the frustration of the moment, and carries well beyond "its natural period," because it is aimed not at a present provocation but at memories of past injuries. It is anger; that is, retaliation where there is no real threat, unease without a definite object, or with too many diffuse objects. It will be added to the recollection of failures, and list of grievances, that are heaped together in the midden of memories that is oneself.

In Hartley's analysis of the origins of anger, there are initial specific causes for feelings of unease; other causes create the same feeling and compound it; the child attempts to defend himself against an initial cause and then uses the same response to ward off the threat from other "causes" that are associated with the now generalized feeling of unease. Among these are other real or imagined threats of harm, denials of gratification, and the "signs and tokens" linked to such threats and denials; all these trigger the same generalized feeling of unease. By striking out, talking loud, and making threats in response to both perceived threats and denials of gratification, the child "goes on multiplying perpetually, by farther and farther associations, both the occasions of anger, and the expressions of it; and particularly associates a desire of hurting another with the apprehension, or the actual receiving, of harm from that other." This multiplication of occasions and expressions of anger may develop into a continuous chain reaction of threat and counterthreat in which anger breeds anger. If trapped within this cycle, the little child may grow into a larger but stunted one, the source of threats and harm to others: "Our threatening harm merely from a motive of security, leads us to wish it really; wishing it leads us to threaten and inflict it, where it can afford no security or advantage to us." The result is a condition of "pure disinterested cruelty and malice." Persecuted becomes persecutor, the abused the abuser, the frightened child the unprovoked bullying adult, capable of seemingly motiveless attacks upon others, especially those who reveal the vulnerability the attacker once felt so acutely himself. The child's face mirrors his first tormentors' frown of hate.

An angry self is what Hartley terms "factitious": such a personality is something *made,* a construct that develops out of the interpersonal exchanges that the growing child both endures and creates. In Sterne's *Tristram Shandy* the narrator says of Locke's *Essay* that the work is "a history... of what passes in a man's own mind." Hartley's short essay on the angry self is equally a history of what passes into and becomes a person's "understanding"—if one can apply the word to something so disturbed. Like Locke before him, Hartley relies upon the concept of association to explain how such a state of disturbance can come to be. Locke attributed the "madness" that is "opposition to reason" to the accidental association of ideas, caused to adhere to each other by custom, habit, or personal trauma; it was thanks to such associations that "this wrong Connexion in our Minds of *Ideas* in themselves, loose and independent one of another, has such an influence, and is of so great force to set us awry in our Actions" (*HU* 2.33.9). To a rational observer, the "long train of associated remainders of painful impressions" that are wrought into the angry child's history of his self is made up of events and memories that are "loose and independent of one another"; there is no causal connection between the teacher's intervention at the computer and the threats the child remembers receiving on the playground or at home. The contingent and circumstantial workings of association, then, seem to be the key to factoring the sum of accidents and mistakes that is a self.

Looked at more closely, however, association is only one element in a larger story of development. The transformation of threatened child into threatening adult involves a succession of substitutions, whereby an emotion linked to one object or event is *transferred* to another and at times *transformed* by the transference. The associations among the current experiences and memories that constitute a person's history provide the synaptic junctions, as it were, over which such transferences can be made; but it is the actual occurrence of such transferences and substitutions that effects the successive transformations of the self. Hartley's analysis begins with a basic reflex: when the child is actually struck, he raises his arm in an attempt to ward off the blow. But the pain of the blow is both felt and remembered; the memory is "a miniature trace of that harm" initially endured. Pain thus transfers from a physical experience to a memory of this experience. Moreover, the fear of being harmed is also transferred from the "actual attack" to any "appearance, idea, [or] approach" that may signify the likelihood of such an attack—from an upraised hand to an expression on a parent's face or to an inanimate object, say, an empty bottle of gin. The child may react to the sight of any of these, having learned "to ward off or remove the causes of uneasiness or pain." Note here the transformation: what began as a gesture of defense, an attempt to "ward off" the infliction of pain, has now also become an attempt to "remove the causes of uneasiness." An act of defense has altered into an anticipatory and perhaps preemptive act of removal, and painful memories of beatings have transmuted into a generalized and indefinite "uneasiness." On the one hand, the child learns a whole repertoire of actions intended to remove the causes of unease; on the other, the feeling of unease is transferred to an expanding collection of people, things, and circumstances. And here Hartley adds new elements to the list: the uneasiness may transfer either to actual denials of gratification or to symbols ("signs and tokens") of such denials, so that a denial or its symbol may elicit this generalized uneasiness as easily as would the anticipation of an actual harm. At this point the person has become unpredictably violent, a powder keg liable to be set off by even the slightest token of opposition. He is seldom freed from situations of conflict; by his own responses to others, he "goes on multiplying perpetually... both the occasions of anger, and the expressions of it." With one final transference, the deformation of character is complete. Among the repertoire of actions that are at first intended to "remove" a cause of uneasiness are those that cause actual harm to another person; but the successful removal of uneasiness brings about pleasurable feelings of relief, triumph, power. Consequently, the performance of acts that harm others becomes a source of pleasure; and when pleasure adheres to such acts, the person will perform them even in situations "where it can afford no security or advantage." For such a person, the original defensive nature of responses to fear and uneasiness vanishes to nothingness; to be gratified, the desire to harm requires not perception of a threat but rather the perception of weakness.

7. "The Free Agent"

Two general implications follow from Hartley's account of the genesis of anger. First, the concept of human agency becomes problematic. Rational people, Hartley notes, do not get angry with effects but if at anything with causes: "their resentment passes from the inanimate instrument to the living agent" (OM 1.4.4.97); rational people do not smash their computers when they malfunction. Similarly, a rational person does not get angry with the abusing adult when he makes the acquaintance of the abused child cowering within. "As we improve in observation and experience," Hartley writes, "and in the faculty of analysing the actions of animals, we perceive that brutes and children, and even adults in certain circumstances, have little or no share in the actions referred to them; but are themselves under the influence of causes, which are therefore to be deemed the ultimate ones. Hence, our resentment against them must be much abated in these cases, and transferred to the ultimate living cause, usually called the free agent, if [it] so be that we are able to discover him." *If we are able to discover him.* The conditional calls into question the degree to which we are ever able to discover in adults, and especially in irrational, disturbed, damaged adults, "free agents" who are responsible for their actions. It calls into question whether such adults ever perform actions—or only exhibit behaviors.

In this view of human nature, an individual's anger and violence can be interpreted as symptoms of deformative social forces; they indict not the aggressive individual but the aggressions of a society that has repeatedly hammered him. Moreover, they are as inevitable an outcome of causative social forces as earthquakes and floods are of causes in nature. This interpretation of the "doctrine of philosophical necessity" became a central article in the creed of philosophical radicals including William Godwin and, for a time, Samuel Taylor Coleridge. In *An Enquiry concerning Political Justice* ([3d ed., 1798] 1976), Godwin affirmed that "in the life of every human being there is a chain of events, generated in the lapse of ages before his birth, and going on in a regular procession through the whole period of his existence, in consequence of which it was impossible to act in any instance otherwise than he has acted" (1976, 351). It was for its contribution to our understanding of how this chain forms that the radicals conferred a canonical status upon the *Observations*. Coleridge had his portrait painted holding a copy.

To the philosophical radicals, Hartley's work was most emphatically a gospel, despite what might at first appear the fatalism of the doctrine of necessity. For although the "chain of events" forms, in this corrupt world, the "mind-forg'd manacles" that Blake detected "in every voice, in every ban," Hartley's analyses of the processes that form human beings were at heart intended to show how we are so framed as to learn ultimately to love one another. Anger is never the termination of development, and Hartley's goal is not to describe how the self turns itself into a prison of manacles and stone. Rather, his goal is to point the way towards liberation.

What liberates a person from the prison of self? To begin to answer this, we need to attend to a second implication of Hartley's account of anger: the importance of what Hartley terms "counter-associations" (see §8.3). A lifetime of cruelty endured and inflicted produces a cruel character, a person with "long trains of associations" that, like organic compounds, wreathe and bind the elements of experience into that twisted knot, the person's character. A therapy that sought to undo "disinterested cruelty and malice," or any similar disorder of character, would involve a process of counterassociation—of dissociation and differentiation—by which experiences are decoupled, liberated from the compacted mass, set free from their fixation within particular clusters of associations. The planet Mars does not appear to support life today because its ancient atmosphere has turned to stone: its free atmospheric oxygen long ago was locked into calcium carbonate. In contrast, the earth continues to have an atmosphere thanks to the subduction of its tectonic plates: as a plate dives under another and into the depths of the earth, heat and pressure undo the effects of the eon spent on the surface, and the gases locked in its solid compounds are again released into the air. If not counteracted, an uninterrupted process of association would turn a person into stone; and it is a person's stoniness—her inflexibility, her lack of differentiation between experiences, and her inability to see the present as anything other than a repetition of the scenes, scripts, and failures of the past—that is the mark of an illness of the soul. Locke spoke of the "madness" that comes when a mind is in bondage to connections of ideas "wholly owing to Chance or Custom" (*HU* 2.33.5). Coleridge elaborated upon this theme when he wrote of the "tyranny of association" (*C* 1:47). Hartley, so often described as the father of association psychology, was equally aware that association alone would drive a person mad.

In one place, Hartley suggests that our dreams help keep us sane, for they provide counterassociations that preserve us from such stony madness: "The wildness of our dreams seems to be of singular use to us, by interrupting and breaking the course of our associations. For, if we were always awake, some accidental associations would be so cemented by continuance, as that nothing could afterwards disjoin them; which would be madness" (*OM* 1.3.5.91). A therapy, then, that would undo the calcification of a person would need to be a lengthy dream-work, in which the crust of character is submerged and reduced to its elements by forces of pressure and heat. In such a process, a dream would not be the enigmatic expression of a secret wish; it would rather act as a solvent in a psychological chemistry. As an acid or heat will liberate oxygen and carbon dioxide from a carbonate, the dissociative power of such a dream-work would dissolve the bonds that cement memories and would liberate spirit from a stony self. The person could then begin the long work of learning to love.

In the nineteenth century, James Mill and his associates credited Hartley's lead in explaining how, through "association," complex thoughts are developed out of the elements of experience. They said nothing about the complementary and equally important process by which our complexes of thought and character undergo decomposition. And they say nothing about the transformations a person may experience, as the reciprocal dynamic of association and counterassociation leads to the transcendence of the self.

Today, the factors that the school of associationist psychology chose to ignore—his interests in neurophysiology, in development, in the social expression of emotion, in spirituality and religion, in the transcendence of the ego or, in his terms, "annihilation of the self"—are exactly the topics that make him interesting and vital to us. For his psychology is grounded in the body; it pays great attention to growth in the early stages of life; it is always attentive to the social context of personal development; and it equally assumes an ascent toward that which is beyond the little self to be an essential aspect of the human psyche. Let us renew our acquaintance with David Hartley.

2

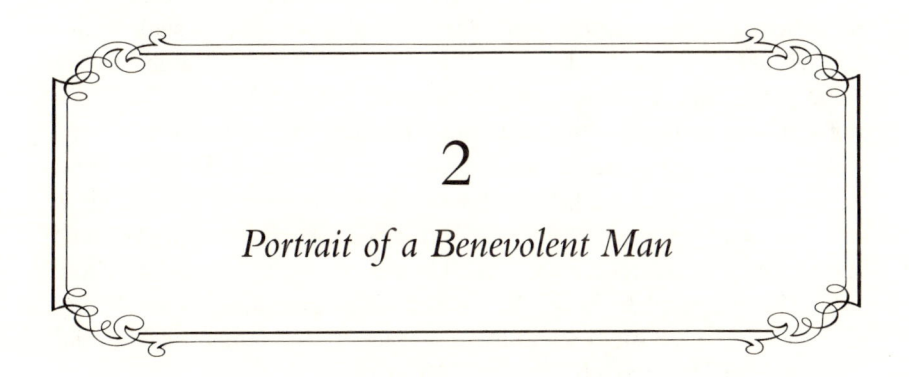

Portrait of a Benevolent Man

I have heard from himself, that the intention of writing a book upon the nature of man was conceived in his mind, when he was a *very little boy*. He was not a boasting man, nor ever spoke an untruth; but in many conversations that I have had with him about his book, he has told me, that when he was so little as to be swinging backwards and forwards upon a gate... he was meditating upon the nature of his own mind; wishing to find out how man was made; to what purpose, and for what future end; in short, (as afterwards he entitled his book,) 'the Frame, the Duty, and the Expectations of Man.'

—Mary Hartley, 18 July 1795[1]

1. "He Is So Much Thinner"

On 9 March 1736, David Hartley walked across the floor of Richard's Coffee-house, at no. 8 Fleet Street, London, and reintroduced himself to John Byrom.[2] Hartley was thirty years old, Byrom forty-five; Hartley, of medium height, Byrom, at 6'4" one of the tallest men in England. Few people in the coffeehouse could have told you the younger man's name.

David Hartley on Human Nature

...ter man was well known in London and Cambridge as the teacher of a system of shorthand and as a member of the Royal Society. His friends also knew him to be a self-described "disciple" of Nicholas Malebranche and William Law and an assiduous purchaser of books of spirituality and mysticism. Some may have known of his extensive collection of geometric drawings, of which some are apparently diagrams of Elizabethan theaters; a few would know him to be a Jacobite.[3]

On Thursday, the 11th, two days after the meeting, Byrom wrote to his wife Elizabeth, at home in Manchester: "to-morrow I shall breakfast with Dr. Hartley, he that found out our shorthand at Cambridge by some papers and questions, &c. I met with him at Richard's, and did not know him, he is so much thinner. He lived at St. Edmund's Bury, where he married a second wife, £7,000 for him, &c. He has a mind to learn of me" (B 2.1.10).[4] Hartley had been admitted to Jesus College in 1722 as a Sizar—a student who performed menial labor in exchange for a reduction in fees. He received his B.A. in 1726, became a Fellow in 1727, and a M.A. in 1729.[5] Byrom, who graduated from Trinity College in 1712, visited Cambridge in May 1723, January 1728, and November 1729 through March 1730 in order to promote his shorthand. Although Byrom does not mention Hartley in his journal entries from 1723 through 1730, his comment suggests that the two had become acquainted and that Hartley had expressed an interest in learning shorthand. The phrasing of Byrom's letter also suggests that Hartley's name was familiar to Elizabeth Byrom; his comment about "he that found out..." has the character of a reminder.

"I did not know him, he is so much thinner." Hartley had changed so much that Byrom did not recognize the man who approached him in Richard's Coffee-house. We can imagine a moment's awkwardness and confusion, as Hartley greets a person who looks at him as if at a stranger; then, perhaps, Hartley says his name, and the other's face alters, as he connects the man before him with the image stored in memory. But how did the change in Hartley affect Byrom? Did it please him, so that he laughingly explained his momentary confusion, while telling Hartley how much better he looked? Or did it pain him, so that he struggled to conceal his disturbance?

A novelist could place Byrom's lack of recognition in one of several narratives. If Hartley had been grossly overweight from obsessive overeating and drinking, like his friend and fellow physician George Cheyne, then his thinness could be a sign of health. Cheyne was famous as the author of *An Essay on Health and Long Life* (1724) and *The English*

Malady (1733) and especially for reducing his own weight from 32 to 9 stone—approximately 450 to 125 pounds.[6] In this story, Hartley adheres to Cheyne's regimen of a "vegetable diet" and is similarly transformed.

In May 1736, Byrom, Hartley, and their mutual friend Benjamin Hoadley, M.D., discussed the sensitivity of "vegetable livers" to heat and cold; Byrom complained of the heat, and Hoadley commented that vegetarians had difficulty bearing it, but "Dr. Hartley thought it was cold they could not bear so much, that for his part he was like an old man, choosing the sunny side of the way" (*B* 2.1.165). If Hartley adopted the vegetable diet in order to control his gluttony, he may have found the need to choose the sunny side of the way a small price to pay for at least partial freedom from an addiction. Hartley made a practice of writing out his prayers, and a collection of these were published fifty years after his death (Hartley 1810). In several prayers from 1733 and 1734, Hartley writes of struggling with desires for sensate gratification, of himself as "the slave of the gross pleasures of sense" (1810, 14; summer 1734). In October 1736, he writes of a partial release from such bondage: "I was once afflicted in body, mind, and estate; my vices and follies had led me into all kinds of perplexity and misery; and I grew every day more and more the servant of sin. But blessed be Thy goodness, which gave me a heart to pray, and to endeavour to repent and amend" (1810, 31); nonetheless, despite his knowledge that "pain, sickness, and death are the punishments peculiarly appointed by Thee for the correction of luxury and intemperance of all kinds," his conduct does not always conform to his conviction: "And yet, notwithstanding this my knowledge and conviction, I am utterly unable to regulate my conduct in these matters. I find a foolish and vicious self-indulgence prevailing over me every day; and I am assured by repeated experience, that I have no power of myself to help myself" (1810, 33). Still, the prayers are evidence that Hartley struggled against such self-indulgence. Moreover, in a letter of 2 March 1735, to his elder sister Elizabeth Booth, from Bury St. Edmunds, Hartley writes that "Mr. Walton and I manage our house tolerably well. We are both very abstemious, and neither drink ale nor wine" (Warner 1817, 100). In this story, Byrom is delighted at Hartley's thinness, for it vindicates the vegetable diet that both men follow; it indicates that Hartley is resisting his hunger for fat geese and ale, roast beef and claret.

Lest one think that Hartley was simply being neurotically scrupulous, too harsh with himself, the writer of this narrative could conduct the reader's attention away from Hartley and Byrom and to the people around them, drinking coffee or wine; eating meals. "The goose is a silly bird," said one writer; "too much for one, not enough for two." Some of the patrons of the coffeehouse have the look of men who would not find a goose all that silly.

The narrator could also direct the reader out of the coffeehouse and onto the pavement, for a tour of the city. Richard's was one of more than five hundred coffeehouses,[7] but outnumbering these were establishments selling spirits, particularly gin. For one or two pence, a man or woman could buy enough to reach oblivion; some of the gin houses provided a room full of fresh straw, in which their patrons could pass out in comfort. Such places were littered with the poor; gentlemen would not be found lying there. Nonetheless, the man staggering down the street could as well be dressed in silk as in a workman's clothes or a beggar's rags. In London the yearly consumption of spirits—not counting wine or beer—came to fourteen gallons per adult male (Rudé 1971, 70).

Hartley and Byrom stick to their dishes of coffee; no goose and claret for them. Still, a narrative of the triumph of the vegetable diet is not the only one that can be told. In an alternate story, Hartley's face is unrecognizable for its gauntness; his thinness is a sign that he is suffering from calculus of the bladder—the chronic, painful disease that tortured him, that he worked to cure, and that caused his death at the age of fifty-two. He later reported that he first experienced symptoms of the stone at "beginning of the year" 1736, while drinking the waters at Bath. The stone can cause frequent stoppages during urination, ulcers in the bladder and urethra, nephritis, and death. In this story, when Byrom looks up from his dish of coffee, he sees the shrunken countenance of a man living in constant pain.

It is also possible that neither story fully illuminates what Byrom saw that day in March. A third novelist could place Hartley's thinness and Byrom's blank look within a different narrative, one less tied to the body. Instead of treating Hartley's altered appearance as a medical symptom, this third writer could thread it into a story that speaks of larger transformations—of a changed life. In fashioning this story, the storyteller would seek to draw the connections between that life's physical, social, and spiritual dimensions, and to show those dimensions to be parts of one whole, possibly even different ways of speaking about the transformations of the psyche.

2. "That Inherent Love of Virtue"

On Friday, March 12, Byrom went to the Hartleys' for breakfast: "went to Dr. Hartley's who was gone out, so I stayed for him in his study according to his order, and there read Dr. Stukeley's *Palæographica Sacra,* that the Bacchus of the Heathens was the Jehovah of the Jews; the Doctor coming in we had a little talk, and he went out again and I stayed there; and he came in again and we had a shorthand lecture; Dr. Hartley began and paid five guineas" (B 2.1.11–12). Hartley's goings out and comings in are probably attributable to his medical practice; he was being called out, or keeping appointments, to see patients. The book Byrom read was a newly published work by William Stukeley (1687–1765), physician, divine, scientist, astrologer, and antiquary, who wrote an important early work on Stonehenge (1740). As a student at Cambridge, Stukeley studied medicine, attended dissections, and conducted chemical experiments with his lifelong and then "inseparable" friend, Stephen Hales (Gunther 1937, 222; Allan and Schofield 1980, 11–12). Stukeley's aim in *Palæographica Sacra* was to situate secular history within the sacred, the stories of the ancient world within the alpha to omega defined by the biblical narrative; doing so required the demonstration that pagan mythology was a derivation from, and a garbling of, the original Judaic (Mosaic or Adamic) knowledge. Stukeley's project would have appeared completely sound to Hartley and Byrom. The Bible defined the boundaries of time, and the idea that the Bible could be fit within a larger secular history, and thus itself historicized, was scarcely imaginable.[8] Moreover, many philosophers, including Sir Isaac Newton, told the story of human history as one of misunderstanding and loss, as ancient peoples literalized symbol into thing; the scattered generations forgot a God who refused to be imaged and built instead a god which was only an image, an idol; their covenant with Jehovah degenerated into their worship of Bacchus (see Rattansi 1988; Manuel 1963). The task for modern philosophers, then, was one of recovery, especially by means of seeing *through* images. Stukeley sees through Bacchus—and detects the faint, primordial memory of Jehovah; Newton sees through the Ptolemaic system of crystalline spheres circling the earth—to the true system of celestial mechanics, once known to Moses and now revealed again. To the extent that they succeeded, they would help bring the long, sad history of mistakes to an end.

After the shorthand lecture, Byrom went with Hartley "in his chariot" to the house of a mutual friend, George Lloyd (see *B* 1.2.440), who was not at home; the two went from there "to St. James's, where he went to Court and I took a turn in the park" (*B* 2.1.12). Following their separate diversions, the two returned to Hartley's house for dinner, along with "one Dr. Battely, a clergyman of St. Edmund's Bury"; they had "pancakes and toasted cheese"—no meat—and, "Mr. Battely going, we drank coffee, and Mrs. Hartley (Packer that was) having a mind to begin with the Doctor, Dr. Hartley's lady began, and the Doctor going a visit I gave her a lecture upon shorthand till he came in, and she seemed much pleased with it."

Elizabeth Packer—now Mrs. Hartley—was one of the five children of Robert Packer and Mary Winchcombe, and the couple's only daughter. The Packers were an important family, with estates in three counties; in 1736 her brother Winchcombe Howard was lord of the manors at Donnington and Bucklebury, in Berkshire; at Little and Old Sodbury, in Gloucestershire; and at Shellingford, in Oxfordshire. Her father was M.P. for Berkshire from 1710 until 1727; he died in 1731. One ancestor, John Packer (d. 1649), was clerk of the Privy Seal and secretary to George Villiers, Duke of Buckingham, one of Charles I's closest advisers. Despite his connection with the Court, John Packer had refused to lend money to Charles I during the Civil War, and as a result Donnington Castle, which he had purchased some years before, was occupied by a Royalist garrison. Parliamentary forces besieged the castle, but the defenders held out for eighteen months, until it was apparent to all that Charles I had lost the war. On the king's instructions, they surrendered the castle in April 1646. When the defenders marched away, both the castle and the village of Donnington, lying below it, were in ruins.[9]

Mary Winchcombe, Elizabeth Packer's mother, was the daughter of Sir Henry Winchcombe, Bart., lord of the manor at Bucklebury, Berkshire. Although blind since childhood, Sir Henry lived a full and active life; he served as M.P. for Berkshire from 1689 to 1695. At his death in 1703, the Bucklebury estate passed to Mary's elder sister Frances and her husband, Henry St. John, politician, rake, and literato, the associate of Swift, Pope, and Arbuthnot. The couple were married in 1701; St. John was appointed Secretary of State in 1710, and made Baron St. John and Viscount Bolingbroke in 1712. Although his marriage brought him an income of nearly £3,000 a year from the Bucklebury estate, it did not temper his character; he was never faithful to Frances. In 1715 he fled to France, having been implicated in Jacobite maneuverings, after the death of Queen Anne, to have the Old Pretender succeed to the throne. When Frances died in 1718, Bucklebury passed to her sister Mary; after her death a year later, it became the property of her eldest son, Winchcombe Howard Packer, then a minor.

The Packers were not enchanted with the prospect of Elizabeth marrying Hartley. David and Elizabeth's daughter Mary, writing in 1796 to the Rev. William Gilpin, stated that "her family were much against the match, and did for some time retard it" (Warner 1817, 107). It is not difficult to imagine why they would. In George Eliot's *Middlemarch,* for instance, Dr. Lydgate marries, under circumstances full of delusion, Rosamund Vincy. Lydgate is a dedicated and progressive young doctor, new to a country town and, at the beginning of his career, dependent upon patronage. Despite his very modest and uncertain income, there is no social or class barrier to the match, for the Vincys are themselves only moderately successful manufacturers. But imagine Lydgate wanting to marry Dorothea Brooke—or, to change the venue, Mr. Darcy's sister in *Pride and Prejudice.* Elizabeth Packer was the only sister in a very wealthy family; her brother Winchcombe Howard owned a collection of estates in three counties. Although the £5,000 she was left in her father's will amounted to only a fraction of the total wealth of the Packer holdings, it still represented a substantial sum at a time in which, for example, a country vicar would count himself fortunate to have a church living of £100 a year.

Hartley, in the eyes of the Packers, would have been a nobody. He was the orphaned son of an obscure Yorkshire clergyman; a charity student at Cambridge; a nonconformist in religion, perhaps even an Arian or Socinian; a "doctor" without a medical degree, struggling to establish a practice in a country town—and not helping his career by publishing a pamphlet advocating the unpopular and controversial practice of variola inoculation for smallpox. To make matters worse, he had a young son (and heir) by his first wife. To Elizabeth's brothers, Hartley could very possibly have had the look of a fortune hunter, an opportunist who, under circumstances full of delusion, had secured a promise of marriage from their sister.

I do not know what Elizabeth Packer was doing in Bury St. Edmunds, or when she and Hartley met, or the circumstances of their gravitation toward each other, or the proportions of illusion and clear-sightedness in their decision to marry. Mary Hartley writes that she believed her parents met "at the house of one of her relations, who lived in Suffolk." Neither do I know how much effort the brothers spent in remonstrating with their sister, or in attacking Hartley, or how long they succeeded in retarding the match, or what finally caused them to relent. Mary simply states that her mother "was her own mistress, and she followed that inherent love of virtue, which taught her, that the affection of a heart like my father's was of more value than wealth or titles." She adds that "her brothers thought not so."

What we do know is that all parties signed a marriage contract—an "Indenture Quadripartite"—on 1 August 1735.[10] It is a large and impressive document. The purpose of it is twofold. First, after appointing John Willis and Henry Packer as trustees, it states that Elizabeth's £5,000 "shall not be paid to the said Elizabeth Packer or the said David Hartley or as either of them shall direct or appoint but the same shall ... be paid into the hands of the said John Willis and Henry Packer ... that they ... lay out and vest the said sum of £5000 in lands and hereditaments." Note that the principal shall *not* be paid to either or as either shall direct. Although Elizabeth and David will receive the income from the investments, the trustees will manage the principal. Hartley has no say in the matter; he has no direct control over the principal, and neither can he cajole his wife into making investment decisions that would suit his interests. Second, the document goes on to state that, if the marriage takes place, "it shall and may be lawful to and for her the said Elizabeth by any deed or deeds writing or writings under her hand ... and as well without or with the privity and consent of the said David Hartley ... to limit, appoint, or dispose [of the estate] ... as the said Elizabeth Hartley shall think fit." Elizabeth, in other words, gets to write her own will. If she and Hartley have a child, the child would of course inherit her estate; but in the event that she has no children, or they die while she is still living, the document stipulates that Elizabeth retains the right to leave her estate to whomever she wishes. Hartley has no right to veto the terms of the will, or even to know what those terms are: she can make up her will "as well without or with [his] privity and consent." She is under no obligation to leave her portion of the Packer property to her husband or stepson.

The marriage contract was signed by all the parties at the beginning of August. The records of the parish church in Nowton, Suffolk, a village outside of Bury St. Edmunds, contain an entry, dated 26 August 1735, for the marriage of "David Hartley, A.M. of Bury St Edm^{ds} and Eliza Packer of ye same wth Licence." The license signifies that they were not residents of the parish, and hence that there had been no reading of the banns.[11] The license also specifies that Hartley was required to post a surety bond of £2,000—ten times the usual amount for a marriage by license. I do not know the reasons for the choice of this little village church, or how to picture the event—whether David and Elizabeth were, in their countenances, radiant or grave; whether any of her family were there, now reconciled, or grim, or wreathed in suppressed snarling contempt; or whether Hartley's son, David Jr., aged five, was limping about, with his club foot. We do know that David had just turned thirty, but not how thin he was; he had been born in June 1705, a year after Newton had published his *Opticks*. Elizabeth was eight years younger. Their determination to marry had prevailed over her family's opposition.

Now, seven months later, after a dinner of pancakes and toasted cheese, Elizabeth Hartley is seated with John Byrom in the Hartleys' house on Princes (today, Wardour) Street, near Leicester Fields. She is about five months pregnant with her first child, who will later be named Mary, probably after her grandmother, who died when Elizabeth was five. While Hartley is out for the fourth time that day, she listens to Byrom's lecture on shorthand, which she has decided to learn alongside her husband, and is "much pleased with it."

3. "The Fundamental Doctrine Both of Reason and Scripture"

When Hartley returned, he and Byrom went out again to attend a lecture: "We went to the Temple Exchange coffeehouse to hear Mr. Whiston's lecture upon the globes; . . . We drank a dish of coffee with Mr. Whiston after the lecture, who saluted me and talked away after his manner. The Doctor and I had a talk about the Christian religion, which he said he was persuaded of by reasoning, and about his notion of αιωνιος, which I could not come into. We parted from the Temple Exchange, and he went with Mr. Whiston and another gentleman, and I to Will's and to Abington's [coffeehouses], and had no supper." William Whiston (1667–1752) had in 1701 been Newton's hand-picked successor as Lucasian Professor of Mathematics at Cambridge University; in 1710 he had been expelled from the university for his criticisms of the Athanasian doctrine that Jesus embodied two natures—human and divine—in one person. Unlike his predecessor, he was unable to keep his theological convictions to himself. He supported himself, after his expulsion, by giving lectures in London coffeehouses. His early lectures on comets followed from the speculations in his *New Theory of the Earth* (1696) and *Astronomical Principles of Religion* (1717), and caused a great stir of interest. The lecture "on the globes" that Hartley and Byrom attended may have concerned Whiston's attempts to devise a method of determining longitude. He had played an important role in securing the passage in 1714 of the act of Parliament that established the Board of Longitude and that promised a prize of £20,000 to the person who could perfect a system for determining it (see Force 1985, 21–23; Farrell 1981, 133–35; Howse 1980, 45–56). When Hartley and Byrom listened to his lecture "on the globes," Whiston was at work on his third solution of the problem, which this time was based upon the eclipses of the moons of Jupiter (Whiston 1738; Farrell 1981, 164–65; Howse 1980, 197–98).[12]

The topic was significant; a nation that was becoming the world's dominant seapower had a compelling interest in devising a method that would enable ships at sea to determine their exact locations and cartographers to draw accurate maps. Navigators and cartographers could, at this time, ascertain their latitude by measuring the altitude of the sun or Pole Star, but a method for determining positions relative to east and west eluded them. Because the earth rotates on its axis, there is no way to establish one's longitude by direct reference to the heavens; as the hours of night pass on, the constellations sweep through the sky.

The key to determining longitude is to know exactly what time it is; more precisely, it depends upon knowing what time it is in two places—the first, at a fixed location on the earth, and the second, at your position at this moment. If you know what time it is "now" at the Greenwich Observatory near London and at your present location, you can then calculate your position relative to Greenwich as a direct function of the difference in time; you will be so many hours, minutes, and seconds east or west of Greenwich. Longitude could in theory be determined by the method Whiston proposed, at least on land. If one knew, for example, that an observer at Greenwich would see one of Jupiter's moons eclipsed at exactly 10:00 P.M. on 8 May 1736, he could, by observing the eclipse himself, determine how far ahead or behind Greenwich Mean Time he was, at his present position. At sea, however, the method would only work on clear, still nights; imagine keeping a high-powered telescope fixed on Jupiter from the rolling deck of a ship.

Despite his years of effort, Whiston never received the prize money, which eventually went to John Harrison in 1773 for work on a marine chronometer, which he first started in 1737. Harrison's method requires that a ship keep on board an extremely accurate clock, set to Greenwich

Mean Time; given such a clock, there is no need to calculate the current time in Greenwich from the eclipses of Jupiter's moons or from any other astronomical point of reference. Still, their different approaches to the problem are both reliant upon a fundamental theoretical discovery that was progressively developed and articulated by Christian Huygens, Robert Hooke, and Sir Isaac Newton—that of the mechanism of isochronous vibration. For a vibrating medium, whether a flexing spring, a cycloidal pendulum, or waves of light and sound, the vibrations' periods are constant for any given wavelength; for a correctly constructed clock, using either a pendulum or balance wheel, the period of vibration is a function of the length of the "arm" and is independent of how far the pendulum or wheel swings. Waves of light and sound are dynamically equivalent to a pendulum; for each, frequency varies directly with wavelength, and consequently the velocity of propagation of each will remain constant in any given elastic medium. Were there not a mechanism that guaranteed that vibrations are isochronous, neither Whiston's nor Harrison's methods of calculating longitude would work; Whiston's method requires a constant velocity for light, and Harrison's a constant "frequency" for any given "wavelength." As we shall see in the next chapter, Hartley also attempted to use a theory of "vibrations" to account for the transmission of neural impulses—and hence for the basic mechanism of the mind.

It is important to note here that, insofar as the principle of isochronous vibration reveals a fundamental mechanism of the universe, to think that the world could be understood as operating like a clock—as a clockwork universe—is to get the analogy backward. To Newtonians of Hartley's era, the central and liberating insight was not that the physical world was a big clock; it was rather that clocks could be manufactured that could be made to run according to the mechanism that already ran the world. Before the work of Huygens, Hooke, and Newton, it was unimaginable that the completely regular harmonic motions present in vibrating media could be used as the measure of time, velocity, or distance. To the people gathered in the Temple Exchange coffeehouse in 1736, it was thanks to the fundamental regularity of the universe that it was possible in theory at least to construct mechanical devices that replicated it.

As they sat over their coffee, Hartley and Byrom began to discuss Christianity. They had just heard Whiston's lecture on the measurement of time, and Hartley now began to explain "his notion of αιωνιος"— sometimes translated as "eternity." That the discussion would take this turn makes sense, for in an essay entitled "Reason and Philosophy no Enemies to Faith" Whiston had argued that the punishments of the wicked after death shall continue "through all those αἰῶνες των αἰώνων, long and undeterminate Periods of Being, to which their Lives shall be preserved by the Divine Power; so that nothing shall put an end to their Torment, but what shall do so to their lives, and their State for ever also" (1709, 220). Unlike the saved, who will forever enjoy the full benefits of the resurrection, the unrepentant wicked will eventually be annihilated (see Walker 1964, 96–101). That Byrom "could not come into" Hartley's explanation of his own interpretation of αιωνιος could mean either that he did not understand it or that he could not subscribe to it. In any event, in the Temple Exchange coffeehouse, after a day spent in each other's company, Hartley began to explain to Byrom a concept that was central to his thinking and to his life.

The New Testament writers speak of the "eternity" of punishment that will be the fate of those who reject Christ or do evil. In Matthew 25:41, for example, Jesus says to the goats at the Last Judgment, "Depart from me, ye cursed, into everlasting fire [τὸ πῦρ τὸ αἰνώιον], prepared for the devil and his angels." At the end of the chapter Matthew writes (v. 46), "these shall go away into everlasting punishment" [κόλασις αἰώνιος]. In the common interpretation, the situation of the damned, like that of the blessed, will be permanent; their suffering will continue forever (see Walker 1964, 19–23). Those descending into Dante's hell, for example, read an inscription telling them to "abandon all hope"; as depicted in the thirty-third canto, Ugolino will forever gnaw at the back of Archbishop Roger's head, as both remain immobilized, frozen up to their necks in the lake of ice in the ninth circle at the bottom of hell. This immobility, for the damned, is the essence of eternity. In *Mimesis*, Erich Auerbach writes of Dante's conception of hell: "[F]rom the fact that earthly life has ceased, so that it cannot change or grow, whereas the passions and inclinations which animated it still persist without ever being released into action, there results as it were a tremendous concentration. . . . It is precisely the absolute realization of a particular earthly destiny in the place definitively assigned to it, which constitutes Divine Judgment" (1953, 192). Ugolino's face will always be pressed against Roger's scalp; his teeth will always turn to bloody pulp the head of the man who starved him and his sons to death. There is no end to Ugolino's hunger, now ravening upon the man who caused it; there is no way for the two to disengage; the dreaded resurrection of the body will only intensify these souls' hatred and pain. Then, the blood that spreads across the ice will be real.

The image of frozen torment was one that Hartley could not bear— or believe. A benevolent God could not witness such carnage and be unmoved; God could not maintain a system that perpetuated it without end, without hope of change. Hartley came to the conclusion that God did not will the endless continuance of suffering, and hence that the term αιωνιος did not signify "forever." The day after his conversation with Byrom in the Temple Exchange coffeehouse, Hartley wrote to his friend and schoolmate at Bradford Grammar School and Cambridge, the Rev. John Lister. Although Lister was to later move back to Shibden Hall, the Listers' ancestral home outside of Halifax, he was in 1736 the proprietor of a grammar school in Bury, Lancs., and Hartley's letter is addressed to him there. It ends with a paragraph on "eternity":

> As to my Proposition viz. That Universal Happiness is the Fundamental Doctrine both of Reason & Scripture I hope & believe it is so. The Word *eternal* in the New Testamt. seems to be quite indefinite & to vary with the Circumstances; & the whole Tenor of both old and new Testamt. is Repentance & Redemption, that God is a Father & Friend, & that he will restore the Jews to the Land [of Israel], i.e. all Mankind to Heaven and [. . .]. And undoubtedly nothing is so irreconcilable [with] Reason as eternal Punishmt., nothing so contrary to all the Intimations God has given us of himself in his Works. Have you read Sr. Is. Newton's Commt. upon Danl. & the Apocalypse? It affords great Light to many Passages of the old & new Testamt. (*L* 2; 13 March 1736)[13]

Hartley's discussion of αιωνιος with Byrom the day before probably also concerned the ways in which the specific meanings of this word, itself indefinite, varied with the circumstances of its use. And as he did to Lister, Hartley may have suggested to Byrom that particular references to the "eternity" of punishment need to be interpreted in a manner congruent with "the whole Tenor" of the Old and New Testaments—the fundamental themes of "Repentance & Redemption." Rather than imagining that the Fall had produced a permanent fragmentation of the universe into a realm of bliss and a realm of endless pain, Hartley believed that all of creation, and all the beings in it, angels, humans, and possibly even animals, would ultimately return to paradise. Over a dish of coffee, Hartley was attempting to share his liberating vision of a time when the ice will melt.

4. "A Fair Calculation According to the Doctrine of Chances"

For fifteen centuries, the Christian peoples of Europe had lived within a text that absorbed the world.[14] For most of those centuries, most people in Western Europe lived within a distinctive interpretation of that text—an interpretation that privileged imperial and juridical categories. As retold by Augustine and Anselm, by Dante and Milton, the biblical story begins with creation, fall, and expulsion from paradise and ends with an apocalypse. In it, a primal crime—and all the crimes that follow—demand judgment and retribution, for the upholding of divine justice. But, as Anselm tells us in his *Cur Deus Homo* (1.20), as we stand in the dock in the divine court, our situation is hopeless: there is no way for us to make restitution for our crimes, for all our acts of charity are only what a just God rightly expects us to do in the first place. There is no way for us to be better than we ought to be, and hence to pay the fine, restore the balance. Consequently, there is nothing the prisoner can plead on his own behalf. It is only because the one truly guiltless and unique man offers himself as our substitute that we escape our just and permanent sentence. Thus, a primal crime is canceled by a triumphant self-sacrifice. And that act of self-sacrifice and the triumph of new life that follows it form the center point upon which human history turns, and by which it is transformed. Now, people can hope that, in the great settling of accounts that will be the end of history, their debts will be forgiven them.

It is possible that a person could keep to this juridical interpretation and also affirm universal salvation; in such an interpretation, Christ's sacrifice cancels all debts: all the prisoners are reprieved, regardless of their crimes or their attitudes toward their crimes. But such a revision of the story is deeply problematic; it writes in an absolutely happy ending, but the ending seems artificial, disconnected from the blighted histories of human beings. It seems to suggest that my actions have no ultimate consequences; I may stagger through a life of cruelty and oblivion, feel nothing for the people I have harmed, and yet think that in the end I will not be held to account.

It is not enough to tack a new ending onto an old story; the story itself must be recast so that the ending makes sense. For a scriptural story that ends with "universal happiness" to make sense, the text must absorb the world in a different way. If God is to "restore . . . all mankind to heaven" in a way that is not arbitrary, then the dynamic culminating in that restoration must be shown to be at work in the histories of human beings. A cosmic and supernatural narrative must be given a psychological and natural dimension. God's action is not to be imagined as something that imposes itself on human life from the outside—a last judgment in which the natural order of the world is ripped to pieces; rather, it is awaiting to be discovered naturally at work within human experience, transforming consciousness.

The key, for Hartley, to this natural and psychological dimension is the connection between "happiness" and "benevolence"—between, that is, a subjective state of well-being and actions that advance the well-being of others. Hartley articulates the connection in a series of four letters to John Lister, written on 13 March, 15 May, and 2 December 1736, and 16 January 1737. In the first of these, written the day after his meeting with Byrom, he states:

> In all Enquiries into the Foundation of Morality the first thing to be determined seems to be what Definitions we shall give to the Terms *Moral Good* & *Moral Evil*. . . . Now this may be done by making *Moral Good* coincide either with private Happiness, with Public Happiness or with the Will of Good [God]. . . . Let us first make it coincide with private Happiness & call those Actions morally good wch promote the Happiness of the Agent in the best possible Manner, & then if it can be shewn from Observations made upon the Course of Nature that the fairest Probability of obtaining private Happiness always arises from our endeavours to promote public, if also it can be shewn that God is infinitely benevolent & therefore must will that we shd be too, & the Result upon the whole will be that the supposed Coincidence of Moral Good with private Happiness will draw after it a consequential one both with public Happiness & with the Will of God. And so the three Definitions of Virtue will coincide with each other ex omnia parte, just as if A shd. define a Triangle from its 3 sides, B from its 3 Angles, & C from the perpetual Equality of its Angles to

2 right ones. Nevertheless as in the Definitions of a Triangle one serves better than another for demonstrating its Properties, so the first Definition of Moral Good from private Happiness seems best accommodated to the Purposes of a Teacher of Morality, because he will by that means engage the Attention of his Readers. Most Men have indeed some Regard both to public Happiness & the Will of God, but every Man intuitively regards his own Welfare. (L 2)

Hartley's starting point is similar to that of Aristotle in the first book of the *Nichomachean Ethics*. Aristotle defines the "good" as "that at which an action aims," and then points out the flexibility of the formula. What appears to be a definition of the term *good* turns out to be an observation of how people use the word in their everyday lives. Everyone wants *eudaimonia*—happiness, well-being, to be blessed by the gods—for himself, but everyone specifically wants what he senses is missing, and thus the sick man calls health "good," while the poor man speaks of wealth. It is the task of the teacher of morality to lead people from their private definitions of good to an understanding that can be shared. In a rhetorical tactic similar to Aristotle's, Hartley begins his disquisition on ethics by offering the somewhat shocking definition of moral good or virtue in terms of "those actions which promote the happiness of the agent." The advantage of identifying the moral good with private happiness, *agathon* with *eudaimonia*, is its appeal to each person's "intuitive" interest in his own welfare. Hartley points out in his next letter that the definition is intended to "engage the Attention of my Reader" (L 3; 15 May 1736).

For Hartley as for Aristotle centuries earlier, identifying the good with happiness is only the starting point for an ethical theory. In his work, Aristotle quickly points out that ethics is a branch of politics, the science that concerns the well-being of the *polis*. People achieve a good life by performing their tasks or functions with skilled competence, but it is the welfare of the community that must determine what those tasks or functions ought to be. Similarly, in Hartley's theory, it is true that actions that promote the agent's happiness are morally good—when they promote that happiness "in the best possible manner." But it is the furtherance of the well-being of others that defines the "best possible manner," and indeed the only possible manner, in which actions can promote the agent's happiness: "observations made upon the course of nature" show that "the fairest probability of obtaining private happiness always arises from our endeavours to promote public" happiness. The first definition of moral good thus coincides with the second. Happiness is inseparably connected with benevolence. It is also connected with the third; God, as an "infinitely benevolent" being, desires the happiness of all persons, and hence desires that we be benevolent, both for our own sakes and for the sake of each other.

The equivalence of the three definitions of moral good is, of course, not recognized by all. There are many who think that another's loss can be their gain, and there are some who imagine that they can attain private, solitary happiness through the suffering of others. In Hartley's theory, such people are living an illusion. To the extent that they act upon that illusion, they harm both the community and themselves. In his letter of 15 May 1736, Hartley writes to Lister that "any Man who hopes to gain private Happiness by aiming at it directly is toto coelo mistaken upon a fair Calculation according to the Doctrine of Chances. The Epicure palls his Taste & plunges himself in Offensiveness & Disease, the Ambitious exposes himself to disgrace, & the Covetous tortures himself with an imaginary real Poverty; whereas the Temperate, the humble & the generous have in general all they can wish or enjoy, with an Immunity from both bodily & mental Pain" (*L* 3). Note that Hartley does not claim that virtue is its own reward and vice its own punishment in every individual instance. The observation is based upon "a fair calculation according to the doctrine of chances"—that is, upon a truth known to students of probability theory: that as the number of events increases, the ratios of the observed outcomes approach the theoretical probability distribution in a measurable way. The chance of rolling a six is 1 in 6 on any given throw of a die, and with a sufficient number of throws the number of sixes will converge on one sixth of the total; in Hartley's day, the Huguenot refugee Abraham De Moivre demonstrated in his *Doctrine of Chances* (1718) how to achieve a fair calculation of this convergence. Here, Hartley is saying that, although the epicure may not find the fish and fowl and flesh and wine before him wearisome and a danger to his health, it is almost mathematically predictable that after a sufficient number of such dinners he will find the pleasures of dining nearly extinguished and the consequent pains much more acutely felt.

The coincidence of the three definitions means that, in Hartley's view, people live within a world structured as a self-correcting system. There is no need for a last, external judgment, because our every action embodies its own judgment within itself. The process is continuous, incremental, inescapable; pain is an inevitable symptom of sickness, whether physical or moral. But pain may also be a consequence of therapy, as the person is gradually cured of his disease. Hence, the process also carries within itself the potential for transformation. Although a person may feed his selfish and vicious cravings for a very long time—perhaps even an eon, counting both this life and an afterlife—at some point he will recognize that his participation in a war of all against all has been futile. It has brought him nothing. He may then realize that there is no happiness for an island self; that private happiness can only come from acts of benevolence to his neighbor—from, that is, doing the will of God. And although a person's character is the cumulative residue of his history, the accumulation of all the judgments he has unconsciously passed upon himself, he may, once granted this realization, undergo a transformation into something he never before has been; he may be released from the endless repetition of the past. When Ugolino realizes that gnawing at Roger's skull does nothing but bring them both more pain, he may leave off. The two of them, together, may begin to find a way to break free of the ice.

5. "A Man Who Disregards Himself"

In his letter to Lister of 15 May 1736, Hartley affirmed "that a Man who disregards himself, who entirely abandons Self-Interest & devotes his Labours to the Service of Mankind, or in that beautiful and expressive Phrase of the Scriptures, *who loves his Neighbour as himself* is sure to meet with private Happiness" (L 3). This is Hartley's core conviction, an insight that he labored to communicate to others. At Cambridge in June 1735, nearly a year before their meeting at Richard's coffeehouse, Byrom read a copy of "Dr. Hartley's paper upon benevolence, never to sacrifice a greater pleasure for a less" (B 1.2.634). And writing to Lister on 2 December 1736, Hartley comments:

> I have wrote two small Treatises abt. a year & half ago, but without any Design of publishing them in their present Form. I call them, The Progress of Happiness deduced from Reason —— & from Scripture. The first begins with shewing that all our Intellectual Pleasures & Pains are formed either immediately or mediately from sensible ones by Association, i.e. that they are meerly Compositions of a variety of Sensations &

all Reflection ultimately resolvable into Sensation. It then proceeds to show that Benevolence is the best means of obtaining private Happiness, that this naturally leads us to the love of God, that our Natures are so formed & so adjusted to the System of things that we must from the Law of Association at last become benevolent, & consequently that all must some time or other be happy. The 2d. endeavours to show that if we interpret Scripture in the large & unconfined sense according to wch. our Saviour & his Apostles interpret the old Test. . . . its great Doctrine will be universal Salvation. (*L* 4; cf. *T* 236)[15]

If the "paper" Byrom read at Cambridge in June 1735 was the first treatise, then he would have been familiar with Hartley's theses concerning benevolence and universal happiness; he would also have encountered Hartley's account of how the "Law of Association" brings us to recognize that private happiness, the public good, and the love of God are three terms for the one reality. To support and amplify his ethical and religious principles, Hartley had begun to explore how "our Natures are so formed & so adjusted to the System of things"—to develop a psychology.

Hartley also sought to devote his own "Labours to the Service of Mankind," to make benevolence the guiding principle of his life. In addition to his medical practice and to participation in the meetings of the Royal Society, Hartley devoted himself to various philanthropic projects. He supported the Society for the Encouragement of Learning, an organization that was founded on 14 May 1736, primarily "to assist authors in the publication, and to secure to them the entire profits of their own works."[16] Hartley joined the society on 14 January 1737, regularly attended the society's meetings, and reviewed, along with Thomas Birch, one of the proposals the society decided to publish, *The Necessity of Revelation* (1738) by Archibald Campbell, Professor of Ecclesiastical History at the University of St. Andrews. Hartley mentioned the work to Lister; in the work, he writes, "it is shewn that no sect of Philosophers came by their Notions of God, Providence, and a future state from their philosophy and reasoning, but had all this from tradition, and then corrupted tradition by philosophy."[17] Campbell's thesis is another expression of the outlook articulated by Newton and Stukeley.

Hartley was also involved in facilitating the publication, by subscription, of Nicholas Saunderson's *Elements of Algebra* (1740).

Saunderson (1682–1739) was the successor of Newton and Whiston as Lucasian Professor of Mathematics. He had been blinded in infancy; "when twelve months old," according to his son John, he "was deprived by the small pox, not only of his sight, but his eyes also, for they came away in abscesses" (1740, ii). Saunderson was educated privately, and in 1707, at age twenty-five, he moved to Cambridge. Although he had no university degree and no official place in a college, he soon became a valued teacher; students paid a fee to attend his private lectures on Newton's *Principia, Opticks,* and *Arithmetica Universalis.* Scholars at Cambridge knew that the *Principia* in particular was a work of supreme importance, but Newton's use of the language of geometry to present his discoveries made the work incomprehensible to all but a few. Saunderson's talent for explaining what Newton was saying won him a following. Even Whiston, who at the time held the Lucasian chair and was also lecturing on Newton's philosophy, supported Saunderson's activities: "As a good-natured man and an encourager of learning," John Saunderson writes, "[Whiston] readily consented to the application of friends made in behalf of so extraordinary a person" (1740, iv–v). When Whiston was deprived of the Lucasian chair and expelled from the university, Saunderson was the popular candidate for the chair. His lack of a university degree presented an impediment, but this was removed when the university, with Queen Anne's approval, granted him an M.A. on 19 November 1711. He was appointed Lucasian Professor of Mathematics the next day.

By 1738, although he had been teaching for more than thirty years, Saunderson had published no major work of his own. In addition, his poor health raised concerns about the financial security of his family. Friends encouraged Saunderson to complete his *Elements of Algebra* and also canvassed for subscribers—people who would purchase the book before publication. Hartley, in a letter of 5 June 1738, wrote to Lister: "I now send you proposals for Saunderson's Algebra, and beg you to do him all the service you can. It has been with much difficulty that he has been prevailed with to finish this work, and if it does not meet with proper encouragement the world will be a greater loser, because he has so many beautiful useful treatises which only want the last stroke" (*L* 6; cf. *T* 238). When a book was published commercially, the publisher would purchase the copyright from the author for a fixed sum; if the book sold well, the publisher enjoyed profits upon which the author had no claim. However, because the costs of production were borne entirely by the publisher, the more costly the production the greater the financial risk and the greater the likelihood that the publisher would seek to negotiate a low payment for the copyright—assuming, that is, that he was willing to undertake the project. Publication of Saunderson's *Algebra* by subscription resolved both difficulties in a way that simultaneously benefited the author, the publisher, and the public. Because a known number of copies were sold in advance, Saunderson or his heirs could receive a payment for the copyright that was proportionate to the success of the book; in addition, Cambridge University Press did not have to assume the entire risk of producing an expensive quarto edition of nearly eight hundred pages that contained numerous geometrical figures, all of which had to be engraved. Publication of the *Elements of Algebra* the year after Saunderson's death thus represented a gesture of thanks by those who benefited from his teaching and also a means of providing for his family. In addition to these private benefits, publication of the work also contributed to the public good; subsequent abridged editions of this beautiful and useful treatise introduced students to the study of algebra throughout the century.[18]

There is a hazard in biographical writing that derives from the contingencies of documentation: the writer is tempted to emphasize those matters that are amply documented while passing over other matters about which the record is largely silent; the reader in turn is led to infer that the writer's modulations of emphasis reflect the contours of care, interest, and effort in the subject's life. I have written two paragraphs about Saunderson; besides the fact that Hartley attended his lectures at Cambridge, they contain one of the few documented facts I know about their relationship—that Hartley asked Lister to subscribe for the book. In addition, that Lister collected some subscriptions and also that Hartley was in personal contact with Saunderson can be inferred from a line in Lister's letter to Hartley of 6 November 1738: "In my next [letter] I design to send you a small bill with the remaining receipts for Dr. Saunderson, to whom I beg my best services" (*L* 10; cf. *T* 243). Nonetheless, I do not know what quality their personal relationship possessed, the degree to which Hartley knew the "many beautiful useful treatises which only want the last stroke," whether he personally encouraged Saunderson to put that last stroke to the *Elements of Algebra*, or whether his letter to Lister represents a lone request or one of many he made to potential subscribers.

Thanks to the wealth of detail in Byrom's journals, I could, in contrast, fill the next ten pages with a history of Hartley's efforts to promote Byrom's shorthand. Were this a Shandean text, filled with voices, a reader could here interject—Please don't!—but I would assure her that, though the prospect may at first seem dreary, the story would be interesting, even fascinating; it would combine elements of intellectual history, suppressed personal conflict, and possibly political intrigue. But I would also caution the reader that the relative quantities of information do not constitute a ratio by which we may decide that Byrom's shorthand played a greater part in Hartley's life than Saunderson's mathematical instruction.—Please go on.

Upon learning Byrom's shorthand, Hartley became convinced that "it would be universally practised if known" (B 2.1.136). Moreover, the shorthand would be much more than a useful tool for stenographers. Seventy years earlier, founding members of the Royal Society, including John Wilkins, the society's first secretary, had attempted to advance knowledge and diminish error through the creation of a "philosophical language" that would be denoted by a "real character" (see §6.8; Wilkins 1668). Their attempt to formulate a philosophical language came to nought—it was based on the creation of tables in which all living things could be systematically arrayed, like beetles pinned in a specimen cabinet, and the profuseness of life defeated them—but nonetheless the idea of a "real character" that would accurately represent spoken language retained its power. Robert Hooke, for example, recommended Wilkins's character as one that "seemeth to be wanting nothing to make it have the utmost perfection, and highest Idea of any Character or language Imaginable, as well for Philosophical as for common and constant use" (1679, 31). Despite Hooke's recommendation, Wilkins's character never came into common use; its perfection apparently went unappreciated by others. In Hartley's eyes, in contrast, Byrom's shorthand "character" possessed the perfection Wilkins's and other characters lacked; it could both adequately express spoken language and be written with economy and ease—and hence it could answer both for philosophical and for common use. This reformed system of writing possessed the potential to facilitate communication and to further the advancement of human knowledge; its general adoption would thus contribute greatly to the public good.

There was, however, a difficulty in ensuring that public good coincided with private. To become a common method of writing, the system needed to be made public. But publication of the system, which could be accomplished in a pamphlet, risked putting an end to Byrom's livelihood, for it was not possible to copyright or patent a shorthand. Byrom would have no way of proceeding either against a pirated edition or against someone who set himself up in business as an independent teacher. When David and Elizabeth Hartley began their lessons, Byrom had for more than ten years earned his bread by giving private tuition in the system he had invented. He charged five guineas per person and required each student to promise that he would not teach the system to someone else. Private tuition provided Byrom with an income, but it limited the number of people who knew the system, and it meant that only people who learned the system from Byrom could use it communicate with each other. Hence the dilemma: as long as Byrom profited from his invention, it would never realize its potential to become a common method of communication; the moment it was made public, Byrom could no longer earn his livelihood.

Hartley wished the system to be made accessible to all, and he encouraged Byrom to pursue various strategies for making it public in a way that would also be profitable to its inventor. Two months after their meeting in Richard's coffeehouse, on 20 May 1736, Byrom wrote in his journal that Hartley "was about recommending the King." The entry continues: "(At Dr. Hartley's Thursday afternoon): here I am come from Westminster, where I went with the Doctor, but was tired of staying there, the King not coming to the parliament till very late" (*B* 2.1.45). The entry suggests that Hartley intended to introduce Byrom to George II, presumably with the hope of securing the king's patronage for Byrom's shorthand. A year later, in March and April 1737, Hartley on several occasions tried, without success, to elicit Byrom's interest in having a book demonstrating the system published by the Society for the Encouragement of Learning (see *B* 2.1.95, 107, 119–20, 127, 132–33). Hartley then proposed that the book be published by subscription; Byrom agreed to this, and Hartley set about writing a prospectus for the book—which, Byrom notes, "was to be a paper of my scholars, not mine" (*B* 2.1.136)—and also organizing an informal shorthand society that would see to the business of raising the subscription. The society first met on 2 May 1737, decided to announce its existence with an advertisement in the *Daily Advertiser* of 7 May, and read Hartley's draft of the prospectus (*B* 2.1.145). After seemingly endless tinkering, the prospectus was finally published in November 1739, eighteen months after the society's initial meeting (see *B* 2.1.289–94 for the text of the proposal). The project did not succeed in raising a sufficient number of subscriptions. However, in June 1742 a special act of Parliament granted Byrom the exclusive rights, for twenty-one years, to publish and to teach his shorthand (see *B* 2.1.320, n.1, and 2.1.324–26 for the text of the act). No book demonstrating his system appeared during his lifetime; Byrom's manual, *The Universal English Shorthand,* appeared in 1767, four years after his death.

There is something puzzling about the record of events recorded in Byrom's journal, for in them Byrom appears to be most diffident about taking action to promote his own cause. In 1723 and 1724, at the beginning of his career as a shorthand writer, he actively solicited endorsements for a proposal to publish his shorthand by subscription; he also tried to find someone who could cut the type for the system (*B* 1.1.48–78). In 1736 and after, however, he forfeited the opportunity of an introduction to the king; refused even to explore the possibility of having his shorthand published by the Society for the Encouragement of Learning; made Hartley write and rewrite the prospectus in order to palliate his sensitivities concerning the exact wording; and declined to solicit subscribers once the prospectus was published. There may be obvious, or good, reasons for Byrom's noncooperation. As one who had kissed the hand of King James III of England, the thought of humbly begging the favor of the Elector of Hanover may have been most distasteful. Given the lack of copyright, he may have had cause to fear that a cheap pirated edition would ruin the market for a more expensive edition published by the Society for the Encouragement of Learning (see *B* 2.1.133).

There are, in addition, other, obscurer factors at play here. In a journal entry of 13 February 1739, Byrom indicates that he and Hartley virtually came to an argument over the matter: "After some time the Dr. talked about shorthand, and the same as of old, very friendly, but none of us seemed to be a whit nearer; he would Mr. [Martin] Folkes, &c. subscribe his paper that he had drawn up, and Mr. [George] Lloyd and Dr. [Robert] Smith and Mr. [William] Chaddock; I said that Mr. Chaddock must be excused, and that he was not a known person, and besides he could not be at the meetings, . . . we had long disputes about this matter, and I was justifying myself that the delay was not through me, and that I had and would do all that I could, but that I could not solicit; Dr. [Peter] Shaw seemed to think me not courageous, which indeed is very true, for I am tired of a subscription, if I knew how to act properly in it I would escape from it" (*B* 2.1.221–22). Peter Shaw leaves, and Byrom then objects that "Mr. Folkes had said that, through 'the request of friends,' yet it would look quackism, and I said I could not ask him, that to be sure it was more graceful for me to say the truth, that I was requested, which was the truth, but that it was more difficult for me to act than they imagined, because of the different sentiments of friends; that I believed I should be forced to do the thing which I was always unwilling from the first to do, that is, to take it upon myself, that the agreement with me was to have no care of subscriptions; Dr. H. said it would not do without my stirring." William Chaddock was a friend of Byrom's who married Byrom's mother's sister (B 2.1.314, n. 1); it is not clear why Byrom objected to having Chaddock's name in the prospectus. Particularly unclear is the matter of Byrom's "friends." Byrom wanted the text to say that he "was requested" to make his system public—though not "at the request of friends." To his friend Hartley he alludes to other, unnamed "friends" whose "different sentiments" made it "more difficult for me to act than they imagined."[19]

Hartley and Byrom then discuss which bookseller to approach; Hartley suggests Harding, but Byrom insists upon Hutton, and Hartley agrees. Then Byrom notes:

> When we talked, he often said, Well come, this is losing time, we must be in the magazine; and I quoted Mr. [George] Whitfield, the mower losing no time while he was whetting his scythe. I told him that I wanted a Mæcenas still, that the man was not yet risen that was to make shorthand flourish by way of patronage, that he might have been the man if Mrs. Stephens had not come in the way; he said that would be over shortly, and then, said he, I am all yours. "You talk," says I, "of my family, I have more blood than all of you," so proud was I; for though these gentlemen are friends, they have done none such mighty effects as they talked of to me, but yet their friendship should not be measured by events; all I wish and desire is, that, as I am obliged to them, they should not tease me about an affair which themselves had undertaken and not succeeded in so far as they might, I think, and no harm done; that I only desired not to be limited in the time, and for the rest would do anything. (B 2.1.222-23)

This is a knot. Byrom is resentful that his supporters have not succeeded as well as they said they would, but at the same time will do nothing to help them, and is not keen to have the system published at all, so there is "no harm done" by the fact that they have not succeeded. In his comment about "blood" Byrom was unsubtly reminding Hartley of the fact that he, of a aristocratic family, was dependent for patronage upon a person who owed his wealth and influence to having made a fortuitous marriage.

The conversation took place the evening of Monday, 13 February. The next evening Byrom wrote a letter to his wife from the house of William Chaddock—"Cousin Chad's"—in which he comments that "I am here writing out a paper of Dr. Hartley's, to give him tonight to show to Mr. Folkes, &c. about shorthand, one his old ones with some alterations." On Wednesday, Byrom was again at the Hartleys' for dinner. He stayed for the evening, listening to Hartley and another guest play music "till nine o'clock." (Hartley played the violin.) The guest then leaves, "and we to supper, and came away soon after, the Dr. being sleepy" (*B* 2.1.226).

On this occasion, Byrom did not record what he and the Hartleys ate; on other occasions he lists toasted cheese, pancakes, apple dumpling, messes of spinach—the meals tend to be simple, even abstemious. It would seem that the Hartleys understood that an overstocked larder can be as much a threat to a healthy life as an empty pantry. The principle applies as well to writing a life. Concerning Hartley's activities on behalf of Saunderson, the lack of documentation makes writing a sustained narrative difficult; concerning his relationship with Byrom, the difficulty arises from the plenitude of material in Byrom's journal. Specific incidents need to be selected from the mass and drawn together into a larger whole. But without some sense of the whole, we lack a principle of selection. There is more: without some sense of the whole, we are at a loss to say what a "specific incident" *is*—that is, to identify its character, the constituents of what medieval philosophers called its 'thusness,' its *haeceitas*. On more than one occasion in his *Observations*, Hartley says that a sensation cannot be a "monad"; the term is Leibniz's, and Hartley uses it to make the point that through our hands and ears and eyes we take in continuous, complex, and ever-varying flows of pressure, sound, and light. The picture of a single datum or impression of sensation existing in isolation, like the letter *m* at the end of *datum*, is an abstraction, captivating to those for whom writing is the archetype of thought, who, dwelling among books, imagine sensory ideas pressed upon the mind like letters on paper. But the flows of touch and hearing and sight come before any attempts to make them stand still, just as orality precedes literacy, the music of speech the writing down of words. And when we gaze at words, descriptive of life, silent and still upon the page, it is as if the words need to be reanimated, suffused with *anima*, if we are to hear and comprehend the thusness of which they are the record.—" 'You talk,' says I, 'of my family, I have more blood than all of you,' so proud was I."—How discordant was this? Did it sting? One could expect Hartley to be sensitive about the point; his wife's brothers would not let him forget it: "though my father was the kindest of brothers to them," Mary Hartley wrote, "they treated him always with *hauteur*" (Warner 1817, 107–8).[20] Did Hartley flinch? Snap back? Suppress with effort feelings of anger and frustration? Maintain a demeanor of indulgent calm? Or, putting self aside, understand the conflicted feelings of dignity and dependency that prompted the outburst, and feel unaffected sympathy for his friend? And on Wednesday, would the other guest at dinner have sensed any awkwardness? We do not know; to answer these questions, we would have to hear the silence speak. And here we may reach the limit of narrativity, for it may be that neither Hartley nor Byrom were fully conscious of what animated them and spoke through their words. It may be that, possessing only a confused and contradictory sense of the whole, neither could say the incident happened *thus*.

6. "The Cruelty of This Distemper": The Cure for the Stone

In March 1736, thanks to his pamphlet of 1731, Hartley was known to other campaigners for variola inoculation, such as Sir Hans Sloane, president of the Royal Society, and James Jurin, M.D., secretary of the Royal Society from 1721 until 1727 and later to be president of the Royal College of Physicians.[21] He also enjoyed the support of important families in Suffolk, notably of Lords Townshend and Cornwallis; in contrast to the hauteur displayed by his brothers-in-law, Mary Hartley writes that "the old Lord Townshend (then Secretary of State) treated him with as much kindness as if he had been an additional son, and all the sons and daughters as an additional brother."[22] He was soon to be inducted into the Royal Society, and to become a physician for Thomas Pelham-Holles, Duke of Newcastle, and his wife Henrietta, the eldest daughter of Francis, Earl of Godolphin, whose London home was close to the Hartley's house on Princes Street. He had the opportunity to go Court, and could at least hope to "recommend" Byrom to George II.

Nonetheless, as Hartley traveled about London in 1736, going to the homes of his patients, attending the Thursday afternoon meetings of the Royal Society, meeting his friends and colleagues in one or another of the city's coffeehouses, he may have circulated largely unrecognized, known neither by face or name. He was another recent emigrant to London—a country physician come to the city. And it was a city that was continually necrotic. In London at this time deaths exceeded births by over two to one; life continued to flow along its arteries only thanks to a continuous and sustaining transfusion of newcomers.[23]

By 1740, Hartley was known to every physician in London, and indeed to everyone who kept up with the news, as it was disseminated through pamphlets, newspapers, and coffeehouse conversations. For starting in 1738 he was at the center of a major medical controversy. During their argument, Byrom complained to Hartley, "[T]he man was not yet risen that was to make shorthand flourish by way of patronage, that he might have been the man if Mrs. Stephens had not come in the way." He was referring to Hartley's campaign to effect, once again, the coincidence of private happiness and public welfare—this time through the "publication" of the recipe for Joanna Stephens's medicine for the stone.

Uroliths—kidney or bladder calculi—are commonly calcium or magnesium salts of phosphate or oxalate that form about an organic matrix. Calcium and magnesium salts are generally insoluble in water; they give hard water its hardness, build up as scale in kettles, and form the scum that floats on the top of tea or soapy water. Their presence in the kidneys or bladder can be extremely painful and potentially life threatening; basically, they can stop the flow of urine. Hartley describes their symptoms: "The Symptoms of a Stone in the Bladder are Pain and Difficulty in making Water, a sudden Stoppage in full Stream, Forcings to go to Stool, violent Pain at the Neck of the Bladder upon Motion, especially on Horse-back, or in a Coach over Stones, with bloody Water upon the same occasions. And I do not know any Disorder, besides a Stone in the Bladder from whence all these Symptoms can arise. But it is best that the Patient be searched by a Catheter, which may be done with very little Pain and no Danger" ([1740], 60–61). A bladder stone, which can grow a large as an egg, can function as does a ball-cock in a toilet tank; urination can be suddenly interrupted when the stone is drawn down upon the top of the urethra.

In Hartley's day, the standard treatment for the stone was lithotomy—surgical removal of the stone by a lithotomist, a surgeon who specialized in the procedure. In an age that lacked anesthetics and had no concept of bacterial infection, cutting open a person's bladder could be fatal. William Cheselden, the foremost surgeon in England, probably had the best record of success: he lost twenty out of the three hundred and twelve persons upon whom he performed the improved "lateral operation" (Viseltear 1967, 198).[24] For less-skilled surgeons, the rate of fatalities would have been higher. Consequently, the medical world and the public took notice when in the first months of 1738 Hartley raised the possibility of an effective alternative to surgery. In *Ten Cases of Persons who have Taken Mrs. Stephens's Medicines for the Stone* (1738a), Hartley suggests that Joanna Stephens may have developed a lithontriptic, that is, a medicine that could dissolve or break up a stone in the bladder and hence allow it to be gradually voided.

Of the ten case histories discussed in the pamphlet, by far the most detailed is Hartley's own. What strikes the reader is Hartley's complete forthrightness concerning his own case. Hartley first experienced symptoms of the stone at the beginning of 1736. *Ten Cases* contains "A Diary, as I took the Medicines" of Hartley's first course of treatment with Stephens's medicines, starting on 18 July 1737 and continuing until the end of November of that year. The diary does nothing to minimize the suffering that attended the treatment. After noting that he began to void bits of matter in his urine soon after starting the treatment, he notes that, from 20 to 31 July, "I was in great Pain all this time." The pain eased for two weeks and then returned, possibly even worse than before. The entry for 21 August, for example, records: "Water the same [foul, with sediment]; very grievous Pain. It was so intolerable, I sent for Mrs. *Stephens,* to acquaint her, I was not able to endure: She said, I must have Patience, I should in a little time be easier; and I might take an Opiate to make me rest in the Night." Hartley endured the agonies of the treatment through the rest of August and through September, with, for example, "very cruel pain all this Night" on 25 August, and "excessive Pain this Night" on 1 September. He continued taking the medicines all through the autumn, with some good days and others bad, with clear or foul urine, sometimes with a stoppage, but with a gradual lessening of the pain. Finally, on 28 November 1737 he records: "I walk'd abroad as far as the Custom-house, having confined myself for Twenty Weeks, taking the Medicines regularly, without stirring out of Doors." In addition to his openness, what is equally remarkable about Hartley's account is that, although the other nine cases contain reports of success, in his own case he does not claim that Stephens's medicines have cured him. After twenty weeks of at times agonizing pain, he thinks his condition has improved, but he does not say that he is free of the stone.

Hartley's purpose in publishing *Ten Cases* was not simply to report on the effectiveness of the medicines. Stephens's recipe was one of her own devising, and she offered to reveal it to the public in exchange for a payment of £5,000. As he did with regard to Byrom's shorthand, Hartley thought that Stephens was entitled to payment for her invention and that the price was worth paying, given the potential benefit to the public. He, along with other supporters of Stephens, sought to raise the money through a public subscription. The *Gentleman's Magazine* of April 1738, for example, carried a notice that £500 had already been deposited with the banker who was to collect and hold the subscription money.

Hartley's actions on behalf of Stephens were immediately challenged. An anonymous letter "To Mr. David Hartley" appeared in the May 1738 issue of the *History of the Works of the Learned*—a monthly review of scientific, medical, philosophical, and theological literature that ran from 1735 until 1742. The writer begins:

> As soon as I heard you intended shortly to publish more Cases of Persons, who have taken Madam *Stephens's* Medicines for dissolving the Stone in the Bladder, I determined publickly to inform you, that you might justly expect to be deemed only a Puff-scribbler in Favour of an old Woman's Quack-medicine, if you continued to publish the Cases of Persons only, who received Benefit from those Medicines, without taking the least Notice of the Cases, either of those, who received no Benefit after many Months of taking them, or of such who received great Injury from the Use of them. (Anon. 1738a, 373)

The writer goes on to accuse Hartley of ignoring or suppressing clinical evidence. "I wonder," he writes, "you did not mention, that you had met with some Persons" in whose cases the medicine was ineffective or harmful; he lists eight cases of this sort. He also adds his own testimonial in favor of the medicines of Joshua Ward: "I shall only just hint to say, that some People think, if you had taken a Quarter of the Pains to serve Mr. *Ward*, as you have done to serve Madam *Stephens*, you must have been convinced, that his Medicines, which her late Majesty was graciously pleased to countenance, are preferable to Mrs. *Stephens's*, inasmuch as they are not nearly so nauseous, and that they always bring away exactly the same sort of small soft and rotten Parts of Stones as hers does, and never produces any ill Symptoms, . . . and much seldomer fails of Success." Joshua Ward, who had claimed to have invented a panacea that could cure all types of ailments, had been the subject of medical and public controversy in 1735 and 1736; an analysis of his three kinds of pills had shown that they were composed of compounds of antimony, arsenic, and cobalt (Anon. 1763). Tartar emetic, an antimony compound used as a mordant in dyeing and as an insecticide, was used in medicine as an expectorant, emetic, and diaphoretic. "Her late Majesty," Queen Caroline, the wife of George II, had suffered from an umbilical rupture; she died on 20 November 1737 when her bowel burst. If she had "countenanced" Ward's pills by taking them, they might have contributed to her death.

Hartley responded in the June issue of *History of the Works of the Learned* with a fourteen-page "Account of the Contribution for making Mrs. Stephens's Medicines public; with some Reasons for it, and Answers to the most remarkable Objections made against it" (1738c). He opens his account by noting that "the false Pretences to Methods of dissolving Stones in the Urinary Passages have been so many, and some of them so pernicious, that Physicians of Character and Experience seem for some time to have left off inquiring into the Nature and Efficacy of Medicines said to dissolve stones" (443)—limiting themselves to recommending "opiate and lenient Remedies" or to surgery in those cases in which the patient is healthy enough to endure it. This opening comment may constitute a general and indirect response to the anonymous critic of the previous month; no "Physician of Character and Experience" would recommend the false and pernicious medicines of Joshua Ward. Hartley, however, goes on to say: "But still the thing is not impossible; the active Principles discovered in Stones have always afforded some Hopes to the careful Inquirers into Nature, that a safe Dissolvent might at last be found; and, what is above all, Matters of Fact may justly claim a Fair Hearing, especially in a Case of great Importance." He then points out that it was for the purpose of gaining such a fair hearing for Stephens's medicines that he published his *Ten Cases*. A concern for fairness also fixes the terms of the subscription to raise the £5,000 to purchase Stephens's "secret"; a committee headed by the Archbishop of Canterbury will act as "Trustees and Judges between the public and Mrs. Stephens." Once the subscription has been raised, Stephens will "discover her Medicines. They will then be . . . tried in the Hospitals, in the most strict and authentic Manner, upon Persons who are to be examined by the Catheter, both before and after taking them." The trustees, in other words, will oversee clinical trials upon "as many Patients as [they] shall think fit" (450); if the trustees are satisfied that the treatment is effective, Stephens will receive the money; "and if this

Evidence does not answer, she gives up all Title to the Reward, and each Contributor shall have his Contributions returned." Hartley argues that this is the most expedite and advantageous way to proceed. The alternative of raising the subscription only after clinical trials have proved the efficacy of the medicines, for example, would be attended with "several Inconveniences" that derive from the fact that as long as the medicines remain a secret, they will be in short supply, since Stephens is the only person able to manufacture them: she is already hard pressed to make enough for her current patients; the number of hospital trials would be severely limited; there would need to be a second set of trials, after publication of the recipe, to ensure that she had accurately disclosed the composition of the medicines. But to Hartley "the principal Reason for contriving a Method, which admitted of an immediate Publication" is the fact that "there are in all Parts of the World many unhappy Persons, either dying or living in Pain, thro' the Cruelty of this Distemper, whose Misery calls for the most speedy Relief; so that if these Medicines should be effectual, their Publication ought not to be deferred a Moment longer than necessary" (451). Hartley here confronts the dilemma of how to balance testing and distribution of a promising but unproven treatment for an otherwise incurable condition. It is important to verify the efficacy and safety of the drug, and that requires testing; but testing takes time, and the longer it continues, the more will people suffer and die who might today be alive had they received the treatment. Raising the subscription prior to testing would result in immediate publication; and immediate publication would allow for simultaneous widespread testing and use of the medicines. The effectiveness of the treatment could be evaluated independently throughout Britain and Europe, and not just at one or two London hospitals; in the meantime, treatment would no longer be limited to those who personally picked up their packets of medicine from Joanna Stephens. Unhappy persons "in all parts of the world" could determine for themselves whether the treatment relieved them of their misery.

Concerning the potential for an effective lithontriptic, Hartley notes that the "prevailing Notion" is that "Stones of the urinary Passages cannot be dissolved by any Liquid, except such as is too acrimonious for the passages themselves" (445). He adds, however, that the notion is "plainly a Mistake; for Monsieur [Alexis] *Littre*, a Member of the Royal Academy of Sciences at *Paris* [see Sturdy 1995, 312–14], found, that the common Waters of *Paris,* one of which leaves great Incrustations upon the Pipes thro' which it runs, dissolved Stones, even without

Heat.... Dr. *Hales* also wasted several Gravel-Stones both in warm and cold water." Hartley repeated the experiment with water from various sources, including the Thames. The point of these experiments is not to suggest that these various waters possess some special medicinal quality; it is rather to show that bladder stones are themselves unstable. That they will dissolve in "mere Water only" indicates that "there seem therefore to be in Stones themselves some Principles, which have a great Tendency to Putrefaction and Dissolution." These are the "active Principles" mentioned in the opening paragraph of the "Account." In Hartley's view, bladder calculi are not inert structures; thanks to the "active principles" in them, it is not necessary to introduce into the bladder some "acrimonious" liquid to act upon them; they would come apart of their own accord, if a continuous stream of water could be made to pass through the bladder.

Although "a Rill of warm Water passing through the urinary Passages would indeed waste all the Stones lying in them by degrees," such a continuous dialysis is "what no Art can procure" (446).[25] Consequently, "the great Question is, Whether Urine, which naturally increases Stones... can be so changed by any Medicines, as to dissolve Stones in the same manner as common Water has been shewn to do." Because frequently repeated injection of any liquid through a catheter was not practical, the question needs to be further qualified: Is there any medicine which, when taken orally, can change the chemical composition of the urine in such a way as to dissolve stones and then prevent their recurrence? From his investigations into its effects upon other people, and from his own experiences with it, Hartley thought that Stephens's medicine did alter the urine in the way desired. To verify the medicine's effectiveness, he conducted in vitro experiments using his own urine, "altered by taking the Medicines." He placed various bladder calculi in the urine, "in a Heat equal to that of the Urine in the Bladder; and found, that they were dissolved entirely by lying in it, much in the same manner as the corresponding Pieces in common water; and that at the same time that other corresponding Pieces were increased by lying in common Urine with the same Heat." After repeating the experiment using the medicated urine of another person, Hartley reached the conclusion that "those who take Mrs. *Stephens's* Medicines, have evidently a Liquid running through the urinary Passages, which is a Solvent for Stones in a Heat no greater than that of those Passages. And this is a Presumption in Favour of Mrs. *Stephens's* Medicines, as few others can pretend to from Theory." Nonetheless, despite this apparent experimental confirmation that Stephens's medicines do alter the composition of the urine in the required manner, Hartley still remained scrupulous about not claiming that they were effective in his own case: "As it seems to me, both that I have a Quantity of Stone somewhere in the Passages, and also that this is coming away gradually, tho' very slowly, I go on with the Medicines, hoping that they will at last be effectual, and not knowing what else to do. And it would be very unreasonable for me to conceal a Medicine of great Importance to Mankind, because I myself have as yet received no Benefit from it" (445).

A second criticism of Stephens and Hartley appeared in the July 1738 issue of the *History of the Works of the Learned,* this time in a letter addressed to the "Author" of the periodical. This letter, like the one in May, is anonymous; although it is not clear whether the two letters are or are not by the same person, they are similar in tone. The second letter begins: "Since you have been pleased to endeavour to promote the Reputation of an old Woman's Medicines, by publishing a Quack Paper concerning them, sign'd by one *David Hartley,* whom you have presumed to dignify with the Title of *Doctor;* . . . I hope you will not now refuse to publish the following Account of those very Medicines, which have been so lately puffed by you; and also some Observations on their Effect on the human Calculus" (Anon. 1738b, 57). The writer then begins his "Account" by divulging the contents of the medicines—that they consist of powder made of slaked lime and of a drink made from "a Decoction of Burdock, Parsley and Chamomile Leaves" into which is dissolved a ball that is mainly soap. He says that Stephens freely gave him the instructions for making the drink, and that it was only the "Secret of her Powder" that she seemed "to be desirous of concealing." Upon tasting the powder, he "immediately supposed it to be a weak *Calx Viva*" (58). He then writes that the simple experiment of placing a mixture of the powder and some of the soap on the back of his hand "convinced me, that I was not mistaken in my Guess; for Lime and Soap mixed, every Surgeon knows, makes a gentle Caustic." Having thus let "the World know, *gratis,* what those pretended Stone-dissolving Medicines are" (59), the writer goes on to claim that they are "to most Constitutions, dangerous and pernicious Medicines." To support this claim, he states that he is personally acquainted with twenty-four of "this Doctress's Patients," of whom "only three now pretend to have received any real Benefit." Several of the others died, and many were made worse by the treatment. In addition, he reports on three in vitro experiments, in which stones taken from bladders were immersed in the urine of patients taking Stephens's medicines; in these experiments, the stones actually gained in weight.

It is clear that the author of the July letter knew some things about both Hartley and Stephens. His comment about "one *David Hartley*, whom you have presumed to dignify with the Title of *Doctor*" indicates that he knew that Hartley, although a practicing physician, had never been granted a degree in medicine.[26] He also had talked to Stephens about her medicine, correctly guessed the contents of her "powder," and claimed he knew a number of her dissatisfied patients. His claim that "I have now given you an Opportunity of letting the World know, *gratis,* what those pretended Stone-dissolving Medicines are" is at least in part true. Still, Hartley and his colleagues eventually won the fight; although the subscription campaign was able to raise only £1,356 by December 1738, in itself a considerable sum but far short of the £5,000, the whole amount was a few months later pledged by the government through a special act of Parliament.[27] Joanna Stephens disclosed her "secret" in June 1739 and received the reward the following March, after the trustees had verified to their satisfaction that the medicines worked as claimed.[28]

There are a number of factors that contributed to Hartley's success as an advocate for Stephens's treatment for the stone. The first concerns public perception of the qualities of character he and his opponents displayed. Writers of intemperate and abusive letters do not stand forth as persons of good character and credible testimony, especially when they hide behind the veil of anonymity. In the names they call others, such writers often describe themselves. The author of the first (May) letter warns Hartley "you might justly expect to be deemed only a Puff-scribbler in Favour of an old Woman's Quack-medicine," but by his own recommendation of the truly poisonous pills of Joshua Ward, the author reveals that he himself is the one guilty of such scribbling. The second (July) letter makes no mention of Ward and may or may not be by the same person; but its language echoes that of the first: "an old Woman's Medicines...a Quack Paper concerning them...those very Medicines...puffed by you." Hartley's response to the second letter, in the August 1738 issue of the *History of the Works of the Learned*, was to say, very calmly, "Surely it is needless to say, that I endeavour to be impartial in a Case where my own Life and Health are so nearly concerned. If the Author of that Letter will name himself, the twenty-four Persons whose Cases he mentions, or those who made the Experiments,

I shall be extremely obliged to him; but the World may demand the Authority upon which his Facts are founded" (1738d, 126). The writer's response, that "it will not be long before I acquaint [Hartley] with the Reasons for my treating him in the Letter to you last *July* as a Q—— &c. and then he'll have no Difficulty finding out who I am, if he pleases to endeavour it by Recollection" (Anon. 1738c, 222), was hardly adequate, for he still refused to let the public know who he was or to identify the disputed cases. The critic's credibility was further undermined by a letter from "M.S.T." in the August 1738 issue of the *History*. "I was surprised to find, in the Letter to you dated from *Pall-Mall* the 15th of Last Month," M.S.T. begins, "some very material Omissions of what I had desired to be inserted in it, particularly of Part of the Accounts of my Experiments made on human Calculi" (154). M.S.T. charges the anonymous critic with misrepresentation of his findings, for "Reasons best known to himself, which I fear he wont be able to prove to be very honourable or just ones." Although it is true that he found that stones show an increase in weight when immediately taken out of the vials of medicated urine, M.S.T. attributes this increase largely to "a Quantity of Urine remaining unexhaled in them." When dried, the stones weighed slightly more or, in one case, less, than they did before the experiment.[29]

We should note, however, that Hartley responded to his critic's complaint concerning his *Ten Cases* that he would be "deemed a Puff-scribbler" if he "continued to publish the Cases of Persons only, who received Benefit from those Medicines." For in 1739 Hartley published *A View of the Present Evidence for and against Mrs. Stephens's Medicines, as a Solvent for the Stone*—a work which he dedicated to "The President and Fellows of the Royal College of Physicians." The title acknowledges Hartley's desire to be evenhanded in his approach. The work itself, which runs to over two hundred pages, is an inventory of 155 cases of people who have undergone treatment by Stephens. It also contains an account of in vitro experiments Hartley conducted upon bladder calculi. Hartley could no longer be accused of special pleading.

A second factor concerns the impressive degree of support Hartley was able to marshal in aid of the cause. Of the fifteen trustees originally named to evaluate Stephens's medicine, the only physicians were Hartley and Peter Shaw. (Shaw was the editor and translator of philosophical and medical works by Bacon, Boerhaave, Boyle, Hoffman, and Stahl and the author of *A New Practice of Physic* [1728], a work "formed on the model of Dr. [Thomas] Sydenham"; in 1752 he became physician to George II.) The other trustees were, in addition to the Archbishop of Canterbury, "the Right Hon. the Earl of *Godolphin,* Lord Privy-Seal; his Grace the Duke of *Richmond* and *Lenox;* his Grace the Duke of *Montague;* the Right Hon. the Earl of *Pembroke;* the Right Hon. the Earl of *Scarborough;* the Right Hon. the Lord Viscount *Lonsdale;* the Right Rev. the Lord Bishop of *Gloucester;* the Right Rev. the Lord Bishop of *Oxford;* the Right Hon. the Lord *Baltimore;* the Right Hon. *Arthur Onslow,* Esq., Speaker of the House of Commons; the Right Hon. *Stephen Poyntz,* Esq.; and the Hon. *Thomas Townshend,* Esq." (Hartley 1738c, 444). The trustees appointed by Parliament included all of the above, with the exception of the Earl of Godolphin and Thomas Townshend; the committee was also expanded to include Philip Lord Hardwicke, Lord High Chancellor of Great Britain; the Earl of Wilmington, Lord President of the Council; Lionel Duke of Dorset, Steward of His Majesty's Household; Henry Hyde, Viscount Cornbury; Sir Robert Walpole, Chancellor of the Exchequer; Stephen Hales; five members of the Royal College of Physicians, including Thomas Pellet, president of the College; and three surgeons, including William Cheselden, the foremost surgeon in Britain and the author of a standard text on anatomy and also of a work on lithotomy. The committee of trustees was thus composed of leading members of the political, religious, and medical establishments. Stephens could not have asked for a more distinguished group of judges.

The composition of the trustees, however, also points to an inherent liability in the method of evaluation. The presence on the committee of such a constellation of men of high reputation and status suggests to me that, by the time Parliament passed the act, there was already an institutional momentum in favor of the effectiveness of Stephens's medicine; I suspect that all the people who agreed to serve as trustees expected that the clinical trials would prove successful—and thus that they would be spared the embarrassment of having to put a brake to the process. Although it was upon Joanna Stephens's medicines that the trustees were charged with passing judgment, a negative conclusion would also have been an implicit judgment upon the medical and scientific competence of those who urged Parliament to pass the act, upon the wisdom of Parliament in listening to them, and upon the credulity of the trustees themselves for lending their names to the proceedings. Four clinical trials were conducted by the physicians and surgeons on the committee, and these proved sufficiently successful to warrant a unanimous recommendation on 5 March 1740 that Parliament approve the award. Given the earlier extensive documentation of similar case studies, it is likely that the trustees would have been most dumbfounded if the trials had produced negative or equivocal results.

Besides the evidence of the previous case studies and testimonials and of the four clinical trials, the trustees may have had what seemed to them a further good reason to think that Stephens's medicines were effective. A third factor in the successful conclusion of the proceedings may have been that the discovery of a lithontriptic represented the practical application to medicine of the latest and most advanced chemical theory. By the time Hartley turned to the problem of the stone, the theoretical basis and some of the experimental groundwork for liberating the "active principles" in bladder calculi had already been set forth by Stephen Hales.

7. "That Thereby This Beautiful Frame of Things Might Be Maintained"

Stephen Hales (1677–1761) is remembered today as the father of plant physiology and for his work on the measurement of blood pressure. His *Vegetable Staticks* appeared in 1727; in 1733 it was combined with its companion, *Haemastaticks,* in his *Statical Essays* (3d ed., 1769). In his own time, he was also esteemed for his work on ventilation in ships and prisons, for his active participation in the Society for Promoting Christian Knowledge, and for his tireless campaign against gin drinking. According to his biographers Allan and Schofield, "in nearly all of Hales's technological achievements, [the] three criteria [of] importance, intent to apply scientific theory, and effectiveness combine . . . to justify his contemporary reputation as an eminently successful and public-spirited scientist" (1980, 91).

Hales's research into "statics" concerned a fundamental aspect of plant and animal physiology: the ways in which living beings maintain states of functional equilibrium. A thriving plant neither wilts nor splits apart from the pressure of the fluids within it; similarly, a healthy animal neither faints nor bursts a blood vessel. The flow of sap within a plant or of blood through the circulatory system of an animal enables the organism to sustain a dynamic yet static condition, even as variable environmental and physiological demands are placed upon it.

To investigate such states of functional equilibrium, Hales conducted numerous ingenious experiments upon plants and animals. In the experiments upon plants, for example, he sought to quantify rates of water uptake, respiration, and growth. Hales's experiments guided the manner and direction of further scientific work and hence represented the "concrete scientific achievement" that Kuhn (1970, 72) intended by the term *paradigm* to designate. As Allan and Schofield note, the *Vegetable Staticks* "introduced the study of experimental plant physiology, was essential in the foundation of pneumatic chemistry, and provided the eighteenth century with a prototype of experimental science" (1980, 30).

Hales's own understanding of what he was doing—the theoretical basis of his experiments—drew upon a theory of dynamic corpuscularity that he learned from Newton, the brothers John and James Keill, and John Freind (Allan and Schofield 1980, 14–19, 39–40). John Keill, in a 1708 paper in the *Philosophical Transactions,* and Freind, in his *Praelectiones Chemicae* (1709), had proposed a model, deriving from suggestions in Newton's *Principia* and particularly in query 22 of the 1706 Latin edition of the *Opticks,* according to which fundamental particles exhibiting nongravitational forces of attraction cohere into the complex aggregates or associations that constitute all observable physical objects. In this model, the microarchitecture of objects bears some resemblance to the solar system: not in the sense that some of the constituent corpuscles orbit others, but in the sense that even the minutest grains of sand are structures in which infinitesimal particles act upon each other across the void of space.

The force by which such infinitesimal particles act is, in the work of Keill and Friend, that of attraction. But Newton had originally suggested that forces both of attraction and repulsion are at work in matter, and Hales, according to Allan and Schofield, "was the first person, after Newton, to see the necessity of both attraction and repulsion in an active, organized universe" (1980, 41). In proposing the thesis that "air abounds in animal, vegetable, and mineral substances," Hales writes:

> If all the parts of matter were only endued with a strongly attracting power, whole nature would then immediately become one unactive cohering lump; wherefore it was absolutely necessary, in order to the actuating and enlivening this vast mass of attracting matter, that there should be every where intermixed with it a due proportion of strongly repelling elastick particles, which might enliven the whole mass, by the incessant action between them and the attracting particles: and since these elastick

particles are continually in great abundance reduced by the power of the strong attracters, from an elastick to a fixed state; it was therefore necessary, that these particles should be endued with a property of resuming their elastick state, whenever they were disengaged from that mass in which they were fixed, that thereby this beautiful frame of things might be maintained in a continual round of the production and dissolution of animal and vegetable bodies. (Hales 1769, 1:314–15; cf. Allan and Schofield 1980, 41)

A seemingly inert grain of matter, organic or inorganic, thus contains within itself a world in which the forces of attraction and repulsion are in a dynamic equilibrium; as long as it remains stable, the grain neither collapses into the subatomic equivalent of a neutron star nor explodes into a micronova. And yet such infinitesimal compactions and explosions occur continuously in nature; the materials within the bodies of living things are formed and dissolved and formed again—"that thereby this beautiful frame of things might be maintained."

In Hales's conception of matter, a "considerable a quantity of matter, as we find plentifully interspersed in animal, vegetable and mineral bodies, [is] endued with this double capacity, of changing *pro re nata* from a strongly attracting fixed state, to a permanently and vastly elastic state, and *vice versa*" (1769, 2:278). Some particles possess an attractive force, others a force of repulsion, and many others have the "double capacity" of being either in an attracting or repelling state. Drawing further on the work of Newton, and of Roger Cotes and William Whiston on pneumatics and hydrostatics, Hales came to identify "air" as consisting of the "strongly repelling elastick particles" that keeps the universe from collapsing (Allan and Schofield 1980, 16–17, 41–42). Moreover, in his view, "air" is itself chemically active; "may we not," he asks, "adopt this now fixed, now volatile Proteus, among the chymical properties, and that a very active one?" (1769, 1:317). Although as a gas or mixture of gases, particles of air are in an elastic and repelling state, they can undergo a state change into attractors that become fixed in solid substances. Air thus enters into the composition of most if not all physical objects; through chemical interactions, particles of air are rendered "unelastic" and are locked into the relatively stable structures that are complex physical objects. Hales confirms this model experimentally in a series of investigations described in the sixth chapter of *Vegetable Staticks*. In these investigations into the nature of "factitious airs," Hales sought to liberate the air in various substances either by "fermentation" or by "distillation"—that is, through chemical reactions or through heating. He tested a variety of organic and mineral substances and measured the volumes of "air" produced or absorbed during the experiments; he also probably produced a variety of different gases, "including carbon monoxide and dioxide, nitrous and nitric oxide, ammonia, sulphur dioxide, hydrogen and oxygen" (Allan and Schofield 1980, 42). Although he never sought to identify the various distinct elements or compounds he produced, he did suggest that "air" is not a uniform substance but a composite of various kinds of particles (1769, 1:314). Consequently, "it is reasonable to conclude, that our atmosphere is a *chaos*, consisting not only of elastick, but also of unelastick air-particles, which in great plenty float in it" (1769, 1:316).

Of all the various substances tested, Hales discovered that, when heated, "vegetable tartar" (i.e., acid potassium tartrate) and stones taken from the human bladder released the greatest volumes of air proportionate to their volumes; according to his calculations, "vegetable tartar, *viz.* that of wine, contained five hundred times its bulk in air, which was a great deal more than I found, bulk for bulk, in any fluid or solid parts of vegetables." He adds that this discovery "put me upon trying whether it was the same with animal tartar, *viz.* the *calculus humanus*" (1769, 2:186). Bladder stones also proved to produce large volumes of air: from a stone of "something less in bulk than 3/4 of a cubick inch ... arose ... very briskly, in distillation, a bulk equal to 645 times the bulk of the stone" (Hales 1769, 1:194; cf. Allan and Schofield 1980, 93). Although less air was liberated through chemical reactions, the experiments proved to Hales that both vegetable tartars and bladder stones were composed largely of air: "from the great quantities of air that are found in these tartars," he writes, "we see that unelastic air particles, which by their strongly attracting property are so instrumental in forming the nutritive matter of animals and vegetables are by the same attractive power apt sometimes to form anomalous concretions, as the stone, &c. in animals" (1769, 1:197–98). He also suggests that "this great quantity of strongly attracting unelastic air particles, which we find in the *calculus*, should rather encourage than discourage us, in searching for some proper dissolvent of the stone in the bladder, which ... is to be found well stored with active principles" (Hales 1769, 1:198; cf. Allan and Schofield 1980, 93). Because they are difficult to dissolve chemically, the attractive forces within organic "anomalous concretions" must be exceptionally strong in order to render "unelastic" the proportionally great quantity of naturally repelling air particles; nonetheless, in Hales's conception, could we view matter microscopically, we would see all nature trembling or vibrating with tension: "For as all the parts of this system are in a constant oscillatory motion, so all matter seems to be agitated by a repulsive and attractive force" (1769, 2: 276). Consequently, could the right agent be found, "the brisk action" of chemical interaction would "so shake and rouse these air particles, as to make them fly off into an elastick state, and thereby dissolve the union of the part of the stone" (Hales 1769, 2:193). Today, one treatment for vesicle calculi is ultrasound; an induced vibratory state can cause the stones to disintegrate. In his day, Hales was in effect envisioning a kind of chemical ultrasound. Bladder stones consisted of highly active principles, both attractive and repulsive, fixed into a static and inelastic configuration. Contact with the appropriate chemical agent could apply forces of attraction and repulsion to the internal components of the structure, push and pull at them, and set them vibrating with sufficient vigor to cause the structure to break apart. The air, returned to its elastic state, would fly off and the stone would fragment and disappear.

In 1739, the year Parliament promised Joanna Stephens the reward for disclosure of her medicines, the Royal Society awarded Hales its Copley Medal, in large part for his experiments "towards the discovery of medicines for dissolving the stone in the kidnies and bladder" (Allan and Schofield 1980, 93). It is noteworthy that although it was Hartley who appears to have done much of the legwork in relation to Stephens's medicines—writing of his own case, assembling the ten and then the 155 case studies, organizing the subscription committee of lords and bishops, possibly personally lobbying members of Parliament—the commendation of the Royal Society went to the person who developed the theory that explained how bladder stones could be dissolved and who also conducted the first experiments upon them.[30]

For Hartley and Hales, the publication of Joanna Stephens's "secret" was but one stage in the search for an effective lithontriptic. The recipe Stephens divulged was what people of the time called "empirical"—that is, it included ingredients, some derived from folk medicine, selected and combined through a process of trial and error. It consisted of a powder made from eggshells and the shells of garden snails, calcined and slaked; of pills made from Alicant soap mixed with more calcined snail shells and with "Wild Carrot Seeds, Burdock Seeds, Ashen Keys, Hips and Hawes, all burnt to a blackness"; and of a drink made from more Alicant soap, honey, chamomile, sweet fennel, parsley, and burdock leaves (see Viseltear 1968, 203). If the treatment worked, it worked for reasons that its inventor could not explain or even understand. And because the combination was empirical, it probably contained both effective and useless elements. The task of the scientist, then, was to analyze and improve upon the concoction an unlettered healer prepared in her kitchen. Laboratory research would rationalize the product of farmyard, hedgerow, and garden.

Hales, in collaboration with Hartley, set about locating the chemically active principle or principles in Stephens's medicines. Simultaneously in France, the apothecary and chemist Claude-Joseph Geoffroy (1685–1752) and Sauveur-François Morand (1697–1773), chief surgeon at the Invalides, also began their own investigations into the medicines.[31] Geoffroy and Morand were both members of the Académie Royale des Sciences, and they read their generally positive reports to the Académie in December 1739 and November 1740 respectively. Hales published his results in *An Account of some Experiments and Observations on Mrs. Stephens's Medicine for dissolving the Stone*. The English and French researchers were clearly working in tandem, for Hales refers to "the learned Chymist Mons. *Geoffroy,* in a Memoir which he sent to Dr. *Hartley*" ([1740], 12), and Morand in turn published a translation of Hales's *Account* in 1740; the date of publication suggests that Morand did the translation while performing his own experiments on Stephens's medicines. In 1741 Hartley's Latin account of his search for a solvent for the stone, *De Lithontriptico,* was published in Leiden and Basel. The results of the research were now available to physicians throughout Europe.[32]

The four researchers appear to have immediately disregarded the vegetable ingredients—all of which were well-known diuretics, and at any rate had been "burned to a blackness"—and to have focused instead on the slaked lime and soap, both individually and in combination. Hales found that stones quickly dissolved when boiled in soap-lye—in this instance, caustic potash or potassium hydroxide (KOH), produced by the reaction of an aqueous solution of potassium carbonate with slaked lime.[33] This discovery was, however, of no therapeutic use, for caustic potash is "of so exceeding corrosive and caustic a nature, that it will not only instantly destroy any animal substance which is thrown into it while boiling, but will also corrode copper, brass, and iron" (Hales [1740], 3). An effective remedy for the stone would have to be something that a person could tolerate taking; in addition, it would have to pass through the system in such a way as to change the chemical composition of the urine. Hence the importance of the soap. Soaps in general are alkaline salts of fatty acids and are usually produced by heating either sodium or potassium hydroxide with tallow or a vegetable oil. Alicant soap—the kind specified in the recipe—was manufactured by boiling caustic potash and olive oil.[34] In Hales's view, then, the soap was a tolerably ingestible vehicle for the delivery of the active ingredient, the alkaline salt. In addition, Hales was confident that the alkaline salt did indeed pass into the urine:

> It is well known that the Urine of those who take the Medicines is strongly impregnated, with the alcaline Salt of Soap-lees, as is manifest by its fermenting with acid Spirits, which the Urine of other Persons will not do in any Degree; as also from the Effect, which Dr. *Hartley's* medicated Urine had in dissolving several *Calculus's*. Mons. *Geoffroy*, in the Memoir above mentioned, in analysing chymically the Urine of those who took the Medicines, found in it also a considerable quantity of fix'd Salt, such as is in Soap-lees; on which having poured some Oil of Vitriol, the same kind of neutral Salt, called *Glauber's* Salt, was formed, as when poured on Soap-lees. A plain proof that the alcaline lixivious Salt of the Soap-lees, passes in plenty through the Blood into the Urine of those who take the Medicines for some Time. (Hales [1740], 24–25)[35]

In addition, Hales experimented with calcined eggshells and other sources of lime; he found that lime was also effective in dissolving bladder stones ([1740], 28–29). Thus were the two effective ingredients identified. In his contribution to the discussion, the Quaker physician John Rutty commented that Stephens's "Medicine, as communicated to the Publick, is a Composition operose and troublesome, several Parts of it being of little or no Use, and others plainly calculated to disguise the rest. The Ingredients of which it consists have lately been examined by the ingenious Dr. *Hales* and Dr. *Hartley*, who have with much Judgment rejected the superfluous Parts, and reduced this pompous Medicine to a slacken'd Powder of calcin'd Egg-shells, and a Solution of Soap" (Rutty 1742, ii–iii).[36] To us, using lime and soft soap to treat uroliths may appear another instance of the foolishness that preceded modern medicine. But this would not have been the experimenters' view. To them,

Stephens's recipe, once rationalized, brought together "the two most powerful active agents in the universe: the attraction of cohesion [from the alkaline salt] and the repulsive elasticity of air released in fermenting lime" (Allan and Schofield 1980, 97–98). To Hartley, Hales, and their colleagues, the discovery of a lithontriptic came about through the alliance of chemical theory and experimental medicine: according to the theory, the medication should work; according to the clinical histories, the medicine did work as the theory predicted.[37]

Hartley believed in the effectiveness of the medicine throughout his life, despite the fact that it never left him free of the stone. In the October 1752 issue of the *Gentleman's Magazine*, he published his own recipe for the production of a "lithontriptic mass and electuary," in which Alicant soap and oyster-shell lime are boiled together, exposed to air, and then formed into pills or into an "electuary" or paste.[38] Hartley writes that "the generation of gravel and gravel-stones may be entirely prevented by this medicine: It is likewise of great service in disorders of the stomach and bowels arising from, or attended with acidities, there, and gouty habits" (1752, 465). Hartley's publication of his recipe follows shortly after an important endorsement of the soap and lime treatment by Horace Walpole. In two letters read to the Royal Society on 24 January 1750 and 28 May 1752 and published in the *Philosophical Transactions*, Walpole (1751, 1752) reported that a course of treatment involving Alicant soap and lime had succeeded in curing him of the stone. His testimony would have been especially important because his father, Sir Robert Walpole, had died of an obstruction of the bladder in March 1745, while being treated for the stone by James Jurin, who was administering his own version of the soap and lime medication. Walpole's death had become the occasion of a pamphlet war initiated by John Ranby, Principal Sergeant-Surgeon to George II, against Jurin and Sir Edward Hulse, First Physician to George II, the physicians who were called in when Walpole had refused the option of lithotomy (see Viseltear 1967). Horace Walpole writes that when he first considered beginning the treatment himself, "my relations, touch'd with the fatal effects, which Dr. Jurin's *lixivium* had had upon the late lord Orford, would not suffer me to follow my own inclinations" (1751, 45). That he went against their advice, persisted in the treatment, and was apparently cured would have been an especially weighty testimonial to the effectiveness of the treatment.

8. "The Manifold Imperfections of My Best Desires"

To an acquaintance aware of only its outward aspect, Hartley's life would by 1741 appear to be one of progressive success: in the previous five or six years he had gone from being an unknown country physician in straitened circumstances to being an important figure in London, a name known in medical and scientific circles not only in England but throughout Europe. As a physician, he attended upon the wealthy and powerful, including the Duke of Newcastle; he went to Court and could at least plan to recommend Byrom to George II; he was now known for his championing of Stephens's lime and soap remedy and as the author of books on the stone. He was also known to be active on behalf of Byrom's shorthand and Saunderson's book on algebra, and as a member of philanthropic societies such as the Society for the Encouragement of Learning and the Society for the Promotion of Christian Knowledge (which he joined, on Hales's recommendation, in January 1741).[39] Moreover, the acquaintance might have heard of writing projects of a philosophical, ethical, or religious nature: Hartley's manuscript "on benevolence" had been read by Byrom in 1735; he had mentioned his two treatises on the "progress of happiness" to Lister in late 1736. Some of his friends would also be aware of an essential element in his thinking: that the time was soon approaching for the public proclamation of universal salvation. In addition, the acquaintance might surmise that a key factor in Hartley's success was his marriage; were it not for his wife Elizabeth's fortune and family name, Hartley might not have had as easy entry to the houses of the great or as much time to devote to the selfless exercise of benevolence.

The acquaintance would thus observe a practitioner of benevolence and the vegetable diet keeping to the sunny side of the street. But what that observer probably would not have sensed were the shadows, and indeed the darkness, that accompanied him. Neither would we, were it not for the collection of Hartley's prayers and meditations, which were first published in 1810, more than fifty years after his death. The entries date mainly from the 1730s, with the earliest dated Spring 1733. Several of these, cited at the beginning of this chapter, record Hartley's struggle with and experience of slavery to "the gross pleasures of sense"—pleasures that so controlled him that he found himself "utterly unable to regulate" his conduct. Overall, Hartley's prayers and meditations offer a different perspective on the events recounted thus far in this chapter.

Parliament passed the act that promised Joanna Stephens her reward on 14 June 1739. Hartley had triumphed, both personally and in terms of bringing about the coincidence of public and private happiness. Yet on 17 June he composed a prayer, which begins:

> O GOD, whose unerring Providence conducts all things, both in heaven and earth, I humbly bless and praise thy name for the success which Thou hast given to my late endeavours. I humbly implore thy forgiveness for the manifold imperfections of my best desires and designs; for the want of due modesty, meekness, and charity; and for the actual selfishness and self-will, the impatience of contradiction, and fondness for applause, which I am abundantly conscious of in this matter. I have not had the respect and forbearance towards others, which both reason and religion require; not even when I have been sensible of this obligation; but have suffered myself to run into hastiness and bitterness; to give unfavourable constructions and representations; and, in many instances, of thought, word, and deed, to be guided by jealousy, pride, and passion. (1810, 48)

Hartley had conducted an effective political campaign; he had marshalled support for his cause, had bested his critics, and had prevailed in having Parliament promise the £5,000 Stephens required for her secret. But at the moment of success he was most conscious of his own failings, of his "impatience of contradiction, and fondness for applause." To the extent that his effort on behalf of Stephens became a public contest of wills, a competition in which reputations could be won or lost, it seems that to some degree his purpose shifted, so that winning the contest became the end in itself. With that shift, Hartley is aware, the person is diminished; respect and forbearance evaporate, and unfavorable constructions and representations of the actions and arguments of others become weapons of debate. Indeed, fractious debate crowds out fair discussion; at its worst, giving the appearance of a fair weighing of the evidence for and against the issue itself becomes a tactic, another arrow in the quiver. As Lister noted, "your unpolite adversary shewed his best sense in concealing his name, and you took the best method for your own praise and giving satisfaction to the Public by concealing your anger, if you were angry" (*L* 10, 6 November 1738; cf. *T* 242).

Hartley was also troubled by his "fondness for applause." He believed that active benevolence was the key to private happiness, and prayed in the spring of 1733: "Almighty Parent and Governor of the world, Thou hast placed me in the various relations of this life, that I, as a part, may, in my proper station, contribute to the beauty, order, and good of the whole. Let me ever pursue this great end with unfeigned and unwearied zeal, courage, and constancy; let me earnestly seek all occasions of producing happiness, and avoid all of producing misery" (1810, 8). A truly benevolent person would be happy when he did contribute to the "beauty, order, and good of the whole," regardless of whether or not anyone applauded him for his contribution; he would be content with not letting the right hand know what the left was doing, as long as the giving had its intended effect. And yet Hartley was aware of his longing for a prominent place among the worshippers in the temple; it troubled him that his happiness derived not so much from *being* benevolent as from *being thought* benevolent by others:

> As to my desires of the riches and honours of this world, I sometimes flatter myself that I am in this respect arrived at some degree of perfection: but alas! I then forget what are my daily and hourly thoughts and pursuits. For I am still anxious and fearful; solicitous to place myself in the most advantageous light; and desirous to *appear* skilful and compassionate, rather than to *be* so. I am eager after the opinion of mankind; and fond of the glory of discovering, or executing, what may be of service to them: but not sincerely and devoutly earnest with Thee, that thy kingdom may come. Even my prayers and religious meditations are infected with some secret folly of this kind. (1810, 39)

Hartley wrote this on 18 March 1737; he would start taking Stephens's medicines in May, and would begin his diary of the effects of treatment in July. It is possible that a reader might think that perhaps Hartley was here being too hard on himself. Wanting to be esteemed skilful and compassionate, such a reader could suggest, is a normal and inevitable consequence of being a social being; we want others to think well of us, to respect us for our good qualities and actions—and it is a good thing that we do, for such desire makes us biddable. The issue is one of proportion; some degree of concern with others' perceptions of oneself is normal, part of what it is to live a life; but an exclusive concern with *being thought*, at the expense of being, is a common element in the pain of being fourteen years old; in an adult it represents a disordering of priorities, a sign of falseness, a dishonesty in which the persona overwhelms the person. We cannot measure the proportionality of Hartley's wanting "to *appear* skilful and compassionate" and of his desire "to *be* so," and we thus cannot determine the degrees to which this prayer is symptomatic of overscrupulous self-reproach or is an accurate assessment of a flaw of character. Still, for Hartley it was an issue; concern with how others apprised him was a source of anxiety and fear; and, as with overindulgence in the pleasures of sense, his solicitousness to present himself to the best advantage was something he struggled to overcome.

9. "The Near Approaches of Death"

What was *not* a matter of scrupulosity or solicitousness were Hartley's fears concerning his own and his wife's health. In the meditation written on 18 March he acknowledges, "I am terrified above measure at the prospect of pain and death" (1810, 37). He had recently experienced the first symptoms of the stone, and he was in a little over six weeks to begin taking Stephens's medicines. But it is possible that his greatest terror concerned the prospect of the death of his wife. In March 1736, when Byrom first visited their home, the Hartleys had been married for not quite six months; Elizabeth Hartley was about five months pregnant. She gave birth to her daughter, Mary, in July, and there is evidence that giving birth nearly killed her. On 20 July 1736 Hartley wrote a prayer of thanksgiving, thanking God for the deliverance of his wife. It says in part: "Accept, therefore, O merciful Father, of my most humble and hearty acknowledgments for the life of the dear partner of all my hopes and happiness. It is thy command that we should fly to Thee in every desire and distress. This I did, and thou sawest the bitterness and anguish of my soul, and had mercy upon me" (1810, 29).

Exactly five years earlier, in July 1731, Alice Rowley, Hartley's first wife, died giving birth to their son. They had married a little more than a year earlier, on 21 May 1730, in her home town of Saffron Walden. Alice was buried on 22 July 1731 at St. Mary's church in Bury St. Edmunds. Their child, David, was baptized privately a day later.[40] According to Mary Hartley, writing in 1796, Hartley was "extremely in love" with Alice and "extremely afflicted" by her death; he "remained attached to her memory all his life" (Warner 1817, 106). In an intricate and intense Latin poem that he composed but did not use for her epitaph, Hartley writes: "Heu vidi hisce oculis tristi te cedere fato, / Audivi gemitus quos moritura dabas. [But alas! with these eyes I saw you yield to your sad fate, / And I heard the sighs you were giving when you were about to die.]"[41] Hartley transcribed the epitaph in a letter of 16 March 1743 to John Lister. After writing the lines, he adds that "it has cost me some tears to write them over for you." Although never engraved on a monument, the epitaph still mattered to him twelve years after Alice's death; in his next letter to Lister, Hartley includes a revised beginning to the poem (*L* 32; 13 April 1743).

It is not difficult to appreciate the terror Hartley felt in March 1736, in anticipation of Elizabeth's coming to term, and the anguish that he felt in those hours or days when it seemed that she too might not survive childbirth. Despite his profession as a physician, despite his faith in the benevolence of God, Hartley had lost one wife after little over a year of marriage. Now it was possible that he would lose another—on the fifth anniversary of the loss of the first. Both Alice Rowley and Elizabeth Packer would then have shared the fate of his own mother, Evereld Wadsworth, who had died three months after she had given birth to him. As he had done, both his son and daughter would grow up never knowing the mothers who bore them.

Elizabeth Hartley did not die in 1736, but she did suffer further near encounters with death. She was severely ill during June, July, and August 1738—the months when the public could read all about the abuse of her husband and the controversy over Stephens's medicines in the *History of the Works of the Learned*. Byrom noted on 22 June 1738 that "Mrs. Hartley has been very ill, is better, but very weakly" (2.1.208), and on 24 July Hartley, while treating the Duke of Newcastle for what appears to have been a stroke, wrote to the Duchess: "My wife is just recovered of a very dangerous illness at Kensington, but I hear she grows better every day, & so I propose staying here till I have satisfied both your Graces fears and my own."[42] A prayer of 11 September 1738 concerns his wife's health and his own conflicted feelings of gratitude and continued anxiety: "Thou hast already afforded me instances of thy compassion, in the repeated deliverance of my wife from the near approaches of death, as call for the warmest returns of gratitude and obedience; but alas! I find myself unable to persevere in the good attempts which I sometimes make; and the uncertain condition of her health compels me once more to call myself to account, and to apply to Thee, my only friend and protector" (1810, 46). Although we do not know the cause of the repeated "near approaches of death," it is clear that Elizabeth's condition persisted, for the Hartleys eventually moved out of London and settled in Bath. Writing to Lister from Bath on 26 May 1742, Hartley states that "I am come with my family to settle on account of the many illnesses, and particularly some affecting the lungs, which my wife has had in town. We have got a very pleasant house in the new Square, where we breathe good country air, and I hope it will please God to give my wife a confirmed state of health" (*L* 27; cf. *T* 262).

Even in the good country air of Bath, it appears that Elizabeth did not escape at least one other life-threatening illness. The Hartley family papers contain an undated letter from Elizabeth Hartley to her children; the letter is a last request, written "whilst I have any being," and in it Elizabeth charges her children Mary and Winchcombe to "Love, Honour, and obey your Father, to comfort and support him to the utmost of your Power in every Thing," and, when they come of age, "to make a handsome Provision" for him; the children are instructed to "consider also with brotherly Affection" their half-brother David, to "let him never want such Assistance or addition to his fortune as will suit the Relation he bears to you," and also to provide for their "poor Relations in Yorkshire"—that is, their uncles, aunts, and cousins on their father's side.[43]

Elizabeth's letter was probably written no earlier than the end of 1746. We noted, earlier in this chapter, Mary Hartley's comment that Elizabeth's brothers "treated [her husband] always with *hauteur.*" She adds further:

> My uncles were men of the world, and men of pleasure. They knew not my father's value; and were even offended with him for the true kindness he shewed them, in giving them good advice. They drank hard, ... that compelled him, both as a physician and a moralist, to endeavour to dissuade them from. At such interference they would sometimes be angry; but when they were in their best humour with him, they would say, "You foolish dog, can'st you see, that the sooner we kill ourselves, the better it will be for you and your family." (Warner 1817, 108)

The brothers succeeded in their aim; Winchcombe Howard Packer died on 21 August 1746, at age forty-four; his younger brother Henry John Packer followed him two months later (two other brothers had died some years earlier). Both were unmarried, and all of the Packer and

Winchcombe estates passed in trust to Elizabeth's six-year-old son, Winchcombe Henry Hartley. Mary notes that although her mother "inherited the *settled* estate," her brothers "left from her the unsettled part, and gave it to my brother W.H. over her husband. This was a disrespect to my mother, which I think she must have felt" (Warner 1817, 108).[44] Hence Elizabeth's instructions to her children: because of her brothers' "disrespect" for her, she could not make her own provision for her husband and stepson, and instead had to instruct her children to do so. Still, it was the children of David Hartley and Elizabeth Packer—of the marriage the Packer brothers tried to prevent—who inherited the family's wealth.

Finally, Hartley's core belief in the "fundamental doctrine" of universal salvation was more than just a theory, a way of interpreting Scripture that amounted to a stroll down the sunny side of a theological and metaphysical street. It also represented an emergence out of shadow. In a letter of 2 March 1735 to his elder sister Elizabeth Booth, written from Bury St. Edmunds prior to his second marriage, Hartley stated:

> I have lately gained the knowledge of some things in physic, which have been of great use to me; but the chief of my studies are upon religious subjects, and especially upon the true meaning of the Bible. I cannot express to you what inward satisfaction these contemplations afford me. You remember how much I was overcome by superstitious fears, when I was very young. I thank GOD, that He has at last brought me to a lively sense of his infinite goodness and mercy to all his creatures; and that I see it both in all his works, and in every page of his word. This has made me much more indifferent to the world than ever, at the same time that I enjoy it more; has taught me to love every man, and to rejoice in the happiness which our Heavenly Father intends for *all* his children; and has quite dispersed all the gloomy and melancholy thoughts which arose from the apprehension of eternal misery for myself or my friends. (Warner 1817, 100–1)[45]

The little boy swinging on the gate pondered the nature of his own mind; he was also subject to "superstitious fears"—beset by the anxiety that, should they die, he and his family and friends would burn in hell forever. I do not know, specifically, who his guides were in the "chief of [his] studies," or in what works upon religious subjects he discovered "the true meaning of the Bible"—the promise of "the happiness which our Heavenly Father intends for *all* his children." The source of the transforming idea could have been Newton and his circle. Newton, Locke, Samuel Clarke, and William Whiston all disbelieved in eternal punishment; the quiet convictions of the first three presumably would have been known to careful inquirers at Cambridge, and Whiston had in print affirmed his belief that αιωνιος does not signify eternity. Hartley's source of inspiration could also have been Peter Sterry and Jeremiah White, both religious mystics, Cambridge Platonists, and chaplains to Cromwell (Walker 1964, 104–21). And there is also a hint that Hartley's liberation from superstition had its origin in a sector of religious thought that may appear to us much stranger than the enlightened and politely rational world of Cambridge Arians and Platonists. In a journal entry for 25 May 1736—two months after they met at Richard's—Byrom notes that Hartley "sat with me in Abington's coffeehouse till three o'clock talking about the time approaching for the preaching of the everlasting gospel" (*B* 2.1.50). The phrase is from Revelation 14:6, the text of which appears on the title page of White's *Restoration of all Things* ([1712] 1779): "And I saw another Angel flie in the midst of Heaven, having the Everlasting Gospel to Preach unto them that dwell on the Earth, and unto every Nation, and Kindred, and Tongue, and People." It was apparently put there by the volume's editor, Richard Roach (Walker 1964, 121). Roach (1662–1730) was the leader of the Philadelphian Society for the Advancement of Piety and Divine Philosophy, a group that drew its inspiration from the visions and divine communications of Jane Lead (1623–1704). Central to Lead's prophecies was the new and final revelation of the everlasting gospel: that "the whole lapsed Creation" would be restored to its original harmony with God (Thune 1948, 76). Whatever the source, the effect upon Hartley was one of release from the grey oppression of "gloomy and melancholy thoughts."

If we find such fears remote and even mildly distasteful, let us recall at least how chilling they once were. They turned men's blood to ice. Bunyan had for years staggered under the conviction he was among the damned. Besides Hartley's campaign on behalf on Joanna Stephens's medicines, 1738 also was the year of John Wesley's reception of the "blessed assurance" that he was saved; in Byrom's journal entry for 14 June 1739, in which he notes that the bill favoring Stephens has passed and that he, Hartley, Hales, and Roberts are "putting her account in writing," Byrom also notes that Wesley's fellow Methodist George

Whitefield, famous for preaching to thousands in the fields, "is the chief topic of private conversation" (*B* 2.1.245). And let us also recall William Cowper, whose conviction that he was destined for hell became the expression of a lasting sickness that wasted his mind; it was in Richard's coffeehouse, where Hartley reintroduced himself to Byrom, in "about 1763, that Cowper first exhibited symptoms of mental derangement" (Lillywhite 1963, 192). Although this fear of Hartley's may seem remote to us, it is important to remember that, in his age, the fear did not chill him alone.

10. "Meditating upon the Nature of his Own Mind"

If this were all that there is to the story, this book would not exist. Hartley would be a minor figure in the history of medicine, the protagonist in a controversy over a supposed cure for the stone. A few might know him as one representative of a certain temper of mind. In a letter of 29 August 1738, at the height of the controversy and the day after he had submitted to being "searched" for the fourth time for the stone, Hartley wrote to Lister that, because of his illness, "I cannot bear to read so much as I have done sometimes, and what I do apply to is chiefly Physick and Divinity" (*L* 7; cf. *T* 239). A historian who looked into Hartley's reading and activities would recognize them to be representative of the liaison of Newtonian science, liberal religion, and practical benevolence that was one characteristic of the first half of the eighteenth century.

Still, this book is here before you. It is here because Hartley accomplished something that was more than simply typical or representative of his age. We have his daughter's testimony that "when he was so little as to be swinging backwards and forwards upon a gate... he was meditating upon the nature of his own mind; wishing to find out how man was made; to what purpose, and for what future end." Hartley continued to swing on that gate; his achievement was to extend and apply his studies in physick and divinity to the matter of his childhood meditations. We noted above that Byrom read his "paper on benevolence" in 1735, and that Hartley mentioned having written at this time two treatises on "the progress of happiness" in a letter to Lister. In November 1738 he sent Lister a package containing what may have been a more developed version of these two, but now placed within a larger framework: "My first design," he writes, "was to have confined myself to the plan of the 2 Papers I send you: since I have enlarged my design and propose to call it 'An Introduction to the History of Man in Four Parts,' considering him in his corporeal, mental, moral, and religious capacities."[46] This history eventually became the *Observations on Man*.[47] In this, Hartley's great work, the elements of physics, chemistry, mathematics, medicine, religion, and philosophy combine to form a psychology—a new compound that illuminates our physical frame, our moral duty, and our religious expectations.

As we shall see in the coming chapters, Hartley's psychology contains accounts of: the "doctrine of vibrations," whereby the forces of attraction and repulsion enable a sensation of touch to pass from fingertip to brain; the chemistry of perception according to "the doctrine of association," as sensations of touch, hearing, sight, etc. combine to generate ideas; the algebra of language, with its potential for becoming ever more "philosophical"; the transformations of emotion, whereby our painful experiences and memories, like the particles of air, change from a repellant to an attractive state when fixed within strongly coherent compounds of experience; the development of the self, as the person struggles to place a concern with being above the satisfactions and anxieties of being thought; and the progress of happiness, whereby we may all be confident that—though it may take an αιων for some—"our Natures are so formed & so adjusted to the System of things that we must from the Law of Association at last become benevolent, & consequently that all must some time or other be happy."

3

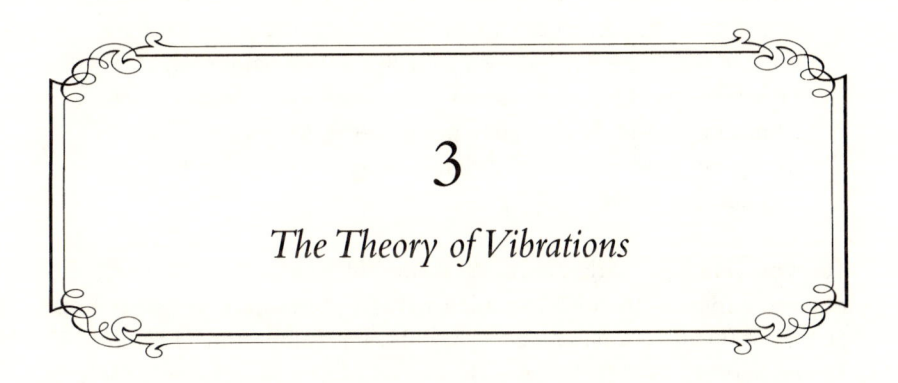

The Theory of Vibrations

> Theological inquiries excepted, there is no employment wherein Mankind is so much and so generally concern'd, as 'tis in the study of Natural Philosophy. And those great transactions which make such a noise in the World, and establish Monarchies or ruin Empires, reach not so many Persons with their Influence as do the Theories of Physiology.
>
> —Robert Boyle (1663, 2:5)[1]

At the start of his *Observations on Man,* Hartley defines his project in reference to one of Sir Isaac Newton's speculative hypotheses concerning the fundamental properties of matter:

> Sir Isaac Newton supposes, that a very subtle and elastic fluid, which he calls *aether,* for the sake of treating upon it commodiously under an appropriated name, is diffused through the pores of gross bodies, as well as through the open spaces that are void of gross matter. He supposes likewise, that it is rarer in the pores of bodies than in open spaces, and even rarer in small pores and dense bodies, than in large pores and rare

bodies; and also that its density increases in receding from gross matter; ... To the action of this aether he ascribes the attractions of gravitation and cohesion, the attractions and repulsions of electrical bodies, the mutual influences of bodies and light upon each other, the effects and communication of heat, and the performance of animal sensation and motion. My business in these observations is only with the last; but the reader will do well to consult what Sir Isaac Newton has himself advanced concerning the existence of this aether, and the properties and powers which he has ascribed to it in the last paragraph of his Principia, the Questions annexed to his Optics, and a Letter from him to Mr. Boyle, lately published in Mr. Boyle's Life. As to myself, I am not satisfied that I understand him perfectly on this subject. (*OM* 1.1.1.5)[2]

To those familiar with Newton's theory of matter from reading the popular explanations of Newtonian natural philosophy by James Keill (1720), Willem 'sGravesande (1726), Henry Pemberton (1728), J. T. Desaguliers (1734–44), Voltaire (1738), and Colin Maclaurin (1748), or from their own study of the Queries in the third book of Newton's *Opticks* ([1717] 1730), Hartley's summary of Newton's proposal would have been comfortably familiar—and, perhaps, equally comfortably confusing. It would have situated Hartley within what I. Bernard Cohen (1956) has termed "speculative Newtonian experimental science"— within, that is, the paradigm, or penumbra, or swirling currents, of the Newtonian science of his day.[3] At the end of Query 31, and thus at the end of the *Opticks,* Newton had written: "In this third Book I have only begun the Analysis of what remains to be discovered about Light and its Effects upon the Frame of Nature, hinting several things about it, and leaving the Hints to be examin'd and improv'd by the farther Experiments and Observations. . . . And if natural Philosophy in all its Parts, by pursuing this Method, shall at length be perfected, the Bounds of Moral Philosophy will also be enlarged." Hartley's project receives its commission from Newton's statement. His task is, first, to conduct, gather, and record the experiments and observations that will elaborate Newton's "hints" concerning the effects of light upon "the frame of nature"; and second, thereby to enlarge the bounds of moral philosophy through natural philosophy's perfection. Like Stephen Hales, working on plant and animal physiology and on "factitious airs," or Benjamin

Franklin, on electricity, Hartley would be understood by his colleagues in the sciences to be a Joshua to Newton's Moses.

Of the scouts Moses sent out to reconnoitre the land, some returned with clusters of grapes, others with combs of honey. Similarly, Hartley set himself a specific task in natural philosophy: his "business in these observations," Hartley writes, begins with the means by which "the performance of animal sensation and motion" involves "the action of this aether." In taking on this task, Hartley selected one of the projects of exploration that Newton's speculations on the fundamental properties of matter suggested. The result—Hartley's "doctrine of vibrations," as applied to the human person—represents his attempt to construct a modern and comprehensive neurophysiology on the basis of Newtonian physics; it is also the physiological basis for Hartley's attendant psychological theory.[4]

As such, Hartley's observations begin at that place at which Newton's *Opticks* ([1717] 1730) leaves off. This was a common starting point, and the model of matter it assumes was familiar, though not necessarily comprehensible, to scientists in the eighteenth century; Hartley was hardly the only person who had reason to doubt whether he understood Newton perfectly. Still, neither the model itself nor the language in which it is expressed are common elements of discourse today. A "subtle and elastic fluid" called the "aether," which fills space and diffuses itself through the "pores of bodies," to the "action" of which "attractions" and "repulsions" of various kinds, including gravitation, "cohesion," electricity, heat, "the mutual influences of bodies and light," and "the performance of animal sensation and motion," are "ascribed"—what is Hartley talking about? To understand what Hartley is saying, we need to begin with a review of the model of matter that emerges out of Newton's hints, specifically, in the *Opticks*.

1. "A Certain Most Subtle Spirit"

In the seventeenth century, a natural philosophy commonly described as "mechanistic" and "corpuscular" triumphed over older Aristotelian and Scholastic theories of matter. For a quick (and oversimplified) sense of Aristotle's theory, imagine a lump of dough and a collection of cookie cutters; the dough is not any "thing" until cut into shape, and the cookie cutters are idle until they are put to use cutting dough. The dough has the potential to be things, but it needs to be shaped in order to be particular things. A cookie cutter is a "species," an "incorporeal substance"; when dough is cut using a cutter, the resulting object has a "substantial form." The grains of wheat from which real dough is made have one such substantial form, impressed upon a more fundamental "dough." Of course, all objects pressed out from the same cutter are qualitatively alike and belong to the same species. Moreover, in this model, the key to understanding the interactions of things in the world is not the matter of which they are composed but the forms by which they are composed. Each species is qualitatively distinct, but all species are related to each other through their similarities and differences. Aristotelians of the ancient world and then of the Middle Ages—the schoolmen—elaborated upon this model by suggesting that resemblances between species could be symbolic of hidden mutual influences—relationships of sympathy and antipathy, for example—by which objects act upon each other. Physicians took the tripartite lobed leaves of the plants known as *Hepatica* to be an indication of the plants' efficacy in treating diseases of the liver; although the "power" or quality in *Hepatica* for healing the liver was itself "occult" in the sense of being occluded from sight, hidden, concealed, the liver-shaped leaves were nonetheless a symbol of its presence. Mechanists would have none of this. Hobbes, for example, writing in *De corpore* (1655), declared the entire conceptual system of the schoolmen to be vacuous: "For as for those that say that anything may be moved or produced *by itself*, by *species*, by *its own power*, by *substantial forms*, by *incorporeal substances*, by *instinct*, by *antiperistasis*, by *antipathy, sympathy, occult quality*, and other empty words of schoolmen, their saying so is to no purpose" (quoted in Westfall 1971, 110). What was to the purpose, rather, was a philosophy of nature that held out the promise of replacing qualitative descriptions with quantitative ones. Where the older model described a cosmos of symbols, the new model sought to describe the world solely in terms of "matter and motion"—that is, as a system in which all observable change derives from measurable transfers of motion between units of matter. In their passion for simplification, for ridding the cathedral of nature of symbolic elements and the "occult" powers they supposedly reveal, the mechanistic philosophers could be likened to the Protestant reformers of the sixteenth century, who stripped their altars of the seductive and dangerous images that the superstitious foolishly thought could, through some secret sympathy, act on their behalf, to protect and cure.

But also like the reformers, unanimity concerning what they opposed did not forestall dissension over the positive content of doctrine. Mechanism's advocates debated the meaning of their basic articles of faith, matter and motion. What was matter? And how did it move? And what did it mean to say that the two principles described a mechanism? Among forward-looking philosophers, only some accepted the answers Descartes gave in his *Principles of Philosophy* (1644). In Descartes's model, swirling whirlpools of matter fill the cosmic ocean. Space is a function of the matter that fills it; matter, defined primarily in terms of extension, has no limit to its divisibility, so that it may form into particles ranging in size from the sun and stars to the infinitely small; the total quantity of motion is constant; all changes in an object's motion are caused by the physical impacts of other objects; and the total system of motion is ultimately caused and conserved by God.

The philosophy of nature Hartley inherited from Newton differed from the Cartesian on all these points. Newtonian space is absolute, independent of matter; atoms represent a limit of divisibility; the universe would slow down—be subject to entropy—if it were a closed system; and changes in particles' positions are attributable to forces other than contact mechanism.

Two features of the Newtonian model are particularly relevant to the physiological theory Hartley developed in his *Observations*. The first concerns the atomic structure of matter, the second the forces that cause motion. First, matter possesses a complex architecture. The ultimate building blocks of this architecture are atoms—impenetrable, indivisible particles. But atoms cohere into larger units (which Hartley, possibly following the Dutch physician Hermann Boerhaave, terms "molecules" [OM 1.1.2.9]), and these in turn form into still larger aggregates and aggregates of aggregates (which Hartley calls "the molecules of the molecules").

In Newton's model, although the ultimate atomic particles are solid, the "molecular" structures formed from them are not. What appear to us as solid bodies are made up of molecules that are, in their internal structure, highly "porous," that is, filled with empty space. (It is this space that Hartley refers to as the "pores of bodies" in the quotation above.) Newton had suggested in the *Opticks* that, given his thesis that light does not reflect off the surfaces of hard bodies, "we may understand that Bodies are much more rare and porous than is commonly believed" (1730, 242). To help explain this porosity and rarity, he had proposed in Query 31 a model that pictured matter as a fractal lattice, in which atoms cohere into larger entities that in turn crystallize into still larger entities, with the process continuing through successive generations before forming particles of the size involved in chemical operations.[5] Henry Pemberton suggests that, to picture this, we imagine cubic salt crystals arranged so that they are joined at their corners. A sufficient quantity of crystals thus arranged would in turn form a larger cubic crystal, nearly half of which is empty space. Now imagine building a second generation of crystals out of the first, a third out of the second, and so on. The more generations one imagines, the less atomic matter there is in the whole; consequently, the porosity and rarity of matter means that the total amount of actual matter in the entire universe may be very small. Pemberton writes that this model "shews that this whole globe of earth, nay all the known bodies in the universe together, may be compounded of no greater portion of solid matter, than might be reduced into a globe of one inch only in diameter, or even less" (1728, 291). And Joseph Priestley, writing in 1777, states that "for any thing we know to the contrary, all the solid matter in the solar system might be contained in a nut-shell, there is so great a proportion of *void space* within the substance of the most solid bodies" (1777a, 17).[6]

Second, particles of matter are not purely inert lumps that undergo changes of motion only when struck by other particles. Rather, as Priestley notes, "the principles of the Newtonian philosophy were no sooner known, than it was seen how few, in comparison, of the phenomena of nature, were owing to *solid matter*, and how much to *powers*, which were only supposed to accompany and surround the solid parts of matter" (1777a, 17). In respect to his philosophy of nature, the most significant proposal Newton makes in the *Opticks* is that particles exert attractive and repulsive forces upon each other. Again in Query 31 he writes: "Have not the small Particles of Bodies certain Powers, Virtues, or Forces, by which they act at a distance, not only upon the Rays of Light for reflecting, refracting, and inflecting them, but also upon one another for producing a great Part of the Phaenomena of Nature? For it is well known, that Bodies act one upon another by the Attractions of Gravity, Magnetism, and Electricity; and these instances shew the Tenor and Course of Nature, and make it not improbable that there may be more attractive Powers than these" (1730, 350–51). Hartley's mention of "the attractions of gravitation and cohesion" in the quotation at the start of this chapter identifies two such forces: Gravitation acts on the macrocosmic level to draw apples to earth and the planets toward and hence around the sun, while cohesion acts at the microcosmic level to hold atoms together in molecules. According to Stephen Hales, the repulsive forces associated with "strongly repelling elastick particles" are in contrast responsible for keeping the universe from collapsing into "one unactive cohering lump" (Hales 1769, 1: 314; §2.7); things exist in solid and liquid states for as long as the forces of attraction and repulsion within them maintain an undisturbed equilibrium. Repulsive forces are also responsible for the observed property of gases to expand when heated—a property that receives its quantitative expression in Boyle's Law. Moreover, Newton also hints that the "same" force may be either attractive or repulsive, depending upon the distance at which it acts: "And as in Algebra, where affirmative Quantities vanish and cease, there negative ones begin; so in Mechanicks, where Attraction ceases, there a repulsive Virtue ought to succeed" (1730, 370).[7] Newton's suggestion became a key element in Hales's conceptualization of the chemical properties of "air." According to Hales, "this now fixed, now volatile Proteus" (or "Hermes") has the "double capacity" of changing its state from being a repeller to being an attractor (1769, 1: 317; 2:278); strongly repelling "airs" thus have the capacity of being "factitious," that is, of making chemical compounds when they bond with other substances.

The contrast between the Cartesian and Newtonian images of the cosmos could not be more radical: on the one hand, an ocean of continuous inert matter, everywhere eddying and swirling in whirlpools; on the other, a vast empty space in which a walnutful of atomic matter has crystallized into lattices, and ever-larger series of lattices of lattices, which are held in positions of more or less stable equilibrium by forces of attraction and repulsion; on the one hand, all action through physical contact, as particles push at each other; on the other, action at a distance, as particles attract and repel each other across the voids of space, whether cosmic or infinitesimal.[8]

To committed mechanists, Newton's appeal to forces of attraction and repulsion in place of action through contact appeared regressive, a return to the sympathies and antipathies of the schoolmen. Leibniz, for example, sounds a mechanistic note when, in his correspondence with Clarke, he charges that such a force amounts to "a chimerical thing, a scholastic occult quality" of the sort already banished from scientific discourse.[9] But Newton claimed forces did not represent a regression. In Query 31 he drew a distinction between appeal to occult qualities per se and the use of terms that refer to "active principles," where the phenomena the terms name are manifest although their causes are unknown: "It seems to me further, that these Particles . . . are moved by certain active Principles, such as that of Gravity, and that which causes Fermentation, and the Cohesion of Bodies. These Principles I consider, not as occult Qualities, supposed to result from the specifick Form of Things, but as general Laws of Nature, by which the Things themselves are form'd; their Truth appearing to us by Phaenomena, though their causes be not yet discover'd. For these are manifest Qualities, and their Causes only are occult" (1730, 376–77). The "principles" of gravitation, fermentation (i.e., chemical reaction), and cohesion are terms to which we refer observed—and predicted—relationships among phenomena. What recommends them is their economy: use of the concept of gravitation enables the scientist to develop an elegant and powerful mathematical description of celestial mechanics—independently of any particular theory of a gravity-causing mechanism. It enables, in other words, Newton to write the *Principia,* even though he does not know how gravitation works. Similarly, the concept of cohesion, by whatever term one wishes to name it (e.g., the strong force), promises to enter into the description of how fundamental particles form into the lattices, and lattices of lattices, that are the constituents of matter. The term *cohesion* is thus for Hartley and other followers of Newton similar to an X in an algebraic equation: an unknown, yet necessary for the calculation.

In Newton's view, concepts such as gravitation and cohesion serve as points of referral for "manifest qualities" but themselves refer to "causes" that are presently "occult." But this distinction between observed phenomena and hidden cause would appear unsatisfactory to a natural philosopher committed to the Cartesian concept of mechanism. To such a philosopher, making this distinction would amount to abandoning a principal article of the mechanists' confession of faith: that setting matters in motion requires the motions of matter. In place of this symmetry between matter and motion, the Newtonian distinction introduces an apparent asymmetry: matter is observed to move, but not all motion is observably "caused" by matter.

For rigorously Cartesian mechanists for whom Newton's forces represent backsliding, the challenge is to locate causes for the observed motions, causes that can be described in the approved terms of the system. If one affirms the symmetry of matter and motion, such phenomena as gravitation, magnetism, chemical reactions, and the cohesion of bodies must be described in terms of particles of matter interacting through contact. For any apparent "force," there must be some class of particles whose physical presence is the cause of the observed phenomena. And this is what Descartes and other mechanists attempted to provide—through what Westfall has called a "game of imagining invisible mechanisms [that] recognised no limits" (1971, 88). Descartes, to explain magnetic attraction and repulsion, proposed spiral particles, with both right- and left-handed twists, that worked their way through an iron bar like corkscrews.

It is in relation to this difference over basic terms of explanation—forces of attraction and repulsion as opposed to the "pure" mechanist's appeal to the immediate interactions of particles—that we need to situate Newton's comments about the aether, which Hartley recommends we read for ourselves. But this situation is an exceptionally complex one, and the complexity is compounded both by Newton's character and by the nature of the comments. To many of his contemporaries, Newton was a living paradox, combining unsurpassed authority in mathematics and science with equally pronounced habits of concealment and secrecy. William Whiston, Newton's successor as Lucasian Professor of Mathematics at Cambridge, wrote of his one-time mentor: "Sir *Isaac*, in Mathematicks, could sometimes see almost by Intuition, even without Demonstration.... And when he did but propose Conjectures in Natural Philosophy, he almost always knew them to be true at the same Time" (1749, 39). But Whiston adds that Newton "was the most fearful, cautious, and suspicious Temper, that I ever knew" (1749, 294).[10] A reader of the Queries to the *Opticks* could be confident that what Newton presented as a conjecture was true—while doubting whether he had the right key for deciphering it. Newton pointed the way to the promised land of truth. That was certain. But how to interpret the gesture?

Interpreting Newton's hints requires that one place them within a frame of reference. But which one? Ernan McMullin (1978, 79) identifies four such frames, or explanatory models, in connection with Newton's account of gravitation.[11] An account of "how gravitation works" could call upon: (1) an aether, though not the purely material aether Descartes and Huygens had earlier invoked to explain gravitation (see Westfall 1971, 185–88; Hesse 1961, 107–8); (2) light, taken as the source of all activity; (3) an "active principle" or "spirit"; or (4) the direct action of God. The first alternative satisfies the mechanists' desire for a causally explanatory concept; moreover, it avoids a purely positivist (i.e., descriptive) interpretation—an interpretation that McMullin (1978, 101) writes is contrary to Newton's intentions and that Cohen states "robs his work of those qualities of imagination which caused his contemporaries to admire him" (1956, 144). The second derives from Neoplatonism, and the third from Newton's extensive researches in alchemy—researches that Newton kept secret but which obliquely inform the discussions of chemical interactions in Query 31 (see Golinski 1988; Henry 1988; McMullin 1978, 43–47). And the fourth, according to Westfall, represents "the ultimate foundation of Newton's conception of nature" (1971, 396)—his own "innermost thoughts," but thoughts to which "he brought himself only so far as [to give] an evasive and obscure presentation" in the General Scholium of the *Principia* and Queries 28 and 31 of the *Opticks*. In Westfall's interpretation, the *immaterial* aether is "the infinite omnipotent God, who by His infinity constitutes absolute space and by His omnipotence is actively present throughout it" (1971, 396).

An aether as a quasi-material medium, as a Neoplatonic beaming-forth, as an alchemical spirit, as a cipher for the action of God—Hartley had good reason for doubting whether he had understood Newton perfectly. Some of the doubt, along with the suggestion that he is aware of the options, appears in Hartley's discussion. In the context of applying the concept of forces of attraction and repulsion to neural molecules, Hartley comments that Newton means "by attraction and repulsion, a mere mathematical tendency to approach and recede, be the cause what it will, impulse, pressure, an unknown one, or no physical cause at all, but the immediate agency of the Deity" (*OM* 1.1.1.5). The causal alternatives that Hartley mentions correspond to those in McMullin's list. They also correspond to Newton's hints in the *Opticks,* where he in Query 21 suggests that the aether may contain particles "which endeavour to recede from one another (for I do not know what this Aether is)" (1730, 326), and where in Query 31 he writes of "a powerful ever-living Agent, who being in all Places, is more able by his Will to move Bodies within his boundless uniform Sensorium, and thereby to form and reform the Parts of the Universe, than we are by our Will to move the Parts of our own Bodies" (379). Thinking of the aether in mathematical terms, as constituted by particles repelling each other, and thinking of it as a figure for the boundless sensorium of God, are both alternatives that Newton suggests.[12]

For our purposes, the question is not, What did Newton think? but rather, What did Hartley think Newton was thinking? More specifically, what direction does Hartley take, starting from Newton's conjectures concerning the action of the aether in the "performance of animal sensation and motion"? The answer lies in the concept of vibration.

2. "The Doctrine of Vibrations"

Theories of nature abhor a vacuum. In the Newtonian model, the supersaturated solution that is the Cartesian ocean of matter collapses, precipitating out crystalline lattices that contain infinitesimal quantities of matter and leaving behind the vast emptiness of absolute space. However, this conceptual Big Collapse poses new problems for understanding physical reality. Matter acts on matter through forces of attraction and repulsion, such as magnetism and gravitation; it also "glows" with heat, light, sound. But how could bodies attract each other across the distances of space? How could radiant heat reach the earth from the sun, or even a thermometer suspended inside a vacuum?

One way of dealing with these questions is to declare oneself a positivist: "force" is a descriptive concept that calls our attention to "mathematical tendencies to approach and recede"—and no more. But it is difficult for a person hungry for answers to be content with such ascetical fare. If physics is to be more than model building, if it does correspond to reality, then it must explain how things work. It must explain how light reaches the earth from the sun, or how a thermometer or planet grows warm when surrounded by emptiness.

There are, both in classical and modern physics, two alternatives for explaining how one body affects another body at a distance. The first is to imagine that a parcel is mailed from the one body to the other. The second is to imagine that both bodies are placed within a continuous medium or field, like two bowling balls upon a trampoline. The first alternative, of course, is that of the Standard Model of quantum mechanics, in which two classes of fundamental particles—quarks and leptons—exchange quanta of energy, where each quantum is a subatomic particle of some sort. The second alternative is represented by attempts to unify all "forces" in terms of the geometry of space-time—a project that owes much to Einstein's theory of general relativity and that continues in the present in work on the theory of vibrating superstrings (Kaku 1995). The sheet metaphor is the one commonly used to picture how the bending of space accounts for the "force" of gravity: two bowling balls placed on a trampoline will roll toward each other because each creates a depression in the otherwise flat canvas.

Both alternatives were also present in Hartley's day. Light, according to Newton, consisted of streams of "corpuscles" that travel across the emptiness of space and through "pellucid" materials such as air, water, prisms, and possibly nerves. Sound is the vibration of a continuous medium, whether air, water, or an anvil when hit with a hammer. Other natural philosophers such as Hooke, Huygens (1690), and Euler (see Hakfoort 1988, 97–98) thought that light also consisted of waves in a medium, but no one suggested that there were particles of sound.

In his interpretation of Newton's physics, Hartley refers to various fluids or "effluvia" that are made up of particles emitted from bodies. If one heats crystals taken from wine or a stone taken from the human bladder, a quantity of air will be released. Heat a bar of iron until it glows, and streams of light particles will fly off from it. There are similar emissions of "odoriferous particles" and "magnetical and electrical effluvia" (*OM* 1.1.1.5). In addition, "the gross bodies that lie upon the surface of the earth emit air-particles, constituting a thin elastic fluid, of great efficacy in performing the ordinary operations of nature." (Recall that it is because "air" particles can return to an elastic state, according to Hales, that "this beautiful frame of things might be maintained in a continual round of the production and dissolution of animal and vegetable bodies" [1769, 1: 315].) Consequently, Hartley suggests, "it seems not unnatural to expect, that the small particles of bodies should emit a proportionably attenuated air, *i.e.* an aether which may likewise have a great share in the subtle actions of the small particles of bodies on each other." He adds that "it is reasonable to expect" that this aether is comprised of extremely small particles of virtually no mass but with highly repulsive charges toward each other and other forms of matter.

In Hartley's interpretation, latticed forms of matter—molecules and the atoms that comprise them—do not exhaust the inventory of particles in the universe. For the lattices may also emit what we may call "free" forms of matter, which exist as fluids expanding through space. Had we a microscope powerful enough, we could see that any "molecule" in its microstructure has the form of a crystalline lattice-work, in which atoms (and other molecules of "air") are held in a configuration by counterbalancing forces of attraction and repulsion (hereafter, "a/r forces"). Subject the molecule to a chemical reaction or heating, and the a/r forces will be pushed out of equilibrium; if pushed "far" enough, a force may change its polarity from attraction to repulsion, and the molecule will either break apart, releasing some of its components as a gas, or, if the remaining forces of attraction are sufficiently strong, combine with other molecules in a new compound configuration. If our microscope were by several orders of magnitude more powerful still, we would see that the "empty" space around *and within* this lattice is filled with swirling streams of subatomic particles—some emanating from the lattice itself, others arriving from elsewhere—of light, electricity, and in some instances magnetism. We would also see these subatomic particles tug and push at the atoms in the lattice, causing the lattice as a whole to vibrate, although the overall structure of the "crystal" will not disintegrate. Depending upon the kind of molecule it is, and on the frequency and amplitude of the initiating vibration, the molecule will begin to do something—to luminesce, to build up or release a charge of static electricity, to be pulled toward a magnet. And if we looked very closely, perhaps at the first-level lattices out of which all the higher levels are built, we would catch sight of perhaps the smallest particles of all, those of the aether.

Imagine a universe filled with what we could call "aetherinos"—negatively charged counterparts to neutrinos. Hartley points out that the behavior of a fluid consisting of such particles would be the exact opposite of air, which has a much higher ratio of mass to repulsive force. The earth's gravitation keeps the envelope of the atmosphere around the planet, despite the propensity of the air molecules to fly away from each other, with the result that the air is denser at sea level than at a mountain top. The aether, in contrast, is rarest within matter, rarer near matter, and denser farther away from it. Because of their absence of mass, aetherinos, like neutrinos, are able to a degree to penetrate solid bodies, so that the aetherial gas is everywhere, though with pronounced variations in density. Still, again because of their absence of mass, aetherinos are largely unaffected by the gravitational attraction of massive bodies and thus always tend to move away from them and toward empty space. There, aetherinos will crowd together until their density reaches a temporary state of equilibrium, where the pressure on the aetherial gas is equal to the mutually repulsive force of the aetherinos on each other and on whatever "gross" bodies are in the vicinity. But that state of equilibrium would be highly unstable: the aether would be highly perturbable, "elastic, compressible, and apt to receive vibrations" from any distortions in its particles' relative positions. It would, in short, be an ideal vibrating medium.

It is the aether's function as a vibrating medium that is the key to Hartley's interest in it. What Hartley has to say about the aether is, in a sense, simply a platform from which he can develop his real theme: a theory of vibrations. Of the parcel and trampoline alternatives outlined above, his commitment is to the second. Rather than the particles of light, the waves that are sound provide the fundamental interpretive category for the explanation of phenomena; sound is the standard in relation to which all other phenomena and forces are explicable by analogy. If we take Democritus as the emblem of the first alternative and Pythagoras as emblematic of the second, we could say that Hartley is profoundly Pythagorean. On a practical level, this means that Hartley frequently draws on acoustic and musical examples. Had he been a creative artist, he would have been a musician rather than a painter. We noted in chapter 2 that he played the violin. But on a higher level, Hartley's theory of vibrations is resonant with the desire for *theoria*— for, that is, the contemplation of the world's harmony that is, said Aristotle, the essence of a blessed life. As the theory of superstrings does for its proponents today, vibrations held out for Hartley the promise of the unification of all forces and phenomena in a pattern that would be single, simple, and harmonious. Michio Kaku, who has contributed both to the development and popularization of superstring theory, has stated that "our bodies are essentially symphonies. They are made out of vibrating strings. The universe obeys the laws of physics, and the laws of physics are nothing but the laws of harmony" (McKay 1995). Like Newton, Hartley would have agreed completely; and we can understand everything he has to say in the *Observations* concerning the twin "doctrines" of vibration and association as contributing to his working out the laws of harmony for the symphonies that are our bodies and minds.

The intuition that "the laws of physics are nothing but the laws of harmony" is of course an ancient one; it has its beginning, the story tells us, in that moment when Pythagoras walked past a blacksmith's forge and observed that two anvils were ringing an octave apart (see Gregory 1702, v).[13] In time Pythagoras's discovery of the harmonic ratios of the musical scale became the principle, the key, for picturing the order of the cosmos. As long as people saw the earth at the center of nested crystalline spheres carrying the moon, sun, planets, and fixed stars, they heard, or believed it was possible to hear, the spheres' music.

After Copernicus and Galileo, the image of the cosmos as a series of nested spheres gave way to the image of the earth and other planets circling the sun. To some, the loss of the former image meant the loss of harmony; John Donne, for example, in the *First Anniversarie* (1612) lamented "freely men confesse, that this world's spent / When in the Planets, and the Firmament / They seeke so many new; they see that this / Is crumbled out again to his Atomis. / 'Tis all in pieces, all cohœrence gone; / All just supply, and all Relation." Nonetheless, the intuition that the laws of physics are the laws of musical harmony retained its hold on people's imaginations. Kepler, writing in *The Harmonies of the World* (1619), affirmed that the planets' elliptical orbits caused each to produce a series of rising and falling notes, radically unlike the supposed monotonous dronings of the Ptolemaic spheres; together, the planets sang in a polyphony that could be heard only by the Composer (see Rattansi 1988, 189). And Newton's perfection of celestial mechanics in book 1 of the *Principia* demonstrated that coherence was not gone, that the movements of the planets in the solar system were ordered according to laws of elegance and precision—laws that, Newton insisted, were known to Moses and Pythagoras. But the ancients spoke in images and symbols that were misinterpreted by later generations. Ptolemy's error was to read the image of the music of the spheres literally and not symbolically; and Newton's rediscovery of the ancient truth would have never been possible, had the old image retained its saturnine power (see Rattansi 1988, 197–200).

In addition to a reimagining or rediscovery of the true import of celestial harmony, the equivalence of the laws of physics and the laws of harmony could also be established through an alternative application of the latter: the laws of musical harmony could be observed not only in the world of the vast but also in the world of the small; not simply in the orbits of the planets, but perhaps more deeply in the infinitesimal vibrations that are tone and color.

A series of discoveries revealed the manner in which these infinitesimal vibrations obeyed the laws of harmonic motion. First, Marin Mersenne published his *Harmonie universelle* in 1636–37. The title itself is significant in its affirmation of universal harmony. In his work Mersenne established the correlation between the pitch of a string and its frequency of vibration. In addition, Mersenne proposed that musical consonance was explicable in terms of the coincidence of two or more vibrations; that is, we hear harmony when the vibrations corresponding to two or more notes are in phase (see Gouk 1988, 115).

Second, in his *Horologium oscillatorium* (1673), Christian Huygens demonstrated that the oscillations of a cycloidal pendulum were isochronous. Specifically, for a pendulum tracing a cycloidal curve instead of the arc of a circle, the time of descent from any point on the curve to the lowest point on the curve bears a fixed ratio to the time of descent along the axis (that is, the length of the pendulum, perpendicular to the lowest point). The period of oscillation for a cycloidal pendulum is thus a function solely of the length of the pendulum and the force of gravity; it is independent of how far out along the curve the pendulum is swinging. The demonstration of this principle enabled Huygens to draw up a design for a precision clock, the true "grandfather" of all pendulum clocks down to the present day.[14]

Third, Robert Hooke, in *De Potentia restituva* (1678b), a lecture enunciating Hooke's Law (that the "power" of a spring varies directly in proportion to its degree of flexure or displacement), articulated "the brilliant intuition that a vibrating spring is dynamically equivalent to a [cycloidal] pendulum" (Westfall 1971, 212).[15] The period of a spring's vibrations are, like the swings of a pendulum, independent of the amplitude of the vibration. Moreover, in *De Potentia restituva* and in his earlier *Micrographia* (1665), Hooke proposed that all matter consisted of vibrating particles. In the 1678 lecture he states that "the particles that compose all bodies I do suppose to owe their greatest part of their sensible or potential extension to a vibrative motion" (1678b, 8). To illustrate this point, he uses the image of a plate of iron one foot square, moving "with a vibrative motion forwards and backwards the flat ways the length of a foot with so swift a motion as not to permit any other body to enter into that space"; such a vibrating plate would appear to us to be a solid cube. In his theory, such vibrations in the particles account for heat, cohesion, the extension of bodies, and the differences between solids, fluids, and gases; vibrations in the aether account for light and color, and may account for gravitation. Hooke employs a musical analogy to describe the interactions of such vibrations: "for particles that are all similar, will, like so many equal musical strings equally stretcht, vibrate together in a kind of harmony or unison" (1665, 15).[16]

Finally, the greatest impetus for a comprehensive theory of vibrations came from Newton. In the second book of the *Principia* Newton improved upon the work of Mersenne, Huygens, and Hooke by working out "the first satisfactory analysis of simple harmonic motion" (Westfall 1971, 496); he demonstrated that vibrations propagated through any elastic medium are isochronous; consequently, just as the period of a pendulum is independent of variances in how far the pendulum swings, so also is the velocity of propagation through an elastic medium independent of variances of frequency. The fact that the velocity through a given medium is constant for any type of vibration—so that notes from tubas travel as fast as notes from piccolos—enabled Newton to calculate the speed of sound in air (see Westfall 1971, 496–98).

The aspect of Newton's work that best expressed the laws of physics in terms of the laws of harmony was his attempt to draw an analogy between the color spectrum and the musical octave. In 1675 Newton sent a paper, *An Hypothesis Explaining the Properties of Light,* to the Royal Society to be read before the society but not published; the paper did not appear in print until it was published by Hartley's colleague Thomas Birch in his *History of the Royal Society* (1756–57). In it Newton continued to maintain that light was corpuscular, but he accommodated Hooke's theory of vibrations by proposing that light particles interact with the aether, inducing density differentials in it that account for the reflection and refraction of light and also inducing vibrations of various frequencies that in turn set up similar vibrations in the optic nerve, which we experience as the various colors (Westfall 1971, 363–69; *Opticks,* Query 13). In addition, he proposed a structural parallelism between the color spectrum and the musical octave, so that the mathematical ratios that describe the intervals between the seven notes of the diatonic scale also describe the intervals between the seven colors of the visible spectrum (Gouk 1988, 118).

Newton's analogy between the color spectrum and the octave is a crucial instance of an attempt to comprehend the laws of physics within the laws of harmony. Concerning the specifics of the analogy, Hartley follows Newton closely; his discussion of the perception of color in proposition 56 details how the ratios of the seven colors' vibrational frequencies match the ratios of the notes in the octave. To begin with, "the frequency ... of the vibrations excited by the extreme red may be to that of the vibrations excited by the extreme violet as 1 to 2" (*OM* 1.2.4.56)—that is, as a note to the note an octave higher, as everyone since Pythagoras knew.[17] But the substance of the analogy, as developed by Newton and affirmed by Hartley, concerned the correlation of the color spectrum to the internal division of the octave. There are several ways of spacing the notes in the octave, all of which are attempts to overcome the flaw in the Pythagorean scale, that a series of seven octaves starting, for example, on C will end on C, while a series of twelve perfect fifths starting on the same C will end on B#. To make the final note a C for the two series of octaves and of fifths requires a degree of fudging, otherwise known as temperament. One such system, termed "just intonation," had been invented by Gioseffo Zarlino in 1588; in just intonation the intervals between two of the notes are slightly extended, so that the octave is made up of tones of two sizes plus a semitone. Newton experimented with finding the best—mathematically most pleasing—form of just intonation, and decided upon a division in which the order of ratios was symmetrical in each direction from the center of the scale. (Starting on D, as Newton did, the ratios are: D to E, 9:8; E to F, 16:15; F to G, 10:9; G to A, 9:8; A to B, 10:9; B to C, 16:15, and C to D', 9:8; see Gouk 1988, 110–11.) Then, in *An Hypothesis* and again in the *Opticks,* he proposed that the color spectrum could be divided in exactly the same way. The color green corresponds to the G in an octave starting on D, with the other six colors arrayed symmetrically on each side of it. Hartley recommends this order for its correlation with the natural world, stating that "it seems to me, that our fixed point ought to be placed in green, from the commonness and purity of the green of the third order, *i.e.* of grass and vegetables in general." In this arrangement, Hartley notes, red, yellow, green, blue, and violet correspond to the five tones, while orange and indigo correspond to the two semitones. He also comments that he has learned "from a MS. paper of Sir Isaac Newton's on music, not yet published" that the proposed order "is the second in absolute perfection . . . and the first in relative, *i.e.* of those in which the semi-tones are at equal distances from the middle or extremes." In other words, both Newton's preferred octave (D, E, F, G, A, B, C, D') and the color spectrum are in the Dorian mode; in comparison to the Ionian mode, or major key, the Dorian mode starting on D is "second" in absolute perfection; but it is "first" in relative perfection among symmetrical scales, presumably because it is the only one that can be played without sharps or flats.

Newton's analogy of octave and spectrum appeared to offer a simple yet powerful way of investigating the phenomena of light and sound, and specifically of replacing qualitative descriptions with precise quantitative analyses. It suggested that the seven primary colors, like distinct tones, could be shown to consist of specific frequencies of vibration, and all "compound" colors to be various blendings and combinations—that is, associations—of these seven.

The demonstration that color and sound derive from vibrations and the further discovery of their structural correlation suggested to Hartley that, by the extension of the analogy, the other senses could also be explained in terms of vibrations: "If the differences of the primary colors arise from the specific differences of vibrations, it is easy to see, that the differences of tastes and smells may have a like origin" (*OM* 1.2.4.56). Moreover, the structural parallel between the octave and the spectrum also suggested the possibility of again reducing processes that appear to be qualitatively distinct to quantitative variances of a single process. He proposed that the different types of sensations might form a spectrum, in which the vibrations responsible for heat, light, smell, taste, touch, and sound are arranged in order, from the highest frequencies to the lowest, or, which is the same thing, from the shortest wavelengths to the longest (*OM* 1.2.1.24, 1.2.3.49). Unlike the spectra of colors and tones, which order qualities we already perceive as belonging together, Hartley's sensation spectrum would thus demonstrate the underlying unity of qualities that at first appear distinct, in the way the spectrum of electromagnetic radiation integrates the "distinct" phenomena of cosmic rays, gamma rays, x-rays, ultraviolet light, the visible spectrum, infrared radiation, microwaves, and radio waves.

In hypothesizing the existence of a sensation spectrum, Hartley notes that the vibrations corresponding to the sensation of heat, etc. are not simply the continuation in the nervous system of the vibrations that are their physical causes: "It is to be observed, that [sound waves] may excite much more frequent vibrations in the auditory nerve, than those of the sounding body, to which they correspond; just as the vibrations from friction are much more numerous than the strokes of friction; and the tremor of the particles of an anvil much more numerous than the strokes of the hammer" (*OM* 1.2.3.49). The vibrations of the sensation spectrum thus probably possess higher frequencies than the forms of energy that excite them.

Hartley also conjectures that the vibrations of the sensation spectrum differ from those of light, sound, etc. in another important respect. As we noted above, Newton had worked out the laws of simple harmonic motion, which demonstrate that vibrations in any elastic medium are dynamically equivalent to the movement of a cycloidal pendulum or to a flexed spring: because degree of force (and hence of acceleration) is directly proportional to degree of displacement, the period of oscillation remains constant for a pendulum of a given length, or any vibration of a given wavelength. The farther the pendulum is displaced, the faster it accelerates as it swings down to what would be its resting position, and consequently the tick-tocks are all isochronous. However, in his discussion of the sensation of heat, Hartley notes that this is true only of a specific kind of pendulum:

> We may conceive further, that all the vibrations of the small particles of the medullary substance, and interjacent aether... grow quicker as they grow shorter, *i.e.* weaker; or... that in declining they tend to those which impress the sensation of heat. For vibrating motions of different lengths [amplitudes]

can be isochronous only according to one law, *viz.* that of the accelerating force being in the simple proportion from the middle point of the vibration, as when a heavy body vibrates in a cycloid; whereas, if the accelerating force be any less ratio than this, short vibrations will be quicker than long ones. (*OM* 1.2.1.24)

Huygens had determined that the cycloid was the curve of isochronous motion in order to overcome the problem that had thwarted the development of an accurate clock: the tendency of pendulums to speed up as they ran down. Here, Hartley is suggesting that the vibrations in the brain and nervous system may exhibit the same tendency to increase in frequency as they "decline." Like the oscillations of cycloidal pendulums, the vibrations of light and sound remain constant, uninfluenced by such declines in amplitude; light waves do not shift toward the violet as they diminish, and sound waves do not rise in frequency as they grow softer. But the vibrations excited by light and sound and carried along the nerves to the brain do not, according to Hartley's conjecture, exhibit this isochronous constancy. For them, accelerating force may not be in direct proportion to the degree of displacement, and thus, like medieval pendulum clocks, their periods of oscillation may shorten as the oscillations grow "weaker." Such shifts along the sensation spectrum, Hartley suggests, may account for sensations of taste leading to experiences of varying degrees of heat; the first bite of the vindaloo burns, while the second or third is pleasingly warm.

More generally, Newton's analogy of spectrum and octave held out the promise of a science that could discover the fundamental "harmonic" principles that structured all physical reality, including the brains and nervous systems of living organisms. Just as it revealed the mathematical and harmonic principles underlying the perceived differences in sound and color, the analogy also suggests a potential for a much more extensive unification of phenomena—indeed, for future integration of all forms of vibrations in one "grand unified theory." Hartley writes:

To sum up in one . . . : as the attractions of gravitation, electricity, magnetism, and cohesion, with the repulsions which attend upon the three last, intimate to us the general tenor of nature in this respect; *viz.* that many of its phaenomena are carried on by attractions and repulsions . . . so the pulses of the air, the tremours of surrounding bodies, the propagation of sounds both through the air, and along contiguous solid bodies, the oscillations of electric bodies, and the phaenomena of electricity, may, in like manner, serve as a clew and guide to the invention, and afford a presumption, that other reciprocal motions or vibrations have a great share in the production of natural phaenomena.

Nor is it an objection to this, but rather a confirmation of it, that these principles of attraction and repulsion of the several kinds, and of vibrations, are dependent upon and involved within each other, since this is also agreeable with the tenor of nature, as it is observed in the body, in the mind, in science in general, and in the several branches of each science in particular. Each part, faculty, principle, &c. when considered and pursued sufficiently, seems to extend itself into the boundaries of the others and, as it were, to enclose and comprehend them all. Thus magnetism mixes itself with the gravitation both of bodies upon the surface of the earth, and with that of the moon to the earth: a polar virtue of the same kind seems to have a principal share in the formation of natural bodies, especially those whose parts cohere in regular figures: electricity may also extend, without being excited by friction or otherwise, to small distances, and join with the just-mentioned polar virtue in making the parts of bodies cohere.... A repulsion which should throw off indefinitely small corpuscles with indefinitely great velocity from all the bodies of the universe (a thing that would be very analogous to the emission of light, odoriferous particles, and magnetical and electrical effluvia ...) might cause the gravitation of all the great bodies of the universe to each other, and perhaps other kinds of attraction. Some of these corpuscles, by stopping each other in the intermundane spaces, or other mutually repulsive corpuscles lodged there from causes not yet discovered, may compose a subtle vibrating medium. The vibrations of this medium, being continued to the great bodies of the universe, may so far agitate their small parts, as to give their attractive and repulsive powers an opportunity to exert themselves with great vigour; ... However it is not impossible ... but future ages may analyse all the actions of bodies upon each other, up to a few simple principles, by making such suppositions as the phaenomena shall suggest, and then trying and modelling them by the phaenomena. (*OM* 1.1.1.5)

A comprehensive theory of vibrations, then, is methodologically significant, for it provides a warrant for treating all forms of vibrating media as dynamically equivalent. It thereby justifies the extensive use of analogical reasoning in science. A series of imaginative leaps enabled Newton to build upon Huygens's work on pendulums and Hooke's work on springs in determining the laws of simple harmonic motion for any elastic vibrating medium. By making similar leaps, Hartley argues, other scientists should be able to extend the results of these researches to further areas of inquiry. Moreover, the theory suggests that "vibration" promises to be the fundamental principle that will, in future ages, enable scientists to unify all the forces of attraction and repulsion; when this is accomplished, the people of the future will understand how such forces as "gravitation, electricity, magnetism, and cohesion" are quantitatively distinct aspects of an underlying unity, in terms of which "all actions of bodies upon each other" are explicable. But "all actions" includes the motions of a mite, or a man, as well as of a solar system or a galaxy. This prospect of future unification—of seeing that the universe consists of vibrating particles—also provides a warrant for the present use of the principle as a heuristic in seemingly opaque areas, such as that concerning the transmission of impulses along the nerves and into the brain. In other words, the theory supports the development of a neural harmonics that would show that the laws of physiology are the laws of physics, which are the laws of harmony.

3. Neural Harmonics

The foremost anatomist and physiologist of Hartley's day was Hermann Boerhaave (1668–1738), professor of botany, medicine, and chemistry at the University of Leiden.[18] Boerhaave was an advocate of the application of the "mechanistic" approach to chemistry and physiology. For example, his 1703 oration at the University of Leiden, "On Mechanistic Reasoning in Medicine," begins: "Mechanists are those who, by mathematical calculation based on rational premises or on observation, explain the operations [*vires*] of bodies from their mass, configuration, and velocity" (quoted in King 1978, 121; cf. Boerhaave [1703] 1983, 94). Boerhaave applied this axiom with great thoroughness in his masterworks, *Institutiones Medicae* (1713) and *Elementa Chemiae* (1732). The crucial operating principle in the latter work is that chemical interactions be modeled as changes in the relative positions, and hence the configurations, of particles; that is, as changes in *molecular* structure: "Boerhaave ... argued that the changes produced in bodies by chemistry must be mechanical, that all the operations of chemistry produce 'alterations in bodies which are owing intirely to motion.' Chemistry can be distinguished from ordinary mechanics because the latter deals with the motion of translation of a body from one place to another, whereas the former deals with the motions of the 'different kinds of corpuscles' that make up bodies. By motion of the parts of bodies, chemistry is employed 'either in uniting, or in separating; there is no third [chemical] operation in nature'" (Cohen 1956, 224, quoting Boerhaave).[19] In other words, a chemical interaction involves either the compounding of a new molecule out of previously discrete particles, the breakup of a molecule into two or more parts, or the reconfiguration of the internal structure of the molecule itself.

Hartley had no quarrel with Boerhaave's general outlook; Peter Shaw, his colleague in making the case for Stephens's lithontriptic, was co-translator of the unauthorized edition of the *Elementa Chemiae* (1724; English trans., 1727, 2d. ed. 1741), and in the official edition of 1732 Boerhaave attempted to incorporate Hales's work on air (Allan and Schofield 1980, 124). However, although Hartley's numerous references to Boerhaave's observations and hypotheses maintain a consistently respectful tone, most of these references draw attention to points at which Hartley differs from the great teacher.

The main point of difference concerns the anatomy of the nervous system. In his *Passions of the Soul* (1649) and *Treatise on Man* (1664), Descartes had proposed a model of neural physiology according to which the brain filters out of the blood "a certain very fine [*subtil*] wind, or rather a very lively and pure flame, which is called the *animal spirits*" (Descartes 1985, 1:100); the nerves, in turn, are composite structures that consist of hollow tubes each with a thin filament within, in the manner of a catheter inside of an artery. The filaments, acting somewhat like bell pulls, transmit stimuli from the relevant sensory receptors to the brain; when a filament does so, it opens a valve at the point where the nerve joins the brain, animal spirit flows into the nerve, and thence into the muscles in the area adjoining the sensory receptor, causing them to contract (Descartes 1985, 1:332–34). I have read nothing that suggests that Boerhaave accepted Descartes's specific model of tubes with filaments inside them. However, Boerhaave does advocate a general model of the body as composed of solids and fluids, with the latter running through channels or canals, and he does follow Descartes in taking the brain to be a gland that produces a "nervous fluid" or "animal spirit" that flows through the hollow tubes that are the nerves (*OM* 1.1.1.5; cf. Boerhaave 1713, 89–120; 1983, 101).[20]

During Descartes's lifetime, Hobbes, Gassendi, and Mersenne challenged his physics and by extension the physiology based upon it. To those who sided with them, physical reality consisted of indivisible atoms in empty space, and not of a continuous plenum of infinitely divisible matter. A century later, the debate continued among those committed to mechanistic reasoning in physiology and medicine, concerning which model of mechanism to adopt. Many followed Boerhaave; Hartley calls Boerhaave's position "the common doctrine concerning the powers of the nervous system" (*OM* 1.1.1.5). But there were some who accepted the "Newtonian doctrine of vibrations"; they understood the nerves to be "solid capillaments" and the vibrations of their "infinitesimal particles" the means of the transmission of sensory and motor impulses.

Hartley, always open-minded and careful to present his criticisms in the gentlest possible manner, acknowledges "many, or even most, things in the Boerhaavian doctrine concerning the structure and functions of the brain, to be beautiful, just, and useful." He also hopes that there may be a convergence between the Newtonian and Boerhaavian hypotheses, in which "all that is probable in the received doctrines concerning the nervous fluid, and the animal spirits . . . and all the arguments which Boerhaave has brought for his hypothesis, of a glandular secretion of a very subtle active fluid in the brain, may be accommodated to the Newtonian hypothesis of vibrations" (*OM* 1.1.1.5). Nonetheless, the disagreement is fundamental. The brain is not a gland, and the nerves are not hollow. Hartley notes that the tubular hypothesis has been disproved experimentally: in attempts to inject fluids into the nerves or brain, the "best injectors [have] never penetrated farther than the grosser order of vessels in the cortical substance"; the "finer orders of the vessels of the cortical substance" and the still finer vessels of the medullary substance are therefore even more resistant to such injections. Hartley draws the inference that "the medullary substance consists of a texture of vessels so small and regular, as that it may have no vacuity or interval in it, sufficient to interrupt or disturb the vibrations of the aether, and concomitant ones of the medullary particles." In other words, nothing—no physical fluid, no animal spirits—flows through a nerve. Nerves are made up of infinitesimal particles, which at one point Hartley terms "the component molecules of the brain, the molecules of the molecules, &c" (*OM* 1.1.2.9). As we noted above, a molecule's lattice-like structure fixes a small quantity of atomic matter within a relatively large space; thus, although the molecules within a nerve are porous and permeable to fluids of subatomic particles, such as those of the aether, nerves themselves are not themselves tubular in structure.

According to G. S. Rousseau (1991b, 129–31; see also Edwin Clarke 1968), the doctrine that nerves were hollow tubes was a focal point of the dispute between mechanists and "animists" over the relation of the soul to the body. Thomas Willis, Locke's teacher at Oxford, published a series of works on the brain in the 1660s and 1670s; in them, he was "the first scientist clearly and loudly to posit that the seat of the soul is strictly limited to the brain, nowhere else" (Rousseau 1991b, 128). But if the soul is so limited, then it can experience sensations and initiate actions in the rest of the body only through the nerves; consequently, nerves must be hollow tubes through which circulates the animal (or vital) spirit produced by the brain. Mechanists, following Willis, thus argued and sought to demonstrate that nerves were hollow. Their vitalist opponents, in contrast, most notably Georg Ernst Stahl (1660–1734) and his followers, argued, as Hartley notes, for the existence of "a rational agent presiding over the fabric of the body, and producing effects that are not subject to the laws of mechanism" (*OM* 1.2.8.78).[21] They sought to vindicate their position by challenging the anatomical correlate of their opponents' model—that is, by demonstrating that nerves are solid. "For if the nerves were solid fibres rather than porous hollow tubes," writes Rousseau, "no avenue existed by which to explain the brain's control over the rest of the body—not, at least, until the discovery of electricity in the mid eighteenth century" (1991b, 130). In the light of Rousseau's comments, Boerhaave's position appears to be the more conventionally mechanistic one. We can imagine that to the many physicians who studied under Boerhaave at Leiden, the position of Newton and Hartley could at first sight appear to be suspect as insufficiently mechanistic. However, a careful reader would note that Hartley affirms Willis's central tenet; because "all the vibrations which belong to ideas, and intellectual affections, must reside in the brain . . . not in the spinal marrow or nerves," it follows that "the brain is therefore the seat of the rational soul, *i.e.* of the soul, as far as it is influenced by reasons and moral motives" (*OM* 1.1.2.14). Moreover, in Hartley's otherwise generous and inclusive text, Stahl is one of the few who receive direct criticism. The view of "Stahl and his followers" concerning the relationship between involuntary and voluntary actions is "diametrically opposite" to his (*OM* 1.1.3.21), and of their supposition that a "rational agent" presides over the body by nonmechanical means, Hartley states that "this is *gratis dictum*" (*OM* 1.2.8.78). By offering an account of how the brain can receive sensations and induce actions via nerves composed of solid fibers, Hartley is in effect pursuing another avenue of explanation—one that, by providing an alternative explanation of the transmission of nerve impulses, frees the overall theory of mechanism from dependence upon the hollow nerve doctrine. And as we shall see below, "electricity" plays a role in Hartley's thinking concerning the transmission of nerve impulses.[22]

The question is, then, how does a solid nerve receive and transmit an impulse? The process must be in some sense "mechanical": "External objects," Hartley writes, "being corporeal, can act upon the nerves and brain, which are also corporeal, by nothing but impressing motion on them" (*OM* 1.1.1.4). This statement is consistent both with Newtonian physics and with Boerhaavian chemistry. But "motion" here needs to be understood in a specific sense. Motion is not grossly kinetic, on the analogy of a series of marbles cracking into each other. Nor is it a continuation of the external signal in the form in which it is received: the optic nerves do not transmit light in the manner of fiber optic cables. And it does not involve the entire nerve in a "single" motion: a nerve does not vibrate along its length like the string of a violin—a notion Hartley discounts as "highly absurd" and that he emphasizes was never "asserted by Sir Isaac Newton, or any of those who have embraced his notion of the performance of sensation and motion, by means of *vibrations*." Rather, the interior motion that constitutes the reception and transmission of an impulse along a nerve consists of the temporary and progressive disturbance of the molecular structure of the nerve, along its length. This reconfiguration is, taking the term in the broadest sense available to a reader of Hales and Boerhaave, chemical.

Or more precisely, the reconfigurations are subchemical, insofar as they do not cause permanent alterations in the composition of the affected molecules. Hartley states that the vibrations in the nerve are those of the "infinitesimal" particles, "and not those biggest particles, on which the operations in chemistry, and the colours of natural bodies, depend, according to the opinion of Sir Isaac Newton" (*OM* 1.1.1.4). By emphasizing that the infinitesimal particles constitute the vibrating medium, Hartley may be responding to an objection to the vibration hypothesis raised years earlier by William Cheselden. In the chapter on

The Theory of Vibrations

the brain and nervous system in his *Anatomy* (4th ed., 1730), Cheselden reviews the "hot dispute [which] has arose... whether sensation and motion are occasioned by a vibration communicated to the nerves, which these gentlemen suppose entirely solid and tense, or by a liquid contained and moved in them" (1730, 218). Although Cheselden comments that he is "rather incline[d] to" the tubular hypothesis, his presentation is balanced, exploring the pros and cons of each side in the dispute:

> That the nerves are instruments of sensation, is clearly proved from experiments, but how they convey those sensations to the brain, is a matter of great dispute. The most general opinion is, that they are tubes to contain animal spirits, by whose motions these sensations are conveyed: And diligent enquiry has been made to discover their cavities, but hitherto in vain; and if each nerve is distinct from its origin, ... and too small to be the object of the best microscope, I do not see how such cavities are likely to be discovered. However, I think the nerves may be tubes, and that a fluid, whose cohesion is very little, and whose parts are perhaps no finer than light, may move very freely in them. Those who deny animal spirits in the nerves, suppose that the sensation is conveyed by a vibration. To which it is objected, that they are slack, moist, and surrounded by soft parts, and are therefore unfit for vibrations, as indeed they are for such as are made on the strings of a musical instrument; but the minutest vibrations ... may be as sufficient for this end, as the impulse of light upon the Retina, is for the sense of seeing. So that for ought I can discern, sensations may be conveyed either, or both ways, tho' the advocates for each opinion, have chiefly insisted upon the improbability or impossibility of the other opinion. (1730, 236–37)

In Cheselden's view, if nerves are tubes, their internal cavities will be so small as to be virtually unobservable, and the "fluid" that flows through them will have to be as aetherial as light. If nerves transmit vibrations, the "vibrations" will have to be exceptionally minute and will have to occur *within* the slack and moist nerves. Cheselden points out that both models are problematic; both represent at best imperfect approximations of the process by which nerves actually transmit impulses. Compared to phenomena observed in ordinary life, the models are as much disanalogies as analogies: if there is a fluid, it bears little resemblance to anything wet running through a pipe; if nerves vibrate, their motions are nothing like the movements of a fiddle string.

To accommodate Cheselden's criticism requires more than a disclaimer. If it is "highly absurd" to imagine that nerves behave like fiddle strings, it is necessary for the proponent of the theory to explain the manner in which they do vibrate. If the assertion is that a nerve vibrates with an interior motion, the proponent must describe the mechanism of internal vibratory motion and then show how nerve impulses are explicable in terms of it.

According to Hartley, the molecular reconfigurations that constitute the "vibration" of a nerve are brought about by means of changes in the relative strength of the positive and negative charges that together form the molecules' "spheres of attraction and repulsion." In Newton's theory, as Hartley restates it, at the level of the very small, the world is one of lattices or constellations of particles surrounded by fluids or fluxes: that is, of "infinitesimal" particles caught up in, and together constituting, fields of force, by virtue of the attractive and repulsive forces the particles exert. This is true of the space between the stars, of the spaces within the "anomalous concretion" that is a bladder stone, and also of the infinitesimal interior spaces within a living body. An atom in a nerve is charged, both positively and negatively; it is the interactive sum of individual atoms' "spheres of attraction and repulsion" that determines the configuration of the molecule they form; this configuration determines the molecule's "sphere of attraction and repulsion," and consequently the manner in which it will interact with other molecules in forming the still larger "molecules of molecules" that Boerhaave and Hartley consider the operative units in chemical interactions per se. Finally, it is the totality of the interactions involving all the constituent corpuscles' spheres that determines the internal structure of the nerve.[23]

Assuming that the corpuscles' spheres of attraction and repulsion do not undergo spontaneous changes, the molecules in a nerve will assume a stable configuration, a resting state, in which the nerve is quiescent. This resting state is the condition of a nerve prior to the reception and transmission of a stimulus. But a stimulus of the right kind would disturb this state, resulting in the transmission of an impulse along the nerve. To understand how Hartley thought this happened, we need to examine, first, how a nerve can function as a receptor to an external stimulus, and second, how the nerve transmits the signal it has received.

To answer the first part, we should begin by noting that Hartley held that nerves are specialized: "each nerve and region is fitted to receive, and, as one may say, sympathize with, such vibrations as are likely to be impressed upon them in the various incidents of life" (*OM* 1.1.1.6). The optic nerve is "fitted to receive" vibrations deriving from light, while the auditory nerve is able to transmit those deriving from sound.

But how do nerves initially receive the appropriate impulses? How, for example, do the nerves in the retina manage to respond at all to Newton's particles of light? Hartley states: "First, then, We are to conceive, that when external objects are impressed on the sensory nerves, they excite vibrations in the aether residing in the pores of these nerves, by means of the mutual actions interceding between the objects, nerves, and aether. For there seem to be mutual actions of all the varieties between these three, in all the senses, though in a different nature in different senses. Thus it seems that light affects both the optic nerve and the aether; and also, that the affections of the aether are communicated to the optic nerve, and *vice versa*" (*OM* 1.1.1.5). Then he adds: "Secondly, We are to conceive, that the vibrations thus excited in the aether will agitate the small particles of the medullary substance in the sensory nerves with synchronous vibrations, in the same manner as the vibrations of the air in sounds agitate many regular bodies with corresponding vibrations or tremblings." The task, for Hartley, is to give an account of how light can be transferred to a non-optic medium, the nerve, in terms of a neural harmonics.

In the case of sight at least, it is the aether that provides the connecting link. Newton had hypothesized that, although light itself was corpuscular, the aether was involved in its transmission and was responsible for such observed phenomena as reflection, diffraction, and color. As a stone thrown into a pond causes waves to ripple and spread in circles from the point of impact, so also do the streams of particles that are light create more complex patterns of ripples in the aetherial pond. Then, as light sets the aether vibrating, the aether, which permeates space and is also able to penetrate the spaces between and inside the molecules of a nerve, sets these in motion with "synchronous vibrations," in a way analogous to the way a note played on the D string of a violin can cause the same string on another instrument to tremble.

In this account of the transmission of light, the vibration of the aether itself, outside the nerve, continues through to the aether within the nerve and sets particles of the nerve in motion. But in addition, the streams of light corpuscles, which are already vibrating on account of their interactions with the aether, may "excite vibrations in the small particles of the optic nerve, by a direct and immediate action" (*OM* 1.1.1.5). To the extent that this occurs, light would be similar to sound, for which there is a direct action of the vibrating external medium upon the relevant anatomical structures. The vibrations of the air act mechanically upon the tympanum, and are transmitted through the small bones of the inner ear, to the colchea, and hence unto the nerves (*OM* 1.1.1.5). Here, a genuinely mechanical impulse is transformed into a quasi-mechanical one: the "vibrations" of the molecules and localized aether in the auditory nerve.

A nerve's capacity for receiving an impulse needs to be viewed as a process by which relatively large vibrations are transformed into much smaller vibrations of the atomic particles; the anatomical structures of ear, obviously, and eye, less obviously, are designed to do this. The physical vibrations of the air are refined and transformed, in their progress through the outer and inner ear, into the high-frequency vibrations of both the particles and aether that is a nervous impulse. Hartley suggests an analogous process occurs in the sense of smell and in the perception, by touch, of heat. But the meaning of "vibration," in the context of the microstructure of a nerve, can only be one of analogy to the vibrations of sound, light, and heat. And to make sense, the analogy needs to be developed and articulated in a model that has its own internal coherence and explanatory force. We have now arrived at our second question: In what way can the transmission of an impulse along a nerve be pictured as a kind of vibration?

Imagine an individual atom A in a molecule. In its state of equilibrium, E, it is held in position by the array of a/r (attractive and repulsive) forces that determine the molecule's structure. If a force "pushes" the atom to the right (position y) and then releases, the atom will seek to return to E. However, its momentum will carry it beyond E to position x on the left, at which point it will reverse direction and again move toward E. The movement from E to y to x to E constitutes one full cycle of an oscillation about a point of equilibrium. The atom is the functional equivalent of a bob on a pendulum.

But a single oscillation does not constitute a vibration. A violin string, for example, in order to create a tone, must be continuously pulled from its position E to y, released, and pulled again. In this instance, the static friction of the bow, as it is drawn over the string, pulls the string away from E to y—where y is the point at which the ratio of the downward force of the bow to the tension of the string is greater than the coefficient of static friction. The bow can no longer hold the string away from *E;* the string slips and moves back toward *E,* goes as far as *x,* and on its return to *E* is pulled again toward *y.* The string is now vibrating at its resonant frequency, and the player hears the note to which the string is tuned.

For the note to continue, the force upon the string must not move it beyond its elastic limit—the point at which the note gives way to a shriek and at which further "stretching" would cause a nonreformable deformation of the vibrating medium. Pulled too far, and the string will be permanently stretched out of shape, or will snap. A particle forced beyond its elastic limit will not return to its original point of equilibrium but will occupy a new point of equilibrium instead.

Now, in what comparable sense could the particles in a nerve be said to vibrate? Because the vibrating particles are embedded within apparently stable "molecular" lattices, the vibration cannot result from physical contact. Nor can it be so strong as to affect the anatomical integrity of the nerve, for example by setting off wholesale chemical interactions among the molecules. Instead, the bow that sets the infinitesimal particles in motion must be "aetherial" in the broad sense of being a flowing medium that itself resonates by virtue of the interactions of the attractive and repulsive forces that its constitutive particles possess. And this resonance is, in turn, transferred to the particles in the nerve, through the interaction of the a/r forces of the aether with the a/r forces of the particles in the sensory receptors of the nerve. Once this transference occurs and the particles in the sensory receptors are motion, the oscillations of one particle or lattice of particles will cause the ones next to it to vibrate, and so forth down the length of the nerve, as each particle seeks to maintain its point of equilibrium—its appropriate distance—relative to its neighbors. A nerve does not vibrate, in this sense, perpendicular to its length, as does a violin string; rather, the overall direction of its vibratory motion is parallel to its length. Transmission of a nervous impulse is thus a kind of "chemical" activity, but one that stops short of permanently disrupting the physical integrity of the nerve. The transfer of energy from the source of stimulation is strong enough to temporarily unbalance the equilibrium of a/r forces in the nerve, but not so strong as to cause the nerve to boil away into a factitious air.

Imagine a kind of a game of musical chairs, with the chairs stretched out in a long line. Person A attempts to push B off his chair, and almost succeeds, before B pushes back and in turn almost pushes A off his chair. But when A pushes B, B in turn pushes against C, who also pushes back, as each person strives to maintain his point of equilibrium, his seat on his assigned chair. Thus, a push at the start eventually involves pushing and counterpushing along the whole line. This game of musical chairs provides us with a simplified model of an alternating electrical current. As the back-and-forth movement of electrons creates a current along a copper wire, so also the similar oscillations of the infinitesimal particles within the nerve create a "current" that sends an impulse—an "action potential"—along it.

A violinist plays an A; the vibration of the string creates a vibration in the air, which strikes the eardrum, and which is transformed in its passage through the bones of the inner ear, etc., into a sequence of changes of the a/r forces belonging to the infinitesimal particles in the auditory nerve. These repeated changes in force cause the particles in the nerve to oscillate. In this form the signal travels to the brain. The listener hears the note.

4. Complex Vibrations

In real life, listeners seldom hear a single, simple note. When a person draws a bow across the D string of a violin, for instance, the sound produced is a composite of the fundamental and a number of overtones. Moreover, a skilled listener hears the D as the opening note of a well-known tune; she observes that it is slightly flat, held too long, and played without confidence. It is Caitlin's first appearance at a recital. In addition to her pupil's tentative beginning, Mrs. Laurie also hears, simultaneously, a clock ticking, the wind outside, and two of her other pupils whispering to each other. Finally, for Mrs. Laurie, listening to Caitlin's first public performance of "The Skye Boat Song" may not be the most pleasurable moment of the day. She may feel a contrary wish to sink the bonny boat. But at the same time Caitlin's tentative squeakings are, to her hopeful and encouraging parents, magic.

After stating that "the theory of sounds deduced from the nature of an elastic fluid . . . becomes to us a guide in all inquiries into the vibrations of other elastic mediums, such as the aether," Hartley writes:

> The doctrine of sounds does also furnish us with an answer to one of the principal and most obvious difficulties attending the

supposition, that all sensation, thought, and motion, is performed by vibrations in the medullary substance. For it may be objected, that such a number of different vibrations as seems to be required ... can scarce exist together.... Thus it is not uncommon for a person to receive a series of sensations, carry on a train of thought, and perform a course of external actions, which have little connexion with each other, at the same time. Now to this we may answer, that vibrations as different from each other do, in fact, exist together in common air, in such a manner as to be perceived distinctly. Thus a person may listen to what part he pleases in a concert of music, and masters in the art can listen to more than one. They can also at the same time receive, attend to, and understand the vibrations of the air, arising from the discourse of other persons. (*OM* 1.2.5.68)

Hartley points out that a crowded concert hall is filled with sounds; the air overflows with the vibrations produced by violins and cellos, oboe and bassoon, and by the "discourse" of the audience. Analogy suggests a related fact: that the nervous systems and brains of the concertgoers are filled with a symphony of vibrations. In the midst of that symphony, an experienced musician can discriminate discrete sequences and sources of sound: both the parts played by the principal players and the whispered conversation of the couple seated behind him.

Hartley's observation makes clear that the mechanism involved in the transmission of auditory (or visual) signals must be highly complex. My earlier example of atomic musical chairs was intended provide an image of how one particle can set the one next to it vibrating, and so on along a given line; but to accommodate Hartley's example of the concert room, we would need to picture the auditory nerves as forming a corridor in which a multitude of games were going on simultaneously, and the brain as the central location where the auditory—and all other—corridors meet. One option would be to view a nerve as carrying a multitude of simultaneous impulses in a manner analogous to a fiber optic cable. Concerning this option, Hartley would have been aware of Cheselden's observation that nerves appeared to be composed of bundles of fibers, "not communicating with one another," in which "every the minutest nerve, terminating in any part, is a distinct cord from its origin in the brain, or spinal marrow" (1730, 235–36).[24]

Moreover, Hartley's concert hall raises another issue, which is key to understanding his psychology: the difference between the reception of sensory stimuli and perception. "There is," Hartley adds to the passage quoted above, "a difficulty in performing... the things here mentioned; that confusion does often arise; and that where any person is remarkable for doing more than one thing at once, it is in consequence of great practice, and also of exquisite mental powers." What to the novice is an undifferentiated mass of sound possesses, for the expert, both logic and passion. By dint of "great practice," the expert has developed his mental powers so that he is able to comprehend the interior structure and dynamics of the music, and also to attend to the specifics of the performance. Although musical expert and novice may sit side by side in a concert hall and be the recipients of the "same" vibrations, they do not *hear* the same things.

In other words, Hartley's model of the reception and transmission of an impulse is only the starting point for a full physiological and psychological theory. And here, the first point to recognize concerning this model is that there is no direct and immediate route from sensation to perception. Although our sensory receptors are obviously stimulated by sound, light, etc., the "vibrations" that are sensory stimuli do not package themselves into discrete data of sense that are ready-made objects of our attention. The emergence of perceptions out of sensations—of, as Gerald M. Edelman puts it, a repertoire of labels from an "unlabeled" world (1992, 99)—requires the continuous construction and reconstruction of perceptual and conceptual categories. It is, in short, a matter of *making sense* of the world.

To integrate the "doctrine of vibrations" into a psychological model of how we make sense of the world, the simplified account of the transmission of a single impulse along a nerve needs to be complemented by further observations that provide refinements or elaborations of the model. Hartley makes four such elaborations, concerning (1) the difference between what Hartley terms a "natural" and an "induced" state of a nerve; (2) the affective dimension of sensory experience; (3) the means by which sensory stimuli are transformed into perceptions and concepts; and (4) the integration of perception and physical movement. We turn to the first and second of these in the remainder of this chapter and to the third and fourth in the next. To put this in terms of our example, we now turn to the beginning of Hartley's account of how Caitlin can, during music practice, perceive that a note is flat; take pleasure in the sound of her violin; perceive the tune as a tune, as a whole and not as random notes; and learn new tunes first by following a printed score while listening to someone play and then by practicing the tune herself. By exploring these issues, we will see how the "doctrine of vibrations" grounds, and expands into, the "doctrine of association."

5. Natural and Induced States: Vibrations and Vibratiuncles

Section 1 of chapter 1 of the *Observations* concerns the application of the doctrine of vibrations to sensations; section 2 extends the discussion to "ideas"—which Hartley, at the very start of the *Observations*, defines very broadly as including all "internal feelings" that are not sensations. The second proposition in the section states: "Sensory Vibrations, by being often repeated, beget, in the medullary Substance of the Brain, a Disposition to diminutive Vibrations, which may also be called Vibratiuncles, and Miniatures, corresponding to themselves respectively" (*OM* 1.1.2.9). In the text that explicates this proposition, Hartley states that "it will much establish and illustrate the doctrines of vibrations and association, to deduce it directly, if we can, from the nature of vibratory motions, and of the animal body; and not only from the relation of sensation and ideas." Hartley is not content with simply arguing that, because we know, first, that sensations leave "vestiges, traces, or images" of themselves, which we call the "simple ideas of sensation" (*OM* 1.1.2.8), and second, that sensations correlate with changes of state in the brain and nervous system, which may be modeled as "vibrations," we may conclude that ideas are also correlated with "vibrations" of some sort, here termed "vibratiuncles" (from *vibratiuncula*, the Latin diminutive). Such an argument, although it is consistent with the propositions that precede it, introduces the latter as purely hypothetical entities; it can be criticized for multiplying entities beyond necessity, insofar as postulating the existence of vibratiuncles adds nothing to our knowledge of sensations and ideas. As a deduction from sensations and ideas, proposition 9 thus fails as a scientific hypothesis, because it offers no guidance for the inquirer; it promises no illumination of phenomena that are poorly understood, overlooked, or presently undetected. Hence Hartley's desire to "deduce it directly... from the nature of vibratory motions, and of the animal body." Such an independent deduction may involve the creation of a physical model that does lead to the discovery of new facts about sensations and ideas, and possibly to a reformulation of our ways of thinking about them.

Hartley begins his "deduction" by drawing the reader's attention to what he terms the *natural vibrations* present in the brain and nervous system of a foetus: "If we admit vibrations of the medullary particles at all, we must conceive, that some take place in the *foetus in utero*, both on account of the warmth in which it lies, and of the pulsation of those considerable arteries, which pass through the medullary substance" (*OM* 1.1.2.9). The natural state of the nervous system in an animal body is thus not featureless or inactive. Rather, a developing foetus is stimulated by and responsive to the circumstances of its environment and its own autonomic and homeostatic processes—the warmth that surrounds it, its own heartbeat and circulation, and, we should add, the heartbeat of the mother.

And then the child is born into the Jamesian "blooming, buzzing confusion" (James 1890, 1:488) of the world. Here, "external objects act upon it violently, and excite vibrations ... which differ from the natural ones, and from each other." These new vibrations Hartley terms *preternatural*, to distinguish them from the natural ones present in the foetus. Some initial order arises out of the confusion from the fact that each type of nerves—optic, auditory, etc.—sends its signals to the specific regions of the brain that have "such a texture to receive, with the greatest facility, [its] specific vibrations." Even though the newborn has never before seen anything (except light and darkness), now the regions of its brain connected with vision receive a flow of preternatural vibrations from the optic nerves, and ultimately from the world. The same holds true of the other senses as well; blooms and buzzes are sensed separately. The infant "sees" and "hears," although what it sees and hears may make less sense to it than would a gamelan orchestra to a fan of country and western music.

At this point in Hartley's deduction, the newborn animal, whether person or piglet, still has no *idea* as to what is going on within or around it. Nonetheless, it would be misleading, on two counts, to picture the newborn's "mind" as a tabula rasa, waiting to be inscribed with the impressions of the objects of sense. First, the newborn does not have a "mind" as such, if "mind" is taken to refer to a preexisting empty space, a blank sheet of paper. Second, though not yet a mind, the newborn is a body; it possesses a brain and nervous system that is already humming with the vibrations of its "natural" state, and it is immediately responsive to pleasure and pain. Being warm or cold, dry or wet, hungry or full—a newborn responds to these feelings. Her nervous system is attuned to them. Her comfort—and her life—depends upon that attunement.

For the next step in his presentation, Hartley notes that, over time, certain sensory stimuli will recur, and that their recurrence will effect changes in the infant's brain and nervous system:

The Theory of Vibrations 119

> Representing now the natural vibrations by *N*, and the preternatural ones ... by *A, B, C*, &c let us suppose the first object to impress the vibrations *A*, and then to be removed. It is evident from the nature of vibratory motions, that the medullary substance will not, immediately upon the removal of this object, return to its natural state *N*, but will remain, for a short space of time, in the preternatural state *A*, and pass gradually from *A* to *N*. Suppose the same object to be impressed again and again, ... it seems to follow, that the medullary substance will be longer in passing from *A* to *N*, after the second impression than after the first, after the third impression than second, &c till, at last, it will not return to its natural original state of vibration *N* at all.... This state may therefore be fitly denoted by *a*, and, being now in the place of the natural state *N*, it will be kept up by the heat of the medullary substance, and the pulsation of its arteries.... For the alterations which habit, custom, frequent impression, &c. make in the small constituent particles, can scarce be any thing besides alterations of the distances, and mutual actions, of these particles; and these last alterations must alter the natural tendency to vibrate. (*OM* 1.1.2.9)

Recall that at the level of its molecular or atomic structure, the component particles in a nerve are arranged in a nested sequence of lattices within lattices, in a configuration determined by the interactions of the a/r forces among the several orders of particles. A force disturbs the atomic or molecular structure of a nerve by causing changes in the relative strengths and hence shapes of the particles' spheres of attraction and repulsion; it thus acts upon a nerve, displaces particles from their points of equilibria, and causes them to vibrate. At various points of fetal development, the component parts of the nervous system are, as it were, switched on by such forces, particularly by those associated with the body's own metabolic and autonomic systems. Because these stimuli are continuous and regular, they produce in the nerves "continuous" tones, like those of a bagpipe's drones, which Hartley terms "natural vibrations" and designates as *N*. At birth, other forces, deriving from light, sound, external heat and cold, etc., act upon the relevant parts of the nervous system, causing the further vibrations *A, B, C,* and so forth.

Now, the key physical fact, which Hartley notes, is that an elastic body, when repeatedly displaced from its original resting state, will gradually become fatigued: it will lose its elasticity, so that its return to its initial point will be delayed. In the next section, we shall see that, in his discussion of sensate pleasures and pains, Hartley uses this observation to explain the diminishment of hedonic intensity that results from repeated exposure to a sensory stimulus. Here he points out that fatigue—the loss of elasticity—will eventually result in a nonreformable deformation of the body. If pushed into a position often enough, an elastic body will eventually learn to occupy that position. To illustrate the point, he uses the example of a musical string: "Musical strings always accommodate themselves to, and lean towards the state into which they were last put. Thus the tone of a musical string either rises or falls upon altering its tension, according as the preceding tension was greater or less than its present tension. Now the small component parts of a musical string must recede from, and approach to, each other, *i.e.* must oscillate lengthways, during every transverse oscillation of the string. And this must arise from the mutual influences of the component particles tending to their last superinduced state."

For a string to be pulled in a transverse direction, perpendicularly to its length, there must be some slight give in the string; the component particles must be pulled away from each other along the string's length. Although the string as a whole vibrates transversely, the individual particles also oscillate very slightly back and forth along its length. Now, for a string to vibrate when repeatedly pulled and released, the degree of give must be limited, so that the component particles snap back into positions that are nearly identical to their original ones; the string is made out of metal and not taffy, and it generally maintains its internal structure after repeated playing. However, the fact that there is give in the material at all, which is required for vibration, also means that the material will have some susceptibility to nonreformable deformation; the repetition of longitudinal displacements will cause the component particles to remain in "their last superinduced state"; give gives way to stretch. Consequently, other things, such as the expansion or contraction of a wooden instrument's body, being equal, a metal string will, whenever struck or bowed, vibrate at the frequency to which it is tuned—and gradually go flat. And further tuning is accomplished by modulating the tension on the string. Relaxing the tension will cause the string to go flat, while increasing the tension will cause it to go sharp relative to the "superinduced state" of the string when the instrument was last played.

Hartley then applies this point to the microstructure of a nerve: if we could observe a nerve vibrating at frequency A, we would find no transverse movement; at the molecular level, however, we would detect rapid changes in the shape and size of the a/r spheres of the component particles. Such is the nature of neural vibration. Repeated vibration at A will cause a chemical reformation of those spheres so that they remain in an induced state, designated a, when the external stimulus ceases. The nerve "learns" to vibrate in a particular manner, as its initial state of vibration N is superseded by the induced state a. In this manner, a nerve is tuned to vibrate at a certain frequency, much as a musical string is, the difference between them being that the vibration in a nerve is exclusively molecular and longitudinal. And as would a violin string when the instrument is in its case, the state a would be quiescent, until again stimulated to vibrate, at which point it would vibrate at frequency A.

To generalize: according to Hartley, a sensory stimulus, especially when repeated, can effect a reconfiguration of the molecular structure of the brain and nervous system. Such a reconfiguration is localized in the nerves relevant to the sensation and in the region of the brain involved in processing the signals received from the sensory receptors. Now, to continue the analysis of Hartley's theory, we should note that such reconfigurations have two important consequences. First, sensory stimuli induce responses of pleasure and pain. And second, a reconfiguration is, in effect, the nervous system's memory of the stimulus. The presence of such "memories" in an animal's brain and nerves bring it to the threshold of having "ideas." The first consequence is the subject of the remainder of this chapter, the second of the chapter to come.

6. Good Vibrations and Bad: Pleasure and Pain

In Hartley's world, talk about pleasures and pains was commonplace. What is distinctive about Hartley's account is the way in which he provides a physiological explanation for them within the context of the theory of vibrations. Hartley begins his discussion of sensate pleasure and pain (*OM* 1.1.1.6) by observing that "the doctrine of vibrations seems to require, that each pain should differ from the corresponding and opposite pleasure, not in kind, but in degree only; *i.e.* that pain should be nothing more than pleasure itself, carried beyond a due limit." Vibrations, according to his theory, differ from each other in four ways: degree (i.e., amplitude), kind (i.e., resonant frequency), place of origin, and "line of direction" (i.e., through which part of the nervous system they are received and travel to the brain). For any given sensation—eating a chili pepper, for example—the kind, place, and line of direction will remain the same; whether or not the experience is pleasurable or painful depends upon the amplitude of the signal and intensity of the vibrations it effects. An apparently qualitative difference in the experience of a sensation is thus shown to be a quantitative one.

That a pleasurable sensation becomes painful when it exceeds its "due limit" suggests, in turn, that the boundary between pleasure and pain is determined by a physiological event. If three chilies in a stew make it pleasingly hot but the addition of a fourth renders it painfully so, the increase in the amplitude of the signal must cause the nervous system to shift from one mode of response to another; the point where this shift occurs marks the pleasure/pain boundary.

Hartley's explanation of this shift in mode of response relies upon the concept of the "solution of continuity"—a medical term of art that referred to the displacement, rupture, or dissolution of previously connected physical structures. A separated shoulder or dislocated knee are examples of muscular-skeletal solutions of continuity; other "evident" or "manifest" solutions of continuity occur in burns, wounds, and contusions. All are painful, and the vibrations that stream towards the brain from them are "violent."

There are, however, subtler solutions of continuity that derive, not from accidents, but from the activities of daily life. The bodily frame is a system of "situations and connections" including the skeleton, muscles, joints, tendons, and ligaments. In movement and exercise, these are capable of extension and contraction, and of some degree of "distention"—that is, of loosening, stretching, and enhanced flexibility, such as results from a routine of warm-up exercises. Hartley notes, first, that "a moderate degree of distention in the parts is necessary for their growth and pleasurable state," and, second, that "all great distentions are attended with pain for a considerable time before they are raised to such a pitch as to cause a visible solution of continuity." On the one hand, it feels good to stretch; on the other, pain in a muscle or joint acts as a warning that an injury is about to occur through overextension.

To account for these two observed phenomena, Hartley proposes that the application of the concept of the solution of continuity be extended from those structures in the body we can see to those we cannot. What is true of the frame of muscles and joints is also true of the minute frames of particles that constitute all larger anatomical structures: "It seems not improbable, that in preternatural and painful distentions, the small particles are perpetually separating themselves from their former cohesions, and running into new ones; so that a minute and invisible solution of continuity is carried on during the whole distention, till such time as this degree of distention becomes familiar to the parts, and the situation and mutual actions of the small particles be accommodated to it.... Every manifest solution of continuity does therefore ... include within itself an infinite number of minute invisible solutions." At one level of magnification, the "small particles" are the cellular components of soft tissue, particularly the muscle fibers. When we tear a muscle, the individual muscle fibers "separate themselves from their former cohesions, and run into new ones." In addition, Hartley uses the solutions of continuity in muscle fibers and capillaries to explain inflammation in tissues adjacent to a wound or burn.

At a higher magnification, solutions of continuity also occur at the molecular level, among the particles that are the constituents of the nervous system. It is these molecular solutions of continuity that, Hartley proposes, determine the boundary between pleasure and pain:

> Hence we may ask, whether this minute invisible solution of continuity in the infinitesimal medullary particles of the brain be not that common limit, and middle point, which separates pleasure from pain? ... It is some presumption in favor of this position, that all conjectures concerning invisible things ought to be taken from visible ones of the same kind; also, that it is particularly suitable to the doctrine of vibrations; inasmuch as ... one may easily conceive how moderate and pleasant impressions may agitate the medullary particles in so moderate a degree, as that they shall again return to their former situations and connexions, when the agitation is over; whereas violent and painful ones may force the particles from thence, and give rise to new ones, *i.e.* to the solution of continuity. (*OM* 1.1.1.6; cf. Hartley 1959, 14)

As we saw above, in Hartley's theory the reception of energy from an external source causes the particles within a nerve to oscillate about their points of equilibrium. The nerve vibrates and sends its vibrations along to the brain. Such activation of the system is itself pleasurable, provided that the particles' oscillations remain within their elastic limits. If, however, sufficient force is transferred to the particles, they will begin to oscillate beyond their elastic limits and even begin to enter into a state of molecular disruption. The organism will then experience pain.

The following illustration may help to clarify the transit from pleasure to pain in a manner consistent with Hartley's theory. A musical sound has three components: pitch, loudness (amplitude), and timbre (tone color, determined by the combination of overtones). As a bow is pulled with ever more pressure and speed across a violin string, or as one puts more breath into blowing across the mouthpiece of a flute, the note played will grow louder while the pitch will remain constant—as long as the string (or air column) continues to oscillate at its resonant frequency. However, at a certain point, the force of friction from the string (or breath) will force the vibrating medium to move beyond its resonant frequency and elastic limit. At this point, the medium will enter a state of chaotic oscillation: the violin screams, the flute shrieks. Now, to apply this analogy to Hartley's harmonic vibrations of the nervous system, we could say that, as anatomical solutions of continuity mark the point at which a bodily structure becomes nonfunctional, a solution of continuity at the molecular level occurs at that point at which a nerve's vibrations become chaotic. As increasing amplitude can eventually cause a musical tone of a given pitch to degenerate into noise, so also can increasing amplitude cause a nervous signal of a given frequency to degenerate into pain. This degeneracy would be the physiological event that marks the boundary between pleasure and pain.

In many instances, such moments of pain are temporary and cease as soon as or shortly after the "scraping" stops. The body's mechanisms for maintaining its integrity ensure that the degeneracy leaves no lasting effects: "As the body is so formed, that great and visible solutions of continuity may be healed again, and the parts restored, in great measure, to their primitive integrity and perfection, by the power of nature ... so we may suppose, that the power of nature restores all minute solutions of continuity in the constituent infinitesimal particles almost instantaneously, and so that the body receives no perceptible detriment from single instances." As long as there is no anatomical solution of continuity, pain will cease fairly quickly after the removal of the stimulus: hit your thumb with a hammer and it will continue to hurt, but pinch it and it will stop hurting shortly after you stop.

In instances involving chronic pain, nervous solutions of continuity can both signal and cause permanent damage: when there are "frequent repetitions" of these, "pain, by often returning, impairs the faculties, both bodily and mental." Similar impairment may also occur if a solution of continuity is particularly severe. In some cases of impairment, the nerves may be disrupted to a point at which they are no longer able to transmit impulses at all: "old age, inactivity, inflammation, [and chronic] pain" may induce "such a degree of condensation, fixation, and callosity, in the medullary substance, as must end at last in insensibility and death."

Between these two limiting conditions—of nearly immediate recovery from a solution of continuity, and of the complete breakdown of a nerve's capacity for receiving and transmitting signals—are many instances in which single or especially repeated solutions of continuity have lasting effects upon nerves and brain. What is notable, in Hartley's view, about these instances, is the manner in which the repetition of a particular stimulus leads to a diminishing sensibility to it.

In general, the "power of nature" acts in a living body to repair the damage that is the correlative of pain, even when it cannot restore the nerves and brain "to their primitive integrity and perfection." As noted above, when a "solution of continuity" occurs on the neurological level, the healing powers of nature can cause disrupted particles to "run into" new connections, as they accommodate themselves to their new positions. The healing process does not reknit the now-severed connections but rather causes the disrupted parts to establish new linkages with each other. Given their new linkages, the reconfigured neurological structures may be "accommodated" to a particular impression and hence are no longer forced into a solution of continuity by it.

But what does it mean, in terms of Hartley's model of the physical structure of the nerves and brain, to say that neurological molecular particles "run into" new connections? We noted above that repetition of a stimulus A can lead to the creation of an induced state a in place of an original state N. The transit from N to a requires that the particles in the nerve adopt a new configuration, in which they occupy new points of equilibrium. This is achieved through a change in the values of the forces that define the shapes of the particles' spheres of attraction and repulsion: interaction with the a/r forces of the particles of light, etc. that carry the external signal, and then with each other, causes a modulation of the shapes of the particles' spheres of attraction and repulsion and consequently a reconfiguration of the relative positions of the particles within the molecules they comprise. Although a nerve's coming to rest at a involves a nonreformable deformation of an existing configuration, it would follow from Hartley's theory to say that such a reconfiguration will not cross over the pleasure/pain boundary as long as the transit from N to a is gradual—as long, that is, as the nervous particles' limits of oscillation are gradually stretched without at any point causing the particles in the nerve to enter a state of chaotic oscillation. They may, however, enter that state at any time, provided that A be "loud" enough. Such chaotic oscillation would force the nervous particles beyond their elastic limits and thereby disrupt the microarchitecture of the nerve.

To the question "what general tendencies in the small medullary particles might dispose them to undergo such changes [as are involved in a gradual adaptation to a stimulus]?" Hartley answers, "it appears to me, that a change of the spheres of attraction and repulsion in these particles, upon every change in their situations, so as always to lean towards the situation last superinduced, might be sufficient for this purpose." Repeated impressions of a sensory stimulus A gradually induce a resting state a in place of the natural state N, because after each impression of A the nerve returns to one of a series of intermediate states a_1 a_2 a_3 etc., which are progressively farther away from N and closer to a. Here the new "situations and connections" of the particles to each other that represent the series of induced states affect the manner in which further impressions of A will be received and transmitted. A certain quantum of energy is required to effect the change of state from N to A; moreover, the distance a nerve at N has to move to vibrate at the A frequency, at a given amplitude, may distend its oscillation beyond its normal limits and create a solution of continuity. But repetition of A will eventually induce the nerve to occupy resting states intermediate to and ending at a, and because the distance from a_1 a_2 a_3 etc. to A is progressively less than that from N to A, vibration at the frequency and amplitude represented by A will gradually start to fall within its normal limits of oscillation, and involve fewer and eventually no episodes of degeneracy into chaos (i.e., solutions of continuity), *even though* the quantum of energy imparted through the impression remains constant.

We shall see in the next chapter that a nerve's adoption of an induced state, its learning to vibrate at A, can lead to an increase in acuity. A nerve in resting state a will vibrate at A even in the presence of a weak or indirect stimulus. But adoption of a new resting state also serves to account for what at first may seem to be the opposite phenomenon, the diminishing tendency of a signal to cause pain—or pleasure:

> It is not unsuitable to the doctrine of vibrations, that the frequent repetition of the same external impressions should have

> the power of converting original pains into pleasures, and pleasures into mere sensations, *i.e.* into evanescent pleasures; as we find it has in fact. For this may be effected by such a change in the organ and brain, as that organ shall send weaker and weaker vibrations perpetually to the brain, upon every successive renewal of the same impression, and the brain become perpetually less and less disposed to receive strong vibrations, though the power of communication from the impressions should continue the same. (*OM* 1.1.1.6)

With repetition, sensations lose their intensity; pains diminish until they fall within the "limits of pleasure," and pleasures diminish until they fall within the "limits of indifference." A person learns to enjoy eating chilis, and a stew without them seems insipid. Alternatively, the first chocolate truffle is wonderful, but after the third or fourth or fifth, the pleasure vanishes. Just as repeated playing of a violin string will cause it to stretch slightly and consequently vibrate at a lower frequency, so also will the repeated stimulation of a nerve; in both cases, repetition will cause the "string" to go flat.

In his discussion of the "pleasures and pains of imagination" in a later chapter of the *Observations,* Hartley points out that if a body is "indisposed" to pleasure, either through physical illness or numbing of the nervous system, "it is possible to force it into a state of pleasure by the vivid introduction of various and powerful circumstances" (*OM* 1.4.1.94). He adds that "this unnatural state cannot last long." He also notes that "where the disposition to pleasure is preternaturally prevalent, as after wine and opium, and in certain morbid cases, the least hint will excite profuse joy." A nervous system that has become nonresponsive to stimuli at normal levels of intensity can be forced temporarily into an extreme state of pleasure and even of elation through the introduction or administration of "powerful circumstances" of some form or other. Repeated recourse to intoxicants or opiates, of course, will only further depress the nervous system's responses and diminish the person's capacity for experiencing pleasure.

Hartley also makes the comment that "it is easy to see how the doctrine of vibrations, which appears to be the only one that admits of permanent states of motion, and disposition to motion, in the brain, suits these last remarks in a peculiar manner." The conceptual advantage of the theory of vibrations over the theory of animal spirits is that it offers an account of the neurophysiological basis of learning: the nerves adapt to stimuli by undergoing micromolecular reconfigurations and thus by remaining in induced states; it is these "permanent states of motion, and dispositions to motion" that account for a person's capacities to recognize the flavor of cinnamon, to learn to enjoy eating chilis, and to become dependent upon wine and opium for fleeting minutes of profuse joy. According to Hartley, an adequate theory must model both the transmission of an impulse along a nerve and into the brain and also the manner in which the nerve and brain *retain* a memory of that impulse. His claim is that the theory of vibrations does precisely this, and that theories of animal spirits flowing through tubular nerves do not.

7. From Sensate to Intellectual Pleasures

In Hartley's theory pleasure and pain are types of events or states in the brain and nervous system; the terms refer to the ways in which the nerves and brain respond to stimuli. Accordingly, states of pleasure and pain can occur in the absence of perceptual categorizations, concepts, or any of the other elements of higher consciousness. The discussion of pleasure and pain appears in section 1 of chapter 1 of the *Observations*, prior to the initial discussion of ideas in section 2 and of voluntary motion in section 3. Pleasure and pain are thus the common property of all biological organisms possessed of some form of neural organization. Moreover, at least among the mammals, the body responds to pain in a typical way. "The action of crying," Hartley writes, "is in all animals, but especially young ones, the natural and necessary consequence of pain" (*OM* 1.2.1.35). With the sudden onset of pain, "violent vibrations excited in the injured part will pass up to the brain, and over the whole muscular system, immediately," with the result that all muscle groups, including the groups of antagonist muscles, are put "into a state of contraction." But in any pair of antagonist muscles, the stronger will "overpower the weaker, for a certain time, and then give place to them for a certain other time, and so on alternatively." Hartley gives a detailed anatomical account of how the alternating dominance by antagonist muscles in the chest and diaphragm, throat, and face causes a young child to break into fits of spasmodic sobbing.

Consistent with this emphasis on physiological response, the sources of pleasure and pain for a newborn person are much the same as those for a newborn puppy. The nervous systems of both hum with pleasure when they are warm and dry, safe, and either feeding or fed. But as person and puppy grow, "compound or mental [pleasures and] pains will arise from simple bodily ones by means of words, symbols, and associated circumstances" (*OM* 1.2.1.33), and their new sources of pleasure and pain will diverge, reflecting their different intellectual capacities and paths of development. Despite this growing complexity and differentiation, the pains of feeling are fundamental, and Hartley remarks that, "the greatest part of our intellectual pains are deducible from them" (*OM* 1.2.1.33; see §1.6 for such a deduction regarding anger). And among humans at least, the combination of smell and taste remains the foundation of our "intellectual" pleasures; thanks to their "greatness and constant recurrency, from our first infancy to the extremity of old age," the pleasures of taste "introduce and keep up pleasurable states in the brain, and . . . connect them to foreign objects" (*OM* 1.2.2.44). If Hartley's slavery to "the gross pleasures of sense" centered upon taste, his comment here may be an acknowledgment both of the power of those pleasures and of their capacity for transmutation into "intellectual" pleasures of an entirely different kind, when successfully connected with "foreign objects."

Both people and puppies mature; both develop their capacities for experiencing "intellectual" pleasures and pains. Hartley's account of the development of intellect relies upon two central concepts: first, "association," the process by which "ideas" emerge, form larger composite structures, and make skilled motor activity and voluntary action possible; and second, "transference," the process by which the pleasures deriving from taste and the pains deriving from feeling are invested in the "intellectual" categories of experience, thereby creating "compound or mental" pleasures and pains. The first concept, association, is the subject of chapters 4 and 6; the second, transference, of chapters 7 and 8.

4

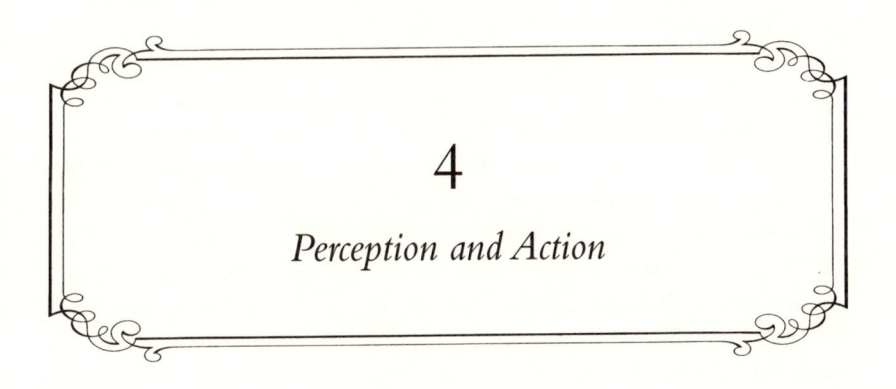

Perception and Action

>   Superior beings, when of late they saw
>   A mortal Man unfold all Nature's law
>   Admir'd such wisdom in an earthly shape,
>   And shew'd a Newton as we shew an Ape.
>   Could he, whose rules the rapid Comet bind,
>   Describe or fix one movement of his Mind?
>
>   —Pope, *An Essay on Man* (1733)

Pope's epitaph for Newton—"God said, *Let Newton be!* and all was *Light*"—represents the man not as a second Adam but as a second Creation. The first words God spoke, *Fiat lux, Let there be light,* initiated the days of creation. But the children of the first parents only dimly understood what God had accomplished—until God, echoing his originating words, spoke again, *Let Newton be!* Only in the light of this second creation could the first be comprehended. The second *Fiat* initiates the age of knowledge, of enlightenment.

Still, Pope, in a more skeptical mood, recognizes that the light cast by this second creation is also partial, more a lantern at night than a sun. And Locke, his thoughts turning to "other creatures" dwelling in "other mansions" of this "vast and stupendous universe," imagines them to be "intelligent beings, of whose faculties" we have "as little knowledge or apprehension, as a worm shut up in one drawer of a cabinet, hath of the senses or understanding of a man" (*HU* 2.2.3). To such superior beings, Newton may have discovered the rules that bind the comets—and for this they acknowledge the man as we do a trained ape—but Newton is no more able to explain *how* he made this discovery than the ape can tell how it learned to mimic a man. We can imagine the looks, the smiles the superior beings exchange with each other, as they show off their pet: he has discovered the laws of mechanics that control the motions of the planets and stars through the depths of space, but he knows not the first thing about the even greater depth of space that is enclosed within his skull.

We now think that the human brain has on the order of 100 billion (10^{11}) neurons, with each neuron making several thousand synaptic connections with other neurons. Consequently, "the number of possible different combinations of synaptic connections among the neurons in a single human brain is larger than the total number of atomic particles that make up the known universe" (R. Thompson 1993, 3). The superior beings are right after all: the space within is greater than the space without. And we are still, despite our knowledge of neuroanatomy and physiology, a far way from describing "one movement" of our minds. No one can describe the patterns of neural organization by which you remember your name.

Lack of knowledge does not, however, signify the impossibility of knowledge. Who in 1600 could have anticipated the discoveries in celestial mechanics that would be common knowledge a century later? And who, living in 1730, could predict which of Newton's "hints" could be most fruitfully "examin'd and improv'd by . . . farther Experiments and Observations"? Many accepted Newton's invitation, proffered in the closing paragraph of the *Opticks,* to investigate such hints and thereby expand the bounds both of natural and of moral philosophy. Among them was Hartley, whose self-assigned task was to confront directly the agnosia that caused Pope's superior beings to exchange smiles, as they showed their wise ape: he would attempt to "describe or fix the movements of the mind" on the basis of a neural Newtonianism.

In chapter 3, we examined Hartley's "doctrine of vibrations," according to which he used Newton's theory of matter and of forces of attraction and repulsion to model a nerve's reception, transmission, and

Perception and Action 133

memory of impulses. In this chapter, we turn from the doctrine of vibrations to its partner, the "doctrine of association." We begin here with his account of perception, paying particular attention to the importance of "joint impression" for turning sensory inputs into meaningful perceptual categories. We then turn to Hartley's account of how the coordination of perception and motor activity contributes to the learning and perfection of actions.

At the time Hartley wrote, the science of physics had just undergone rapid growth and was approaching an adult's stature. The sciences of chemistry and biology, in contrast, were barely in their infancy. Superior beings, observing the man as he worked away at his book, must have smiled at Hartley's attempt to describe the movements of the mind on the basis of a neural Newtonianism, without benefit of basic concepts in chemistry and biology. But how do we interpret their smiles? As smiles of weariness, the sad result of watching someone labor at a task one knows is futile? Or as smiles of wonder, the smiles of beings who, seeing the work, remark how much is done with the materials at hand, and delight in seeing the illumination, however partial, of another of nature's realms?

1. From Simple to Complex Ideas

In Hartley's neurophysiology, the "corporeal" explanation of the reception, transmission, and memory of impulses in the nerves and brain extends to the subjective, experiential dimension of the lives of living organisms:

> Since therefore sensations are conveyed to the mind, by the efficiency of corporeal causes of the medullary substance, ... it seems to me, that the powers of generating ideas, and raising them by association, must also arise from corporeal causes, and consequently admit of an explication from the subtle influences of the small parts of matter on each other, as soon as these are sufficiently understood. (*OM* 1.1.2.11)

Projects such as Hartley's that situate awareness and action within the processes that order "the subtle influences of the small parts of matter on each other" are confronted with several problems. One, perhaps most resistant to explanation, concerns the relationship between "corporeal causes" and consciousness, between physical events, neurological events, and subjective experience. "How," asked Humphrey Ditton in his *Discourse concerning the Resurrection of Jesus Christ*, "is this Reciprocal Agitation of an *Eye* or an *Ear*, my apprehension of the Thing seen or heard?" (1712, 497; quoted in Yolton 1984, 124). A related problem concerns the capacities minds have to order the flow of experience: that is, to step out of, or rise above, the flow of physical events so as to abstract from them, classify them, and generalize about them in ways that enable the living being to experience the world in a coherent manner. If "observers themselves are 'things,' like the rest of the objects in their world," asks Gerald Edelman (1992, 11), "How do we account for the curious ability of observers . . . to carve up their world into categories of things—to refer to things of the world when things themselves can never so refer?" A third problem concerns the introspective availability of consciousness to itself: when a conscious mind seeks to observe itself, how reliable are its observations? When it carves itself into categories of "things" such as *memory, will,* and *ideas,* to what do the words refer?

Let us begin to explore Hartley's thinking on these matters by asking: what, to Hartley, is an *idea*? On the first page of the *Observations,* Hartley defines "ideas" as referring to all "internal feelings" that are not "sensations." The broadness of the definition is, I think, purposive. An idea is any "internal feeling" that is not a sensation; in terms of the physiology underlying the doctrine of vibrations, it would thus seem to make sense to say that an idea is the correlate of any molecular reconfiguration within the nervous system and brain—that is, of any induced neural state a, which is ready to vibrate in a distinctive way when stimulated.

As we noted in §3.3, Hartley proposed that the repetition of a sensory stimulus A causes a change in the shapes of the "spheres of attraction and repulsion" of a nerve's atomic particles and hence in the morphology of the molecular lattices the particles form. The natural state of the nerve gives way to an induced state, as the nerve is tuned to vibrate at a specific frequency. Once tuned, the nerve will vibrate at the a frequency whenever stimulated by a signal with the correct harmonic resonance. Nerves that have been trained to vibrate at specific frequencies are thus the fundamental "corporeal causes" from which "the powers of generating ideas . . . arise."

And first among the ideas thus generated would seem to be the "Vestiges, Types, or Images" of sensations, "which may be called, Simple Ideas of Sensation" (*OM* 1.1.2.8). The notion of simple ideas derives, of course, from Locke's *Essay Concerning Human Understanding,* first published in 1690. According to Locke, such simple ideas are categories that identify the general and unchanging qualities that a sensing being recognizes as it interacts with its world: "Though the qualities that affect our senses, are, in the things themselves, so united and blended, that there is no separation, no distance between them; yet 'tis plain, the *ideas* they produce in the mind, enter by the senses simple and unmixed.... The simple *ideas* thus united in the same subject, are as perfectly distinct, as those that come in by different senses. The coldness and hardness, which a man feels in a piece of *ice,* being as distinct ideas in the mind, as the smell and whiteness of a lily; or as the taste of sugar, and smell of a rose" (*HU* 2.2.1). Each category is basic: it identifies a quality that cannot be further decomposed, confused with another category, or changed. I take an ice cube out of the tray in the freezer. It is roughly cubic in shape, cold, smooth, and dry at first. In Locke's account, the object "produces" in my mind a set of separate, enumerable ideas, as the mind surveys the qualities the object manifests. Although the object is a compound of qualities, each quality is a distinct and static perceptual category. "Nothing could be plainer to a man," comments Locke, "than the clear and distinct perception he has of those simple *ideas;* which being each in it self uncompounded, contains in it nothing but *one uniform appearance.*" Such simple ideas range from the most general, such as the ideas of unity, solidity, and motion, to the highly specific, such as the fragrance of a violet or the flavor of cinnamon.

Locke understood the need for a physiological account of sensation, an explanation how bodies act upon the nerves to produce in them "some motion" that is "thence continued to the brains or seat of sensation, there to *produce in our minds the* ideas *we have of them*" (*HU* 2.8.12). It might seem obvious that Hartley's account of "induced states" could be taken as providing this account.[1] An infant is given a bath and dried in a white towel. As she splashes in the water, the sensory vibration *Wet* travels along the nerves from skin to brain, and in the brain it causes certain other nerves to configure into the induced state *wet.* Similarly, the blend of sensory vibrations deriving from the sight of the towel includes, among others, the vibration *White,* which also configures other nerves in the brain into the induced state *white.* (This example assumes that the child has not already gained the induced states *wet* and *white* from other experiences.) The induced states *wet* and *white* are now feature detectors; when activated, the child will recognize wetness and whiteness, in raindrops and puddles, in clouds and sheets of paper.

A glass of milk will elicit in the child's mind the uniform and simple ideas of *wet* and *white,* among others.

We should recall, of course, that this is just the beginning of the story. A mind that perceived only simple ideas would scarcely be a mind at all. Such a "mind" would be like the optical nervous system of a frog, which is programmed to respond only to movement; because it is unable to see motionless objects, a frog would starve to death while surrounded by newly swatted flies. What distinguishes our minds from the nervous systems of frogs are, in Locke's psychology, our capacities for mental action. Although "the mind is wholly passive in the reception of all its simple *ideas,*" writes Locke, "so it exerts several acts of its own, whereby out of its simple *ideas,* as the materials and foundations of the rest, the other[s] are framed." These actions include our abilities "to unite [ideas] together, or to set them by one another, or wholly separate them"—in other words, our powers to combine simple ideas into "complex" ones, to identify relationships between ideas, and to abstract an idea from its constellation of circumstances (*HU* 2.12.1). The child's mind combines the simple ideas of *wet* and *white,* along with others, to produce the complex idea *milk*—which is in time set beside the complex idea *cow* and utilized in the further production of generalizations such as *food* or *liquid.*

Viewed in terms of this story, Hartley's *Observations* could be taken to be a further development of Locke's psychology—a detailed exposition of the process of construction, by which the mind builds ever more complex structures (and higher states of consciousness) out of the "materials and foundations" of simple ideas. In this interpretation, Hartley's innovation appears to be his identification of association as the fundamental mechanism of construction: it is through association that "the simple ideas of sensation must run into clusters and combinations" and each of these clusters in turn "coalesce into one complex idea" (*OM* 1.1.2.12). "The several acts" by which Locke thought the mind "frames" complex ideas, relations, and abstractions out of "the materials and foundations" of simple ideas are thus reduced to one: the mechanism of association recurring over and over again—an operation generating complexity out of "simplicity" through repetition. Given this reduction, moreover, Locke's distinction between the "passive" reception of simple ideas and the "acts" of framing simple ideas into complex ideas, relations, and abstractions would also seem to break down; association could be taken to be as spontaneous or automatic a process as sensation, and the mind as "passive" before the objects of its experience.

In this interpretation of Hartley's theory, the process of association is one that builds up compounds out of simple ideas, atoms of sensation. In this regard, Hartley, like Locke before him, appears to be guilty of the "one huge error" against which William James conducts a sustained critique in his *Principles of Psychology:* "that of the construction of our thoughts out of the compounding of themselves together of immutable and incessantly recurring 'simple ideas' " (1890, 1:553). It is their reliance upon this psychological atomism, this "brickbat plan of construction," that leads James to "impeach the entire English psychology derived from Locke and Hume, and the entire German psychology derived from Hebart, so far as they both treat 'ideas' as separate subjective entities" (1890, 1:196). James adds that such supposedly simple and separate ideas are the "pailsful, spoonsful, quartpotsful, barrelsful, and other moulded forms of water" that some philosophers and psychologists dip out of the flowing "free water of consciousness" (1:255).

Writing seventy years prior to James, Coleridge questioned in his *Biographia Literaria* (1817) whether such a plan of construction could build anything at all.[2] Association, he states, if understood as a purely passive process, could never form the minds we know ourselves to have. But such passivity, he then argues, is a necessary feature of a process of association that is grounded upon a neural physiology: "the *material* hypothesis" of the theory of vibrations, which is the foundation of Hartley's system, "constrained" Hartley to represent "the principle of *contemporaneity* ... as being itself the sole *law*" (C 7:110) governing the ordering of our thoughts.[3] Coleridge then asserts that, from the sole law of contemporaneity, it "results inevitably, that the will, the reason, the judgment, and the understanding, instead of being the determining causes of association, must needs be represented as its *creatures,* and among its mechanical *effects.*" The result is contradicted by the facts of human experience: it is, according to Coleridge, the consequence of Hartley's theory "that our whole life would be divided between the despotism of outward impressions, and that of senseless and passive memory" (C 7:111). And such despotism would render experience incoherent; such a law "would indeed be mere lawlessness":

> Consider, how immense must be the sphere of a total impression from the top of St. Paul's church; and how rapid and continuous the series of such total impressions. If therefore we suppose the absence of all interference of the will, reason, and judgment, one or other of two consequences must result. Either

the ideas (or relicts of such impression) will exactly imitate the order of the impression itself, which would be absolute *delirium*: or any one part of that impression might recal any other part, and . . . *any* part of *any* impression might recal *any* part of any *other*, without a cause present to determine *what* it should be. . . . There is in truth one state to which this theory applies at all, namely, that of complete light-headedness; and even to this it applies but partially, because the will, and reason are perhaps never wholly suspended. (C 7:111–12)

Hartley's "sole law" of association, in Coleridge's view, fails because it makes the active powers of the mind the "mechanical *effects*" of a physical process. Such mechanical effects can have no causal efficacy. But if we deny causal efficacy to the mind—if we deny that the terms *will, reason,* and *judgment* refer to the "several acts" which Locke thought the mind performs "of its own"—then, Coleridge argues, we have no way of accounting for intentionality and for the selectivity of attention that are essential for experiencing the world. How would we find our way down from the top of St. Paul's? A purely passive mind would be no mind at all.[4]

In the context of the story presented in the previous paragraphs, both Locke and Hartley could be found guilty of the huge error for which James impeaches them. And to the degree that Hartley reduces the "several acts" by which Locke thought the mind "frames" complex ideas to a purely passive process, his theory would fail in the manner Coleridge describes, for it would be hard pressed to explain how such a being could choose to climb to the top of St. Paul's and there attend to the landmarks in London. However, the above story is not the only one Locke and Hartley tell. There is another, which recognizes that the presence in the mind of simple ideas is no simple matter, and which is much closer in spirit to James's description of the "free water of consciousness" than he appears to recognize. This second story is, in turn, part of Hartley's more comprehensive account of how humans and other animals perceive their worlds and act within them. In this account, "the powers of generating ideas, and raising them by association" do "arise from corporeal causes." This is not, however, to reduce our conscious experiences of ourselves and our worlds to epiphenomena. "A man," Hartley writes, "may speak, handle, love, fear, &c. entirely by mechanism" (*OM* 1. Conclusion). The mind of a person, or for that matter of a cat, may be described as a mechanism—*and* the person, at least, speaks, acts, loves, and fears. Hartley offers an account of how we perceive, act, speak, and love that is grounded upon the fact that we are physical beings. Coleridge is exactly right in stating that the psychological dimension of Hartley's system cannot be separated from "the *material* hypothesis"; Hartley was "too coherent a thinker" (C 7:110) for that. But Coleridge was incorrect in thinking that a psychology based on "the *material* hypothesis" would divide life "between the despotism of outward impressions, and that of senseless and passive memory." Hartley knew full well that people perceive, act, speak, and love; his aim was to explain how we, as living physical beings, do so.

Appreciating Hartley's account requires that we read the *Observations* as a coherent whole; it is not enough to read the first dozen or so propositions in book 1. Of the chapters to come, chapter 6 focuses on Hartley's discussion of language, and chapters 8 and 9 are largely concerned with his extensive treatment of the forms of love. But this chapter is entitled "perception and action." Let us begin our investigation of Hartley's account of perception by turning to the second story Locke and Hartley tell.

2. The Natural History of Ideas

Locke included in his *Essay* a query which William Molyneux had sent him. Molyneux had asked Locke whether a person born blind, who had learned to discriminate by touch between a sphere and a cube of the same size, would, upon gaining his sight, be able to identify them by sight alone (*HU* 2.9.8). Locke agreed with Molyneux that the person would not be able to do so, and he took the proposed absence of visual identification as an illustration that, in perception, "the ideas we receive by sensation, are often in grown people alter'd by the judgment, without our taking notice of it." Although we think we *see* a "globe" of "gold, alabaster, or jet," Locke remarks that "'tis certain, that the *idea* thereby imprinted in our mind, is of a flat circle variously shadowed, with several degrees of light and brightness coming before our eyes." According to Locke, the newly sighted person's inability to identify objects is evidence that what we take to be "the perception of our sensation" is often "an *idea* formed by our judgment; so that the one, *viz.* of sensation, only serves to excite the other" (*HU* 2.9.9). The rays of light that reach the eye from the globe do not convey to the mind a coherent image of the object; such an image, of a separate, three-dimensional object, is an artifact of the mind, which the rays of light only serve to activate.

George Berkeley, in his *Essay Towards a New Theory of Vision* (1709), further develops Locke's point that all we receive from the sensation of sight are variations in color and brightness. "All that is properly perceived by the visive faculty," he writes, "amounts to no more than colours with their variations, and different proportions of light and shade: but the perpetual mutability and fleetingness of those immediate objects of sight, render them incapable of being managed after the manner of geometrical figures" (§156). To illustrate this point, Berkeley discusses the visual comprehension of a person who possesses only sight—that is, whose body is born 'blind' in feeling (i.e., lacking pressure touch, kinesthesia, and proprioception). Such a "disembodied" but seeing being, Berkeley argues, would not have "any idea of distance, outness, or profundity, nor consequently of space or body" (§152). Moreover, his lack of ideas of "space or body," his incapacity for "managing" visual sensations "after the manner of geometrical figures," would extend to include both solid and plane geometry (cf. §158): not only unable to see Locke's "globe" of gold, alabaster, or jet, he would also be equally unable to discern the "flat circle variously shadowed," which Locke suggested would be evident to the newly sighted person. Totally lacking the comprehension of geometry, he would be consequently unable to distinguish any distinct and separate objects whatsoever within his field of vision.

In 1728 William Cheselden provided important experimental confirmation of these thoughts (Cheselden 1728). Cheselden—the physician and surgeon who examined Hartley for the stone in 1737—reported to the Royal Society on a young man of thirteen or fourteen who, thanks to a successful cataract operation, gained his sight after having been blind from birth. As Molyneux, Locke, and Berkeley had predicted, he was unable to visually identify objects:

> He knew not the shape of any Thing, nor any one Thing from another, however different in Shape, or Magnitude; but upon being told what Things were, whose Form he knew before from feeling, he would carefully observe, that he might know them again; but having so many Objects to learn at once, he forgot many of them; and (as he said) at first he learn'd to know, and

again forgot a thousand Things in a Day. One Particular only... I will relate; Having often forgot which was the Cat, and which the Dog, he was asham'd to ask; but catching the Cat (which he knew by feeling) he was observ'd to look at her steadfastly, and then setting her down, said, So Puss! I shall know you another Time. (1728, 448)

The boy's learning to see which was the cat and which the dog required a conscious forging of associative links between his new visual impressions and the knowledge of the animals he already possessed through touch, hearing, and smell. That he looked steadfastly at the cat also could be taken to suggest that a visual image was apparent to him, and that his difficulty lay in remembering what this and a thousand other visual ideas *meant*. In this interpretation, the boy's situation could be compared to that of a person learning a second language, and his steadfast gaze at the cat to the preparation of a mental flash card containing a picture and a word. Cheselden's report, however, suffers from the lack of a clear temporal sequence, and his comment that the boy was ashamed to ask once again about the animals suggests that the conversation with the cat took place some time after the surgery. Other observations in the report indicate that the boy's perceptual deficits were at first much more profound. Berkeley had claimed that a being whose sense of sight was dissociated from his sense of touch would not have "any idea of distance, outness, or profundity, nor consequently of space or body." Cheselden's account confirms this, for the boy's not knowing "the shape of any Thing, nor any one Thing from another, however different in Shape, or Magnitude" derives from the initial absence of any perception of "distance, outness, or profundity": "When he first saw, he was so far from making any Judgment about Distances, that he thought all Objects whatever touch'd his Eyes, (as he express'd it) as what he felt, did his Skin" (448). At first, the boy could not *see* a *thing* at a *distance*.

Even after several months of seeing, the young man found it difficult to fathom basic aspects of the architecture of visual perception. He could not, at first, see a picture as a representational image: "We thought he soon knew what Pictures represented, which were shew'd to him, but we found afterwards we were mistaken; for about two Months after he was couch'd, he discovered at once, they represented solid Bodies; when to that Time he considered them only as Party-colour'd Planes, or Surfaces diversified with Variety of Paint" (449). Prior to the shock of recognition, he had no idea that a portrait contained the image of a person. But this sudden discovery led to a further puzzlement: "Even then he was no less surpriz'd, expecting the Pictures would feel like the Things they represented, and was amaz'd when he found those Parts, which by their Light and Shadow appear'd now round and uneven, felt only flat like the rest; and ask'd which was the lying Sense, Feeling, or Seeing?" (449). And in addition to not understanding why some visual images should not be accompanied by the tactile impressions he was laboring to associate with them, he was also baffled by the fact that visual representations can vary in size: "Being shewn his Father's Picture in a Locket at his Mother's Watch, and told what it was, he acknowledged a Likeness, but was vastly surpriz'd; asking, how it could be, that a large Face could be express'd in so little Room, saying, It should have seem'd as impossible to him, as to put a Bushel of any thing into a Pint" (449). Relative magnitudes continued to elude him: "At first, he could bear but very little Sight, and the Things he saw, he thought extreamly large; but upon seeing Things larger, those first seen he conceiv'd less, never being able to imagine any Lines beyond the Bounds he saw; the Room he was in he said, he knew to be but Part of the House, yet he could not conceive that the whole House could look bigger" (449). In a sense, the boy was correct, for the room I am in fills my visual field and is the largest thing I see. But what a normally sighted person can do, and what the boy could not, is to imagine a spatial geometry of lines beyond the bounds of sight—and thereby to place the room within the house, and the house on the street or in the landscape.[5]

The clear conclusion, to a philosophically and medically informed person of Hartley's day, is that even as important a sense as sight is unable, in isolation, to produce the ideas we habitually and unconsciously attribute to it. According to Locke, the primary qualities that are simple ideas "enter [the mind] by the senses simple and unmixed"; in addition, they would appear to a newly sighted person as if they were arranged on a flat, two-dimensional surface—"a plain variously colour'd, as is evident in painting" (*HU* 2.9.8). It is the mind's task to make the leap from plane to solid geometry, and to blend and unite ideas of primary qualities into representations or images of solid objects. Berkeley goes beyond Locke and asserts that a being blind in body, relying on the sense of sight alone, would be incapable of seeing the world as if it were a painting. Such a being would lack understanding of both plane and solid geometry; it would be unable to see either spheres or circles, and consequently it would be hard pressed to discriminate any constant demarcations or boundaries whatsoever in the free water of visual sensation. Lacking such boundaries, this disembodied being would be unable to see either objects or flat "pictures" of objects, and it is questionable whether such a being would be able to identify the recurrent, invariant, and distinct qualities that are simple ideas. On Locke's account, Cheselden's young patient would at least see the world as a flat painting; he would perceive circles though not spheres. On Berkeley's account, the young man's incapacity would be much more fundamental and his task of fashioning a coherent visual world all the greater; it is not apparent that he would be able, by sight, to discriminate anything at all. And, despite its obscurities concerning the development of the young man's sense of visual perception, Cheselden's account appears to confirm that Berkeley was nearer to the mark than Locke. At first, the young man could make nothing out of the impressions sight conveyed to him: "he thought all Objects touch'd his eyes, . . . as what he felt, did his skin." He could not see the world as a painting, and it was some time before he could see a painting as a representation of the world.[6]

Although "nothing could be plainer" than that I do perceive "simple" ideas, such as those of *white* and *wet,* and also that I am able to see a geometrical world filled with objects, how I do so is thus far from a simple matter. The contributions of Molyneux, Locke, Berkeley, and Cheselden warrant rejection of the assumption that the perception of simple ideas and of objects is a passive and nearly automatic process; their contributions require the recognition that a living being actively conceives its world through perceptual categories that are meaningful to it.

John W. Yolton, discussing "the way of ideas" in his *Perceptual Acquaintance from Descartes to Reid* (1984), argues that "Descartes, Arnauld, Locke, and the tradition stemming from their writings, were developing a psychological account of perceptual awareness, a cognitive psychology. . . . It is the role of meaning in perceptual acquaintance that has been overlooked in the standard discussions and histories of the way of ideas" (16). Yolton notes that, in some readings of Locke, the notion that the mind perceives its own ideas and not the things themselves is taken to mean that ideas are incorporeal objects that are capable of being present to a nonmaterial mind in a way that physical objects can never be. But in Yolton's interpretation, ideas are not substitutes for physical objects. He writes: "To cognize the world is not to have objects literally in our minds, nor is it to have special objects that stand proxy for objects in the world: to cognize the world is to be aware of the world" (101). The thesis that ideas are themselves objects is that of Malebranche, and it is, according to Yolton, explicitly rejected by Arnauld and Locke. Instead of a threefold division of physical objects, incorporeal ideas, and nonmaterial minds that perceive only the latter, Yolton proposes that, to Arnauld and Locke, ideas are the mind's "semantic and epistemic responses" to physical sensations.

I see Hartley firmly within the tradition of the "way of ideas" as Yolton describes it. I also think that he makes some innovative contributions to it. As we shall see in this and the following chapters, these include emphases on: (1) the role of the "joint impression" of sensations from the different modalities of touch, hearing, sight, etc. in the formation of ideas; (2) the importance of motor activity in perception and in learning to perform skilled actions; (3) language, as a mechanism for generating ideas and not simply as a means of labeling ideas that already exist; and (4) mind as a dynamic construct, the totality of physiological and psychological processes. The language used by philosophers in the seventeenth and eighteenth centuries bears within itself an implicit model of mind, and even those who, like Locke, articulate a quite different understanding of how minds work are often taken to be advocating it. This model generally suggests that the mind is a nonmaterial entity that knows the world by looking at the images that appear on the retinas of the eyes. In contrast, the being Hartley observes is the human infant or young child: a living physical organism that moves, explores its environment, and learns to handle cups and spoons and toys; that coordinates flows of sensation deriving from physical movement, taste, smell, hearing, and sight; that listens to the speech of others and learns to speak; and that, through these activities, develops a "mind" filled with words and memories and capacities for perceptual discrimination and skilled motor activity—in other words, ideas. For such a being, ideas are clearly "semantic and epistemic" responses, as Yolton suggests; but they are not simply the responses of a disembodied mind to visual stimuli; rather, they are the meanings an embodied, active, and speaking being develops through interaction with its social and physical environments.

Yolton writes of "the de-ontologizing of ideas" (1984, 221) as the distinctive feature of the "way of ideas." Locke writes that ideas of such things as solid objects are "formed by our judgment" (*HU* 2.9.9). He is, however, at pains to dispel the notion that terms such as *judgment* or *will*, as designations of *faculties*, name separate and independently acting agents within the person. He emphasizes that the term *faculty* is synonymous with *ability* or *power*—and that such faculties, abilities, or powers are "relations, not agents" (*HU* 2.21.19). It is the person who judges or wills, not the faculty of judgment or will. Hence to say that ideas are "formed by our judgment" is the equivalent of saying that a person's ideas are "formed by the person's ability to form ideas." In other words, the statement that "ideas are formed by our judgment" itself explains nothing; it merely states that ideas are *formed,* and not just passively and effortlessly *received.* The process by which ideas are generated remains to be discovered and explained.

3. Association and the Formation of Ideas

"The ideas of sensation," writes Hartley, "are not entirely simple, since they must consist of parts both co-existent and successive, as the generating sensations themselves do" (*OM* 1.1.2.8). A living being's sensations of the world are constantly and continuously blended; they form what James calls a "stream of consciousness." At any moment, within any single sensory modality, the nerves transmit a continuous and variable flow of "vibrations" to the brain; as I write this, for example, I hear the hum of the computer's hard drive, the wind, water flowing through the radiator next to me, an airplane flying overhead, a car driving past on the road, the clicks of the keyboard, the faint sound of my own motions. I name these separately, because I have *learned* to discriminate among them, to place them in separate categories of sound. Moreover, what I name is not in many of these cases a static and uniform thing; some predictable trajectory or function of change through time is part of the idea. For example, a continuous increase and then falling away of volume is part of my idea of the sound of a car driving down the road; my idea of that sound is made up of "parts both co-existent and successive."[7]

There are no grounds for me to assume that an infant lying next to me will be automatically able to make the same auditory discriminations I do; she may not be able to differentiate, as yet, between the sound of a car, the sound of an airplane, and the sound of the wind. Sensation does not of its own accord spontaneously parse itself into a set of uniform, static, simple ideas. As the reader of Locke, Berkeley, and Cheselden knows, the formation of such ideas is an achievement, not a given.

Hartley in effect abandons Locke's distinction between the passive reception of simple ideas of sensation and the active production, by our judgment, of perceptual categories, such as are involved in the identification of geometric figures by sight. In this regard, the starting point of Hartley's psychology is not that simple or basic ideas can be linked by association; rather, it is that a process of association *generates* ideas, including our categories of perception. In proposition 11, Hartley states that "ideas, and miniature vibrations, must first be generated... before they can be associated." He adds:

> But then (which is very remarkable) this power of forming ideas, and their corresponding miniature vibrations, does equally presuppose the power of association. For since all sensations and vibrations are infinitely divisible, in respect of time and place, they could not leave any traces or images of themselves, *i.e.* any ideas, or miniature vibrations, unless their infinitesimal parts did cohere together through joint impression, *i.e.* association. (*OM* 1.1.2.11)

This idea is stated somewhat more fully in the *Conjecturæ quædam de Sensu, Motu, & Idearum Generatione,* the Latin précis Hartley published in 1746, three years before the *Observations.* In the text explicating proposition 11, Hartley writes:

> Certainly it can be said... that the power of association always requires the power of generating ideas and miniature ideas and that the latter faculty... supposes the former. For neither ideas nor miniature vibrations can be excited by association, unless they are first generated. And, in turn, the faculty of generating ideas and miniature vibrations always requires the power of association. For how would sensations generate ideas, or vibrations generate miniature vibrations, unless parts of the sensations or vibrations, which are infinitely divisible in respect of place and time, did cohere together through joint impression, i.e. association? Further, there is need of an association, that is to say a cause, which will make the brain lean successively in this or that direction, i.e., that will make one part or another of the very complicated miniature vibrations... especially prevail over the rest. (Hartley 1959, 28–29)

Ideas are associated, but first ideas are generated by a process of association that sets limits to the potentially infinite divisibility of sensations and vibrations. By stating that "all sensations and vibrations are infinitely divisible, in respect of time and place" Hartley is in effect elaborating on and generalizing the point made earlier by Berkeley, that a being that possessed only sight would be unable to perceive a geometrically ordered world. To such a being, sensation would be "infinitely"—i.e., arbitrarily—divisible; unable to see spheres or circles, cubes or rectangles, it would not perceive which divisions mark patterns and boundaries in the flowing and fluctuating stream of vision. Moreover, and perhaps equally importantly, it would not know which patterns and boundaries are meaningful: its brain would be unable to "lean" toward the features in the "very complicated miniature vibrations" that are significant. A being handicapped in this way would, in other words, be unable to focus its attention on anything in particular. For it, as Coleridge claimed, "*any* part of *any* impression might recal *any* part of any *other*, without a cause present to determine *what* it should be" (C 7:112). As a result, the flow of sensation "would not leave any traces or images" of specific and recognizable qualities or things. Vibrations would not generate vibratiuncles, or sensations ideas.

In the passages above, Hartley is in effect asserting that there are no innate perceptual categories, no natural qualities or forms that file before the passively observing mind. Because sensations are infinitely divisible, there are no preexisting data of sensation, none of James's "separate subjective entities," equivalent to the atoms that make up the world. For there to be perceptual categories—ideas, traces, images—at all, the brain and nervous system must be actively involved in fashioning them. A being unable to do so would be trapped in Jamesian infancy, ever feeling "it all as one great blooming, buzzing confusion" (1890, 1:488; see §3.5).[8] To pass beyond this state, a mind must learn to detect whole patterns, and it must also learn to "lean" toward those features of these patterns that are in some way significant.[9]

Specifically, the perception of meaningful features and patterns requires the "joint impression" that constitutes "association." The example Hartley gives in the *Observations,* which immediately follows the statement above, is an illustration of the problem more than an instance of the way in which association is supposed to solve it: "Thus, to mention a gross instance, we could have no proper idea of a horse, unless the particular ideas of head, neck, body, legs, and tail, peculiar to this animal, stuck to each other in the fancy, from frequent joint impression" (*OM* 1.1.2.11). But this is just a first division of the sensation of seeing a horse, and Hartley has just noted that sensations are divisible all the way down. It is thus misleading to think that the "joint impression" of the perceptual units "head," "neck," etc. eventually, through association, cohere into the perceptual gestalt of a "horse." The ideas of "head," "neck," etc. no more represent basic units—natural kinds of objects—than do the ideas of "horse" or "animal." In fact, a child will point to the *horsie* well before she can identify a *neck*. The problem is not one of explaining how *some* patterns form out of the perceptual categories already at hand. It is, as Hartley states it, much more fundamental: to explain how perceptual categories are able to form at all.

How is it, then, that the concept of "joint impression" or "association" accounts for the demarcation of boundaries in the fields of sense—for, in Edelman's terms, labeling an unlabeled world? To answer this question, let us return to what Hartley says about the transmission of neural vibrations to the brain.

We noted in §3.3 that an induced state *a* can be activated—tremble with vibratiuncles, little vibrations—whenever stimulated by a signal with the correct harmonic resonance. But in addition, the induced state may be activated in the *absence* of the parent stimulus, provided that another stimulus triggers it. Hartley makes this point in propositions 10 and 11: "Any Vibrations A, B, C, &c. by being associated together a sufficient Number of Times, get such a power over a, b, c &c. the corresponding Miniature Vibrations, that any one of the Vibrations A, when impressed alone, shall be able to excite in the Mind, b, c, &c. the Miniatures of the rest" (OM 1.1.2.11). *Think of the smell of freshly brewed coffee.* The sight of those words, event *A*, may elicit event *b*, the vibratiuncles that correspond to one's memory of the smell of coffee. It may also call up events *c, d, e*, etc.—a cluster of associations. Though, by reading these words, you cannot sample the actual sensation of drinking coffee, you can enjoy the "little vibration" corresponding to it, and the memories and daydreams it evokes.

When the sight of words evokes the memory of a smell, the part of the brain and nervous system that is specialized to receive and process one type of sensory input (vision) is able to trigger events in another location and functional specialization (smell). To account for this, Hartley proposes that we consider the neural impulses reaching the brain as having both local and global effects. While a vibration involved in one type of sensation directly affects what Hartley terms its "primary seat," it also "diffuses itself all over the medullary substance" and thus interacts with the functional specializations that have their primary seats in other locations in the brain. The interplay of local and global effects allows for the development of a mechanism of cross-signaling between two (or more) types of sensory input, experienced simultaneously:

> Let A and B be two vibrations, associated synchronically. Now, it is evident, that the vibration A (for I will, in this proposition, speak of A and B in the singular number, for the sake of greater clearness) will, by endeavouring to diffuse itself into those parts of the medullary substance which are affected primarily by the vibration B, in some measure modify and change B, so as to make B a little different from what it would be, if impressed alone. For the same reasons the vibration A will be a little affected, even in its primary seat, by the endeavour of B to diffuse itself all over the medullary substance. Suppose now the vibrations A and B to be impressed at the same instant, for a thousand times; it follows ... that they will first overcome the dispositions to the natural vibrations N, and will then leave a tendency to themselves [a, b], which will now occupy the place of the original natural tendency to vibrations. When therefore the vibration A is impressed alone, it cannot be entirely such as the object would excite of itself, but must lean, even in its primary seat, to the modifications and changes induced by B...; and therefore much more, in receding from this primary seat, will it lean that way; and when it comes to the seat of B, it will excite B's miniature a little modified and changed by itself. (*OM* 1.1.2.11)

The repeated simultaneous occurrence of A and B leads to the modification of each by the other; instead of experiencing "pure" versions of A and B, the "animal body" experiences the pattern *(A + B)*— that is, the "joint impression" of *A as modified by B* and of *B as modified by A*. Such joint impressions occur in the brain as complex waveforms (cf. *OM* 1.1.2.13). C. U. M. Smith (1987), commenting on Hartley's hope that the doctrine of association may enable us to "analyse all that vast variety of complex ideas ... into their simple compounding parts" (*OM* 1.1.2.12), states: "But not, let us note, atoms. The simple compounding parts, so far as the physical correspondents were concerned, were unit waves: Fourier elements, not billiard balls" (1987, 130; see §5.4). And not bricks. A living organism experiences the world through all the sensory modalities that are active at any moment. Its brain is filled with complex patterns of vibrations, of which *(A + B)* is the simplest symbolic notation. A "simple" idea *A* or *B*, taken in isolation, is a product of analysis. The joint impression is primary.[10]

Once the memory of the joint impression *(A + B)* has been effected, the animal body will now be able to recognize future joint impressions of *(A + B)*—even allowing for varying ratios between the two signals (a strong *A* and a weak *B*, for example). Although *A* alone and *B* alone are infinitely divisible (that is, lack any definite identifying boundaries), the recognition of the pattern *(A + B)* is thus relatively constant; the organism can detect the "same" pattern, even on the basis of a variable signal presenting an analogue of the pattern, or of an incomplete signal presenting part of it. *(A + B)* is, in consequence, the basis for a perceptual category in the way *A* or *B* alone are not. A young child learns, for example, to discriminate and identify the smell of coffee in particular sensory and social situations. The smell occurs within a constellation of joint impressions—of her mother saying "It's time for a cup of coffee," going into the kitchen, taking a can out of the refrigerator and spooning coffee beans into a mill, grinding the beans, putting the ground coffee into a filter cone, and then pouring the liquid into cups. The constellation of experiences may also include actually having a sip of coffee, and amazement at how adults could enjoy drinking such stuff. (Learning to enjoy it awaits the bonding together of another cluster of associations.) Initially, the entire cluster of joint impressions may be involved in the process of learning to differentiate and recognize the specific olfactory "vibration" *C* that is the physical cause of the experience of smelling coffee, but with further exposure and with the experience of detecting the aroma of coffee in other situations, the child may become more and more able to recognize and respond to *C* even when it is unaccompanied by its customary joint impressions.

There is a particular difficulty in imagining the experience of a person or being who cannot do something we take for granted. Locke and Molyneux ask us to consider what a person born blind would see, upon regaining his sight; Berkeley asks us to imagine something even more difficult, a person or being whose body has always been blind to feelings of touch and movement. But, because we are already at home in a three-dimensional world of separate things, in which we have no difficulty telling apart spheres and cubes, or knowing whether something is wet or white, or recognizing the smell of coffee, it is difficult for us to comprehend what the experiences of beings with such deficits would be, and consequently it may also be difficult to credit Hartley's claim that a process of joint impression or association is necessary for the generation of ideas. What did Cheselden's young patient see? And, if we were to take him out of doors on a clear night, would he not be able to see the moon and stars?

It may help us to understand the centrality of association to consider the effects of the sundering or alienation of one sense from the others, particularly in the cases of sensory agnosia (i.e., mental blindness) described by William James. In what amounts to a restatement of Hartley's position, James also attributes the perception of objects to "association . . . between impressions of different senses": "In fact, the 'objects' of our perception, as trees, men, houses, microscopes, of which the real world seems composed, are nothing but clusters of qualities which through simultaneous stimulation have so coalesced that the moment one is excited actually it serves as a sign or cue for the idea of the others to arise" (1890, 1:555). Moreover, James's account of the physiology underlying such associations also relies on the language of local and global effects, and on the concept of coupling or cross-signaling between separate neural regions. Early in his *Principles of Psychology*, James states that "the brain is essentially a place of currents, which run in organized paths" (1890, 1:70) and which trigger each other.[11]

In some pathological conditions, the currents are blocked. One sensory modality may be sundered from the rest, in which case the alienated sense ceases to make sense to the person; although, for example, the person may continue to see in the sense of receive visual input, he will be blind mentally in the sense of knowing what he sees. James notes that mental blindness "consists not so much in insensibility to optical impressions, as in *inability to understand them*. Psychologically it is interpretable as *loss of association* between optical sensations and what they signify" (1890, 1:48). He writes of a case in which "the patient made the most ludicrous mistakes, calling for instance a clothesbrush a pair of spectacles, an umbrella a plant with flowers, an apple a portrait of a lady, etc. etc"; nonetheless, despite these confusions, "he seemed . . . to have his mental images fairly well preserved" (1890, 1:50). This person's condition is similar to that of Dr. P, the subject of Oliver Sacks's "The Man Who Mistook his Wife for a Hat" (1987, 8–22). Dr. P also suffered from a nearly complete visual agnosia, an inability to identify things by sight, all the while being unaware of his loss. He patted fire hydrants on the head, thinking they were children. But like the patient James describes, Dr. P maintained a good store of (predominantly schematic) visual images—he could recognize cartoon figures and play mental chess, although he could not recognize people's faces—and he continued to make use of an sophisticated descriptive vocabulary. When Sacks presented him with a rose and asked him what it was, Dr. P answered, "A convoluted red form with a linear green attachment" (1987, 13). He could describe it accurately but could only guess at what it was—until he smelled it.

James proposes that, in cases of agnosia, the affected sense has become cut off from the other modalities of sensation with which it is customarily correlated: "It is in fact the momentary loss of *non*-optical images that makes us mentally blind, just as it is that of *non*-auditory images which makes us mentally deaf. I am mentally deaf if, *hearing* a bell, I can't recall how it *looks;* and mentally blind if, *seeing* it, I can't recall its *name*" (1890, 1:50). Upon seeing the red and green object, Dr. P was able to give a precise description of it, though the visual image links with no name. But when he lifted it to his nose and smelled it, he immediately knew it to be a rose. Dr. P's ideas of smell retained their associations with concepts and names, and the worlds of smell and, more importantly for him, of music, kept their internal coherence.

In the cases of Dr. P and of the man James describes, visual agnosia represents a loss of an ability that was previously fully developed. Thanks to his past life, Dr. P possessed a highly articulate visual language, and, as in the instance of the rose, was able to give detailed descriptions of things, without knowing what the descriptions "meant" or what the objects were. Imagine, however, a person born with Dr. P's deficit. Would such a person ever be able to develop a language that could describe what he saw? Could he be trained to respond consistently to specific visual cues—for example, to point to the moon on a clear night? If the answer to these questions is no, then Hartley's and James's claim that association among sensory modalities generates ideas would be upheld, at least with regards to vision, for a person born mentally blind could not be said to have visual ideas at all.

In his account of the *formation* of ideas through association, Hartley is especially indebted to Berkeley, who argues that our visual perception of a three-dimensional world derives from the correlation of sight with touch. This correlation enables visual ideas to function as a language that names the primal world of touch and feeling. Hartley also identifies feeling or touch as "the fundamental source of information in respect of the essential properties of matter" and thus "our first and principle key to the knowledge of the external world" (*OM* 1.2.1.30). Because touch is "the earnest and presage of what other tangible impressions the body... will make upon our feeling in other circumstances," Hartley writes, "it is from this difference that we call the touch the reality, light the representative."[12] In this relationship, because the representative "is much more extensive and expedite than feeling, we judge of tangible qualities chiefly by sight." We are spared having to stick a hand into the fire to know it is there. Given its reliably representative character, the sense of sight "may be considered, agreeably to Bishop Berkeley's remark, as a philosophical language for the ideas of feeling" (see §6.4, 6.8, and 9.4).

Drawing on Berkeley's comments on the situation of a person born blind in bodily feeling, Hartley proposes "that a person born [visually] blind may foretell with certainty, from his present tangible impressions, what others could follow upon varying circumstances; whereas if we could suppose a person to be born without feeling, and to arrive at man's estate, he could not from his present visible impressions judge what others would follow upon the varying circumstances." The problem, as Hartley states it, concerns predictability of variation. With a knife, one can cut a block of cheese in two, while "the picture of a knife, drawn so well as to deceive his eye, would not, when applied to another body, produce the same change of visible impressions." But the person blind in body would be unable to tell the one from the other, on the basis of visual inspection alone.[13] Consequently, for this person the apparently same sequence of variations in the visual field could be followed by inconsistent results. Joint impression would fail. We are spared the difficulty, Hartley notes, because for us "the same qualities are made by means of light to impress vibrations on our eyes, which correspond in great measure to those made on the sense of feeling, so as to vary with their varieties" (*OM* 1.2.1.30).[14]

Hartley's discussion here follows Locke's presentation of Molyneux's question, because it assumes the existence of a coherent, though flat, visual field. But as we have observed, it is more in keeping with the position Hartley and Berkeley developed to say that a person whose visual ideas were disconnected from his awareness of his own movement and feeling would not simply be confused by pictures of knives; rather, he would be unable to understand the picture as a representation of a knife in the first place. It is the correlation of the flows of sensation through two (or more) sensory modalities, so that the sensations of one modality "vary with the varieties" of another, that accounts for the fact that we have ideas—in James's sense of "separate subjective entities"— at all.

4. Hartley and Edelman

A comparison with a contemporary neurological theory may help us further appreciate what is at stake in Hartley's claim that ideas are dependent upon the association of joint impressions. Allowing for the differences in vocabulary and for the development of neuroscience, Hartley's theory bears a remarkable conceptual similarity to that of Gerald M. Edelman, particularly to Edelman's discussion of the role of *reentrant mapping* in the development of perceptual and conceptual categorization. Selection of Edelman's theory for comparison is not arbitrary, for James provides a bridge between the two: Edelman's work refers back to James in a way that corresponds to James's debt to Hartley. In both cases, the later work is to a degree an elaboration of concepts present in the earlier.

Edelman has articulated his Theory of Neuronal Group Selection (TNGS) in his trilogy *Neural Darwinism* (1987), *Topobiology* (1988), and *The Remembered Present* (1989) and also in *Bright Air, Brilliant Fire* (1992). Edelman is critical of "modern psychologists [who] assume one version or another of an idealist or Cartesian epistemology" (1989, 13) as they seek to model consciousness on systems of information processing, whether Turing machines or forms of Chomskian depth grammar. A main failing of such "computer" models of the mind is, in his view, their assumption that experience provides ready-made (and "labeled") data for the mental program to process. In making this point, Edelman is in effect reframing James's earlier criticism of psychological atomism, though now in terms of evolutionary neurology. In his account of the evolution of the units of selection that are neuronal groups, Edelman stresses a point that closely matches one that Stephen Jay Gould emphasizes regarding the evolution of species: although the world imposes constraints upon any population limiting "where" it can go developmentally, evolution is not headed anywhere in particular. In species evolution, argues Gould, there are no ideal forms (or natural kinds) specifying the direction of evolution for that species—despite, for example, all the illustrations of human evolution depicting the "natural" (and implicitly "right" and "inevitable") line of ascent from *A. afarensis* on the left of the page to *H. sapiens* on the far right. Similarly for Edelman, neural groups evolve—that is, establish multiple synaptic interconnections—without the prespecification of what associations those interconnections will make or what patterns they will form. There are no prespecified forms or bits of information that it is the destiny of

Perception and Action   155

neural groups to apprehend and process. Accordingly, just as James described a fundamental task of psychology as that of showing how the twin processes of discrimination and association separate perceptual objects out of the stream of consciousness, Edelman stresses that the task of the neurobiologist, in developing a comprehensive theory of brain development and consciousness, is to give an account of how perceptual and conceptual categorization, language, and all the manifestations of "higher consciousness" come about in the *absence* of prespecification. It is, in Hartley's terms, to explain why certain divisions rather than others are made in the "infinitely divisible" fields of sense.

Edelman lists the requirements of a satisfactory neurobiological theory in an important summary statement:

> We need a theory that rejects the notion that brains and consciousness are based on Turing machines. At the same time, it must be consistent with evolution, population thinking, and biological individuality while accounting for the "Jamesian" properties of consciousness.... The theory should allow phenomenal properties based on values to emerge in each biologically variant individual. It should take account of the ability to categorize a variety of real-world states without prespecification or instructionism. The conditions assumed by the theory should allow the development of semantic capability in each human individual. Moreover, the theory should take account of social interaction and learning in an open-ended manner to yield changes in consciousness and subjectivity. Consistent with the evolutionary assumption, the theory should also consider conscious and phenomenal states as causally significant. (1989, 30–31)

Hartley did develop a theory that does address the requirements Edelman here sets forth. In this and the following chapters, we shall see how Hartley's theory accounts for (1) "phenomenal properties based on values"; (2) categorization without prespecification or instructionism; (3) the development of language ("semantic capability"); (4) the "open-ended" quality of social interaction and learning; and (5) the causal significance of conscious and phenomenal states.

Edelman states that "the fundamental question" addressed by the Theory of Neuronal Group Selection is: "how can a selective system give rise to perceptual categorization and generalization?" (1989, 49).

Categorization here refers to "the adaptive discrimination of an object from background or other objects and events," and generalization to "the treatment... of a more or less diverse collection of such entities as equivalent." A perceptual system has to see the trees for the forest, and also to distinguish beech, birch, and maple. To answer this fundamental question, "The TNGS proposes that any nontrivial categorization must arise through the operation of at least two separate channels carrying signals to [neuronal] maps," in which "each channel (for example, a sensory modality or submodality) samples a particular stimulus domain."

Edelman's term for this parallel, coordinated sampling is "reentrant mapping," with "reentry" defined as "a process of temporally ongoing parallel signaling between separate maps along ordered anatomical connections" (1989, 65). In this model, neurons in a "sensory receptor sheet" in a given perceptual system "map" onto the relevant "higher-order lamina" in the brain. For example, in primates there is a point to point correlation of the ganglion cells in the retina with the cells of the visual cortex, so that the former maps onto the latter; the right half of each eye projects to the left cortex via a relay in the lateral geniculate nucleus in the thalamus, and vice versa. The visual cortex in each hemisphere is made up of a series of visual areas, each of which contains a complete map of the relevant half of the visual field. Information from area V1 is funnelled to area V2, and information from V1 and V2 to V3, etc. The visual areas appear to be involved in the perception of three dimensions, movement, color, and specific shapes (see R. Thompson 1993, 226–49). Edelman offers this summary of the process of reentrant mapping:

> After multiple encounters with a stimulus, particular patterns of neuronal groups will be selected in a mapped area. Following such selection, similar signals in each neuronal channel can preferentially activate previously selected neuronal groups in the repertoires of a neural region [in the brain] to which that channel is mapped. But... each of the higher-order maps to which the independent signals go is mapped to the other. Operations in these different maps that are related to the same perceptual stimulus are linked to one another by reentry.... This coordinate dynamic interaction between maps results in the correlation of the responses to each disjunct sample made by the different channels, each representing different modalities or submodalities. (1989, 50)

The result of such mapping is that a signal can "preferentially activate previously selected neuronal groups" in the brain; the nervous system has "learned" to respond to a particular signal, after repeated exposures to it. But, because animal bodies live in a world of spatial and temporal continuities, they do not receive signals one at a time, in isolation from each other. Instead, the organism simultaneously samples signals through a variety of sensory modalities. And when disjunctive parallel samplings by two or more modalities are mutually correlative, the maps can in turn map onto each other. This is reentrant mapping. It is obviously very close to Hartley's concept of joint impression.

But how does reentrant mapping contribute to an account of categorization and generalization? I take the key feature to be what I term choreography: "disjunctive parallel sampling" involves the coordinated ("co-existent and successive") movement of the inputs of two or more sensory systems. Consider a "classification couple"—reentrant mapping between two maps (Edelman 1989, 48). The first map represents a "higher-order lamina" in the brain, to which neurons in the visual system are mapped, while the second represents a similar lamina onto which are mapped neurons "related to light touch on a moving finger." Extrapolating from this model, we can imagine a young child, say at age ten months, looking at a toy duck and running his finger along its sides. The child's sensory systems are registering a varied and continuously varying swirl of inputs, visual, auditory, tactile, etc., out of which it is the task of the brain and nervous system to discern pattern and order. Pattern recognition relies upon the detection of significant variances; it involves, in other words, knowing which variances in input mark the boundaries of the pattern and hence differentiate it from the background. But the absence of prespecification means that, in the child's brain, there is no innate schema for toy ducks, and hence no predisposition to see the toy lying on the floor as a separate object at all; or, when seen as an object, to see it as the *same* object if it is put away and brought out again; to see it as one of a class of objects, *ducks* or *birdies*; or to draw any connection between the toy and the mallards on the pond—all of which the child will be able to do in relatively short order. Now, Edelman's point is that, if the child had to rely upon the inputs of a single sensory system, he would be unable to determine which variances in input were significant for demarcating the pattern of the object. The visual world, for example, would appear like one of the "magic pictures" that have recently become popular, but with no promise that an image would ever emerge from the background pattern. But the choreography of two or more sensory modalities supplies the essential factor that makes such demarcation possible: variances in one sensory input modulate consistently with variances in another, so that two sets or sequences of variances can be correlated with each other. In Hartley's terms, the one "varies with the varieties" of the other. Because a change in color, in this example, occurs regularly in tandem with a change in tactile sense, a boundary is marked, and on the basis of such correlative demarcations the child's brain is able to construct simultaneous visual and tactile images of the duck. What causes the picture to emerge, the pattern to appear, the object to stand out from the background, is the choreography of variation in two sensory modalities: the child handles the duck while looking at it, and it is the choreography of touch and sight that provides the foundation for both a perceptual category and generalization from that and related categories to such classifications as *ducks, toys,* and *birds.*

Because sight impressions "vary with the varieties" of impressions of touch, the two senses appear to cooperate in the "temporally ongoing parallel signaling" that Edelman defines as reentry. However, there is an asymmetry between sight and feeling, and a complexity to the latter, that suggests a further parallel between the theories of Hartley and Edelman.

We noted above that Hartley, like Berkeley before him, considers touch to be "our fundamental source of information in respect of the properties of matter" and "our first and principle key to the knowledge of the external world." Visual impressions become ideas—gain boundaries and meanings—through their correlation with the impressions of touch. But Hartley uses the words *touch* and *feeling* interchangeably and also includes under this heading several senses that we class separately: on the one hand, touch proper, which registers the pressure of the fingertips, etc., against objects, and which accounts for our perceptions of things as smooth and rough, oily or dry; on the other, the proprioceptive and kinesthetic senses, which monitor bodily position and motor activity.

Now, if we take *feeling* to refer foremost to the senses involved in monitoring and controlling motor activity, Hartley's emphasis on its primacy and its asymmetry relative to sight (and by extension, hearing) correlates not so much with the local mapping of reentry but with what Edelman calls "global mapping." In global mapping, multiple local maps map to each other and "interact with non-mapped regions such as those of the brain stem, basal ganglia, hippocampus, and parts of the cerebellum" (1989, 54). But these nonmapped regions are responsible for the coordination of sensation and motion and for the control of position and movement, and thus at the heart of the concept of global mapping is the integration of sensory and motor processes in one dynamic structure: "The concept of global mapping takes account of the fact that perception depends upon and leads to action. In this view, categorization does not occur solely in a sensory area that then executes a program to activate motor output. Instead, the results of continual motor activity are considered to be an essential part of perceptual categorization.... Neuronal group selection in global mappings occurs in a dynamic loop that continually matches gesture and posture to several kinds of sensory signals" (1989, 54). The ten-month-old infant with the duck is, in Hartley's terms, an "animal body" crawling about the floor, or, in Edelman's, a *"moving organism,* actively sampling its environment." He crawls toward the duck, runs his fingers over it, picks it up, chews on it, waves it around, lets it fly, crawls over to it again. Here the parallel disjunctive sampling of the world through the senses of sight, etc. is linked to the body's awareness of itself through kinesthesia and proprioception. Continuous flows of signals of sight, touch, hearing, and smell are associated "in a dynamic loop" with a continuous flow of signals deriving from, and monitoring, position and motion. And once again, the linkage, the association, is precisely choreographed: variations in the composition of the visual field, for example, occur in tandem with changes in physical position: "the results of continual motor activity" are thus "an essential part of perceptual categorization." Through their continuous, looping, dynamic interactions, sensations and movements perfect the choreography by which they vary with each other's variances.

As a result of this choreography of sensory and motor modalities, "the process of global mapping ... creates a spatiotemporally continuous representation of objects and events" (Edelman 1989, 56). Thanks to its ability to move about within the world, and to move things within it, the infant animal body is able to develop a "representation" of the world as a place in which a toy duck may be *next to* the sofa, or *behind* it, and in which the disappearance of the duck behind the sofa comes *after* the physical motion of letting it fly. Given the ability to experience such a world—given the order, general patterns, schemas such experience of the world offers—perceptual categorizations come into relief and become generalized.

They also enter into memory, which Edelman conceives of not as "a store of fixed and coded attributes to be called up and assembled in a replicative fashion as in a computer," but as rather resulting from "a process of continual recategorization, which ... must be procedural and involve continual motor activity and repeated rehearsal" (1989, 56). In a sense, memory is performance, and the choreography of sense and movement must be performed—rehearsed—to be remembered. The memory of a dance is not a matter of its being recorded in a notation, or of being videotaped; it exists fundamentally in the bodies of dancers, as they perform it now. Here, any rehearsal will be *perceived* by reference to the embodied memory of previous performances of the dance, but in addition the memory of those previous performances is dependent upon, and is "recategorized" by, this latest rehearsal. As the constituents of memory, previous global mappings of sense and movement create the space in which any further new experiences will occur, so that the world the organism experiences *now* is always "the remembered present." But simultaneously, the present that one remembers also redefines the past that is memory.

Finally, another question arises: why put the effort into learning the choreography at all? "Necessary as all these processes are for categorization of an unlabeled world," Edelman writes, "they cannot serve the adaptive needs of the organism unless learning takes place" (1989, 56). Clearly, as any teacher knows, people do not learn whatever they are presented with. What needs to be incorporated within the model is something to account for selectivity, for explaining why someone learns this and not that. Edelman writes: "Perceptual categorization and memory are ... considered to be necessary for learning but obviously are not sufficient for it. The sufficient condition is provided by the synaptic linkage of particular global mappings to the activity of hedonic centers and to the limbic system in a fashion that will satisfy homeostatic, appetitive, and consummatory needs" (1989, 57). Out of the infinity of things we could learn and remember, we focus upon certain ones because of their connections with the various forms of hunger and satisfaction; it is their association with our appetites and affections—with our pleasures and pains—that guides our attention to particular thoughts and actions, that leads us to rehearse them, perform them, remember them.

In sum, Edelman models the biology of consciousness as a series of increasingly inclusive dynamic interactions between parts of the brain. There is, first, the linkage between two or more local maps to which sensory inputs are referred; this reentrant mapping coordinates the disjunctive sampling of environmental stimuli that is the basis for labeling an unlabeled world. Second, these local linkages are incorporated into systems of global mapping, which connect and coordinate local sensory maps with the parts of the brain responsible for registering and controlling movement. The dynamic loops connecting sensation with motor activity are essential for perceptual categorization, generalization, and memory. Third, the further connection of global mappings to the centers of the brain involved in the maintenance of the organism in pleasurable states of comfort and safety is essential for the selectivity of attention and retention present in learning. The result, consciousness, is thus a grand choreography of movement, in which the ongoing flowing pattern of the dance is continuously created and maintained through the dancers' communication with each other. The whole dynamic interplay, the entire pattern, rises out of the dancers' exchanges; each cues and is cued in return, continuously and reciprocally, through the subtleties of glance and gesture, through the slightest modulations of bodily movement.

To summarize the parallels between the theories of Hartley and Edelman: (1) Hartley affirms the "infinite divisibility" of sensation; Edelman, the absence of prespecification. (2) Hartley proposes the association of joint sensory impressions as the basis for ideas as correlates of objects and events; Edelman proposes reentrant mapping as the basis for perceptual categorization and generalization. (3) Hartley emphasizes the integration of sensory impressions and processes of motor activity, as necessary both for the comprehension of spatial and temporal frameworks and for the development of skilled action; Edelman stresses that global mappings involving local sensory maps and motor activity are necessary for perceptual categorization and memory. (4) Hartley emphasizes the connection between ideas and affections (pleasures and pains), and, as we shall see in the following chapters, places transformations in affective orientation at the center of his model of psychological development; Edelman asserts that learning depends upon the connection between global mappings and the hedonic centers of the brain and the limbic system. Further parallels can be drawn concerning Hartley's and Edelman's views of the development of the constituents of higher consciousness, particularly language, consciousness of self, and the efficacy of conscious states.

Earlier in this chapter, I suggested that the tradition of psychology deriving from Locke tells two stories. The first is of the "brickbat plan of construction" that, according to James, constitutes the "one huge error" of psychological atomism. The second explores how the process of association, or joint impression, is responsible for the generation of ideas. In Locke's *Essay*, one can read both stories. In Hartley's *Observations*, there are elements suggestive of the first story; Hartley uses Lockean language when he writes that simple ideas "run into clusters and combinations" (*OM* 1.1.2.12) and subsequently form complex ideas. The theme of this chapter, however, is that the second story is the one that more fully articulates the fundamental themes in Hartley's work. This second story is, to begin with, more fully associative: it connects Hartley's thesis that joint impression generates ideas with Locke's discussion of the Molyneux problem, with Berkeley's emphasis on the dependency of vision on touch, with core themes in James's psychology, and with the work of Edelman. No one, in this tradition, thinks that sensations arrive in the mind already labeled, in separate and distinct bits. In addition, while the first story is, after all, based on a rather simple concept, the ideas woven together in the second are much more complex. If the first story takes us to the building site to watch the bricklayers, the second takes us first to the brickyard, to watch the firing of the kiln, and perhaps even out to the fields to observe the mining of the clay.

Put another way, the second story allows us a richer and more inclusive reading of Hartley's work—a reading that attends to the ways in which his many and various topics combine to form a complex whole. Concerning the topic at hand, this story alerts us to the fact that our minds are not mirrors, static and immobile reflectors of whatever light falls upon them. We discriminate and identify and remember and desire (or fear) the things of our world in the manner of living animals, on the move, exploring, touching, tasting, and watching our environments. A full discussion of how we create and combine ideas must be mindful of that animal life. As Edelman stresses and as Berkeley affirmed, the qualities of our perceptions are essentially bound up with our movements. Let us, then, continue the story by examining Hartley's observations concerning bodily movement, and specifically concerning how we learn repertoires of skilled action through the association of sensory impressions and motor activity.

5. Repertoires of Action: Complex and Decomplex Movements

In Hartley's theory, learning to perform a "decomplex movement"— e.g., playing Chopin's Prelude No. 4 in E Minor on the piano—requires that a person first develop a skilled repertoire of "complex movements."

In his *Conjecturæ* (1959, 42), Hartley states that complex movements involve the "synchronous" associations of "motory vibratiuncles" with other sensations, ideas, or movements, while decomplex movements involve "successive" associations between motory vibratiuncles and further sensations, ideas, and especially movements. A "complex movement" is thus a conditioned reflex; a "decomplex movement" is a sustained sequence of action.

A perfected complex movement will also be what Hartley terms "secondarily automatic." The beginning piano student plays scales—with the hope some day of playing Chopin. But the performance of such complex movements as hitting the right key, for the right length of time, at the sight of a given note in turn requires that a person first gain control of specific automatic actions, so that they can become "voluntary," and then perfect these so that they become "secondarily automatic." Skilled repertoires of action are thus themselves artifacts, and as such they are dependent upon our capacities for memory. Just as the present of perceptual awareness is for Edelman "the remembered present," so also for Hartley any repertoire of action a person performs or plans to perform, to be voluntary, must also be remembered: "All our voluntary powers are of the nature of memory" (*OM* 1.3.4.90). The question, then, is: How do we remember what to do?

Hartley begins his account of action in the *Observations* with a discussion of muscular contraction, and specifically with forms of muscular contraction that are purely "automatic" reflexes. We saw in §3.7 with regard to Hartley's description of crying that a sufficiently sharp stimulus leads to a generalized muscular contraction in which the sets of antagonist muscles work against each other. More generally, drawing on research into muscular contraction by Stephen Hales, Leeuwenhoek, Richard Lower, and Henry Pemberton (*OM* 1.1.3.16), Hartley models the movement from sensation to automatic action as involving a circuit by which an impulse travels up the sensory nerves to the brain and then from the brain down the "motory" nerves to the muscles (*OM* 1.1.3.19).[15] After ascending to the brain and passing over to the motor nerves, "vibrations descend along the motory nerves... in some such manner as sound runs along the surfaces of rivers, or an electrical virtue along hempen strings" (*OM* 1.1.3.16). The vibrations then agitate "the small particles" in the muscular fibers, and "the vibrations thus excited in the fibres, put into action an attractive virtue, perhaps of the electrical kind" so that "each muscular fibre is made shorter by this increase of attraction."[16] This is contraction. Touch a hot poker with your finger, and your hand will jerk back. But such reflex contractions last only for a limited time, for muscular contraction "impedes" the vibrations that are descending along the motor nerves, and as a result "the contraction of a muscle, when carried to a certain degree, must check itself, and bring on a relaxation" (OM 1.1.3.17).

In his account of automatic muscular action, Hartley discusses both reflex actions, including the contraction and dilation of the iris,[17] and the autonomic processes including heartbeat, respiration, and peristalsis. He differentiates between the two types of action and attempts to account for the latter by noting the continuous or recurrent sources of their stimuli, in part deriving from the vibrations emanating from the autonomic processes themselves. (Peristaltic motion, for example, is partly a response to respiration and the circulation of the blood, but is largely triggered by "the impressions which the aliment, bile, and faeces, make upon the villous coat" [OM 1.1.3.19].) Although he reports on experiments involving animals that show, for example, that a frog's heart will continue to beat for some time after being taken out of the body, he lacked a means of conceptualizing how this process can be self-sustaining. In addition, Hartley also notes, with regard to reflex actions, that the response is not necessarily limited to the muscles corresponding to the location of the stimulus. Touch your finger to a hot poker, and you—and not just your finger—jump back (see OM 1.1.3.18).

Because the vibratory circuit runs from sensory nerves to brain to "motory" nerves to muscles, it is possible for vibrations to be patched into the circuit in the brain, so that a muscular action can be triggered by vibrations or vibratiuncles from any source. The vibrations may be sensory stimuli from a source that is arbitrarily related to the action, so that "particular motions of the body may . . . be made to depend upon sensations, with which they have no natural or original connexion" (OM 1.1.3.20): Pavlov's dogs salivated at the sound of a bell, and a pianist taps the appropriate key at the sight of a note on a staff. Or the source may be ideational, so that "ideas may therefore excite muscular motions of the same strength with the automatic motions." Anticipation of speaking in public activates "little vibrations" in the brain that induce in some the physical symptoms of stage fright. Or the source may be muscular, so that a muscular action itself becomes both the response to and the stimulus for other muscular actions: to Hartley, such self-sustaining action/reaction sequences account in part for autonomic processes, and they are also involved in coordinated continuous actions such as walking. Moreover, the muscular actions that occur in response to these stimuli can, besides further muscular actions, also activate ideas. Hartley sums up the variability of the circuitry in a theorem: "If any sensation A, idea B, or muscular motion C, be associated for a sufficient number of times with any other sensation D, idea E, or muscular motion F, it will, at last, excite d, the simple idea belonging to sensation D, the very idea E, or the very muscular motion F" (*OM* 1.1.3.20).

Hartley's theorem accounts for the transit of action from automatic to voluntary and then to secondarily automatic. Hartley gives a detailed analysis of the initial stage of this transit in his account of the process by which a child learns to grasp objects:

> The fingers of young children bend upon almost every impression which is made upon the palm of the hand, thus performing the action of grasping, in the original automatic manner. After a sufficient repetition of the motory vibrations which concur with this action, their vibratiuncles are generated, and associated strongly with other vibrations or vibratiuncles, the most common of which, I suppose, are those excited by the sight of a favorite play thing which the child uses to grasp, and hold in its hand. He ought, therefore, according to the doctrine of association, to perform and repeat the action of grasping, upon having such a play thing presented to his sight. But it is a known fact, that children do this. (*OM* 1.1.3.21)

At first the action is purely automatic response to a sensory stimulus: touch an infant's palm with your finger and the infant will grip it. But with repetition the motor vibratiuncles for the grasping reflex are generated—the child will now possess the motor idea of grasping. Whereas the automatic grasping reflex can be triggered only by a sensory stimulus to the hand, the motor idea can be activated by stimuli from modalities other than touch. The child's hand grasps, in a "complex" movement, at the *sight* of a favorite toy.

The substitution of associated visual and other perceptions for physical touch of the palm extends the range of stimuli that can prompt the child to grasp with his hand. In addition, the mastery of the motor idea of grasping, especially in connection with the sight of desired objects, will enhance hand-eye coordination and refine the child's motor control of his hands. However, such grasping is still in direct response to sensory stimuli. To qualify for being called voluntary, a further development is required:

> By pursuing the same method of reasoning, we may see how, after a sufficient repetition of the proper associations, the sound of the words *grasp, take hold,* &c. the sight of the nurse's hand in a state of contraction, the idea of a hand, and particularly of the child's own hand, in that state, and innumerable associated circumstances, *i.e.* sensations, ideas, and motions, will put the child upon grasping, till, at the last, that idea, or state of mind which we may call the will to grasp, is generated and sufficiently associated with the action to produce it instantaneously. It is therefore perfectly voluntary in this case; ...

Note the elements that enter into the development of the voluntary action of grasping: the *sound* of relevant words, especially commands such as *Hold my hand when we cross the street;* the *sight* of the adult's hand, when, at the curb, it closes over her own; the generalized idea of a hand; and the child's idea of her own hand in the state of grasping. Like the bricklayers at the beginning of Wittgenstein's *Philosophical Investigations,* for the child learning the words and learning the action are two aspects of one process. And eventually, in this process, the "idea, or state of mind which we may call the will to grasp, is generated and sufficiently associated with the action." Complex actions become voluntary when the idea, *the will to ...,* enters into the complex.

The voluntary action of grasping is dependent upon the cementing of a connection between *Grasp!* and the motor idea that is the act of grasping. But for the act of grasping to be put to practical use in the activities of life, as in, e.g., holding and swinging a baseball bat, the voluntary action must itself become secondarily automatic:

> After the actions, which are most perfectly voluntary, have been rendered so by one set of associations, they may, by another, be made to depend upon the most diminutive sensations, ideas, and motions, such as the mind scarce regards, or is conscious of; and which therefore it can scarce recollect the moment after the action is over. Hence it follows, that association not only converts automatic actions into voluntary, but voluntary into automatic. For these actions, of which the mind is scarce conscious, and which follow mechanically, as it were, some precedent diminutive sensation, idea, or motion, and without any effort of the mind, are rather to be ascribed to the body than the mind, *i.e.* are to be referred to the head of

automatic motions. I shall call them automatic motions of the secondary kind, to distinguish them both from those which are originally automatic, and from the voluntary ones. (*OM* 1.1.3.21)

A young girl wants to play softball, and to do so she must learn how to swing a bat. When she begins to learn such a sequence, she has to follow—or cue herself with—a series of separate commands: *Keep your hands together. Choke up a little on the bat. Keep the bat off your shoulder. Swing level; don't chop.* She first heard these from her coach, and now, bat in hand, she repeats them to herself. By relying upon such commands, she consciously monitors and attempts to control how she holds and swings a bat. For her, batting is a composite sequence of voluntary actions, each of which she tries to monitor and correct. Over time, the process becomes habitual and continuous, and the need for such explicit cueing and conscious monitoring diminishes and then disappears. Swinging a bat becomes secondarily automatic.

"And, in the same manner," writes Hartley, "may all the actions performed with the hands be explained, all those that are very familiar in life passing from the original automatic state through the several degrees of voluntariness, and then repassing though the same degrees in an inverted order, till they become secondarily automatic on many occasions, though still perfectly voluntary on some, *viz.* whensoever an express act of the will is exerted." Once perfected, swinging a bat is on most occasions a secondarily automatic action, dependent "upon the most diminutive sensations, ideas, and motions, such as the mind scarce regards." The player's mind no longer regards the act of batting; rather, her attention is focused upon the ball approaching her, and her "express act of will" concerns her decision to swing, or not swing, at a particular pitch. The more a complex action becomes secondarily automatic, the less does the agent attend to the action, and consequently the more can the agent's consciousness be focused upon the circumstances in which the action occurs. The player stops going after bad pitches.

Conversely, it is when secondarily automatic actions become defective that the agent may again need to exert an "express act of will" in order to perform them. The softball player will need to exert such an act of will when her batting average starts to slip and the coach suggests a way to correct the quirk in her swing. Similarly, and more seriously, for people with neuromotor deficits, what a normal person takes as a continuous movement may fragment into discontinuous and recalcitrant particles. A person with Parkinson's disease may suffer an ataxia of gait. He may even shout to his right leg, *Move!*, but remain rooted to the spot. He may, however, sustain a relatively coordinated sequence of steps if prompted with external sensory stimuli—for example, by being verbally cued by another's saying *Right, Left,* or, if stuck, by having a yardstick placed on the floor in front of him. For such a person, walking depends upon the repeated and timed intervention of ideas of "will," and when the person is unable to provide them for himself, they may be provided by another, for as long as the connections between taking a step and such stimuli remain to some degree secondarily automatic.

Coleridge criticized Hartley's "the material hypothesis" and the linked theory of association for reducing "the will, the reason, the judgment, and the understanding" to "mechanical *effects.*" Were such a reduction true, he argued, "our whole life would be divided between the despotism of outward impressions, and that of senseless and passive memory" (see §4.1). For Coleridge, and for those who share his view, mechanism is despotism—the opposite, the enemy, of human freedom. To the extent it is true, mechanism is something to overcome.

What Hartley's account of automatic, voluntary, and secondarily automatic actions shows, however, is that to him the mechanism of mind and body is not a despotic given; rather, in a sense, it is an achievement. "All our voluntary powers are of the nature of memory." But our memories are in our bodies; how to swing a bat should "rather to be ascribed to the body than the mind." A person's ability to do anything voluntarily depends upon a repertoire of secondarily automatic processes that operate "mechanically," that is, independently of attentive conscious monitoring. Rather than being in opposition, voluntary and "mechanistic" (i.e., secondarily automatic) actions are in alliance. In general, the more "mechanistic" the action, the more voluntary the choice of when to perform it (see §5.5).

Moreover, what really matters in life are the decomplex movements that enable people and other animals to conduct themselves in the world. And when it comes to decomplex movements, whether playing softball or playing Chopin on the piano, the more secondarily automatic the complex movements the better. Overall, in the perfection of any of the skilled repertoires of action required for the performance of decomplex movements, the greater the expertise developed through practice, the less must the performer direct his attention to the movements themselves, and the fewer the interventions of ideas of will. Hartley makes this point in relation to the process of learning to play the harpsichord:

Suppose a person who has a perfectly voluntary command over his fingers, to begin to learn to play upon the harpsichord; the first step is to move his fingers from key to key, with a slow motion, looking at the notes, and exerting an express act of volition in every motion. By degrees the motions cling to one another, ... the acts of volition growing less and less express all the time, till at last they become evanescent and imperceptible. For an expert performer will play from notes, or ideas laid up in memory, or from the connexion of the several complex parts of the decomplex motions, some or all; and, at the same time, carry on a quite different train of thoughts in his mind, or even hold a conversation with another. Whence we may conclude, that the passage of the sensory, ideal, or motory vibrations which precede, to those motory ones which follow, is as ready and direct, as from the sensory vibrations to the original automatic motions corresponding to them; and consequently, that there is no intervention of the idea, or state of mind, called will. (OM 1.1.3.21)

The virtuoso plays, it seems, effortlessly. But the novice student of the piano peers at the music and says to himself, "The bottom line of the staff is E, and let's see, E on the piano has no black key to its right." The tune proceeds slowly, as the student gradually gains a voluntary control over the movements of his hands relative to the keyboard. After some practice, the actions of striking the keys are triggered automatically by the associated visual signals, without any calculation on the student's part. Playing the piano thus becomes a matter of creating multiple direct links between visual, auditory, ideational, and motor elements. The better one learns to play, the more tightly are these links drawn together, and the less need is there for recourse to "intervention of the idea, or state of mind, called will." With enough practice, one sits down at the piano and plays Chopin. Or perhaps more accurately: one sits down at the piano, and the music plays.

As a skill is perfected, which sensory modality is most important may shift, and one that has been primary may cease to be regarded—at least once the action is under way. Hartley notes, in a later proposition, that when learning how to dance, "the scholar desires to look at his feet and legs, in order to judge by seeing when they are in their proper position. By degrees he learns to judge this by feeling; but the visible idea left partly by the view of his master's motions, partly of his own, seems to be the chief associated circumstance, that introduces the proper motions" (*OM* 1.2.7.77). On the one hand, learning to dance is a matter of a gradual shift from a reliance on imitation of action guided by visual cues to a performance of the action as monitored by the flow of kinesthetic information, correlated with the music. (Such a shift is a requirement for dancing well; a person who continues to rely on visual cueing will dance slightly behind the beat.) On the other, the "visible ideas" of the dancing master or of the dancer himself often remain the "associated circumstances" that enable the dancer to "introduce the proper motions." To begin a quadrille, the dancer may need to follow a visual cue, either sensed or remembered.

"Associated circumstances," interpreted broadly to include both an action and elements of the situation in which the action takes place, are, in Hartley's view, necessary for the initiation of any complex or decomplex action. "It is necessary, according to the theory of these papers," he writes, "that every semi-voluntary, voluntary, and secondarily automatic action should be excited by an associated circumstance" (*OM* 1.2.5.70). We do not count a reflex action to be voluntary, and neither would we consider voluntary an action sequence that has the potential for occurring without warning. Like Christopher Smart's dropping to his knees in the street, the latter would be an affliction and not an instance of voluntary control. Voluntary actions are those for which, as Hartley notes, the initiating "associated circumstance" is an idea rather than an externally impressed sensation, and particularly an idea that is itself not compelled. Voluntary action thus requires a conscious state with a particular kind of causal efficacy—the efficacy of reflexivity. Statements of the form *I will practice my music today* are paradigmatic instances of such initiating associated circumstances.

Hartley's theorem in proposition 20 describes a single event that exists only as one moment abstracted from a flux or stream of action: through association, one sensation, idea, or motion excites another idea or motion. When the associations include motion and are synchronous, the movement is complex. But association also functions to create and sustain decomplex movements such as dancing or playing a musical instrument—continuous and self-sustaining processes that integrate sensory, ideational, and muscular activity. And here it is important to note that, although the voluntary power of playing a Chopin prelude relies upon memory, that is, upon secondarily automatic actions formed out of the joint impression of kinetic, auditory, visual, and emotional progressions, the remembered present that is the performance of the

Perception and Action   171

decomplex action involves the dynamic interplay of memory with *present* kinetic, auditory, visual, emotional, and interpersonal flows of perception. The "associated circumstances" involved in playing the prelude constitute a continuously interactive system rather than a simply linear sequence of causes. Moreover, although complex movements are essential for human and animal life, decomplex actions are, as noted above, what matter most. The sight of the sparrows through the window sets my cat's teeth chattering; but if she had to fend for herself, her survival would depend upon her skills at stalking and pouncing. Rather than the isolated event of sensation A exciting motion F, we should take for our paradigm of association the entire flowing, cascading, decomplex process it creates—a process that, at each moment, is itself a response to antecedent stimuli and a source of further stimuli that recursively sustain and guide its own continuation.

6. Experiencing Ideas

Perception and action involve ideas. But the term *idea* must be very inclusively defined, if the adjectives *simple, complex,* and *decomplex* are to meaningfully precede it. We noted above that, on the first page of the *Observations*, Hartley defines ideas very broadly as referring to all "internal feelings" that are not "sensations." Although we may at first think of an idea as a vestige or trace of a sensation, Hartley's statement that "no sensation can be a monad" (*OM* 2.1.4) and his emphasis on joint impression alert us to the fact that an animal body does not experience the separate pure sensations A and B, but rather the synthetic compound $(A + B + \ldots + N)$, where the input of each sensory modality is modified—one could say colored or tinted—by the others. Because it is the regular conjunction of sensory impressions that accounts for perceptual discrimination, it must be to the compound induced neural state $(a + b + \ldots + n)$ that an idea, as a basic fact of perception, corresponds.

That any perceptual idea is a synthesis, a joint impression involving elements from different modalities of sense and movement, has as a consequence that there will be a difference between a person's primary *experience* of an idea $(a + b + \ldots + n)$ and the various elements that went into the composition of it. Recall John Stuart Mill's comment, that "it was reserved for Hartley to show that mental phenomena ... may form a still more intimate, and as it were chemical union—may merge into a compound, in which the separate elements are no more distinguishable as such, than hydrogen and oxygen in water, the compound having all the appearance of a phenomenon *sui generis*" (1859, 294; see §1.1). In the first corollary to proposition 12, Hartley writes: "If the number of simple ideas which compose the complex one be very great, it may happen, that the complex idea shall not appear to bear any relation to its compounding parts, nor to the external senses upon which the original sensations . . . were impressed" (*OM* 1.1.1.12) Hartley notes that a "compound medicine," for example, "has a taste and flavour of its own, which appears to be simple and original, and like that of a natural body." Hartley also mentions what would have been to his readers the fundamental instance of the disjunction between appearance and underlying associative compounding—white light, which "is vulgarly thought to be the simplest and most uncompounded of all colours, while yet it really rises from a certain proportion of the seven primary colours, with their several shades or degrees." We see a white swan or brown sparrow, not the spectrum of colors reflecting from them.

A further consequence of the notion that perceptual ideas are analogous to chemical compounds is that conscious awareness of an idea is not necessarily a reliable indicator of its presence in my mind. The problem here derives from the common tendency to take visual images as the paradigm of ideas: it is difficult to think of having a mental visual representation without being aware of it. However, because consciousness at any moment is a matter of selective focus upon one part of comprehensive processes of association, the experience of an idea as an evident mental image or representation is only one, and perhaps not the most important, indicator of its existence. Equally important is recognition. Hartley notes that we lack the power to call up "evident" ideas of smell (*OM* 1.2.3.52); but we "reconnoitre" smells, and recognition of a smell is as clear an indicator of the presence of an idea as would be an internal visual image or "olfactory representation" (if there be such). I have the idea of the smell and taste of Laphroig whiskey if I can correctly say "That's Laphroig" when given a dram. Moreover, because our ability to discriminate and categorize perceptions depends upon the association of different sensory and motor modalities, it follows that the richer the total combination of associated circumstances, the better are we to make ever finer perceptual discriminations. "We are," for example, "prepared to receive and distinguish the several smells more readily, and more accurately, on account of the previous influence of these associated circumstances. And, conversely, the actual smells of natural bodies enable us to determine them . . . by suggesting their names, and visible appearances" (*OM* 1.2.3.52). When an idea is proving elusive, any number of circumstances will finally elicit it. Recalling a particular memory, recognizing a particular sensation, is often a matter of hunting though the constellation of associated circumstances for the key that unlocks memory's door (cf. James 1890, 1:585–86). Knowing the names, places of origin, and labels of single malt whiskeys helps one to distinguish between Laphroig and Lagavulin. And the taste of Laphroig can evoke an image of the label—and much else besides.

In addition to being expressed as a perceptual idea (an evident image or a recognition event), a neural state $(a + b + \ldots + n)$ can also, when activated, manifest itself as a complex action. A higher-level neural state can also be expressed as a decomplex movement, a sustained sequence of secondarily automatic actions. A *motor idea* could thus be the correlate of a neural configuration that is the memory of, and hence the guide or control for, a complex movement—or for an entire decomplex movement as a whole. For example, while I was researching Hartley's role in the promotion and assessment of Joanna Stephens's medicine for the stone, I discovered the music for "The Birks of Invermay" printed in the November 1737 issue of the *Gentleman's Magazine*.[18] "The Birks of Invermay" is a lovely strathspey, and in Scotland one can hear it played at dances to this day. Initially I needed the notes in front of me, but now I play the tune from memory on my button-key accordion. Although it would be a challenge for me to figure out how write it out in musical notation, and at the moment I write this I cannot tell you even what note it begins on, I do have the idea for the tune: were I to pick up my "box," my hands would find it. For me, this strathspey's "primary seat" lies in a muscular or kinesthetic memory. I know the tune "from the connexion of the several complex parts of the decomplex motions" (*OM* 1.1.3.21)—that is, as a sequence of specific muscular positions and motions, as these are associated with a flow of sounds, so that the sounds "vary with the varieties" of the motions. Continued practice of the tune has created in my brain and nervous system an induced state—however we will eventually model it—that can be activated and sustained when I pick up the instrument and say to myself, "Now for 'The Birks of Invermay.' "

Motor ideas occur in contexts that are saturated with associated circumstances. The writing of this sentence is itself but one moment in a continuing flow of activities, which are more or less connected with each other. Such connections between acts and their initiating stimuli can be multiple, and indeed the initiating conditions can be so "diminutive" and the connection so spontaneous as to escape conscious attention. The experience of an idea reveals only one part of a totality, much of which remains submerged below the threshold of consciousness. A dancer may be unaware of the faint and fleeing visual images that accompany her movements. Playing "The Birks of Invermay" may depend upon "the most diminutive sensations, ideas, and motions, such as the mind scarce regards." And much of what a person does in the course of daily life falls under this description. What I write now is prompted by what I have already written, and it in turn prompts what I shall write next. It is also connected with the physical act of writing: I sometimes do not know what I want to say until I put pen to paper; in such situations the physical act of writing the words down itself becomes a source for ideas of what to say. In addition, I am partially aware of any number of "associated circumstances"—as I write this, I look over at the coal fire in the grate, at the rain upon the fields, the line of books on the shelf in front of me, and I wonder what secret influences these have on what you are reading now. Although it is possible to make distinctions between the multiply interconnected streams of sensations, motions, and words that constitute decomplex actions and the apparently accidental associations, such as the fire and the rain, that surround them, the boundary between them is imprecise.

The "internal feelings" that are ideas may thus be expressed as representations, as acts of recognition, or as decomplex actions. In all cases, their "associated circumstances" possess depth both in terms of synchronicity and of temporal flow. Hartley suggests, for example, when we read or speak, that "faint miniatures of the sounds of words [which] pass over the ear" (*OM* 1.2.5.70) are associated circumstances of the action of reading or speaking, but that the reader or speaker is usually unconscious of them. To the objection that, if they exist, we should be conscious of them, he replies that we sometimes are, and also that, when reading, "visible trains do not appear as objects of consciousness and memory, till we begin to attend to them." In Hartley's view, we only become conscious of something when we attend to it and "watch the evanescent perceptions of our minds." What we are then conscious of, as we go about our activities, is dependent upon the "diminutive sensations, ideas, and motions" beneath the surface of our attention. My capacity to bring an idea above the threshold of consciousness, in terms of one dominant modality—e.g., a tune as a sequence of sounds, or St. Stanislaus Church in Milwaukee as a visual image—remains dependent upon the submerged joint impressions and associated circumstances that are indissoluble aspects of that idea, and that define its contours, stability, and mass.

"All our voluntary powers are of the nature of memory." And: "It is necessary, according to the theory of these papers, that every semivoluntary, voluntary, and secondarily automatic action should be excited by an associated circumstance." According to the theory, we are beings of memory and circumstance. A person's ability to do anything—to make a conscious choice and then to carry out a decomplex act—depends, as it were, upon all that mind has turned over to body. But what, then, is left of mind?

5

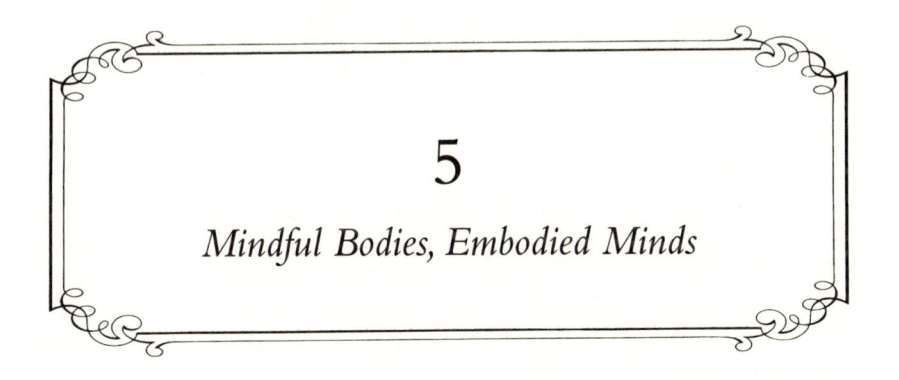

Mindful Bodies, Embodied Minds

1. "This Train of Folly and Extravagance"

On the morning of 29 March 1737—a year after the newly married David and Elizabeth Hartley had taken up residence in London—Joseph Butler stopped by their house. The Hartleys were drinking tea with John Byrom and another friend, George Lloyd. Byrom reports that the four were discussing "Dr. Hartley's illness, which he described to us, and indeed he seemed to be in a very bad way; he was searched by Cheselden for the stone" (*B* 1.2.96). Hartley introduced Byrom to Butler, and the topic of conversation quickly shifted to Byrom's shorthand and particularly to the possibility of interesting William Augustus, the Duke of Cumberland and the youngest son of George II and Queen Caroline, in becoming one of Byrom's students. The duke would in a few years gain the title the "Butcher" for his ruthless suppression of the Jacobite rebellion of 1745. But in late March 1737 the duke was about to celebrate his sixteenth birthday, and according to Butler he was a thoughtful young man. Butler was at the time the Clerk of the Closet to Queen Caroline, and in this capacity he met with the queen every day from seven to nine P.M. to discuss philosophical and religious issues. Butler reported that one evening, when he was reading Hobbes to the queen, she asked her son, "Well, what do you think of this?"—to which he responded "that there must be right and wrong before human laws, which supposed right and wrong; and besides, wherever was there that state of nature that he talked of? who ever lived in it?" The queen then asked, "but if you was left to yourself, what would you do?" And the duke said, "I cannot tell what pleasure, &c., might do to blind me, but unless it did, so and so, &c." Byrom does not complete the sentence.

After this anecdote, the conversation turned to religion. They "talked of Sir Is. Newton having writ his books with a view to religion," and of Pascal. Then, Byrom writes, "we entered into a kind of dispute about prophecy, and I said I thought the Old Testament for prophecy and the New for miracles ... upon which arose an argument and talk about reason and authority, they being for reason and I for authority, that we had reason indeed to follow authority, viz. the consent of the Christian Church" (B 1.2.96–97). The discussion continued for nearly two hours; Byrom's summary of it runs to more than two pages in his journal. Butler, Byrom writes, "talked with much mildness, and myself with too much impetuosity."

When he dropped by the Hartley's home on this spring morning in 1737, Joseph Butler was forty-five years old; he had enjoyed a reasonably successful career in the Church of England. In the remaining fifteen years of his life, he would ascend to the heights of the ecclesiastical establishment. After Queen Caroline died on 29 November 1737, George II respected his wife's wishes concerning Butler's advancement; Butler became the bishop of Bristol the following year, and then in later years dean of St. Paul's and bishop of Durham. Contributing to his success was the publication in 1736 of his *Analogy of Religion, Natural and Revealed, to the Constitution and Course of Nature,* for the book quickly became one of the most widely admired works of the century. The *Analogy* owes its influence at least in part to its apparent capacity to balance and harmonize our knowledge of the natural world and of ourselves as moral and social beings. Central to it is an affirmation of the compatibility of scientific and religious knowledge; Butler states that his aim is to compare "the known Constitution and Course of Things, with what is said to be the moral System of Nature" and thereby to demonstrate "that both may be traced up to the same general Laws, and resolved into the same principles of divine Conduct" (1736, viii–ix). God is both the designer and the moral governor of the world. "As the manifold Appearances of Design and of final Causes, in the Constitution of the World, prove it to be the Work of an intelligent Mind," he writes, "so the particular final Causes of Pleasure and Pain distributed amongst his Creatures, prove that they are under his Government: what may be called His natural Government of Creatures endued with Sense and Reason" (1736, 44). There is, in Butler's view, no inherent conflict between what reason discovers in nature and authentic moral truths, as these are taught by religious authorities and enforced by the natural allocation of pleasure and pain.

Within the context of the analogy between the natural and the moral worlds, Butler preserves what I will call the standard account of human nature.[1] According to this account, there are in the universe two kinds of substance, immaterial and material, which are respectively active and passive, causes of movement and inert targets of movement. A person houses an immaterial substance—mind or soul—in a material body. The mind is a self-conscious unity, aware of its freedom, that directs the body to act; the mind moves the body, but except in instances of delirium, madness, or irrationality, the body does not move the mind. The mind is also immortal; moreover, it knows that, because of the moral governance of the universe by God, its free actions in this life on earth will determine whether it will spend eternity in heaven or hell. Finally, it knows that popular belief in God's moral governance—that every hair on one's head is numbered, that every action, no matter how secretly performed, will be counted in the final reckoning—maintains civil society. Were people to think that life ended with the death of the body, or were they to think they could escape from the sight of an all-knowing and perfectly just God, nothing could restrain their heedless descent into sensuality, vice, and criminality.

Butler suggests that the arguments supporting the standard account are so strong as to make rational dissent impossible. In his discussion of our "future state," Butler asserts that although "the Simplicity and absolute Oneness of a living Agent cannot, from the Nature of the thing, be properly proved by experimental Observations," nonetheless, because such observations *"fall in* with the Supposition of its Unity, so they plainly lead us to *conclude* certainly, that our gross organized Bodies, with which we perceive the objects of the Senses, and with which we act, are no Part of ourselves" (1736, 17). Consequently, "it is easy to conceive, that we may exist out of our Bodies as in them." Writing a half century later, Thomas Reid echoes this point: "A person is something indivisible, and is what LEIBNITZ calls a *monad*" (1785, 317).

According to the standard account, I am my immaterial, immortal spirit, possessing a fundamental simplicity and oneness—this I can infer with near certainty from experimental observations. And further, although there are some who entertain "so absurd a Supposition as that of universal Necessity" (Butler 1736, 104), I am also aware that free will is an essential quality of spirit: God, the absolute spirit, directs the movements of the cosmos; a person is a finite spirit, which freely directs the movements of the body. Moreover, I am or at least I should be aware that God has fashioned a world in which the system of nature and the moral order are in harmony. Although Butler is careful not to claim that the moral order is self-evident, he is convinced that the probability of the evidence is sufficient to convince any right-thinking person. However, not everyone thinks rightly. Butler acknowledges that there are some "who indulge themselves in vain and idle speculations, how the World might possibly have been framed otherwise than it is" (vi). Some imagine "that the whole method of Government by Punishment should be rejected, as absurd; as an awkward round-about method of carrying things on; nay as contrary to a principal Purpose, for which it would be supposed Creatures were made, namely Happiness" (vii). But a mind that knows its own nature will not follow "this Train of Folly and Extravagance."

Imagine how Hartley's *Observations* would appear to a reader who accepted the standard account, as Butler articulates it. On the one hand, Butler and Hartley have much in common. Both are broadly interested in giving an account of morality that is congruent with, and to a degree reliant upon, the methods of scientific reasoning. Central to this account is reasoning from analogy (see §6.5); in his discussion of revealed religion Hartley credits Butler with showing that "the word and works of God, are in all things most wonderfully analogous" (*OM* 2.2.28). Because analogies are always matters of degree, both are also interested in the theory of probability and on reasoning from probabilities; Butler's *Analogy* begins with an Introduction that is devoted to a discussion of probabilistic evidence.

Both Hartley and Butler are also interested in showing how God's system of moral governance can be detected within the structure of the natural world, and especially in the manner in which human beings are framed. We noted above Butler's assertion that "the particular final Causes of Pleasure and Pain distributed amongst his Creatures, prove that they are under his Government." The distribution is such that pleasure is correlated with virtue, and vice with pain, so that "in the of attractive force. But unlike a celestial body, a molecule also manifests a force of repulsion. While the force of attraction draws molecules together, the force of repulsion pushes them apart. These forces define the molecule's "sphere of attraction and repulsion."

At some distance from the center of a molecule, the two forces cancel each other out; this distance marks the boundary of indifference, the threshold or horizon at which the molecule manifests neither an attracting or repelling force. In the absence of other outside forces, molecules in a local environment will arrange themselves so that they meet at their boundaries of indifference. Like that of bubbles of soap, this arrangement will be a state of stasis.

The state of stasis is dynamic. The two forces give the molecule both a degree of elasticity and also a capacity for forming and breaking bonds or associations with other molecules. In certain circumstances molecules' forces of attraction overcome their forces of repulsion; they then fuse into larger molecular compounds, and these in turn may be grouped together into the physical structures we observe about us. In other circumstances the forces of repulsion may overbalance the attractive forces. When heated, for example, or placed in acid or caustic potash, some stones will decompose into gases. Consequently, as Hartley notes, the concept of "a single thing" is a relative one: "By a single thing, . . . I mean one that is so comparatively; so that I call not only a single part of an animal (which yet is a thing decompounded, perhaps without limits), but a whole system of animals, when compared with other systems, a single thing" (*OM* 2.1.4). And beings existing in other worlds, and at different scales from our own, may have very different notions of what constitutes single things.

Picture a nerve fiber—a long thread of linked molecules, perhaps extending from retina to brain, or from fingertip to spine. Because the molecules comprising the fiber are in a state of dynamic stasis, stillness easily gives way to motion; like the glassy surface of a pond on a quiet night, the fiber will ripple with motion when a pebble of stimulation is dropped upon it. When stimulated, the fiber vibrates. The vibrations are not transverse, as are those of a violin string or of light, but are rather longitudinal or axial, like the waves of sound that move through air and water. A wave travels along the medium as the molecules comprising it jostle back and forth.

In a living being, a nerve fiber is never completely still; it vibrates continuously at a constant frequency, its natural state of vibration. In theory, if one had an instrument sensitive enough, one could measure this frequency; one could determine that, in its natural state, a given number of waves per second flow along a particular nerve fiber.

When a stimulus is applied to a fiber, the frequency and amplitude of vibration change. We can suppose that the stimulus leads either to an increase or to a decrease, so that when a fiber enters into an induced state of vibration the frequency and amplitude are either higher or lower than they are in the natural state. For "sensory" fibers specialized to register light, sound, aromatic substances, physical pressure, or the position of the body, the stimuli are those of the relevant physical media. For fibers wholly within the nerve-brain system or for the "motory" fibers that travel outward to the muscles, the stimuli are imparted by other fibers.

Although nerve fibers tend to return to their natural states when no longer stimulated, after a particularly intense stimulus, or after repeated stimuli, a nerve fiber may undergo a nonreformable deformation at the molecular level. The configurations of the "spheres" of its molecules' forces of attraction and repulsion may be permanently changed. When this deformation occurs, the fiber will adopt a new natural state; it will in effect be tuned to vibrate at a different frequency and/or amplitude. This tuning is, on the level of the single fiber, the basis of memory. Any further changes in vibration will be changes relative to this new natural state.

When a change in frequency or amplitude occurs, and a signal is sent axially along a nerve fiber, a stress is placed upon the fiber's molecular stasis. In certain instances the stress causes "a minute invisible solution of continuity," a condition in which the molecules are forced to oscillate beyond their elastic limits. Such a breakdown of molecular structure will disrupt the transmission of vibrations along the fiber. Instead of sounding a note or registering changes in pitch, the nerve will shriek with a chaos of frequencies. And the organism will flinch in pain.

In sum: Taken as a single thing, a nerve fiber is a vibrating medium (1) that temporarily changes its frequency and amplitude in response to the stimuli it receives; (2) that, through changes in the shapes of its molecules, bears the imprint of induced changes in frequency and amplitude, so that it vibrates in a new way; (3) that possesses a pleasure/pain threshold; that is, a limit, itself variable, at which harmonic vibrations break down into noise; and (4) that forms links to other nerve, brain, or muscle fibers, in which it in turn induces further vibrational changes.

And taken together as a single thing, the brain and nerves comprise a vastly complex system for responding to, recording, and transferring stimuli. This system can also be taken to have its natural state; Hartley thought such a state of equilibrium and stasis would be that of a sleeping foetus. But this system is organized to be exceptionally sensitive to any changes in vibrational frequencies and amplitudes; any such change in one fiber or set of fibers will ramify throughout the system, changing the vibrations of other nerves and effecting changes in the other bodily systems. It will also leave its imprint upon the system itself; individual fibers will now be predisposed to vibrate in certain ways, and associative connections between fibers or groups of fibers will be made or strengthened.

The world Hartley imagines is one in which vibrant physical entities are capable of sensing—interacting with—each other, according to the laws of acoustic, or optical, or neural harmony. In addition, the overall thrust of Hartley's work is to show that "the whole superstructure of ideas and associations observable in human life may, by proceeding upwards according to analysis, and downwards according to synthesis, be built upon as small a foundation as we please" (*OM* 1.1.2.11). For Hartley, the foundation is indeed a small one: all that nerve fibers do is vibrate, change their frequencies or amplitudes of vibration, and transmit those changes to other fibers. But thanks to the vast number of associative connections between fibers, this simple and fundamental mechanism is able to generate all the complexities of action we observe in living beings. The spider darts along its web toward the struggling fly; the rabbit bolts for its hole at the whisper of danger; the chimpanzee comforts a distressed infant; the man comes up with the next sentence in the paragraph—however dissimilar these actions seem, they are all the observable manifestations of a fundamentally simple neural mechanism that relies, at bottom, upon the fact that a change of state in one nerve fiber causes changes of state in others.

3. An Entertainment

"It may afford the reader some entertainment," Hartley writes, "to compare my hypothesis with what Des Cartes and Leibnitz have advanced, concerning animal motion, and the connexion between the soul and body. My general plan bears a near relation to theirs" (*OM* 1.1.3.21). He then adds that "Des Cartes might have had success in the execution of his, as proposed in the beginning of his Treatise on Man, had he been furnished with a proper assemblage of facts from anatomy, physiology, pathology, and philosophy." A reader could take Hartley to be suggesting that his *Observations on Man* succeeds more fully in being the work the *Treatise on Man* had the potential to be; to the degree that it incorporates the scientific advances of the intervening century, and thanks particularly to the advance in natural philosophy brought about by the replacement of the Cartesian concept of contact mechanism by the Newtonian theory of vibrations.

However, as we saw in chapter 3, Descartes and Newton modeled "matter in motion" in fundamentally different ways. To Descartes, change in the motion of any body requires the physical impact of another moving body. Newton, by contrast, describes a universe largely devoid of matter but filled with forces of attraction and repulsion, forces that account for and manifest themselves in the vibrations of sound, light, the aether—and of the components of the nerves and brain. Now, in terms of Descartes's concept of motion, there is no way to account for self-initiated "animal motion"; all physical actions are *re*actions, completely predictable if one could with sufficient precision specify the antecedent causal contacts. As Coleridge argued, there is no way for a material body, understood in this way, to be capable of intentional action: "our whole life would be divided between the despotism of outward impressions, and that of senseless and passive memory" (*C* 7:111; see § 4.1). Creativity, novelty, flexibility—as displayed by a child, once she learns her native tongue and begins to generate a profusion of decomplex movements—must be attributed to something outside the closed system of interactions that mechanism describes: to, that is, a substance whose essence is thought. But matter, ever passive, cannot think. Hence the disjunctive dichotomies of Cartesian dualism: matter or spirit, body or soul, mechanistic or rational, passive or active, animal physiology or human consciousness.

Such disjunctive either/ors are not an essential part of the Newtonian model. The terms *passive* and *active* lack a meaningful application to the various forces of attraction and repulsion that are gathered together in the general theory of vibrations. In neural harmonics—the theory of vibrations applied to neurophysiology—there is no inherent requirement that the state of "mind" and "body" involved in playing or even composing Chopin's Prelude No. 4 in E Minor be described as *either* mechanical *or* rational. The one frame of reference does not exclude the other. To interpret Hartley's statement that "the powers of generating ideas . . . arise from corporeal causes" (*OM* 1.1.2.11) as reducing of "mind" to "matter" depends upon a dichotomizing of matter and consciousness that an advocate of neural Newtonianism would not be obliged to accept.

Of the followers of Newton and Hartley, it was Joseph Priestley who understood this clearly. We read, in his abridged edition of the *Observations,* "that . . . man does not consist of two principles, so essentially different from one another as *matter* and *spirit*" (Hartley 1775, xx). Rather, taking the active forces of attraction and repulsion to be the defining properties of matter, Priestley proposes that "the whole man is of some *uniform composition,* and that the property of *perception,* as well as the other powers that are termed *mental,* is the result . . . of such an organical structure as that of the brain" (xx). We will return to Priestley in chapter 11.

What kind of "entertainment," then, does Hartley think a comparison of his own work with that of Descartes and Leibniz would provide? Perhaps this is another example of Hartley's habitual generosity, of his avoidance of philosophical and religious faction, of his search for common ground. Although himself a committed Newtonian, he is offering some praise of Leibniz, Newton's bitter rival. Still, the term *entertainment* seems charged. His work "bears a near relation" to theirs, but this nearness is that of figures on opposite sides of the chasm separating Newton's and Descartes's models of matter.

The "near relation" and the distance within it are both evident in Hartley's comments on Descartes's theory of animal motion. In his section of "The Intellectual Faculties of Brutes" (*OM* 1.3.7.93), Hartley writes that "though I suppose, with Descartes, that all their motions are conducted by mere mechanism, yet I do not suppose them to be destitute of perception, but that they have this in a manner analogous to that which takes place in us; and that it is subjected to the same mechanical laws as the motions. . . . I always suppose, that corresponding feelings, and affections of mind, attend upon them, just as in us. And the brute creatures prove their near relation to us, not only by the general resemblance of the body, but by that of the mind also." The Cartesian dichotomies are absent. From the fact that a being can be described mechanistically, it does not follow that it lacks perceptions, feelings, and affections; and from the fact that a being displays intelligence, it does not follow that something exists within it that cannot be described mechanistically. Animals can be described in terms of physical mechanisms—*and* they have minds, are conscious, perceive and feel. Symmetrically, people have minds, are conscious, perceive and feel—*and* possess bodies and brains that can be described in terms of physical mechanisms. Bodily mechanism and mental consciousness, the two realms Descartes (and Butler and Coleridge as well) would keep separate, are aspects of a single reality, and they apply equally to animals and to human beings. As we shall see in §6.1, Hartley does list significant differences between humans and animals, concerning relative brain size, neurological structure, capacity for language, reliance on instinct, and forms of life. But all these differences are matters of degree; none of them constitute an absolute separation of human beings from the rest of the animal kingdom. None of them demonstrate the presence in humans of some thing that animals lack: animals prove their "near relation" both in body and in mind.

4. A Hypercomplex Idea

How, then, shall we explain that aspect of body called mind? What is mind, if it is a common property of humans and other animals, both a mechanism and a capacity for conscious perception, feeling, and thought? It is clearly not a "thinking substance." We noted in §3.3 that Hartley rejects the Stahlian notion of "a rational agent presiding over the fabric of the body, and producing effects that are not subject to the laws of mechanism" (*OM* 1.2.8.78). Further, in his discussion of memory, Hartley writes that "some people seem to suppose, that the soul surveys one object, the old for instance, and comparing it with the impressions which a similar new one would excite, calls the old one an object remembered. But this is like supposing an eye within the eye to view the pictures made by objects upon the *retina*" (*OM* 1.3.4.90). Just as there is no eye within the eye, there is no interior watcher that stands detached from a person's perceptions, feelings, thoughts, and actions. The mind is not a separate agent that presides over the body's fabric, and neither is it an observer that registers the results of the fabric's doings.

In his *Essay*, Locke famously calls the mind "white paper" (*HU* 2.1.2) upon which ideas—"the object[s] of the understanding when a man thinks" (*HU* 1.1.8)—are impressed, like strokes of a pen. In another image, Locke calls the brain the "presence-room" of the "mind," the place where ideas of sensation are conducted by the nerves for their "audience" with the regent (*HU* 2.3.1). The images suggest, if not mind as a detached observer, then mind as a preexisting space that becomes filled with the doodlings or bric-a-brac (and perhaps essays or artworks) of sensation and reflection. In an infant this space, although empty, already awaits the filling.[4]

In the opening words of the *Observations*, Hartley states that "man consists of two parts, body and mind" and adds that the latter "is that substance, agent, principle, &c. to which we refer the sensations, ideas, pleasures, pains, and voluntary motions." *To which we refer.* The nominal definition, coupled with the indefinite series of nouns that the *&c.* suggests, introduces what I take to be a purposive indeterminacy: *mind* is an unknown, an *X* to which are equated the formulae of a physiological and psychological algebra.

We noted in §4.2 that Locke emphasized that terms such as *will* and *understanding* designate "relations, not agents"; it is the person who wills, not the will that wills, and the term *will* refers to the relation between the person and the relevant action. Similarly, we may interpret Hartley as extending Locke's analysis of faculties to the mind itself, so that the term *mind* also refers to a set of relations, and not to some thing or substance—whether presiding agent, observer, or space waiting to be filled. In other words, it is the living being that perceives, feels, thinks, and acts, and the term *mind* refers to the totality of these processes. In this interpretation, the continuing processes of sensation, perception, feeling, action, and thought, understood both physically and subjectively, *are* the mind. Or, to extend the sequence of simple, complex, and decomplex: if simple ideas are the individual and largely imperceptible neural events that register sensory stimuli, if complex ideas are our primary categories of perception, emotion, and action, if decomplex ideas are the sequences we form out of complex ideas, then the mind could be said to be a hypercomplex idea. As I focus upon a small spot outside my window, light of various wavelengths from red to violet strikes my eyes; I see a brown sparrow hopping on the ground; I write this sentence, using the words *brown, sparrow, hopping.* And I want to communicate a thought to *you,* as one hypercomplex idea to another.

What is it like to be a hypercomplex idea? The key factor is that wholes are greater than the sums of their parts: the higher levels of organization denoted by the terms *complex, decomplex,* and *hypercomplex* each possess qualities that the lower levels do not. The sequence points to the way in which ideas incorporate other ideas, much in the way sparrows incorporate proteins and proteins incorporate carbon and other elements. The sequence also points toward the possibility of analysis. In the second corollary to proposition 12, Hartley writes: "One may hope, therefore, that, by pursuing and perfecting the doctrine of association, we may some time or other be enabled to analyze all that vast variety of complex ideas, which pass under the name of ideas of reflection, and intellectual ideas, into their simple compounding parts, *i.e.* into the simple ideas of sensation, of which they consist. This would be greatly analogous to the arts of writing, and resolving the colour of the sun's light, or natural bodies, into their primary constituent ones" (*OM* 1.1.1.12). The psychological theory holds out the hope that complex and decomplex ideas may be analyzed in a manner analogous to those by which analyses are conducted in linguistics, physics, chemistry, and biology. However, it is essential to keep in mind that analysis does not signify reduction, a complete description of a higher level of organization in terms of the processes that constitute a lower: a chemist cannot explain the manner in which sparrows build their nests.

In Hartley's discussion in the corollaries to proposition 12, the linguistic analogy is the most fully developed: simple ideas are analogous to phonemes, complex ideas to words, and decomplex ideas to sentences: "This coalescence of simple ideas into complex ones," he writes, "may be illustrated, and farther confirmed, by the similar coalescence of letters into syllables and words, in which association is likewise a chief instrument." And once again, it is important to emphasize that Hartley is not advocating here a brickbat plan of construction. He states in corollary 10 that in language meaning pertains to the whole: "the decomplex idea belonging to any sentence is not compounded merely of the complex ideas belonging to the words in it." Just as when people speak the primary experiential unit of language is the well-formed utterance, so also do people primarily experience decomplex and complex ideas. The fact that a linguist can analyze the speech of another into its constituent phonemes does not mean that the speaker is assembling what he intends to say out of them (see §4.3); rather, the speaker wishes to say something about his cat. Similarly, that Hartley thought it may be possible some day to analyze all ideas into the equivalent of sensory phonemes does not mean that he thought people assembled their ideas out of atomistically "separate subjective entities" (James 1890, 1:196). They rather think about their pets—and then leave off their business to play with them.

5. "Associated Circumstances"

There is, in Hartley's view, more to the mechanism of the mind than the fact that physical causes generate ideas. "By the mechanism of human actions I mean," he writes, "that each action results from the previous circumstances of body and mind, in the same manner, and with the same certainty, as other effects do from their mechanical causes; so that a person cannot do indifferently either of the actions *A,* and its contrary *a,* while the previous circumstances remain the same" (*OM* 1. Conclusion). A fundamental presupposition of Newtonian natural philosophy is that occult causes have no place in the explanation of physical systems. Hartley remains true to this axiom in his account of living beings: actions result from antecedent mental and bodily circumstances *in the same manner* as effects do from mechanical causes. There are no hidden causes for actions, causes that are independent of the total system of interchanges. All causes, in other words, were once effects; all actions add to the sum of events that constitute the mental and bodily "circumstances" that function as initiating and sustaining conditions for still further actions. In addition, Hartley claims that actions follow circumstances *with the same certainty* as effects follow causes: there is no uncertainty principle at work in human actions, introducing a fundamental indeterminacy into the mechanisms of an individual organism or of the total system in which that organism lives. The state of a system at any moment is determined by the sum of the system's "previous circumstances," so that no particle or person can do "indifferently" an action or its contrary, the antecedent circumstances remaining constant.

Hartley's affirmation that "each action results from the previous circumstances of body and mind, in the same manner, and with the same certainty, as other effects do from their mechanical causes" raises a question concerning the manner in which the hypercomplex ideas we call minds function in the world. Late in the eighteenth century the astronomer Pierre-Simon de Laplace proposed that, if an observer could determine both the positions of all the particles in the universe at a given moment and all the laws governing their movements, that observer would be able to describe the entire history of the universe, past and future. Among these particles, of course, would be those constituting a person's bones, muscles, nerves, and brain. Does this mean that Laplace's observer could have predicted that I would write the sentence about the brown sparrow, a few paragraphs back? That I did so seemed to be a happy coincidence. I happened to look out the window and noticed the sparrow, which was going about its own business. I then decided to use it as an illustration of the point I was attempting to express. Is it true that, given the conspiracy of circumstances, there could have been no other outcome?

Some of Laplace's contemporaries were willing to answer, no other. "In the life of every human being," according to William Godwin, "there is a chain of events, generated in the lapse of ages before his birth, and going on in a regular procession through the whole period of his existence, in consequence of which it was impossible to act in any instance otherwise than he has acted" (1976, 351; see §1.7). Godwin here states a rigorous version of the "doctrine of philosophical necessity"—a fundamental article in the creed of political radicalism and a legitimation for the social engineering attempted by, among others, Robert Owen at New Lanark and New Harmony, Indiana (see §11.5). Philosophical radicals acknowledged themselves indebted to Hartley for articulating this doctrine and for demonstrating its truth.

There are passages in the *Observations* that do seem to support Godwin's interpretation of necessity. In one place, Hartley writes: "Virtue and vice, merit, and demerit, reward and punishment, are applied to voluntary actions only.... Hence they are esteemed inapplicable to involuntary ones" (*OM* 2.1.15). Then he adds: "But involuntary actions are necessary by a necessity *ab extra,* which is generally seen; and because the necessity *ab intra,* which causes voluntary actions, is seldom seen, these are supposed not to be necessary." Voluntary actions are *supposed* not to be necessary: because we do not see *ab intra* necessities, we suppose them not to exist. An adult, Hartley notes in another passage, calls the child *willful* when she *will not mind*—for no reason that is satisfactory or apparent to the adult. But this says more about the adult's inattention to or ignorance of the child than it does about the child's state of mind. It is significant, Hartley notes, that adults start calling children willful at about the time they learn to walk: "When [a child] is arrived at such a perfection in walking, as to walk readily upon being desired by another person, the action is esteemed still more voluntary. One reason of which is, that the child, in some cases, does not walk when desired, whilst yet the circumstances are apparently the same as when he does. For here the unapparent cause of walking, or not walking, is *will*" (*OM* 1.2.7.77). Or so it seems. Hartley notes that the idea that the child is being willful occurs to the adults when she refuses

Fifth, to say that "all our voluntary powers are of the nature of memory" also suggests a capacity for transcendence; it points to the way in which a person can develop a *relation* to her environment, and indeed to her own thoughts and passions. Hartley offers a definition of willing that matches the one Jonathan Edwards presented in his *Freedom of the Will*, published five years after the *Observations*. "The will is as the most apparent good is," according to Edwards ([1754] 1957:143); Hartley writes that "the will is therefore that desire or aversion, which is strongest for the present time" (*OM* 1.3.3.89). But the strongest desire or aversion may be that which enables a person to *resist* the motives "of sensuality, ambition, [and] resentment" (*OM* 1. Conclusion) In his *Nichomachean Ethics,* Aristotle locates *arete* (i.e., virtue) in *hexis*—not, that is, in how a person immediately thinks or feels in response to a situation, but in the stance or relationship the person takes to her own spontaneous thoughts and feelings. It is not what I feel, but what I take a feeling to mean, and consequently how I deal with what I feel, that is the measure of my character.

The practice of an ethic thus creates among our desires and aversions subjective and self-referential elements. At times such associated circumstances as the statements *I will not let the sun go down on my wrath* or even *I will order a salad instead of the fettucine alfredo* represent the victories that combine to define "the most apparent good" for us. A person may feel set in motion by sensuality, ambition, and resentment, or by anger, contempt, and despair—such, both Hartley and Aristotle would agree, commonly follow "mechanistically" from their associated circumstances; but it is thanks to the mechanism of the mind, or to the power of what Aristotle calls *ethos*, habit, that the consistent practice of sympathy, of charity to others and oneself, can enable a person to resist such motives and eventually be free of the pains they cause.

People do confront *ab extra* necessities; they are embodied beings, present to their environments. But the forms that presence takes, and the ways in which they respond, depend upon necessities that are *ab intra;* for people are also storehouses of memory. Moreover, their *ab intra* necessities consist of emotional, cognitive, and semantic responses that are qualitatively different from *ab extra* stimuli. People concern themselves with what things mean—a fact that in itself should have discouraged Owenite attempts to institute social harmony. And from those meanings they over time develop traits of character—new models of the self. Their acts, in turn, contribute to the substance, shape, and meaning of the sets of circumstances that are their personal environments. Although it is true, in Hartley's theory, that a stream of outward experiences flows continuously around and through each person, people are not swept along before the current. They learn how to swim. Or more strongly: the practice of an ethic can redirect the flow of the stream of experience. How one swims in part directs the flow of the stream.

Of course, such resolutions as *I will not let the sun go down on my wrath* have their own associated circumstances, some of which lie in "the secret springs of action." A person's imperfect consciousness of the desires and aversions that motivate another, or himself, may render the other's or his own behavior a cipher. Viewed one way, Hartley's comment concerning the secret springs of action could be taken to indicate his awareness of the repressed unconscious drives that have become the specialty of psychoanalysis. But viewed another way, such secret springs may flow from another source entirely. And viewed in this way, "philosophical necessity" takes on a vastly different meaning from that attributed to it by such as Godwin and Owen.

"For all is God's," Hartley writes; "he is the only cause and reality; and the existence of every thing else"—including ourselves—"is only the effect, pledge, and proof, of his existence and glory" (*OM* 2.3.7.71; see §9.5). The sixth dimension of "associated circumstances" consists of the motions whereby, in the words of Fénelon, the "Eternal and Allpowerful Word of the Father speakest in the very Bottom of Souls" (1735, vi). This dimension is the subject of chapter 9.

We noted above a similarity between Hartley's and Jonathan Edwards's definitions of the will; "the will is," in Edwards's formulation, "as the most apparent good is." Hartley's position also bears a close resemblance to that which Peter Sterry articulated in his *A Discourse of the Freedom of the Will* (1675). Sterry identifies two definitions of liberty. The first, which he affirms, is that "*Liberty* is a *relation* or *harmony* between the *essence* or *nature* of each thing, and its *operations*" (1675, 2); this is "the liberty of acting from an *internal*, essential, universal Principle of *inclination* or love" (8). The second, which he rejects, involves the concepts of "*Libertas contradictionis, & libertas contrarietatis; Liberty of contradiction and of contrariety*"—according to which "the Will of this intellectual Spirit without any change in any circumstance, in any degree, may *act* or *not act* . . . or act either one way or *another*" (8). Like Sterry, Hartley denies that people possess *libertas contradictionis* and *libertas contrarietatis*—and he does so in order to affirm the possibility of harmony between essence and operations. But the human essence is grounded in that which speaks at the bottom of souls: the "*internal,* essential, universal Principle of *inclination* or love." This universal principle is the ultimate circumstance from which actions—and hypercomplex ideas—proceed. "Every Creature," writes Sterry, "is an *emanation* or *stream* from the Divine Essence.... The *Being* of the Creature is the *beaming* forth from God, like light from the Sun" (63). Compare Hartley's statement, quoted above, that God "is the only cause and reality; and the existence of every thing else is only the effect, pledge, and proof, of his existence and glory." In Hartley's estimation, "every thing else" would include the sparrows of the fields and all those who love them.

6. Popular Liberty and Philosophical Necessity

Let us grant that people do not possess "*Libertas contradictionis, & libertas contrarietatis; Liberty of contradiction and of contrariety.*" The "previous circumstances of body and mind"—however extensively these are understood—determine how a person acts, so that "a person cannot do indifferently either of the actions *A,* and its contrary *a,* while the previous circumstances remain the same." In what sense is a person a free agent? Keeping in mind that these circumstances include a person's memories, meanings, model of self, and principle of love, how are we to assess our common experiences of choosing among alternate courses of action and of following through upon one such course, without compulsion? We experience ourselves making such choices continuously, as we encounter events we cannot anticipate. Brown sparrows are always flying into our fields of perception.

Hartley proposes that, concerning human freedom, there are "two different methods of speaking, and ... two different languages; the one popular, ... the other philosophical" (*OM* 2.1.15).[5] The former is the language in everyday use; because of their familiarity, its usages often seem self-evident to us. According to this way of speaking, once past the age of reason, a human being is said to be a being possessing both reason and free will; and a free and rational individual is held responsible for the actions he or she deliberately chooses to perform. The philosophical way of speaking exists much more as a promise or goal than it does as an accomplished reality. According to it, a person's mind is a neural symphony, a complex constellation of dynamic processes, a hypercomplex idea. Whenever we try to use a philosophical language, and thereby to develop and refine it, we find ourselves saying things that are unfamiliar and often seemingly absurd—"vain and idle speculations" from the point of view of the popular way of speaking.

While affirmation of the regularity and certainty with which actions follow previous circumstances rules out a "philosophical" conception of free will, it simultaneously supports a "practical" understanding of freedom as voluntary action. Hartley asserts that if we think of free will as "the power of doing what a person desires or wills to do, of deliberating, suspending, choosing, &c. or of resisting the motives of sensuality, ambition, resentment, &c.," then free will thus defined, "under certain limitations, is not only consistent with the doctrine of mechanism, but even flows from it" (*OM* 1. Conclusion). A mechanistic theory, in other words, provides a much more coherent explanation of how a person deliberates, chooses, and resists base motives than does a theory that detaches mind from body, active spirit from passive matter. We experience ourselves as free, capable of voluntary control of our actions and hence responsible for them, *because* actions follow predictably from psychological, neurological, and environmental causes. Rather than impeaching our common awareness of personal freedom and moral responsibility, the language of mechanism and necessity makes available an understanding of psychological processes that accounts for them. "A man," Hartley writes, "may speak, handle, love, fear, &c. entirely by mechanism."

Hartley proposes a paradox: the popular language speaks of free agency, the philosophical language speaks of "necessity," and both languages are, in their own spheres of usage, true. And Benjamin Rush affirms it: "However strange it may sound, necessity does not infringe in the smallest degree upon free agency. On the contrary, as we act most *necessarily* when we act most *freely*, so we act most *freely* when we act most *necessarily*. The doctrines of necessity and free agency therefore are alike true" (1981, 529). In the standard account, the contrasts are exclusionary: either spirit or matter, either free or necessary. Or, if there are gradations of freedom and necessity, the more the one, the less the other. But in the theory presented by Hartley and affirmed by Rush, freedom and necessity do not exclude each other. Rather than confronting each other on the same level, the two languages rather offer two distinct ways of speaking about the one reality.

In Hartley's view, an approach that respects both languages promises a fuller and more coherent account of human action than can a theory that attempts to affirm the one by canceling the other. The language of "philosophical necessity" is, in this regard, much better able to account for the observed qualities of human voluntary action than is the notion of philosophical liberty, which assumes, as Butler stated, that "our gross organized Bodies ... are no Part of ourselves." According to the "philosophical" aspect of Hartleian psychology, it is from "from the mechanism of our natures" that our "voluntary and semi-voluntary powers of calling up ideas, of exciting and restraining affections, and of performing and suspending actions, arise." It is precisely because a person, swimming in the stream of experience, can be confident of the reliability and consistency of his responses to his "circumstances" that he is able to perfect secondarily automatic actions and to initiate and perform decomplex voluntary ones. When I play "The Birks of Invermay," performance of this decomplex action depends upon an initiating condition, upon my memory of the tune, and upon a reserve of secondarily automatic actions. Conversely, if I found myself responding unpredictably to what I am experiencing and doing, I could not be certain that I would persevere in any course of action. If I started playing "The Birks of Invermay" and swerved into playing "On Wisconsin," I would not experience this as an exercise of the freedom of my will; I would wonder what imp of contradiction and contrariety had intruded into my thoughts.

But is it possible that Hartley intends the philosophical language to be to the popular language as knowledge to opinion, science to "folk psychology"? We noted in the first chapter Hartley's observation that "many persons are apt to be offended even with stocks and stones, with brutes, with hurts merely accidental and undesigned, and with punishments acknowledged to be justly inflicted"—but that "as we improve in observation and experience, and in the faculty of analysing the actions of animals, we perceive that brutes and children, and even adults in certain circumstances, have little or no share in the actions referred to them; but are themselves under the influence of other causes, which therefore are to be deemed the ultimate ones. Hence, our resentment against them must be much abated in these cases, and transferred to the ultimate living cause, usually called the free agent, if so be that we are able to discover him" (*OM* 1.4.4.97). Will a person who thinks philosophically, who becomes skilled at analyzing the actions of animals, and who perceives the ultimate causes that drive brutes, children, and even adults, ever discover the free and responsible agent? Or will a philosophical perspective abate all resentment?

"The ultimate living cause, *usually called* the free agent"; the "mind, . . . the substance, agent, principle, &c. *to which we refer* sensations, ideas, pleasures, pains, and voluntary motions" (but, note, not the faculties of reflection, reason, or will); "the state of mind called *will*"—by employing these nominal definitions, Hartley points out that the choice of words involves a manner of speaking. This is not to say, however, that the popular language creates an illusion, while the philosophical language describes the reality. Hartley argues that the fact that we use the two languages is itself not a problem, provided that we keep the languages separate and use one or the other consistently. Difficulties in our accounts of human agency arise when elements of the two languages are mixed. He writes "that the notion of popular liberty is sufficient to obviate these difficulties, while we keep to the popular language alone; also, that the philosophical language does of itself obviate these difficulties, while we keep to it alone; but that, if we mix these languages, then, and not till then, insuperable difficulties will arise" (OM 2.1.15). For example, when the "notion of popular liberty" applied to humans is combined with a notion of "philosophical necessity" that emphasizes *ab extra* necessities, the result is incoherent: humans are held responsible, according to the popular notion, for actions caused by their "real circumstances," according to the philosophical notion. An equally insuperable difficulty arises for those who think that the "popular notion of liberty" requires grounding in a concept of "philosophical liberty," defined as "the power of doing different things, the circumstances remaining the same"—the "*Liberty of contradiction and of contrariety*" that Peter Sterry criticized. People deliberate among alternatives, sometimes resist the temptations of a lesser good for the sake of a greater, and resolve upon courses of action, which they then carry out. But were a person a being possessing a philosophical liberty—were there another simple and uniform agent "inside" the person's body, observing the person's associated circumstances but capable of disconnecting itself from these at will—then, "though there be a desire sufficient to cause the exertion of the will, this exertion may or may not follow; also, . . . though the voluntary powers depending upon this exertion be completely generated by association, they may or may not follow it in fact." The person could not be sure what her next behavioral event would be. Sitting down to the piano, she may announce, "I will now play Chopin's Prelude No. 4 in E Minor," but the exertion might not follow the desire, were the interior agent to indulge its liberty of contradiction. Or "On Wisconsin" might occur, were the agent to exercise its liberty of contrariety.

For Hartley, an explanation of voluntary action must concern itself primarily with the fact that people perform actions rather than with the fact that they differentiate between actions that are voluntary and involuntary. For a person to choose to play the Chopin prelude is dependent upon the fact that she has learned to perform this highly decomplex action. With regard both to such learning and to making the choices that initiate such actions, we exhibit varying degrees of appropriateness, consistency, and novelty. For those, like Butler and Coleridge, committed to a philosophical conception of freedom, novelty is crucial: the capacity to act or not act, and to act either one way or another, without any change of circumstance, is proof that the agent is above circumstance and hence morally responsible for actions freely chosen. For Hartley, the primary considerations are not novelty but consistency and appropriateness: how is it that people learn to perform highly decomplex actions and to persevere in carrying them out at the right times and places? How do people gain the power of doing what they desire or will to do—"of deliberating, suspending, choosing" and even "of resisting the motives of sensuality, ambition, resentment"? Answering these questions requires a focus not upon the agent's detachment from circumstance but rather upon the person's engagement with, and immersion in, his world: for how can a person develop a history, a character, a mind, but through the deposition of experience in memory?

7. *The Resurrection of the Body*

Butler's comment on ""the Simplicity and absolute Oneness of a living Agent" appears in the context of his discussion of our "future state." Hartley's reservation concerning the "chasm" between sensation and the "material organs" appears in proposition 86 of book 2, "It is probable from the mere Light of Nature, that there will be a Future State." Like Butler, and like virtually everyone else in his world, Hartley believed that personal identity continues beyond death.

Adherents of the standard account equated personal identity with the "one being" of mind or spirit; the equation neatly explains the continuity of personal identity—immortal spirit cannot be destroyed by the mere death of the body—but it renders human nature and human psychology opaque. Hartley, seeking to create a coherent psychology, thought that the personal identity of a human being is that of an embodied being. The foundation of identity is memory, and memories exist as changes in the molecular structure of the brain and nerves. A person's capacities to sense, to feel pleasure and pain, to perceive meaningful categories, to perform skilled voluntary actions, to learn to love—in short, to function fully as a conscious being—are the capacities of a body that fills with memories. The psychology is internally coherent, in the sense that it does not need to explain how an immaterial substance can remember the sound of a lark or move one's hand to pet the cat. But a theory of human nature according to which, as Priestley puts it, "the whole man is of some *uniform composition*" (Hartley 1775, xx) has a particular difficulty in explaining how the "whole man" can hope for life beyond death.

Hartley's task in proposition 86 is to show that a future state is "probable from the mere Light of Nature"—that is, without direct appeal to the authority of religious revelation.[6] He begins his first point by stating that, because "it is not possible to produce any evidence against a future state," the initial odds, according to the doctrine of chances, must be even. In this context he warns against our predilection to conclude, "that because what we see *is*, so what we see not, *is not*." To think this is to "make our ignorance of the means by which our existence is preserved after death, and of the manner in which we are to exist, an argument against it. But this is utterly inconclusive. Our ignorance is a nothing, and therefore can be no foundation to go upon." Having thus shown that the probability of the negative can be no better than 1/2, he then assembles the considerations he thinks might "turn the scale, in some measure, in favour of a future state." The second of his ten considerations concerns the possibility of an immaterial substance:

> The subtle nature of sensation, thought, and motion, afford some positive presumptions for a future state. The connexion of these with matter, and their dependence upon it, are perhaps more fully seen in the foregoing account of vibrations and association, than in any other system that has yet been produced. However, there remains one chasm still, *viz.* that between sensation, and the material organs, which this theory does not attempt to fill up. An immaterial substance may be required for the simplest sensation; and if so, since it does not appear how this substance can be effected by the dissolution of the gross body at death, it remains probable, that it will subsist after death, *i.e.* that there will be a future state. (*OM* 2.4.3.86)

Mindful Bodies, Embodied Minds

In this passage, Hartley admits no more than the possibility that an immaterial substance may be required for sensation, thought, and motion.

The admission follows a reminder that the overall tendency of his work is to ground psychology in neurophysiology; in his account of vibrations and association, the bodily character of perception, thought, and action is revealed "more fully . . . than in any other system that has yet been produced." Moreover, after admitting the possibility of an immaterial substance, Hartley turns to a speculative alternative—an "elementary infinitesimal body in the embryo, capable of vegetating *in utero*, and of receiving and retaining such a variety of impressions of the external world, as corresponds to all the variety of our sensations, thoughts, and motions." Reid thought that "a person is something indivisible, and is what LEIBNITZ calls a *monad*"; such a monad, to Reid as to Leibniz before him, is a spiritual entity. Hartley is here proposing a kind of material monad: to use a contemporary analogy, the "elementary infinitesimal body" would be an organic object, a seed, that resembles the hypothetical memory chip that some have suggested could be implanted in a person, to record and store all of that person's experiences. Like a grain of wheat, such an elementary body would survive the dissolution of the body at death, and it would be the basis of the restoration of one's identity, when it exercises "its power of vegetating again" (cf. 1 Cor. 15:37–38).[7]

It is important to note here that, for Hartley, neither an immaterial substance nor an elementary body is constitutive of personal identity. The first is a bare possibility acknowledged only in passing, and the second, which interests Hartley much more, is a device for the preservation of memory, without which the continuation of personal identity is impossible. "Neither the elementary body, nor the immaterial principle," he writes, "can exert themselves without a suitable set of organs" (*OM* 2.4.3.90). What guarantees the continuation of personal identity in a future state is the promise, in Christian revelation, of resurrection into a "glorified body" (cf. *OM* 2.4.3.87, 89, 90). Hartley suggests that the "soul," encapsulated within the elementary body, "is reduced to a state of inactivity by the deposition of the gross body"; at least this can be "conjectured from its entire dependence upon the gross body for powers and faculties" (*OM* 2.4.3.90). This state of inactivity may not be total: "motion, and consequently perception, may not cease entirely in the elementary body after death; just as in the seeds of vegetables there is probably some small intestine motion kept up, during winter, sufficient to preserve life, and the power of vegetation, on the return of spring." Though not necessarily entirely "insensible," this state of dormancy is probably a "passive one, somewhat resembling a dream." Hartley speculates that this dream state will cease at the resurrection, when the dormant seed of soul will be "roused to [activity] by the fire of the conflagration"—in the same manner in which the seeds of some plants require fire to germinate. "For," Hartley comments, "analogy seems to intimate, that the resurrection will be effected by means strictly natural. And thus every man may rise in his own order, agreeably to the words of St. Paul."[8]

To account for personal immortality, defenders of the standard account affirmed a dualism of spirit and body that rendered human nature inexplicable, if not miraculous, and a physiological psychology impossible. Hartley, and Priestley after him, to affirm the "whole man of uniform composition," deny the dualism of mind and matter; matter has properties that, when sufficiently organized, become mind. To affirm the continuity of identity in a future state, Hartley appeals to a hypothetical material monad, a seed of soul. He hints at a naturalistic explanation of the resurrection: the sleeping seeds of soul will germinate in the fire to come.

6

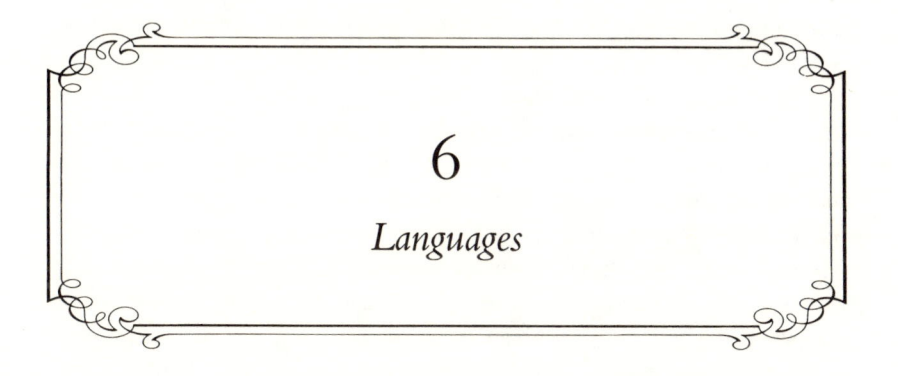

Languages

Hartley, le précurseur de la psychologie anglaise moderne, a parfaitement reconnu la véritable constitution de ce qu'on appelle le mot.

—Jean-Martin Charcot (1887, 1:468)

We think in words ... and invent chiefly by means of their analogies.

—David Hartley (*OM* 1.3.1.83)

1. Animals and People

It may seem odd to begin a chapter on language with the "near relation" (*OM* 1.3.7.93) humans bear to other animals. Language and by extension reason are commonly taken to distinguish us from them. Although everything else said to this point, about neurophysiology, about perception, about becoming skilled in repertoires of actions, about ideas, holds true of humans and at least all other mammals, no other species of animal can read this book.

In his *Discourse on Method* ([1637] 1985) Descartes had contended that the creative flexibility we display in speech and action points to the presence in us of rational souls that "cannot be in any way derived from the potentiality of matter, but must be specially created" (1985, 1:141). Animals, in contrast, are "mere" mechanisms; their behavior can be explained exclusively in terms of physiological events; the attribution to them of thought or consciousness explains nothing that cannot be described mechanistically. Animals thus have, in Descartes's view, no inner lives, no subjectivity. They are entities whose being is limited to what is observed.

Hartley, in contrast, emphasizes that "the brute creatures prove their near relation to us, not only by the general resemblance of the body, but by that of the mind also" (*OM* 1.3.7.93). And he comments that we commonly underestimate animals' capacities for reasoning. "It ought always to be remembered in speaking on this subject," Hartley writes, "that brutes have more reason than they can shew, from their want of words, from our inattention, and from our ignorance of the import of those symbols, which they do use in giving intimations to each other, and to us." Because they do not speak our language, we make no effort to understand their systems of communication. In important ways, our inattention serves our interest.

Hartley begins his discussion of animals by commenting that "the laws of vibrations and association may be as universal in respect of the nervous systems of animals of all kinds, as the law of circulation is with respect to the system of the heart and blood vessels." This point concerning the universality of the twin theories of vibration and association is critical for orienting the comparisons that follow. Although humans possess a capacity for language that is unmatched in the animal kingdom, this capacity is a specialized development of neurological and psychological processes that are common to all beings with sufficiently complex nervous systems. Just as all vertebrates have hearts that pump blood, so also do all vertebrates have nerves that respond to and transmit vibrations and brains that function to establish associative connections between sensory vibrations, the vibratiuncles or "little vibrations" the vibrations induce, and the impulses that travel along the motor nerves to the muscles. In light of the universality of the laws of vibrations and association, language is a functional specialization of a very complex kind, itself dependent upon the distinctive anatomical structure of the human brain. Contrary to Descartes's claim, it is not evidence that a separate nonphysical entity inhabits the brain.

Hartley lists five points in relation to which animals differ from humans. The first and second concern brain anatomy; the third and fourth, language and instinct; the fifth, form of life. Animals' brains are, first, proportionally smaller than human brains, and, second, exhibit different anatomical structures. Third, animals are deficient in the capacity to speak and understand language, so well developed in humans; but, fourth, the absence of language is in many cases compensated for by innate instinctual repertoires of action, which animals possess but which humans generally lack. And fifth, the lives of animals differ from ours in their "events and incidents," so that animals and people experience the world differently: the variable lives of people can "enlarge" their understandings, while the repetitious lives of most animals leave their minds running in narrow channels. Let us examine the first four of these points in more detail.

In his discussion of the first two points, Hartley suggests that the brains of humans differ from those of animals both by being larger overall in proportion to body size and by allocating a larger proportion of their mass to those functions involved in "intellectual" activities. In those animals, for example, whose exploration of the world is primarily through smell, "the internal parts [of the brain] belonging to the olfactory nerves, and, perhaps, those belonging to the nerves of taste, take up, probably, a greater proportional part of the medullary substance of the brain than in us." For such animals, "there will therefore be still less room for the variety of intercourses between the auditory and optic nerves in . . . the brain." However, "the eye and ear, with their associations, are the chief sources of intellect"; and as we shall see, it is the associations between hearing, sight, and the motor activities of producing sounds that are the basis for language.

To put this into modern terms, Hartley is in effect saying that the auditory and visual areas of the sensory cortex are proportionally larger in humans than they are in animals who rely primarily on other sensory modalities, and, further, that the association cortex is also larger. Neither Hartley nor any of his contemporaries had a way of proving this experimentally, and in fact Hartley's proposal concerning brain anatomy rests on an inference from behavior: for animals who sense the world primarily through sight, or hearing, or smell, or their whiskers, the part of the brain "belonging" to the relevant sense will have to be proportionally larger in order to process the extensive and nuanced flow of sensation coming from that source. Still, Hartley's conjecture is correct; there is a direct proportionality between the importance of a sensory modality to an animal and the amount of the brain devoted to it.

Hartley further suggests that animal brains differ from ours in their microstructure, "in the very constitution and texture of the nervous system." An animal's nervous system tends toward a greater "fixedness... in its dispositions to vibrate" than does a person's. We noted in §3.5 that sensation can effect a lasting change in the shape of the molecules in a nerve. This change, from the natural state N to the induced state a, is the nerve's memory of the stimulus. In §4.3 we also noted that sensations from separate sensory modalities occur simultaneously; this "joint impression" is essential for perceptual discrimination and categorization. In this model, the neurological substrate of an idea is the induced state $(a + b + c \ldots + n)$—where the letters represent different sensory modalities or motor commands and the + the associative links between them. This state can be activated, made to vibrate, when stimulated either by a stimulus corresponding to any of its component parts, or by other sensations, induced states, or motor actions that become associatively linked with it. Now, in Hartley's model of the human brain, there are very few *natural* states with this structure. The brain of a newborn human is exceptionally plastic; the nerves in it are not tuned to vibrate in any specific ways, and associative links have yet to be formed. By proposing the "fixedness" of animal nervous systems, in contrast, Hartley is suggesting that newborn animals are born with such structures already in place. Newborn animals are disposed to recognize certain preselected perceptual categories when presented with appropriate stimuli and to respond in specific ways to them.

Young animals' brains are thus more readily "able to retain miniatures than those of children." They recognize and respond quickly to what they are predisposed to know. This neurological predisposition to retain certain "miniatures" has its price, for the "fixedness" required for such prestructuring diminishes the brain's flexibility. When animal brains possess what are in effect the neurological substrates of innate ideas, "this texture will unfit them for receiving a variety" of new ones. Every "fixed" structure that exists in an animal's brain eliminates the possibility of its forming a different structure in that place. For most animals, this tradeoff between fixedness and flexibility is worthwhile; preselected perceptions and responses have a high adaptive value, especially when they compensate for "the shortness of their lives, and consequently of their ascent to the summit of adult age." Most animals do not enjoy a long and protected childhood in which to learn to ways of the world. The newly hatched chick does not have the luxury of *learning* that it should dive for cover when a hawk passes overhead.

In humans, the general lack of neurological prestructuring means that young children are potentially capable of learning any variety of new things. This flexibility of learning, combined with the amount of the brain devoted to hearing, sight, motor control of the larynx, tongue, and lips, and the establishment of associative links between these, means that young children are well equipped to learn any spoken language rapidly and easily.

The condition of the deaf illustrates the centrality of language to reasoning. "The mental improvement of persons born deaf," Hartley writes, "is extremely retarded by their incapacity of having things suggested by articulate sounds, or the pictures of these, and also by their not being able to solve the inverse problem, and denote their own trains of thought by adequate symbols.... Persons born deaf cannot therefore make any great progress in the knowledge of causes and effects, in abstracted and philosophical matters; but must approach, as it were, to the state of brute creation." (Hartley's comment, of course, pertains to the situation of deaf persons in Britain before the invention of primary languages appropriate to them; see §6.3.)[1] Conversely, Hartley notes that domestic animals, to the extent that they form associations with words and symbols, "become more sagacious than they would otherwise be. And, if particular pains be taken with them, their docility and sagacity, by means of symbols, sometimes arise to a very surprising degree."

Such "sagacity" is the result of social interaction between humans and animals, and particularly of deliberate training. And even with such training, domestic animals like dogs and horses never do more than respond to specific commands or symbols. But this lack of language ability is, for animals, "no imperfection on the whole." The ideas that animals do have "may be perfect in their kinds; and consequently the memory, and short direct ratiocination depending thereon, as perfect also as the analogous things in man." Moreover, in animals generally, the presence of prespecified neurological structures and hence of innate ideas is expressed through instinctual patterns of action, which fulfill the function of knowledge.

Because they have fewer ideas overall, animals are capable of a more limited range of voluntary motions than humans; nonetheless, "they may arrive at a greater perfection in the automatic ones, and the small number of voluntary ones which they do perform." These perfected automatic motions "very much resemble the rational faculties of mankind. Animals, in preparing and providing for themselves and their young, in future exigencies, proceed in much the same manner as a person of good understanding, who foresaw the event, would do."

Given the ability to perform actions necessary for the continuation of life with dedication and apparent foresight, animals offer a contrast to human beings: "Man is distracted, as it were, by the endless variety of his ideas, and voluntary motions: and it is notorious, that none besides extraordinary geniuses arrive at perfection in any considerable variety." People tend to be jacks of all trades, doing many things not very well. Animals, demonstrating the perfection of their instinctual repertoires of action, resemble rather savants, "persons not much removed from idiotism, who could perform arithmetical operations by memory, far better than men of good understandings, well versed in those operations." Like savants and other "persons of narrow capacities and acquisitions," animals are also subject to a limitation from which normally "distracted" people are free. They can continue to act as if they had foresight, in their preparations and provisions for themselves and their offspring, "even though they be a little put out of their way"; but to the extent that their repertoires of action are instinctual and fixed, they will be "quite lost and confounded" if put much out of their way by novel events or circumstances.

By acting as if they had foresight, animals act more wisely than they know; they demonstrate a wisdom that they have not learned, and that, if they could speak, they would not be able to explain. This wisdom represents "a kind of inspiration . . . mixing itself with, and helping out, that part of their faculties which corresponds to reason in us." This inspiration in animals "might be called natural, as proceeding from the same stated laws of matter and motion as the other phaenomena of nature"—in contrast to the inspiration of the writers of sacred scripture, "which appears to be of a much higher source, so as to be termed supernatural properly, in contradistinction to all knowledge resulting from the common laws of nature." But having said that, Hartley adds a fascinating qualification. The distinction between natural and supernatural may, "after the facts are once settled," turn out to be "merely verbal." What people now take to be supernatural inspiration may in fact "result from some higher laws of nature"—laws of which we are presently unaware, just as the robin is unaware of the reason why it builds its nest.

In inspiration as in everything else, animals bear a nearer relation to human beings than many people acknowledge. The "doctrines of vibrations and association" apply to all; our bodies, brains, and nervous systems are explicable in terms of these laws, as are theirs, and the "corresponding feelings, and affections of mind, attend upon [the vibrations in their brains], just as in us." Like animals, people are bodies; like people, animals are perceiving, feeling, and to a degree thinking, minds. The differences between animals and people are differences of degree, not of essence. We speak, learn much, and are "inspired" to do little; they communicate short of language, commonly learn what they are neurologically prepared to learn, and act much more from the inspiration of instinct.

Lacking the abstracting and symbolizing powers of language, animals do differ from people in that they "seem scarce ever able to arrive at any proper self-interest of the abstract and refined kind, at [self-] consciousness, so as to compare and connect themselves with themselves in different situations, or at any idea and adoration of God." Were animals able to enter into our minds, they would find our capacities for self-consciousness, for connecting ourselves with ourselves in different situations, for contemplating and loving the being St. Anselm called an "inaccessible light" to be unfathomable; perhaps as unfathomable as the inaccessible light would be to us, were we to enter therein.

Hartley ends his discussion of animals by writing that "we seem to be in the place of God to them, to be his vice-regents, and empowered to receive homage from them in his name." He does not, however, pull out the conventional conclusion that our mandate as vice-regents gives us the license to make use of animals for our convenience; their value is not a measure of their utility as suppliers of labor, skin, meat, or sporting entertainment. Rather than saying that animals live at, and for, our pleasure, Hartley concludes: "we are obliged, by the same tenure, to be their guardians and benefactors."[2]

In the remainder of this chapter, we turn to the capacities in humans that make us the guardians and benefactors of the animals and each other: our abilities to speak and to reason. We will examine both the promise and the perils these abilities hold for us.

2. How Does a Child Learn to Speak?

Speech is a very complex motor skill that enables people to perform an unlimited variety of decomplex movements. To speak, the young child must gain control of the motor activity of larynx, tongue, and mouth and correlate that activity with the auditory activity of discriminating and recognizing sounds. On the basis of this association of motor activity with hearing, the child learns to perfect a flexible repertoire of "secondarily automatic" action sequences—phonemes, morphemes, words, sentences. The child is then equipped to say whatever he wishes.

Like learning to grasp, learning to speak has its origin in a purely automatic, reflex action. A newborn, Hartley writes, "is not able to produce a sound at all, unless the muscles of the trunk and larynx be stimulated thereto by the impression of pain on some part of the body" (OM 1.1.3.21). For newborns, all sounds are cries of pain or discomfort. But, as we noted in §4.5, the same reflex action can be triggered by various sensations, motions, or "associated circumstances," if these are patched into the stimulus-response loop. In the first few months of life, "the frequent returns of this action [of crying] facilitate it; so that it recurs from less and less pains, from pleasures, from mere sensations, and lastly from slight associated circumstances." The child, as it gains facility in crying, starts to produce sounds in response to a wide range of pains, pleasures, sensations, and "slight" circumstances that have become associated in one way or another with the act. Some of these circumstances may be the child's own urge to babble. At the same time, the variety of vocalizations also increases, as "the muscles of speech act occasionally, in various combinations." The infant now no longer simply cries, but also laughs (see §7.1), coos, gurgles, babbles. And as she does so, the child produces a variety of sounds that will be "articulate" or "inarticulate" in relation to the language spoken by her parents and caregivers: "It is evident, that an articulate sound, or one approaching thereto, will sometimes be produced by this conjoint action of the muscles of the trunk, larynx, tongue, and lips; and that both these articulate sounds, and inarticulate ones, will often recur." Hartley's account is here consistent with modern studies of language acquisition; infants appear to babble all of the roughly ninety phonemes out of which all languages are formed (R. Thompson 1993, 390–91).

In addition to making sounds, the infant also hears them, and it is the association of hearing with vocalization that is crucial for the development of articulate speech. The child hears his own voice whenever he vocalizes, so that "the impression which these sounds, articulate and inarticulate, make upon the ear, will become an associated circumstance ... sufficient to produce a repetition of them." Babbling becomes a self-sustaining action sequence. Moreover, the auditory sensation or memory of a sound becomes the stimulus for the production of that particular sound; "and thus it is, that children repeat the same sounds over and over again, ... the impression of the last sound upon the ear exciting a fresh one, and so on, till the organs be tired." In other words, the joint impression of the child's own vocalizations and his hearing of these sounds itself begins to introduce regularity into the child's babbling: *ba ba ba ba*. We can imagine that a hearing child brought up even in the land of the deaf would be able, through the association of hearing and vocalization, to select certain sounds for repetition. To the extent that he habitually linked certain sounds with specific states, particularly experiences of pleasure and pain, he would come to exclaim some version of *Umm!* and *Ouch!*

Most children grow up in lands of the hearing. As they listen to others' speech, prelingual infants hear a subset of the phonemes they are already vocalizing; hearing an "articulate" sound uttered by others provides a further stimulus for vocalizing that sound. Consequently, "if any of the attendants make any of the sounds familiar to the child [from listening to himself babble], he will be excited from this impression, considered as an associated circumstance, to return to it." The result is a kind of linguistic natural selection: out of the total set of potential phonemes, the infant will gradually come to respond to and repeat those it commonly hears and to neglect those it hears only when he makes them: "the child's articulate sounds will be more and more frequent every day—his inarticulate ones grow into disuse."

The associative process by which a set of phonemes is selected is one that combines the parallel development of auditory discrimination and of motor control of the vocal tract. In Hartley's account, the child hears—that is, recognizes—others making the sounds she already makes, and in turn vocalizes the sounds she hears others make. The joint impression of hearing and speech leads to the refinement of each: auditory perception of the sounds of a given language and the motor skill of uttering the sounds of that language are thus mutually dependent and mutually reinforcing processes. But along with increasingly refined discriminative abilities, this joint development of auditory perception and motor skill also enables the child to master the complexity of her native tongue: she can identify and speak, in addition to the core set of phonemes, an ever-increasing number of the language's morphemes, words, and sentences. Here as well, the process is one of a natural selection, as meaningful combinations of phonemes are reinforced and retained, while meaningless combinations are discarded: as the child "compounds these simple articulate sounds, making complex ones, which approach to familiar words at some times, at others such as are quite foreign to the words of his native language," hearing others speak will again cause "the first [to] get an ever-growing balance in their favor." Association with environmental stimuli, with "visible objects, actions, &c.," provides further reinforcement that enables the child to master the language of her people.

What she learns, however, is not simply a repertoire of meaningful sounds. A vast distance separates the songs, howls, mews, or barks by which various species say *Ummm* or *Ouch, Come here* or *Go away* and the flexible and creative speech of one person conversing with another. Despite Hartley's wry comment that children are often like parrots, "having many words with very little knowledge annexed" (*OM* 1.3.7.93), people do not repeat by rote what they hear, and neither are they limited to specific repertoires of song; rather, they make up new sentences from the elements of their language to express their intentions, desires, and thoughts.

How does language take shape? Hartley comments that he "perceives himself to be still a mere novice in these speculations," and adds that the topic's reflexivity creates a special difficulty, for "it is difficult to explain words to the bottom by words; perhaps impossible" (*OM* 1.3.1.80). Throughout the discussion, he emphasizes the tentative nature of his observations, and on various occasions he suggests that a full treatment of the topic awaits completion by other researchers. His own approach to the question relies, once again, upon the concept of joint impression.

"Words," writes Hartley, "may be considered in four lights" (*OM* 1.3.1.79). We know words as (1) perceived or (2) created sounds—"impressions made on the ear" and "actions of the organs of speech"—and (3) perceived or (4) created visual images—"impressions made upon the eye" and "actions of the hand in writing." As we have already noted, joint impressions of hearing and vocal action are essential for a child's learning to speak; the first and second of Hartley's four "lights" are basic to language, while the third and fourth are subsidiary.[3]

For language learning to occur, associative connections must also be made between perceived and created sounds, on the one hand, and features of the child's world, on the other. Hartley describes the process of learning the vocabulary and syntax of a language as one involving both differentiation and generalization. His first example is that of a nursing infant learning the word *nurse*. The initial association between the sound and the person is established when the nurse is present, particularly when the word is "sounded in an emphatical manner, when the child's eye is directed to the nurse with earnestness and desire" (*OM* 1.3.1.80). Repetition of this joint impression between a sound and a visual impression eventually "overpower[s] all the other accidental associations"—e.g., the fire in the hearth—that attend the appearance of the nurse, and the child differentiates the nurse from the associated circumstances present in his environment. The conditioning that links the sound of the word firmly with the presence of the nurse "go[es] on with an accelerated velocity" when "the child has gained so much voluntary power over his motions, as to direct his head and eyes toward the nurse upon hearing her name."

Although the word is now linked to the person, the child's idea of the person will itself contain a congeries of sensations. If the nurse always wears the same dress and sits in the same chair by the fire, the idea raised in the child's mind by the word *nurse* may include both the dress and the situation by the fire. The meaning of *nurse* will only become dissociated from the dress and the position by the fire insofar as "the nurse often changes her dress, and the child often sees a fire in a different place, and surrounded by different visible objects"; given such changes, the variable associations counteract each other, while "his idea of that part which is common, and which we may call essential, continues the same."

Hartley also notes that the part that is "common" and "essential" to the child may not match that understood to be so by the adults around him. Words are primarily associated with the strongest correlated impressions; given the importance of vision for humans, "in common cases," Hartley writes, "the visible idea is strongest, or occurs most readily at least." But then he adds that "in the present instance, it seems to be otherwise." The impression that elicits the infant's "earnestness and desire" is not the sight of the nurse; it is rather "an idea, or nascent perception, of the sweetness of the nurse's milk." To the infant, the sound *nurse* is primarily linked to the experience of nursing. The child learns the verb before the noun, and perhaps the imperative mood before the indicative.

Over time, the process of differentiation (and dissociation) leads to the beginning of a process of generalization. The child will eventually learn that the noun *nurse* is not the name of a unique individual but a term for any one performing the same function. He will also learn that the term can be applied to people who perform various caregiving functions, such as nursing in a sickroom. Such generalization is again the outcome of differentiation between common and variable properties. The child learns the generalized meaning of *nurse* in the same way as he learns the meaning of the color term *white*, through its association with what is common to "the visible appearance of milk, linen, paper."

We need to note, however, that Hartley comments that, in many instances, the process of learning the meaning of words is not as simple and clear as this example suggests. "We must ... observe," he writes, "in respect of appellatives, that sometimes the idea is the common compound result of all the sensible impressions received from the several objects comprised under the general appellation." In such instances, the process of differentiation does not occur, or occurs only imperfectly, and the learner associates the word with a domain of experience that is simultaneously both highly specific and highly indefinite. Further, even in cases in which some degree of generalization has occurred, a word may still be linked to specific personal ideas, as "different associations [are] transferred upon the same words by the difference in the accidents and events in our lives." In later years, the word *nurse* may continue to evoke memories of smell, touch, sight, constellated around the image of one person seated in the blue chair beside the fire. Hartley attributes many of the misunderstandings that impede communication to such differences in private associations. Especially frustrating distortions of communication involve general or abstract terms for which "the miniatures excited in [a person's] nervous system by a word, are not always suitable to his definition, *i.e.* are not the same with those which the words of the definition would excite." In such an instance, the person's public definition of a word such as *justice* or *God* is at odds with the private memories and images the world evokes: "if then this person should pretend, or even design, to reason from his definition, and yet reason from his idea, a misapprehension will arise in the hearer, who supposes him to reason from his definition only." The hearer may not understand why the speaker spits out the word *justice* with such bitterness.

Moreover, learning a language is not simply a matter building up of one's stock of words—*nurse, fire, toy*. Recall Hartley's comment that "the decomplex idea belonging to any sentence is not compounded merely of the complex ideas belonging to the words in it" (*OM* 1.1.1.12; see §5.4). Similarly, Hartley emphasizes that people do not learn a language by accreting basic units into larger wholes. People usually do not say single words to infants; they speak to them in sentences, and it is the task of the child to comprehend the meaning of the semantic units. As they learn their native language, "both children and adults learn the ideas belonging to whole sentences many times in a summary way, and not by adding together the ideas of the several words in the sentence" (*OM* 1.3.1.80). This summary method is the primary one; it is doubtful that David and Elizabeth regularly said *Nurse!* or *Fire!* or *Toy!* to Mary and Winchcombe, when they were infants.

Words like *nurse* and *fire* can be correlated with ideas that have sensory associations; someone learning English can show that she understands the meaning of *fire* by pointing to the glowing coals or to the picture of a forest in flames. However, no one can point to anything corresponding to *however*. The participles, pronouns, and other parts of speech that are essential for a language's grammar form no such correlations. The meanings of these words, and frequently the meanings of abstract terms, are learned through an "analysis" of the sentences in which they occur—sentences whose general meaning is, again, first understood in a "summary" way. Such terms "answer... to x, y, and z, or the unknown quantities in algebra, being determinable and decypherable ... only by means of the known words with which they are joined."

The deciphering of such terms involves a process that is as much dissociative as it is associative. Hartley points out that the repetition of sentences containing the words *I walk, nurse walks, brother walks* (and *she walks, he walks*) at first "can suggest nothing permanently for a long time but the action of walking"—once, that is, that the word has become associated with the action. But when the core word *walk* is a known one, the child can begin to differentiate among the varying semantic units containing the element *walk* and to associate these variances with specific experiences and social contexts. Through this process of differentiation and association, the child learns "what difference he is to expect in his sensible impressions according as this or that pronoun is used"—e.g., to look to the speaker for the performance of the action whenever he says "*I walk*," whether the speaker is another person or himself.

Learning the rules governing the use of the relevant parts of speech is thus a process involving observation and social interaction. It is also a process involving much trial and error. Hartley notes that children frequently have difficulty with pronouns; they "are much at a loss for the true use of the pronouns and particles for some years, and ... they often repeat the proper name of the person instead of the pronoun." He also notes that children learn general rules of grammar and usage before they learn the exceptions to the rules, and thus apply the rules in ways that are consistent but incorrect: "children, while yet unacquainted with that propriety of words and phrases which custom establishes, often make new words and constructions, which, although improper according to common usage, are yet very analogous to the tenor of the language in which they speak." The child will say, for example, *I digged in the garden.*

Over time, as the child masters her native language, speaking becomes both secondarily automatic and voluntary. The child is able both to decipher and to produce the decomplex movements of articulate speech effortlessly and spontaneously. Unlike a person who is struggling to learn a second language through formal instruction, the child has no need to stare at the spelling of a word before pronouncing it: when learning to read, although children are able to sound out some words "in an elementary way" by combining the "letters and syllables of which they are composed," they also learn other words "in a summary one," that is, "by associating the sound of entire words, with their pictures." Further, and again unlike someone learning a foreign language, the child has no need to compose a grammatical sentence in her head before uttering it. But as speakers of their native tongues, preliterate children are also unable to "separate sentences into the several words which compound them"—a skill that, Hartley goes on to say, "those unable to read are unable to do, even when arrived at adult age." The "summary" performance of the decomplex movements of speaking remains fundamental.

3. Language and Thought

Given the capacity of language for symbolic abstraction, our conversation is not limited to immediate concerns revolving around food, sex, and safety. We may converse about the curve of isochronous motion, or the theory of vibrations, once we have the required words.

It is thanks to attention to the contexts of usage that children gain "their first imperfect notions" of the meanings of general terms—including "the names of intellectual and moral qualities," terms of art, and words such as *identity* and *existence,* which are "used in the abstract sciences." However, although children learn the meanings of *existence,* or, to use our earlier example, of *justice* or *God* in the same way that they learn the meanings of *she* or *however,* the two classes of words differ insofar as the meanings of abstract terms can be specified through definitions, while the meanings of the latter cannot. The meaning of *existence* or *justice* can be clarified through a "description, or any other way of explaining a word by words"; the meaning of *she* or *however* can be described or explained only in the sense that one can specify the rules of usage in English, as one might do for a native speaker of another language.

Hartley combines the distinction between abstract terms and parts of speech with a distinction between words with and without sensory correlates to produce a fourfold typology. Words can be divided into those (1) that "have ideas only"; (2) that "have both ideas and definitions"; (3) that "have definitions only"; and (4) that "have neither ideas nor definitions" (*OM* 1.3.1.80; see also 1.1.2.12). The names of "simple sensible qualities" such as *white* or *sweet* fall into the first class. Included in the second class are "the names of natural bodies" such as *apple* or *melodeon*, as well as the names of geometrical figures. The third class comprises "algebraic quantities, such as roots, powers, surds, &c.," scientific terms of art, and "abstract general terms" of the kind mentioned in the previous paragraph. The fourth class contains the parts of speech, prepositions, participles, pronouns, etc.

Hartley acknowledges that this classification is not one of absolute and rigid demarcations. "It is difficult," he writes, "to fix precise limits to these four classes, . . . ; and, if we consider these things in the most general way, there is perhaps no word which has not both an idea and a definition, *i.e.* which is not attended by some one or more internal feelings occasionally, and which may not be explained, in some imperfect manner at least, by other words." Still, the fourfold classification does differentiate words according to the varying importance of ideas and definitions for their shared, public meanings. I may have very specific ideas associated with *trigonometry*—the classroom in my high school where I learned it, my classmates, the fact that, that year, I and the other boys wore corduroy trousers all the time—but none of these memories and images have anything to do with the meaning of the word. The only ideas that could be relevant to its meaning are the decomplex movements involved in doing trigonometric calculations. What matters most is the definition, the explanation of the word with other words. Similarly, I may try, through the use of various analogies, to explain the difference between *red, green,* and *blue* to a person born sightless. I may also explain the relative frequencies of the colors in the visible spectrum. But the analogies and explanation would only very imperfectly communicate the qualities of these colors. Neither analogies nor explanations are satisfactory substitutes for the ideas, derived from sight.

One category of words it is particularly difficult to place in the four classifications consists of the words for emotions. Hartley states that words "denoting the passions do not, for the most part, raise up in us any degree of the passions themselves, but only the ideas of the associated circumstances." Although a person who sees the word *red* may think of an apple, a sunset, a cardinal, or a Chinese dragon, she will also be able to picture to herself redness as a red light. The word can raise up the "evident" idea of the color. But a person who sees the word *anger* will not necessarily see red. The word will elicit associated circumstances—memories of situations in which she or someone else became angry—but the memories will not necessarily induce her to become angry all over again. According to Hartley, there is not an evident idea of anger that is equivalent to a person's idea of a color. Thus, the words for emotions do not fall into the first or, by extension, the second classes, for there is no direct association of the word for an emotion with an evident idea of that emotion. What people do associate with words for the emotions are highly variable sets of associated circumstances. The ideas a person may associate with *love* or *anger* may be as specific to him and unknown to others as the images I associate with *trigonometry*—and as unpromising a basis for mutually comprehensible communication between people. And yet it seems odd to suggest that the meanings of words such as *love, hate, affection,* and *anger* are exclusively given in definitions, in the way algebraic terms are. It appears that words for the emotions can be given publicly shared meanings neither through linkage with "simple sensible qualities" nor through exact definitions; their meanings will always remain linked with the circumstances, both bodily and social, we associate with them. Consequently, Hartley suggests that agreement concerning their meanings depends upon agreement concerning the circumstances that most clearly involve them: "We are supposed to understand the continued discourse into which these words enter sufficiently, when we form true notions of the actions, particularly the visible ones, attending them." *Love* is as love does; we understand the meaning of the term when we form a "true notion" of the actions that are emblematic of it, or more emphatically, that are it. But discerning what that true notion might be is no simple matter, and agreement difficult to reach. As we shall see in the chapters to come, one person's notion may be laughable, or baffling, to another.

It may be useful here to compare Hartley's observations concerning language with Locke's discussion of the subject. The two accounts are in some ways similar. First, both Locke and Hartley turn to the nursery to observe "by what steps we enlarge our *ideas* from our first infancy" (*HU* 3.3.7), and both offer similar explanations of how a child learns to generalize the meanings of *nurse* and other words that at first are taken to be proper names. Although their overall accounts of the process of generalization are broadly the same, Hartley's observations in the nursery do differ from Locke's in one respect: for Locke, ideas are primarily or even exclusively derived from vision, so that the ideas linked to the proper names *Nurse* and *Mamma* "are well framed in [children's] minds . . . like pictures of them there"; Hartley, in contrast, recognizes that the sound *nurse* can be associated with various sensory modalities, of which vision may not be the most important. The word *nurse* may most strongly evoke memories of hunger and satisfaction, the act of nursing, and the sweetness of the nurse's milk.

A second point of comparison concerns the relative importance of ideas and definitions in establishing the meaning of general terms. According to Locke, general terms for basic sensory qualities such as light and color derive their meanings exclusively from their denotation of simple ideas. Locke notes that an explanation of the cause of light, no matter how accurate, would never enable a blind person to understand what a sighted person sees. A thorough scientific explanation of the corpuscular nature of light as "a great number of little globules, striking briskly on the bottom of the eye . . . would make the *idea,* the word *light* stands for, no more known to a man that understands it not before, than if one should tell him, that *light* was nothing but a company of little tennis-balls, which fairies all day long struck with rackets against some men's fore-heads" (*HU* 3.4.10). According to Locke, all general terms referring to simple ideas "are incapable of being defined" (*HU* 3.4.7). Hartley would agree. We noted above that, for Hartley's first class of words, association with sensory experiences are essential. With complex ideas, in contrast, Locke comments that "it is in the power of words, standing for the several ideas, that make that composition, to imprint complex *ideas* in the mind, which were never there before, and so make their names be understood" (*HU* 3.4.12). It is for the purpose of imprinting complex ideas on the mind that, Locke adds, "*definitions* . . . ha[ve] place, and *may make us understand the names of things,* which never came within the reach of our senses." Hartley would again agree. Words in his second and third classes of words derive their meanings at least in part from definitions. We could refine the parallel by suggesting that Hartley's second class, comprising words having both ideas and definitions, contains terms for complex ideas that require denotations to complement or complete their definitions. As Hartley notes, words for "natural bodies, animal, vegetable, mineral" (which Locke terms the "ideas of particular sorts of substances" [HU 2.23.3]) are in this class; a blind biologist may have a thorough definitional understanding of what a falcon is, but no comprehension of what one looks like in flight. Terms for what Locke calls "simple modes," which include the ideas of space, place, motion, and duration, are even more dependent upon the ideas they denote. Locke points out that attempts to provide definitions of these terms produce tautological expressions that only make sense if one already understands what they are meant to signify (HU 2.13.15; 3.4.8–9). Although we can imagine the blind biologist writing a chapter on falcons for her book on raptors, it is difficult to imagine a disembodied being, blind in body, being able to make any sense of the languages of spatial and temporal measurement; neither is it easy to imagine such a being writing a treatise on "geometrical figures," since the terms for such figures, which fall into Hartley's second class of words, are dependent upon the ideas of space and place for their comprehension.

However, despite the parallels between Hartley's and Locke's thinking on the sources from which terms derive their meanings, there are significant points of difference between the two over the nature of language, and particularly over the relationship between language and thought. First, we noted in chapter 4 that perceptual categorization and generalization involve the cross-signaling, or joint impression, of streams of sensation from coordinated but distinct modalities. Hartley agrees with Berkeley that visual perception of objects and of the geometry of space depends upon the correlation of visual impressions with those deriving from touch and movement (§4.2 and 3). As a result, all visual (and other) ideas are "complex" in the sense that they are formed through joint impression—which renders the applications of the terms *simple* and *complex* problematic. It is important to note that in his discussion of the four classes of words, Hartley does not employ the language of simple and complex ideas to elucidate the properties of the first, second, and third classes; drawing the parallels above occurs in this book, not in his.

Second, in Hartley's classification, there is no place for terms relating to Locke's "ideas of reflection." Locke had proposed that ideas originate either through sensation or reflection. As the second "fountain, from which experience furnisheth the understanding with *ideas*," reflection "is the *perception of the operations of our own minds* within us" (*HU* 2.1.4), and as such, it functions as an introspective equivalent of sensation, "an internal sense." It is through this introspective reflection that we "sense" the realities to which we assign the words "*perception, thinking, doubting, believing, reasoning, knowing, willing*, and all the different actings of our own minds." These are, according to Locke, words for simple ideas, and hence undefinable; I understand the meaning of words such as *perceive* or *will* by observing the relevant action in myself.

Hartley writes that Locke's appeal to reflection as a "distinct source" of ideas is an "error"—a very strong criticism for Hartley, and one that he immediately moderates by commenting that the error is "of little consequence" (*OM* 1.3.2.88). But it is of consequence. No person determines the meaning of a word such as *will* by correlating the word with an act that he views with his "internal sense." Rather, in Hartley's account, the word *will* is, in sentences beginning *I will...*, one of the associated circumstances that enter into the initiation of action sequences; in sentences of the form, *What a willful child*, it signals the speaker's inattention to or ignorance of the child's "real circumstances" and attendant motivations (see §5.6). Instead of being a name for an introspectively observable act or faculty, the word *will* is a counter used either to get things moving or to express one's bafflement and vexation at things not moving as they ought.

In his explanation of why Locke made this error, Hartley suggests that Locke did not always carry his analysis far enough: "We may conceive, that he called such ideas as he could analyse up to sensation, ideas of sensation; the rest ideas of reflection, using reflection, as a term of art, denoting an unknown quantity." He then adds that the words which "stand for ideas of reflection, are in general words, that... have no ideas, but definitions only." Words such as *perceiving* and *thinking* do not denote acts or processes that are introspectively evident. The words may be correlated with certain situationally relevant complexes of sensation and recollection, but these complexes would be associated circumstances similar to those associated with and evoked by terms for the emotions; in neither case do the words derive their meanings from the associated circumstances. Instead, they derive their public, shared meanings from definitions—not in the sense of dictionary definitions, but in the broad sense of "explaining a word by other words," that is, through the practice of a "continued discourse." To employ a current philosophical idiom, the meanings of psychological terms are fixed by our agreements concerning their use.

At the heart of Hartley's criticism of ideas of reflection is an understanding of the relationship of mind and language that is radically different from Locke's. To think that the "mind" can observe its own operations itself depends upon picturing it in terms of spatial and visual images. If we picture the brain as the mind's "presence-room," the place where ideas are brought for an "audience" (*HU* 2.3.1), we can image that the "mind" may be seated on a throne within that room, watching the procession of courtiers or monkeys that file in before it, and issuing commands for some to approach, others to withdraw. Similarly, if the mind is a "white paper" (*HU* 2.1.2), then the figures painted upon it must be visual images, most probably iconic representations of things.

It also follows from the images of an audience room or a sheet of paper that ideas are first placed within or inscribed upon the mind and then later badged or marked with words. In other words, it is the presence within the mind of distinct and stable ideas that makes a meaningful language possible: "The use then of words, is to be sensible marks of *ideas;* and the *ideas* they stand for, are their proper and immediate signification" (*HU* 3.2.1).

Language, for Locke, is a dictionary, consisting mostly of nouns, each of which marks an idea that is known prelinguistically to the speaker; for, "words being voluntary signs, they cannot be voluntary signs imposed by [the speaker] on things he knows not.... Till he has some *ideas* of his own, he cannot suppose them to correspond with the conceptions of another man; nor can he use any signs for them: For thus they would be signs of he knows not what, which is in truth to be signs of nothing" (*HU* 3.2.2). Moreover, because "it is beyond the power of humane capacity to frame and retain distinct *ideas* of all the particular things we meet with" (*HU* 3.3.2), the mind must form "abstract ideas," largely from iconic memories, in order to keep the crowd of ideas from overflowing the audience chamber. Present to the observing mind are some icons that represent individuals who exist independently of it, but most icons, such as those marked by *courtier* or *monkey,* exist within its space alone. And just as the mind cannot hold a boundless multitude of individuals, so also would language be impossible if all words were proper names for single individuals; consequently, the ability to assign names to ideas requires that the mind's capacity for abstraction and generalization be prior to and independent of language:

general terms depend upon abstract ideas. To communicate successfully with another, then, to command the presence of certain icons in another's mind, those icons must first be limited in number, present in my audience chamber, and properly marked. If I use words that I have heard, "before the *ideas* are known for which they stand," I will speak them "no otherwise than parrots do"—as "so much insignificant noise" (*HU* 3.2.7).

Locke tells a story of images, likenesses of individual things, filing into the audience chamber of the mind; the mind surveys them, compares them, and on the basis of these comparisons creates general icons of its own; it dismisses most of the individuals, to keep the room from getting overcrowded; it then assigns words to the icons and individual images; and when the mind wishes to communicate with another, it arranges a selection of words and sends it along to the mind that rules the neighboring kingdom, hoping that his neighbor's collection of icons, and system of labeling, corresponds to his own.

Hartley tells the story of an animal. Once born, it begins to taste, smell, touch, hear, and see the world around it. Out of the initial confusions of sensation, certain patterns emerge, thanks to the regular joint impression of, say, sensations of smell and hearing, touch and sight. Among the things it senses are certain sounds, which it either makes or hears. It has a great capacity to discriminate among sounds and to associate them with feelings—*Ouch!*—and with the objects of its earnestness and desire—*Mommy!* This double capacity for discrimination and association, combined with an equally great plasticity of action, enables the animal to carry out specific actions in response to particular sound sequences—*Comehere!* or *Pointoyerear!* or *Timeforawalk*. But what sets this animal apart from other species is her ability to grasp, with rapidity, the rules by which these sound sequences are made. Although she learns the sequences "in a summary way," as units of meaning, she quickly differentiates between *Pointoyer ear!* and *Pointoyer nose!* and *Nowpointo Daddysear!*—and between *Blowout thecandle!* and *Blowyer nose*. Thus, although she is not especially aware that these sounds are made up of individual units called words, she learns how to follow the rules to put together new sound sequences that make things happen, if used at the right moment: *Gowalk now!* As she becomes ever more competent in speaking her language, she learns that a sound used in one context can be applied in a number of others: *Point to your ear,* but also, *The scissors has a sharp point,* and *The point is . . .* and *The lighthouse is on the point*. From hearing a sound used variously by others, and from attempting further applications herself, the young animal eventually understands the kind of situations in which application of the sound is appropriate. As she does with sentences, she learns the use of individual sounds "in a summary way"; but through repeated summations she grasps what we call the "abstract idea," concept, or point of having or being... a point.

To summarize: In Locke's view, minds contain ideas, ideas are marked by terms, and terms are combined into sentences to express the thinker's thoughts. Just as mind preexists the ideas in it, as the space they come to fill, ideas preexist words: if you do not have the ideas present before you speak, you are parroting. But for Hartley, the sequence is reversed: the hearing and speaking of language comes first, as the child is born into a family, a tribe. Sentences are the units of meaning, learned "in a summary way"; we then learn the meaning of expressions and words, in the context of their use in social interactions. Then, the achievement of language marks the emergence those processes, so richly developed in humans, that we call mind.

Reversal of the sequence means that, for Hartley, the capacity for abstraction is dependent upon language; we are able to understand the various uses of the word *point* because we grow up among people who use the word when playing a game with infants, urging care with scissors, confirming their understanding of what others intend, and giving directions to the lighthouse. Hartley remarks that persons who grow up in isolation from a community of heard and spoken language generally evidence a severely limited capacity for using symbols to discover the similarities among discrete things or experiences. We have already noted Hartley's connection with Nicholas Saunderson, the blind Lucasian Professor of Mathematics at Cambridge, and his interest in the experiences of the blind and the deaf. In this context, he writes that "observations that are made upon persons born deaf, and continuing so" serve to "verif[y] abundantly" the fact that "the use of words adds much to the number and complexness of our ideas, and is the principle means by which we make intellectual and moral improvements" (*OM* 1.3.1.80). Although Hartley considers it probable that the deaf "make use of some symbols to assist the memory, and fix the fancy" and adds that "they must have a great variety of pleasures and pains transferred upon visible objects from their associations with one another," he concludes that "they are very deficient in this [capacity for transference], upon the whole, through the want of the associations of visible objects, and states of mind, &c., with words." Because words "collect ideas from various quarters, unite them together, and transfer them both upon other words, and upon foreign objects," they are the essential elements that allow a language speaker to effect virtually unlimited connections, transferences, and extensions of meaning. I mention a lighthouse and scissors, and you get the point. A person who is locked out of language would not. The lack of access to an ample system of symbols restricts the intellectual development of deaf persons who lack language competence; as we noted above, in his discussion of animals Hartley comments that, lacking language, "persons born deaf... must approach, as it were, to the state of brute creation" (*OM* 1.3.7.93). In addition, as we shall see in the next chapter, the transference of pleasures and pains to and through symbols is the key process that accounts for psychological and spiritual development; the inability of the deaf to use language thus inhibits "the enlargement of our affections" that is necessary for human growth "as spiritual beings" (*OM* 1.2.5.69).

Blind persons, such as Nicholas Saunderson and Sir Henry Winchcombe, the grandfather of Elizabeth Packer, do not suffer from the same limitation; even though they cannot correlate words with any visual sensations, they can associate words with ideas derived from the other senses and with pleasures and pains in their natural and symbolic varieties; moreover, because "they are capable of learning and retaining as great a variety of words as others, and perhaps greater, ... they fall little or nothing short of others in intellectual accomplishments, and may arrive even at a greater degree of spirituality and abstraction in their complex ideas" (*OM* 1.3.1.80). We should note, in this context, that to Hartley it is the impediment to learning a primary language, and not, as many of his time thought, a fundamental mental deficiency, that keeps deaf persons from attaining to an equal degree of spirituality and abstraction. He comments, concerning deaf persons, that "learning to read must add greatly to their mental improvement," although he adds that even then "their intellectual capacities cannot but remain very narrow." The reason for this, we now know, is that the written form of a spoken language does not, for deaf persons, answer the requirements for a primary language in the way that systems of gestural signs can. In one place Hartley writes that "an accurate inquiry into the mental progress of persons deprived of the advantages of language, by being born deaf, would be a still better test of the theory of these papers, than a like inquiry concerning persons born blind" (*OM* 1.2.5.69). When such an accurate inquiry was undertaken by such pioneers in deaf education as the abbé de l'Epée (1712–89), the abbé Sicard

(1742–1822), and Roch-Ambroise Bébian (1789–1825), it proved to be more than a test of a theory; it led toward the creation of a fully symbolic language of gestural sign that enabled deaf persons to attain intellectual capacities of abstraction and spirituality as extensive as those of the hearing (Lane 1984a, 1984b; Sacks 1989). And it was Roch-Ambroise Sicard, director of the National Institution for Deaf-Mutes in Paris, founding member of the Society of Observers of Man (established in 1800), and author of *Cours d'instruction d'un sourd-muet de naissance* (1800), the account of his education of the congenitally deaf Jean Massieu, who performed the service of translating Hartley's *Observations on Man* into French.

Reversal of the sequence also means that there is a great deal of babbling in our use of language. As a child learns to use her native language, she hears words commonly used that are of uncertain meaning. She understands what she is supposed to do when her mother tells her, *Thank Auntie Jane for your present,* but she is unclear about the expression she hears much more frequently, *Now let's thank God for our food.* Who is she supposed to thank, and why? She was with her mother when they picked up the pizza. Still, she says the table grace along with her mother, and also says her prayers, as instructed, at bedtime. As noted above, Hartley grants that children are often like parrots, "having many words with very little knowledge annexed"—although we should add that, unlike parrots, they can learn to mean what they say. But unlike Locke, Hartley does not seem to be too greatly troubled by the way in which speaking can outrun thinking; instead, he seems to consider it an essential and important aspect of what it means to be a human being. To clarify this point, let us consider what he says about language as an algebra.

4. Language as Algebra

In corollary 2 to proposition 80, Hartley compares "language to geometry and algebra, the two general methods of expounding quantity" (*OM* 1.3.1.80) The first class of words, with ideas but no definitions, "answer to propositions purely geometrical, *i.e.,* to such as are too simple to admit of an algebra." He gives as an example statements "concerning the equality of the angles at the basis of an Isosceles triangle." The second class, with both ideas and definitions, corresponds "to that part of geometry which may be demonstrated either synthetically or analytically." In the first, synthetic method, "the learner's imagination shall go along with every step of the process painting out each line, angle, &c. according to the method used by the ancient mathematicians." In the alternative, analytic method, the mathematician "shall operate entirely by algebraic quantities and methods, and only represent the conclusion to his imagination, when he has arrived at it, by examining then what geometrical quantities the ultimately resulting algebraical ones denote." The third class of words, which have only definitions, "answer to such problems concerning quadratures, and rectifications of curves, chances, equations of the higher orders, &c. as are too perplexed to be treated geometrically." Hartley, in other words, correlates the third class of words to the branches of mathematics that are strictly "algebraic" in the sense of being capable of being expressed only in a symbolic notation. Finally, the fourth class of words, with neither ideas nor definitions, correspond to "the algebraic signs for addition, substraction, &c. to indexes, coefficients, &c"—that is, to the elements of mathematical notation.

The question of the proper uses of "synthetic" and "analytic" reasoning was a vital one in Hartley's time. In Nicholas Saunderson's *Elements of Algebra* (1740)—the posthumous work that Hartley helped to publish—Saunderson's son John writes in the Preface: "As to the *geometric* and *analytic* methods of reasoning, each of which have their advocates and favourers among the mathematicians of the present age: our professor, I think, did justice to them both, in allowing each the advantage on different occasions. . . . The *geometric* being the most intuitive, and conveying the strongest and clearest ideas to the mind, he allowed preferable, where equally obvious and easy of application. But as it was often otherwise, the *analytic* advancing us in science much faster and farther than we could have gone by all the methods of the ancients, and being the very art and principle of invention, he thought the moderns were greatly assisted by the use of it" (xv). We should note here that "synthesis" is correlated with the geometric method, and "analysis" with the algebraic, and that algebra is very broadly defined as "the art of computing by symbols, that is, generally speaking, by letters of the alphabet" (49). Saunderson illustrates the relative merits of the algebraic and geometric methods by solving problems both ways; for each problem, an "analytic" demonstration, relying exclusively on an algebraic notation, is followed by a "synthetic" one, complete with a geometric diagram.

Hartley, echoing his teacher, comments that the geometrical is "the most satisfactory and affecting," while the algebraic is "the most expeditious, and not less certain, where due care is taken." Often, we are able to picture things to ourselves geometrically and also treat of the same things in a symbolic notation. Consider, for example, a cycloidal curve—the curve of isochronous motion discussed in the second chapter. The curve can be pictured: on the wheel of a bicycle, mark the point at which the wheel touches the ground, and move the wheel one full revolution forward. The curve traced by the marked point is a cycloid. But in addition, the curve can also be given in a formula: $x = a(\phi - \sin \phi)$, $y = a(\phi - \cos \phi)$. Although a picture of the curve will most clearly show a person with little mathematical training what a cycloidal curve is—in the sense of what such a curve looks like—the formula will show a mathematician what the curve is—in the sense of what the curve does, of how it can be utilized in various contexts, including those relating to isochronous motion. A person not trained in mathematics will be unable to "see" the curve in the formula, and consequently the picture will give that person a better "idea" of a cycloid. But, because he does not see the curve in the formula, the untrained person will also have difficulty seeing how the curve could apply to problems concerning the flexing of springs, the movements of pendulums, and the speeds of sound and light. A person who can work with the mathematics, in contrast, by linking this formula with others, will be able to move from these to new statements that will solve other real-world problems. Use of algebra, of a symbolic notation, enables the mathematician to discern an analogy or equivalency among phenomena, whereby they can be subsumed under one law, that the untrained observer would not deduce from the curve traced by a point on a bicycle's wheel.

At a time when conventions of mathematical notation were in the process of being established, it was often an open question whether a particular problem would be best solved synthetically or analytically, geometrically or algebraically. Robert Hooke's essay on springs, *De Potentia Restituva* (1678), for example, is written from a geometric standpoint; the few formulas are almost always given in words, and the argument proceeds by way of visual images. Hooke's account of isochronous motion—by which he shows how "the Vibrations of a Spring, or a Body moved by a Spring, equally and uniformly shall be of equal duration whether they be greater or less" (16)—is presented synthetically, with reference to a geometrical diagram. If the essay's form of exposition reflects Hooke's process of discovery, it is a wonder that he reached the insights he did. An even greater source of wonder, to Hartley's contemporaries, was Newton's *Principia* (1687). Written in the language of geometry, the work defeated the comprehension of readers lacking the requisite mathematical preparation; the opacity of the *Principia* led many to the hypothesis, probably incorrect but nonetheless encouraged by the author, that Newton had used the "expeditious" calculus to do the mathematics and had then written up the results in geometrical form (Roche 1988, 50).

Baffled by the diagrams and demonstrations, students at Cambridge attended the lectures of Whiston and Saunderson, Newton's successors, for enlightenment. Readers throughout Britain turned to the more accessible parts of the *Opticks* or to one of the popular explanations of Newton, such as those by Pemberton (1728) and Maclaurin (1748). These latter works, however, share a limitation with contemporary works of popular physics such as those written by Stephen Hawking (1988) and Michio Kaku (1995)—that of presenting concepts developed through purely mathematical reasoning in terms of the nonformal geometry of everyday experience. Kaku (1995, 37–43), for example, shows how a space of N dimensions can be described with ease by utilizing Reimann's metric tensor; even when warned that no one can visualize what space of four (or ten) dimensions looks like, the reader wants to know, if our universe is indeed one of ten dimensions, "where" the missing six are. The views of Saunderson and Hartley on the relative merits of geometry and algebra thus identify a problem confronting popularizers of the eighteenth century, or of the present day: if physicists use the "expeditious" methods of an algebraic mathematics to define and solve problems and to communicate with each other, and then represent the results to the public in an "affecting" pictorial language, the latter language will conceal the means by which those conclusions were reached. But if the primary language of reasoning is inaccessible, communication in a second language is in jeopardy; if a person is in the dark concerning the process by which another arrives at a result, he has cause to doubt whether he grasps what the picture drawn for him is meant to indicate.

The difficulty would not arise, of course, if one language could answer all our needs by being simultaneously affecting and expeditious—by, that is, on the one hand "painting out each line" in a way that leads "the learner's imagination . . . along with every step," and, on the other, possessing an economy and elegance that facilitates the processes of thought and discovery. Hartley was greatly interested in systems of formalizing, writing, and reforming language that promised to better satisfy one or both conditions. He was, as we noted in §2.5, a dedicated promoter of Byrom's shorthand—a system that gives its practitioner a rapid and highly abbreviated method of writing. He was also interested in the art of memory, and he recommends the system developed by Richard Grey in his *Memoria Technica* as enjoying an advantage over earlier systems based on the visualization of a memory theater: "The visible *loci* make a stronger impression upon the fancy, and therefore excel the audible ones [i.e., Grey's] in that view; but the audible ones have a much more ready and definite connexion with the things to be remembered" (*OM* 1.2.5.70).[4] The distinctions between vision and hearing, geometry and algebra, here illuminate the relative merits of the differing approaches to the art of memory. The visual systems, relying upon the detailed memorization of the architecture of a location, such as the interior of a cathedral, into which images can be placed, are the more intuitive and affecting; they allow one "to bring to view, at pleasure, the principles and materials of knowledge for meditation, inquiry, and more perfect digestion by the mind." Grey's method, in contrast, is algebraic; it involves the creation of "technical words" that combine names and sounds for numbers. Although it is neither affecting nor intuitively obvious, Hartley argues that it makes up for these deficiencies by virtue of its speed and accuracy; the words "make short and definite impressions upon the ear" and also "preserve the order of the figures without danger or error."

With regard to mathematics, Hartley acknowledges that satisfying the one goal requires the diminution of the other; the more affecting a language system is, the less expeditious, and vice versa. He comments that "geometrical figures may be considered as representing all the modes of extension in the same manner as visible ideas do visible objects; and consequently the names of geometrical figures answer to the names of these ideas." He then adds, "Now, as all kinds of problems relating to quantity might be expounded by modes of extension, and solved thereby, were our faculties sufficiently exalted, so it appears possible to represent most kinds of ideas by visible ones, and to pursue them in this way through all their varieties and combinations" (*OM* 1.3.1.80). The representation of nonvisual ideas by visual ones would take place through a "character" that "represent[ed] objects and ideas immediately" (discussed in the following proposition, *OM* 1.3.1.81), of the sort developed by John Wilkins in his *Essay towards a New Character, and a Philosophical Language* (1668). However, although Hartley believes that in theory all mathematics could be "expounded by modes of extension"—expressed geometrically—"were our faculties sufficiently exalted," in fact our faculties fall far short of the necessary level of exaltation;

only a Newton could have used the geometry of the *Principia* to discover the principles expressed therein, and most people cannot even follow the demonstrations in the form they are presented. Similarly, although a character that represented "all objects and ideas immediately" was to Hartley also a theoretical possibility, attempts to create such a character had made very limited progress. Hartley concludes that just as geometry is best "confined to problems, where extension, and motion, . . . are concerned, using algebraic methods for investigating all other kinds of quantity, so it seems best also to use visible ideas only for visible objects and qualities . . . and to denote all other qualities by words considered as arbitrary signs"—words of the sort, that is, that make up English and other human languages.

Still, "the representation of other quantities by geometrical ones, and of other ideas by visible ones, is apt to make a more vivid impression upon the fancy, and a more lasting one upon the memory." Hence an "affecting" language maintains its appeal and its power; over and over again, we observe how "in similes, fables, [and] allegories, visible ideas are used . . . to denote general and intellectual ones." And, reflecting for example on whether the mind can be pictured as a white paper or blank slate, we also note how deeply insinuated are such similes, fables, and allegories into even the most general and philosophical of discourses.

In general, natural languages contain large collections of general terms, and these often designate variable and/or unknown qualities and quantities. Consequently, a language "itself may be termed one species of algebra; and, conversely, algebra is nothing more than the language which is peculiarly fitted to explain quantity of all kinds." The parallelism suggests to Hartley that "the difficulties and perplexities attending the theory of language" may be elucidated by "the corresponding particulars in algebra, where everything is made clear"—provided, of course, that a skeptic does not "call the rules of algebra into question," for there is no way of demonstrating the rules "but by using words." The explanation of language in terms of algebra and then of algebra in terms of words leaves us with "no independent point wherein to stand."

Hartley is not overly concerned with the skeptic's challenge to mathematics. If the skeptic were to "allow only that simple language, which is necessary for demonstrating the rules of algebra, the thing would be done." Moreover, any reasonable person will allow this language and the resulting demonstration, for "it seems impossible to become acquainted with this, and at the same time to disallow it." The much more significant issue concerns the sheer indeterminacy of reference that the correlation with algebra reveals in language. If language is taken to be a species of algebra, then most of the general terms in it stand as x's and y's in relation to realities. What they designate is variable and/or unknown.

In the expeditious use of mathematical algebra, it is possible to verify the truth of the conclusion in two ways: first, by ensuring that "due care" is taken when working through the steps of the calculation, and second, by representing the conclusion geometrically to the imagination. But the calculations we perform with the algebra of language follow a much more open-ended set of rules; we are able to compose all sorts of grammatically correct formulas, using x's and y's we have picked up in our conversation or reading, while we have only an indistinct sense of the meaning of the terms or of the statements in which they appear. Moreover, such statements can at times be represented to the imagination only indirectly, through analogy, metaphor, fable, or allegory. In many instances, we are like the "blind mathematician" that Hartley, remembering Saunderson, mentions, who must "use words" algebraically "when he reasons on colors": we are like blind men reasoning upon colors when words such as *impression* or *association* appear in our algebra, not to mention *forces of attraction and repulsion, gravitation, justice, benevolence,* or *God*. How, then, do we know we are using our x's and y's correctly in the formulas, and then manipulating the formulas to solve the problems set for us in the algebra of language?

Let us begin to explore Hartley's answer to this question by turning to his observations concerning analogy, one of the topics discussed in proposition 82, in the first section of chapter 3, on "Words, and the Ideas Associated with them."

5. Analogy

We noted above that an infant may take the word *nurse* as a proper name; the sound is associated with one person, and it may even be linked primarily with something as specific and concrete as the experience of nursing and the taste of milk. Over time, the child hears the word used in conversations about people other than her nurse; the word, she learns, can be applied to any person who acts as a nurse. And acting as a nurse involves a variety of functions: a wet-nurse is a nurse, but so is someone who tends a child generally or who tends an adult who has become dependent through illness. Early in her life the child also learns that she has a *mouth*. So do the cat and the dog. So also do goldfish, and grasshoppers and caterpillars. The mouths of insects do not look like a person's, but one can watch them chewing on a leaf. But she also stands, with her parents, at the *mouth* of a cave, and they walk together along the sand at the *mouth* of a river. And her parents smile at her when she says that tea comes out of the *mouth* of the teapot.

Experienced users of a language distinguish between literal and figurative uses of words. The usage is literal when a word applied to people or things who are alike in appearance or function, figurative when a primary meaning can be distinguished from a secondary one. When the usage of language is being pushed and extended, however, as it is for a child learning the language, or for a science in the process of development, every novel use of a word is at first figurative. The child's calling someone other than her nurse a *nurse* is figurative, as is her using the term to refer to someone tending her grandmother. Later, she will learn that all of these are literal uses of the term; what was figurative for her becomes literal. But the same shift from figurative to literal would happen to "a people so rude in language and knowledge, as to have names only for the parts of the human body, and not to have attended to the parts of the brute creatures" (*OM* 1.3.1.82). For such a people, the "application [of words for mouth, eye, hand, etc.] would have at first the nature of a figure; but when by degrees any of these words, the eye for instance, became equally applied to the eyes of men and brutes, it would cease to be a figure, and become an appellative name." Humans, other mammals, and insects have mouths literally. And as words continue to be used in their broader applications, "many or most common figures pass so far into literal expressions by use, *i.e.* by association, that we do not attend at all to their figurative nature." Are we aware that we are using a figure of speech when we refer to a river's mouth? Or, if it is a very large river, its *delta*?

What makes the extension of meaning possible is analogy, which Hartley defines in a way "more enlarged and practical" than the "restrained sense" of analogy in use in mathematics. "Analogy," he writes, "is that resemblance, and in some cases sameness, of the parts, properties, functions, uses, &c. any or all, of A to B, whereby knowledge, concerning A, and the language expressing this knowledge, may be applied in the whole, or in part, to B, without any sensible, or, at least, any important practical error." There is an analogy between two things if language that is used to describe or explain or analyze the first can be applied to the second. Because in biology I can discuss the *mouth* of a person or of a goldfish without in either case introducing an "error," there is an analogy between the mouths of people and goldfish—an analogy that sustains the literal sense of the word when applied to both classes of animal. The analogy diminishes, becomes much more partial, when an animal's mouth is compared to that of a river, and we consequently consider the latter application to be more figurative.

Figurative applications of words are prompted by perceptions of resemblance; when more closely examined, resemblances may in some cases contain analogies, which in turn enable figurative applications to become literal ones. "Now analogies ... some more extensive, some less so, present themselves to us every where in natural and artificial things; and thus whole groups of figurative phrases, which seem at first only to answer the purposes of convenience ... and of pleasing the fancy ... pass into analogical reasoning, and become a guide in the search after truth, and an evidence for it in some degree." Hartley expands upon this comment by listing a wide range of examples of analogical reasoning. Much of what he mentions concerns the analogies of morphology and function that are the goal of investigation in comparative anatomy, both in botany and zoology. And to Hartley as to many thinkers of his time, plants and animals occupy just some of places on the great chain of being. "There seems to be," he writes, "a perpetual thread of analogy continued from the most perfect animal to the most imperfect mineral, even till we come to elementary bodies themselves." He further elaborates the point in proposition 87: "The analogous natures of all things about us are a great assistance in decyphering their properties, powers, laws, &c. inasmuch as what is minute or obscure in one may be explained and illustrated by the analogous particular in another, where it is large and clear. And thus all things become comments on each other in an endless reciprocation" (*OM* 1.3.2.87). It is thanks to the "endless reciprocation" that occurs along the "thread of analogy" that the sciences of comparison have a warrant to investigate the "comments" that all things make about each other; Stephen Hales discovered, and measured, blood pressure by conducting experiments on dogs and farm animals; his conclusions were directly applicable to humans.[5]

When they pass into analogical reasoning, "whole groups of figurative phrases ... become a guide in the search after truth, and an evidence for it in some degree" (*OM* 1.3.1.82). At times they do. Nonetheless, "the mind being once initiated into the method of discovering analogies, and expressing them, does by association persevere in this method, and even force things into its system by concealing disparities, magnifying resemblances, and accommodating language thereto." The algebraic freedom of language, whereby we invent x's and y's and apply these unknowns in novel and creative ways, is a gift of great promise and great peril. It enables us, through the search for analogies, to discern real relations and identities. It also enables us to signify nothing, to fantasize vast and hidden systems of correspondences. For there is a disjunction between the elements of a language and the things of the world which language bears to us: Hartley's "endless reciprocation" of analogies are in nature; the lexicons of language are human social conventions. This means that, unlike things, languages have histories; they are archives or museums that accumulate both a people's collective knowledge and their collective illusions, both their wisdom and folly, their common sense and common senselessness. Figurative phrases drawn from a culture's archive can become "a guide in the search after truth"; they can also suggest relations between things that, "by concealing disparities" and "magnifying resemblances," force things into a system that exists only within language—a tower supposedly reaching to heaven, built solely of words. A language, as an archive, does not only convey truth, the clear and harmonious music expressive of the plenitude of being; it also produces cacophonies of prejudice, superstition, and mystery.

How, then, can we know if a figure of speech is a reliable guide? How do we determine whether a verbal analogy does or does not echo one of the "comments" that things make about each other "in an endless reciprocation"? Hartley's exploration of these issues appears in second section of the chapter, "Of Propositions, and the Nature of Assent."

6. Probabilities

A reader of Locke's *Essay* would know of its author's assertion that "Intuition and Demonstration"—"are the degrees of our knowledge," and that "whatever comes short of these . . . is but faith, or opinion" (*HU* 4.2.14).[6] For Locke, the ultimate criterion of knowledge is certainty: you may be certain that two apples added to two apples brings the total to four because you can see the four apples; the total number of apples is intuitively obvious to you. Such intuition is the surest and most immediate guarantor of certainty: it reveals a necessary truth. In contrast, it may not be intuitively obvious that, for a right triangle, the square of the long side is equal to the squares of the other two sides;

still, although you may not immediately *see* the equivalence, the relationship can be demonstrated. A mathematician could start with a diagram of a right triangle and proceed by drawing a sequence of further diagrams, each of which is intuitively obvious when it follows upon the previous diagram, that show the equivalence. Although at first you did not see it, after following the demonstration the relationship may become intuitively apparent. But in addition, a truth that is either intuitively or demonstratively certain to others may be beyond your reach, given your present level of training. You may not be able to either see the truth of Kepler's law, that a planet in an elliptical orbit traces out equal areas in equal times, or follow the demonstration; yet credible people who can see this, or who have worked through the demonstration, assure you that it is true, and you accept their testimony. They have knowledge of this, while you have an opinion; you accept the assertion of Kepler's law because it is what Locke calls *probable*—it comes to you on good authority. Finally, there are a great many matters in life that "come short" of intuitive or demonstrative verification. Although "God has set some things in broad day-light," writes Locke, "in the greatest part of our concernment, he has afforded us only the twilight ... of *probability*, suitable ... to that state of mediocrity and probationership, he has been pleased to place us in here"—a state that is meant "to check our over-confidence and presumption" (*HU* 4.14.2).

There is nothing new here. Locke's notions of knowledge and opinion, of intuition, demonstration, and probability, would have been as familiar to a university student of the thirteenth century as to one in the seventeenth. Similarly, at first sight Hartley also seems to be reaffirming the commonplace that intuition provides knowledge at its most immediate and certain. He comments that the "instantaneous and necessary coalescence of ideas, which makes intuitive evidence"—and which "takes place only in mathematics"—"may be considered as the highest kind of induction" (*OM* 1.3.2.87). However, a more attentive reading of Hartley's comment reveals the distance between his outlook and the earlier tradition concerning daylight and twilight, knowledge and opinion. To say that intuitive *evidence* supplies the highest kind of *induction* is to say something that, at the time, represented a new way of thinking about thinking.

Proposition 86 in the *Observations* concerns "the nature of assent and dissent." In it Hartley distinguishes between rational and practical assent. Rational (or verbal) assent follows from "a close association of the ideas suggested by the proposition, with the idea, or internal feeling, belonging to the word truth; or of the terms of the proposition with the word truth." Practical assent is a "readiness to act in such a manner as the frequent vivid recurrency of the rational assent disposes us to act." Although it is usual for practical assent to be "the natural and necessary consequence of the rational," Hartley notes that there are instances in which "the practical assent is sometimes generated, and arrives at a high degree of strength, without any previous rational assent, and by methods that have little or no connexion with it." In these instances, rational assent may derive from the practical. For example, "the frequent recurrency of an interesting event, supposed doubtful, or even fictitious, does, by degrees, make it appear like a real one, as in reveries, reading romances, seeing plays, &c. This affection of mind may be called the practical assent to past facts; and it frequently draws after it the rational." What applies to the construction of the past also applies to the projection of the future, so that there may be a practical assent to future facts: "the sanguine are apt to believe and assert what they hope, and the timorous what they fear" (cf. James [1896] 1992, 473).

Overall, the impression that emerges from proposition 86 is that people are likely to assent to (or dissent from) any number of propositions, which are to them well or poorly understood, for good reasons or bad, or for no reasons at all. Locke had written how, thanks to "the schools, disputes, and writings, the world has been fill'd with," students are "lost in the great wood of words" (*HU* 4.3.30). Hartley adds that even in mathematics and science, "terms or words are absolutely necessary to the art of reasoning," and, further, that "our assent is here also, in every step of the process, deducible from association." But here as in other circumstances of life, our associations are heightened by memory and authority, by the familiarity and imaginative vividness of ideas, and by our interest in seeing things one way rather than another. Depending upon the circumstances, writes Hartley, "sometimes truth may recur, and unite itself with the proposition under consideration, sometimes falsehood." Those lost in the great wood of words are, in their attempts to find their ways about, liable to turn right or left, depending.... Regardless of which path they determine to follow, Hartley notes, "the foundation of assent is still the same. I here describe the fact only."

How, then, can we begin to find our way about? To decide which pathways lead... where? Some of Hartley's reflections on this matter appear in the following proposition, "To deduce Rules for the Ascertainment of Truth, and Advancement of Knowledge, from the Mathematical

Methods of considering Quantity" (OM 1.3.2.87). The mathematical methods with which Hartley is primarily concerned are the theory of probability and the calculus—two areas of mathematics that, in Hartley's day, were the scenes of fundamental developments.

We noted above that *probability*, in its older sense, referred to the reliability of testimony; something was probable if persons of probity attested to it. Such a notion is in no way quantitative, and it does not guarantee that a supposition is even true. Gibbon, for example, could write in his *Decline and Fall of the Roman Empire* that "such a fact is probable but undoubtedly false" (quoted in Hacking 1975, 19). According to Ian Hacking, "probability"—in its mathematical sense, concerning the determination of stable frequencies of occurrences—"began about 1660" (1975, 18); more precisely, he notes that *probability* was first "used to denote something measurable" in 1662, "in the concluding pages of the Port Royal *Logic*—the most successful logic book of the time" (1975, 73).[7] In addition to Antoine Arnauld, co-author of the *Logic*, Pascal, Fermat, Huygens, and Jakob Bernoulli also made fundamental contributions to probability theory. In England, the best-known writer of the subject was Abraham De Moivre (1667–1754), who contributed both to the development of the theory and to its exposition in his "De mensura sortis," published in the *Philosophical Transactions* of January, February, and March 1711, and in *The Doctrine of Chances* (1718), an expanded version of the earlier work.

Hartley employed the "doctrine of chances" in his 1733 pamphlet, *Some Reasons why the Practice of Inoculation ought to be Introduced into the Town of Bury at Present*, to argue in favor of inoculation with the smallpox virus, even though such inoculations could result in the deaths of some people who might not otherwise have contacted the disease. If four in one hundred people die from contacting the "natural" smallpox and one in one hundred die from smallpox contracted through inoculation—assuming, that is, that deliberate inoculation is a safer way to contract smallpox—then it is obvious that lives would be saved, were the entire population of Bury St. Edmunds to be inoculated. The more difficult argument to make is one that would convince any individual person that inoculation is in his or her own self-interest. Why consent to be inoculated, when one may never contract the natural form of the disease?

In the *Observations*, Hartley's discussion of probability first concerns a mathematical formalization of the issue of the role of evidence in determining the probability of a proposition. If "evidences brought for any proposition" are dependent upon each other, so that each is necessary for the support of the next and "the failure of any one... renders all the rest of no value," the probability grows progressively less as the number of evidences increases. When the evidences are independent of each other, so that each can "be applied directly to establish the proposition," the probability of the proposition grows stronger as the number increases. In the case of dependent evidences, for any proposition p, if the probability of each evidence be $1/a$, the probability of p will be $1/a^n$. For independent evidences, if the "common deficiency" or probability of failure in each be also $1/a$, then the probability of *not p* will be $1/a^n$.

Hartley's general point is well known in law. Hearsay is not allowed in evidence in court, while corroboration of events by independent witnesses is often crucial. What the mathematical formalization of this principle adds to it is the possibility of attaining some degree of precision in determining how probable or improbable a proposition is. For example, Hartley considers "the principal facts of ancient history" to be "not less probable practically now, than ten or fifteen centuries ago, nor less so then, than in the times immediately succeeding; because the diminution in evidence in each century is imperceptible." Although historical accounts are often dependent upon prior accounts, we can be confident of the "principal facts" if $1/a$ is close to 1 for the first and all succeeding elements in the series—if the original report is highly probable and if succeeding generations of historians have been careful to reproduce it accurately in their accounts. In addition, in situations in which numerical probabilities can be assigned to independent evidences, that the probability that a proposition is not true is $1/a^n$ would assist the inquirer in determining how many independent evidences—e.g., trials of an experiment—there need to be, to reach a satisfactory degree of probability. As Hartley notes, "after a point is well settled by a number of independent [evidences], all that come afterwards are useless, because they can do no more than remove the imperceptible remaining deficiency." Because for independent evidences the probability of falsehood decreases exponentially, the probability of p approaches asymptotically to 1. The practical challenge is to determine the point at which further testing becomes "useless."

Fundamental issues concerning the convergence of numbers of trials upon stable frequencies are central to the two other topics in probability theory Hartley discusses. The first concerns the convergence of trials upon a known probability distribution, while the second concerns the converse problem of the determination of an unknown probability distribution from the observed trials. Of the first problem, Hartley writes: "M. De Moivre has shewn, that where the causes of the happening of an event bear a fixed ratio to those of its failure, the happenings must bear nearly the same ratio to the failures, if the number of trials be sufficient; and that the last ratio approaches to the first indefinitely, as the number of trials increases." Imagine, for example, one of a pair of dice. Assuming the die is unbiased, the probability of rolling a one is 1/6 on any trial. But as gamblers never seem to learn, because there is no causal connection between the separate rolls, the probability is 1/6 for each roll of the die; consequently, even though a snake eye has come up on two successive rolls, the probability of rolling another on the next roll remains 1/6. However, it is also intuitively obvious that over a large number of rolls, the frequencies of the events will approach their probabilities; over some n of rolls, the numbers of times the die comes up 1, 2, 3, etc. will even out, with each number accounting for very nearly 1/6 of the rolls. But what intuition cannot answer are the questions, How rapid is this approach of frequencies to probabilities? And, after some n number of trials, how close to the probability distribution can we expect the observed frequencies to be? Jakob Bernoulli attempted to answer these questions, and part of De Moivre's fame rests in the fact that he improved upon Bernoulli's answer. De Moivre developed a theorem that allows for the determination of the degree of convergence between the frequency of the observed events and the underlying probabilities, for any finite number of events. More specifically, he was able to assign a probability to a probability—that is, to determine, for any n, the probability with which the ratio of observed "successes" to "failures" will lie within assigned limits on either side of what Hartley calls the ratio of the "causes of the happening of an event . . . to those of its failure" (if r is the ratio, let q and s be the ratios that represent the higher and lower limits). He was then able to show that the divergence of the observed ratio from the ratio of the "causes" decreases in inverse proportion to the square of the number of trials—or, in other words, that for any given degree of probability, for every increase of n, the values of q and s will converge exponentially on r. Hence, as n increases, the probability that the observed ratio will match the underlying ratio approaches asymptotically to 1.

De Moivre's solution was first made available to the public in a supplemental section, "A Method of Approximating the Sum of the Terms of the Binomial $(a + b)^n$ expanded in a Series, from whence are deduced some practical Rules to estimate the Degrees of Assent which is to be given in Experiments," printed in the third edition of his *Doctrine of Chances* (1st ed., 1718), published in 1756. In this work De Moivre states that the section represents "a Paper of mine which as printed *November* 12, 1733, and communicated to some friends, but never yet made public" (1756, 243; cf. Archibald 1926). Given that the *Observations* was published in 1749, Hartley must have read the paper. He was either one of the friends to whom De Moivre communicated his discovery, or at least a member of the group of people among whom such discoveries circulated.

In his paper, De Moivre acknowledges that it would be possible to reverse his method of reasoning, so that one could infer the underlying probabilities from the observed events. "As, upon the Supposition of a certain determinate Law according to which any Event is to happen," he writes, "we demonstrate that the Ratio of Happenings will continuously approach to that Law, as the Experiments or Observations are multiplied: so, *conversely*, if from numberless Observations we find the Ratio of the Events to converge to a determinate quantity, ... then we conclude that this Ratio expresses the determinate Law according to which the Event is to happen" (1756, 251). This comment, with its mention of "numberless" observations, is clouded with the vague and limitless immensity that his own work had done much to dispel. Throw a die enough times, and the frequencies of the results will converge closely upon the underlying probabilities. It was De Moivre who clarified "enough," who determined the rate of convergence. But here he is saying, in effect, toss a die "numberless" times, and the results will tell you how many sides the die has, and whether it is biased. But he did not work out how many throws this would take, or how probable the "determinate Law" would be, after a given number of throws.

After his discussion of De Moivre's work, Hartley comments that "an ingenious friend has communicated to me the solution of the inverse problem, in which he has shewn what the expectation is, when an event has happened p times, and failed q times, that the original ratio of the causes for the happening or failing of an event should deviate in any given degree from that of p to q." The person who is credited with solving this "inverse" problem, and hence with providing a possible foundation for the concept of statistical inference, is Thomas Bayes (1702–61). His "Essay Towards Solving a Problem in the Doctrine of Chances" was published posthumously in 1763 in the *Philosophical*

Transactions, after Richard Price (see §11.1), his literary executor, sent the paper to the Royal Society.[8]

I do not know of any information that links Hartley and Bayes directly; however, given the uniqueness of Bayes's theorem, it is hard to imagine who else the "ingenious friend" might be. There are, in addition, some points of commonality between Hartley and Bayes. Of the two works Bayes published during his lifetime, the first, *Divine Benevolence* (1731) is, according to its subtitle, *An Attempt to Prove that the Principal End of the Divine Providence and Government is the Happiness of His Creatures*; the work is, in other words, an argument in favor of the universality of salvation—a position that, as we saw, Hartley also embraced at about the time Bayes published his book. Bayes's second work was *An Introduction to the Doctrine of Fluxions* (1736)—a defense of Newton's calculus against Berkeley's criticisms in the *Analyst*.

If Bayes is the "ingenious friend," then he had developed his solution to the problem, and communicated it to Hartley, at least before 1749. Hartley was thus familiar with, and appreciative of, one of the most significant contributions to probability theory in his century. And Bayes's theorem continues to exercise fascination, invite application, and generate controversy to this day. (Lorraine Daston's work on classical probability contains a lucid explanation of the theorem [1988, 253–67] as well as discussion of Hartley [203–06, 245].)

Hartley's interest in the "inverse" problem of inferring laws from data carries over into his discussion of Newton's calculus, which follows upon the mention of the work of his "ingenious friend." Bayes's work dealt with determining the probabilities with which probability ratios could be inferred from observed outcomes (hence it is also a work in the probability of probabilities). With regard to the calculus, Hartley is interested in the analogous problem: given some number of points with determinate positions relative to the x and y coordinates of a graph, to determine the function that draws the curve that best connects the points. Although the standard problems the calculus addresses are those of integration and differentiation—of finding the area under a curve, and the rate of change at any point on a curve—it is the techniques for solving problems of curve fitting that Hartley thinks may be compared with, and also suggest improvements in, methods "of arguing from experiments and observations, by induction and analogy": "Now here we may suppose the given ordinates . . . to be analogous to effects, or the results of various experiments in given circumstances, the absciss analogous to all possible circumstances, and the equation afforded by the differential method to that law of action, which... produces the given effects." The analogy enables the experimenter to model the relationship of experimental data to the "law of action" in a way different from that suggested by the "doctrine of chances"—or, as we now say, the theory of probability. In the work of such as De Moivre and Bayes, the trials are all identical; a person does the same thing over and over—throws a die—and keeps track of the frequencies of the outcomes. In the experimental calculus that Hartley proposes, the trials are not identical; they are, rather, systematically varied so as to match some number of points on the abscissa. The purpose of this method of experimentation is to systematically vary the trials in a way that represents a significant subset of "all circumstances," to observe how the results vary with the variations in the trials, and to infer the "law" governing the results from the way in which they do vary with the variations of circumstances. We can imagine someone at work in an attempt to determine the effectiveness of a medicine for the stone. Because there are a number of variables in this research, several separate graphs could be plotted. The points of the x axis could be made to represent varying combinations of ingredients, of strengths of dosage, or types of bladder calculi. Careful observations of variations in the effects of varying combinations of ingredients, strengths of dosage, and kinds of calculi could, if properly coordinated, suggest to the experimenter the optimum composition and dosage of a medication for a particular variant of the condition. And if there were no variances observed in the results—if the graph were flat—the experimenter could conclude that the medication is useless.

This notion of one thing varying with the varieties of another came up before, in the discussion of joint impression in chapter 4. There we noted that the concept plays a central role in Hartley's account of perception; it is, for example, thanks to the fact that visual inputs vary with the varieties of touch that we are not in the position of Cheselden's young patient, but are able to organize the world we see according to meaningful categories. In the light of Hartley's comments upon the calculus, we can now say that it would be consistent with his theory to model touch as the abscissa, sight as the ordinate axis, and a given perceptual category as the function that governs the manner in which the varieties of the one sense vary with the varieties of the other. One factor that this model suggests is that, just as a function can, once it has been defined, be identified on the basis of any number of sections cut out of the curve it draws, so also can a defined perceptual category be recognized on the basis of any number of sensory inputs. A variety of shapes and colors can prompt one to say, "That's a cat." In other words, in this interpretation of Hartley's theory, an idea is not a reproduction, a static representation, a snapshot of something sensed. Rather, an idea is a function that predicts how sensations can change and still remain sensations of the same thing or place.[9] And it was the absence of such a perceptual calculus that left Cheselden's patient frequently baffled by his visual impressions; he had few rules, few functions, that told him how impressions could change predictably.

To return to the present context: Probability theory and the calculus both offer models of the way in which a person can, on the basis of partial sets of observations, form propositions that reveal the patterns underlying the sets. Here it is important to note that the tasks of determining a probability ratio from observed events, and of determining which curve best fits the known points on a graph, are matters of inference, not deduction. Problems such as these cannot be solved by applying some simple rule, which will automatically produce the best result. Instead, they involve guesswork, and they thus may be grouped with the other mathematical methods of approximation that Hartley discusses, in order "to shew how analogous methods may be introduced into the sciences in general to advantage."

7. Framing Hypotheses

Hartley draws four additional parallels between mathematical and scientific methods of discovery. The "means [by which] we are to form these general conclusions [in the sciences], and discover their evidences" resemble: first, the *regula falsi*, the rule of the false position in arithmetic; second, the use of symbols for unknown quantities in algebra; third, "the algebraic methods of finding the roots of equations of higher orders by approximation"; and fourth, cryptography. The first of these is an ancient method of solving problems in arithmetic; an arbitrary number is posed, giving an erroneous answer, and the correct answer determined on the basis of the discrepancy between the actual and the intended results. Hartley suggests that, similarly, "it is useful in inquiries of all kinds to try all such suppositions as occur with any appearance of probability, to endeavour to deduce the real phaenomena from them; and if they do not answer in some tolerable measure, to reject them at once; or if they do, to add, expunge, correct, and improve, till we have brought the hypothesis as near as we can to agreement with nature."

Hartley is, in effect, recommending the method that was later to be termed *abduction*, whereby a likely hypothesis is proposed as a means of guiding experiment and observation—and the formation of further hypotheses with increasingly greater explanatory power.

"I frame no hypotheses."—Thus had Newton famously, and disingenuously, written in the *Principia*. Hartley responds directly to this statement. "It is in vain," he writes, "to bid an inquirer form no hypothesis" (*OM* 1.3.2.87). Detecting a pattern in the arrangement of things, and giving an explanation of why things are as they are, are universal human activities. They are unavoidable, for beings possessed of symbolic thought. The question, for Hartley, does not concern whether one should or should not frame hypotheses; people will do this. Rather, the question concerns people's relationships to the patterns they detect and the explanations they give. Will their hypotheses arise willy-nilly, be formed unconsciously and believed as soon as formed? Or will a person become self-aware that he is forming hypotheses—always on the basis of partial evidence—and adopt a critical attitude toward them? Were people to take to heart the resemblance between the formation of hypotheses and the use of the *regula falsi*, the resulting critical method "would much abate that unreasonable fondness, which those who make few or no distinct hypotheses, have for such confused ones as occur accidentally to their imaginations, and recur afterwards by association. For the ideas, words, and reasonings, belonging to the favourite hypothesis, by recurring, and being much agitated in the brain, heat it, unite with each other, and so coalesce in the same manner, as genuine truths do from induction and analogy. Verbal and grammatical analogies and coincidences are advanced into real ones." A person who embraces his favorite hypotheses unconsciously and uncritically will "entertain a confused inconsistent mixture of all, of fictitious and real, possible and impossible: and become so persuaded of it, as that counter-associations shall not be able to break the unnatural bond." But a person who understands that his hypotheses are often no more than first attempts at explanation, very much in need of revision and sometimes replacement, "forms hypotheses [self-consciously] from the first, tries them by the facts, and rejects the most unlikely ones; and, being freed from these, is better qualified for the examination of those that are probable. He will also confute his own positions so often, as to fluctuate in equilibrio, in respect of prejudices, and so be at perfect liberty to follow the strongest evidences." Such a habit of mind is of course a distinctive achievement, for it requires that the inquirer learn to think in a way that runs counter to a natural tendency of thought. Thanks to the processes of association, we tend to accept as real the "ideas, words, and reasonings" which "being much agitated in the brain... unite with each other, and so coalesce"; we tend to affirm, and insist upon, the compounds of ideas that appear to us most vividly and are most firmly cemented together. But when it comes to distinguishing genuine analogies from the merely verbal, the real from the fictitious, and especially when it comes to freeing oneself from one's own dearest hypothesis, it is the *counter-associations* that must be allowed to work, to break the bonds that compound our ideas together. Normally, and perhaps for reasons of self-preservation, we tend to protect our associations from that which threatens dissociation; once we detect the pattern, we tend to ignore those other evidences which would cause our perception of the gestalt to break down. "This method of making definite hypotheses, and trying them," writes Hartley, "is far too laborious and mortifying for us to hope that inquirers will in general pursue it." Nonetheless, the practice remains essential for the process of discovery in the sciences. Making progress there requires detecting both patterns and the breakdown of patterns, both building up and taking apart; it requires giving both associations and counter-associations the weight due them. A century and a half later, William James wrote in "The Will to Believe" of the importance of both belief and doubt in the practice of the sciences: "The most useful investigator, because the most sensitive observer, is always he whose eager interest in one side of the question is balanced by an equally keen nervousness lest he become deceived. Science has organized this nervousness into a regular *technique*" ([1896] 1992, 471).

For those who desire to develop this habit of mind, despite the labor and mortification, Hartley recommends that they begin by proposing "hypotheses for the phaenomena, whose theories are well ascertained... and see how they are gradually compelled into the right road, even from wrong suppositions fairly compared with the phaenomena." The recommendation is the kernel of an experimental method of education: students should learn a science not as a collection of facts but as a process of discovery. By first practicing their craft in areas in which fundamental discoveries have already been made, they are like sailors learning the art of navigation in well-charted waters, before venturing out into unknown and boundless seas.

Hartley mentions two further benefits that accompany the formation of this method and habit of mind. The first concerns the development of what he terms "factitious sagacity"—the practical, and nonformalizable, knowhow that derives from continued practice of a skill. He writes that "the frequent attempts to make an hypothesis that shall suit the phaenomena, must improve a man in the method of doing this; and beget in him by degrees an imperfect practical art, just as algebraists and decypherers, that are much versed in practice, are possessed of innumerable subordinate artifices... [that] can scarce be explained or communicated to others." Hartley attributes the development of such sagacity to "impressions often repeated, with small variations from the general resemblance." Whether one is a mathematician or cryptographer, a chess master or skilled automobile mechanic, years of practice lead to the formation of a vast web of memories, in which all the "small variations from the general resemblance" have their places. A newly encountered problem, code, pattern of chessmen, or sound under the hood will evoke memories of others that are familiar, and even old friends; the new will be recognized as yet another small variation on the old, and the skilled expert, possessing factitious sagacity, will know which subordinate artifice to employ in order to deal with it.

To an old hand, novel events are seldom entirely new; there is usually some place in the web of memory into which a newly encountered situation will fit. Such an integration of the novel into the familiar is the basis of the knowhow that enables a practiced hand to get on with the job. But in addition to the gradual development of such factitious sagacity, the practice of the method Hartley recommends can also lead to a seemingly opposite result: "The frequent making of hypotheses, and arguing from them synthetically... would suggest numerous phaenomena, that otherwise escape notice, and lead to *experimenta crucis*, not only in respect of the hypothesis under consideration, but many others." It is the person who is already familiar with many things who may know where to look for something new; it is the person who knows what to expect who may be most sensitive to the appearance of the unexpected. An experienced hunter of wild mushrooms finds mushrooms where others cannot; in addition, finding a particular kind of mushroom in the "wrong" place may reveal to her how a forest is changing—and also suggest further avenues of exploration that would disclose more about the causes, extent, and direction of that change. It is an essential point, and today well known, that theory guides observation; having a hypothesis—a hunch about something—both tells you where to look and discloses the significance of the previously overlooked. And at times what it discloses may be the key that opens the portal on another of nature's realms. Newton was not the first person to notice that a prism produced a rainbow of light; but he was the first person to direct the violet light from one prism through a second—and to explain what this crucial experiment revealed.

Hartley's second parallel, to the use in mathematics of letters for unknown quantities, follows upon his discussion in proposition 80 of language as "a species of algebra." To a young child, many if not most general terms are at first *x*'s and *y*'s—the child learns their meanings by hearing them used, and using them, in various circumstances. A child experiments with words, in order to determine their boundaries of meaning, whether literal or figurative. And as the child marks these boundaries, the words suggest correlations and resemblances, as well as distinctions, that might not otherwise be noticed. People have two *legs* and two *arms*, cows four *legs*, ants six; a daddy longlegs has eight. Chairs also have *legs* and sometimes *arms*, but seals have *flippers* where their legs (or arms?) should be, and starfish have *arms* but no *legs*. When it comes to adventuring onto uncharted realms, inquirers in the sciences are like children, or like Ogden Nash, conversing with a creature of the sea: "Tell me, Oh Octopus, I begs, / Is those things arms, or is they legs?" Their task is to seek the patterns among unknown things: "Things that are quite unknown have often fixed relations to one another, and sometimes relations to things known, which, though not determinable with certainty and precision, may yet be determinable in some probable manner, or within certain limits." To discover the unknown relations in worlds that are new to them, inquirers, like children new to the world, use words of indefinite meaning in order to discern similarities, correlations, patterns in the objects of their study, which would otherwise remain unobserved. "Bringing an unknown quantity into an equation," writes Hartley, "answers, in philosophy, [to] the art of giving names, expressing nothing definite . . . and then inserting these names, or indefinite terms, in all the enunciations of the phaenomena, to see whether, from a comparison of these terms with each other, something definite in manner, degree, or mutual relation might not result." When some set of observations has been correlated with an indefinite term, the term can then be substituted for any or all of the observations in the set in subsequent discussions. And once a vocabulary of such terms has been created, inquirers can use the language to expedite thought. "Comparison of the terms"—as the terms are discussed, correlated, contrasted, formed into propositions—suggests deeper comparisons of the sets of phenomena for which they are the shorthand symbols. A vocabulary of indefinite terms is thus to the phenomena under consideration as the hare of algebra is to the tortoise of geometry: ideal for rapid analysis, and awaiting completion through synthesis. For the hare's problem is not simply that of overconfidence; the hare is capable of darting off in any number of directions, but it is the tortoise who ultimately knows the route of the race.

Still, to maintain the virtues of speed and flexibility, it is important that the hare travel light: "In philosophy we must give names to unknown quantities, qualities, causes, &c. not in order to rest in them, as the Aristotelians did, but to have a fixed expression, under which to treasure up all that can be known of the unknown cause, &c. in the imagination and memory, or in writing for future inquirers." Common terms, for example, have the advantage of familiarity over neologisms. To interpret the octopus's reply as indicating that they is arms is already to have some notion of their function. But such familiarity can also be misleading. The difficulty with using known terms such as *arm* or *leg* is that one's interlocutors will have various constellations of meanings, and secondary associations, already attached to the words, which may, by assimilating new to old, lead one to overlook the distinctive features of the new. A sagacious and scientifically minded octopus would inform the questioner that neither alternative is desirable, that either conceals more than it reveals about the function of the body parts under consideration. Consequently, Hartley writes that purposely indefinite terms "should have no more of secondary ideas from prior associations, than the terms x and y in algebra." Further, "if we use old terms excluding the old associations, the reader should be made aware of this." Newton, he adds, used the old terms *attraction* and *aether* in this way, "not resting in them." He also recommends Joseph Mede's *Clavis Apocalyptica* (2d ed., 1650) as "an instance of the proper manner of reasoning concerning the knowable relations of unknown things."

Hartley's comments on the third and fourth points of comparison, concerning the extraction of roots and cryptography, correlate with his specific interests in probability theory, the calculus, the rule of false position, and the "innumerable subordinate artifices" that comprise factitious sagacity. What is common to all these topics is that they are all instances of situations in which there is no single formula, or deductive method, for the solution of problems, and hence in which a person has to approximate a solution through a process of guided and self-correcting trial and error. With regard, for example, to the extraction of roots, there is a formula for the solution of quadratic equations, but extracting the roots of cubic, quartic, and quintic equations relies on a variety of methods—and the ingenuity of the mathematician. One such method, relying on approximation, is in effect a more sophisticated version of the rule of false position. As Hartley explains it: "Here a first position is obtained, which, though not accurate, approaches, however, to the truth. From this, applied to the equations, a second position is deduced, which approaches nearer to the truth than the first; from the second a third, &c. till the analyst obtains the true root, or such an approximation as is practically equivalent, every preceding discovery being made the foundation for a subsequent one, and the equation resolving itself, as it were, gradually." Hartley adds that "this is indeed the way, in which all advances in science are carried on; and scientific persons are in general aware, that it is and must be so." He then points to Newton as an exemplary practitioner of this method. Newton's *Opticks* ([1717] 1730), *Chronology of the Ancient Kingdoms Amended* (1728), and *Observations on the Prophecies of Daniel* (1733) "abound in instances to this purpose." It may seem odd to us today that works of ancient history and biblical interpretation should be paradigms of the correct practice of the method of science, but this sense of oddness should make us aware that for Hartley and his readers the words *science* and *philosophy* treasured up much; they served as algebraic symbols for more expansive domains of phenomena than they do for us today. Hartley thought that Newton's mathematical expertise made him particularly suited to carry out research into ancient chronology. We may consider their view overly broad and insufficiently scientific. They would probably consider ours to be fragmented, stunted, needlessly constrained.

The general point of Hartley's observations concerning mathematics is that we have no single method by which we come to certain, demonstrative knowledge of the world. As we try to understand some aspect of a pattern in things, we make guesses—frame hypotheses—using terms whose meanings are not precisely defined; these hypotheses then suggest that we look for certain features or patterns in the phenomena, evidences that will confirm or disconfirm the hypothesis. If we are scientifically honest, intellectually flexible, not so besotted of our own hypotheses as to refuse to admit any evidence to the contrary, we will acknowledge that the fit between hypothesis and data is approximate: the evidence indicates that the probability distribution we propose is itself probable to a certain degree, within a broader or narrower set of limits; the points on the graph are more or less close to the function with which we propose to join them. Then, after one trial, we make another; we try another variant of the function, to see if it better fits the known points, and we also note that, if this function is approximately correct, then we should expect to find as yet unobserved points farther out along the curve. We find some of the latter *near* where they are supposed to be, and the process of refining the hypothesis and looking for new evidences recurs. (Note the mutuality: a hypothesis relies on evidence for support, but what counts as evidence is defined by the hypothesis.) In addition, because the sets of observations always fall far short of a complete enumeration of "all circumstances," the hypotheses formed to account for them are always open to revision, as more information comes to light. Our assent to them is always more or less qualified, and our understanding of what it is we are saying about the world is more or less precise.

8. A Philosophical Language

In Hartley's view, we are algebraic beings living in a geometric world. The world is one of "fixed relations," but our relations to it are unfixed. Although the world possesses a complete geometric coherence and regularity, we lack the mental capacity to apprehend it synthetically. Because our knowledge of the world is through our use of languages, we have to speak in order to tell ourselves what we think. But because our languages are algebraic, we speak with unknowns, and we do not know clearly and distinctly what we say. Our explanations are probabilistic and symbolic, and hence always to some degree distanced and indeterminate. Still, there is always the potential that, as a science develops, "the knowable relations of unknown things" will over time lead us to a deeper understanding of the things themselves: "from the due comparison of [terms such as *attraction, aether,* etc.] with each other, and with such as farther observation and experiments shall suggest, their laws and action will, perhaps, be discovered hereafter; so that we may be able to predict the phaenomena." The fact that vibrations of a given frequency are isochronous, for example, opens up a way of investigating dimensions of the world that was, a century before Hartley wrote, unimaginable. And as those investigations produce results, the meaning of *vibration* became both richer and more precise. As a science grows in explanatory and predictive power, its indefinite terms will gradually gain in detail and definiteness, as inquirers discover more and more about the "fixed relations" that exist amongst the phenomena that are "treasured up" under them.

The development and continuously refined application of scientific vocabularies marks, in other words, the potential for the convergence of the algebra of language upon the geometry of the world. Just as De Moivre had discovered the law that described the asymptotic path by which observed frequencies approach a given probability distribution, so also did Hartley hope that a language could be so reformed and rationalized so as to follow a similar path of approach toward the plenitude of being. Such a language, in which algebra converged upon geometry and in which all verbal analogies were expressive of natural ones, would be what Hartley and his contemporaries called *philosophical*.

Hartley's design for creating a philosophical language begins with a biblical account of the origin of language and writing (*OM* 1.3.1.83).[10] Adam and Eve spoke a philosophical, though "very narrow" language, which changed after the fall to meet their new experiences, especially of pain, and which was later miraculously confused at Babel. The first parents and their children also practiced a form of "picture-writing." However, given the summary way in which people learn to speak, Hartley doubts that ancient humanity could have possessed of itself the capacity for analysis that would be necessary to make the leap from characters to letters—which supports the "presumption, that [alphabetical writing] is not a human invention" (*OM* 1.3.1.80, Cor. 8). Left to themselves, people would develop an extensive fund of characters, which would remain in common use even as the languages that people spoke gradually diverged from each other. And this is what happened in China and the surrounding countries, where Hartley, following "Mr. Whiston and Mr. Shuckford," supposes that "Noah, his wife, and their postdivulian posterity" settled, "so as to be cut off from Shem, Ham, and Japheth": "And thus we may conceive, that the postdivulian posterity of Noah might all write the same characters, and yet speak different languages; also that their character would be very extensive, and always the immediate representative of objects and ideas" (*OM* 1.3.1.83). In contrast, the first person to gaze upon letters was Moses, on Mount Sinai: by writing on the tablets of stone, God gave Israel the double gift of the law and of that powerful means of abstraction and analysis, the alphabet.[11]

Next, Hartley expresses the hope that the fall of language which accompanied the fall of man could be reversed. Such a language would need to enable people to "denote all their conceptions adequately, i.e. without any deficiency, superfluity, or equivocation"; it would also depend "upon a few principles assumed, not arbitrarily, but because they were the shortest and best possible, and [would grow] on from the same principles indefinitely, so as to correspond to every advancement in the knowledge of things" (*OM* 1.3.1.84). Such a language "would as much exceed any of the present languages as a paradisiacal state does the mixture of happiness and misery, which has been our portion ever since the fall." It would be akin to "the language given by God to *Adam* and *Eve*, before the fall"—though, thanks to its potential for growth and development, it would be incomparably more comprehensive and powerful.

Three projects for creating such a language follow. The first is to produce a completely phonetic character or script and then to determine all the simple and complex ideas that correspond to these sounds. Hartley does not think this is practicable, and suggests, as an alternative, that we take words from existing languages, select the best rules of etymology and syntax available, and create a new language, something like an Esperanto. As a last resort, he suggests the use of a reformed Hebrew, the one language that must bear within itself the most traces of the one spoken in Eden.

By Hartley's day the idea of a philosophical language already had a long history. Ramon Lull (1236–1315) and the Moravian bishop John Amos Comenius (1592–1670) had sought to develop universal sign systems that would enable people to resolve religious disputes and to reestablish contact with God.[12] And the immediate influence on Hartley may have been the project to create a philosophical language that had been undertaken by founding members of the Royal Society, led by John Wilkins, its first secretary, and including John Ray and Samuel Pepys. The result of their labors was Wilkins's *Essay Towards a Real Character, and a Philosophical Language* (1668). The work has a twofold purpose: Wilkins thought that the "design will ... contribute much to the clearing of some of our Modern Differences in *Religion*," and also that "the reducing of all things and notions to such kinds of Tables as are here proposed ... would prove the plainest way for attainment of real knowledge" (1668, "Epistle Dedicatory"). "Tables" is the key to the project. Wilkins's assigned task was to invent a character, that is, a system of signs, that would in itself *show* the exact interrelationships between the ideas the character signified. Such a character would be a system of visual analogies.[13] When these signs were arranged on a table, the table itself would be a visible representation of the structure of ideation—and of the "perpetual thread" of natural analogies. Wilkins's colleagues had the task of developing the tables upon which all the things of the world would be arranged. Once these tables were completed, all that would remain would be the assignment of correspondences between the elements of the character and the things in the tables. For such a scheme to work, Wilkins and his friends had to assume that there were manageable numbers of things, all amenable to a spatially systematic arrangement. Although Wilkins designed the character, his friends never did finish their tables. They encountered unexpected multitudes of things. Their inability to do so did not, however, stop Robert Hooke from recommending the use of Wilkins's character. In his *Description of Helioscopes,* he writes that the character is one "in which I could wish, that all things of this nature were communicated, it being a Character, and Language so truly Philosophical . . . that there seemeth to be nothing wanting to make it have the utmost perfection, and highest Idea of any Character or Language imaginable, as well for Philosophical as for common and constant use" (1679, 30–31). Hartley felt the same way about Byrom's shorthand: "If we were possessed of a philosophical language," he writes, "it ought to be denoted by this character."

Wilkins related signs to things. Were the tables of signs able to map onto the tables of things, the language itself would *be* knowledge. Hartley, knowing this had not succeeded, suggested three alternatives for creating a philosophical language. The aim remained the same: the formation of a purified language that would embody and display the "perpetual thread" of relationships among things. Language and the world would match each other perfectly, luminously. The perfection of the algebraic language would be the perfection of synthetic representation. Algebra would become geometry.

9. The Wood of Words

Locke spoke of students lost in the wood of words. As woods go, it is an odd one. It is swarming with gardeners, who, although they often have difficulty describing what the trees, bushes, and plants look like, nonetheless are ceaselessly busy digging up and moving about plants both large and small, forming and reforming them into clusters. Moreover, the gardeners think the *oaks* and *orchids* and *lichens* in this wood bear a relationship to things in another forest; they say their purpose for creating arrangements is to call attention to features of or relations among things in this other forest. Such features and relations, when observed, are taken to be evidences of the aptness and accuracy of the gardeners' designs.

There are two conditions that define limits to the gardeners' activities, two boundaries to the relations between the wood of words and the forest of things. On the one hand, given the fluency of speech, the richness of word associations in any living language, and the antiquity of the archives of words, it is possible for a gardener (or guild of gardeners) to construct a proprietary wood of words that is distant from, and virtually independent of, the world all hold in common. We noted above Hartley's observation that "the ideas, words, and reasonings, belonging to the favourite hypothesis ... unite with each other, and so coalesce in the same manner, as genuine truths do from induction and analogy. Verbal and grammatical analogies and coincidences are advanced into real ones." The "coincidences" among words form a thicket so dense and intertwined and yet familiar that the gardeners who plant and tend it become convinced that it is natural—and hence patterned on an archetype. That others find their thicket impenetrable is, to the committed, evidence that Sleeping Beauty really does rest in the castle at its center. And the adherents of this vision are often ready to dispute, or fight, those who assert otherwise, or who promote thickets of their own. "Religious controversies concerning abstract propositions," Hartley writes, "arise generally from the different degrees of respect paid to terms and phrases, which conduce little or nothing to the generation of practical faith" (*OM* 1.3.2.86).

On the other hand, at the other limit is "that instantaneous and necessary coalescence of ideas, which makes intuitive evidence, [and which] may be considered as the highest kind of induction, and as amounting to a perfect coincidence of the effect concluded with those from which it is concluded" (*OM* 1.3.2.87). Hartley adds that "this takes place only in mathematics." We know that 2 plus 2 makes 4 "only from prior instances of having actually perceived this, and from the necessary coincidence of all these instances with all other possible ones of 2 and 2." Ultimately, the basis of the intuition that $2 + 2 = 4$ is *necessarily* true is the fact that the "coalescence" of ideas ends in their merger. The formula asserts an equivalence, but in the final analysis the equivalence is an identity: a person *sees* that "2 + 2" and "4" are two expressions for one quantity. In this "highest kind of induction," the names for two or more seemingly distinct kinds of plants are discovered to converge upon the same thing. When that convergence occurs, the distinct ideas associated with the names must instantaneously and necessarily coalesce.

Existing in the space between imaginary thickets and intuited identities is the realm of partial but real analogies. Animals, for example, have stomachs. But how much can one infer about the physiology of digestion in one animal from what one knows about the stomach of another? "If we argue from the use and action of the stomach in one animal to those in another, supposed to be unknown," Hartley writes, "there will be a probable hazard of being mistaken, proportional in general to the known difference of the two animals, as well as probable evidence for the truth of part, at least, of what is advanced, proportional to the resemblance of the two animals." What we learn from studying the stomachs of pigs probably tells us more about our own digestive systems than would study of the stomachs of crayfish. We understand the point as a general rule, in the same way that we understand that, over time, a tossed coin will turn up heads half the time. Determining with some preciseness the probability of the evidence or hazard of error requires the creation of a scale, table, or clade that specifies the proportionality of the resemblances between people, pigs, crayfish—and many other living things. (Such were the tables that Wilkins and his colleagues attempted to frame.) But even when one possesses such a scale, there remains, in Hartley's formulation, an asymmetry between doubt and confidence. The "probable hazard of being mistaken" is "proportional to the known difference of the two animals"; in contrast, the degree of "resemblance of the two animals" provides only "probable evidence for the truth of part, at least, of what is advanced." Given known differences between two species, a biologist will be cautious about transferring conclusions reached about one to the other. Given known resemblances, the researcher can be confident only that *some part* of what she has learned of the one species can be "advanced" concerning the other.

Because of its potential for inventiveness, its algebraic capacity to form novel combinations, "analogy may also, in all cases, be made a guide to the invention." It is the basis of both creative discernment and fantasy. On the one hand, we noted above that Hartley perceived in the world "a perpetual thread of analogy continued from the most perfect animal to the most imperfect mineral, even till we come to elementary bodies themselves" (*OM* 1.3.1.82), and that this perpetual thread is "a great assistance in deciphering" the properties of things, which thus "become comments on each other in an endless reciprocation" (*OM* 1.3.2.87). It is this "endless reciprocation" of natural analogies that fills verbal analogies with the potential for representing real relations. Just as Stephen Hales's experiments on dogs and other animals led him to conclusions that were directly applicable to humans, one can similarly learn much about human digestion from a study of the stomachs of pigs, and possibly something as well from crayfish. On the other hand, in his discussion of figurative language, Hartley wrote that "the mind being once initiated into the method of discovering analogies, and expressing them, does ... even force things into its system by concealing disparities, magnifying resemblances, and accommodating language thereto" (*OM* 1.3.1.82). Natural analogies are based on selective resemblance; features or aspects of one thing match like features or aspects of another. The difficulty arises from dissimilarities that go unnoticed, either because they are unapparent or because the observer's passion to force everything into the system leads to their being overlooked. When a treatment that succeeds for one patient fails to help a second, the physician must ask how the two, seemingly peas in a pod, in fact differ. As long as thought operates through analogy, the selectivity of analogy will ensure that there will be some degree of incompleteness and uncertainty to our conclusions, some probability of the hazard of being mistaken.

Nonetheless, as a figurative use of words can become literal, so also can resemblance ascend from analogy to the higher level of induction. As we noted above, we use the word *mouth* literally when speaking of the relevant anatomical parts of goldfish and caterpillars, but figuratively when referring to the point at which a river enters a lake or the sea. The reason for this is that the mouths of goldfish and caterpillars are, in the respects that are important, equivalent, while the river's mouth is not. Similarly, if one could be certain that the points of comparison between one thing and another comprised a nearly exhaustive list of all the truly significant features or factors, then the transfer of a conclusion from the first thing to the second would be a matter of induction, not an argument from analogy. "Where the instances ... are alike," writes Hartley, "to that under consideration, at least in all things that affect the present inquiry, it affords the highest probability, and may be termed induction, in the proper sense of the word" (*OM* 1.3.2.87). If all the members of a class of objects, which we have encountered, have the features *a, b, c, d,* and *e,* and if we are satisfied that this is a sufficient list of significant features, then we infer, through what we take to be induction, that if a new object has the features *a, b, c,* and *d,* then it will also have *e.* "Thus we infer that the bread before us is nutritive and wholesome, because its smell, taste, ingredients, manner of composition, &c. are the same as those of other bread, which has often before been experienced to be so."

Hartley gives another example of the passage from analogy to induction. Referring to his own work, he writes that "if it could be shewed, that the human understanding is entirely dependent upon association, the many analogies and connections between the understanding and the affections, as these terms are commonly understood and contradistinguished by writers, would make it very probable, that association presides in the same manner in the generation of the affections." Such would be an instance of analogous reasoning. "But, if it now be shewn farther, that the understanding and affections are not really distinct things, but only different names, which we give to the same kind of motions in the nervous system, . . . then all the arguments from analogy are transformed into one of induction; which, however, is stronger than the united force of them all." It is as if the observer of man were working through two massively complex mathematical equations; as he labors with them, he sees that there are areas of similarity between the two, and these areas of similarity enable him to use what is large and clear in the one to illuminate what is minute and obscure in the other. But at some point he discovers that both equations are equal to a third; and when he sees this, he has the sudden insight that he has all along been working on two different versions of the one equation. The apparent similarities between the two are not analogies, but evidences of the equations' identity. Like "2 + 2" and "4," language concerning the "understanding" and language concerning the "affections" converge upon—while revealing different aspects of—the same thing.

For the observer of man, the third equation, which defines the point of convergence, concerns "motions in the nervous system." And in Hartley's day, such motions were purely hypothetical entities, themselves unobservable. Hartley could not record or measure the vibration passing along a nerve. Because the point of convergence they mark was itself undefined, although the discourses concerning the understanding and the affections could gravitate toward each other, they could never completely coalesce into an intuition of unity. In addition, there was no language that could give expression to such an intuition.

Although Locke thought that intuition was possible in mathematics, he doubted whether such knowledge could ever be had of the physical world. Too much of the universe is too remote, or too minute, to be directly apprehended:

> If . . . far the greatest part of the several ranks of *Bodies* in the Universe, scape our notice by their remoteness, there are others that are no less concealed from us by their *Minuteness*. . . . Our want of precise distinct *Ideas* of their primary Qualities, keeps us in an incurable Ignorance of what we desire to know about them. I doubt not but if we could discover the Figure, Size, Texture, and Motion of the minute Constituent parts of any two Bodies, we should know without Trial several of their Operations one upon another, as we do now the Properties of a Square, or a Triangle. Did we know the Mechanical affections of the Particles of *Rhubarb, Hemlock, Opium,* and a *Man,* as a Watchmaker does those of a watch, . . . we should be able to tell before Hand, that *Rhubarb* will purge, *Hemlock* kill, and *Opium* make a Man sleep. (*HU* 4.3.25)

Locke grants that our understanding of the "mechanical affections" of particles of matter could, if we could but see minutely enough, be as intuitively and demonstratively certain as our comprehension of the properties of a square. But our ignorance in this matter is "incurable"; the limitations of our sensory systems, designed to help us live our lives at the scale to which we are suited, bar us from perceiving the world of the very small.

Hartley, in contrast, is very cautiously optimistic. Although he cannot claim to have invented a superior microscope that would enable people to observe the "mechanical affections" of the particles in rhubarb or in a man's nerves directly, he clearly is willing to develop hypotheses about the manner in which such particles vibrate and thereby send signals to each other. Such hypotheses are the first tentative steps toward a "philosophical" description of the fundamental processes at work in the world. Given that people *will* form hypotheses, an inquirer's object should be to articulate the "best that we can form" in the circumstances; such a hypothesis "ought to be preferred to all others"— if "it is most conformable to all the phaenomena," and even if, because of the nascent state of a science, it "will amount to no more than an uncertain conjecture." Students of the sciences, if they adopt Hartley's recommendation to try to discover laws that are already established, will, after all, experience how "even from wrong suppositions fairly compared with the phaenomena" they will be "gradually compelled into the right road." A wrong supposition or a failed experiment can teach us much. They help to define the path; they suggest revisions of the hypothesis, new models and analogies, refinements in the methods of experiment, new kinds of phenomena to seek out, and reinterpretations of existing observations that bring to light a significance that went previously unremarked.

Instead of a hard and fast demarcation between knowledge and opinion, between truths known through intuition and demonstration and hypotheses arrived at through conjecture, there is, in Hartley's understanding of the search for knowledge, a continuous space that stretches between the boundaries of fantasy and intuition. This is the space, or field, of language. We move about in it. Attuned to patterns of similarity and difference, we articulate analogies. In doing so, the words we use and the propositions we form are often, like good bamboo, relaxed, flexible, algebraic, resonant with possible meanings, suggestive of possible relations among things. And it is good that they are so, for such words are useful for invention and discovery in a way that words, rigidly braced with the ashen rods of clarity and distinctness, often fail to be.

Hartley transforms the wood of words into a garden. Some gardeners, their imaginations brimming with their articulations, approach the boundary of fantasy; they build follies, construct thickets about imaginary castles, stake out plants in beds and patterns that are found nowhere else. Other gardeners, observant, open, questioning, carefully note the features of the plants around them, and arrange wood, leaf, and flower into globes, or models, or symbols that image the geometries of the vast, or of the vastly small. Such gardeners approach the garden's other boundary. Their goal, ultimately, is the creation of a philosophical language.

That other boundary is a very long way off. Yet there is no internal wall built across the garden—or angel with a flaming sword—that keeps us from it. An argument from analogy can become more precise; it can be formulated into a hypothesis that, like a function in calculus, accounts for the variations in a variety of phenomena—and alerts us where to look for phenomena yet to be observed. An argument from analogy can also be transformed into an induction, as seemingly distinct phenomena are discovered to be manifestations of one underlying cause or force. In addition, induction can also gradually approach becoming intuitive evidence, as one learns how to magnify the remote and the small:

> Thus also inductions may be taken from the smell and taste of bread, to prove it wholesome; which would be transformed into one simple argument stronger than both, could we see the internal constitution of the small parts of bread, whence its smell, and taste, and wholesomeness, are all derived. Thus, again, all the arguments of induction for the manner of extracting the square root in numbers vanish into the single demonstrative proof, as soon as this is produced. And the great business in all branches of knowledge is thus to reduce, unite, and simplify our evidences; so as that the one resulting proof, by being of a higher order, shall be more than equal in force to all the concurrent ones of the inferior orders. (*OM* 1.3.2.87)

Because there is no theoretical barrier to perceiving "the internal constitution of the small parts of bread"—or of the human frame—we are not permanently incapacitated from gaining intuitive knowledge of the "mechanical affections" that pattern the natural world. Hence the "instantaneous and necessary coalescence of ideas, which makes intuitive evidence," does not, for Hartley, represent a different kind of thinking, limited to mathematics; intuition presents us with "evidence," as do analogy and induction. Direct intuition is a limit condition toward which thought can aspire. To the extent that such intuitions are achieved and shared, analysis converges upon synthesis, the fluid algebra of language upon the geometry of the world.

7

The Emergence of the Self through the Transference of Emotion

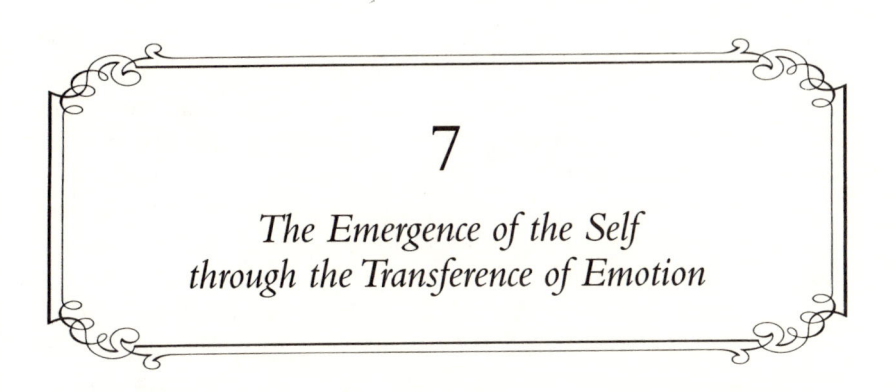

> But as far as the 'scientific psychology' of the emotions goes, I may have been surfeited by too much reading of classic works on the subject, but I should as lief read verbal descriptions of the shapes of rocks on a New Hampshire farm as toil through them again. They gave one nowhere a central point of view, or a deductive or generative principle. They distinguish and refine and specify *ad infinitum* without ever getting on to another logical level. Whereas the beauty of all truly scientific work is to get to ever deeper levels. Is there no way out from this level of individual description in the case of the emotions? I believe there is a way out, if one will only take it.
>
> —William James (1890, 2:448–49)

At the center of Hartley's *Observations* is a theory of the emergence and then transcendence of the self—a theory which relies upon a "generative principle" of emotion. I use the term emergence because, in Hartley's theory, the self, as a complex psychological structure of memories, thoughts, and especially dispositions, arises out of a ground of purely physical responses to one's circumstances. And it does so by means of a generative psychological operation: namely, the "transference" of emotion.

1. The Transference of Emotion

We noted in chapter 3 that, according to Hartley, we experience physical sensations as being neutral (or "indifferent"), pleasurable, or painful, and that we seek pleasurable sensations and avoid painful ones. We also noted that Hartley thought that indifference, pleasure, and pain were quantitatively rather than qualitatively different: for any type of sensation, there is a continuum of intensity, with the transitions from indifference to pleasure and from pleasure to pain marking thresholds along the continuum. On the one hand, pleasure carried beyond its limit—at which point it causes a neurological "solution of continuity"—becomes painful: children squeal with delight when being tickled—up to a point. On the other hand, if a painful experience is sufficiently diminished, it will fall within the limits of pleasure. Eating a chili pepper would be painful, and yet adding the chili to the stew turns an insipid dish into a pleasurable one. In addition, Hartley suggested that the thresholds between indifference, pleasure, and pain are variable and responsive to experience; an organism may adapt to a painfully disrupted state by establishing a new muscular or neurological continuity, so that previously painful excitations of its nervous system no longer cause a solution of continuity and hence are not experienced as painful. After a number of bowls, a person begins to enjoy his chili hot.

As well as being surrounded by circumstances and events, people live in memory and in anticipation, and the pains attending an injury, for example, may color one's memory of it or one's anticipation of future injuries. "The appearance of the fire, or of a knife, especially in circumstances like those in which the child was burnt or cut, will raise up in the child's nervous system painful vibrations of the same kind with, but less in degree than, those which the actual burn or wound occasioned" (*OM* 1.2.1.33). Here an emotional charge has been detached from the sensation of pain and attached to perceptions of its cause, the fire or knife; similarly, this charge, which Hartley calls a "miniature pain," may also be attached to the child's memory of the original injury or fantasies of future injuries. In the process, a sensate pain becomes what Hartley calls an "intellectual" one. It is important to note, in this context, that intellectual pleasures and pains are not the exclusive possession of human beings; recall Hartley's comment that animals "prove their near relation to us, not only by the general resemblance of the body, but by that of the mind also" (*OM* 1.3.7.93; see §6.1). For us and all our relations, the images that fill the mind, that are the elements of memory and imagination, are charged with what we call emotions and what Hartley and his contemporaries more commonly termed "affections."

In Hartley's theory, emotion is a fluid like electricity or water; it jumps or flows from one experience, memory, word, or cluster of words to another. Hartley calls such a jump a *transference* of emotion, and he generally suggests that such transferences can occur between any two (or more) items that are linked with each other. The current will flow wherever it can.

Hartley did not invent the concept of transference. In his "Preliminary Dissertation" to the English translation of William King's *Essay on the Origin of Evil* (1731), John Gay had utilized the concept, and Hartley credits Gay as the one from whom he first learned of "the possibility of deducing all our intellectual pleasures and pains from association" (*OM* 1. Preface). Gay's main thesis is "that our Approbation of Morality, and all Affections whatever, are finally resolvable into *Reason* pointing out *private Happiness*, . . . and that whenever this end is not perceived, they are to be accounted for from the *Association of Ideas*, and may properly enough be call'd *Habits*" (1731, xxxi). According to Gay, "The Case is really this. We first perceive or imagine some real Good, *i.e.* fitness to promote our Happiness, in those things we love and approve of. Hence . . . we annex Pleasure to those things. Hence those things and Pleasure are so ty'd together and associated in our Minds, that one cannot present itself but the other will also occur. And the *Association* remains even after that which at first gave them the Connection is quite forgot, or perhaps does not exist" (1731, lii). Gay's point is that the connections frequently *are* forgotten: we become attached to, and take pleasure in, things and ideas even after their connections with real goods are no longer noticed. Gay uses the example of a miser: although money has value only as a means to accomplishing various ends, which are the real goods we perceive or imagine promoting our happiness, a miser takes pleasure directly in the possession of money itself; such an annexation of pleasure to stamped bits of metal (or computer printouts) paradoxically inhibits him from using his hoard to achieve any of the ends for which it was initially valued.

Although Hartley acknowledges that Gay "put me upon considering the power of association" (*OM* 1. Preface), he develops an account of association's power that differs from the one Gay sketches out. According to Gay, a person perceives or judges some thing to be a real good and, on the basis of this judgment, annexes pleasure to the thing. This is reason "pointing out" private happiness. The feeling follows the judgment. According to Hartley, as toddlers we make no such judgments; we simply do not *reason* about happiness: "The young child learns to grasp and go up to the play-thing that pleases him, and to withdraw his hand from the fire that burns him, at first from the mechanism of his nature, and without any deliberate purpose of obtaining pleasure, and avoiding pain, or any explicit reasoning about them" (*OM* 1.3.3.89). In Hartley's genetic account, the logic of Gay's initial suggestion is reversed: the initial, direct connection is between the thing and the feeling of pleasure or pain. The feeling precedes the judgment, and the child's approach or avoidance is an automatic reaction to a stimulus. Only with repeated experience and "the instruction and imitation of others" will the child learn "to pursue every thing which he loves and desires, fly from every thing which he hates; and to reason about the method of doing this." Hartley's point here is not that children have to learn how to pursue and fly from objects; they reach for and pull back from things automatically. Rather, the point is that it is inaccurate to ascribe the states we call *love* and *hate* to the infant, as if they were native dispositions, and then to imagine that a child pursues one thing *because he loves it,* and flees another *because he hates it.* It would be truer to say that, with repeated experience, instruction, and imitation, we learn to love those things we pursue and to hate those things we flee from. The ability to pursue something *because* one loves it is an achievement. A greater achievement is the ability "to reason about our method of doing this"—to reason out why the thing is loved.

A person must, in other words, accumulate a fund of associations and habits in order for reason to point out private happiness. Before the associations are compounded and the habits established, *reason* cannot point out happiness. And neither can *happiness* be pointed out. The passage in the preceding paragraph continues:

> And because mankind are for the most part pursuing or avoiding something or other, the desire for happiness, and the aversion to misery, are supposed to be inseparable from, and essential to, all intelligent natures. But this does not seem to be an exact

or correct way of speaking. The most general of our desires and aversions are factitious, *i.e.* generated by association; and therefore admit of intervals, augmentations, and diminutions. And, whoever will be sufficiently attentive to the workings of his own mind, and the actions resulting therefrom, or to the actions of others, and the affections which may be supposed to occasion them, will find such differences and singularities in different persons, and in the same person at different times, as no-way agree to the notion of an essential, original, perpetual desire of happiness, and endeavour to attain it; but much rather to the factitious associated desires and endeavours here asserted. (OM 1.3.3.89)

As adults, we observe ourselves and others constantly engaged in the pursuit of this and the avoidance of that, and we imagine that behind these various actions there is one general goal. Aristotle, in the first book of his *Nicomachean Ethics,* identifies *eudaimonia,* usually translated as happiness, as the "final end" of human life: although there are many conceptions of what it is and of the means of obtaining it, everyone longs to be happy. But Hartley in effect denies that happiness functions as a final end or cause, in the Aristotelian sense. Our intellectual affections are what Hartley terms "factitious"—that is, "generated by association." They are not evidence of an innate teleological drive for happiness or completeness, and they are not necessarily internally consistent. Rather, as factitious constructs, they are decomplex ideas; like piano concertos with space left for cadenzas, they "admit of intervals, augmentations, and diminutions." A person's longing for happiness, like her ability to pursue something because she loves it, is a development that owes its existence to a generative power of association.

We may amplify Hartley's idea by saying that the habits of character derived from the intellectual pleasures and pains represent factions of desires, and the self a parliament in which these political parties, though themselves internally diverse, pursue their own immediate goals and form various alliances to achieve them. "The several powers of the little world within a man's own breast," Hartley writes, "are at variance with one another, as well as those of the great world" (OM 2.2.24). The fluctuating internal conflicts, negotiations, contests, alliances, and compromises result in pronounced "differences and singularities"—both between individuals and within the same person in varying circumstances and at different stages of life.

Hartley learned from reading Gay that the affection attached to one thing can jump to another: the pleasure one takes in what money can buy can transfer to the coins themselves. But in the *Observations*, this notion of transference receives a further, crucial elaboration. Most importantly in Hartley's theory, people are users of language, and our memories, fantasies, and hence senses of self are themselves largely formed through narratives or other verbal constructs. In his discussion of memory (*OM* 1.3.4.90), Hartley comments that, because "we think in words[,] both the impressions and the recurrencies of ideas will be attended with words"; hence, "when a person relates a past fact, the ideas do in some cases suggest the words, whilst in others the words suggest the ideas." Consequently, the charge of affection attached to an experience may also be transferred to the *words* used to articulate the memory of it: "By degrees these miniature pains will be transferred upon the words, and other symbols, which denote these and such-like objects and circumstances" (*OM* 1.2.1.33). Emotion, originating in the attractive or aversive qualities of physical sensation, is variously transferred onto and concentrated upon words, both individually and in associated clusters. In addition, the emotion now adhering to words can also be transferred back onto things or actions; our evaluations of our experiences and our own conduct are largely determined by the emotions attached to the words we use to describe them. We noted in the previous chapter that, according to Hartley, "we think in words... and invent chiefly by means of their analogies" (*OM* 1.3.1.83)—and also that our capacity for invention leads both to the discovery of real relations among things and to the fabrication of imaginary ones.

What is true with regard to the outer world that is the object of scientific inquiry is also true of the inner world that is the self. Hartley writes that "the properties, beauties, perfections, desires, or defects and aversions, which adhere by association to the simile, parable, or emblem of any kind, are insensibly, as it were, transferred upon the thing represented" (*OM* 1.3.1.82). When the "thing represented" by similes, parables, emblems, or narratives is one's sense of self, of being a person with a unique constellation of memories, "the passions are moved to good or evil. Speculation is turned into practice, and either some important truth felt and realized, or some error and vice gilded over and recommended." The transference of emotion from "things," whether sensed, remembered, or imagined, to words and from words back to "things" is thus a mechanism both of discovery and deception, of insight and rationalization; moreover, it is the mechanism by which is made that knotty combination of discovery and deception that is the self.

Because "the words suggest the ideas," in personal narratives, "many mistakes in the subordinate circumstances are committed in the relations of past facts, if the relater descends to minute particulars. For the same reasons these mistakes will be so associated with the true facts after a few relations, that the relater himself shall believe that he remembers them distinctly" (OM 1.3.4.90). Hartley is describing the construction of memories in personal experience narratives—and pointing out the fact that a narrative, when repeated frequently enough, itself forms the memory. Because words suggest ideas as easily as ideas suggest words, people remember the events described in the stories they tell. But how then can we distinguish true from false memories? Hartley states that, often, we cannot: "many persons are known by relating the same false story over and over again, *i.e.* by magnifying the ideas, and their associations, at last to believe, that they remember it." Our personal histories are formed of our memories; but our memories are formed by the stories we tell, and by the emotions we attach to them.

The transference of emotion is thus the key to Hartley's theory of psychological development. Indeed, as the concept of natural selection is to Darwin's theory of the origin of species, transference of emotion is the generating principle that explains the origin and evolution of individual human personalities.

Consider, to begin with, Hartley's account of the origin of laughter in children. Hartley observes, first, that newborns do not laugh. But when they do begin to laugh, "The first occasion of doing this seems to be a surprize, which brings on a momentary fear first, and then a momentary joy in consequence of the removal of that fear, agreeably to what may be observed of the pleasures that follow the removal of pain" (OM 1.4.1.94). In other words, laughter is at first a purely physical response to a stimulus: it is occasioned by a split second's moment of fear immediately followed by a feeling of relief. It is the result of passing back over the threshold that separates pleasure from pain. Hartley adds that "this may appear probable, inasmuch as laughter is a nascent cry, stopped of a sudden; also because if the same surprize, which makes young children laugh, be a very little increased, they will cry."

A related source of laughter, which illustrates the same principle, is tickling. A child that is tickled also experiences "a momentary pain and apprehension of pain, with an immediately succeeding removal of these" (OM 1.4.1.94; cf. 1.2.1.33). But the squeals of delight that accompany the pleasure of being tickled can turn to sobs, if the tickling is too hard or continues for too long. But careful adults usually do not cross the limits of tickling or surprise. The customary practice, as anyone who has played endless games of peekaboo knows, is to stop and "repeat the surprize" (*OM* 1.4.1.94).

The laughter that originates in the passage from fear to relief, or in the almost painful experience of being tickled, soon shifts its focus from immediately physical to more social occasions. "The progress in each particular is much accelerated," Hartley writes, "and the occasions multiplied, by imitation. [Children] learn to laugh, as they learn to talk and walk; and are most apt to laugh profusely, when they see others laugh." Laughter is thus "a principal source" of the later-developing pleasures of "sociality and benevolence" (*OM* 1.2.1.33).

With the learning of language the objects that prompt laughter shift from the physical to the symbolic:

> As children learn the use of language, they learn also to laugh at sentences or stories, by which sudden alarming emotions and expectations are raised in them, and again dissipated instantaneously. And as they learnt before by degrees to laugh at sudden unexpected noises, or motions, where there was no fear, or no distinguishable one, so it is after some time in respect of words. Children, and young persons, are diverted by every little jingle, pun, contrast, or coincidence, which is level to their capacities.... And this is the origin of that laughter, which is excited by wit, humor, buffoonery, etc. (*OM* 1.4.1.94)

The transit from fear to relief still remains the occasion of laughter, but now the fear and relief derive from scary stories or incongruous wordplay. Or more accurately, scary or incongruous to a point: a story that arouses "sudden alarming emotions and expectations" that do not dissipate may cause nightmares; and although an incongruity that tests the limits of logic and decorum will be experienced as humorous, one that destroys or disregards "continuity" altogether will be absurd and frightening. Many children are disturbed rather than amused by *Alice in Wonderland*.

As we mature, we continue to be pleased, surprised, delighted by activities in which we push ourselves to, and step back from, the threshold of fear and pain. Some climb vertical walls of rock or shoot rapids in canoes. Others prefer simply to view what is fearful from a vantage point of safety. A crowd gathers in the theater featuring the latest film about flesh-eating aliens. As Hartley notes, "representations of battles, storms, wild beasts, and other objects of horror, in pictures" can be highly pleasurable, when the "near alliance" they have with pain combines with "the secret consciousness of our own security." And the thresholds we choose to test contribute to the definitions of who we are.

2. Defining the Self

As language comes more and more to form our minds, the words we and others say become the cores of our personalities, of our senses of identity as selves. Because such intellectual pleasures and pains are themselves creations of words and symbols, the self that is fashioned from them is also a compound or construct of verbal and symbolic elements.

Imagine a person who has been badly burned in a fire. He flinches at the recollection of it, at the memory of the long and painful process of treatment and recovery, and possibly at the thought of what would have become of him had he not been pulled from the burning building. In addition, a whole "cluster" of words has become charged for him. He may find it difficult to say, or perhaps even to think, *burn, dressing, skin graft, hospital, physical therapy, scar, mirror.* As Hartley notes, "compound or mental pains will arise from simple bodily ones by means of words, symbols, and associated circumstances" (*OM* 1.2.1.33).

Now, Hartley states that the pain transferred to a word "from a single cause" must be less than pain originally felt. The physical pain derives from an immediate and actual "solution of continuity" in the body and nervous system; certain words—*Ouch!*—are expressions of this disruption, while others are the bearers of the memory of the experience. However, as we noted in §6.3, according to Hartley words "collect ideas from various quarters, unite them together, and transfer them both upon other words, and upon foreign objects" (*OM* 1.3.1.80); they thus allow a language speaker to effect virtually unlimited connections between words, transferences of affection, and extensions of meaning. But in addition, because *understanding* and *affection* are, like *electricity* and *magnetism,* "not really distinct things, but only different names, which we give to the same kind of motions in the nervous system" (*OM* 1.3.2.87; see §6.9), the connections, transferences, and extensions thus effected are simultaneously emotional and ideational. Because words collect, unite, and transfer the emotional responses to particular experiences, emotional charges become concentrated in those words that stand out, for whatever reason, as targets for repeated transferences. Words are like Leyden jars, the early electrical condensers that fascinated scientists and the public in Hartley's day. The single term *dressing* may function as an emotional condenser that accumulates the charges transferred to it each time the bandages are pulled off and replaced. Hartley notes that in children words themselves can cause pain even when they are "not formed into propositions or threatenings." It is often the same for adults: "The very words, *burn, wound,* &c. seem even in adults, tho' not formed into propositions, or heightened by a conjunction of circumstances, to excite . . . a perception of the disagreeable kind" (*OM* 1.2.1.34). We experience a shock when we touch them.

Still, it is when words are wired together, like Leyden jars in a series, that they are capable of delivering the most painful shocks: "Since a great variety of particular miniatures are transferred upon each word, since also the words expressing the several pains of feeling affect each other . . . , it comes to pass that the various verbal and other symbols of pains of feeling, also of other pains bodily and mental, excite a compound vibration . . . which exceeds ordinary actual pains in strength" (*OM* 1.2.1.33). Propositions, threatenings, narratives of scenes remembered or anticipated, and even inarticulate clusters of words associated with the same trauma are able, according to Hartley, to induce states of mental suffering or joy that surpass individual instances of physical suffering or joy.

Hartley's notion of "clusters" of words, memories, and images resembles the concept of "feeling-toned complexes" later developed by C. G. Jung. According to Jung, a complex is "the *image* of a certain psychic situation which is strongly accentuated emotionally and is, moreover, incompatible with the habitual attitude of consciousness" (1960b, 96). Complexes originate, according to Jung, in emotional trauma and particularly in "moral conflict" (98). They function as "splinter psyches" (97) with "a high degree of autonomy" and even intentionalites of their own. They interfere with the projects of persons' conscious lives. Moreover, they are detected through the word association test, a technique first developed by Charles Darwin's cousin, Francis Galton. The anomalies in a person's responses to a list of words reveal the outline, as it were, of a complex. It is ruptures in the fluency of association—hesitations, delays in response, obvious substitutions, sweating palms, and an increased heartbeat—that speak the unspoken.

Hartley's verbal clusters, like Jung's complexes, frequently originate in trauma and particularly in physical pain. In fact, Hartley states that it is physical pain (the "pains of feeling") from which "the greatest part of our intellectual pains are deducible" (*OM* 1.2.1.33). Further, Jung's description of complexes as "constellations of psychic elements grouped round feeling-toned contents" and as consisting of "a nuclear element and a large number of secondarily constellated associations" (1960a, 10–11) would seem equally applicable to Hartley's description of a cluster of words and images bound together through the transferences of emotion.

However, it is not apparent that Hartley's concept of a cluster needs to be limited to an emotionally accented "*image* of a certain psychic situation" that is "incompatible with the habitual attitude of consciousness." It is true that an associative cluster could have an image as its nucleus and also that it could be an autonomous "splinter psyche" at odds with a person's "habitual attitude." Long after a trauma has occurred and the process of physical healing completed, a person could still be haunted by a hidden image that, when reexperienced, would prompt actions that would be otherwise out of character; Hartley is well aware that "the secret springs of action in men are frequently concealed, both from the by-stander, and even from the agent himself" (*OM* 1. Conclusion). Nonetheless, such a cluster does not necessarily have a single image as its nucleus. In the account of the genesis of anger discussed in chapter 1, the habit of "disinterested malevolence" derives ultimately from primary experiences of physical abuse or threats of abuse, but there is no suggestion that the image of that abuse must be retained as the nucleating element that holds together a number of "secondarily constellated associations." It is consistent with Hartley's theory to suggest that a primary traumatic event or scene may become so overlayered with words, descriptions, narratives, memories of the voices of others, and interior monologues as to decline into oblivion under their accumulation. In addition, over time the "associated remainders of painful impressions" mutually reinforce each other and thereby create a chain reaction that fuels itself, independently of its initiating spark; the child "goes on multiplying perpetually, by farther and farther associations, both the occasions of anger, and the expressions of it" (*OM* 1.4.4.97). Moreover, there is no reason to assume that such clusters are incompatible with a person's habitual attitude; the problem for the child and the people around him is precisely that anger *is* his habitual attitude. Whereas for Jung a complex of words is the means of detecting an image that is concealed from consciousness, for Hartley, in the case of the angry child, words largely form the vast and indefinite clusters that constitute a mode of consciousness and action that conceal that mode's own nature—its "secret springs"—from itself.

Jung speaks of complexes as if they were splinters, bits of a flint flaked off a core, and seems to assume that there is a core to start with—that there is an *I* with a distinctive habitual attitude, over against which a complex can assert incompatibility and autonomy. Nonetheless, the existence of complexes raises for Jung a question concerning "the possibilities of psychic disintegration" (1960b, 97). Specifically: "The word 'complex' in its psychological sense has passed into common speech both in German and in English. Everyone knows nowadays that people 'have complexes.' What is not so well known, though far more important theoretically, is that complexes *have us*." That such splinters "have us" leads Jung to question the degree to which they *are* the psyche. "The existence of complexes," he continues, "throws serious doubt on the naïve assumption of the unity of consciousness, which is equated with 'psyche,' and on the supremacy of the will" (95–96). In this "more important" theoretical point, this challenge to naïve assumptions, Jung's thinking approaches most closely to Hartley's. I suggested above that, to Hartley, the self is a parliament of intellectual affections. I have also suggested in §5.4 that we interpret Hartley as extending Locke's analysis of faculties to the mind itself, so that the term *mind* be taken, like the term *will*, to refer to a set of relations rather than to some substantial entity. In this interpretation, a cluster of processes constructs the edifice of, or hypercomplex idea that is, mind. Such a mind would not be transparent to itself, the immediately accessible "object of its own contemplation" (*HU* 2.1.8). Contrary to Locke, who proposed that personal identity lies in "Identity of consciousness" (*HU* 2.27.23), Hartley remarks: "It is difficult to know what is meant by the unity of consciousness" (*OM* 1. Conclusion). And in another context he refers to "perpetual alternations of opposite consciousnesses, *i.e.* recollections and judgments on our own actions" (*OM* 1.4.3.96). The existence of complexes does indeed throw doubt on the unity of consciousness and the supremacy of the will. And for Hartley, the self could be said to consist of complexes all the way down.

Or, to change direction, all the way out. Language is foremost a medium of social interaction, and the verbal compounds that enter into the self form like crystals, or concretions, within that medium. A cluster of words thus does not at least initially mark a boundary between me and not-me, between the dry land of self and the sea of social life. Rather, verbal clusters are saturated with experiences of the speech and actions of others. We noted in §6.2 that children learn the meaning of sentences "in a summary way" (*OM* 1.3.1.80), as parents, family, and others speak to them. For the young child, the initial situations of interaction may often involve a use of language that is both generic and idiosyncratic, all-encompassing and amorphous.

The resulting process of language learning (and attendant self-construction) may reflect these paradoxical qualities:

> To give an instance from childhood, the words *sweet, good, pretty, fine,* &c. on the one hand, and the words *bad, ugly, frightful,* &c. on the other, being applied by the nurse and attendants almost promiscuously... the one to all the pleasures, the other to all the pains of the several senses, must by association raise up general pleasant and painful vibrations, in which no one part can be distinguished from the rest; and, when applied by farther associations to objects of a neutral kind, they must transfer a general pleasure or pain upon them.
>
> All the words associated with pleasures must also affect each other by this promiscuous application. And the same holds in respect of the words associated with pains. However, since both the original and the transferred pleasures and pains heaped upon different words are different, and in some cases widely so, every remarkable word will have a peculiar internal feeling, or sentiment, belonging to it. (*OM* 1.3.1.80)

Like a young puppy, the child seeks pleasure and avoids pain; and again like a young puppy, she is able to respond to the emotional content of expressions, even when she has no clear idea what the words mean. She responds differently to a smile and a frown, to an expression of delight and a stern or angry warning. Hence, she tries to elicit words of praise and to evade words of blame, whatever they are and whatever the reason for their bestowal. And the teachers and attendants in the preschool or daycare, in their enthusiasm to further their charges' self-esteem, cooperate with the child through the "promiscuous application" especially of words of praise: "*GOOD JOB*, Jennifer; you've made it down the slide." Because "no one part can be distinguished from the rest" in the use of such terms, all the words of praise or blame tend to create a sense of, and then elicit, "a general pleasure or pain" that can in turn be transferred indifferently upon any neutral thing. The result is praise inflation. But at the same time, since "both the original and the transferred pleasures and pains heaped upon different words are different," Hartley dryly observes, "every remarkable word will have a peculiar internal feeling, or sentiment, belonging to it." No matter how generic, amorphous, and haphazard the nurse's and attendant's use of *sweet, good, pretty, fine,* and of *bad, ugly, frightful,* the child may remember the precise situations in which these words were applied to her. Like the words for the passions, such words also seem to derive their meanings from "the ideas of the associated circumstances" (*OM* 1.3.1.80; see §6.3) and their distinct emotional tones from the "peculiar internal feeling" associated with each. Deriving her sense of the meaning of words from these circumstances, she may habitually associate "a peculiar internal feeling" with being *a good girl* and another such feeling with fearing that she is *an ugly child.* When told, later in life, that she has done a "good job," Jennifer may recall the slide, and reexperience a faint taste of the peculiarly sweet or perhaps astringent feeling that arose when pleasures and pains were first heaped upon these words.

It is important to note that, in Hartley's account, words and symbols are given to the emerging self by others—and, particularly by others in whom the child has complete faith:

> In like manner all the kinds of honour and shame, by being expressed in words and symbols, that are nearly related to each other, enhance each other: Thus, for instance, the caresses given to a child when he is dressed in fine cloaths prepare him to be much more affected with the caresses and encomiums bestowed upon him when he has been diligent in getting his lesson. And indeed it ought to be remarked, that the words and phrases of the parents, governors, superiors, and attendants, have so great an influence over children, when they first come to the use of language, as instantly to generate an implicit belief, a strong desire, or a high degree of pleasure. They have no suspicions, jealousies, memories, or expectations of being deceived or disappointed; and therefore a set of words expressing pleasures of any kind, which they have experienced, put together in almost any manner, will raise up in them a pleasurable state, and opposite words a painful one. Whence it is easy to see, that the fine language expressing praise, and the harsh one expressing dispraise, must instantly, from the mere associations heaped

upon the separate words, put them into a state of hope and joy, fear and sorrow, respectively. And when the foundation is thus laid, praise and dispraise will keep their influences from the advantages and disadvantages attending them, though the separate words should lose their particular influences, as they manifestly do in our progress through life. (*OM* 1.4.2.95)

Because words and symbols, as they become charged with emotion, gain an ever-greater capacity to be further charged with yet more emotion, the child's emotions tend to transfer more and more from experiences to memories to verbal constructs. Commonly, the process of transference is circumstantial and haphazard: pleasant and painful associations are *heaped* upon the separate words. Such transference meets little if any resistance when the child brings to the social interaction the qualities of dependence and trust, when the child has no reason to suspect the gifts of praise and the threats of blame bestowed by "parents, governors, superiors, and attendants." By laying a "foundation" that will guarantee the life-long influence of praise and dispraise, the transference of affection functions as a generative principle that creates an emerging pattern out of the initial heap of verbal and symbolic elements.

3. The Six Classes of Intellectual Pleasures and Pains

In his discussions of the development of our habitual orientations such as laughter or anger, Hartley commonly starts with an automatic physical reflex, moves on to the transference of the pleasures and pains associated with that reflex to clusters of words and ideas, and then discusses how more general dispositions develop out of these clusters.

There is something distinctive, if not paradoxical, about Hartley's account of these transferences and transformations. On the one hand, emotion is volatile and nonselective with respect to its objects; it easily transfers from one word or image to the next, and, apart from the shift from physical to symbolic, it exhibits no disposition to select certain specific paths of transference over others. Just as there is no innate and general desire for happiness, there is no telling, when looking at an infant, what will excite her laughter at age ten, twenty, or thirty, or possibly how habitually angry she will become. On the other hand, a person is decidedly more than a haphazard collection of verbal clusters, memories, emotional states. Although the process of transference tends to be idiosyncratic and nonteleological, Hartley is interested to show how the process can in fact lead to psychic integration—how, that is, the self can emerge with a definite structure and something like wholeness.

The key to the emergence of a structured and to a degree coherent self lies in the capacity of the transference of emotion to bring about fundamental dispositional reorientations. In the example above, although the child receives praise for something she has done, the doing of which is a source of satisfaction and pleasure, the child quickly shifts focus from the action itself to the praise received for doing the action, so that doing the action is secondary to receiving the praise. The result is what counts, and the child will be inclined to perform any action that achieves it. Like a miser with the symbols of value, the child comes to desire, and even hoard, the words used to praise the "real good" that is herself. She will take pleasure in such words, quite regardless of the reasons or occasions of their bestowal.

This shift of pleasure from the material to the symbolic also represents a shift of focus concerning the source of pleasure: "It becomes a matter of praise to a child, to be influenced by praise, and deterred by shame; and a matter of reproach, to be insensible in these respects. And thus it comes to pass, that praise and shame have a strong reflected influence upon themselves; and that praise begets the love of praise, and shame the fear of shame" (*OM* 1.4.2.95, Cor. 2). The child's new concern to *be thought* a good child represents a shift from a direct to a reflected and reflexive source of pleasure; as such, the child's concern to be thought the kind of child who is influenced by praise and deterred by shame marks the appearance of a new category of pleasures and pains. A concern with *being thought* marks, in other words, a change in orientation—and the next stage in the emergence of the structure of the self.

A child learns to laugh at wordplay and at scary stories, and she takes satisfaction in being thought the kind of child who is influenced by praise and deterred by shame. The sequential changes that gradually turn suddenly stopped cries into laughter and that amplify the "reflected influence" of praise and shame represent the emergence of two distinct categories or "classes" of intellectual affections. Hartley terms these "imagination" and "ambition."

Hartley identifies six classes of "intellectual pleasure and pain" in all: imagination, ambition, self-interest, sympathy, theopathy, and the moral sense. Each category is "factitious" and owes its specific content

The Emergence of the Self 281

in the individual to processes of transference that are nonselective and circumstantial. Nonetheless, the six classes represent more than a toilsome typology of the emotions, dreary as "descriptions of the shapes of rocks on a New Hampshire farm": the categories represent fundamental orientations on the part of the person to his world. Moreover, Hartley states that the classes arise as fully developed orientations in sequence out of each other: "As sensation is the common foundation of all these, so each in its turn, when sufficiently generated, contributes to generate and model all the rest. We may conceive this to be done in the following manner. Let sensation generate imagination; then will sensation and imagination together generate ambition"—and so forth (*OM* 1.3.3.89). In addition to being factitious constructs that are "generated by association," the six classes thus also constitute an epigenetic series. The six classes provide a model of the complex and dynamic structure of the self.

I propose that we think of Hartley's sixfold classification in terms of a prism formed between two triangular surfaces, with the farther surface larger than the nearer (see Figure 7.1). Imagination, ambition, sympathy, theopathy—these are all terms that describe what a person loves, and also the manner of that loving. In the first chapter I suggested that Hartley's psychology could be understood as answering the question, How does a child learn to love? We can now sketch out a general

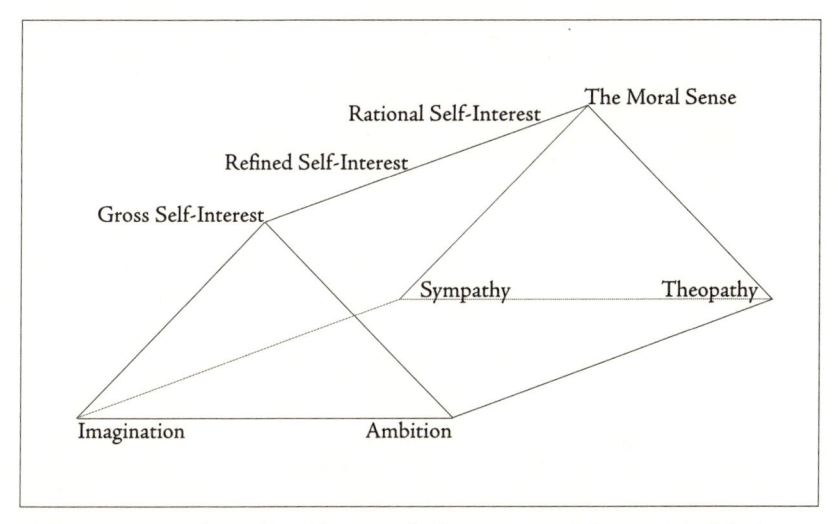

Figure 7.1 Hartley's Six Classes of Pleasures and Pains, Modeled as a Triangular Prism

outline of Hartley's answer. First, the ability to love is something accomplished, the culmination of an associative process of transference; although it derives ultimately from the human organism's responses to physical pleasure and pain, it is not itself an innate disposition or drive. Learning to love, secondly, requires the transference of emotion from physical sources of pleasure to "intellectual," particularly verbal and symbolic, resources. Thirdly, such transferences generate a series of basic dispositions or orientations: the love of objects that is imagination, the awareness of self as an object of approval that is ambition, the love of other selves that is sympathy, the awareness of oneself as loved that is theopathy. Fourthly, the dispositions separate into two kinds: the I-it relationships of imagination and ambition, in which there is a lack of reciprocation between the desiring subject and the desired object, and the I-thou relationships of sympathy and theopathy, to which reciprocity of subjectivity is fundamental. Finally, this separation into two kinds of relationship, and hence into the two end planes of the prism, suggests that the process of becoming a complete person requires movement along the line from self-interest to the moral sense—a movement that represents transformations of one's sense of self-interest and a radically enlarged sense of self. In his philosophical poem "Religious Musings," written in the mid-1790s when he was very much a disciple of Hartley, Coleridge criticizes the "smooth savage" who feels "his own low self the whole; / When he by sacred sympathy might make / The whole one Self!" (ll. 149–58, at 151–53). At the center of Hartley's psychology of development is an account of this transformation—and a challenge to the reader, to put aside the low self for the whole self.

4. The Prism of the Self

Imagination, ambition, and self-interest are the three corners of the first plane. Closest to sensate pleasures and pains are the affections associated with imagination. Under this heading Hartley brings together all the pleasures and pains elicited by our perception of objects. The pleasures, in this case, concern the perception of beauty—however broadly defined—in people, nature, or artifacts. Hartley canvasses the experiences of wonder, delight, and awe people derive from the contemplation of a beautiful person or a grand scene in nature, or from music, painting, and poetry, architecture and manufactures, and such sciences as natural history, astronomy, and philosophy. The child who is delighted by "every little jingle, pun, contrast, or coincidence" is responding to the pleasures of imagination—as is the scientist pursuing the possibility of ancient life on Mars, or the mathematician searching for the most elegant solution to a problem.

In the imaginative orientation, the person's attention is wholly directed outward toward the object, and there may be little awareness of self. A child just emerging from infancy may lack of ego boundaries, a clear sense of self and other; a grey-haired scientist may, through total absorption in her studies, lose herself in the *theoria*—contemplation—that Aristotle (*Nic. Eth.* 1177a12–18) identifies as the noblest of human activities. Ambition, in contrast, represents the contrary orientation. In imagination, the issue is the subject's perception of objects. The pleasures and pains of ambition are the reverse: they concern the subject's perception of others perceiving the self as object. Consequently, imagination and ambition represent two basic orientations: perceiving and being perceived, desiring and being desired, feeling affections and eliciting affections in others.

The pleasures and pains of ambition are those that derive from self-consciousness, from one's awareness of being a separate object of attention for others, and from one's desire to elicit esteem and praise and to avoid scorn, ridicule, and condemnation. The shift, then, is from consciousness directed toward things to the self-consciousness that derives from awareness of being watched, assessed, sized up. As Hartley states, "The opinions of others concerning us, when expressed by corresponding words and actions, are principal sources of happiness and misery" (*OM* 1.4.2.95). The child for whom it has become "a matter of praise ... to be influenced by praise, and deterred by shame" has made the pleasures and pains of ambition a source of her happiness and misery. If they become her principle source, ambition will be what Hartley terms her "primary pursuit" (*OM* 2.3.2.50).

A perfect example of someone for whom ambition is a primary pursuit is Gwendolen Harleth in George Eliot's *Daniel Deronda*. Eliot describes her thus: "She meant to do what was pleasant to herself in a striking manner; or rather, whatever she could do so as to strike others with admiration and get in that reflected way a more ardent sense of living, seemed to please her fancy" ([1876] 1995, 39).

The key element in Hartley's analysis of ambition concerns the difference between "being" and "being thought"—between actually possessing a quality and being perceived as possessing it. To Gwendolen Harleth, it is to the latter that she owes "a more ardent sense of living."

This was also the issue that so troubled Hartley at the beginning of his medical career in London. "I am still anxious and fearful," he confessed, "solicitous to place myself in the most advantageous light; and desirous to *appear* skilful and compassionate, rather than to *be* so" (1810, 39). In the *Observations* he notes that, with regard to "external advantages and disadvantages" as a source of the pleasures and pains of ambition, *being* is irrelevant; it is *being thought* that counts: "Now it is evident, that these external advantages and disadvantages become such by being made known to others; that the first gain men certain privileges and pleasures; and the last subject them to inconveniences and evils only ... when they are discovered to the world" (*OM* 1.4.2.95). Discovery is everything.

As fundamental orientations, imagination and ambition are unreliable sources of pleasure. Whether they give a person pleasure or cause him pain is contingent upon the events in the person's life. People succeed and fail, experience triumphs and disappointments. And vexingly, the ambitious find that even the same discovered quality invites the admiration of some, the scorn of others. Gwendolen Harleth cannot get Daniel Deronda's apparent disapproval out of her mind. What is more, imagination and ambition are demanding, always hungering for more; a person for whom either has become a "primary pursuit" will have trouble knowing when to say *enough*. For the avid collector, how many acquisitions are enough? And for the person hungry for admiration, yesterday's praise is stale. Imagination and ambition do not understand the economics of pleasure: that an allocation of resources that maximizes total return demands that certain projects go unfunded. Neither will they be able to resolve the conflicts that occur when their demands for pleasure are at odds. For a person to function consistently, he must attain a higher perspective; to avoid being beset at every moment by immediate and conflicting demands for pleasure, a person must develop a third orientation that exercises an executive function over imagination and ambition. Hartley calls this third orientation gross self-interest.

Hartley identifies three forms of self-interest—gross, refined, and rational. Gross self-interest relates to "the pursuit of the means for obtaining the pleasures of sensation, imagination, and ambition" (*OM* 2.3.5.65; cf. 1.4.3.96). Its business is to guide a person's conduct so as to maximize the supply of pleasures and to minimize the occurrence of pains. To do so, it must be economical; on occasion, it must countermand the immediate demands of imagination and ambition. Gross self-interest thus represents the "ego" (though Hartley never uses the word) as it seeks to secure the means of satisfying the pleasures of sensation, imagination, and ambition.

Refined self-interest, in turn, concerns "the pursuit of the means of obtaining the pleasures of sympathy, theopathy, and the moral sense" (*OM* 2.3.5.65; cf. 1.4.3.96). Refined self-interest thus represents a higher development of the ego, for it is concerned with securing the pleasures and avoiding the pains that derive from the orientations that form the farther plane of the prism.

Like imagination, sympathy also involves the outward direction of attention and care, though here the person's attention is directed toward other persons, other selves, rather than toward objects. George Eliot describes Daniel Deronda thus: "Daniel had the stamp of rarity in a subdued fervour of sympathy, an activity of imagination on behalf of others, which . . . was continually seen in acts of considerateness that struck his companions as moral eccentricity" ([1876] 1995, 178). Where imagination basically delights in the beauty of the object, sympathy delights in what is good for the other. When it *acts* to further the well-being of other persons, sympathy manifests itself as benevolence.

Similarly, like ambition, theopathy comprises the feelings that derive from one's sense of being a subject of perception and affection; but where ambition focuses on other people's attitudes toward oneself, theopathy is concerned with one's standing in the presence of a divine other—an other whom, in the Judaeo-Christian tradition, we love "because he first loved us" (1 John 4.19). However, in neither sympathy nor theopathy does awareness radiate in one direction only, from observer to observed. Sympathy and theopathy are fundamentally intersubjective, I-thou rather than I-it relations. The low self of the first plane can be a lonely self; the "smooth savage," wrote Coleridge, feels "his own low self the whole." But "sacred sympathy," he continued, makes "the whole one Self."

Also concerned with the prism's farther plane is rational self-interest, which concerns the "pursuit of the means"—in this instance of "such things, as are believed to be the means for obtaining our greatest possible happiness" (*OM* 2.3.5.65; cf. 1.4.3.96). Rational self-interest places one's life within the longest view, the largest possible perspective. For all those who believe that death is not extinction, the perspective is that of eternity. For such, rational self-interest looks to the limitless future and asks, What means must I pursue, to secure eternal happiness? It asks, in a Christian context, What must I do to be saved? At its best, rational self-interest may be a further development of the self, as far beyond refined self-interest as refined is beyond gross. But note the qualification: *as are believed to be*. As we shall see in the next chapter, Hartley describes rational self-interest as often stunted and distorted by what a person believes about death and God, and about what she believes she must do to obtain the greatest possible happiness. For those beset by certain forms of belief and fear, rational self-interest is a torment.

Finally, at the far end of the prism, beyond rational self-interest, there is the moral sense. It grows out of and guides sympathy and theopathy. Serving as "their substitute upon emergent occasions" (*OM* 2.3.8.74), the moral sense is a "monitor" that directs how the person shall act, when prompted by love of neighbor and love of God. When properly developed, the moral sense functions to guide sympathy and theopathy toward their fullest and most effective ends.

5. The Moral Sense

The concept of the moral sense was one that had gained currency in the first decades of the eighteenth century. The term was used by Anthony Ashley Cooper, third Earl of Shaftesbury, in his *Characteristics of Men, Manners, Opinions, Times* ([1711] 1963). The notion was further developed by Francis Hutcheson in his *An Inquiry into the Original of our Ideas of Beauty and Virtue* (1725) and *Essay on the Nature and Conduct of the Passions and Affections, with Illustrations on the Moral Sense* (1728). In their writings, the moral sense is at the heart of a strikingly elegant ethical theory: that good and virtuous actions manifest a beauty to which the natural affections of the human heart spontaneously respond. Our approval of virtue and disgust at vice relies on no inference that the action produces good or bad effects; rather, we possess a capacity to perceive directly the moral quality of actions that is as spontaneous as are our aesthetic perceptions of physical beauty and deformity. Thus, Hutcheson defined the moral sense as "a Determination of our Minds to receive amiable or disagreeable Ideas of Actions, when they shall occur to our Observation, antecedently to any Opinions of Advantage or Loss to redound to our selves of them" (1725, 124). And Shaftesbury writes that in the "characters or pictures of manners, which the mind of necessity figures to itself..., the heart cannot possibly remain neutral; but constantly takes part one way or other. However false or corrupt it be within itself, it finds the difference, as to beauty and comeliness, between one heart and another, one turn of affection, one behaviour, one sentiment and another; and accordingly, in all disinterested cases, must approve in some measure of what is natural and honest, and disapprove of what is dishonest and corrupt" (1963, 1:252). Although Shaftesbury acknowledges that a person's heart can be "false and corrupt," he believes that we "find the difference" between moral beauty and ugliness naturally—and at times despite ourselves. It is said that it is difficult to get a person to see something when his livelihood depends upon his not seeing it; to this point an advocate of the moral sense could reply that the power of a virtuous action can move a person even when he thinks it is his interest to remain insensitive to it.

In the theory developed by Shaftesbury and Hutcheson, the good is lovely, and it is in our nature to love it. It is not the case, however, that the term *good* is merely an expression of emotional approval, a slightly more articulate equivalent of *yumm*. Theirs, in other words, is not an emotivist and relativist theory of ethics, in which personal likes and dislikes, affections and disaffections, are taken to determine what counts as goodness. Rather, that goodness and virtue do manifest a beauty to which we respond is itself a feature of the moral order of the world. Shaftesbury calls himself a "perfect Theist," certain "that everything is governed, ordered, or regulated for the best, by a designing principle or mind, necessarily good and permanent" (1963, 1:240). It is thanks to the governance by this "designing principle" that people can be confident of their responses to moral qualities. Unless they are hopelessly corrupted, their spontaneous moral affections will lead them aright. It is true that, in the absence of a "necessarily good" designer, a theory of the moral sense could decay into an emotivism that isolated individuals within their private assessments of what is good for them; in a culture that abandoned reference to such a designer, *good* could be equated with whatever "feels good to me," and what feels good could be taken to be solely a matter of personal opinion—sealed off, no matter how perverse or self-serving, from public discussion, consensus, or guidance. Carried to an extreme, in such a culture it would become impossible for one person ever to charge another with being perverse or self-serving; making such a charge would be seen as a perversely intrusive expression of personal preference and self-interest. But Shaftesbury's intention is exactly the opposite. Because there is a moral order to the world, the moral sense functions to draw people out of themselves and into a commonality of shared perceptions of value. Each individual has a specific, concrete, and usually limited understanding of his or her present self-interest, and often these definitions of interest are at odds, so that one person's gain is thought to be another's loss. Nonetheless, what we all share in common, according to Shaftesbury and Hutcheson, is a sense that perceives moral qualities whether we want it to or not; "however false or corrupt" a person's heart may be, as a result of the corrosions of selfishness, the person's moral sense "finds the difference, as to beauty and comeliness, between one heart and another." Because it does so, the moral sense sets up "a new trial or exercise of the heart" in the perceiver: he must now follow either the moral perceptions he shares with all human beings or his distorted private preferences (and their privacy will be a measure of their distortion). He will "either rightly and soundly affect what is just and right ... or corruptly affect what is ill and disaffect what is worthy and good" (1963, 1:252).

Theorists of the moral sense envisioned humans living within a providential order; this order guarantees that, by directly sensing the moral qualities of actions and by acting upon that sense without any calculation of profit, a person will be drawn out of selfish isolation and into a common moral world. As she or he is so drawn, a person may at some point realize that the trial of the heart need not be continuous; the person may realize that the affections of the moral sense guide us all toward our own true interest, which is the good we share in common. The person may, in short, comprehend what Hartley affirmed in his letters to John Lister, quoted in chapter 2: that private happiness, public good, and the will of God are three terms for the one reality. "The wisdom of what rules," Shaftesbury writes, "and is first and chief in Nature, has made it to be according to the private interest and good of every one to work towards the general good, which if a creature ceases to promote, he ... ceases to promote his own happiness and welfare. He is on this account directly his own enemy, nor can he any otherwise be good or useful to himself than as he continues good to society, and to that whole of which he himself is a part" (1963, 1:338). We are all parts of the main, and we diminish ourselves whenever we ignore this fact.

By stating his conviction to John Lister that private happiness, public good, and the will of God coincide like three different definitions of a right triangle, Hartley was expressing his allegiance to an ethical theory already articulated by Shaftesbury and Hutcheson. And by making the moral sense the "monitor" of sympathy and theopathy, the apex of the farther plane of the prism, he affirmed his conviction that a person could, and ultimately should, transcend all forms of self-interest. Such transcendence is an aspect of what he terms the "annihilation of self" (see chapter 9). Still, a difficulty with the theory of the moral sense was that Shaftesbury and Hutcheson appeared to offer no account of how the moral sense comes to be; in their writings, it sounds as if the moral sense were simply an instinct. John Gay, although he acknowledged "the Matter of Fact, *i.e.* that the generality of Mankind do approve of Virtue, or rather virtuous Actions, without being able to give any Reason for their Approbation," nonetheless thought that "this Account seems still insufficient, rather cutting the Knot than untying it, and if it is not akin to the Doctrine of *Innate Ideas,* yet I think it relishes too much of that of *Occult Qualities*" (1731, xxx). The fact that people are generally unable to give reasons *for* their approbations does not mean that the reasons *why* people approve what they do are inexplicable or inaccessible. Rather, the fact that people approve of virtue without being able to give reasons for their approbation is precisely what needs explaining. As we noted above, Gay recommended untying the knot by resolving "our Approbation of Morality, and all Affections whatever" either into "*Reason* pointing out *private Happiness*" or into "the *Association of Ideas,*" in which case such affections "may properly enough be call'd *Habits*" (xxxi). Hartley, in turn, took up Gay's brief suggestion and attempted to develop it systematically, though, again, in a way quite different from the one Gay originally suggested. He wrote, he informed Lister, "two small Treatises" in 1734, which he entitled "The Progress of Happiness deduced from Reason —— & from Scripture." He added that "the first begins with shewing that all our Intellectual Pleasures & Pains are formed either immediately or mediately from sensible ones by Association." That we love and can reason about our loving are capacities that are themselves generated by the power of association. Hartley continues: "It then proceeds to show that Benevolence is the best means of obtaining private Happiness, that this naturally leads us to the love of God, that our Natures are so formed & so adjusted to the System of things that we must from the Law of Association at last become benevolent, & consequently that all must some time or other be happy" (*L* 4; see §2.5).

Hartley thus sought, in his 1734 treatises, to account for the development of the moral sense. Where Shaftesbury had simply affirmed his belief in the moral governance of the world, and where Gay had appealed first to "reason pointing out private happiness," Hartley wished to demonstrate how, through a psychological law as uniform in operation as is the law of gravitation in celestial mechanics, "our Natures are so formed & so adjusted to the System of things" as to eventually become benevolent and consequently happy—even though, it is important to note, our actions and thoughts cannot be attributed to "an essential, original, perpetual desire of happiness, and endeavour to attain it; but much rather to the factitious associated desires and endeavours here asserted" (*OM* 1.3.3.89). Hartley, in other words, sought to explain the growth of the prism without appealing to a teleological principle. Our natures are so formed that we will become whole selves, embodiments of sympathy, theopathy, and the moral sense, but that condition is neither understood nor desired by the infants we once were or the low selves we become.

Hartley's *Observations* was published fifteen years after he had written his two treatises on the progress of happiness. The continuity and consistency of his thinking is worth noting; the two sentences describing the plan of his first treatise are equally applicable to the *Observations*. Thus, one way to read the *Observations* is to see it as an extended and detailed account of how sympathy, theopathy, and the moral sense come to full development. We noted above that Hartley can be understood as answering the question, How does the child learn to love? We can now refine this by saying that Hartley's work can be understood as answering the question, How does the person learn to love the good—and to act upon that love? As we shall see, the process is a highly complex one, filled with paradox, conflict, and indirection.

6. The Self as Dynamic System

Hartley suggests that the six classes of intellectual pleasures and pains represent an epigenetic sequence. It would seem to follow from this that the six classes should appear in chronological order. However, Hartley does not say that infants are first aware of things, then of themselves as objects of attention, then of others as other selves, and then of the other Self that is God. Very young children play with their favorite toys, are pleased when they are praised, cling to their mothers and fathers, and are taken to church and taught to say their prayers. As we observed above concerning the emergence of imagination and ambition, Hartley includes in his discussion of each class an account of the first appearance of pleasures and pains of that class in early childhood. Imagination, ambition, self-interest, sympathy, theopathy, and the moral sense are all simultaneously present in their "nascent" forms in the earliest

The Emergence of the Self

stages of life. At every stage of life, the prism that stretches from the plane of imagination, ambition, and gross self-interest to the plane of sympathy, theopathy, and the moral sense is the matrix of the self.

In what sense, then, are the six classes epigenetic? Although the matrix is a structural constant, the crystal of personhood that grows upon it forms and then forms again, as the fluid of experience accretes into the material of the self. As the years pass, first one facet and then another becomes the dominant feature of the crystal. In a young person, imagination and then ambition will be primary pursuits (*OM* 1.4.1.94). Later in life, sympathy and theopathy may gain prominence—if they do gain prominence. (Because it "rises late," refined self-interest "is never of any great magnitude in the bulk of mankind,... and in some it scarce prevails at all" [*OM* 1.4.3.96].) But for an orientation to be a functionally effective primary pursuit that defines the character of the person, that orientation must attain a complete form. This is especially true of sympathy and theopathy. An attempt, for example, to accomplish an "annihilation" of self, whether in an ashram or monastery, may only harm a person whose sense of self-interest is incomplete. The facets of imagination and ambition must develop, as must the self-interest that manages them, so that facets of sympathy and theopathy may later reach completeness.

The six classes of intellectual affections thus represent an epigenetic sequence of development—but a sequence that arises out of elements that are present simultaneously, as structural elements, throughout virtually all of a person's life. In the metaphor used above, these elements are the matrix upon which the crystal grows. But this is just a metaphor. It is essential here to note that the self of a person, in Hartley's theory, does not have the rigidity we normally associate with a crystalline structure. Imagination, ambition, sympathy, and theopathy do not constitute closed sets of affections that have no influence on each other. Because they are epigenetic, each class exists in reference to the classes from which it is "generated." But because they are simultaneously present, each class also reciprocally affects the others related to it. Imagination generates ambition, but one's ambitions in turn affect how one experiences imaginative pleasure. To use Hartley's language, each class, working in concert with sensation and the other existing classes, "generates" and "models" the next class in the sequence; but so also does each class "new-model" (*OM* 1.3.3.89) the other classes. The image of the prism, in other words, is not static but internally dynamic; the self it models needs to be understood as a complex and dynamic system, in which each orientation interacts with the others at all times. Its six elements are similar to the hexagrams in the *I Ching*. In the hexagrams, the movement of one line from solid to broken or vice versa effects a permutation into another pattern, another interpretation of *ming*; in Hartley's six classes, movement in any one class has the potential to stimulate movement in all the others—and thereby to effect a transformation of one pattern of self into another, which may bring with it a radically new understanding of one's destiny.

Consider, for example, what Hartley says about the first stirrings of sympathy in childhood. And as you read this, think of the Hartleys' children; think of what David, Mary, and Winchcombe saw and suffered, when they witnessed their mother repeatedly ill, possibly with asthma, and their father clenched by the pain of the stone:

> Compassion . . . in children seems to be grounded upon such associations as these that follow: The very appearance and idea of any kind of misery which they have experienced, or of any signs of distress which they understand, raise up in their nervous systems a state of misery from mere memory, on account of the strength of their imaginations; and because the connexion between the adjuncts of pain, and the actual infliction of it, has not yet been sufficiently broken by experience, as in adults.—When several children are educated together, the pains, the denials of pleasures, and the sorrows, which affect one, generally extend to all to some degree, often to an equal one.—When their parents, attendants, &c. are sick or afflicted, it is usual to raise in their minds the nascent ideas of pains and miseries, by such words and signs as are suited to their capacities; they also find themselves laid under many restraints on this account.—And when these and such-like circumstances have raised the desires and endeavors to remove the causes of these their own internal uneasy feelings, or, which is the same thing, of these miseries of others (in which they are much influenced, as in other like cases, by the great disposition to imitate, before spoken of) . . . the child may properly be said to have compassion. (*OM* 1.4.4.97)

The child's compassion is initially dependent upon the pains of imagination. It is grounded in the child's own memories of misery: the appearance of misery in another evokes a memory of the child's own experience of pain or illness, and a flood of misery again whelms the child. Such sympathy depends upon the close connection of, and inability to distinguish between, image and reality, so that the misery and fear attending the "actual infliction" of pain are spontaneously transferred to the "adjuncts" of it. It includes the "restraints" the child is put under, on account of another's incapacity. And it relies especially upon the absence of ego boundaries that is characteristic of imagination; lacking such boundaries, the child will associate all experiences of pain and misery with all others. Fundamentally, the child feels compassion for the other because the child does not sharply differentiate self from other: when confronted with suffering, children endeavor "to remove the causes of these their own internal uneasy feelings, or... of these miseries of others"—"which is the same thing."

As the child grows, she develops other motivations for sympathetic actions. A disposition toward "benevolence" is reinforced by the "high degree of honour and esteem annexed to it, [and from the fact that it] procures us many advantages, and returns of kindness, both from the person obliged and others; and is most closely connected with the hope of reward in a future state, and with the pleasures of religion, and of self-approbation, or the moral sense." Hence, the sympathetic passion of benevolence gains reinforcement from "the honour and esteem annexed to it" that constitute one of the pleasures of ambition, and from the "many advantages" that delight the child's sense of gross self-interest. And eventually, "benevolence," like all the genuine sympathetic passions, will direct the maturing person toward theopathy and the moral sense and provide reinforcement for them in turn.

There is, then, an imaginative version of sympathy, based on spontaneous imitation and identification, upon the absence of clearly demarcated ego boundaries; an ambitious version, based upon a person's gratification at being praised for sympathetic acts and upon her desire to be thought sympathetic, so that such praise will continue; and a self-interested version, derived from a person's calculation that being thought sympathetic can be profitable in his dealings with others. In each instance, there are pleasures and pains that can be considered sympathetic, even though these sympathetic affections are subsidiary to the person's quite different primary pursuit.[1]

Finally, though, there is genuine, fully developed sympathy—the true form that emerges when sympathy itself becomes one's primary pursuit. And Hartley states that it should be one's eventual goal to make this authentic form of sympathy one's spring of action. This goal is attainable, again, through the transference of affection. For a person at the requisite level of development, the pleasure that derives from being thought sympathetic, or from the profits that accrue from acting in a sympathetic manner, may transfer themselves directly to the acts that flow out of *being* sympathetic. Although one may begin acting in a sympathetic manner in order to obtain the pleasures of imagination, ambition, or self-interest, when the person becomes habituated to the actions and attitudes of sympathy, those actions and attitudes may become expressions of one's character—and a direct source of pleasure. And when one has been too long mired in the tangled and fragmenting and arid conflicts generated by imagination and ambition, finally making true sympathy one's primary pursuit will be a solution to the crisis of the self—and a pleasurable relief. On this point, Hartley's theory is consistent with Aristotle's observations that "moral virtue is formed by habit [*ethos*]" (*Nich. Eth.* 2.1, 1103a15) and, further, that it is in the character of the virtuous person to enjoy acting in a virtuous manner. Through the transference of affection that comes when the practice of sympathy becomes habitual, one attains the "love that seeketh not itself to please" that characterizes the Clod of Clay in Blake's "The Clod and the Pebble," and one loves with that love simply for the sake of building "a heaven in hell's despair." One loves others for their own sakes—and for the sake of the good in them.

But equally importantly, when the goal of genuine sympathy is attained, the quality of one's imagination, ambition, and self-interest are also "new-modeled" and transformed. There is thus, in Hartley's theory, a upward movement, as each class comes to be "generated," and a downward movement, as each new class transforms or "new-models" all the others below it. Just as there are imaginative, ambitious, and self-interested versions of sympathy, there are also sympathetic forms of imagination, ambition, and self-interest. Turn the prism of self so that the smaller end is facing you. The smaller, closer surface will now be framed within the body of the prism, as it expands toward the larger, farther plane.

That imagination is new-modeled by sympathy does not mean that the person of sympathetic character no longer delights in beauty. Rather, such a person gains, through the chemistry of affection, a new quality of imagination. What gives imaginative pleasure is now different from what gave pleasure when imagination was a primary pursuit. The beauty of the world is perceived in a new light; what was dark before may now be luminous. Physical beauty may now be discovered shining forth in people and things previously passed over with indifference or contempt.

What changes then, as the child's black locks or flaxen ringlets gradually turn white, are the qualitative contents of the six classes and the distributions of emotion amongst them. As we saw above, each class is largely constituted through and mediated by language; imagination, ambition, etc. are "clusters," or clusters of clusters, analogous to the "molecules" and "molecules of molecules" that form a nerve or indeed any physical object. Although every person possesses the orientations represented by the six classes, memories and words are continuously added to and constellated in each class, so that the crystalline form of each person's self will be unique—and subject to transformation. In addition, what counts as pleasure and pain in a given orientation is variable, changing, and dependent upon the evaluation supplied by the person's current sense of self-interest. Pleasures of imagination can extend from pretty dolls and plastic action heros to attempts to come to grips with the theory of superstrings, Thomas Bayes's contribution to the theory of probability, or the issue of whether Gerald Edelman's theory of neuronal group selection is a good way to model the biological basis of consciousness. Similarly, the pains of ambition can be felt in response to being thought poor, or plain, or dim, or deviant.

New discoveries mean new affections, and these provide the material for further associations and transferences. The process is continuously interactive: the ascent upward that models the classes and the subsequent descent by which the lower classes are new-modeled are repetitive and dynamic. Just as new discoveries of beauty lead to new affections, so also do the transformed senses of ambition and self-interest; and the new qualities of affection that derive from these may be transferred to one's sympathy, further refining it. But the cycle may again repeat, as that refined sympathy will in turn work upon imagination, ambition, and self-interest. In this process, a new quality of perception or action at any level can act transformatively upon the other classes. And out of this process, "At last, by the numerous reciprocal influences of all these [six classes] upon each other, the passions arrive at that degree of complexness, which is to be observed in fact, and which makes them so difficult to be analyzed" (*OM* 1.3.3.89).

It is no wonder that a person's passions and motivations are so resistant to analysis. Some are original and primitive, others late developing and refined, still others new-modeled, reformed. Together, these form the facets of the prism of the self. And the self thus formed is not only structurally complex; it is also vibrating with pleasures and pains, as the six classes transform, and are transformed, by each other. It is no wonder that one's *self* is so resistant to analysis.

8

Transformations of the Self

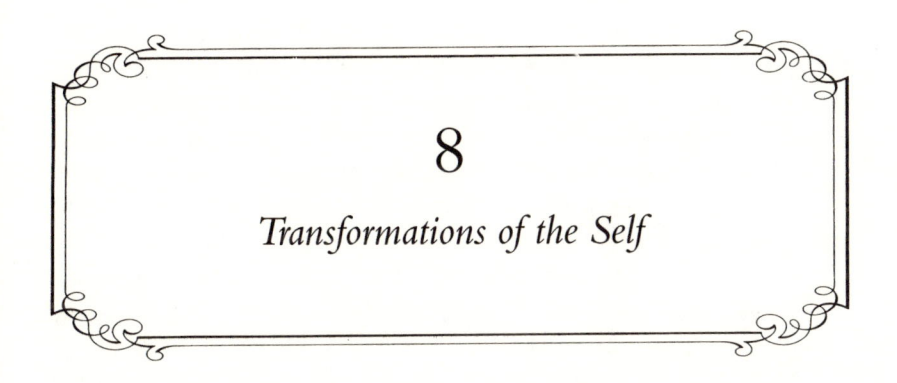

As anyone familiar with Stephen Hales's chemical experiments would have known, even the hardest pebbles bind within themselves huge amounts of air. If observed minutely, such concretions, seemingly static, would be seen to tremble with internal tensions. The observer would understand that their condition of stasis depends upon an equilibrium between the forces of attraction and repulsion within them. The observer would also understand that a change in these forces' "spheres of attraction and repulsion" could effect fundamental reconfigurations of their structures—and hence in the qualities they display.

These observations also hold true of the prism of self. In Hartley's psychological chemistry, a simple repetitive process generates a dynamic system: transferences of emotion among clusters of words, narratives, and symbols create the orientations of imagination, ambition, and self-interest, of sympathy, theopathy, and the moral sense. The crystal grows.

Like any pebble, the crystalline prism of self also vibrates with internal tensions, for it too is held in a state of semi-stasis by the equilibrium of the forces of attraction and repulsion within it. But there is a profound difference between pebbles and people. We are conscious beings, gifted with language. We are capable of understanding and affection. And because "the understanding and affections are not really distinct things, but only different names, which we give to the same kind of motions in the nervous system" (*OM* 1.3.2.87; see §6.9 and 7.2), what we understand is guided by what we feel, just as what we feel depends upon what we understand. The emotional tensions with which we vibrate are tensions of meaning.

As conscious beings, we remember—what matters. When we plan to do something, we remember the future, and when things are done, we "new-model" the past—including the past sense of self. The "numerous reciprocal influences" (*OM* 1.3.3.89) of our highly complex passions enable us to say *self* in new and often elaborate ways. Discovering and articulating new senses of the self is thus an essential aspect of having a self; a person who lacked the capacities for discovery and articulation would be unable to learn from his experiences, evaluate the meaning of what he felt, reevaluate his sense of self, and thereby extend the horizons of his concern. A person who fossilized into a truly perfect and immobile pebble would be condemned to a rigid and impoverished life, lacking in understanding and affection.

So, how do we develop and change? Broaden and enrich our awareness? Redefine our senses of self-interest? Comprehend tensions of meaning? New-model ourselves? Learn to love?

1. Imagination

Laughter, according to Hartley, is "a nascent cry, stopped of a sudden" (*OM* 1.4.1.94). And as we noted in §7.1, although children originally laugh in response to physical stimuli, the range of stimuli rapidly expands to include those that are social and symbolic: "As children learn the use of language, they learn also to laugh at sentences or stories, by which sudden alarming emotions and expectations are raised in them, and again dissipated instantaneously." The alarm is dissipated because the disruptive element in the story, like the "representations of battles, storms, wild beasts, and other objects of horror" that pleasingly appall even adults, is not an actual threat; "the secret consciousness of our own security" protects us from the passions that would flood over us were we to face the realities the representations depict. Because we know we are secure, the things that could cause fear "by degrees pass into pleasures by suggesting the security from pain." Part of the pleasure of being high up a mountainside comes from knowing it is a long way down—and that you are safely on top of the situation.

More generally, imaginative pleasure derives from the presence of an element of disruption within an overall context of order. An element of surprise or fear in a context of security is one such source of pleasure; another is the interplay of "uniformity and variety" in poetry. Both music and poetry set up patterns, or rely upon rules—which are "violated at proper intervals." In music the disruptions are achieved through the introduction of discords, which "are originally unpleasant, and, therefore, . . . may be made use of to heighten our pleasures." With repeated hearing, these "become less and less harsh to the ear, and at last even pleasant, at least by their associations with the concords"; consequently, for the experienced musician, "more harsh discords, are perpetually required to give a relish, and keep the sweetness of the concords from cloying." Although poetry also derives some of its beauty from the interplay of uniformity and variety in meter and rhyme, it above all relies on figurative language, in which words "seem to strike and please us chiefly from that impropriety which appears at first sight, upon their application to things denoted by them, and from the consequent heightening of the propriety, as soon as it is duly perceived." We are at first surprised by an unexpected and at first glance inappropriate use of a word or image; only with a second or third or fourth reading does the "heightening of the propriety" occur, when we realize that the figure is exactly right.

The dynamics of surprise and security, disruption and order, variety and uniformity are common to the child who laughs at jingles, the youth with a passion for horror films, and the adult who derives his supreme delight from reading Shakespeare or listening to Beethoven. All experience the pleasures of imagination. Accordingly, Hartley cautions against applying too rigid a standard of aesthetic judgment, and especially against universalizing the standards of one's own time and place: "According to the foregoing history of the pleasures of imagination, there must be great differences in the tastes and judgments of different persons; and that no age, nation, class of men, &c. ought to be made the test of what is most excellent in artificial beauty; nor consequently what is absurd."

Hartley, however, does not conclude that within a culture all such pleasures are indifferently equal; he would not agree with Bentham's remark that "push-pin is as good as poetry." An adult, for example, who persisted in a child's delight in "every little jingle, pun, contrast, or coincidence" would become a crank, a Tristram Shandy or a Mr. Bennet in Austen's *Pride and Prejudice*. Such a person, "by the perpetual hunting after apparent and partial agreements and disagreements, as in words, and indirect accidental circumstances, whilst the true natures of things themselves afford real agreements and disagreements," would eventually "pervert his notions of things themselves, and become unable to see them as they really are." It is this concern with the perception of things "as they really are" that displays the scientific cast of Hartley's imagination. In one conversation with John Byrom, Hartley mused that people of a future age may "think that that book that does not inform them of the nature of the world is all babble"—and then averred that even in the present age "all that taste mathematics quit poetry and such nonsense" (*B* 2.1.109–10). In Hartley's view, gaining the knowledge of things, through patient investigation and inquiry, affords a quality of pleasure that verbal contrasts of uniformity and variety can never attain. Hence the aesthetics of scientific inquiry, which derives both from the struggle to discover a deep and previously unthought pattern and also from the awareness that this pattern is indeed dis-covered, real, not just apparent. The scientist knows, with Heraclitus, that "hidden harmonies are sweetest." But what is most striking about these harmonies is how discordant they often appear at first to be. "The novel, the grand, and the marvellous" are, Hartley writes, "most conspicuous in the works of nature." The artist, poet, or storyteller must search for the original but appropriate disruptions that at first surprise but then heighten the propriety. But the explorer of the realms of nature is continually compelled to marvel at the way in which new discoveries disrupt present expectations. The "phaenomena of nature" strike us as objects of wonder "by seeming to exceed all bounds of credibility, at the same time that we are certified by irrefragable evidences of the truth of the facts." No human art, Hartley seems to say, can match nature's capacity for heightening the propriety. Why *do* quarks come in six colors?

2. Ambition

The pleasures of sensation and imagination in turn generate the pleasures of ambition. Hartley makes this point through an analysis of the significance of dress. He states that "fine cloaths please both children and adults, by their natural or artificial beauty; they enhance the beauty of the person; they excite the compliments and caresses of the attendants in a peculiarly vivid manner" (*OM* 1.4.2.95). In addition to being perceived as objects or enhancements of beauty, clothes also take on a symbolic character: "they are the common associates of riches, titles, and high-birth; they have vast encomiums bestowed upon them; and are sometimes the rewards of mental accomplishments and virtue," so that "these pleasures and pains, which thus attend a person's being actually dressed in fine cloaths... will, by farther associations, be transferred upon all the concomitant circumstances, the possession of fine cloaths, the hopes of them, or the fear of rags; and particularly upon all narrations and symbols, whereby others are first informed of the person's dress...; so that the person shall have his vanity gratified, or his shame excited, by all such narrations, and by all the concomitant circumstances and symbols." A pleasure of imagination is thus first extended to a variety of "concomitant circumstances" and then transformed into a pleasure of ambition. The pleasure of wearing a beautiful garment is transferred to "narrations and symbols, whereby others are first informed of the person's dress": from the cloth to the designer's label, and, for those who set the fashion, to the narrations about themselves in the relevant magazines. Just as the child in the nursery praises himself for being thought the kind of child who can be influenced by praise, here the fashionable admire themselves for their being thought to be fluent in and responsive to the symbolic language of fashion.

Because items of clothing are often the "common associates of riches, titles, and high-birth... and are sometimes the rewards of mental accomplishments and virtue," they also function as emblems of status that link with "narrations and symbols" that have a significance that far surpasses the self-referential language of fashion. The emblems of status a person is able to display are "marks" that stand for associated clusters or complexes of ideas that refer to the "privileges and pleasures" that are the property of the marked status. Wearing a stethoscope around one's neck may, for a physician on her rounds, be a matter of convenience; but it is also a "mark" that signals an entire complex of privileges and pleasures—authority based on extensive training, a high position in the hierarchy of a hospital, a commitment to healing, but also possibly a six-figure income and that income's attendant luxuries. And whoever sees the stethoscope may be reminded of some combination of those ideas. Nonetheless, the point remains that an emblem's power depends upon others, and upon what they make of it. An external advantage is no advantage if others do not recognize or respect it. Gulliver receives the title of *Nardac*—the highest honor in the empire of Lilliput—for towing away the Blefuscuian fleet, but the title brings no advantage beyond the borders of that realm; by aggravating the envy and malice of the hero's enemies, it even contributes to the conspiracy against him there.

Many of the pleasures that come from being a physician are initially pleasures of imagination. A condominium in Aspen, or a second home on the Maine coast, could be sources of imaginative pleasure; so also could the continuing process of medical education and research, for one whose imaginative pleasures are centered on "the study of the sciences" (*OM* 1.4.1.94). But, as we noted above regarding the child for whom being thought responsive to praise and blame is itself a reason for praise, imagination generates ambition reflexively, through the transference of affection. The satisfaction derived from vacations in Maine, or the exhilaration that accompanies progress in research, may transfer to the discovery of them and hence to the symbols that enable others to make that discovery. Draping a stethoscope around one's neck may itself become a source of pleasure. If this transference happens, the pleasure of owning the condo or doing research may also shift from *being* to *being thought*—from actually doing so, to being known to do so—in which case the condo and the research attain a symbolic value of their own, as emblems respectively of "external advantages" and "intellectual accomplishments." And here it is possible that someone may transfer much of her emotional capital from her old account to the new one. The person for whom stethoscope, condo, and research project are pleasurable primarily as symbols, as marks that function as means for directing how others shall think about her, has made the pleasures of ambition her primary pursuit.

3. Gross Self-Interest: "This Labyrinth of Error and Anxiety"

It is the task of gross self-interest to secure the means of satisfying the demands of sensation, imagination, and ambition. As the "pursuit of means" of gaining pleasure and avoiding pain, gross self-interest generally is not a separate source of pleasure unto itself. The pleasure a person takes, for example, in winning a lottery derives from her anticipation of the pleasures of sensation, imagination, and ambition that will now be available to her. Moreover, her sense of her own self-interest will depend upon what she conceives to be the sources of pleasure and pain for her: one lottery winner may imagine spending the money immediately on a convertible with leather seats, a brand-new Tudor manor in the suburbs, a few weeks of pampered luxury at an exclusive Caribbean resort; a second winner may pay off what she owes on her Ford Escort, book a whale-watching cruise in Alaska, and start thinking about developing a herd of milking ewes. In either case, gross self-interest functions as an ego that manages the supply of pleasure. It also represents the ego in the sense that it is compounded out of the person's evaluations of what will, in fact, give her pleasure. Her sense of her self-interest—of what constitutes for her the pleasures and pains of sensation, imagination, and ambition—contributes greatly to her sense of self.

The trouble is, the low self that gross self-interest attempts to manage is inherently unmanageable. As primary pursuits, imagination and ambition both demand a continuous supply of pleasure; but it is in the nature of these pleasures to deteriorate; consequently, providing a continuous supply of them will be an increasingly difficult task. In the fable of the grasshopper and the ant, the grasshopper, with the pleasures of the imagination as his primary pursuit, mocks the ant's industry and only learns his lesson when he is left friendless and freezing at the onset of winter. But in a Hartleian telling of the story, the pains that arise from making imagination a primary pursuit are not merely accidents of the weather; they are themselves generated by the exclusive pursuit of imaginative and sensate pleasures. To attempt to overcome these pains by means of the pursuit of still more imaginative pleasures will only multiply the pains endured.

In Hartley's understanding of the physics of vibrating media (§3.5 and 6), the mechanical fatigue that results from continued stimulation will lead to a nonreformable deformation of the medium; in neural harmonics, the creation of such an induced state accounts both for an increase in acuity and for a loss of hedonic intensity. Hence the deterioration, or decay, of pleasure: while one becomes ever more sensitized to the objects of pleasure, the feelings of pleasure derived from these objects progressively diminish. For the cultivated grasshopper who devotes himself to "the study of the polite arts, or of science, or to any other pleasure of mere imagination," the result is the simultaneous hyperrefinement and dulling of experience. The grasshopper develops an ever more acute capacity of discrimination in his area of interest, but the pleasures he takes in his objects of study continuously drop below the threshold that separates pleasure from indifference.

Moreover, although "the frequent repetition of these pleasures cloys" (*OM* 2.3.1.55), the same cannot be said of the pains that accompany their pursuit. It is, in general, the interplay of "unity and variety" that gives imaginative pleasure, but once experienced, the unexpected becomes expected, and variety is assimilated into unity. To maintain the experience above the limit of pleasure, the pursuer of imaginative pleasure must continually search for new surprises, new, more piquant mixtures of uniformity and variety. But when most everything has been experienced and is consequently expected, discovering the unexpected becomes progressively harder, and the remaining sources of pleasure ever more recondite: "And it is not uncommon to see men, after a long and immoderate pursuit of one class of beauty, natural or artificial, deviate into such by-paths and singularities, as that these objects excite pain rather than pleasure; their limits for excellence being narrow, and their rules absurd; and all that falls short of these, being condemned by them, as deformed and monstrous" (*OM* 2.3.1.54). As one's "limits for excellence" grow increasingly narrow, the source of pleasure becomes more and more often the occasion of pain: the audiophile with his thousands of recordings can barely endure his community symphony orchestra; his meticulously selected collection of the truly great recordings sets limits to excellence that render anything less "deformed" and "monstrous." And most of what he hears, when he can bear to listen, is less.

The exclusive pursuit of one type of pleasure thus generates "counterassociations"—in this instance, experiences of pain or indifference where one anticipated pleasure (see §1.7). And thanks to the fact that they do generate counterassociations, the orientations of imagination and ambition tend to be self-correcting. Although a person's "long and immoderate pursuit of one class of beauty" can cause him to "deviate into by-paths and singularities," the thickets of thorns he encounters there push him back toward a common path. It is pleasanter to walk in a place where the limits for excellence are not narrow, nor the rules absurd.

Such counterassociations are analogous to the forces of repulsion in the chemical theory of Stephen Hales. Recall that, in Hales's chemistry, air can be either bound or released. Bladder stones form as air is fixed in a concretion, but drop one into caustic potash and it will "ferment." In Hartley's psychology, there is an analogous binding and release: association cements experiences together into ideas, orientations, senses of self; but counterassociations cause the fermentation of ideas, orientations, one's sense of self. To Hales, the dynamic interaction of the forces of attraction and repulsion in matter maintains "this beautiful frame of things... in a continual round of the production and dissolution of animal and vegetable bodies" (Hales 1769, 1:314–15). To Hartley, the dynamic interaction of associations and counterassociations maintains the beautiful frame of the psyche in a continual round of production and dissolution. Like our dreams, which dissolve the associations that are "cemented by continuance" during the day, counterassociations deriving from imagination and ambition keep us from the rigid and paralytic madness that would encase us, were the cement of association to spread unchecked. As long as the balance is maintained, the person's psychological "frame" also continues in a condition of dynamic semistasis. The self remains sane—and open to transformation.

So, let us imagine a grasshopper with some potential, unlike the foolish one in the original story. Thanks to his counterassociations, he realizes that having the most discriminating taste for the rarest leaves has made most dining experiences unpleasant; ordinary timothy is tasteless, and besides, his grumblings about it are beginning to cost him friends. Imagine this clever grasshopper awakening to the possibilities of higher forms of imaginative pleasure, and also to the pleasures and pains of ambition that go with them. He decides to become someone, a doer and a builder, an intellectually accomplished insect. He settles down to emulate the ant—and wonders how he could have wasted so much time in the tedious tasting of grass. He would agree with Hartley that "it is evident that luxury, self-indulgence, and an indolent aversion to perform the duties of a man's station, do not only bring upon gross bodily diseases; but also... are often apt to lead men into such a degree of solicitude, anxiety, and fearfulness, in minute affairs, as to make them inflict upon themselves greater torments, than the most cruel tyrant could invent" (*OM* 2.3.1.54). When awakened and freed from "this self-tormenting state, this labyrinth of error and anxiety," he sees things in a new way, and what would have been occasions of suffering—long hours of study and labor, or the scorn of the dissolute locusts he once counted as his friends—now pain him no longer. Instead, he realizes that what had seemed to be the sweetest pleasures of his former life were in fact the most insidious forms of self-inflicted torture.

The grasshopper has come to a new way of evaluating his self-interest, and consequently to a new understanding of his self. This higher stage of imagination and ambition, however, although it transcends the fission of experience into the pleasures and pains felt before, also generates new pleasures and pains that are unique to itself. The ant has worries the grasshopper never dreamed of. And these are as unresolvable in terms of the grasshopper's new sense of self-interest as the pleasures and pains of being an epicure of grasses were in terms of the sense of self-interest he left behind. In Hartley's psychology, this continuing splitting of experience into the states of pleasure and pain becomes harder to bear, and the person's gross self-interest has an increasingly difficult task in trying to satisfy and reconcile imagination and ambition's irreconcilable demands. Defining oneself through gross self-interest proves, ultimately, to be a profoundly ineffectual and unsatisfying form of life.

The fissile pleasures and pains of imagination insensibly transfer onto ambition; and the more elevated the form of imaginative interest, the more thoroughly do the attendant pains of ambition cripple the self. "Eminent votaries of this kind," Hartley writes of those who have conducted "a long and immoderate pursuit of one class of beauty," are "peculiarly liable to vanity, self-conceit, censoriousness, moroseness, jealousy, and envy; which surely are uneasy companions in a man's breast, as well as the occasion of many insults and harms from abroad" (*OM* 2.3.1.55). No one, simply put, wants to invite the sniffing gourmet to dinner—including the gourmet himself. This distorting effect on character is even more acute in people who devote themselves not to cooking but to chemistry: Hartley writes of the danger that "the study of science, without a view to God or our duty, and from a vain desire of applause, will get possession of our hearts, engross them wholly, and by taking deeper root than the pursuit of vain amusements, become in the end a much more dangerous and obstinate evil than that. Nothing can easily exceed the vain glory, self-conceit, arrogance, emulation, and envy, that are found in the eminent professors of the sciences, mathematics, natural philosophy, and even divinity itself" (*OM* 2.3.3.60). Ambitions relating to external advantages or to bodily perfections are bad enough, but it is the sensitivities bred of ambitions concerning intellectual accomplishments that can most deform a person's character, make intellectual work a loveless task, and render life a misery for oneself and others.

It may be too much to expect the lottery winner to work this out while she is on a Caribbean beach or on the deck of a ship off the coast of Alaska. But even if she is temperamentally inclined to being an ant, some time after receiving the first payment the lottery winner may begin to realize that there is little happiness in the pursuit of pleasure, no matter how apparently ethical or elevated, when the rewards benefit no one but the self. Looking into the weary eyes of her deferent servants—

the maid who makes her bed, the waiter who brings another glass of wine—she may wonder about their lives, their homes, their families. And she may then begin to see that great wealth brings with it a great responsibility, and that it is now her responsibility to use her wealth in a way that gives something back. She may come to the understanding that her wealth will never truly benefit her until it benefits others besides herself.

When she comes to this realization, her evaluation of the sources of pleasure will have again changed, and her sense of self-interest changed as well. She will become aware of the potentiality of a whole new way of being, a new way that has nonetheless been with her always: the way of fully being the glowing self that sleeps and waits within her. No longer restless and distracted, no longer overcome and exhausted by the pursuit of the means for supplying imagination's and ambition's pleasures, her sense of self-interest will begin to reorient itself and steady itself. As she becomes concerned with "the pursuit of the means of obtaining the pleasures of sympathy, theopathy, and the moral sense" (OM 2.3.5.65; cf. 1.4.3.96), her sense of self-interest will be poised to pass from being "gross" to being "refined."

4. Refined Self-Interest: Aiming at Sympathy and Theopathy

The transition from gross to refined self-interest marks the point at which a person ceases to identify with the low self of imagination and ambition and instead finds a new identity in the whole self of sympathy, theopathy, and the moral sense. After having a taste of what life would be like as a perpetual holiday, the lottery winner undergoes this transformation when she realizes that, to make her life worth living, she must not bury her talents in the earth of selfish consumption; that, to be whole, she must give of herself. This new sense of self, and vision of a life devoted to active benevolence, does not obliterate imagination and ambition as sources of pleasure. Rather, it "new-models" them; she now begins to discover beauty in people and things she never before cared to notice, and her vanity is gratified—somewhat to her discomfort—when she perceives that others admire her selflessness. She now perceives and understands the world and herself in ways that, from the perspective of her earlier life, would have been literally inconceivable. Still, her realization that contributing to the happiness of others is what makes her happy often leaves her feeling uncomfortable, and sometimes miserable. Sympathy, theopathy, and the moral sense can also generate associations and counterassociations, and hence split experience into states of pleasure and pain. Reports of cruelty and injustice, of famine and massacre, make her feel inadequate to the task; she accuses herself concerning the luxuries she allows herself; and she discovers herself feeling resentful and disapproving of the thoughtlessness, triviality, egotism, and wastefulness of all the locusts clattering about her. At times she feels an almost demonic rage: her longing to create a better world almost leads her to wish that this one be burned up. What shall she do? How shall she act, to be a whole self?

The person motivated by refined self-interest has chosen to follow the guidance of sympathy, theopathy, and the moral sense in her actions. But recall Hartley's point that "all our voluntary actions are of the nature of memory" (*OM* 1.2.4.90; see §4.5). What we are capable of doing voluntarily depends upon the repertoires of action we have learned and, more generally, upon the cumulative content of our experiences: acting to shape one's personal future depends upon the presence of one's personal past. Gerald Edelman chose the splendid title *The Remembered Present* for the third volume of his trilogy; our present is always remembered, in the sense that memory is a process involving a dynamic interplay between learned repertoires of action and the ongoing recategorization of those repertoires in present circumstances. We may further elaborate the point by adding that the present carries within itself both memory and anticipation—and hence that it is the future we remember as well as the present, whenever we plan to follow a course of action.

The lottery winner, back from her Alaskan cruise and now possessing a changed understanding of her place in the world, wishes to act responsibly and wisely. She wishes to benefit others, and in addition her experiences among the whales and waters have led her to an awareness of her own dryness; she now longs to drink in a fuller spiritual life. But taking on the qualities of a new sense of self does not annul or efface all her memories of her life, of the selves she has been. Consequently, her passions have "that degree of complexness ... which makes them so difficult to be analyzed." She has determined to act with sympathy and compassion; but often she experiences her compassionate impulses to be childish or compromised. Sometimes she simply identifies with all the soulful puppies at the pet refuge—she knows they are feeling just what she feels; at other times she is annoyed that her friends are not congratulating her for her new orientation to life—and she wonders what she must do in order to be thought a deeply caring person. But she is simultaneously aware that there is no quicker way to invite contempt than to be perceived as putting on a show of benevolence for the sake of applause (cf. *OM* 2.3.4.62). She finds herself hesitating when offered a significant public position in the local chapter of Greenpeace; the organization is controversial, after all, and taking a position of leadership in it might make some other doors harder to open. She is also thinking about once again attending church, after years of absence, but when she imagines going she feels again all the discomfort she felt when she went with her parents as a child. She does not want to put herself in a situation that makes her feel twelve years old. And when she catches herself thinking such things, she is disgusted with herself. She thought she had discovered the key to the treasure, a philosophy that would guide her life toward fulfillment. But now it turns out that sympathy can be painful, and theopathy worse.

Hartley says that when an orientation develops, it "new-models" the others. A person whose self is grounded in sympathy should therefore expect transformed senses of imagination and ambition. The lottery winner finds that this has happened, to a degree. But she also finds herself pulled back into the old models of feeling and thinking and acting. To the extent that a person's sense of self is not fully integrated—and how many are?—a person can find herself responding out of either the old or the new models of her affections. At times she may find herself responding in several modes at once: grasshopper, ant; caterpillar, butterfly; frog, prince.

There is, moreover, no guarantee as to which mode will predominate. Refined self-interest orients a person toward a sense of self that is defined in terms of sympathy, theopathy, and the moral sense. And sympathy, in its positive aspect, is a fundamental good: Hartley states that benevolence should be a primary pursuit that regulates sensation, imagination, and ambition. But the term *sympathy* refers more generally to the orientation of personal intersubjectivity, and as such it includes modes of interaction that are frequently painful and in some cases pathological. Hartley divides his initial discussion of sympathy (*OM* 1.4.4.97) into four sections, dealing respectively with the affections by which we "rejoice at the happiness of others"; "grieve for the misery of others"; "rejoice at the misery of others"; and "grieve for the happiness of others." The first two are healthy manifestations of sympathy, the latter two pathological. The first and third concern pleasure, the second and fourth pain. The good person, the whole person, feels joy at others' happiness; but for such a one grief is unavoidable, and perhaps even a regular companion. There is so much suffering, so much misery. In contrast, a person with a deformed character finds pleasure in another's suffering, pain in another's happiness. But, given that it is possible to be either person, given that both experience pleasure and pain, what determines whether a person shall be whole or deformed?

"Believe me... I was benevolent; my soul glowed with love and humanity." The words are those of a being without a name—the creature brought to life by Victor Frankenstein. From his lengthy and secretive observations on man, in the forms of his "beloved cottagers," the nameless one learns "to admire their virtues, and to deprecate the vices of mankind." And particularly, he comes to know of the miseries they have endured, and of their many kindnesses to each other. "Benevolence and generosity," he remarks, "were ever present before me, inciting within me a desire to become an actor in the busy scene where so many admirable qualities were called forth and displayed" (Shelley 1969, 100, 127). He longed to share in their sympathies, to join in their society. Shaftesbury, Hutcheson, Gay, Hartley—all would approve of his sentiments.

Hartley's account of the development of compassion (see §7.5) appears in the second section of his fourfold typology; compassion originates in the affections we feel when we grieve for the misery of others. Recall Hartley's comment that compassion is grounded in the fact that in children "the very appearance and idea of any kind of misery which they have experienced, or of any signs of distress which they understand, raise up in their nervous systems a state of misery from mere memory, on account of the strength of their imaginations." The appearance of misery in another elicits a memory and a renewed feeling of the misery the child once felt on his own account. Such a rudimentary and self-referential sense of compassion can contribute to the development of benevolence, and "when benevolence is arrived at a due height, all our desires and fears, all our sensibilities for ourselves, are more or less transferred upon others by our love and compassion for them" (*OM* 2.3.6.68). At this due height, we "forego great pleasure, or endure great pain, for the sake of others"—even though "there may be no direct, explicit expectation of reward, either from God or man, by natural consequence, or express appointment" (*OM* 1.4.4.97). From his hiding place in the woods, the nameless being would emerge to cut wood and do other labor for the family he observed.

A rudimentary imaginative compassion can develop into a pure disinterested benevolence that has no care for itself and expects no reward. But in addition, as we noted in chapter 1, a threatened child may learn to threaten harm, as a means of warding off the expected blow; over time, the perpetual multiplication of "the occasions of anger, and the expressions of it" lead the child to associate "a desire of hurting another with the apprehension... of harm from that other"—in which case "threatening harm from a motive of security" leads him "to wish it really," and "wishing it leads [him] to threaten and inflict it, where it can afford no security or advantage." Fearful attempts to ward off one's own suffering, a rudimentary method of self-defense, develop into a pure disinterested malevolence that brings with it neither safety nor benefit. A creature thus deformed rejoices at the misery of others.

Similarly, theopathy and the moral sense are goods; Hartley states they should also be primary pursuits. Yet theopathy and the moral sense can also be painful and in some instances pathological. We shall examine what Hartley says concerning both the love and the fear of God more extensively in the next section; here it is enough to note that, on the one hand, a "pure disinterested love of God may... arise to such a height, as to prevail over any of the other desires interested or disinterested" (*OM* 1.4.4.97); at this height, "the love and contemplation of his perfection and happiness will transform us into his likeness, into that image of him in which we were first made" (*OM* 2.3.7.71). On the other, in a person afflicted by an excessive fear of God, the superstitions that cluster about a "mistaken opinion concerning the severity and punishments of God" can fuel "a great tendency to sour the mind, to check natural benevolence and compassion, and to generate a bitter persecuting spirit" (*OM* 1.4.4.97). And the moral sense can likewise contribute to this pathology. Although it is the function of the moral sense to act as the "substitute" of benevolence and piety "upon emergent occasions," and hence to serve as "a ready monitor to us on such occasions," Hartley counsels that "it should not descend to minute and trifling particulars; for then it would check benevolence, and turn the love of God into a superstitious fear" (*OM* 2.3.8.75).

The pains of sympathy, theopathy, and the moral sense can be as sharp as those of imagination, ambition, and gross self-interest. Moreover, the pathological forms of these orientations possess a great potential for destructiveness. Pathologies of the lower self can produce a self-indulgent, narcissistic lout, a not-so-smooth savage. But the pathologies of the higher self produce a much more savage character. Anger masquerading as smiling sympathy, contempt for others as love for God, a bitter persecuting spirit as a defense of moral values—all these mark out the inquisitor, ready to pluck out the eye that tears with the smallest mote.

We are, according to Hartley, rescued from the futility of gross self-interest by a reorientation toward refined self-interest. But what protects us or liberates us from the demonic potentials of a self-interest that has become refined? Hartley's initial answer to this question concerns the third form of self-interest, which he terms "rational."

5. Rational Self-Interest

We left the grasshopper an ambitious insect, a wunderbug climbing the haystack of success. Let us imagine that he has now discovered a new vocation of service to the poor, the ill, the outcast, when shocked into awareness of suffering. He grieves at the misery of others. And he thinks of the final winter to come and asks himself, what profit is there in gaining the whole stack, if it costs me my whole self? He asks, that is, the central question posed by rational self-interest.

A form of self-interest designated "rational" sounds promising; reason is the capacity philosophers often praise as the noblest and most divine in human beings. Reason is, Plato said, the "soul's pilot" (*Phaedrus* 247d), the charioteer who controls and guides the gentle horse of spirit and the unruly horse of appetite. In Hartley's account, however, the form of self-interest called rational has its genesis in some of the most primitive matter in the human psyche—the fear of death and the fear of God. It is as if the charioteer, before being given the reins, had spent his infancy listening to the cries of the sick crazed souls locked in Bedlam.

We noted in §7.4 that, like the gross and refined forms, rational self-interest also concerns the "pursuit of the means"—in this instance of "such things, as are believed to be the means for obtaining our greatest possible happiness" (*OM* 2.3.5.65; cf. 1.4.3.96). And we noted the qualification: *as are believed to be*. The fundamental difficulty, according to Hartley, is that we do not know what this happiness is, or what the means are that will enable us to attain it. We pursue the means "at the same time that we are ignorant, or do not consider, from what particular species of pleasure this our greatest possible happiness will arise." We are thus ignorant because, according to Hartley, we possess no innate orientation toward the "greatest" happiness. We noted in §7.1 that Hartley claimed that there exist "such differences and singularities in different persons, and in the same person at different times, as no-way agree to the notion of an essential, original, perpetual desire of happiness, and endeavour to attain it" (*OM* 1.3.3.89). There is, in other words, no instinct or drive within the human breast that leads the person unerringly along the path toward the greatest possible happiness. The existence of an "abstract desire of happiness, and aversion to misery, which is supposed to attend every intelligent being during the whole course of his existence" is, Hartley states, "a supposition" that "is not true in the proper sense of the words" (*OM* 1.4.3.96). Rather, any general orientation toward a "greatest" happiness is itself a factitious construct, generated out of the miscellany of a person's narratives, symbols, actions, and memories. In terms of Aristotelian causality, a general and abstract desire for the greatest happiness lacks both a formal and a final cause—it lacks, that is, both blueprint and goal; the efficient causes of association and transference and the material causes that are the specific contents of personal experiences together produce "differences and singularities" both between people and within a person at various times and in diverse circumstances. Even when a person does develop a verbal and shapeless concern for "the greatest possible happiness," the person's sense of that happiness will be built out of lesser material, and the person will *believe* that such happiness relates to any number of things. Rational self-interest is thus the pursuit of the means of obtaining the greatest possible happiness—"without any partiality to this or that kind of happiness, means of happiness, means of a means, etc." (*OM* 1.4.3.96).

Still, the fact is that "very general desires do frequently recur to the mind, and may be excited by words and symbols of general import." Once a person has learned that he has a *rational self-interest*, he may become greatly concerned to identify something that corresponds to the words; furthering this something, whatever it is, may become a major motivation in his life. But again, there is a deep difficulty here, for such a general desire is not itself a consequence of, or response to, the perception of the desired object. The desire is built up out of transferences from various other sources of desire, circumstantially related to it, and it is excited by words and symbols of general import, which happen to have had considerable funds of emotion transferred to them. Hence, the words and symbols name, as it were, the presumed location but not the identity of the desired object, and such words may simultaneously excite both desire and distress: desire, in this instance, to attain ultimate happiness, and distress concerning doubts about the kind of happiness, or means of happiness, one ought to prefer. When the path toward ultimate happiness remains obscure, thinking about one's greatest hopes for happiness may make a person very unhappy; it may tumble him into a mire of frustration and fear.

Consider the development of the ideas clustered about another word of general import, which is closely connected with our general desires for the greatest happiness. In his comments concerning "the idea of God, as it is found in fact amongst men, particularly amongst Jews and Christians," Hartley suggests that we "inquire what associations may be observed in fact to be heaped upon, and concur with this word" (*OM* 1.4.5.98). He then describes four stages in this heaping. First, "since many actions and attributes belonging to men are... in common language, applied to God, children, in their first attempts to decypher the word *God*, will suppose it to stand for a man whom they have never seen, and of whom consequently they form a compound fictitious idea." Second, although they first imagine God to be another person whom they have not yet met, they soon realize that adults say things about God that are true of no living person of their acquaintance: "When they hear or read, that God resides in heaven, (*i.e.* according to their conceptions, in the sky, amongst the stars,) that he made all things, that he sees, hears, and knows all things, can do all things, &c.... vivid ideas, which surprise and agitate the mind, (lying upon the confines of pain,) are raised in it; and if they are far advanced in understanding, as to be affected with apparent inconsistencies and impossibilities in their ideas, they must feel great perplexity of imagination, when they endeavour to conceive and form definite ideas agreeable to the language of this kind." The child is thrown into a state of cognitive incongruity; she is asked to picture God as a person, but as a person who can do things it is impossible for a person to do. These "inconsistencies and impossibilities" create a "great perplexity of imagination" when the child tries to reconcile them into a logically coherent concept. The child's picture or concept of God has become less clear, while at the same time the emotional intensity of the idea has, thanks both to its semantic inconsistency and indeterminacy and to the solemn circumstances in which it is used, become more intense. Thus "this perplexity will add to the vividness of the ideas, and all together will transfer upon the word *God* ... such secondary ideas, as may be referred to the heads of magnificence, astonishment, and reverence."

Third, perplexity and emotional vividness increase when the child learns that God, besides doing things no person can do, also has qualities which it is impossible for any human being to have: "When children hear that God cannot be seen, having no visible shape, no parts; but that he is a spiritual infinite being; this adds much to their perplexity and astonishment, and by degrees destroys the association of the fictitious visible idea before-mentioned with the word *God*." The word no longer immediately calls up the picture of an old man with a white beard, living in the sky. "However," Hartley adds, "it is probable, that some visible ideas, such as those of the heavens, a fictitious throne placed there, a multitude of angels, &c., still continue to be excited by the word *God*, and its equivalents." The image of the old man may have been destroyed by the emphasis of religious instructors that God is a "spiritual infinite being" with no shape or parts, but other images of the cluster may not fade as completely. Although it is now empty, the throne still stands in the palace, and the angels still hover about. And we may add that even in a secular age, and among adults who know better, St. Peter stands guard at a gate in the clouds.

Finally, even as the visual imagery associated with *God* becomes progressively indistinct, the emotions the word excites become more vivid and intense. This process is particularly accentuated "when the child hears, that God is the rewarder of good actions, and the punisher of evil ones, and that the most exquisite future happiness and misery (described by a great variety of particulars and emblems) are prepared by him for the good and bad respectively." By associating the very concrete idea of an inescapable judge with whatever notions such terms as *spiritual infinite being* raise in his mind, the child "feels strong hopes and fears arise alternately in his mind, according to the judgment which he passes upon his own actions, founded partly upon the previous judgment of others, partly upon an imperfect moral sense begun to be generated in him."

Summarizing these steps, Hartley concludes that "it will appear, that, amongst Jews and Christians, children begin probably with a definite visible idea of God; but that by degrees this is quite obliterated, without anything of a stable precise nature succeeding in its room; and that, by farther degrees, a great variety of strong secondary ideas, *i.e.* mental affections, (attended indeed by visible ideas, to which proper words are affixed, as of angels, general judgment, &c.) recur in their turns, when they think upon God." At this point Hartley ends his account of the genesis of the idea of God. The generality of Jews and Christians, in other words, whether children or adults, do not have a stable and precise idea of God at all. They have as it were a general visual picture, but with the central image in that picture erased, leaving a cluster of peripheral images surrounding a blank space. With this space they associate clusters of general and often abstract words—*infinite, almighty, all-knowing, eternal, spiritual*—which, as terms for qualities that lack limits, are all incompatible with any concept of a person derived from one's interactions with human beings. At the same time, they also transfer very powerful feelings upon *God*—feelings that derive partly from their perplexities and, more importantly, from their sense that this infinite being, this eternal enforcer of the law, cares deeply about their individual conduct, sees and remembers everything, and will reward or punish them accordingly. People are thus in the situation of transferring a great charge of emotion upon a word that names a location from which an image, a "compound fictitious idea," has been erased.

Because "the most exquisite future happiness or misery . . . are prepared by him for the good and bad respectively," they understand that God holds the key to "the greatest happiness possible"; that it is in their most vital and rational self-interest to be among those God counts as *good*. But because their ideas of God are without form and void, they are in doubt as to what means to pursue, out of the available alternatives, to secure the greatest possible happiness.

Thoughts about God are involved in a person's sense of his rational self-interest. Equally involved are thoughts about death and about what follows death—thoughts that can increase the doubt and confusion a person may experience regarding the greatest happiness possible. Hartley writes: "Death is certain, and necessarily attended with many terrifying associations; and a future state must, even upon the slightest presumption of its reality, be a matter of the greatest concern to all thinking persons. Now the frequent recurrency of these fears and anxieties must embitter all guilty pleasures, and even the more innocent trifling amusements; . . . And thus men live in bondage all their lives through the fear of death; more so than they are aware of themselves . . . and still much more so than they own and express to others" (*OM* 2.3, Cor. 3). People live in fear, and the fear is one they cannot acknowledge. Such fear lies or is pushed below the threshold of consciousness, and yet from its submerged position it affects what consciousness takes in. Hartley states that it embitters pleasures, whether guilty or innocent; and we can add that it can also make a person's search for pleasure more desperate—and futile.

As Hartley describes it, this bondage "through the fear of death" is composed of two related elements. The first is a natural fear of death and physical corruption, and the second consists of the anticipatory fears expressed in and compounded by the stories and images people create concerning a future state. Concerning the natural fears, Hartley writes: "All our first associations with the idea of death are of the disgustful and alarming kind; and they are collected from all quarters, from the sensible pains of every sort, from the imperfection, weakness, loathsomeness, corruption, and disorder, where disease, old age, death, animal or vegetable, prevail, in opposition to the beauty, order, and lustre of life, youth, and health" (*OM* 1.4.3.96). It may be important here for us, who live in a world in which death occurs mostly to elderly people in hospitals and nursing homes, to remember that in Britain in 1749, as in much of the Third World today, associations with the idea of death were indeed "collected from all quarters." People lived within a world in which the lustre of youth and health was continually shadowed by the loathsomeness of corruption and disorder. A slight wound—pricking one's finger on a thorn—could lead to sepsis, blood poisoning, gangrene. A case of smallpox could leave an infant literally without eyes. People fell ill and died at all ages; any young man, robust with health, could be rapidly reduced to a blood-coughing invalid by tuberculosis; the lovely girl before you today, radiant with youth, could tomorrow be a corpse. And it was particularly children and their mothers who died. We noted in the second chapter that, in London between 1730 and 1749, of the children who were christened, three out of four died before the age of five (Rudé 1971, 6). What is more, illness and death were not sealed up within institutions; when someone fell ill, the family lived on intimate terms with the disorder. When Hartley's mother died three months after giving birth to him, she probably died at home; when Alice Rowley died in childbed a year after marrying him, she died in his arms. Given all the differences and singularities that contribute to our individuality as persons, speculations concerning what a person long dead "must have" thought or felt are impossible to prove; still, with that caution in mind, it would not be unreasonable to imagine that, for a newly married couple such as David Hartley and Elizabeth Packer, even the powerfully cohesive force of sexual desire may have been disturbed by counterassociations, by thoughts of intimacy's potentially deathly consequences. But this we do not know. What we do know, thanks to the publication of Hartley's prayers in 1810, is that when the "life of the dear partner of all my hopes and happiness" was threatened by childbirth in July 1736, Hartley turned to God: "It is thy command that we should fly to Thee in every desire and distress. This I did, and thou sawest the bitterness and anguish of my soul, and had mercy upon me" (1810, 29). Both Elizabeth and their newborn daughter Mary survived this near encounter with death.

The "terrifying associations" that accompany the natural fear of death are in turn often drawn into still larger and more powerful complexes of fear. Given the "slightest presumption" that personal existence continues beyond death, the quality of this state must be "a matter of the greatest concern to all thinking persons"; consequently, "the hopes and fears relating to a future state, or to death, . . . may be considered as proceeding from a rational self-interest, in the highest and most abstracted sense that the terms admit of practically" (*OM* 1.4.3.96). Keep in mind that *abstract* is not for Hartley a term of praise. Self-interest is here rational in "the highest and most abstracted sense" precisely because "we have no definite knowledge of the nature and kind of happiness or misery of another world." Like the idea of God with which people commonly end up, our rational interest in life after death places a great fund of emotion, much of it transferred from our natural fears of death, upon . . . nothing. The space is again blank. And given our lack of definite knowledge, of any stable and precise idea of an afterlife—given, in other words, the total abstraction of our interest—the bare thought of an afterlife could itself add to the anxieties concerning death, much in the same way that words like *infinite* and *omnipotent* can add to the perplexities and confusions that swirl about the blank space that demarcates the idea of God.

What compounds the fear even more are the images and narratives of torment with which religions have filled the blank. Hartley notes that the natural fear of death is often encouraged by other persons, particularly those in authority, who, for purposes of control, draw the natural fears into larger, religious narratives of fear. "When children begin to have a sense of religion and duty formed in them, these do still farther heighten and increase the fear of death for the most part." Such accentuation of fear may aid in the child's preservation; "it is necessary, that the heedlessness and inexperience of infancy and youth should be guarded by such terrors, and their head-strong appetites and passions curbed, that they may not be hurried into danger and destruction before they are aware." At any rate, that is the policy "parents and governors" commonly adopt; they are "more apt to have recourse to fear than to hope (in general, I suppose with reason, because hope is too feeble to withstand the violence of the natural appetites and passions)." Hartley's tone suggests he has little enthusiasm for this policy; he *supposes* that parents and governors have reason for following it. Moreover, he immediately draws the reader's attention to the negative consequences that result from amplifying the narratives of fear: "And it is to be added to all, that adults, by discovering... much more fear and sorrow in the apprehensions or prospect of death, than of hope and comfort,... propagate and increase the fear still farther in one another, and in children, infecting all around them.... And by this means, it comes to pass, that the fear of death does in some circumstances... grow to a most enormous size, collecting and uniting every disagreeable idea and impression under the associations belonging to death; so that such persons live in perpetual anxiety and slavery to the fear of death." Such fear, he adds, "is much increased by the exquisiteness of the punishments threatened in a future state, and by the variety of the emblems, representations, analogies, and evidences, of natural and revealed religion, whereby all the terrors of all other things are transferred upon these punishments." It is still further increased by belief in the eternity of such punishments, which Hartley states was the "general tradition previous to the appearance of Christianity," and which has continued to be "the doctrine and opinion of the Christian world ever since, some very few persons excepted." At least in the Western world as he knew it, many people are chronically sick with fear; such compactions or matrices of fear grow into painful masses within them. Like carriers of a contagious disease, the afflicted infect all around them, including the children, with what they suppose to be a rational self-interest.

A "perpetual anxiety" that fills the imagination with the inflexible punishments of hell; a habit of transferring "all the terrors of all other things... upon these punishments"; a conviction that at death one faces a judge who knows one's every crime and failure—if these are the concomitants of rational self-interest, then rational self-interest is a sickness, and it would seem reasonable to think that we would be better off without it. A person adopting this view could further conclude that rational self-interest and its accompanying religious illusions ought to be kept from developing in the first place, if possible; but that for those who suffer from them, the goal of therapy should be the psychological equivalent of lithotomy.

Hartley is well aware that rational self-interest and religious ideas do make us ill, physically as well as mentally. However, he is also aware that curing such an illness may not be a simple matter, for the site of the illness may be hidden deep within the person. Consider his comments concerning "religious persons under bodily and mental disorders, which fill their minds with disproportionate fears and scruples" (*OM*

2.4.4.93). He remarks first that it is "proper to comfort" such persons; we ought to remind them that such afflictions are both signs of and occasions for spiritual growth. But then he adds that "such persons are to be admonished, that a great degree of fearfulness and scrupulosity often proceeds from some self-deceit and prevarication at the bottom. There is probably some secret sin, some sin that circumvents them more easily and frequently than the rest, of which they may not perhaps be fully aware, and yet about which they have great suspicions and checks, if they would hearken to them fully and fairly." The "disproportionate fears and scruples" that disorder the bodies and minds of some religious persons are devices that simultaneously conceal and express the secret sins that "circumvent" their understanding and control. Their sensitivities to their various physical and mental afflictions distract them from the true causes of their unease: their fears and scruples are mechanisms of self-deceit. But those same fears and scruples are simultaneously among the "great suspicions and checks" that consistently point to the true causes. The disorders that conceal also reveal: though "they may not perhaps be fully aware" of their secret sins, the symptoms of bodily and mental disorders would disclose much, "if they would hearken to them fully and fairly." In such instances, it would not be enough to dampen or eliminate the symptoms; curing oneself of the disease requires rather that one heed what the symptoms are saying.

6. Self-Interest as a Primary Pursuit

Further complicating the task of developing a complete self is the possibility that one or another of the forms of self-interest may itself become a primary pursuit.

Gross and refined self-interest concern "the pursuit of the means" (OM 1.4.3.96) by which we attempt to obtain the pleasures, and avoid the pains, of sensation, imagination, and ambition, or of sympathy, theopathy, and the moral sense, respectively. Rational self-interest, in turn, attempts to look toward and beyond the boundaries of human life—to death and to what may lie beyond death; it attempts, from an imagined perspective outside of earthly human awareness, to determine and pursue the means of securing our "greatest possible happiness."

All three forms of self-interest are means for regulating the economy of pleasure. It is the business of self-interest, so far as it is able, to maintain a steady return of pleasure from whatever orientations are the person's primary pursuits. Over time, a person learns that particular actions, accomplishments, and possessions will maintain and perhaps increase the overall flow of pleasure, and she determines to secure for herself the resources necessary for performing these actions and gaining these accomplishments and possessions; she also tries to sustain the flow of pleasure through the prudent expenditure of the resources she has secured. The resources are predominantly symbolic: gross self-interest concerns itself with the resources that signify wealth and position, very broadly understood; refined self-interest looks to the qualities of character that enable the person to love other people and God; and rational self-interest collects and discards images of the unimaginable.

Managing the economy of pleasure is difficult. In the case of gross self-interest, much of the trouble derives from the fact that the pleasures deteriorate. The pleasures of imagination and ambition decline in intensity even as they become hyper-refined, as their limits of excellence narrow and their rules become absurd. Moreover, the problem of deterioration cannot be resolved within an orientation itself. An ambitious seeking for the "applauses of the world," for example, "must produce endless inquietude, resentment, envy, and self-conceit" (*OM* 2.3.4.64). Such seeking generates the counterassociations that thwart it.

The arrangement of gross, refined, and rational self-interest along the expanding prism of self suggests that the problem of the deterioration of pleasure within one configuration of self can be resolved by attaining the higher viewpoint of a more inclusive configuration. A self defined by gross self-interest cannot rescue itself from the pains of imagination and ambition, but one defined by refined self-interest can. The futility of taking imagination and ambition as one's primary pursuits can only be overcome by committing oneself to a new sense of self, in which sympathy and theopathy are one's primary pursuits. Moreover, this progression of self-interest from gross to refined to rational would appear to represent psychological progress, as the self attains ever higher and more inclusive levels of integration. And the achievement of a higher level of integration would appear to represent, in turn, increases both in wisdom and happiness. Now, it is true that a self defined by refined self-interest will not be beset by the pleasures and pains of imagination and ambition, as these are experienced by a self defined by gross self-interest. However, what is striking about Hartley's description of psychological progress is how increasingly difficult, painful, and potentially destructive that progress is. As we have already observed in this chapter, the pains of sympathy and theopathy can be at least as intense as those of imagination and ambition, and the pains attending the fears surrounding the concerns of rational self-interest can be still worse. Every new-modeling of the self appears to open and subject the person to further pains, greater internal conflicts, and more destructive forms of deformation.

Compounding the difficulties involved in the gross, refined, and rational pursuits of the means of pleasure is the possibility that pleasure may transfer to the pursuit itself, so that the person learns to love the pursuit of the means for its own sake. In such a person, the love of the means "so engrosses and absorbs all their passions and pursuits, as that from being considered as the representative, standard, common measure and means of obtaining the commodities which occur in common life, it shall be esteemed the adequate exponent and means of happiness in general, and the thing itself, the sum total of all that is desirable in life" (OM 1.4.3.96). During one Christmas season in the mid-1980s, the *Wall Street Journal* ran a swinish advertisement on the radio in which it suggested that a subscription to the *Journal* would make the ideal present for the person who could not "relate"—that was the word they used—to anything but the pursuit of the means. The ideal subscriber, it would seem, would be one who loved his bank account, but not for anything it enables him to buy; or even more, who would love above all the fact that he can maintain a rate of asset growth that exceeds the growth rate of the S&P 500—*that* would be the "adequate exponent" of happiness.

The pleasures that flow from imagination and ambition to the pursuit of the means can collect in the latter; this channeling of emotion to gross self-interest has the potential to make the "pursuit of the means" itself a primary pursuit. The transference of pleasure thus acts as a form of drainage; a channel is cut from imagination and ambition to gross self-interest, so that the fluid of emotion runs off into a new reservoir. To change the metaphor to an economic one, we could say that here the funds of pleasure that gross self-interest is charged with managing are transferred to the account of the manager. The part of the self assigned the task of managing the economy of pleasure then becomes the dominant part of the economy.

As a general example of the means by which such a transference can come about, consider Hartley's comment concerning the gratification of the will:

> Since the things which we pursue do, when obtained, generally afford pleasure, and those we fly from affect us with pain, if

they overtake us, it follows that the gratification of the will is generally attended or associated with pleasure, the disappointment of it with pain. Hence a mere associated pleasure is transferred upon the gratification of the will; a mere associated pain upon the disappointment of it. And if the will was always gratified, this mere associated pleasure would... absorb, as it were, all our other pleasures; and thus by drying up the source from whence it sprung, be itself dried up at last: and the first disappointments, after a long course of gratification, would be intolerable. (OM 1.3.3.89)

Because of the associative channel between "the things we pursue" or "fly from" and the sense we have of *willing* the pursuit or flight, the gratification of the will tends to drain and absorb all the pleasures that attend acts of successful capture or flight. What is most gratifying to a person is the fact of gratification, and what is most frustrating is gratification's denial. What pleases most is, in the end, simply the fact of getting one's way.

The problem is that, unlike sensation, imagination, and ambition, which do serve as primary sources of pleasure, the will does not have its own aquifer beneath the surface, the source of its own springs of pleasure. The will is a desert. When pleasures are poured upon its sands, they vanish into it; were all lakes and streams diverted into it, it would eventually suck them dry. Then, knowing of no spring or oasis, the person dwelling there would be tortured by the first sign of thirst. Denials of gratification would be intolerable.

The result can be the devastation of a person. Making gross self-interest a primary pursuit reduces a person to "a condition lower than the mere sensual brutal one, in which he was born" (OM 2.3.5.65). An infant, as a living and sensual animal, at least derives pleasure from being cuddled and fed, but "gross self-interest, when indulged, devours many of the pleasures of sensation, and most of those of imagination and ambition." As with the gratification of the will, the pursuit of the means of obtaining a particular pleasure can, when it becomes itself a source of pleasure, devour or dry up "the pleasures from which it takes its rise." It devours the sources from which pleasure flows into it, and at last is empty of pleasure itself.

The condition is an extreme one. Fortunately, the tendency of gross self-interest to become a primary pursuit is checked by a number of factors. One is the continuing strength of the pleasures of imagination and ambition; in intellectually dedicated persons, for example, a desire for "mental accomplishments, learning particularly ... often checks" the "vicious" versions of the pleasures of sensation, imagination, ambition, and also "the love of money" (OM 2.3.5.67) that is a symptom of taking gross self-interest as one's primary pursuit. Also checking gross self-interest are situations in which gross self-interest fails to be gratified: "it seems probable," Hartley writes, "that the love of money would at last devour all the particular desires, upon which it is grounded, was it not restrained by counter-associations; just as ... the pleasure of gratifying the will would devour all the particular pleasures, to which it is a constant associate, did not repeated disappointments preserve us from this enormous increase of wilfulness" (OM 1.4.3.96). Gross self-interest is also checked by the counterassociations deriving from sympathy and theopathy, even in their lesser forms. "Gross self-interest, being avowedly contrary to them, is often stifled by the increase of benevolence and compassion, of the love and fear of God, and of the sense of duty to him" (OM 2.3.5.65). The clever grasshopper, while still climbing the haystack, and the lottery winner, on beach or boat, do not need to worry unduly about the drought that comes from making gross self-interest a primary pursuit.

In contrast, consider the potential for dryness that faces the person who has undergone the transition from gross to refined self-interest, whose sense of self is now defined in terms of sympathy, theopathy, and the moral sense, and who is tempted to make refined self-interest her primary pursuit: "refined self-interest has, like the gross, a tendency to destroy the very pleasures from which it took its rise; ... it cannot afford happiness, unless the mind and body be properly disposed; it does not, in fact, make men happy; but is the parent of dissatisfaction, murmurings, and aridity; and, being professedly the pursuit of a bare means, involves the absurdity of having no real end in view." What is more, "refined self-interest, when indulged, is a much deeper and dangerous error than the gross, because it shelters itself under sympathy, theopathy, and the moral sense, so as to grow through their protection." At its extreme, "the pride attending on refined self-interest ... is of an incorrigible, and, as it were, diabolical nature.... As gross self-interest, when it gets possession of a man, puts him in a lower condition than the mere sensual brutal one, in which he was born; so refined self-interest, when that gets possession, depresses him still farther, even to the very confines of hell." This is the hell of spiritual narcissism. It is the pebble in Blake's poem that states that love, seeking "only Self to please," "builds a Hell in Heavens despite." Here we may add a Hartleian gloss to Blake's lines: it is not sensual or imaginative or even ambitious love that does this; hell is built of sympathy and theopathy and moral sense, drained of all passion; at the very bottom of hell is the diabolical spirit that devours them and sucks them dry—a refined self-interest, frozen in the ice of its own intolerable thirst.

Still, exposure to the psychological elements will cut back refined self-interest, and such exposure is provided by the third form of self-interest. What is at first surprising about rational self-interest is how irrational it is, at least in its beginnings. It is initially compounded out of ignorance and fear—ignorance regarding what does await us after death, and fear of an astonishing and unimaginable being, a person who is not a person, about whom many terrifying stories are told. But such have their purpose, for they are the storms that prune back or even uproot the self-interest that clings like a parasitic vine to sympathy and theopathy. However, rational self-interest is also a form of an orientation that is dedicated to the management of the pursuit of happiness—even though it often does not know which way to turn in that pursuit—and it is also vulnerable to the tendency of itself becoming a primary pursuit. Thus, while rational self-interest is useful as a check upon our lower senses of self, and especially upon our tendencies toward hellish pride, it is at the same time a burden and a danger:

> We may see from the reasoning used in respect of gross and refined self-interest, that a constant attention to that which is the most pure and rational, to the most general hopes and fears, would extinguish our love of God and our neighbour, as well as the other particular desires, and augment the ideas and desires, which centre immediately and directly in *self*, to a monstrous height. Rational self-interest may therefore be said to lie between the impure motives of sensation, imagination, ambition, gross self-interest, and refined self-interest, on the one hand, and the pure ones of sympathy, theopathy, and the moral sense, on the other; so that when it restrains the impure ones, or cherishes the pure, it may be reckoned a virtue; when it cherishes the impure, or damps the pure, a vice. (*OM* 2.3.5.65)

Whether gross, refined, or rational, the sense of self-interest has the potential of enslaving the psyche and of making the other orientations its servants. A self-referential sense of self is always a danger, and the higher or nobler the sense of self, the greater the danger of a demonic possession of the psyche. The brightest angels become the most monstrous, when they fall.

7. Transcending Self-Interest: The Shelter of Sympathy and Theopathy

As it pursues its pleasures and flees its pains, the self ruled by gross self-interest creates a "labyrinth of error and anxiety." Refined self-interest extends this labyrinth into a place of hellish confinement. To complete the image: Rational self-interest engenders the monstrous self that hides and hungers there.

Such is a possible outcome; in describing it, Hartley obviously thought that some people were intimately familiar with this labyrinth's interior. Yet Hartley also believed in universal salvation, a cardinal article of the "everlasting gospel." He believed it was no one's fate to be confined in hell forever. No matter how deeply entombed in the interior of such a maze a person may be, a liberating power can reach him. "No time, place, or circumstance of life," he writes, "can deprive us of—no height, depth, or creature of any kind, can separate us from—the love of God" (OM 2.3.7.71). The reach of divine love is such that it will build a heaven in hell's despair.

It is not enough, however, to imagine that God, out of love, simply shatters the gates of hell. In Hartley's theory, hell does not exist somewhere "out there," a supernatural realm analogous to a physical one. The confines of hell are fashioned within human consciousness: each of us builds this labyrinth, when we make one or another form of self-interest our primary pursuit. Release, then, must also occur within human consciousness, as a transformation of consciousness (see §2.4). The psychological processes that construct the labyrinths of hell must also have the potential to build the mansions of heaven.

Consider again Hartley's observations concerning self-interest. As noted above, the tendency to make gross self-interest into a primary pursuit receives a variety of checks; negating it are the counterassociations deriving from continuing pleasures of imagination and ambition, its own failures, and the pleasures and pains of sympathy and theopathy. In contrast, the reason why refined self-interest can "depress" a person "to the very confines of hell" is that nothing checks it. Refined self-interest "shelters itself under sympathy, theopathy, and the moral sense, so as to grow through their protection" (*OM* 2.3.5.65). But sympathy, theopathy, and the moral sense define the farther plane of the prism of the psyche; accordingly, they ought to be our primary pursuits. Refined self-interest is so potentially destructive, and also so difficult to overcome, precisely because it adheres to them. The worst in us haunts the best in us.

In proposition 68 in book 2, Hartley states that the pleasures of sympathy ought to be a primary pursuit. Such pleasures "improve those of Sensation, Imagination, Ambition, and Self-Interest; and unite with those of Theopathy and the Moral Sense; they are self-consistent, and admit of an unlimited Extent" (*OM* 2.3.6.68). The pleasures of sympathy "improve" the lower pleasures by new-modeling them. They "unite" with the pleasures of theopathy in the sense that "we are led by the love of good men to that of God, and back again by the love of God to that of all his creatures in and through him." But what is most important, for our purposes here, is that the pleasures of sympathy are "self-consistent" and "admit of an unlimited extent," for it is their consistency and limitlessness that makes sympathy a perfect shelter for refined self-interest. The pleasures of sensation, imagination, ambition, and gross self-interest are not self-consistent; one form of pleasure can negate another, and all forms of pleasure are unstable. In contrast, acts of benevolence, which are practical expressions of sympathy, do not negate each other. Rather, "the self-consistency of benevolence appears from the peculiar harmony, love, esteem, and mutual co-operation, that prevail amongst benevolent persons." Benevolence is not something benevolent people quarrel about. Neither are benevolent acts inherently unstable; the pleasures that derive from them do not necessarily generate painful counterassociations. In addition, unlike the pleasures of sensation, imagination, and ambition, acts of benevolence are not self-limiting. Acts of benevolence are performed for the sake of others in need, and Hartley reminds us that there is no lack of such others: "It is very plain, that [a benevolent] person would have a very large field of employment." An unlimited field. And finally, benevolence is exempt from the dulling of pleasure that is typical of sensation, imagination, and ambition: "It does not appear from the experience of those who make the trial, that the relish for these pleasures languishes, . . . but, on the contrary, that it gathers strength from gratification. We hear men complaining frequently of the vanity and deceitfulness of the other pleasures after possession and gratification, but never of those of benevolence, when improved by religion, and the moral sense. On the contrary, these pleasures are greater in enjoyment than expectation; and continue to please in reflection, and after enjoyment." It is a contradiction in terms to speak of a dissipated connoisseur of benevolence.

Overall, sensation, imagination, and ambition provide poor shelter for gross self-interest; the roof is full of holes, and the building is continuously falling apart. The pleasures that rain upon them lead to the shelter's further deterioration. Sympathy and theopathy, in contrast, are like two great, living trees: the more they are watered, the better they flourish. "When cultivated as they ought to be," benevolence and theopathy "must receive fresh recruits upon every gratification, and . . . increase perpetually."

Refined self-interest can entangle a person in a hellish confinement precisely because it shelters under sympathy, theopathy, and the moral sense. Like a parasitic vine, refined self-interest clings to them and draws nourishment from them. One of the most crippling and demonic potentials of the self derives its strength from its adhesion to the most vital and radiant dimensions of the psyche. And whether a person becomes crippled or whole, demonic or radiant, appears to depend on one of the subtlest of distinctions: Does the person derive gratification from the success and progress she achieves as she strives to be sympathetic, theopathic, and morally aware—or, simply and directly, from being sympathetic, theopathic, and morally aware? Given the ease with which a sense of gratification can insensibly transfer from the reality to the means used to accomplish it, how can one nourish the tree without feeding the vine? How can one be happy in one's wholeness without being pleased with one's progress towards wholeness? How be a whole self without sheltering the aspect of self that labors to accomplish this? How can one attain wholeness if striving for wholeness is a primary obstacle to attaining it?

In Hartley's psychology, a person's development does not end with the composition of a song of myself, no matter how inclusive and articulate. It does not end with the development of self-interest, of an ego, no matter how refined or rational. According to Hartley, a person's moral and psychological growth will remain short of its full height as long as he or she is encumbered with the vine of self-interest. Hartley acknowledges that "we do, and must, upon our entrance into this world, begin with idolatry to external things, and, as we advance in it, proceed to the idolatry of ourselves" (*OM* 2.1.4). He then adds that these forms of idolatry "are insuperable bars to a complete happiness in the love of

God." Overcoming them requires the "annihilation" of the self. It requires, in other words, that one cut away the vine of self-interest altogether. But how is this possible for the psychological being Hartley describes?

9

Annihilation of Self

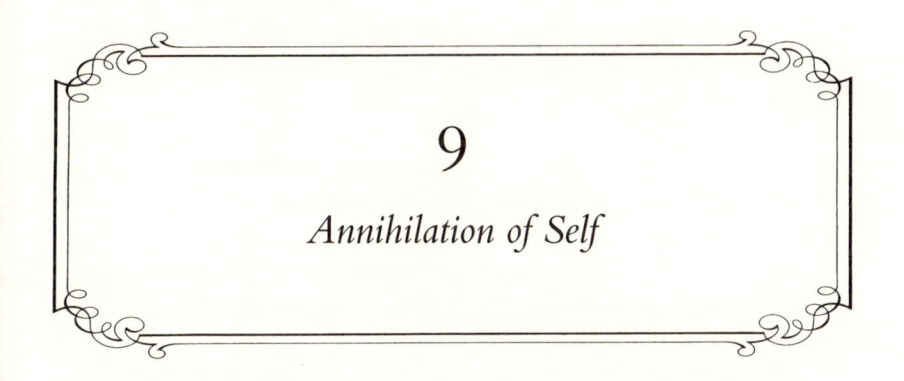

O Saviour pour upon me thy Spirit of meekness & love:
Annihilate the Selfhood in me, be thou all my life!

—Blake, *Jerusalem* 5.21–22

Annihilation is another Term used by the *Mysticks,* and ridiculed by their Adversaries: It cannot be supposed to mean *the reducing to nothing,* in a *physical* or natural Sense; but only *the doing away* of such bad Dispositions as hinder the *divine* Operations on the Soul, or which are Obstacles to the *Union* between God and Man.

—"A Letter Concerning Mr. Marsay, and other Authors of that Class" (Marsay 1749, 10)

1. Two Opinions

Hartley's discussion of the snares of self-interest appears in proposition 65 of book 2, "The Pleasures of Self-interest ought not to be made a primary Pursuit." A few pages later, in proposition 67, on "Practical Observations on Self-Interest and Self-Annihilation," Hartley writes:

"Self-interest being reckoned by some writers the only stable point upon which a system of morality can be erected, and self-annihilation by other writers the only one in which man can rest, I will here endeavour to reconcile these two opinions" (*OM* 2.3.5.67). The reconciliation is one that acknowledges the developmental necessity of beginning with gross self-interest and then of passing through the refined and rational forms. Hartley outlines the manner in which the progressively higher forms of self-interest "check" the lower. Then he adds that the most effective checks do not derive from self-interest at all. They are rather those of sympathy, theopathy, and the moral sense, when these are fully developed:

> The virtuous dispositions of benevolence, piety, and the moral sense, and particularly that of the love of God, check all the foregoing ones, and seem sufficient to utterly extinguish them at last. This would be perfect self-annihilation, and resting in God as our centre. And upon the whole, we may conclude, that though it be impossible to begin without sensuality, and sensual selfishness, or to proceed without the other intermediate principles, and particularly that of rational self-interest; yet we ought never to be satisfied with ourselves, till we arrive at perfect self-annihilation, and the pure love of God.

Those who reckon that self-interest is the "only stable point upon which a system of morality can be erected" are in a sense right: to erect such a system, one must begin with self-interest. It is, however, incorrect to think that self-interest is "stable": there are, in Hartley's reckoning, three forms of it, and each form is a parasitic vine. Although self-interest may be the point, or points, upon which a "system of morality" may begin to be erected, Hartley clearly sides with those who believe that "self-annihilation" points toward the truly stable point "in which man can rest."

What is "self-annihilation"? In Hartley's psychological theory, annihilation is not a transcendent amnesia—an experience whereby one's sense of being a person is annulled. As the anonymous author of the "Letter Concerning Mr. Marsay" states, self-annihilation "cannot be supposed to mean *the reducing to nothing*, in a *physical* or natural Sense." Rather, in Hartley's theory, "perfect self-annihilation" occurs when benevolence, piety, and the moral sense "check" and "utterly extinguish" the dispositions of sensation, imagination, ambition, and self-interest as primary or independent sources of pleasure and pain. It occurs, in other words, when one's sense of being a person detaches from the lower face of the prism of self and derives wholly from one's identification with the farther. It occurs when sympathy and theopathy flow without restriction—when the person without restriction loves others and loves God.

It is important to keep in mind that, in the terms of Hartley's psychology, *self* is not a substance or thing. *Self* is a location; it is a complex of complexes, a latticed molecular compound of associations, a hypercomplex idea. *Self-interest* is a definition; it is a schema that defines a particular set of relations among orientations; it both defines and is part of the network of channels along which emotions are transferred. As such, self-interest both regulates the symbolic economy of pleasure and is a part of that economy. If it becomes a primary pursuit, *self* becomes the vine that drinks up the sap of emotion. In terms of this understanding of *self*, Hartley's recommendation that self be annihilated can be interpreted thusly: for the sake of *being* a loving person, it is best for one to move beyond reflexive reference altogether; that is, in order to make sympathy and theopathy fully efficacious primary pursuits, it is best to fill in, or sever, the channels whereby emotion flows into the self complex.

When a person does so, he does not disappear; he remains a conscious being with all the memories that comprise his personal history, including the definitions of self-interest through which he has passed. What has changed for such a person is that self-interest is no longer a part of the economy of pleasure.

There is more: self-interest ceases to be part of the economy when the person attains the realization that there *need not be* an economy of pleasure. Economics is the science of scarcity; it concerns the totality of transferences by which scarce items of value are allocated within a system. But when it comes to love, there is no scarcity; there is nothing to regulate. The pleasures of sympathy, theopathy, and the moral sense are self-consistent and unlimited. Genuine and unrestricted love of others and of God is never the cause of irreconcilable internal conflicts, and neither is such love something we can ever use up. The pleasures deriving from benevolence and theopathy "receive fresh recruits upon every gratification, and ... increase perpetually" (*OM* 2.3.6.68). A person who helps others and loves God will discover that the pleasures that flow from such help and love never pall and never fail. A person who has awakened to this realization sees in *self-interest* a temporary expedient.

Self-interest, she could say, is a technique for managing scarce resources of love and affection—for only so long as the illusion of scarcity lasts. And when the illusion is ended, the expedient can be abandoned, and the self annihilated.

2. "The Ancient and Modern Interior Christians Called Mystics"

In the passage quoted above, Hartley refers to "perfect self-annihilation, and resting in God as our centre" and then to "perfect self-annihilation, and the pure love of God." By affirming that we should never be satisfied with ourselves until we arrive at this state, he identifies himself with those writers who reckon that self-annihilation is "the only [state] in which man can rest." What writers did he have in mind? And what did "the pure love of God" mean to them? How, in other words, are we to understand the religious world in which Hartley developed his theory of psychological transformation and transcendence?

To begin with, it is important to remember that the later seventeenth and earlier eighteenth centuries marked an era of religious awakening throughout Europe and America (see Bruneau 1998, 147). Pietists flourished in Germany, Quakers and Methodists in England and America, Hasidim in Poland and Russia. Hartley was a contemporary of Hume; he was also a contemporary of William Law, Jonathan Edwards, John and Charles Wesley, Nicholas von Zinzendorf, and Israel ben Eliezer, the Baal Shem Tov. To understand Hartley fully, commonalities with the latter may be more important than comparisons to Hume.

Moreover, although the terms *self-annihilation* and *the pure love of God* may be less than familiar to readers today, they are representative of a well-established pattern of thought. The pattern appears in Kabbalistic and Hasidic Judaism and in Sufic Islam and well as in Christianity, and it is not clear to me to what extent these should be described as separate traditions, despite their distinct histories. Were they to read the relevant sections in the *Observations*, it is likely that followers of Symeon the New Theologian, of Isaac Luria and Dov Baer, and of Ibn al-Arabi and Jalal ad-Din Rumi would all be familiar with the pattern of thought Hartley sought to express.

I do not know whether or not Hartley would have recognized any of the five names in the last sentence. It is not impossible. There were, in Hartley's day, Christian students of the Kabbalah, and there were also some, like Hartley's friend John Byrom, who read Arabic. But there are also sources that are closer culturally to Hartley. To take one example from the books in Hartley's library, in the *Imitation of Christ* Thomas à Kempis writes: "Oh what might there is in the pure love of Jesus; when unmixed with any self-interest or self-love" (2.11.1, Challoner trans.). In addition to à Kempis, Hartley's language would have reminded readers in his day of more nearly contemporary writers. Christian readers may have thought first of those ardent advocates of pure love—Saint Francis de Sales and his disciple, Jean-Pierre Camus, author of *Défense du pur amour* (1640).[1]

More generally, Hartley's use of a distinctive vocabulary would have led devoted readers to associate Hartley with the practice of what Saint Teresa of Avila and Saint Francis de Sales called "mystical theology." In her *Life,* Teresa writes that she "used unexpectedly to experience a consciousness of the presence of God of such a kind that I could not possibly doubt that he was within me or that I was wholly engulfed in him. This was in no sense a vision: I believe that it is called mystical theology" (1960, 1.10). Francis, in his *Traité de l'Amour de Dieu,* writes: "Prayer and mystical theology ... are identical. Prayer is called theology, because it deals with God as speculative theology does.... Prayer is called mystical, because of the hidden nature of the conversation: ... After all, prayer, or mystical theology, is simply a loving talk between the soul and God, where the topic of conversation is the attraction of God's goodness and how to achieve union with him" ([1616] 1962, 218–19). Hartley's "resting in God as our centre" is the goal of those who experience "the attraction of God's goodness" and who long "to achieve union with him." And here, in the language of mystical theology, as the author of "A Letter Concerning Mr. Marsay" notes, "perfect self-annihilation" refers only to *"the doing away* of such bad Dispositions as hinder the *divine* Operations on the Soul, or which are Obstacles to the *Union* between God and Man."[2]

More specifically, given Hartley's advocacy of the spiritual practices of voluntary silence (*OM* 2.3.3.64) and of mental (i.e., wordless) prayer (*OM* 2.3.7.73), contemporary readers would have discerned Hartley's sympathy for a controversial religious "movement," which was termed "Quietism" by its critics and suppressors.[3] The most important figures identified as Quietists are Miguel de Molinos (1640–97), Jeanne-Marie Bouvier de la Mothe Guyon (Madame Guyon, 1648–1717), and François de Salignac de la Mothe Fénelon, Archbishop of Cambrai (1651–1715). Before and during Hartley's lifetime, the movement attracted adherents throughout Europe and Britain; among the figures associated with it are

Antoinette Bourignon (1616–80); Pierre Poiret (1646–1719), a disciple first of Bourignon and then of Guyon; Charles-Hectore de Saint-George de Marsay (1688–1755); and, in Scotland, another follower of Bourignon, George Garden (d. 1717) and his circle, including George Cheyne (for discussion, see Bruneau 1998, Chevallier 1994, and Gondal 1989). One of the more remarkable members of the group was Andrew Michael Ramsay (1686–1743)—Chevalier Ramsay—a Scot who studied in Holland with Poiret, lived in Fénelon's household from 1710 until the archbishop's death, and then assisted Madame Guyon during her last years (see Henderson 1952). In addition to Ramsay, a number of the adherents in Scotland, such as Alexander the 4th Lord Forbes of Pitsligo, were Jacobites, as was the English admirer of Bourignon and close friend of Hartley, John Byrom.

As a group the Quietists today are only dimly remembered, and even in their own time some of them, outside of their own circles, may have been poorly understood or little known. One such is Charles-Hectore de Saint-George de Marsay (1688–1755), the leader of a group of people who called themselves "Associates *à l'enfance de Jésus*" (Marsay 1749, 41) and the subject of the letter from which one of this chapter's epigraphs is taken. George Cheyne wrote to John Byrom on 22 August 1742 (B 2.2.330–32) concerning Marsay's *Témoignage d'un enfant de la vérité et droiture des voies de l'esprit,* a series of biblical commentaries "consisting of eight or ten octavo volumes," which Cheyne sent to Byrom's mentor William Law, for his opinion of them. "For as to [Marsay's] essentials," Cheyne writes, "his directions, and his explications of Holy Scripture, I have not the least demur, well knowing them to be entirely the same with those of *Taulerus, Johannes à Cruce, Bernier, Bertôt* and *M. Guyon,* and all the most approved ancient and modern interior Christians called mystics." Still, Cheyne is worried about "his specialities, his new scriptural manifestations and discoveries about the states of glory of the invisible world and the future purification of lapsed intelligences, human and angelical." Cheyne ends the letter by saying: "Lord Huntington has them from me, and I am getting your good friends and mine, Dr. Hartley and his lady, to read them, and though I cannot promise they will swallow them so eagerly as I have, yet I believe their honest and sincere hearts will relish them in the main, at least the essentials." Appended to the letter was a shorthand note from Hartley, inviting Byrom to visit them in Bath. The note ends with this line: "I pray God direct and bless us all, that we know and speak and act the truth as it is in Jesus."

Although we have no evidence indicating whether or not the Hartleys accepted Marsay's directions and explications as eagerly as did Cheyne, it is clear at least that Marsay's "specialities" and "new scriptural manifestations and discoveries" did not cause Hartley to dismiss him from his mind. To some degree he did at least "relish ... the essentials." The catalogue of Hartley's library lists four of the volumes of Marsay's *Témoignage*: *Explication de la Genèse* (1738); *Explication d'Apocalypse* (1739); *Explication de L'Épître aux Romans* (1739); and *Vie des Patriarchs* (1740).[4] In addition, Hartley apparently made an effort to discover what he could about the author. The only English translation of Marsay's work, a selection of his writings entitled *Discourses on Subjects relating to the Spiritual Life*, was published in Edinburgh in 1749, the year of the publication of the *Observations*. The volume contains the anonymous "Letter Concerning Mr. Marsay, and other Authors of that Class," addressed "To J.F. Esq." (Let us call the author of this letter "Marsay's editor.") The volume also contains "A Letter, giving some Account of the Author" (1749, 39–42). This brief biographical account, we are told, was composed by "Dr. H——'s Friend at *Aix*, who is intimately acquainted with him." Appended to it is a brief "Addition to the above Account sent Dr. C——" (42).

There is a story here. Would that we knew what it is. Unfortunately, I do not know the identities of "Dr. H——'s Friend at *Aix*," of Marsay's editor, or of "J.F.," to whom the letter is addressed. It appears that Hartley, Cheyne, or one of their associates corresponded with Hartley's "Friend at Aix" and asked the man for information concerning Marsay, with whom he was "intimately acquainted," and that the friend obliged. The letter appears in the volume. If the letter was originally sent to Hartley, it would probably be more likely than not that Hartley consented to its publication—as, apparently, did Cheyne, to the subsequent letter sent to him. I do not know of any extant letters between Hartley and his "Friend at Aix," or whether there was any direct exchange of letters between Hartley, Cheyne, or J.F.'s correspondent and Marsay.

What is clear, however, is that Hartley and Marsay had much in common, at least concerning their essentials. Hartley was an advocate of self-annihilation and the pure love of God. "According to this Author," Marsay's editor states, "the Essence of Sin consists in *Self-Will*; that is, in willing without Regard to the *divine Will*. . . . He says plainly, 'If there was no *Self-will*, there would neither be Hell nor Devil'" (1749, 19). The editor adds: "This doctrine is inculcated by Mr. *Marsay* almost in every Paragraph: It may be called *the Burden of his Song*."[5]

Similarly, Hartley held, as a fundamental article of his faith, the doctrine of universal salvation. Marsay affirmed "the universal Restoration of all Spirits; when an End shall be put to all Sorrow, all Disorder, and Rebellion against God" (29). And in a second preface to the 1779 edition of Jeremiah White's *Restoration of All Things,* "J.D." (presumably John Denis, the publisher) mentions Marsay's *Discourses* and notes that "Mr MARSAY, in different Parts of his Works, speaks of his having several Revelations made to him of Spiritual Things, and in particular mentions, That he was under a Necessity to assert the *Universal Restoration of all Things*" (White 1779, xxxvi).

Such commonalities are not necessarily indicators of direct influence; they suggest no more than that both Hartley and Marsay shared a pattern of thought. Recall Cheyne's comment to Byrom that he knew Marsay's essentials "to be entirely the same with those of *Taulerus, Johannes à Cruce, Bernier, Bertôt* and *M. Guyon,* and all the most approved ancient and modern interior Christians called mystics." Cheyne here mentions the well known, such as Johannes Tauler and Saint John of the Cross; one person known today at least by name, Jeanne Guyon; and those who are today obscure, known only to specialists, such as Claude Bernier, S.J. (1601–55; see de Certeau 1992, 265–70) and Jacques Bertot, who was one of Guyon's spiritual associates. Overall, Cheyne's letter illustrates the difficulties of categorization and of tracing affiliations.

Hartley, Cheyne, and Byrom were experienced readers of "all the most approved ancient and modern interior Christians called mystics." Both Hartley and Byrom assembled extensive libraries of their works; Hartley, to take one example, owned both Latin and French editions of the complete works of John of the Cross. In addition, although Hartley, Cheyne, and Byrom maintained some affiliation with the Church of England, boundaries of religion, nation, and language apparently meant little to them; in addition to the people Cheyne lists as examples of "approved" writers, Byrom was also at this time purchasing copies of works by Jan van Ruysbroeck (1293–1381) and Angelus Silesius (1624–77), who had converted to Roman Catholicism. And in his record of a long conversation with William Law in May 1743, Byrom notes that Law said that Cheyne "was always talking in the coffeehouses about naked faith, pure love; that Dr. Cheyne was the providential occasion of his meeting or knowing of Jakob Behmen [Boehme], by a book which the Dr. mentioned to him in a letter, which book mentioned Behmen" (B 2.2.363). Equally importantly, Cheyne's letter to Byrom suggests that he and his friends discussed these works among themselves, and thereby developed their own methods and standards of interpretation and evaluation, whereby they could winnow the kernel of spiritual truth out of the husk of idiosyncratic "specialities." Mystical theology was for them a way of life.

Consider another further complication—and possible affiliation. In the "Conclusion" to the second part of the *Observations,* Hartley makes some remarks concerning "the temporal evils and woes, which will probably fall upon the nominally christian states of these western parts, the christian *Babylon,* before the great revolution predicted in the scriptures, before the kingdoms of this world become the kingdoms of our Lord, and of his Christ" (*OM* 2. Conclusion). Hartley addresses his remarks to "the attention of the present christian world; at least of those good *Philadelphians,* who are desirous to keep themselves and others from that hour of temptation, which is coming to us all." Hartley echoes the text of Revelation 3.10, in which Jesus says to the church of Philadelphia: "Because thou hast kept the word of my patience, I will also keep thee from the hour of temptation, which shall come upon all the world." The "good Philadelphians" to whom Hartley addresses himself may be intended to include all those, such as Cheyne and Byrom, Law and Marsay, for whom Christianity is more than nominal. It would seem inconsistent of him to limit his closing address to the members of any one party in the "christian *Babylon.*"

Nonetheless, there is the possibility that Hartley's choice of biblical reference was not simply coincidental. In directing his remarks to "those good *Philadelphians,*" he may have been addressing a specific audience; or at least, he may have been aware that he could be taken to be doing so. When the author of the "Letter Concerning Mr. Marsay" noted that Marsay affirmed "the universal Restoration of all Spirits," he immediately adds: "This Opinion is not *Marsay*'s alone, it was espoused by the *Philadelphians* in the last century; Doctor *Thomas Burnet* has asserted it with many Arguments; Mr. *Murhalt* says yet more of it; and some other Foreigners have maintained it of late. Long ago it was adopted by *Origen,* though in not so clear a Way" (1749, 30). The reference to the Philadelphians is to a religious group that was particularly notable for its "specialities"—the Philadelphian Society for the Advancement of Piety and Divine Philosophy. The Society was founded by John Pordage (1607–81), who was instrumental in the introduction of the works of Jakob Boehme into England. It is most closely identified with its major prophet, Jane Lead (1623–1704), and then with her disciples Richard Roach (1662–1730) and Francis Lee (1661–1719), who helped establish the Society in Holland and Germany.[6] Lead recorded her extensive revelations from God in a series of books, beginning with *The Heavenly Cloud New Breaking* (1681). Her next work, *The Revelation of Revelations* ([1683] 1884), discloses that "the Spirit of the Lord hath searched and found out a cure, which will bring the broken and divided estate of the first Adamical birth into unity, harmony, and pure liberty" (4), thereby accomplishing "the reducing of every divided property into unity" (6). In *The Enochian Walks with God* (1694) she reveals the everlasting gospel of universal salvation, and in *A Fountain of Gardens* (1696–1700) she speaks of the necessity of "Self-Annihilation" (quoted in E. P. Thompson 1993, 37).

The "everlasting gospel" of universal salvation, self-annihilation, a return to a paradisiacal state where "every divided property" shall be reduced "into unity"—there seem to be strong affinities between Lead's revelations and central themes in Hartley's work. However, on the one hand, it seems difficult to entertain the notion that Hartley was deeply influenced by her writings. Her revelations are interminable; the being who speaks to and through her is garrulous and repetitive. Moreover, there is a problem with the dating. Lead died in 1704, and Thune comments that, in England after 1706, "there are no traces to be found of a public appearance of the Philadelphian Society" (Thune 1948, 137). The society appears to have disappeared as an organization, at least in England, at the time of Hartley's birth. (In an exchange of letters in 1709, Chevalier Ramsay and a friend write of "the old Philadelphian friendship"; see Henderson 1952, 20). On the other hand, Thune (1948, 138) also notes that Richard Roach continued to be a faithful exponent of Lead's teachings up to his death in 1730. It is possible that Hartley and Roach could have crossed paths, or that Hartley knew of Roach's own writings (1725, 1727) or of the preface he wrote for Jeremiah White's *Restoration of All Things*. In addition, the society did continue in Germany—in the district in which Marsay lived. In 1730 Count Casimir von Wittgenstein and his mother invited Count Nicholas von Zinzendorf (1700–60), the refounder of the Moravian church, to the neighboring towns of Berleburg and Schwartzenau in order to settle disputes among the local "interior Christians" and to revitalize the Philadelphian Society. Although the society did not survive for the long term, it did succeed with the publication between 1728 and 1742 of the eight volumes of the "Berleburger Bible"—"a translation of the Holy Scriptures with special prefaces and notes as a help in understanding the mystic implication of the Holy Writ" (Thune 1948, 149).

Marsay lived for a time in Schwartzenau, and the volumes of his *Témoignage* were published in Berleburg. According to the report prepared by Hartley's "Friend at Aix," Zinzendorf lived with Marsay for several months: "At first Mr. *Marsay* received him with open Charity, but soon began to discern a Spirit of Party and Singularity, if not Pride and worldly Views, in him, which when he found he could not reclaim, he dismissed him" (Marsay 1749, 41).

For all their specialities, the Philadelphians were particularly critical of the "Spirit of Party and Singularity," and for this reason they called themselves a society and not a church. Like Hartley, they believed that all denominational differences were chaff. In England they continued to participate in Anglican services, and they criticized the Quakers for setting themselves apart. One of their documents asserted that their "Peculiar Principles" consisted of "none but that single Opinion, That the Coming of Christ was near at Hand; and therefore they think it their duty to warn and awaken the World, that they may prepare for that great and solemn Time, with a good Life, universal Charity, and Union amongst the Protestant Churches" (*The State of the Philadelphian Society* [1697, 2], quoted in Thune 1948, 93). Taking "good Philadelphians" to refer to Byrom, Cheyne, Marsay, and all believers in the everlasting gospel would thus be consistent both with the original principles of the Philadelphian Society and with Hartley's own conviction that the creeds and articles that divide Christians into factions are about to be "carried away like the chaff of the summer threshing floors" (*OM* 2.3.9.76). In this interpretation, all who "worship God *in spirit and in truth*" are "good Philadelphians." However, it is also possible that, despite the apparent disappearance of the group in England, there were in the 1740s some people who still thought of themselves as Philadelphians in a special sense. If so, Hartley may, in the closing pages of the *Observations*, be addressing them.

3. "The Soul of Our Soul"

Given their wide reading, large libraries, and active discussion of the literature of mystical theology, and also given the extensive personal contacts among the "interior Christians," we should be cautious about suggesting that any particular book or author is the single or original source of a term or idea in the writings of Hartley and his friends. Thus, although it is true that Francis de Sales and Jean-Pierre Camus are notable proponents of pure love, it is possible that Hartley encountered the doctrine in the writings of Guyon and her followers, and it is also possible that Cheyne—who "was always talking in the coffeehouses"—converted Hartley to it, just as Hartley had tried, in the Temple Exchange coffeehouse, to bring Byrom around to his interpretation of αιωνιος Hartley does not say, and we just do not know.

With this caution in mind, let us turn to an examination of the Quietist version of mystical theology—taking *Quietism* very broadly, as a term of convenience, to refer to the particular articulation of the ancient pattern of thought that would have been most readily available to Hartley and his friends. To summarize very broadly, the Quietists emphasized three fundamental themes. First, they took seriously those biblical passages that indicated that the goal of human life is union with God—but a union in which the person comes to recognize that God is already and always present within the soul. In the Gospel of Luke Jesus says that "the kingdom of God cometh not with observation: . . . for, behold, the kingdom of God is within you" (17.20–21). And in the Second Epistle of Peter the Apostle writes that we are given "exceeding great and precious promises: that by these ye might be partakers of the divine nature, having escaped the corruption that is in the world through lust" (1.4). The Quietists believed that the kingdom of God is indeed *within* us—to be found within the human heart or soul—and that when a person discovers it there, he or she does come to partake of the divine nature. In *The Archbishop of Cambray's Dissertation on Pure Love*, a compilation of Quietest materials published in England in 1735, the anonymous author of the one-hundred-thirty-page "Apologetic Preface" quotes Fénelon's *Oeuvres Spirituelles* (Antwerp, 1718): "By *Scripture* 'tis certain that the Spirit of God dwells in us; that it acts there; that it prays there continually; that it groans there; that it desires there; that it asketh for us, what we know not to ask for ourselves; that it excites us, animates us, speaks to us in *Silence,* suggests all Truths to us, and unites us so to itself, that we become *One Spirit with God"* (Fénelon 1735, iv). It is important to attend here to the strength and extensiveness of Fénelon's claim. Note the increasingly inclusive progression of the verbs in the sentence: the Holy Spirit *dwells, acts, prays continually, groans, desires,* and *asks what we do not know to ask.* Then it *excites, animates,* and *speaks* to us, *suggests all Truths,* and finally *unites us to itself.* In this progression, the Holy Spirit goes from being something that dwells within the person, to being the principle that animates the person, to being the being of the person.

Fénelon criticizes those who "suppose the outward written Law, or at most a Light drawn from *Scripture* and Reasoning, to be what enlightens us inwardly" (iv–v). People who suppose this, he adds, "set not enough by the *inward* Teacher, the HOLY SPIRIT, who does all this. He is the Soul of our Soul. We cannot frame a Thought, or create a Desire, but through Him. Alas, how great then is our Blindness! We make account as if we were by ourselves in this *inward* Sanctuary, but on the contrary, God is there more nearly and intimately, than we ourselves are" (v).[7] We may add that, to take the thought to its logical conclusion, God is "more nearly and intimately" present in the "inward sanctuary" than "we ourselves are" because our *selves* are, in the ultimate ratio of things, an illusion. Compare Fénelon's statement with the following by Marsay: "It is God who invites us to forsake ourselves and our own Actings, that he may himself become our Life and all our Operation; yes, to the end that he may banish *Self*, in order to make his Abode in us, and become the Soul of our Soul, and the Life of our Life, which can never be, if we do not abandon our own Operations when it is Time to quit them" (1749, 95). For both Fénelon and Marsay, God is the "soul of our soul," and the conceit that we are independent agents is a mark of our blindness.

Students of comparative religion and philosophy could interpret the statements of Fénelon and Marsay as expressions of a thought or insight that has been expressed in other idioms. Those who study the Kabbalah may think of the words of the Besht's successor, Dov Baer, the Maggid of Mezritch, who advised: "Think of yourself as Ayin [nothingness] and forget yourself totally.... If you think of yourself as something, then God cannot clothe himself in you" (quoted in Matt 1996, 71; see also Uffenheimer 1993). Or, more generally, they may be reminded of the shattering of the vessels and of *tiqqun*, the process of mending by which the sparks of divinity return to their source. And perhaps the insight has been most thoroughly articulated by the Vedanta school in Hinduism. In his commentary on the *Vedānta Sūtra*, for example, Śaṁkara writes: "That same highest *Brahman* constitutes—as we know from passages such as 'that art thou'—the real nature of the individual self, while its second nature, i.e., that aspect of it which depends upon fictitious limiting conditions, is not its real nature. For as long as the individual self does not free itself from ignorance in the form of duality... and does not rise to knowledge of the Self [*Ātman*]... which expresses itself in the form 'I am *Brahman*'—so long it remains an individual self" (Radhakrishnan and Moore 1957, 514–15). The empirical self, Self, and Ultimate Reality are three names for the one reality: anatman is Atman is Brahman. The sorrow of human life stems from the fact that people do not recognize the divine reality that they are: they mistakenly think the empirical self [anātman], which is the outcome of "fictitious limiting conditions," to be a substantial and independently existing entity, when in fact the experience of independent selfhood is a factitious associative construct, made up of complexes all the way down. But release comes from seeing through the illusory duality: "Because the non-difference of all selves is essential and their difference due to ignorance only, the individual self after having dispelled ignorance by true knowledge passes over into unity with the highest Self" (538). In Fénelon's and Marsay's terms, the person who realizes that God is the soul of his soul, more intimately present than his own sense of self, will recognize his unity with the divine nature. Such a person will be making progress toward the *annihilation* that, according to Marsay's editor, constitutes "*the doing away* of such bad Dispositions as hinder the *divine* Operations on the Soul, or which are Obstacles to the *Union* between God and Man."

It is unlikely that Fénelon or Marsay would have known about the religions and philosophies of India; Quietism has no direct debt to Vedanta, or Fénelon to Śaṁkara, despite their apparent affinities. Fénelon would, however, have been familiar with Saint Augustine, who called God "the Life of the life of my soul" (*Confessions* 10.6). And like Augustine, Fénelon was directly and explicitly indebted to Plato, and particularly to the account, in the *Phaedrus* and *Symposium,* of the ascent of the soul toward the idea of the true, good, and beautiful. He writes, approvingly: "*Plato* often says, that the Love of BEAUTY is the *summum bonum,* or whole Good of Man: That Man of himself cannot be happy, and that what is most divine in him, is to deny and go out of himself for *Love:* . . . His Glory and Perfection is to go out of himself, to forget himself, to be lost and absorp'd in the pure Love of INFINITE BEAUTY" (1735, 9–10). And Fénelon, following upon the many earlier Christian appropriations of Platonic and Neoplatonic teaching, identifies the "infinite beauty" that we naturally love and into which we desire to be absorbed with the Logos that is the *Archē*—the mind of God and the pattern of the cosmos, manifested in Jesus Christ. The author of the "Apologetic Preface" draws the conclusion: "From the *Premises* now laid down, it follows that REASON is the *Light* of the Soul, the Fountain of Wisdom; the Inspirer of the Prophets and Apostles, and of all holy Souls from the Creation of Man to this very Time: . . . Whoever therefore truly obeys and follows REASON, they obey and follow God; they

Annihilation of Self

are led and guided by the Light of CHRIST, and thereby become *Christians*, as *Justin Martyr*... told the Emperor *Marcus Antoninus*, in his Apology for the Christians" (1735, xx–xxi). In the light of this interpretation, Fénelon's statement that "we cannot frame a Thought, or create a Desire, but through Him" is literally true: our reasons are particular expressions or manifestations of the ultimate Reason; every time we form a thought in words, the Word speaks through us.[8]

The second theme of Quietism concerns the means by which the person should seek to discern the inward operation of God. The "Eternal and All-powerful Word of the Father," writes Fénelon, "speakest in the very Bottom of Souls" (1735, vi); it is, moreover, "certain... that we are inspir'd continually" (vii), for God "continually strives to communicate Himself" (ix). Our objective should be to be open to this inspiration, this communication, so that the Word may speak through us—or more, so that we may discover that the Word is "more nearly and intimately" present in the inward sanctuary "than we ourselves are." And doing so is not accomplished by piling more words onto the heap of words that compound the empirical self; rather, it is accomplished through the mental practice of "orison"—the letting go of words and concepts altogether (see Bruneau 1998, 143). The practice of orison, in turn, does not require that one enter a cloister; stillness can be achieved by any person, in the ordinary circumstances of life. Near the beginning of her *Moyen court et très facile de faire oraison* ([1685] 1995, 68–69), Jeanne Guyon recommends that people who are illiterate begin simply by saying the Lord's Prayer—a phrase at a time, and very slowly. The aim is not to meet a quota of repetitions but rather to let the words fill one's consciousness. Between petitions, they should remain quiet. Then, "if they feel an inclination to peace and silence, they should not continue but should wait for as long as the state lasts" (69). People more experienced in this "little method without method" (59) can do without the specific words, and indeed without formal meditative techniques altogether. Such people can find their way directly, as it were, to the "presence of God" (70), which they then enjoy in a state of contemplation. In this state, the Word resonates within them, though not necessarily in an articulate manner. Guyon reports that, early in her life, "There was made in me, without the sound of Words, a continual Prayer, which seem'd to me, to be the Prayer of the Lord Jesus Christ himself, a Prayer of the WORD" (Fénelon 1735, 21).

For such a "continual Prayer" to be the soul of one's soul, so that one lives at all moments in the presence of God, requires finally what

Guyon calls "l'abandon et la donation de tout soi-même à Dieu" ([1685] 1995, 73)—the surrender, renunciation, or "annihilation" of self, and the gift of one's whole self to God.

On the subject of "mental prayer," without words, Hartley writes: "Words are of great use in most private prayer, because of the associations transferred upon them, and which therefore they excite in the mind. But then, as there are internal sentiments and combinations of these, to which no words can correspond, we must not confine the noble privilege of prayer and praise to our languages, which are the offspring of the confusion at Babel. There are therefore proper seasons and occasions for mental prayer, for the tendency and aspiration of the heart to God without words" (OM 2.3.7.78). In the next paragraph he adds that "forms of prayer, composed by persons of devout spirit" are useful, particularly at the beginning of a course of religious instruction. But then he adds that "it would be a great hindrance to the growth and perfection of our devotion, always to keep to the forms. The heart of every particular person alone knows its own bitterness, its desires, guilt, fears, hopes, and joys; and it will be impossible to open ourselves without reserve ... unless we do it of ourselves, in such words as the then present state of mind, when under a vigorous sense of the divine presence, shall suggest." Words, and recited compositions, help a person to pray, but prayer is ultimately a matter of opening oneself "without reserve" to the "divine presence." A complete, unreserved opening would require that one pass beyond formal prayers and then beyond words altogether. Concerning those who have done so, Hartley writes: "Times, forms, and rules of devotion, are schoolmasters that serve to bring us to Christ. As for those persons who are so far advanced, as to walk with God continually, who sanctify the minutest actions by a perpetual dedication of them to God, I do not presume to instruct them. *Their anointing teaches them all things*" (1 John 2.27).[9]

The third theme is that the Word speaks through every one—to the degree that each person has learned to quiet the voice of self and to cease hindering "the *divine* Operations on the Soul." In a sense, every person already partakes in the divine nature simply by virtue of being human; differences among people depend upon the degree to which they become aware of this. The author of the "Apologetic Preface" quotes Justin Martyr (c. 100–c. 160), who wrote: "We have ... been taught that CHRIST is the first Begotten of God; and we declar'd before that He is the [LOGOS] REASON, of which *all Mankind* are partakers; and that those who live according to REASON are Christians" (1735, xxi; cf.

Justin Martyr, *First Apology*, 46). John Byrom personally impressed this point upon David Hartley on 22 May 1736. While the two were walking through London to Bloomsbury, where Hartley was scheduled to dine with Robert Smith, author of *A Compleat System of Opticks*, at the home of Charles Townsend, Lord Lynn, "we had much talk about reason, enthu., and I parted from him saying, No reason but the Λογος = J.C., that reason was nothing if it was but a grammatical term and different in every man, but the true Reason was the Λογος, Jesus Christ" (*B* 1.2.48). Byrom's parting comment is a virtual paraphrase of the quotation from Justin Martyr.

Three consequences follow from this affirmation. First, if every person may become a vessel filled with "continual prayer," then even within a Christian nation, the ecclesiastical and political authorities do not have a monopoly upon speaking the truth. Rather, it is the responsibility of every man and woman—or better, it is the "Glory and Perfection" of every one—to encounter the Word within his or her own soul. The people who do so, and who then speak prophetically so as to enable others to discern the light within themselves, may be archbishops, like Fénelon, or they may be laywomen like Jeanne-Marie Guyon and Antoinette Bourignon. Hartley writes, concerning the ability to "explain and illustrate" both the "word and works of God": "But we are not to confine this blessing to those who are called *learned* men, in the usual sense of this word. Devotion, charity, prayer, have a wonderful influence upon those who read the Scriptures, and contemplate the works of creation, with a practical intention; and enable persons otherwise illiterate, not only to see and feel the important truths therein manifested, for their private purposes, but to preach and inculcate them upon others with singular efficacy and success" (*OM* 2.3.3.60).

Recall as well Hartley's comparison of animal instinct and prophetic inspiration, discussed in §6.1. Animals' instinctual repertoires of action, such as birds building nests and tending their young, are "a kind of inspiration . . . mixing itself with, and helping, out that part of their faculties which corresponds to reason in us." He adds that such inspiration "might be called natural . . . whereas the inspiration of the sacred writers appears to be of a higher source, so as to be termed supernatural. . . . And yet it may result from some higher laws of nature. . . . and indeed, all differences in these things, after the facts are once settled, will be found, upon due inquiry, to be merely verbal" (*OM* 1.3.7.93). On the one hand, Jeanne Guyon can be taken as an example of a person who can preach important religious truths thanks to the "wonderful influence" of devotion, charity, prayer, and reading the scriptures. On the other, when she gives expression to the continual prayer within herself, she can also be understood to be acting as instinctually as a bird building a nest, but according to "higher" laws of nature, which we have yet to discover.

The second consequence concerns the partial and provisional nature of religious language. Hartley believed that "creeds, articles, &c. seem to have no use now" and indeed that "now they grow old, and seem ready to die away, and to give place to the worship of God *in spirit and in truth;* in which there is no Papist, Protestant, Lutheran, Calvinist, Trinitarian, Unitarian, Mystic, Methodist, &c. but all these distinctions are carried away like the chaff of the summer threshing floors" (*OM* 2.3.9.76). Hartley's comment that creeds and articles "have no use now" could be taken to suggest that they once did have a use. It would be truer to his overall theological stance to say that, for him, creeds and articles never served a legitimate purpose. He states: "The Apostles' Creed is so plain and clear, except in the three articles concerning the descent of Christ into hell, the holy catholic church, and the communion of saints, that no one who believes the truth of the Scriptures can hesitate about it; . . . It is quite useless, therefore, to require an assent even to these articles. As to the metaphysical subtleties, which appear in the subsequent creeds, they can at best be only human interpretations of scripture words; and, therefore, can have no authority. Words refer to words, and to grammatical and logical analogies, in an endless manner, in these things; and all the real foundation which we have is in the words of Scripture, and of the most ancient writers, considered as helps, not authorities."

And lest we think Hartley substitutes a biblical absolutism for a creedal one, we need to note the beginning of the next paragraph: "Nay, it seems needless, or ensnaring, to subscribe even to the Scriptures themselves." In Hartley's understanding of language, all the words of common speech are terms in an algebra; as such they enable us to formulate statements that are greater or lesser approximations of reality. Just as the languages of physics and chemistry are to the direct intuition of the "mechanical affections" of matter, so are the books of the Bible to the apprehension of God the "everlasting gospel" promises. Despite, or because of, the centrality of the everlasting gospel to him, Hartley nowhere states its "articles": it is not something that can be circumscribed in definitions. And here he warns that a captious oversubscription to the Scriptures can be a snare, keeping a person from "the worship of God *in spirit and in truth*" (John 4.24).[10]

The third consequence concerns the unity of the human race. Concerning this unity, the author of the "Apologetic Preface" quotes the author of a life of Fénelon: "By this Principle [of pure love] a Man no longer looks upon himself as an independent Creature made for himself, but considers the universal Lump of Mankind as one great Family, of which all Nations are but so many Branches, and all Men either as Fathers, Brothers, and Children of one common Father, who would have us prefer the general Good of his Family to our own particular Interest" (1735, 2). People of all nations are members of the "one great Family," whether in Europe, India, Asia, Africa, or the Americas. Insofar as they "prefer the general Good of [the Father's] Family," they follow the light of the Logos within themselves. And to the degree that they become vessels for that light, they may discover that "the universal Lump of Mankind" has the potential for a unity that is more closely knit than that represented by a family: the potential unity of the "universal Lump" may be more fully symbolized by the image of a universal man.

4. Albion's Bosom

It is near the beginning of his epic poem *Jerusalem* that William Blake prays for the annihilation of selfhood. The poet needs to do so in order to write the poem—to complete the "great task" of opening "the Eternal Eyes / Of Man inwards into Worlds of Thought: into Eternity / Ever expanding in the Bosom of God" (5.18–20). But this annihilation of selfhood is also what is required of Albion. In Blake's system of symbols, Albion is the "Eternal Man" (*Four Zoas* 1.484), the Adam Kadmon of the Kabbalah, who "anciently contain'd in his mighty limbs all things in Heaven & Earth" (*Jerusalem*, "To the Jews"). When he falls into the deadly sleep of jealousy and selfhood, his primordial unity is shattered; the result is a prolonged nightmare in which the various aspects of the universal man separate from Albion and come into conflict with each other. Thus, Albion splits into the four Zoas—the four "beasts" of Revelation 4.6–9, and also the four "living creatures," each with the four faces of man, lion, ox, and eagle, that appeared to Ezekiel by the waters of Babylon, surrounding the chariot of God (Ezekiel 1.4ff). Blake names these Tharmas, Urizen, Luvah, and Urthona; they represent respectively the body, reason, emotion, and imagination. Also split off from Albion are his "emanation" (in Jungian terms, anima alienated from psyche) and his "spectre" (the power of reason, ever negating). Jerusalem, his emanation, shelters in Beulah, the night realm where the "Sexes wander in dreams of bliss" (*Jerusalem* 79.73) and the "daughters of inspiration" dwell. His Spectre becomes "the Great Selfhood, / Satan, Worship'd as God by the Mighty Ones of the Earth" (32.17–18). These splinter aspects of the whole self then descend, like the gods of Hinduism, into their own avatars, which can split again into emanation and spectre.

Albion's Spectre, Blake tells us, "when separated / From Imagination and closing itself as in steel in a Ratio / Of the Things of Memory, It thence frames Laws & Moralities / To destroy Imagination, the Divine Body, by Martyrdoms & Wars" (74.10–14). It is this destruction of the "Divine Body" by martyrdoms and wars among the splinter aspects of the whole self that Blake describes in his prophetic books. But as well as disintegration and alienation, Blake also depicts the striving of the universal man for reintegration and wholeness. The history of the world is the nightmare that occurs during Albion's sleep, but this history culminates in Albion's awakening. When he awakes, all the unconscious and splintered aspects of his being rise "into Albion's Bosom" (96.41–42). Jerusalem awakes. Albion draws his bow and shoots down his Spectre from the sky (98.1–7). With this final act of "Self Annihilation," Albion attains his authentic and complete form in a renewed Paradise.

In Blake's own time and after, those who knew of him at all commonly regarded his prophetic books as a private and impenetrable mythology. To such, the books stood alone, as disconnected from the real world of men as, for example, Ezekiel's madly detailed plans for the reconstruction of the temple in Jerusalem. But in our time scholars such as Kathleen Raine (1968) and E. P. Thompson (1993) have done much to recover the traditions of thought that inform Blake's prophecies. The story Blake tells in *Jerusalem* is another expression of the ancient pattern of thought, another version of the theme, or prophecy, Jane Lead announces in *The Revelation of Revelations* (1683): that "the Spirit of the Lord hath searched and found out a cure, which will bring the broken and divided estate of the first Adamical birth into unity, harmony, and pure liberty." And concerning the divided estate of the "first Adamical birth," consider this passage from Peter Sterry's *Rise, Race, and Royalty of the Kingdom of God in the Soul of Man*, also published in 1683:

> The Divine Nature, which lies hid at the bottom, and in the center of the Soul, lives there to itself with its Heavenly, and Earthly Image, as in the Secret of its own twofold Paradise, whereof one was never yet revealed in any Creature until Christ; the other withdrew itself hither from the sight of the Soul at the Fall. This Divine Nature, as to the Soul itself, whose Root it is, of whose Being it is the only Life, and Truth, lies slain by the Life of Sin, and buried in its own Ruines beneath the Darkness, and Confusion of the Corrupt, the Fleshly, and the Hellish Image. (Sterry 1683, 500)

In Sterry's theology, regeneration requires the reintegration of the Heavenly and Earthly Images. The Heavenly Image is revealed in the person of Jesus, but the Earthly Image "withdrew itself" at the Fall; this second aspect of the Divine Nature now lies slain and buried within the "Ruines" of itself, beneath its counterfeit, the Hellish Image. Albion, in other words, lies ruined, dreaming nightmares of martyrdoms and wars, while his Spectre dominates humanity. For the Heavenly and Earthly Images to reunite in the Divine Nature, which is also the true human nature, the Hellish Image must be overcome. For one account of how it is overcome, turn to Blake's description of the mutual self-sacrifice of Jesus and Albion at the end of *Jerusalem* (96.8–37).

Consider also *The Restoration of All Things* ([1712] 1779), a treatise on universal salvation by Sterry's friend and fellow chaplain to Cromwell, Jeremiah White. Chapter 15 is entitled "An Argument for this Hypothesis drawn from the Nature of Man, as each Individual is a Compendium and Abstract of the intire Creation; and so not probable to be cast away for ever." In it White writes:

> Can we think so many *Millions* of such precious souls, each of which is an entire World, each of which is more worth than the whole World of Inferior beings, should be deemed such vile and abject things as to be *eternally abandoned* by God, and lost for ever, never to be visited, never to be recovered to the glory of the Creator that made them? ... For if each Soul be a Unity, a Figure, a Shadow of the Supreme Unity (not a dead but a living Shadow) and that all Lines of Being and Beauty meet in *this Apex,* and unity of the intellectual Spirit; no such individual Soul can be for ever abandoned; *but the whole nature of things*

must suffer therein, as it did when Christ was crucified: ... If so many millions of these intellectual Substances be never look'd upon, or visited with Redemption, not one Saint is *completely Saved*, for if each Spirit be an entire world, all Spirits are in each Spirit; as the Soul is in every part of the Body. ([1712] 1779, 146–47)

Each spirit is an entire world, and all spirits are in each. The idea is ancient. "All Israel are related to one another," according to Moses Cordovero, "for their souls are united and in each soul there is a portion of all the others" ([1588] 1960, 52). From the unity of souls White draws the consequence that it is impossible for one soul alone to be happy. It is also impossible for all but one to be completely happy, if that one remains lost. All souls must rise into Albion's bosom, if universal humanity is to awake.

In the context of White's articulation of universal salvation, to annihilate selfhood is to abandon the illusion of separateness; to annihilate selfhood is to recognize that "all Spirits are in each Spirit." Some supposedly orthodox Christian theologians of the time proposed what has been called the abominable fancy: the notion that part of the satisfactions of the saved in heaven derives from their contemplation of the torments of the damned in hell. Archbishop William King, for example, in his *Origin of Evil* asks rhetorically whether "any more effectual Means [could] be found out to make the Blessed approve themselves in their Choice conformed to the Divine Will, and persevere therein, than the continual Contemplation of those miserable Beings who have done otherwise" (King 1739, 500). White and his fellow universalists would have found repellent this image of the "Blessed" continuously looking down into the pit of hell—and deriving a sense of complacent self-approbation from what they see there. Such an image is one of radical and permanent fragmentation; it suggests that it serves the self-interest of some to observe, distantly, the suffering of others. It denies the unity of humanity.

White affirms "that the Saints are not fully glorified without the rest of Mankind." Then he goes further, to assert: "Nay, that Christ is not full without them, nor the manifestive Glory of God himself full and perfect without the recovering of the whole" (1779, 148). That God is perfect and self-sufficient, complete unto itself, has been a prominent idea within Christianity. Here White declares that even God would be incomplete to the extent that the whole is not recovered. The completeness of the divine nature requires the completeness of human nature. Conversely, the unity of humanity ultimately involves a further unification: in Sterry's terms, this is the union of the soul with the "Divine Nature"; in Blake's, it occurs when Albion converses with Jesus "as Man with Man in Ages of Eternity" (*Jerusalem* 96.6).

The unification of the human and divine natures is also a central point in Marsay's thinking. "The Moment *Adam* disobeyed God," Marsay writes, "he fell into Death, God withdrawing the divine Man which he had breathed into his Nostrils at his Creation; for it was not the animal Life that he breathed into his Nostrils, since God is *Spirit*, and communicated to *Adam* his *Spirit* by his *Breathing*. This was the *spiritual* Man, of the same Nature with God, and his *Image*, seeing *we are Partakers of the Divine Nature*, 2 Pet. 1.4.... this Sovereign, this little God, his inward Man, was taken from him, and God resumed it" (1749, 128). The goal of life, according to Marsay, is the recreation of the complete person, the perfect man, through the reunification of the "divine Man" with "the *terrestrial* Body" and with what he terms, following Boehme, the "*astral* Man... our Mind or Understanding."

Consider also Hartley's affirmation that, because they are self-consistent and limitless, the pleasures of sympathy ought to be a primary pursuit. As we noted at the end of the last chapter, one evidence of the self-consistency of benevolence "appears from the peculiar harmony, love, esteem, and mutual co-operation, that prevail amongst benevolent persons." Hartley elaborates upon this harmony:

> And now a new scene begins to open itself to our view. Let us suppose, that the benevolence of *A* is very imperfect; however, that it considerably exceeds his malevolence; so that he receives pleasure, on the whole, from the happiness of *B, C, D,* &c. *i.e.* from that of the small circle of those whom he has already learnt to call his neighbours. Let us also suppose, that *B, C, D,* &c. though affected with a variety of pains, as well as pleasures, are yet happy, upon the whole; and that *A*, though he does not see this balance of happiness clearly, yet has some comfortable general knowledge of it. This then is the happiness of good men in this present imperfect state; and it is evident, that they are great gainers, upon the whole, from their benevolence. At the same time it gives us a faint conception of *A*'s unbounded happiness, on supposition that he considered every man his friend, his son, his neighbour, his second self, and

loved him as himself; and that his neighbour was exalted to the same unbounded happiness as himself by the same unlimited benevolence. Thus *A, B, C, D,* &c. would all become, as it were, new sets of senses, and perceptive powers, to each other, so as to increase each other's happiness without limits; they would all become *members of the mystical body of Christ;* all have an equal care for each other's; all increase in love, and come to their *full stature,* to perfect manhood, *by that which every joint supplieth;* happiness would circulate through this mystical body without end, so as that each particle of it would, in due time, arrive at each individual point, or sentient being, of the great whole, that each would *inherit all things.* (OM 2.3.6.68)

In chapter 4 we noted that, according to Hartley, perception depends upon the "joint impression" of distinct sensory modalities. The coordinated sensing of touch and sight, for example, enables us to learn to identify the significant boundaries of objects in our visual fields. Alternatively, if a person suffers from an agnosia or aphasia that severs joint impression between senses, the stream of impressions deriving from the severed sense will be unintelligible. Here, Hartley opens to our view a "new scene": the joint awareness of every one that every other is friend, child, neighbor, second self. Were people to attain this loving mutual recognition, they would become "new sets of senses, and perceptive powers, to each other." To the extent that people fall short of this recognition, they suffer from an agnosia; they are unintelligible to each other or themselves, and they are unhappy. When they attain their "full stature" as members of "the whole body fitly joined together and compacted by that which every joint supplieth" (Eph. 4.16), they will enter into a limitless and reciprocal happiness. They will then enter into "perfect manhood," and all become of the one body. And happiness will then circulate throughout that body, so as to reach every "particle" of it.

Hartley repeats his comment concerning "new sets of senses, and perceptive powers" in another context in the *Observations.* At the end of his conjectures concerning a philosophical language, Hartley writes:

Was human life perfect, our happiness in it would be properly represented by that accurate knowledge of things, which a truly philosophical language would give us. And if we suppose a number of persons thus making a progress in pure unmixed happiness, and capable both of expressing their own feelings, and of understanding those of others, by means of a perfect and adequate language, they might be like new senses and powers of perception to each other, and both give to and receive from each other happiness indefinitely. (*OM* 1.3.1.35)

As we noted at the end of chapter 6, the wood of words is bounded by fantasy and by direct intuition, and the scientific inquirer seeks to journey toward the latter boundary. Direct intuition is a limit condition toward which thought aspires, as analysis converges upon synthesis, the fluid algebra of language upon the geometry of the world. And the degree to which a language converged asymptotically upon a direct intuition of reality would be the measure of its "philosophical" character.

Just as a philosophical language could be used to describe things, so also could it be used to express our perceptions of, and affections for, each other. It could thus represent both the perfection of science and the perfection of human happiness. And just as those engaged in scientific analysis aim ultimately at direct intuition, so also will people who set out on the long asymptotic curve toward apprehension of infinite happiness aim, in the end, to become "partakers of the divine nature"—in Christian terms, members of "the mystical body of Christ." They would aim to become vessels that resonate with the "continual Prayer" though which God "strives to communicate Himself." As members of that body, their whole selves would be blessed with a limitless capacity for fusion; by integrating all the sources of pleasure, they would shine forth with an undiminishing radiance. And when the members of that community saw in each other the radiance of "unlimited benevolence," together they would become new senses and perceptive powers to each other; together they would light up the world.

Despite their differences in form and means of expression, Hartley's *Observations* and Blake's *Jerusalem* are two tellings of the same story; both conform to the same pattern. As is Blake's, the story Hartley tells in his psychological epic is one of the recovery of "perfect manhood"— the reintegration of a fallen, fragmented, and self-alienated humanity. Like Sterry, White, and Marsay, both Hartley and Blake point toward what Jane Lead called "the reducing of every divided property to unity"— the awakening and reintegration of Adam Kadmon, Albion, the mystical body "fitly joined together" that includes us all.

10

The Whole Body Fitly Joined Together

> Every Creature is an *emanation* or *stream* from the Divine Essence.... The *Being* of the Creature is the *beaming* forth from God, like light from the Sun.
>
> —Peter Sterry (1675, 63)

> He who reads often, and considers deeply, the demonstration of Hartley...that *"God is infinitely benevolent,"* may find all his difficulties respecting the moral government of the universe gradually disappear.... This is the only philosophy worthy of a Christian!
>
> —Edward Tagart (1855, 276–77)

For the one whose theme is paradise regained, the ending is hardest. He is as a mole surfacing in daylight. Hartley's purpose is to demonstrate, in the terms of the best science available to him, that the process of association "has a tendency to reduce the state of those who have eaten of the tree of the knowledge of good and evil, back again to a paradisiacal one" (*OM* 1.1.2.14, Cor. 9). His psychological epic ends with the paradisiacal state of "perfect manhood," in which all become members of the "mystical body of Christ"—"the whole body fitly joined together"; as members of that body, "all become... new sets of senses, and perceptive powers, to each other, so as to increase each other's happiness without limits" (*OM* 2.3.6.68; see §9.4). But how are we to image perfect manhood, the mystical body, the New Adam, Albion awakened? How are we to say what these new senses and perceptive powers apprehend?

It would require a philosophical language. Hartley's language, in the *Observations,* depicts the variable states of imagination, ambition, and self-interest clearly and perceptively, as it does the ill forms of sympathy and theopathy. What, then, of the person who has become what Hartley says we ought—the person for whom the true forms of sympathy and theopathy have become primary pursuits, whose moral sense is sure, who has annihilated self-interest? Hartley's language speaks acutely of pain and fragmentation; what can it express of happiness and holiness?

1. "The Grand Design and Purport of Human Life"

Joseph Butler criticized those "who indulge themselves in vain and idle speculations, how the World might possibly have been framed otherwise than it is." Hartley argued that we human beings are in fact framed otherwise than we commonly imagine ourselves to be. The "Simplicity and absolute Oneness" of the living, free agent, which Butler takes to be the foundation of a proper understanding of human nature, is to Hartley an entity that introspection is able to discover only so long as it avoids descending to particulars. Like medicines or bladder stones, our minds are compounds, complexes of processes; like the will according to Locke, they are relations, not agents; like a false memory, a person's conviction concerning the simplicity and unity of the immaterial substance that constitutes his identity as a rational, free, and immortal I—is a story made to seem real by the intensity of the emotions transferred and bound to it. Given the limitations of our ability to "watch the evanescent perceptions of our minds" (*OM* 1.2.5.70), we are unable to denominate terms such as *free agent* or *mind* through direct observation of the things they purport to name; all we have are terms that derive their meanings, like the terms for the emotions, from the circumstances commonly associated with them. But such circumstances are not a unity, and the term *unity of consciousness* lacks meaning (*OM* 1. Conclusion). A person's consciousness is generally unable to perceive the complex neurological and psychological processes—the vibrations, associations, and transferences—that generate it.

Yet despite this materialistic line of thought, Hartley's work is suffused with religion—though a religion different from the one taken for granted, at least by Anglican bishops. As an aspect of the "absurd" notion of philosophical necessity, Hartley affirms another position that Butler held up for ridicule: "that the whole method of Government by Punishment should be rejected, as absurd; . . . nay as contrary to a principal Purpose, for which . . . Creatures were made, namely Happiness" (Butler 1736, vii; see §5.1). As we noted in §2.3, Hartley believed that "Universal Happiness is the Fundamental Doctrine both of Reason & Scripture" (*L* 2; 13 March 1736). God had created human creatures precisely for happiness; salvation will ultimately be universal; all sentient beings, including both humans and possibly animals, will be restored to a paradise in which punishments will be no more than a distant memory.[1]

"Benevolence," Hartley writes, "is indeed the grand design and purport of human life, of the present probationary state; and therefore every circumstance of human life must point to it, directly or indirectly, when duly considered" (*OM* 2.3.6.68). Benevolence is the fullest expression of the whole self. We ought to be benevolent, and our goal should be to wish ill of no one. Hartley, however, allows for one exception: "that where wishing evil disposes us to be more benevolent upon the whole, as in the case of what is called just indignation against vice, it may perhaps be tolerable in the more imperfect kinds of men, who have need of this direction and incitement to keep them from wandering out of the proper road." Hartley here seems to be granting one of the points upon which defenders of the standard account insisted: to ensure that "the more imperfect kinds of men" obey the law, it is necessary that they fear God.

John Lister, Hartley's friend from his schooldays, urged exactly this point when he read a draft of the *Observations* in January 1739. "There's a chain of reasoning goes through your observations," Lister wrote, "to which I own I have not been used, but yet I think it is very well connected, and your opinion of an ever increasing happiness made as probable as it is desirable" (*L* 13; cf. *T* 248). Two years earlier, Lister had also concurred, in theory, with Hartley; he began his letter of 14 December 1736 by affirming, "I am much inclin'd to think wth. you concerning Universal Happiness taking Place some Time or other" (*L* 4;

cf. *T* 237). Still, in this earlier letter he insisted that "to argue for future probations or Restorations seems not very pertinent to us in our present State, it being our proper Business here to behave as if our Eternal Fates were to be decided by this one Trial." And in his later letter he expanded upon this theme: "But when I consider the weakness of vulgar minds, there appears great danger lest a security of happiness should of consequence beget carelessness, and thereby greatly retard our progress to it. The influence of things present is so strong, and the impressions of the future so weak, that the terrible threats of endless punishment hereafter may be no more than fit counterbalance against the force of temptation here. . . . On this account I cannot say how proper it would be to trust the public with your 'Observations.' " Six years later, when Hartley announced that he had completed the work, Lister again dissuaded him from publishing it: "I am glad you have finished yr Book, for yr own Ease & Satisfaction. . . . Perhaps it is better not to publish" (*L* 36; cf. *T* 265). In the Rev. Lister's view, although the eternity of punishment in hell is an illusion, it remains nonetheless a needful fiction that the wise must collude in maintaining, lest vulgar minds ruin themselves. Hartley, therefore, should keep his observations to himself.

Of course, he did not. However, in the passage at hand he partially grants the point: what is *called* just indignation is tolerable when it keeps the more imperfect kinds of men from wandering astray. It is tolerable, and no more, to the extent that such indignation acts as a check upon others and as also a restraint upon one's own behavior. "If we allow man to consider himself as the author of his own actions," Hartley writes, "he must also consider virtue and vice according to the popular notions, and conceive of God as endued with the popular attribute of justice, in order to be incited to virtue, and deterred from vice" (*OM* 2.1.15). Both Butler and Lister would agree with this statement, minus the conditional: people *are* the authors of their actions, and God *is* just. But for Hartley, the ab intra necessities render agency problematic. Hence the conditional is crucial, for it indicates that describing oneself as the author of one's actions is one manner of speaking, as are representations of God's justice. There is another. The sentence continues: "whereas, could man really annihilate himself, and refer all to God, perfect love would cast out fear, he would immediately become partaker of the divine nature, and, being one with God, would see him to be pure benevolence and love, and all that he has made to be good." Hartley's apparent materialism places us among the animals and thereby far beneath the position we would enjoy as immaterial essences capable of existing as easily "out of our Bodies as in them." Now this alternative way of speaking would exalt us far above the position we occupy in Joseph Butler's scheme of things. Were we to "annihilate" self, we would become "partakers of the divine nature." We noted above that in Hartley's psychology our sense of self is itself a compound concretion, a complex of relations. Dissolving the concretion, it would seem, would simply reveal that the self can be reduced to patterns of vibrations, to a neural harmonics in which a mind or, better, brain is a highly complex and responsive bit of the natural world. But annihilate the self, Hartley says, and the person will hear "the voice of nature" rise in a "universal chorus of joy and transport" (OM 2.3.3.56); he or she will partake of a oneness with the love that has made all things to be good. Annihilate the self and you will encounter not reduction but transcendence.

2. "A Universal Chorus of Joy and Transport"

In Hartley's day, many people were conscious of the possibility of other realms existing at scales vastly different from our own.[2] Devices such as microscopes and telescopes, which rescale the worlds of the small and the vast, had begun to reveal worlds of which humanity was heretofore ignorant. Using a very primitive microscope, Robert Hooke had in 1665 produced his *Micrographia,* full of images of the veins in leaves, the wings and scales of insects. Such images are proof that what appears to us as a world of things is itself dependent upon our categories of perception. But the images in Hooke's *Micrographia* could be just a beginning. As we noted in chapter 4, perception depends upon the associative synthesis of the joint impressions deriving from touch, hearing, sight, and the other sensory modalities. These supply us with continuous flows of sensation in which there are no innately discrete "monads" of sense. All the flows are "infinitely divisible," both spatially and temporally. And as Hartley remarks, what may be taken to be a "single thing" is "one that is so comparatively; so that I call not only a single part of an animal (which yet is a thing decompounded, perhaps without limits), but a whole system of animals, when compared with other systems, a single thing" (OM 2.1.4; see §5.2). This means that the world we do perceive is of a scale that corresponds to our stature. The things we see depend upon our perceptual capacities and our purposes.

How small, or vast, might other worlds be? "There is not an atom perhaps in the whole universe," Hartley writes, "which does not abound in millions of worlds; and, conversely, this great system of the sun, planets, and fixed stars, may be no more than a single constituent particle of some body of an immense relative magnitude, &c. In like manner, there is not a moment of time so small, but it may include millions of ages in the estimation of some beings; and, conversely, the largest cycle which human art is able to invent, may be no more than the twinkling of an eye in that of others" (*OM* 2.3.3.56). There may be beings in other realms to whom the hair on a Lilliputian's head would be a vast world, and others to whom the palace of Brobdignag would be an infinitesimal speck.

People take pleasure in traveling in imagination with Gulliver. Concerning the pleasures of imagination, Hartley writes that "novelty is a never-failing requisite: we look down, with indifference and contempt, upon what we comprehend easily; and are ever aiming at . . . such objects as are but just within the compass of our present faculties." Once comprehension is easy, the mind grows restless. The moral he draws from "this dissatisfaction to look behind us . . . this endless grasping after infinity" is that "the Infinite Author of all things has so formed our faculties, that nothing less than himself can be an adequate object for them." Augustine had made the same point centuries earlier, when he wrote in his autobiographical letter to God, "You have made us for yourself, and we are restless until we rest in Thee" (*Conf.* 1.1). A consequence of this restlessness is, as Hartley puts it, "that it is in vain to hope for full and lasting satisfaction from any thing finite, . . . since it will itself teach us to conceive and desire something still more so." An exclusively imaginative concentration upon specific objects, scenes, or studies will eventually cease to be a source of satisfaction. However, a transformed power of perception is available to those for whom theopathy has new-modeled imagination: just as "nothing can give us more than a transitory delight, if its relation to God be excluded, so every thing, when considered as the production of his infinite goodness, will gratify our utmost expectations, since we may, in this view, see that every thing has infinite uses and excellences."

The person who perceives all things theopathically, in their relations to God, knows that all things are communicative of God's excellence. But for imagination to apprehend the "infinite uses and excellences" of *all* things would require the capacity to perceive all scales. And given our present stature, this is not possible: "The infinite divisibility and extent of space and time admit of such infinities upon infinities, ascending and descending, as to make the imagination giddy, when it attempts to survey them." Recall that to Hartley physical nature is composed of nested lattices of points of attraction and repulsion. The human imagination can actively ascend or descend part way along these lattices, thanks to telescopes and microscopes; it can speculatively continue the ascent and descent, though at the risk of giddiness. And though God can perceive the excellence of all things at all scales, of both the largest theme and the slightest note of the song, human beings must take on faith that the beauty they do perceive extends throughout the whole, to the limits of the cosmos:

> We may be sure, that the true system of things is infinitely more transcendent in greatness and goodness, than any description or conception of ours can make it; and that the voice of nature is an universal chorus of joy and transport, in which the least and vilest, according to common estimation, bear a proper part, as well as those whose present superiority over them appears infinitely great, and may bear an equal one in the true and ultimate ratio of things. And thus the consideration of God gives a relish and lustre to speculations, which are otherwise dry and unsatisfactory, or which perhaps would confound and terrify. Thus we may learn to rejoice in every thing we see, and in the blessings past, present, and future; which we receive either in our own persons, or in those of others; to become partakers of the divine nature, loving and lovely, holy and happy. (OM 2.3.3.56)

In Hartley's imagination, people occupy a midpoint between the infinitesimally small and the infinitely vast. When we think of the small, we encounter the vibrations that sound or sparkle throughout our brains and nervous systems. When we face toward the vast, we contemplate a whole, a totality, that we cannot grasp. Turning one way and then another, we encounter "infinities upon infinities, ascending and descending." Observe, nonetheless, the sequence in the last sentence of the passage quoted above: when we consider all things in relation to God, we will learn to rejoice in everything we see, in the blessings we receive "in our own persons," and in the blessings bestowed upon others. Then, accustomed to this height, no longer dizzy with vertigo, we "become partakers of the divine nature, loving and lovely, holy and happy."

Hartley turns again to this theme in proposition 71 of book 2. The purpose of this proposition to demonstrate that "the love of God regulates, improves, and perfects all the other Parts of our Nature; . . . [and] is therefore our primary Pursuit, and ultimate End." In it Hartley presents his reasons for affirming "that the love of God affords a pleasure which is superior in kind and degree to all the rest, of which our natures are capable." The love of God does afford this superior pleasure:

> First, Because *God is light, and in him there is no darkness at all;* because he is *love* itself, such love as quite *casts out all fear.* The love and contemplation of his perfection and happiness will transform us into his likeness, into that image of him in which we were first made; will make us *partakers of the divine nature,* and consequently of the happiness and perfection of it. Our wills may thus be united to his will, and therefore rendered free from disappointments; we shall, by degrees, see everything as God sees it, *i.e.* see every thing that he has made to be good, to be an object of pleasure. (*OM* 2.3.7.71)

Through contemplation our ideas become the images of what we contemplate; our love and contemplation of God's perfection and happiness transform us into God's likeness. And as our wills converge upon God's will, and the separate ideas that are our minds upon the one idea that is always present in God, we will approach to a perception of everything "as God sees it"—as good, an object of pleasure, and a source of happiness.

Such convergence is, in Hartley's view, a very gradual process. "It is true," he writes, "that all this, in its perfect sense, in its ultimate ratio, can only be said by way of anticipation: whilst we carry these fleshly tabernacles about with us, we must have crosses to bear, frailties, and thorns in the flesh, to struggle with." Still, he immediately adds that "our strength will at last be made perfect through weakness; and some devout persons appear to have been so far transformed, in this life, as to acquiesce, and even rejoice, in the events of it, however afflicting apparently, to be freed from fear and solicitude, and to receive their daily bread with constant thankfulness, *with joy unspeakable, and full of glory.*"

Hartley then states his second reason for thinking that the love of God provides the purest and highest pleasure:

Secondly, God is our centre, and the love of him a pleasure superior to all the rest . . . because they all point to it, like so many lines terminating in the same centre. When men have entered sufficiently into the ways of piety, God appears more and more to them in the whole course and tenor of their lives; and by uniting himself with all their sensations, and intellectual perceptions, overpowers all the pains; augments, and attracts to itself, all the pleasures. Every thing sweet, beautiful, or glorious, brings in the idea of God, mixes with it, and vanishes into it. For all is God's; he is the only cause and reality; and the existence of every thing else is only the effect, pledge, and proof, of his existence and glory. Let the mind be once duly seasoned with this truth, and its practical applications, and every the most indifferent thing will become food for religious meditation, a book of devotion, and a psalm of praise. (*OM* 2.3.7.71)

In Hartley's psychology, the feeling of pleasure is analogous to a force of attraction in natural philosophy. Such forces of attraction create bonds between previously discrete elements, fusing them into larger unities. Complexes of words and ideas are thus the psychological analogue of the molecules, and "molecules of molecules," of chemistry. In chemistry, Stephen Hales emphasized that "this beautiful frame of things" is maintained by a dynamic equilibrium of the forces of attraction and repulsion; if the forces of attraction operated without a counterpoise, no plant could grow or animal be born; instead, "whole nature would become one unactive cohering lump" (Hales 1769, 1: 314–15; see §2.7). Similarly in Hartley's psychology, there are both pleasures and pains, associations and counterassociations, which also maintain the human psyche in a state of dynamic equilibrium while allowing for its growth and development. There is, however, this difference: in Hartley's psychology, the idea of God, once feelings of fear are dissociated from it, is a universal attractor. It "overpowers all the pains" and "augments, and attracts . . . to itself, all the pleasures." As it does so, all of a person's ideas to coalesce into one idea: "Every thing sweet, beautiful, or glorious, brings in the idea of God, mixes with it, an vanishes into it." Contemplation brings convergence; one's mind becomes the image of what it contemplates. And more: it comes to partake of the nature of that which it images.

3. Happiness

"All this, in its perfect sense, in its ultimate ratio, can only be said by way of anticipation." It is consequently difficult to specify how the world discloses itself to one for whom "every the most indifferent thing" has become "food for religious meditation, a book of devotion, and a psalm of praise." Anticipation, however, does not necessarily signify complete inaccessibility. There is a paradoxical sense in which we already possess what we anticipate, in which we already are what we long to be.

In Hartley's vision of the cosmos, human consciousness occupies but one level, and hardly the highest, within a vast scale of being. We exist in the midst of "such infinities upon infinities, ascending and descending, as to make the imagination giddy, when it attempts to survey them." The realms that ascend above us include much more than we know, especially if we countenance "the instrumentality of beings superior to us, men divinely inspired, good angels, evil spirits, and many other influences, of which our present philosophy can take no cognizance" (*OM* 2.2.28). Throughout much of this book, we have looked downward and asked how human agency may be fit into the realms of the small. But we may also attempt to ascend in imagination to vaster scales of space and time and ask how our experience of ourselves can be described in the languages appropriate to them.

When we do so, we confront another paradox concerning the "previous circumstances" of our actions, a paradox that again suggests that the reality of our own lives may be described in two languages, the one popular and the other philosophical. But here the philosophical language aims to speak of the instrumentality of another being—the soul of our soul. The paradox concerns the experience of happiness.

Hartley writes: "Eminently pious and benevolent persons seem to be in possession of some great secret, some *Catholicon,* or philosopher's stone. They pass through life unhurt, as to the peace of their minds, by the evils of it; and find abundant matter for praise and thanksgiving to God in it. All which appears to be owing to their being guided by the true principles of action" (*OM* 2.3.8, Cor. 3). The true principles of action, according to Hartley, are benevolence toward others and resignation concerning the events and circumstances that enter into one's own life. The annihilation of self-interest is expressed through both: people who are whole, who pass through life unhurt, will engage themselves selflessly in loving action on behalf of others and will also accept the misfortunes that befall themselves as expressive of God's will.

Hartley's advocacy of resignation as a true principle of action brings him up against a fundamental problem: if God is an "infinitely benevolent" being who wills the happiness of all people, how can one claim that concrete instances of suffering are also expressive of that will? If God wills the happiness of Alice Rowley and her husband David Hartley, how can it be God's will that she die in childbirth at the age of twenty-five, after one year of marriage? Why should Hartley be resigned to this? These questions are the ones that bedevil all attempts to construct a theodicy that justifies the ways of God to man.

The core belief affirmed in the everlasting gospel is that God wills the happiness of every person; if a supreme and sympathetic intelligence is able to accomplish what it wills, it would follow that such an intelligence, contemplating the world, would perceive no cause for distress and hence would be happy—to the extent that our idea of happiness could be ascribed to such a being. But what help would this thought be to David Hartley at the deathbed of Alice Rowley? And what help would it be to him, when he prayed in "bitterness and anguish" for the life of Elizabeth Packer, that she might survive the birth of their daughter? How could he be resigned to these events, as events a benevolent God could look upon with satisfaction? Hartley writes of those who "pass through life unhurt, as to the peace of their minds, by the evils of it; and find abundant matter for praise and thanksgiving to God in it." Guided by "the true principles of action," they possess "great secret, some *Catholicon,* or philosopher's stone." Did he clasp some catholicon, some philosopher's stone, to himself, to keep his mind at peace during the endless days and nights when the stones in his bladder tormented him with pains he could not endure?

The fourth proposition of the second part of the *Observations* concerns the thesis, "God is infinitely Benevolent." After discussing twelve considerations in favor of the thesis, Hartley turns to a thirteenth, in which he explores what God's infinite benevolence might mean in terms of human happiness. He writes:

We may call that infinite benevolence which makes either,

1. Each individual infinitely happy always. Or,
2. Each individual always finitely happy, without any mixture of misery, and infinitely so in its progress through infinite time. Or,
3. Each individual infinitely happy, upon the balance, in its progress through infinite time, but with a mixture of misery. Or,

4. Each individual finitely happy in the course of its existence, whatever that be, but with a mixture of misery as before; and the universe infinitely happy upon the balance. Or,
5. Some individuals happy and some miserable upon the balance, finitely or infinitely, and yet so that there shall be an infinite overplus of happiness in the universe. (*OM* 2.1.4)

Hartley comments that the first alternative "is not only contrary to fact at first view, but also seems impossible, as being inconsistent with the finite nature of the creatures." The second is also "contrary to the fact, to what we see and feel"; it is, however, consistent with the notion that "pure benevolence can give nothing but pure happiness, and infinite benevolence must give infinite happiness," and consequently it is "with great unwillingness" that Hartley passes it over. The third alternative "is possible in itself; but then it can neither be supported, nor contradicted, by the facts"—at least by the facts as they appear to us, "confined" as we are "within a short distance from the present moment." The fourth is the weakest way of affirming the happiness of all individuals and hence of universal salvation; it is the supposition "to which many thinking, serious, benevolent, and pious persons are now inclined." The fifth alternative is that of the standard account; it supposes the division of humanity into the saved and the damned.

Hartley then turns to "another way of considering the third supposition," which is "a presumption for it, though not an evidence." The key here is the capacity of association to integrate fragmentary experiences of pleasure and pain into states that are, as wholes, pleasurable. "Association has an evident tendency," he writes, "to convert a state of superior happiness, mixed with inferior misery, into one of pure happiness, into a paradisiacal one." A person whose happiness was mixed with misery would, given enough time, gradually fix the specific experiences of fear, suffering, and unhappiness within ever larger associative complexes.

Painful events lose their sting when we incorporate them into narratives of security, health, and happiness. But if the story of a person's life extends beyond death into an infinite future, then the process of conversion can continue without limits. Association, in this long view, thus "tends to convert the state of the third supposition into that of the second," according to which each individual is always finitely happy. The crucial factor here is that association has the capacity to function in a temporal dimension. We noted in §4.6 Hartley's assertion that "no sensation can be a monad, inasmuch as the most simple are infinitely divisible in respect of time, and extent of impression." The statement appears in the section of the *Observations* under discussion; Hartley's point is that what a person experiences as "one sensation" is a function of the person's capacities for associative synthesis (and discrimination), and not of the physical sources of the sensory flow. The same holds true with regard to a person's experience of temporal duration and flow; what is to me "the present" is a psychological matter, not a metaphysical one. Present time, that is, the time present to me, may shrink or expand, depending again upon the extent of my capacities for associative synthesis—or, to put this another way, upon the qualities of my imagination, ambition, sympathy, and theopathy. Hartley continues, in the next paragraph:

> As the enlargement of our capacities enables us thus to take off the edge of our pains, by uniting them with the subsequent superior pleasures, so it confers upon us more and more the power of enjoying our future pleasures by anticipation, by extending the limits of the present time, *i.e.* of that time in which we have an interest. For the present time, in a metaphysical sense, is an indivisible moment; but the present time, in a practical sense, is a finite quantity of various magnitudes, according to our capacities, and, beginning from an indivisible moment in all, seems to grow on indefinitely in beings who are ever progressive in their passage through eternal life. (*OM* 2.1.4)

Through the reach of memory and imagination, I should, according to Hartley, be able to extend the limits of the present time in a practical or psychological sense; in so doing, I would bring more and more of the anticipated future into the practical, psychological present. And if the future bears the promise of pure unmixed happiness, I should, to the extent that that future becomes my present, in some way be always happy "now"—even when my life seems filled with suffering. The third alternative thus converges upon the second.

This convergence embodies a paradox. The third alternative promises only that a person will be "infinitely happy, on the balance, in [his] progress through infinite time, but with a mixture of misery." In this alternative, even in an infinite future I may experience occasions of suffering. For example, though the narrative of my whole life may be one of "superior happiness," I may still flinch at the lash of memory, when I recall bitter or shameful events. With such memories, the greater the trauma, the greater the resistance to ameliorative assimilation; even if isolated, uncharacteristic, atypical—in fact, precisely because isolated, uncharacteristic, atypical—the memory of a single "inferior misery" can persist in causing pain long after the event. But for the third alternative to converge upon the second, it is necessary that the happiness of the paradisiacal state be completely pure and unmixed. Hence the paradox: If I can truly anticipate attaining a state of pure happiness, with no mixture of misery, in the infinite future, I can conclude that, from the perspective of that future state, I will be able to look back upon my present state and perceive integration where now I experience fragmentation. Therefore, I should be able to be finitely happy right now—even when I am troubled yet again by old feelings of bitterness and shame. I should be able to convert them.

Jeremiah White wrote "that the Saints are not fully glorified without the rest of Mankind.... nor the manifestive Glory of God himself full and perfect without the recovering of the whole" (1779, 148; see §9.4) As an individual person, I cannot attain "the recovering of the whole"—complete integration in the future—if I am unable to redeem all of my memories. I will not be able to be achieve "pure unmixed happiness" in the future if images or narratives of pain remain locked fast within memory's prison. If some memories remain imprisoned, my happiness will always be mixed. But if I will be able to redeem *all* of my memories in the future, then I should be able to redeem them all right now.

Moreover, if I am indeed what White calls "an entire World," and *all* of my memories, including those now confined, will fit together into the "Figure" or "Shadow of the Supreme Unity" that shall be the mystical body, perfect manhood, Adam Kadmon, or Albion of my whole and complete and fully awakened self, then the fact that I do not perceive this wholeness, this integration right now is owing to the fact that I am asleep and that what I take to be my waking life is in reality a nightmare. If all memories are redeemable, then the only things stopping me from liberating them right now are the limitations of my own capacities for imagination, ambition, sympathy, and theopathy—that is, the limitations of my self. But if I understand this, if I anticipate awakening, then I am beginning right now to find a way out of the world of dream and into the light of full consciousness. I am beginning to realize, despite what I seem to see and feel, that the second alternative is true, no matter how paradoxical or counterfactual it may seem: I am always finitely happy at each moment of my life.

The Whole Body Fitly Joined Together

Taken to its limit, the way of thinking that leads the third alternative to converge upon the second in turn leads the second to converge upon the first. The former convergence concerns the expansion of the consciousness of a finite being; the latter concerns the approximation of the consciousness of an infinite being. A person experiences the paradoxical effect of the former convergence as his consciousness of the "present" expands to include all of his life in its progress through infinite time. But to an infinite being, all time, including all lives, is already present:

> And the more we suppose the benevolence and capacities of this [infinite] being enlarged, the greater and more pure will his sympathetic pleasure be, which arises from the contemplation of man. It follows, therefore, that, in the eye of an infinite mind, creatures conducted, as we think, according to the third of the foregoing suppositions, are conducted according to the second, and these according to the first; or, in other words, that the first, second, and third, of the foregoing suppositions, are all one and the same in the eye of God. For all time, whether present, past, or future, is present time in the eye of God, and all ideas coalesce into one in him; and this one is infinite happiness, without any mixture of misery, *viz.* by the infinite prepollence of happiness above misery, so as to annihilate it; and this merely by considering time... as a relative thing, belonging to beings of finite capacities, and varying with them, but which is infinitely absorbed in the pure eternity of God. (OM 2.1.4)

The effect of understanding this second convergence is even more startling and paradoxical than the effect of the first. God, possessing an unlimited capacity for associative synthesis, integrates all experiences and all times into one; to an infinite mind, all ideas coalesce into one idea, and that idea may be named "infinite happiness." Were I able to expand my practical or psychological present to include my whole life, I would observe the third alternative converge upon the second, and I would realize that I am "always" at every moment finitely happy and also "infinitely happy in [my] progress through infinite time." But were I ever able to expand my consciousness to include all of time—were I able to see with the "eye of God"—I would see all times absorbed into "pure eternity," and I would know that from the perspective of eternity,

I and all conscious beings are "always" infinitely happy at every moment in what we experience as time.

At the start of the discussion of these alternatives, Hartley comments that the notion that each individual is always infinitely happy is "not only contrary to the fact at first view, but also seems impossible, as being inconsistent with the finite nature of the creatures." Note the qualification: *at first view*. At the end of the discussion of the alternatives, Hartley states that the first view is not the one we should ultimately adopt. Rather, the last view, the most comprehensive view, is the true one:

> Now the appearance of things to the eye of an infinite being must be called their real appearance in all propriety. And though it be impossible for us to arrive at this true way of conceiving things perfectly, or directly, yet we shall approach nearer and nearer to it, as our intellectual capacities, benevolence, devotion, and the purity of our happiness ... advance. So that now ... we may, in some sort, venture to maintain that which at first sight seemed not only contrary to obvious experience, but even impossible, *viz.* that all individuals are actually and always infinitely happy.... We ought to suppose ourselves in the centre of the system, and to try, as far as we are able, to reduce all apparent retrogradations to real progressions.

Hartley invokes an astronomical metaphor: viewed from the earth, the movements of the planets appear on occasion to reverse direction; their movement then appears to be retrograde. But a person who understands that the sun is at the center of the solar system knows that such retrogradations are merely apparent. Viewed from the sun, all the planets always move forward in their orbits. Similarly, what to us seem to be retrograde events—occasions of suffering—are also only apparent; if we could view our lives through the "eye of God," which sees all time as present time, we would know that they are also real progressions. Audaciously, Hartley claims that, if you could view your own life from the viewpoint of God, if you could see the whole of it at once and in the context of eternity, no matter how miserable you may think you are today, you would realize that you are, right at this moment, infinitely happy.

The nearer and nearer approach to the vision of things as seen through the eye of God, to whom all time is present time, seems to push human capacities to their limit or beyond. Hartley comments that "it is the greatest satisfaction to the mind thus to approximate to its first conceptions concerning the divine goodness, and to answer that endless question, *Why not less misery, and more happiness?* in a language which is plainly analogous to all other authentic language, though it cannot yet be felt by us on account of our present imperfection, and of the mixture of our good with evil." The satisfaction comes from approximating a concept, and it seems that, given our imperfections, approximation is all we will ever be able to accomplish. We attempt to express through an algebraic analogy of language the truth that the supreme being knows through direct intuition. The degree of enlightenment required to perceive directly that I am "actually and always infinitely happy"—no matter how miserable I am at the moment—seems a psychological impossibility. Or at least, it seems to require an annihilation of self that goes beyond the abandonment of self-interest to the transcendence of the sense of a separate self altogether. And such is realized but rarely—perhaps by such as Abraham Abulafia, Meister Eckhart, Jalal ad-Din Rumi; by Buddhist arhats; by those Hindu sannyasis who grasp Śaṁkara's statement that *"Brahman* constitutes... the real nature of the individual self"; by the *sheng tzu* who, according to the Confucians, is the person who unites *jen* and *t'ien,* humanity and heaven.

As Hartley notes, the direct experience of "infinite happiness" seems to be inconsistent with "the finite nature of the creatures." And since a happiness that exists only as a theoretical construct is a nullity, creatures who can never be anything but finite will never encounter it. Infinite happiness does not exist for them, for happiness must be in some way and at some time experienced by the subject to be. The promise of a higher harmony will be a mystery beyond their comprehension; and it will be a promise that some, always sensing the "human tears that have soaked the whole earth through, from crust to core," will feel morally obligated to repudiate. Like Ivan Karamazov, they will "absolutely renounce all higher harmony"—lest they betray the unredeemed "fact" of even "one tormented child" (Dostoyevksy [1880] 1990, 243, 245). Similarly, those who are comfortable with the fourth alternative above, or the fifth, and who emphasize the vast distance between the finite creature and the infinite creator, will judge Hartley's affirmation of the first alternative to be yet another example of the "Train of Folly and Extravagance" that comes from imagining the world to be otherwise than it is. But in contrast, there are some who may accept the paradox that we are "always happy infinitely"—either because they have caught a glimpse of such happiness themselves, or because they take the word of saint, arhat, sannyasi, or sage for it. To them, the paradox may both cover and express one of the most basic truths that it is possible for a person to discover: that, "as we know from passages such as 'that art thou', that same highest *Brahman* constitutes . . . the real nature of the individual self"; or, in the words of Fénelon, the "Soul of our Soul . . . is there more nearly and intimately" within us "than we ourselves are." Affirmation of the paradox requires, in other words, a belief that approximation can converge upon unity.

11

Revolutionary Science

> I do not know what the word "materialism" means. Speaking as a physicist, I judge matter to be an imprecise and rather old-fashioned concept. Roughly speaking, matter is the way particles behave when a large number of them are lumped together. When we examine matter in the finest detail in the experiments of particle physics, we see it behaving as an active agent rather than as an inert substance.... Between matter as we observe it in the laboratory and mind as we observe it in our own consciousness, there seems to be only a difference of degree but not in kind. We stand, in a manner of speaking, midway between the unpredictability of matter and the unpredictability of God.
>
> —Freeman Dyson (1988, 8)

1. "The Whole Man"

It is difficult to determine the extent of the influence of Hartley's *Observations* in the two decades after its publication. Frequent mention in other works is no indication that work provided an accepted paradigm for thought. Controversial works, such as Berkeley's attack upon the calculus, *The Analyst,* or his *Principles of Human Knowledge,* were regularly cited—and dismissed. Conversely, many works that were highly respected and probably widely read, such as the explanations of Newtonian science by Pemberton, Maclaurin, Desaguliers, and 'sGravesande, Robert Smith's *Optics,* and Saunderson's *Elements of Algebra,* generated little controversy and only the occasional reference. What of the *Observations*? Hartley himself had become a public figure in 1738, thanks to his leading role in the controversy over Joanna Stephens's medicine for the stone. When the *Observations* appeared a decade later, readers would have known its author to be one who applied the latest theories in chemistry and physics to medicine. Unlike his writings on the stone, Hartley's *Observations* appears not to have prompted the criticisms and defenses of a controversial literature. One may interpret the absence of controversy as indication that the work was simply accepted as another contribution to the Newtonian paradigm—albeit one with a distinctive religious slant. Alternatively, Hartley's perceived saintliness may have silenced those who in other circumstances might have been critics. But one may also interpret the silence as indication that the book went unread. There was no second edition during the 1750s or 1760s. The next edition of the *Observations* was a German translation, published in 1772.

With the intervention of Joseph Priestley in 1774 and 1775, the situation in Britain changed entirely. In chapter 1, we noted Isaac Kramnick's comment that "Hartley, thanks to Priestley, was everywhere" (1986, 29). But being everywhere was hardly the same as being universally accepted. Thanks to Priestley's efforts, Hartley was canonized by some—particularly Unitarians and other religious dissenters.[1] And thanks to Priestley's efforts, Hartley's theory—though never the man—was by others dismissed.

Publication of Priestley's *Examination* (1774a) and of *Hartley's Theory of the Human Mind* (Hartley 1775), his abridged edition of the *Observations,* ignited a public controversy—first in the pages of *The London Review* and then of the Nonconformist periodical *The Monthly Review* (Anon. 1775–76, 1777; see Yolton 1983, 115–26, 184–85). The debates in the periodical press were extended by the publication of several books criticizing Priestley and Hartley. The first of these was *Letters on Materialism and Hartley's Theory of the Human Mind,* the first work, published anonymously, by the liberal Roman Catholic priest Joseph Berington (1776); Berington's book received a very favorable review in *The Monthly Review* for February 1777. Priestley responded to his critics in three works, *Disquisitions Relating to Matter and Spirit* (1777a), *The Doctrine of Philosophical Necessity Illustrated* (1777b), and *A Free Discussion of the Doctrines of Materialism and Philosophical Necessity, in a Correspondence between Dr. Price and Dr. Priestley* (1778). Thomas Reid, an original target of Priestley's *Examination*, offered his own criticisms of Hartley and Priestley in his *Essays on the Intellectual Powers of Man* (1785).

"I am rather inclined to think," Priestley wrote, in one of the essays prefaced to his 1775 edition of the *Observations,* "that, though the subject is beyond our comprehension at present, man does not consist of two principles, so essentially different from one another as *matter* and *spirit,* which are always described as having not one common property, by means of which they can affect or act upon each other; the one occupying space, and the other not only not occupying the least imaginable portion of space, but incapable of bearing relation to it; insomuch that, properly speaking, my mind is no more *in my body,* than it is in the moon" (Hartley 1775, xx). Priestley proposed instead that "the whole man is of some *uniform composition,* and that the property of *perception,* as well as the other powers that are termed *mental,* is the result ... of such an organical structure as that of the brain" (xx). Commenting on this passage years later, Priestley wrote in his memoirs that "I expressed some doubt about the immateriality of the sentient principle in man; and the outcry that was made on what I casually expressed on that subject can hardly be imagined. In all the newspapers, and most of the periodical publications, I was represented as an unbeliever in revelation, and no better than an Atheist" ([1806] 1970, 113). Hartley had expressed the same reservation; and as Priestley did later, he also suggested that it was the promise of the resurrection of the body, rather than the continued existence of a nonmaterial spirit, that guaranteed personal immortality (*OM* 2.4.3.90; see §5.7). Their critics would have none of it.

To affirm that all mental powers are the result of the brain's "organical structure" is to claim that the objectively observable gives rise to the subjectively observing. Although Hales and Hartley had shown that "elastic" air can concrete into a stone, consciousness seems a much more distinctive quality than the hardness of an organic concretion. It is not like anything at all on the level of the physically observable. We noted in §5.2 Hartley's affirmation that if a material organism "could be endued with the most simple kinds of sensation, [it] might also arrive at all that intelligence of which the human mind is possessed" (*OM* 1. Conclusion). To say that an organism is endowed with even simple sensation is to grant it some form of qualitative consciousness—and once this is granted, the "near relation" of animals and humans is evident: the qualities of consciousness an organism can attain are purely a function of the nature and complexity of its brain and nervous system. But we also noted in §5.2 and 7 that, in the context of a discussion of the future state, Hartley admits that "there remains one chasm still, *viz.* that between sensation, and the material organs, which this theory does not attempt to fill up" (*OM* 2.4.3.86). How then, can "organical structure" endow an organism with consciousness?

To their critics, the answer was that it could not. They insisted upon the chasm. In the first chapter we noted Sir James Mackintosh's criticism of Hartley's attempt "to derive the intellectual operations from bodily causes" and his insistence that making this attempt "overlooks the primordial and perpetual distinction between *the being which thinks* and the *thing which is thought of*—not to be lost sight of even for a twinkling, without involving all nature in darkness and confusion" (1836, 245). For those committed to this primordial and perpetual distinction, the problem with Hartley's theory of vibrations was not that it explained too little but rather that it attempted an explanation. George Henry Lewes, writing in his *History of Philosophy from Thales to Comte* in 1880, comments that "those who point out the defect in Hartley's hypothesis are themselves open to a similar charge, since they assume an immaterial principle to be affected by a material change, and assume the mind to be in connection with the body, following its alterations. But there is this difference between them and Hartley: they do not pretend to explain how the mind is affected by body, he does. They accept, as an ultimate fact, what he attempts to elucidate: and it is his elucidation which they refuse to acknowledge" (1880, 2:369; see also Tagart 1855, 146–47).[2] Lewes's comment is an echo of the criticism Priestley directed at Reid a century earlier: "he goes on accounting for every thing, by telling you, not only that he cannot explain it himself, but that it will be in vain for you . . . to endeavour to investigate it further than he has done" (1774a, xx; see §1.4).

One must admit that the distinction is meaningful, at least with regard to the popular way of speaking: *I* think, and so do *you*, but *axons* and *synaptic clefts* are thought of. To the critics of Hartley and Priestley, the distinction not simply verbal; it was primordial and perpetual in reality. That organical structure could *not* be the cause of consciousness was a truth held to be self-evident. We noted in chapter 1 that Reid criticized Hartley for assuming that "the impressions of external objects upon the machines of our bodies, can be the real efficient cause of thought and perception" (1785, 95). According to Reid, that cause, which is the foundation of our identities as thinking and willing beings, can only be known through the mind's reflexive grasp of itself: "In speaking of the impressions made on our organs in perception, we build upon facts borrowed from anatomy and physiology, for which we have the testimony of the senses. But ... to speak of perception itself, which is solely an act of the mind, we must appeal to another authority. The operations of our minds are known not by sense, but by consciousness, the authority of which is as certain and irresistible as that of sense" (1785, 105; cf. Berington 1776, 141–45). And what the authority of consciousness tells us is that consciousness is a single thing: "A person is something indivisible, and is what LEIBNITZ calls a *monad*" (317). Reid's objection, at bottom, is that taking consciousness to be an emerging property of biological organization displaces personal identity. If the oneness a conscious mind experiences when it is aware of itself is the product of one's neurophysiology, then it is both potentially fallible and certainly contingent: what organization gives, defects of organization can and will take away. If personal identity is to be preserved, both as a self-evident truth and as a metaphysical reality, then it cannot be dependent solely upon the proper functioning of one's brain. If the authority of consciousness is to be "certain and irresistible," a person's consciousness of personal identity must be testimony to the presence of "something indivisible" that *is* the person.

In 1778 Priestley and Richard Price published *A Free Discussion of the Doctrines of Materialism and Philosophical Necessity*. The two men were longtime friends, and the philosophical correspondence they printed in the volume is a model of a cordial and substantive debate, free of bitterness and misrepresentation. Although Price and Priestley thought alike on many things, Price could not accept Priestley's claim that perception and all other mental powers are the result of the "organical structure ... of the brain."

As a key objection to Priestley's theory, Price appeals to our commonsense awareness of the unity of mind: "What experience teaches us, is, that the *exercise* of the mental powers *depends* on the brain and nerves; not that the mind *is* the brain and nerves. Common sense exclaims against such a conclusion as much as against concluding that there is pain in the point of a sword. We are sure the mind cannot be the brain, because the brain is an assemblage of beings. The mind is *one* being" (Priestley 1778, 90). Reid said the same in 1785. And, as we noted at the beginning of chapter 5, Joseph Butler made a very similar point in his *Analogy of Religion* of 1736: after acknowledging that "the Simplicity and absolute Oneness of a living Agent cannot . . . be properly proved by experimental Observations," Butler states that because such observations "*fall in* with the Supposition of its Unity, so they plainly lead us to *conclude* certainly, that our gross organized Bodies . . . are no Part of ourselves" (Butler 1736, 17). Although Butler's "experimental Observations" do not speak with the authoritative certainty and irresistibility of Reid's "consciousness," both observations and consciousness lead to the conclusion that our personal identities are independent of our "gross organized Bodies." Butler, Price, and Reid would all concur that a person's mind, that is, his spirit, is "one being."

Those who thought the mind "*one* being," an indivisible monad, supported the testimony of consciousness with the argument, made repeatedly, that a complex body could not possess properties by virtue of its complexity that were not also properties of its component parts.[3] Joseph Berington states: "The most perfect organization is but the most perfect arrangement of material elements; and evidently, what gives but a new extrinsic relation of parts to parts, can never give capacities, which do not before exist" (1776, 61; also cited in Anon. 1777, 85). Extrinsic relations of parts to parts cannot do so "because the essences of things are eternal and independent; they are what they are, and must ever be so. If *all* matter enjoys not the capacities in question, they are not essential to it" (62). In other words, for a complex material body to be conscious, all the atoms of which it is composed must also be individually conscious; but that is absurd. The conclusion, therefore, is that, granting that the "capacities [of consciousness] exist, . . . their existence must be founded in something"—and that something is something other than any material body, namely, an immaterial substance.

Interestingly, Hartley turns this argument on its head and uses it to challenge the idea that consciousness is a unity. Writing that "the unity of consciousness seems to me an inconclusive argument" for the immateriality of the soul, he states: "For consciousness is a mental perception; and if perception be a monad, then every inseparable adjunct of it must be so too, i.e. vibrations, according to this theory, which is evidently false" (*OM* 1. Conclusion). Consequently, perceptions, including the mental perception of consciousness, are not monads. Such sense as a person has of the unity of his consciousness is, like all other perceptions, the product of association. Moreover, Hartley adds that "it is difficult to know what is meant by unity of consciousness"—which is to question whether people in fact experience a quality of awareness that corresponds to the term.

To anyone with the slightest appreciation of chemical theory—for example, of Stephen Hales's discussion of "factitious airs" in his *Vegetable Statics*—the claim of "nothing-in-the-whole-that-is-not-in-the-parts" would be nonsense. Both vegetable tartars and the stony concretions that form in human bladders are composed of otherwise highly active air. That wholes are more than the sums of their parts is a fundamental principle of Hales's chemical theory, of the force theory of matter upon which it is based, and of Hartley's explorations of the chemistry of ideas. It is an axiom of Halesian, Hartleian, and Priestleian science that compounds, whether atomic, chemical, or psychological, manifest properties that are not present in their component elements. In the view of this science, the dense core of the earth, and all the mountains, seas, and living things upon its surface, may contain no more than a nutshell of solid matter; what seems to us to be earth and water and solid rock is, at the level of the infinitesimally small, forces of attraction and repulsion vibrating in the void of space. Similarly, the perceptions and ideas we have of mountains, seas, and living things, and the pure love we may bear both them and their source, arise harmonically out of neural vibrations.

In "A General View of the Doctrine of Vibrations," the first of the three essays he prefaced to *Hartley's Theory of the Human Mind,* Priestley emphasizes the support chemistry offers for a psychology grounded in physiology:

> I do not expect that this general view of the doctrine of vibrations will satisfy those who are accustomed to consider all matter in the most gross and general manner, as if it was subject to no laws but those of the five mechanical powers, which was a turn of thinking that prevailed very much about a half a century ago; ... But as this system has been abandoned, in consequence of our becoming acquainted with the more subtle and important laws of matter exhibited in chymical operations; so now that we see that the laws and affections of mere matter are infinitely more complex than we had imagined, we may ... be prepared to admit the *possibility* of a mass of matter like the brain, having been so formed by the almighty creator, with such

> exquisite powers, with respect to vibrations, as should be sufficient for all the purposes above-mentioned; though the particulars of its constitution, and mode of affection, may far exceed our comprehension. And it is only the bare *possibility* of the thing that I now contend for. Much light, however, has been thrown upon the *manner* of operation in a variety of particular cases by Dr. Hartley. (Hartley 1775, xviii)

It had been the assumption of previous generations, and particularly of Cartesian mechanists, that any speck of "mere matter" was inert and that all motion was impressed upon it from without, either directly through contact with other bits of matter or ultimately and inexplicably through the influence of a spiritual substance. But once matter is recognized to be chemically active, an explanation of sensation, feeling, perception, thought, and action in terms of highly complex patterns of neural organization and activity becomes in principle possible.

Note as well, in the conventional dichotomy, how easily morally and socially evaluative terms are transferred upon ontological concepts. Like peasants, like serfs, bodies of matter are said to be inert and sluggish, base and imperfect. It is only natural that they should, indeed must, be governed and stirred into action by that which is above them. Just as the masses must be ruled by the princes of the state and the church, so also must mass be ruled by the aristocracy of spirit. And note that the analogy works in both directions: to suggest that matter is itself active is to imply that the sluggish and base masses have the energy and intelligence necessary to organize their own affairs. It is to attack the hierarchical structure of society and the legitimacy of both secular and religious government. It is to suggest, as Priestley did, that those who ruled England had "reason to tremble at an air pump or an electrical machine."[4]

2. "The Only Cause and Reality"

Priestley's critics accused him of being a materialist, the advocate of a theory "which degrades man to a meer machine, and which ... must terminate in absolute *spinozism*" (Anon. 1777, 88). The charge misses the point, for neither Priestley nor Hartley before him were materialists in the sense in which the critics intended. Rather than advocating a material universe devoid of spirit, Hartley imagined an active, spiritual cosmos virtually empty of "inert" matter. Because "mere matter appears quite unable to account for the simplest and most ordinary phaenomena, we must either suppose an immaterial substance, or else suppose that matter has some powers and properties different from and superior to those which appear" (OM 2.1.6). In turn, Priestley challenged the conventional dichotomy between passive matter and active spirit: "The considerations suggested above," Priestley writes in *Disquisitions Relating to Matter and Spirit*, "tend to remove the *odium* which has hitherto lain upon matter, from its supposed necessary property of *solidity, inertness*, or *sluggishness*; as from this circumstance only the *baseness* and *imperfection*, which have been ascribed to it are derived. Since matter has, in fact, no properties but those of *attraction and repulsion*, it ought to rise in our esteem, as making a nearer approach to the nature of spiritual and immaterial beings, as we have been taught to call those which are opposed to gross matter" (1777a, 17; the nutshell of matter appears in the next paragraph).

Of these two alternatives—an immaterial substance, or the attribution to matter of "superior" powers and properties—Hartley adds that "this last supposition is of the same effect as the first, though, on account of the imperfection of language, it seems to be different." The concept of inert matter cannot account for the physical universe we perceive about us and of which we know ourselves to be a part. Consequently, to account for the universe as we perceive it, we must either suppose the activity of an immaterial substance or the presence in matter itself of active powers and properties. But, Hartley tells us, the seeming alternative is owing to the imperfection of language; if we could be free of the imperfection, we would understand that both theses say the same thing. In a philosophical language, there would be only one thesis.

In his discussion of the love of God in proposition 71 of book 2, Hartley writes: "God is our centre, and the love of him a pleasure superior to all the rest . . . because they all point to it, like so many lines terminating in the same centre. . . . For all is God's; he is the only cause and reality; and the existence of every thing else is only the effect, pledge, and proof, of his existence and glory" (OM 2.3.7.71; see §10.2). In §3.1 we noted the ambiguities of Newton's ideas concerning force and matter. According to McMullin (1978, 79), Newton variously attributed the cause of gravitation to an immaterial aether, to light, to an alchemical "active principle," or to the direct action of God. Richard Westfall states that the last of these represents "the ultimate foundation of Newton's conception of nature" (1971, 396); the immaterial aether is "the infinite omnipotent God." However, Newton suffered from having what William Whiston called "the most fearful, cautious, and suspicious Temper" (1749, 294), and he gave what Westfall terms "an evasive and obscure presentation" to this, his "innermost" thought (1971, 396). His followers could not be certain that they were interpreting his hints correctly, or, if they did feel that they understood the truth Newton sought to express in ciphers, of the extent to which they ought to make it available to the public. We also noted in chapter 3 that some of Newton's caution carries over into the earlier part of the *Observations*. In his discussion of the role that the forces of attraction and repulsion may play in the transmission of neural impulses, Hartley states that Newton means "by attraction and repulsion, a mere mathematical tendency to approach and recede, be the cause what it will, impulse, pressure, an unknown one, or no physical cause at all, but the immediate agency of the Deity" (*OM* 1.1.1.5). In this context, at the beginning of the *Observations,* the "immediate agency" of God is listed as one among several alternatives, and there is no explicit commitment to any. The point is that the phenomena of tendencies to approach and recede can be designated by the algebraic variables *attraction* and *repulsion*—"be the cause what it will." Newton did not expressly commit himself concerning this cause, and in this context neither does Hartley.

But now, near the end of the second part of the *Observations,* and in a moral and theological context, Hartley does affirm what at the beginning was one hypothesis among several. Let us take this as our major premise: that when we speak of forces of attraction and repulsion, we are in fact speaking of the "immediate agency" of God. But forces of attraction and repulsion are what make up the universe. According to the "doctrine of vibrations," the theoretical amount of solid matter in the cosmos can be reduced to an infinitesimal minimum, to a nutshell; all material objects are in reality composed of vibrations—that is, of complex interactions between the fundamental forces of attraction and repulsion. Let this be our minor premise. The conclusion, then, is that God at every moment directly causes the universe. Hartley's statement that God "is the only cause and reality" is, in the context in which Hartley presents it, simultaneously a thesis in theology and in physics.[5]

The statement is also a thesis in a psychology of transcendence. In the discussion of the love of God in §10.2, I suggested an analogy between pleasure and the forces of attraction in physics and chemistry.[6] But as we discussed §6.5 and 9, according to Hartley's theory of language it is always possible that analogies may turn out to be identities;

further research and more refined hypotheses may enable us to discover that a figure of speech may be interpreted literally.

If the analogy in this case reveals an identity, then the affection or feeling of pleasure is another manifestation of the forces of attraction postulated in Newtonian natural philosophy. To assert that there is an identity here would be to assert that observations concerning associations and transferences of emotion are as much a part of natural science as are observations concerning chemical interactions or concerning the fundamental forces affecting matter. Psychology would thus be linked with neurophysiology, and with chemistry and physics: these four would be different ways of speaking about one reality. Today, physicists search for the grail of a grand unified theory—a means, first, of discovering and expressing the unity of the strong force, the electroweak force, and gravity, and more ambitiously a means of unifying quantum mechanics and the general theory of relativity. As we noted in §3.2, the theory of superstrings represents one such attempt to subsume the "algebra" of the standard account of quantum mechanics within the multidimensional geometry of space-time. But we also noted in §3.2 that Hartley also spoke of the prospect that "future ages may analyse all the actions of bodies upon each other, up to a few simple principles" (*OM* 1.1.1.5)—principles that he thought would unify all forces in one grand theory of vibrations. Such a theory would show that our articulations of the laws of psychology, physiology, chemistry, and physics all terminate in one center, and that all are various expressions of the fundamental laws of harmony.

The "few simple principles" that Hartley looked to future ages to discover would, however, achieve a unification more inclusive than the one envisioned by today's physicists. For the key to this grandest of unifications would be the discovery of identity within the analogies between natural philosophy and theology. Not only would psychology be linked with the natural sciences of physiology, chemistry, and physics; all the natural sciences would also be understood to be ways of describing the actions of God. The "few simple principles," in other words, would account simultaneously for what we can know about the "actions of bodies upon each other," about ourselves as conscious beings, and about the actions of God. A person who grasped these few simple principles would understand that the languages of natural science, psychology, and theology all terminate in the same center; they do not reference three separate spheres or kinds of action. Such a person would take Fénelon's comment that "we cannot frame a Thought, or create a Desire, but through Him" to be true theologically, psychologically, and physically.

In §3.2 I quoted Michio Kaku's statement that "our bodies our essentially symphonies. They are made out of vibrating strings. The universe obeys the laws of physics, and the laws of physics are nothing but the laws of harmony." I think this statement is consonant with the overall outlook articulated in the "doctrine of vibrations." And also consonant with Hartley's outlook are Fénelon's statements, quoted in §9.3, that the "Eternal and All-powerful Word of the Father speakest in the very Bottom of Souls" (1735, vi); and that God "continually strives to communicate Himself" (ix). If we put the two statements together, we could say: in place of speaking of the universe as originating in a big bang, it would be truer to the physics and theology Hartley affirms to say that the universe began—and is sustained at every moment—by a supreme sound. This sound would be, to coin a term, a hyperchord, a harmony that contains all possible harmonies within itself.

When Jeanne Guyon discerned within the silent depth of her self, "without the sound of Words, a continual Prayer" (Fénelon 1735, 21), she heard perhaps one voice in the vast and intricate polyphony that is the song of God. According to the mystical theology of the Quietists, such a sound without words is present within every person; to discern it, one must still the clattering of speech. This wordless sound is a "continual Prayer," but the prayer is no petition; it is sounded by God, who "continually strives to communicate Himself." This polyphonic prayer, then, is without limits. The song of God can be discerned in every one and in every thing; it sounds in the "very Bottom of Souls" and in the vast depths of space; it is the song that sustains, and is, the cosmos.

3. "The Secret Influence and Guidance" of God

As they did concerning materialism, Hartley's and Priestley's critics objected to philosophical necessity; they thought the doctrine denied personal responsibility and hence the moral economy by which God governed the world. Or more severely, they thought that the doctrine reduced people to automatons—and thereby manifested its absurdity by contradicting what Reid called the "certain and irresistible" authority of consciousness. However, given Hartley's sense of the "only cause and reality," the affirmation of philosophical necessity no more reduces living beings to automatons than the affirmation that "the whole man is of some *uniform composition*" reduces them to figurines fashioned from inert clay.

In Hartley's and Priestley's presentation of it, the doctrine of necessity is a theory of action, according to which a person's actions can be described mechanistically—that is, as a complex of processes in which every event occurs within a matrix of "associated circumstances." As we noted in §5.5, such circumstances exist on several distinct levels: sensory, memorial, emotional, semantic, ethical, theocentric. And in §5.6 we noted the distinction Hartley drew between popular and philosophical ways of speaking about action: although "insuperable difficulties will arise" (*OM* 2.1.15) if the two ways are confounded, the use of each language in its appropriate context will enable us to understand that popular liberty and philosophical necessity are congruent.

In his correspondence with Richard Price, Priestley commented that "no necessarian denies that, in a sufficiently proper sense, men have a power over their own actions, so that they can do what they please; and that without this power they could not be accountable beings, or the proper subjects of rewards and punishments" (1778, xxiv). It is this capacity for explaining how people become accountable for their own actions and responsive to rewards and punishments that is, for Priestley, the central value of the doctrine of philosophical necessity: "that men be *voluntary agents,* or that motives, such as hopes and fears, can influence them in a certain and mechanical manner" makes it "in the highest degree *right,* and *wise* in the Divine Being to lay such motives before them, and consequently to place them in a state of moral discipline, ... And one principal reason why I reject the doctrine of philosophical liberty, is that exactly in the degree in which we suppose the mind *not* to be determined by motives, in that very degree do rewards and punishments lose their effect, and a man ceases to be a proper subject of moral discipline" (1778, xx–xxxi). Affirmation of the mechanism of human actions thus has, for Hartley and Priestley, a moral and theological motive: to affirm philosophical necessity is to affirm the efficacy of God's action.

When does God act in the world? To say, "Only at the beginning," is to side with the deists; "Never" is the response of atheism; saying "On occasion" leaves one with the problem of preferences, of explaining why God should choose to intervene in one situation, in one life, and not in another. These answers, however, all assume a disjunctive contrast: an event or action is attributable *either* to God *or* to natural processes, including human agency. But, as we noted in §5.6, it is precisely this disjunction that the doctrine of necessity contests: recall Benjamin Rush's comment that "as we act most *necessarily* when we act most *freely*, so we act most *freely* when we act most *necessarily*." In regard to the question of God's action, Hartley and Priestley answered, as Sterry and White had previously, "Always." And by answering thus they again question the disjunction (for further discussion of this issue, see Placher 1996, 111f.; Tanner 1988). Priestley writes, in *The Doctrine of Philosophical Necessity Illustrated*:

> We ourselves, complex as the structure of our minds, and our principles of action are, are links in a great connected chain, parts of an immense whole, a very little of which only we are as yet permitted to see, but from which we collect evidence enough, that the whole system (in which we are, at the same time, both *instruments* and *objects*) is under an unerring direction, and that the final result will be most glorious and happy. Whatever men may intend, or execute, all their designs, and all their actions, are subject to the secret influence and guidance of one who is necessarily the best judge of what will most promote his own excellent purposes. To him, and in his works, all seeming *discord* is real *harmony*, and all apparent *evil*, ultimate good. (1777b, viii–ix)

We are both instruments and objects, and neither designation cancels the other. All actions and events are necessary because, as objects, they ought to be referred to God, the "only cause and reality." Nonetheless, we are instrumental in performing them.

Priestley's affirmation of the "real harmony" of all things repeats fundamental themes in Hartley's thought. Recall Hartley's statement that "the true system of things is infinitely more transcendent in greatness and goodness, than any description or conception of ours can make it; and the voice of nature is an universal chorus of joy and transport" (*OM* 2.3.3.61; see §10.2). It was Hartley's fundamental conviction that private happiness, the public good, and the will of God are three terms for the one reality: God wills that all people shall be members of the mystical body, that all shall, in the end, raise their voices in the universal chorus of joy. All shall "become partakers of the divine nature, loving and lovely, holy and happy."

Note the universality of the chorus; as Jeremiah White had said earlier in the century, "no such individual Soul can be for ever abandoned; *but the whole nature of things* must suffer therein, as it did when Christ was crucified" (White [1712] 1779, 147; see §9.4). However, were people possessed of freedom in a philosophical sense, some souls could be forever abandoned, for some could resist God's "secret influence and guidance." The end would be in jeopardy. Not even God could say whether all prodigals will return; some might remain alone—unreconciled, unloving, unlovely. If a person's actions were free in a philosophical sense, the person could act for no purposes at all—and the vast edifice of divine providence would crumble. Discords would not only seem, but be.

To Hartley and Priestley, the harmony is real: "the whole system (in which we are, at the same time, both *instruments* and *objects*) is under an unerring direction" because all events in the system are ultimately the actions of God. But in what sense are we "links in a chain" and "parts of an immense whole"? What elementary philosophical truth might these imperfect phrases contain? We observed in §11.1, among the advocates of the immateriality and philosophical freedom of the spiritual substance, the emphasis on the oneness of that substance in each self. "The mind is *one* being," said Richard Price. And that one being, enjoying a unity of consciousness, must be unique and indivisible—it must be "what LEIBNITZ calls a *monad*," according to Reid. But according to Hartley, consciousness is not a unity, and in fact it is difficult to know what the term means. It is difficult to know this, we may add, because for Hartley the concept of unity is itself provisional. The cosmos is a realm of "infinities upon infinities, ascending and descending," and within this totality, what a person calls "one thing" is relative and provisional: "By a single thing, . . . I mean one that is so comparatively; so that I call not only a single part of an animal (which yet is a thing decompounded, perhaps without limits), but a whole system of animals, when compared with other systems, a single thing" (OM 2.1.4). In §5.2, I quoted this statement in the context of a discussion of molecules within nerve fibers and of nerves within a brain; each molecule and nerve can, for certain purposes, be considered a single thing. In the *Observations,* the statement appears in proposition 4 of part 2, "God is infinitely benevolent"—the proposition that works toward the conclusion, discussed in §10.3, that "all individuals are actually and always infinitely happy." In this proposition, Hartley affirms the view that "the present real constitution of things is best upon the whole," a system in which "every single thing is the most conducive to general happiness, that it can be according to the best of our judgments." The application of the latter statement depends, of course, upon what one takes "a single thing" to be, in any given instance.

"A whole system of animals, when compared with other systems," may be considered "a single thing." But what of a whole system of sentient beings, each of which is aware of its individuality? When we annihilate selfhood, according to Hartley, we shall all become "partakers of the divine nature" and "members of the mystical body of Christ" (*OM* 2.3.6.68; see §9.4). The language is clearly analogical, the "mystical body" a metaphor. There are, however, elements in the *Observations* that suggest that these popular biblical phrases may also bear a philosophical meaning, which at present we barely understand. In the theopathic depth of his imagination, Hartley envisioned "infinities upon infinities": in contrast to the standard account of a single cosmos created once in time, Hartley proposed that it is "most probable, i.e. suitable to the divine attributes, that infinite material worlds have existed from all eternity" (*OM* 2.1.6, Cor.). And within the one world we perceive, the infinities descend and ascend as well; "the whole infinite system of sentient beings" includes the animals, ourselves, and "all the higher orders of intellectual beings" (*OM* 2.1.4). As must be true of the other worlds, in this world "every single thing is the most conducive to general happiness"; that humans are often miserable is "owing to our want of benevolence, i.e. to our moral imperfections, and to that which, according to our present language, we do and must call *ourselves*." But if *ourselves* has an application only in our present language, of what shall we speak when language becomes philosophical? What form shall we all take, when in some future state the elementary bodies of humans (and animals) exercise their "power of vegetating again" (*OM* 2.4.3.86; see §5.7)? At what scale shall perception be, when all attain the "full stature" of "perfect manhood"—and become "new sets of senses, and perceptive powers, to each other" (*OM* 2.3.6.68)?

These questions direct our attention to imagination's horizon; here Hartley's language is at its most algebraic, for the words speak of states of being that are not known. Consequently, when extending imagination to its limit, when speaking of infinities of worlds, "it becomes us," as Hartley points out, "to distrust our own reasonings and conjectures to the utmost" (*OM* 2.1.6, Cor.). Nonetheless, this can be said of the direction of Hartley's thought: just as, by challenging the dichotomy of matter and spirit, Priestley spiritualized matter, so also, by challenging the singularity of that which, according to our present language, we call *self,* Hartley pointed toward the inclusion of ourselves in the "mystical body," the "divine nature," that transcends us.

In "Religious Musings," Coleridge writes of the person who feels "his own low self the whole; / When he by sacred sympathy might make / The whole one Self!" (ll. 149–58, at 151–53; see §7.3). Earlier in the poem he states that "'Tis the sublime of man, / ... to know ourselves / Parts and proportions of one wondrous whole!" (126–28). Then he adds: "But 'tis God / diffused through all, that doth make all one whole" (130–31). And earlier still he imagines the process whereby a person's soul is "attracted and absorbed" into the "perfect Love" of God: "and centered there / God only to behold, and know, and feel, / Till by exclusive consciousness of God / All self-annihilated it shall make / God its Identity: God all in all! / We and our father one!" (40–45). The lines have a footnote, in which Coleridge states: "See this *demonstrated* by Hartley...." I imagine that, were he in a future state to read these lines, Hartley would demur—the verb in the note claims too much. But I also imagine that he would approve of the associations Coleridge's lines express.

4. "To New-Model Opinion ..."

John Lister tried to persuade his boyhood friend not to publish his *Observations.* Lister believed that fear of eternal punishment counteracted "the weakness of vulgar minds"; Hartley's proclamation of universal happiness, by annihilating that fear, posed the danger of begetting "carelessness" (*L* 36). The doctrine in the *Observations* threatened to undermine the foundations of personal morality and social order. But to those who took Priestley as a leading light, in contrast, Hartley's *Observations* contained the key to personal and social betterment. By demonstrating that minds form through association, the *Observations* provided the intellectual warrant for their plans to control association and thereby direct the formation of minds. Hartley had written the "holy book of millennarian perfectionism" (Kramnick 1986, 15).

Consider the following passage: "Action is the result of opinion, and to new-model opinion would be to new-model society. Knowledge is power; it is in the hands of the few, who employ it to mislead the many, for their own selfish purposes of aggrandizement and appropriation. What if it were in the hands of a few who should lead the many? What if it were universal, and the multitude were enlightened?" The passage could have been penned by a number of people. One might seek it in the chapters defending philosophical necessity in William Godwin's *Enquiry Concerning Political Justice* ([1793] 1976). Or perhaps in one of the political and religious pamphlets Coleridge wrote during the 1790s, shortly before or after he named his first son David Hartley Coleridge. Then again, perhaps one should read Thomas Belsham's *Elements of the Philosophy of Mind, and of Moral Philosophy* (1801). Belsham taught at Daventry, the dissenting academy Priestley had attended, and then at Hackney, where one of his pupils was William Hazlitt; his *Elements* contains "the substance of a course of lectures, which the author delivered to his pupils, upon some of the most interesting subjects which can occupy the attention of the human mind" (1801, i). Belsham's guide for the exploration of these subjects is Hartley, and his *Elements* is a straightforward textbook in what its author understood to be Hartleian psychology. One might also look in the essay "On Liberty and Necessity" in Thomas's brother William Belsham's *Essays: Philosophical, Historical, and Literary* (1789). Then again, perhaps the place to look would be the *Essays, Literary, Moral, and Philosophical* by Benjamin Rush, Hartley's disciple in America. In his essay "On the Mode of Education Proper in a Republic," Rush wrote of the need "to effect a revolution in our principles, opinions, and manners" that would "convert men into republican machines"—something that "must be done, if we expect them to perform their parts properly, in the great machine of the government of the state" (1798, 9, 15). Or perhaps the passage is from Robert Owen's *A New View of Society* (1813); Owen, after all, states as his first principle that "Any general character, from the best to the worst, from the most ignorant to the most enlightened, may be given to any community, even to the world at large, by the application of proper means; which means are to a great extent at the command and under the control of those who have influence in the affairs of men" ([1813] 1969, 101).[7]

The words are in fact those of Scythrop Glowry, the hero of Thomas Love Peacock's satirical novel, *Nightmare Abbey* ([1818] 1924, 15). They are the opening lines of a soliloquy Scythrop utters as he ruminates on "the practibility of reviving a confederation of regenerators"—the Sarastros who will select themselves to be the Guardians of the perfect Republic. Condensed within this soliloquy is the intellectual history of a generation. Scythrop is a caricature of Peacock's friend,

Percy Bysshe Shelley. The initial thesis—"Action is the result of opinion, and to new-model opinion would be to new-model society"—is one that was argued at length by Godwin, Shelley's father-in-law, at what seemed the dawn of the new millennium.

There is, however, little justification in Hartley's psychology for optimism that changes in opinion follow upon changes in circumstances, or for fancying that a new-modeling of opinions will lead to a new-modeling of society. Hartley preached the everlasting gospel—a vast history of the world in which all people would eventually become "holy and happy" as "partakers of the divine nature" and members of "the mystical body of Christ." The advocates of social regeneration preached a secular gospel of progress—a gospel that probably would have appeared to Hartley to be a pale imitation of the original. That the reformers read him as providing a warrant for their optimism is an indication that they, too, responded to the "circumstance" that is the *Observations* in a manner consistent with their powers of memory.

What is surprising is how much the later Sarastros missed. In contrast to the profound influence Hartley exerted as a moral and spiritual exemplar for such as Harriet Martineau (see §1.1 and ch. 11, n. 1), it appears that little of what Priestley called this "new and most extensive *science*" entered into the language and practice of psychological inquiry—even as practiced by those who acknowledged a debt to Hartley. Although Hartley was revered both as a saint and as a second Newton, in my admittedly incomplete reading of his advocates I have encountered little or no discussion concerning the concepts of joint impression, of secondarily automatic and decomplex actions, of the transference of emotion, of primary pursuits, of the centrality of language, of the emergence of the self through the orientations of imagination, ambition, and self-interest, of the transformations of the sense of self-interest, of the eventual annihilation or abandonment of self-interest altogether, of the attainment of the higher self defined by sympathy, theopathy, and the moral sense, or of the human capacity for transcendence, for becoming a "partaker in the divine nature." There are, of course, exceptions: the Mills understood joint impression; William B. Carpenter (1874, 16) emphasized Hartley's analysis of automatic and voluntary action; John Jebb endorsed Hartley's model of epigenetic moral development, in which the six orientations successively become primary pursuits (1787, 2: 264–65; see Page 1998); Coleridge wrote of the time when, "all self-annihilated," the soul "shall make / God its identity"; and, as the second epigraph in chapter 10 attests, Edward Tagart warmly endorsed

Hartley's demonstration of God's infinite benevolence and hence of our infinite happiness. Although further research may well reveal that Hartley's followers enjoyed a more acute and comprehensive appreciation of the *Observations* than I have been able to discover, my perception at present is that, in general, both advocates and critics did not discern or fathom many of the core themes in Hartley's thought.

In particular, Priestleian reformers failed to understand how little warrant Hartley offered for thinking that they could direct the course of human perfection. "Action is the result of opinion, and to new-model opinion would be to new-model society." This principle embodies a paradox: Human actions are totally the results of the opinions that themselves are part of our previous circumstances, and yet the actions of some humans can transform opinions and hence shape future circumstance. In this view, a person's sins are never original. Vice and virtue do not have their sources within the collection of opinions a person has at any given moment. Yet people with sound opinions can eliminate defective opinions—and vice—from others. Once they regenerate themselves, free themselves from distorted opinions, the confederation of regenerators will be able to direct and assist the rest of humanity in new-modeling a second Eden, a secular paradise, what Coleridge calls a "universal fraternity of love" (C 1.12).

"Action is the result of opinion"—thus say the regenerators of society, including Godwin, the young Coleridge, Robert Owen. But Hartley does not say this. He states that "all our voluntary powers are of the nature of memory." The difference may seem slight; the difference is everything. Opinions are froth. Godwin writes: "Ideas are to the mind what atoms are to the body. The whole mass is in a perpetual flux; nothing is stable and permanent" (1976, 104). But our memories persist. They are embedded within us. Physically, they exist as configurations of molecules in the fibers of our brains. Psychologically, they make present experience possible; we would be unable to remember any present experience—an old tune, the smell of a pine woods, which is the dog and which the cat—but for them. And as they enable us to remember the present, they also help us, as far as we are able, to imagine the future.

But what do we perceive, and what imagine? In the prism of the self, each of the orientations of imagination, ambition, self-interest, sympathy, theopathy, and the moral sense helps to "generate" and "model" the orientations beyond it, and once modeled so also does each orientation "new-model" (*OM* 1.3.3.89) the ones that come before. In this process of modeling and new-modeling, a new quality of perception in *any* orientation may act transformatively upon the others. The development of a selfless sense of sympathy, or of a theopathy that is free of superstitious fear, may lead to new powers of perception in the orientations of imagination and ambition; but these new perceptions will in turn provide matter for the further modeling and refinement of sympathy and theopathy. The psyche is thus a continuously reciprocating system. "At last, by the numerous reciprocal influences of all these [orientations] upon each other, the passions arrive at that degree of complexness ... which makes them so difficult to be analyzed."

This "degree of complexness" is not only difficult to analyze; it also suggests that people's "opinions" and responses to "circumstances" are not easily managed. The nature of a person's response to circumstances depends upon which memories and orientations are foremost in fashioning the perception and evaluation of the situation. For a person who desires to make sympathy and theopathy primary pursuits, imagination or ambition may at times be the primary mode of response. The Old Adam may eclipse the New. Alternatively, a person of unformed character may, prompted by special circumstances, for a moment experience the awakening of a Self within the self, a heretofore hidden presence, Jerusalem asleep in the land of dreams.

How, then, ought we to perceive the present, and imagine the future? Or better, were our consciousness of present time to expand, how should we perceive our situation now? Hartley believed that we live within a system so vast that we become giddy when trying to comprehend it. Nonetheless, he was confident that "this whole universe is a system of benevolence, or, as St. Paul expresses it, a body, which being *fitly framed and compacted together, increaseth itself in love*" (*OM* 2.2.26; Eph. 4.16). Hartley believed that this body is in a process of reintegration. He did not believe that we control the process. Rather, he saw in the biblical story of God's "everlasting covenant" (Gen. 17.7) with Abraham "the strongest evidences of God's great design to purify and perfect mankind." The story declares God's benevolence, and the design will be accomplished when all people comprehend that "the happiness of Abraham, of his seed, and of all mankind ... must arise from their imitation of God in his benevolence." The everlasting gospel thus reveals that this whole universe is the manifestation of the "boundless ocean of love" (*OM* 2.3.3.56) that is God. Progress is measured by the degree to which we annihilate the selfhood that isolates us from this liquid truth. Our perfection comes with the recognition that, at the bottom of our souls, we are, happily, already part of that ocean.

12

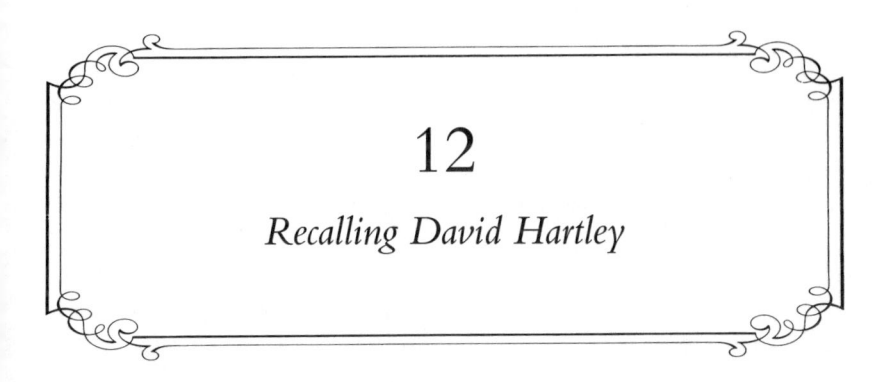

Recalling David Hartley

What are the elements in the synthesis, the colors in the spectrum, in Hartley's *Observations on Man*? When I asked this question in the first chapter, I identified five. We can integrate these into one sentence: Hartley's *Observations* offers a synthesis that begins with a neurophysiology of perception, that ends in spirituality, and that is centered upon a model of development that emphasizes that the self is constructed through language and that includes theopathy as one of the fundamental orientations of the psyche.

Let us rephrase the statement, using some terms Hartley would recognize: the *Observations* offers an account of perception and action that is based upon the doctrine of vibrations; an analysis of the emergence of self through the transferences of affection, which shows that the "self" is factitious, itself formed out of the web of words given in social interactions; and an account of the annihilation of that self, as sympathy and theopathy become more and more a person's primary pursuits.

At the end of the preface I also indicated that I thought that Hartley can provide a resource for thinking today; that a right reading of this "grand work" could show the daughters of memory to be the daughters of inspiration. With that possibility in mind, let us review the elements in Hartley's synthesis.

First, the doctrine of vibrations. The theory is certainly provisional and incomplete; like everyone else in the early eighteenth century, Hartley knew little about human biology and nothing about dendrites and axons, neurotransmitters and synaptic clefts. As we noted in chapters 2 and 3, his theory of vibrations is based largely upon a speculative Newtonian theory of matter and upon the chemical theory Stephen Hales derived from it. Still, if we grant it a charitable interpretation that allows for the limitations in what people knew, what is remarkable is that the theory of vibrations is in a sense correct, at least on a conceptual level. For as long as it is continuously stimulated, a sensory nerve does "vibrate"— in the sense that action potentials travel along it in a regular sequence. In addition, and more importantly, the theory is valuable as a heuristic model, for it opens up the possibility of a type of explanation. In §11.1 we recalled Hartley's comment that, if a material organism "could be endued with the most simple kinds of sensation, [it] might also arrive at all that intelligence of which the human mind is possessed" (*OM* 1. Conclusion)—and hence that "the whole superstructure of ideas and associations observable in human life may . . . be built upon as small a foundation as we please" (*OM* 1.1.2.11; see §5.2). For Hartley, the foundation is a very small one: a nerve fiber vibrates, changes its frequency or amplitude of vibration, and transmits those changes to other fibers. And thanks to the vast number of associative connections between fibers, this simple and fundamental mechanism is able to generate all the complexities of thought and action we observe in living beings.

We also noted in chapter 11 that Thomas Reid, James Mackintosh, and others objected to Hartley's theory of vibrations not because it offered an inadequate answer to a genuine question but rather because it raised a question they thought should not be asked. The theory called into question the validity of Mackintosh's "primordial and perpetual distinction between *the being which thinks* and the *thing which is thought of*" (1836, 245). By suggesting that perception, consciousness, self-consciousness, and such orientations as sympathy and theopathy could be matters of neural harmonics, the theory dispensed with the need to include an immaterial substance in one's explanation of human beings.

In addition to this metaphysical and theological objection, there was also a practical problem that made the theory a difficult one to accept, even for those who were not moved by the objections of Reid and Mackintosh: there did not appear to be a way to put it to use.

George Henry Lewes commented: "To say that vibrations produce sensations throws little light. What is the specific velocity and sweep of each vibration? *That* would be valuable knowledge" (1880, 2:371; see ch. 11, n. 2). Lewes believed there could be such knowledge; he did want "to trace the mechanism of thought," but he did not see in Hartley's "vague theory" any useful indication of how to go about doing so. Today, we can appreciate Hartley's notion that complex, higher-level phenomena could be generated by a system of vibrating and cross-signaling fibers; it is the basis for both our computers and our computer-like models of perception and thought. In Hartley's day and for over a century thereafter, there was no laboratory in which one could begin to put this insight to work.

Second, the account of perception and action. Hartley is again correct regarding the importance of "joint impression" for the formation of perceptual categories. As we noted in chapter 4, the same concept—now called "cross-modal transfer" (Gregory 1974), or "convergent active processing of interrelated networks" (Millar 1994), or "reentrant mapping" (Edelman 1989, 1992)—plays a central role in contemporary discussions of the means by which we learn to label an unlabeled world. Moreover, by grounding his account in his neurological theory, Hartley was able to work through an explanation of perception and action that is deeper and subtler than either supporters or critics have generally recognized. Hartley's name is customarily linked to the phrase "the association of ideas." However, because of their readiness to dissociate "association" from the neurological theory, later writers assumed that Hartley was an inventor of the "brickbat plan of construction" that, according to William James, results when people "treat 'ideas' as separate subjective entities" (1890, 1:196; see §4.1). But Hartley does not assume that "ideas," as the sorts of mental contents even a disembodied mind could have, are preexisting entities upon which "association" sets to work. Rather, a neurological associative process, joint impression, *generates* "ideas." Consequently, what counts as an "idea" must be inclusively understood. In Hartley's theory, as a person's brain and nervous system develops, perceptual categorizations come into being; moreover, repertoires of "complex" actions, such as are involved in learning to speak a language or to play the piano, become "secondarily automatic," and these repertoires enable the person to engage in the performance of "decomplex" actions, such as asking a question or playing a Chopin prelude. Performing a decomplex action is an "idea," as is recognizing which is the dog and which the cat. Playing Chopin the composer and playing with Chopin the cat: A person may have ideas of both.

Third, language. Mastery of a language is itself a paradigm of perceptual categorization through joint impression. A child learns to discriminate among sounds heard and sounds made, and to correlate these with invitations, denials, desires, aversions, tastes, smells, objects, and actions; she perfects secondarily automatic, complex actions, as she learns to speak; and she choreographs the performance, at once intentional and spontaneous, of decomplex actions, as she speaks her mind. My choice of words at the end of the last sentence is deliberate, and the verb transitive.

Fourth, the theory of psychological development. We now live in an age in which models of the psyche and theories charting the course of development are commonplace. We know, from Freud, of the id, ego, and superego, of the unconscious, preconscious, and conscious systems, of the oral, anal, phallic, latency, and genital stages of psychosexual development, and of the importance of resolving the Oedipus conflict. We know, from Jung, of persona, anima, and shadow, of the archetypes of the collective unconscious, and of the lifelong task of individuation. We know, from Abraham Maslow (1968, 1970), that psychosocial development passes through a hierarchy of needs—for physiological satisfaction, for safety, for love, for esteem, and finally for self-actualization. We know, from Erik Erikson (1963), that eight crises define the course of personal development; how a person grows depends on how he or she passes through the first crisis of basic trust versus mistrust, the second crisis of autonomy versus shame and doubt, and so forth. We know, from Lawrence Kohlberg (1969), that children ascend through six stages of moral development, with two stages forming each of the three levels of development, the preconventional, conventional, and postconventional.—Thus far I have named persons whose works have over time become influential in our culture beyond the confines of academic psychology, and whose ideas have been accepted as paradigms even by those who dissent from them or who seek to move beyond them. The list can, of course, be much expanded.

Imagine adding Hartley's name to it. I propose that a Hartleian model of the psyche, of the prism of the self, is as intuitively compelling and as potentially useful as the various models offered by the people named above. In saying this, I assume that the words of a psychological language, rather than bearing reference to empirically observable entities, call our attention to processes, to recurrent patterns that appear within the flowing free waters of consciousness and action. In this sense, a person does not *have* an ego, or an anima. *Ego* and *anima* refer to what a person *does,* and the words are useful insofar as they enable us to understand what is *going on* in ourselves and in other people.

Psychological languages present models, or ways of speaking, that enable us first to recognize and then to explain certain patterns in our thoughts, feelings, actions, and interactions. And no single model is comprehensive; no single way of speaking is able to say everything about what goes on in people. Any model will call attention to some processes and patterns and neglect or ignore others; any single way of speaking will render us both articulate and mute. Which models, then, do we choose to adopt? It depends. For a person for whom imagination, in its intellectual form, is a primary pursuit, that model will most appeal which seems to offer the fullest, deepest, most accurate, and most intellectually satisfying explanation of psychological facts. For a person for whom ambition is primary, the issue will be one of perceived social identity, and the choice of way of speaking will depend upon whose company he wants to be thought to keep. A person who strives to make sympathy her primary pursuit will ask, Is this way of speaking helpful? Will it help me to help others? Will it illuminate the ways and reasons why souls fall ill and suffer, and will it show a way toward healing and wholeness? And a person filled with theopathy will ask, Does it help me understand what I love when I love my God? People, in other words, choose the models that seem to them to reach the farthest—however *reach* is defined.

In my estimation, Hartley's account of imagination, ambition, and self-interest, and then of sympathy, theopathy, and the moral sense, presents us with a far-reaching model, a fruitful way of speaking about ourselves. Although the model is structurally simple, it is dynamically complex. Recognizing that the six orientations both "model" and "new-model" each other gives us a way to investigate "the numerous reciprocal influences" these orientations exert "upon each other" (*OM* 1.3.3.89). I hope that the model and some of the possibilities for its application have been sufficiently explored in chapters 7 and 8 and do not require further elaboration at this point. Here I would like to point out that, like the accounts of Maslow, Erikson, and Kohlberg, Hartley's model describes a process of moral development as a sequence of transformations of the self. It would be fair to say that Hartley was the Maslow or Erikson of his age. In addition, like contemporary transpersonal models of the person (e.g., Hunt 1995; Wade 1996;

Washburn 1988, 1994; Wilber 1983), Hartley's model stresses that self-interest, i.e., the "goings on" of the ego, must be transcended if the person is to realize his or her full stature. And given its emphasis upon transformation and transcendence, Hartley's model also bears a relationship to other ways of speaking that I find also to be rich resources for thought. One, in addition to the Jewish, Christian, Islamic, and Hindu sources already mentioned, is the Confucian philosophy of self-transformation, particularly as it was developed by Mencius (see Hall and Ames 1987).

Fifth, the theopathic dimension. Hartley's specific observations concerning the various forms of theopathy are discussed in chapters 7, 8, and 9. These have value, for Hartley was an attentive and discerning observer. We can appreciate, for example, his account of the stages in which "associations may be observed in fact to be heaped upon" the word *God*, which begin with the "compound fictitious idea" children form when they "suppose [*God*] to stand for a man whom they have never seen" and which end, for many people, when this idea "is quite obliterated, without anything of a stable precise nature succeeding in its room" (*OM* 1.4.5.98; see §8.5).

More importantly, beyond these specific observations is the fact that Hartley makes theopathy a constituent element of the structure of the psyche—that is, one of the fundamental orientations by which people are present to and interact with reality. If Hartley is correct about this, if theopathy is a central aspect of personhood, then observers of humanity ought to recognize it to be one of the most important dimensions of life. As such, it is not a matter to be relegated to a specialized and small subsection of a professional society. If we acknowledge that theopathy names what vast numbers of people take to be a fundamental dimension of their own lives, then we must also recognize that the silence about it, and inattention to it, in academic psychology and in psychoanalysis is itself indicative of a "deficit." It is the symptom of a sickness—a sickness resulting in a massive agnosia. How extensive is this agnosia? People will answer the question differently, depending upon their sense of the intellectual landscape. My sense is that in standard studies of development, of emotion, of cognition, psychologists commonly offer descriptions of human beings from which something very important, indeed central, is simply missing. Hartley observed that in most adults the child's "compound fictitious idea" of God "is quite obliterated"; what seems to be equally obliterated, in psychological writing, is the awareness that people pray and contemplate and sing, that they listen for the quiet voice that "speakest in the very Bottom of Souls" (Fénelon 1735, vi), that they have religious ideas and theopathic affections at all. If we become sufficiently struck by this absence, by what is *not* there, then what will appear odd to us is not Hartley's extensive discussion of theopathy but rather the absence of such discussion from contemporary academic psychology. And Hartley will have done us the service of making us aware of something many of us have forgotten to miss.

Of course, the theopathic dimension is not completely missing from psychology. If it is truly a fundamental orientation of the psyche, it cannot be. James Hillman writes, in the context of a discussion of psychological language, and specifically of Plotinus's image of the soul's revolving around God: "Each new psychological system is but one turning of the soul around the divine inscrutability at its center.... So, our psychological descriptions are also in some way descriptions of the divine. A textbook in psychology is also a kind of textbook in theology" (1972, 155). This duality will be evident especially to those who turn to old theological systems in order to recover a language that speaks of and for the psyche; the conviction that theological texts are also psychological texts guides those, for example, who explore the Kabbalah as a resource for psychology (e.g., Hoffman 1989, 1995). The duality is also evident in the work of those who develop new psychological systems; consider the importance of Buddhist thought in transpersonal psychology (e.g., Engler 1986; Hunt 1995; Wilber 1983, 1986) and also the central position of the mystical theology of John of the Cross in Michael Washburn's *Transpersonal Psychology in Psychoanalytic Perspective* (1994).

And finally, the synthesis of physiology, development, and spirituality. In the preface, I spoke of words as markers in the geography of knowledge. When surveying a long-cultivated landscape, a person interested in the archaeology of settlement can discern features that represent various strata of social organization. In Scotland, for example, the pattern of fields and farms is representative of the enclosures that transformed rural society during the eighteenth century; but in places, in the modern fields of barley and potatoes, one may still see the long lines of runrig—a pentimento of the way of life the Enlightenment replaced. Similarly, there are in Hartley's *Observations* two strata of thought, patterns of meaning, ways of speaking. What people notice first, in the opening chapters of the first book, is the world and language of Newtonian science. Hartley's goal is to extend that language, that way of organizing knowledge, into another of the realms of nature toward which Newton gestured. Hartley wishes to treat the human body as part of the natural world; "its component parts should be subjected to the same subtle laws" (*OM* 1.1.2.9) as other material entities, and the whole system is ideally describable in a language that becomes philosophical insofar as it becomes a consistent and complete nomenclature, "without any deficiency, superfluity, or equivocation" (*OM* 1.3.1.84; see §6.8). But as one progresses farther and farther into the *Observations*, and especially into the second book, one increasingly encounters an older stratum of thought. This is the world as described by the tradition of Plotinus, John Scotus Erigena, the Kabbalists, the Cambridge Platonists, Sterry, White, Guyon, and Fénelon—the world that emanates from and returns to the One, and in which all things are refined by what Jeremiah White calls the "Sparkle" of the fire that flows out from their origin and leads them to their end. Here Hartley's purpose is, again, to show all human beings to be part of the world—of the world in which "the *Being* of the Creature is the *beaming* forth from God, like light from the Sun" (Sterry 1675, 63) and in which "the voice of nature is an universal chorus of joy and transport" (*OM* 2.3.3.56; see §10.2). In speaking of this world, language once again aims to be philosophical, but in a radically different sense: it is philosophical to the degree that it too sparkles with the radiance of being.

To appreciate the synthetic quality of Hartley's psychology, we must understand that for him both ways of speaking are true and also that neither is eliminable or reducible to the other. Further, although Hartley relies upon both ways of speaking, he makes no claim that they refer to two different orders of reality, the one material and the other spiritual. Rather, Hartley's position is that the nature of which we are a part is both material *and* spiritual. The synthesis of physiology, development, and spirituality rests upon the affirmation of both languages: both speak of the complete human person. Those who have no use for the second, or the first, will see in this no synthesis but merely wishful or muddled thinking. Those who bring both to mind and deny neither, or at least are willing to entertain the possibility that both may be held in a creative tension, will find the *Observations* to be a paradigm for a textbook in psychology—that is, both a textbook in science and a textbook in theology.

Hartley fashioned a psychology that is neurological, developmental, and spiritual. The psychology describes a lower self of imagination and ambition that has as its apex the development of a rational self-interest;

the psychology then describes a higher self for which sympathy and theopathy are primary pursuits, and which reaches its completion when selfhood is annihilated. In this psychology, the person who becomes a "partaker in the divine nature" is the same as the one who, as a body, is subject to the "subtle laws" governing the natural world: the pure love of God is a matter of neural harmonics, like all other thoughts and loves. Today, in contrast, much of academic psychology has become blind to theopathy and to the whole self of which it is a constitutive element, while in our religious beliefs, we commonly assume a dualism of body and spirit that ignores how thoroughly personal identity is a matter of the body. But when the works of the inspired authors of the past are read again, this may be set right: we may yet create an age that Benjamin Rush would envy. Recalling the work of David Hartley may inspire us to attempt, in our own ways, to be equally synthetic and comprehensive. Recall that all our voluntary powers are of the nature of memory: the daughters of memory are the daughters of inspiration.

Notes

Chapter 1. Remembering David Hartley

1. For an insightful discussion of Rush's indebtedness to Hartley, see Donald D'Elia 1970.

2. In the first edition of the *Encyclopedia Britannica* of 1771, the entry for "Metaphysics" consists of a discussion of the formation and association of ideas, taken from the pages of Locke's *Essay*. And at about the time Rush wrote to Jefferson, Percy Shelley wrote: "Metaphysics is a word which has so long applied to denote an inquiry into the phenomena of mind that it would justly be presumptuous to employ another" (quoted in Read 1997, 22).

3. Some aim at such completeness—Roger Sperry (1983), John C. Eccles (1979, 1980), and Daniel N. Robinson (Eccles and Robinson 1984). But how many others?

4. For a counterexample, see Robert Marsh (1959a, 1959b, 1965).

5. Mackintosh's review of Hartley is generally sympathetic and perceptive. He recognizes the importance of the "transference" of emotion (1836, 256–57); is interested in the role of such transferences in psychological development; and understands that association functions "chemically" (354).—William Whewell, in his Preface to Mackintosh, comments that "he assents, in great measure, to the explanation suggested by Hume and Smith, but more fully developed by Hartley, of the formation of our passions and affections, and even our sentiments of virtue and duty, by means of 'the association of ideas' " (1836, 34). And Mackintosh writes of "the extraordinary value of Hartley's system"—which, unfortunately, "has been hidden by various causes, which have also enabled writers who borrow from it to decry it. The influence of his medical habits renders many of his examples displeasing, and sometimes disgusting. He has none of that knowledge of the world, of that familiarity with

literature, of that delicate perception of the beauties of nature and art, which not only supply the most agreeable illustrations of mental philosophy, but afford the most obvious and striking instances of its happy application to subjects generally interesting" (253).

6. Priestley writes that the *Observations* "established me in the belief of the doctrine of necessity, which I first learned from Collins; it greatly improved that disposition to piety which I brought to the academy and freed it from the rigour with which it had been tinctured. Indeed, I do not know whether the consideration of Dr. Hartley's theory, contributes more to enlighten the mind, or improve the heart; it effects both in so super-eminent a degree" ([1806] 1970, 76). Priestley was raised in a determinedly Calvinist family. But like Hartley before him, he could not accept that "all the human race . . . were liable to the wrath of God, and the pains of hell forever."

Priestley is also reported to have corresponded with Hartley, prior to Hartley's death in 1757. Jack Lindsay writes that the topic of their correspondence was Priestley's application of Hartley's ideas to education, and that Hartley offered to help subsidize publication of Priestley's writings (Priestley [1806] 1970, 14). The correspondence appears to be no longer extant.

7. This was the elder son, David Hartley, M.P. (1731–1813). A Rockingham Whig, as Minister Plenipotentiary for the British government, he signed, along with John Adams, Benjamin Franklin, and John Jay, the articles ending the American Revolutionary War.

8. Mary Anne Galton Schimmelpenninck adds: "I well remember that in the assembly of these distinguished men [i.e., members of the Lunar Society], amongst whom Mr. [Matthew] Boulton . . . stood pre-eminently as the great Maecenas, even as a child, I used to feel when Dr. Priestley entered after him, that the glory of the one was terrestrial, that of the other celestial" (1860, 32). Mary Anne Galton Schimmelpenninck was the daughter of Samuel Galton and the sister of S. Tertius Galton, who married Erasmus Darwin's daughter Violetta; Sir Francis Galton was the son of Tertius and Violetta, and hence the first cousin of Erasmus Darwin's grandson, Charles.

Chapter 2. Portrait of a Benevolent Man

1. Mary Hartley to William Gilpin, 18 July 1795, in Warner 1817, 92–93.

2. England adopted the New Style, or Gregorian, calendar in 1752. In the Old Style, or Julian calendar, the new year officially began on 25 March, or 1 April, although people sometimes adopted the convention that it began on 1 January. To avoid ambiguity, both dates were often used; 9 March 1736 would be written 9 March 1735/6. In addition, there was by Hartley's time an eleven-day discrepancy between the two calendars, so that 9 March 1735/6 O.S. would

be 20 March 1736 N.S. I have retained the Old Style dating, but give all dates as if the year started on 1 January.

3. See Joy Hancox, *The Byrom Collection* (1992), for reproductions and discussion of the fascinating collection of drawings that were apparently in Byrom's possession.

4. Byrom learned about Hartley's first acquaintance with his shorthand during a dinner with Hartley and Benjamin Hoadley, M.D. (1706–57), the son of Benjamin Hoadley (1676–1761), bishop of Salisbury, on 19 May 1737. Byrom writes: "Dr. Hartley told us how he had found it out, by a paper of Dr. Hoadly's that contained an experiment of Haukesbee's, beginning, '*I took a bottle*,' that the first word he found out was 'jump,' and 'airpump,' that he was three days deciphering, and then was perfectly happy" (B 2.1.165).

5. For fundamental information concerning Hartley's medical training at Cambridge, his practice at Newark-on-Trent and Bury St. Edmunds, and his circle of associates in both places, see the thoroughly researched article by Martha Ellen Webb (1989).

6. From 1733 until his death in 1742, Cheyne advised Samuel Richardson on diet and health. In a letter of 23 December 1741, Cheyne instructed Richardson to keep to the vegetable diet (Cheyne 1943, 77). For more on Cheyne, see Shuttleton 1995; Rousseau 1991a, 78–117; King 1974; and Henderson 1952.

7. According to Lillywhite (1963, 23), there were 551 coffeehouses in London in 1739. Dick's, or Richard's, remained in existence from 1680 until at least 1885.

8. For discussion of the shift whereby the Bible itself becomes placed within history, see Hans W. Frei, *The Eclipse of Biblical Narrative* (1974)—a work that has been profoundly influential for those developing a "postliberal" theology. Frei writes that "one sign of the breakdown of literal-realistic interpretation of the biblical stories was the reversal in the direction of interpretation between the narratively depicted and the 'real' world" (1974, 6). Prior to this reversal, those who, like Luther and Calvin, adopted "precritical" methods of interpretation could say, "We are, as interpreters as well as religious and moral persons, part of the same sequence. We are not independent observers of it from outside the temporal framework in which we have been cast" (36). In this view, the real world is the one the biblical narrative depicts; time is biblical time. But with the reversal, time escapes the biblical paradigm, so that now the Bible must be situated in relation to it. The result is a "split between the explicative meaning and the historical estimation of biblical narratives"—a split that "had crucial consequences for the principles of interpretation" (41). After the reversal, the question becomes, In what sense is the Bible "real"? And its "reality" (i.e., meaning) as a paradigm for religious practice appears both to depend upon and yet to be logically separate from its "reality" as a historical document: *that* the Scriptures are meaningful to us depends upon its historical authenticity, but *what* the Scriptures mean to us is not necessarily identical with what they meant

to those who read them two or more millennia ago. Hartley struggles with the two senses of "real" in the chapter on "The Truth of the Christian Religion" in the second part of the *Observations*.

9. Sources of information: On the Packer family and on the history of Donnington, Millson 1985; Humphreys 1932; and the *Victoria County History, Berkshire*, 4:92–94. On the Winchcombe family and the Bucklebury estate, Millson 1994 and Humphreys 1932.

10. Hartley family papers, Bucklebury, Berks., F82.

11. The marriage license was issued on 25 August 1735 by Nicholas Baker, M.A., through his surrogate James Reynolds, between David Hartley of Bury St. Edmunds St. Mary, widower, M.D., and Elizabeth Packer of Bury St. Edmunds St. James, aged twenty-three, to take place at Nowton. The marriage surety bond was agreed by Hartley and William Walton of Bury St. Edmunds, clerk.

12. For more on Whiston, see Rousseau 1991a, 325–41, and also Whiston's *Memoirs* (1749). For a discussion of public lecturing by Newtonian natural philosophers, see Stewart 1986.

13. The letter is torn, and the words indicated by brackets are missing. In a letter of 16 January 1737 (*L* 5), Hartley states: "Αιωνιος is a Jewish Word & amongst the Jews did always sympathize with the Nature of the Subject to wch it was annexed. Since therefore Punishmt. in the Hands of an infinitely good Being cannot be final but mediate only, αιωνιος when joined to it cannot be more than indefinite. Perhaps something like inconceivable, inexpressible &c amongst us."

14. Writing of "the canonical writings of religious communities," George A. Lindbeck states: "For those who are steeped in them, no world is more real than the ones they create. A scriptural world is thus able to absorb the universe. It supplies the interpretive framework within which believers seek to live their lives and understand reality. . . . It is the text . . . that absorbs the world, rather than the world the text" (1984, 117, 118). For discussion of the postliberal theology of Lindbeck and others, see Placher 1989. For discussion of narrative failure, see Allen 1991.

15. In his reply, written on 14 December 1736, Lister shows himself to be a cautious and conventional correspondent. See §10.1.

16. The statement is from the society's "Articles of Subscription," which appear in the "Memoirs of the Society of the Encouragement of Learning," British Library Add. Ms. 6185. To support the subsidies, the members agreed to pay 10 gns. upon admission to the society, and then 2 gns. annually thereafter. Thomas Birch, for a time secretary of the Royal Society, was the treasurer. The society disbanded at Christmas 1747 because of lack of financial and personal support.

17. *L* 9 (27 Sept. 1738); *T* 242. In a letter of 22 September 1738 (British Library Add. Ms. 6190, f. 44), Hartley and Birch reported in favor of publication of Campbell's work (1739).

18. Five editions of an abridged version of Saunderson's *Elements of Algebra* were published in the eighteenth century, the last in 1792. Saunderson defines algebra as "the art of computing by symbols, that is, generally speaking, by letters of the alphabet" (49), and his *Algebra* covers topics that today are not customarily considered parts of algebra proper. Book 7 is devoted to "proportion" (i.e., the fifth book of Euclid). Book 8, pt. 1, is subtitled "The application of Algebra to plain Geometry"; pt. 2 bears the subtitle, "Of Prisms, Cylinders, Pyramids, Cones and Spheres." In book 8 Saunderson sets problems, first gives an algebraic method of the solution of each, and then follows with "a synthetical demonstration of this construction." He thus shows how problems in geometry can be solved either "analytically" or "synthetically."

19. Joy Hancox, in her highly imaginative biography of Byrom (1994), claims that in May 1737 Byrom "put the brake on Hartley's scheme" at the instruction of Mr. Gardiner, who she states was "a government agent, responsible for other political spies" (144; cf. B 1.2.555, 556; 2.1.153–54). According to Hancox, the government was using Byrom's shorthand as a code, and "Gardiner's intervention in 1737 to stop publication and Byrom's reaction to it are proof of Byrom's role as a double agent" (144–45). If true, Byrom's involvement in espionage would explain why Byrom seemed to resist a plan that Hartley thought would benefit both the public and the man, and also why he would have had to conceal his reasons for doing so in endless quibbling.

According to Hancox, Byrom was the lover of Queen Caroline, wife of George II, and the father of Caroline's son, William, Duke of Cumberland. Hancox further suggests that Byrom was involved in successful conspiracies to poison George I and, with James Jurin, to murder Sir Robert Walpole by means of an overdose of lithontriptic medication. (See Viseltear 1967 for a soberer account of Walpole's last days.) She also insinuates (170–71) that he had a career as a mass murderer, having been active in arranging the deaths, in 1742, of up to a dozen people.

20. Mary Hartley's letter to the Rev. William Gilpin is one of a series concerning her father and mother written in 1795 and 1796.

21. Jurin and Sloane were proponents of variola inoculation for smallpox. For Jurin, see Rusnock 1995. Hartley wrote to Sloane twice from Bury St. Edmunds—on 27 January 1733, when he sent Sloane a copy of his 1731 pamphlet, and on 9 February 1734, to "acquaint you with the success we had in Inoculation. there were only four Persons upon whom the Operation was performed, all had the distinct kind, but one was full. However, he went thro' the distemper very well & with the others is now in perfect Health." British Library, Sloane MS. 4052, f. 264.

22. In Warner 1817, 106. Charles "Turnip" Townshend, second viscount Townshend (1674–1738), was Secretary of State, 1714–1717 and 1720–1730. He married Dorothy Walpole, the sister of Sir Robert Walpole. Their daughter Elizabeth married Charles, fifth lord and first earl Cornwallis (1700–1762).

Their son Charles, first marquis and second earl Cornwallis (1738–1805), surrendered to Washington at Yorktown. It appears that Hartley successfully treated Lady Cornwallis; in a letter of 20 November 1736 to the Duke of Newcastle, Messenger Monsey, another Bury physician, writes: "if you ... can be reconciled to an ingenious young man enquire what Dr. Hartley did for Lady Cornwallis." British Library Addl. Mss. 33065, fol. 113. See also Webb 1989, 629–30. About the Townshend family, Mary Hartley adds: "The same friendly attachment continued to subsist between this family and ours since my father's death."

23. Rudé writes that the shortfall of births to deaths was greatest between 1727 and 1750, "when the waste of lives ... exceeded any that had been known since the great Plague.... The greatest mortality was among children of under five years of age, reaching a figure of three in four of all children that had been christened between 1730 and 1749" (1971, 5–6).

24. Cheselden reports, however, that while he used the older "high operation," he "lost no more than one in seven ...; whereas in the old way, even at Paris, from a fair calculation of more than 800 patients, it appears that more than two in seven died" (1730, 342).—There was some controversy over who deserved credit for developing the "high operation," for the anonymous *Lithotomus Castratu* (1723) charges that Cheselden's treatise on surgery for the stone is a plagiarism of *Lithotomia Douglassiana*. The *Cystitomia Hypogastrica* ([Anon.] 1724) contains a synopsis of three works, including those by John Douglas and William Cheselden. James Douglas's *The History of the Lateral Operation* (1726) critiques the new method, first employed in Europe by Jacques Baulot, known as Frère Jacques. For a further account of lithotomy, and of the sufferers' "aristocracy of endurance, the priesthood of experience," see Richard Selzer 1974.

25. Stephen Hales had already invented a double catheter by which water could be continuously passed into and drawn from the bladder; he had run 900 cubic inches of water through a dog's bladder in four and one half hours (Hales 1769, 2:207–9).

26. Sir George Clark writes that by the 1730s the Royal College of Physicians, which licensed physicians to practice in London, had "ceased to take legal proceedings against irregular practitioners of any kind, whether for practicing without a licence or for malpractice," and that except for two incidents, "it never took an intruder before a judge and jury between 1735 and 1858" (1966, 2:507). Concerning Hartley, Clark writes: "He had been practicing openly in Prince's Street, Leicester Fields, for a couple of years when he was summoned to the *comita minora* [of the College]. He was not well at the time and he was granted six months to take his doctor's degree ([minutes of] 3 June; 1 July; 5 August 1737). Although he never took it and never became a licenciate he seems to have maintained amicable relations with the College, to which he appealed publicly for adjudication of Mrs. Stephens's remedy" (513). It is likely that he never took a medical degree or became a licenciate because there was little

advantage to him in doing so. He already counted the Duke of Newcastle among his patients. He was also allied with Sir Hans Sloane, M.D., president of the Royal Society, and James Jurin, M.D., later president of the Royal College, concerning the issue of variola inoculation. Like Hartley, Jurin suffered from the stone and participated in the search for an effective lithontriptic (see Jurin 1742).

The College's requirement that Hartley take a degree within six months was not impracticable. Mark Akenside, author of *The Pleasures of Imagination,* after studying medicine for three years at Edinburgh, enrolled in the University of Leiden on 7 April 1744—and the next month returned to London with his M.D., after submitting a dissertation which the faculty accepted. Presumably for Hartley as well, a brief stay in Leiden and a Latin dissertation would have served the purpose. Hartley appears never to have traveled outside England; the stone made travel difficult. However, his *De Lithontriptico* was published in Basel and Leiden in 1741; Hartley may, in effect, have "submitted" his dissertation, even though he could not formally enroll in the university.

27. An itemization of the contributors appears in *The Gentleman's Magazine* 9 (January 1739). Among the 189 contributors are the Earl of Godolphin, for £100; Stephen Poyntz, for 50; Ralph Allen, for 21; Stephen Hales, for 1 gn.; and Peter Shaw, M.D., and David Hartley, M.A., for 5 gns. each. Francis, Earl of Godolphin, was the father of Lady Harriet Godolphin, "by Henrietta his wife, daughter of John the great Duke of Marlborough"; Harriet "married Thomas Pelham Holles, created Duke of Newcastle in 1715" (B 2.1.212, n. 3). The bill promising Stephens the reward was passed by Parliament, Stephens accepted the terms, and on 14 June 1739 the formula for the medicines was "put into writing" by Stephen Hales, Hartley, Byrom, and "Mr. Roberts," an apothecary (B 2.1.244). It was published in the *London Gazette* for 16 June and also in the *Gentleman's Magazine* 10 (June 1739): 298–99 (see Viseltear 1968, 202–3 for further details concerning the passage of the act and for a reproduction of the text of her disclosure).

28. *The Gentleman's Magazine* 10 (March 1740), 143, reports that on Monday, 17 March, "Mrs Stephens received the 5000 *l.* Reward for discovering her medicines." The April issue, pages 185–86, reprints from the *Daily Advertiser* of 28 March the report of the trustee's meeting of 5 March 1740. See also Viseltear 1968, 204–6.

29. The critic's abusive tone antagonized some readers. In the August 1738 issue, the "Author" of the *History of the Works of the Learned* introduced Hartley's letter and abstract (1738d) with a comment: "I am sorry that any of my Correspondents should in their Animadversions on others lay aside the Character of a Gentleman . . . especially when they are levelled at a Person, whose Behavior, on these very Occasions, is an Example of Candour and Politeness. I say this with a particular View of the two Letters, addressed to Dr. Hartley and me, published in the History in July; which, by the Complaints of

People wholly disinterested, I find, gave greater Offense to others, than to those against whom they were immediately directed: The Doctor's Behavior under the rough Treatment of his Adversary, as it appears in the following Epistle, bespeaks the Calmness of his Temper, and is a Proof of the Reputation he bears among the better Part of Mankind" (125).

30. Hartley would have learned of Hales's chemical theory and possibly of his experiments on bladder calculi while a fellow at Cambridge; in 1728 he attended the second course of chemical lectures given by John Mickleburgh, Professor of Chemistry from 1718–56 (see Gunther 1937, 469). Mickleburgh was Newtonian in outlook, and his lectures refer to Hales's work (Webb 1989, 621–22). Hales corresponded with Mickleburgh in 1729 concerning calcareous incrustations and in 1731 on incrustations from water (Allan and Schofield 1980, 179, 180).

31. Claude-Joseph Geoffroy (1685–1752) was the younger brother of Étienne-François Geoffroy (1672–1731), famous for his "Table des différents rapports observés en Chimie entre différentes substances" (1718), the first table of chemical affinity published in the eighteenth century. See Sturdy 1995, 331–42 (on Geoffroy) and 409–10 (on Morand); Duncan 1996, 110–19; and Viseltear 1968 for more on Hartley, Hales, Geoffroy, and Morand.

32. Those who thought the medicine effective did not have the field to themselves. Henry Bracken, M.D., a lithotomist with "above twenty years" of experience, wrote *Lithiasis Anglicana: or, A Philosophical Enquiry into the Nature and Origin of the Stone and Gravel, in Human Bodies.... In a Letter to David Hartley, M.D.* (1739). Bracken maintains a generally temperate tone; he does not attack Hartley, and he mentions his own conversations with Hales. Still, he does not accept their claims for the medicine, and he suggests that, for want of experience, they may have misinterpreted their clinical findings. Perhaps the most sustained and serious critique is that of James Parsons, M.D. (1742). Parsons argues that Stephens's recipe is not original, and that all the ingredients appear in earlier medicines for the stone or for cleansing the bladder (138–56). He also questions the design and significance of the experiments by Hartley, Hales, Geoffroy, and Morand (113–16; cf. Viseltear 1968, 216–17).

33. $K_2CO_3 + Ca(OH)_2 \rightarrow CaCO_3 + 2\ KOH$. Potassium hydroxide is a strong base which reacts with various acids and acid oxides, forming salts.

34. British Library Birch ms. 4437, fol. 54 contains a letter from Dr. Cantwell to Dr. Stack, Paris, 30 July 1740, detailing "The Method of Making Alicant Soap": "To make a Pan of Alicant Soap, they take 500 Arroves, that is 125 Quintals of Olive Oil, which they boil by Intervals from 34 to 40 days, and sometimes longer; adding thereto from time to time certain Lixivia which are made in the following manner. The first Lixivium, which is made and put into the Oil by intervals, and which is drawn out of the Boiler or Pan, after it has remain'd a certain time therein, till the Oil has extracted its substance, is composed of sixty Quintals or Barrels of Kali, and sixty of Bourde (a bad sort

of Kali) with four large Cart Loads & half of quick lime, ... The other Lixivium is composed of only forty Quintals of Bourde and one Cart Load & half of quick Lime: and when the Soap appears near being perfectly well boiled, for the last four or five days, they throw into it at different times five or six pounds of Coperas, and two or three pounds of Cinnabar." The resulting soap would probably consist largely of potassium oleate; however, because the recipe calls for kali (caustic potash), "bourde," and quicklime, it is possible that each may react preferentially with one or another of the oleate components in the triglyceride; the calcium may cause some components to precipitate out as scum, and the others would become the soap. Soaps made with potassium hydroxide are generally soft, in contrast to hard soaps made with sodium hydroxide. Castile soap, produced by heating sodium hydroxide and olive oil, is thus the hard equivalent of Alicant soap.

35. Hartley offered this account of the "Alterations the Urine receives from these [Stephens's] Medicines. These are a volatile putrid Smell; a turbid and milky Appearance at the time of making; a copious white Sediment, by the falling of which the Urine becomes clear, and which may be dried into a chalky Substance; and an alkaline Quality, as appears by Trials both with the mineral and vegetable Acids, and also with Syrup of Violets" (1738c, 446–47). He also reported: "Since I have taken Mrs. *Stephens's* Medicines, my Urine has been or a more urinous Smell than usual; turbid at the Time of making, and *alkaline,* that is, it turns Syrup of Violet green, and ferments with the following acid Liquors, Oil of Vitriol, Spirit of Vitriol, Oil of Sulphur, Spirit of Nitre, Spirit of Sea-Salt, Vinegar, and Lemon Juice. And as far as I can judge, the case is the same with all who take these Medicines" (1738d, 127).

36. When Rutty attempted to replicate Hales's and Hartley's results, he found that soap-lye did not work well on hard stones: "Hence we may cease to wonder, that Dr. *Hartley* has taken these Medicines for three Years and a half; and although he has voided Scales and Fragments of Stone during the whole Time, yet has most of his Symptoms remaining, tho' in a less degree" (5). Although Rutty determined that "soap-Lees then thus diluted ... is but a very slow or imperfect Solvent, especially of the harder Stones," he nonetheless wrote that "these Experiments, however, do not conclude against the Efficacy of the Medicine; because, besides the Soap-Lees, the Co-operation of the Powders must also be taken into Account; which in the Section of Lime will appear to be very considerable: And, indeed, if we take for granted the Truth of the Observations of *Morand, Geoffroy,* and Dr. *Hartley,* that the Urine of those who take the Medicines ... did ... corrode and lessen the Weight of several Stones infused in it ... I do not see how can resist the Force of the Evidence of their lithontriptick Efficacy" (7).

37. Uroliths commonly are composed of calcium oxalate, calcium phosphate ($CaPO_4$), or magnesium ammonium phosphate (struvite). Alicant soap is largely potassium oleate, and the slaked lime is calcium hydroxide. If ingesting

these together did increase the alkalinity of the urine, as Hartley suggested and as alkaline salts will do, it is possible that the medication had some therapeutic effect relative to those stones, such as those of calcium oxalate or uric acid, that form in acid urine. However, calculi formed in alkaline urine, such as those composed of calcium phosphate, calcium carbonate, or struvite, require the opposite treatment: the pH should be kept below 7. The medicine may have helped some—and harmed others.

38. Hartley gives the following instructions: "Take five pound of alicant soap, shaved, and one pound of oyster-shell lime; put them in a tin vessel, and pour upon them five parts of water: make the water boil till the soap be perfectly dissolv'd in it, and then strain all into a glaz'd earthen vessel; expose this mass to the air, stirring it every day, till it becomes both mild to the taste, and of a proper consistence to be formed into pills or long pellets. This may be expected to happen in two or three months..." (1752, 465). Heating a fluid containing the soap, which is largely potassium oleate, and the lime, which is calcium oxide, would produce calcium oleate (or stearate)—soap scum—and potassium hydroxide, which in turn would slake upon continued exposure to the air.

39. S.P.C.K., A.L.B. CR1/21, 15703; cf. Allan and Schofield 1980, 155, n. 2, 183. Hartley retained his membership in the S.P.C.K. up till his death. In the last years of his life, Hartley corresponded with Hales and supported Hales's efforts, possibly in an informal connection with the Society for the Propagation of the Gospel (S.P.G.), to distribute religious literature in Jamaica and New Jersey. See the letters from Hales to Hartley in the Hartley Family papers, F79/10 (9 December 1755), F79/11 (24 February 1756), F79/29 (28 September 1757). The letter of 28 September 1757 was written after Hartley's death on 28 August. In it Hales thanks Hartley for his support: "Dr Wilson & I shall be obliged to you for promoting the sending a good number of Dr Leland's *Defense* [?] to America." John Leland was the author of *Divine Authority of the Old and New Testaments Asserted* (1739) and *A Defense of Christianity* (1753).

40. Alice Rowley was the daughter of John Rowley (d. 1758), an attorney and alderman in Saffron Walden, and his wife Alice Arnold (d. 1726). She was baptized on 26 September 1705. Information is from the parish records of Saffron Walden church, Bury St. Edmund's St. Mary's, and Philip Morant, *History and Antiquities of the County of Essex* (1763–68), 2:605.

41. *L* 31; 16 March 1743. Here is the complete text of the epitaph: Dilecti cinneres, vobis dum vita manebat / Haud levis esse olim nostra querala solet: / Tum nitidos lacryma increscens violaret ocellos, / Et cor foeminens molle gravaret amor. / Sospite Te, dulcis Conjux, geminata voluptas; / Sospite Te curae nil valuere graves. / Nunc frustra in somniis iteratâ voce vocaris, / Dum nota amplexus fallit imago meos. / Illa mihi tandem superest [ ] attolor, & amens / Promissam posco somnia vana fidem. / Heu vidi hisce oculis tristi te cedere fato,

/ Audivi gemitus quos moritura dabas. / Et jam tetra jacet monstris informibus esca; / Scilicet hanc legem fert tibi Terra parens / Ecce sequor—varium modo vitae institere cursum / Des atro immunem crimine, summe Pater. / Tum chari accipiant Manes, fessumque [?] reponant / Qua viget aeternum non temeratus Amor.

In English translation: Beloved Ashes, for you, while life remained, / Our complaint was never taken lightly: / Time was, when a gathering tear would sully your shining eyes, / And your wifely love would weigh upon your soft heart. / While you were alive, sweet wife, pleasure matched pleasure; / While you were alive, heavy cares were nothing. / But now in sleep, in vain, you are called again and again, / While your familiar image escapes my embraces. / That image is all I have left. I am carried away, and, crazed, / I demand from vain dreams your promised fidelity. / But alas! with these eyes I saw you yield to your sad fate, / And I heard the sighs you were giving when you were about to die. / And now you lie, black food for formless monsters; / For this is the law mother earth imposes on you. / See, I follow—Supreme Father, grant that I may begin / Another course in life, free from dark crime. / Then may the dear souls of the dead receive me, wearied, / And rest me where Love without fear lives eternally.

I would like to thank John S. Dunne of the University of Notre Dame and David Leach of St. Andrews University for help with this translation.

42. British Library Addl. Ms. 33083, fol. 276.

43. Hartley Family papers, Bucklebury, Berks., F53. This is the only letter by Elizabeth Hartley I have discovered. Because her second child, Winchcombe Henry, was born in May 1740, the letter must have been written after that date, but before August 1757, when David Hartley died.

44. According to A. L. Humphreys (1932, 324), Henry John Packer, in his will, left "all his estates in trust to Penistone Powney, Esquire, and William Le Marchant, his executors, until his nephew, Winchcombe Henry Heartley (sic) ... shall be twenty-one." The will also states that Mary Hartley was to receive £1,000 upon reaching the age of 21—a trifling amount, considering the family's wealth. The will also states that "if his said sister has no child of age before his or her death," the estates would pass to "John Willis of Ipswich, son of my kinsman, John Willis of that place." If Elizabeth's two children were to die in childhood, she (and her husband) would inherit nothing.

45. In a letter of 1 February 1810 to John Adams, second president of the United States, Benjamin Rush writes: "Next to my Bible I find the most satisfaction in reading the works of Dr. Hartley upon both doctrinal and practical subjects. His morality is truly evangelical. His posthumous letters to his sister show him to have been a saint of the first order" (Rush 1951, 1035). The Unitarian periodical the *Monthly Repository of General and Theological Literature* for February 1810 contains two early letters (from 1721 and 1735) from Hartley to his sister Elizabeth (see R. K. Webb 1998, n. 9). The person who

submitted them to the journal—"S.S.Y."—notes that they were previously published in a "little known" work, *A Supplement to the Anecdotes of some distinguished Persons,* compiled by "Dr. Percival of Manchester" and published in 1797. These were later reprinted in Rebecca Warner 1817. If these are the letters to which Rush is referring, either he must have had advance knowledge of the publication in the *Monthly Repository* or he must have known of Percival's volume.

46. *L* 11; 23 November 1738; cf. *T* 244–45. The letter continues: "The 2 pieces I send you are rough drafts of the 3rd and 4th parts, and I have just made a foul over, as it were, of the 1st and 2nd. The first will contain an enumeration of the Phenomena of the Body and its several parts as they are affected by the external objects of Touch, Taste, Smell, Hot, Cold, Diet, Medicines, &c. &c. as they affect and are affected by one another—suppose, for instance, that a stone in the kidneys causes vomiting—and lastly as they affect and are affected by the mind. The 2nd will contain the original of the several senses of Beauty, Honour, Benevolence, &c., with their several parts and the manner in which they rise, with the time of their rise in infancy, &c. as particularly as I can. There are some sketches of this in the largest of the parts which you will receive, for I there assert and explain a little how all our mental Pleasures and Pains are derived from sensible ones, either immediately, or mediately by association."

47. Hartley's *Prayers and Religious Meditations* contains a prayer, dated 2 September 1739, "For a Blessing on the Composition, Publication, and Success of his 'Observations on Man,' " in which Hartley writes: "I . . . humbly implore thy blessing upon my studies, and particularly upon the design which I have now undertaken" (1810, 51). Although Hartley apparently sent his manuscripts to Lister and other friends for their comments, the public would have first read of his psychological theories in *Conjecturae quædam de Sensu, Motu, & Idearum Generatione,* a Latin précis of the *Observations* that appeared as an appendix to the second edition of *De Lithontriptico* (1746). I do not know why Hartley published a Latin version when the much longer English book appears to have been nearly complete. One possible explanation is that a Latin edition would have enabled Hartley to communicate with an audience of educated readers throughout Europe.

Chapter 3. The Theory of Vibrations

1. Quoted in Rousseau 1991b, 110, note 16.
2. In the "General Scholium" at the end of his *Principia,* Newton writes of "a certain most subtle spirit which pervades and lies hid in all gross bodies" (Newton, 1729: Book 3, General Scholium). This spirit, or aether, appears to be a key agent in a variety of seemingly unrelated phenomena: gravitation, cohesion, electricity, various phenomena of light (including the relation of light

and heat), animal sensation and movement. Newton's comment is tantalizing both in its brevity and in its introduction of a range of topics the *Principia* does not address.

3. There is an extensive literature on the social, political, and theological complexities of the eighteenth-century scientific world. See, for example, Jacob 1976, Rousseau and Porter 1980, Schaffer 1980, Shapin 1980, Stewart 1986, and Suzuki 1995.

4. Hartley was not the first to attempt to work out the physiological implications of Newton's hypothesis. George Cheyne had done so in his *Essay on Health* (1724) and *The English Malady* (1733; see note 22 below). In *The English Malady* Cheyne proposed that all parts of the body, including the muscles, nerves, and bones, are made up of solid fibers—"*small, transparent, solid,* and *elastick,* or springy Threads or Filaments" (1733, 60). As Hartley would fifteen years later, Cheyne thus argued against animal spirits and in favor of the aether. In addition, Bryan Robinson, M.D., in *A Treatise of the Animal Oeconomy* ([1732] 1734), also turned to the 24th Query of the *Optics,* where Newton suggested "that the Nerves are solid Capillaments, pellucid when singular—subject to the vibrating Motion of the Aetherial Medium." Robinson proposed: "Muscular motion is performed by the vibrations of a very Elastic Aether, lodged in the Nerves and Membranes investing the minute Fibres of the Muscles, excited by Heat, the Power of the Will, Wounds, the subtile and active Particles of Bodies, and other causes" (87–88). The thesis is developed further in his *Dissertation on the Aether of Sir Isaac Newton* (1743). Robinson's *Animal Oeconomy* appears in the catalogue of Hartley's library. For discussion of Robinson, see Schofield 1970, 108–14, Thackray 1970, 135–41.

5. Newton writes: "Now the smallest Particles of Matter may cohere by the strongest Attractions, and compose bigger Particles of weaker Virtue; and many of these may cohere and compose bigger Particles whose Virtue is still weaker, and so on for divers Successions, until the Progression end in the biggest Particles on which the Operations in Chymistry, and the Colours of natural Bodies depend, and which by cohering compose Bodies of a sensible magnitude" (1730, 370). For further discussion, see Thackray 1970, 53–73 (especially concerning the role of the theory in the debate with Leibniz); and Westfall 1971, 382–86.

6. Quoted in Wylie 1989, 43–44, who also cites Voltaire's *Letters Concerning the English Nation* (trans. J. Lockman, 1733, 147): "examining the vast Porosity of Bodies, . . . [Newton] shows we are not certain that there is a cubic inch of solid Matter in the Universe, so far we are from conceiving what Matter is." Modern physicists' estimates are that, were the earth to be crushed to the density of a neutron star, the resulting lump would be about as large as an apple.

7. Newton's notion that a single force could be alternately attractive and repulsive, depending upon the distance at which it operates, was also made the

basis of a theory of particle interactions by Roger Joseph Boscovitch, S.J. (1711–87), in his *Theoria philosophiae naturalis* (1763). Robert E. Schofield (1970, 236–41) emphasizes that Boscovitch's theory of oscillating particles has much in common with those of other dynamic corpuscularians such as the Keills, Freind, Hales, Maclaurin, and particularly John Rowning and J. T. Desaguliers. For Boscovitch's influence on Joseph Priestley, see Schofield 1961 and Yolton 1983, 109–11; see also McMullin 1978, 116–20; Hesse 1961, 163–66.

8. Westfall writes: "In contrast to Descartes' plenum, Newton's universe was a vast expanse of empty space seasoned with the subtlest suggestion of solid matter.... The immensity of space was now populated solely by limited sections of the slenderest threads. Those threads in turn were composed, not of woven fibres, but of point-like particles . . . laid out in rows and held together . . . by forces of attraction" (1971, 385).

9. *Leibniz-Clarke Correspondence* (1717), quoted in Hesse 1961, 162. Leibniz developed an account of the mechanics of impact, and hence of force, that diverged fundamentally from Descartes's model. Still, Leibniz maintained to Clarke that changes in motion must be attributed to contact: "A body is never moved naturally, except by another body which touches and pushes it; after that it continues until it is prevented by another body which touches it. Any other kind of operation on bodies is miraculous or imaginary" (quoted in Hesse 1961, 160). See also Westfall 1971, 283–322.

10. Whiston's comment occurs in a passage in which he excuses Newton's refusal to support his nomination in 1720 for membership in the Royal Society, of which Newton was president. For Whiston's relationship with Newton, see Manuel 1963, 170–77.

11. McMullin writes: "It is fascinating to follow Newton's thought over the next forty years [following the *Principia*], as he wrestled with the difficulties involved in each of these alternatives.... In point of fact, none of these explanatory models is ever repudiated by him; all continue to play a part in his shaping of the ontological alternative" (1978, 79).

12. Hales suggests that the "double capacity" of matter to change its polarity from attractive to repulsive is inexplicable apart from reference to the action of God: "this wonderful property of [matter] . . . must needs be owing to the direction of an all-wise Being" (1769, 2:278).

13. In his *Astronomiæ Physicæ & Geometricæ Elementa* (1702), David Gregory mentions Pythagoras's discovery and cites Macrobius's commentary on Cicero's *Somnium Scipionis*.

14. Mark the point on a bicycle wheel where the wheel makes contact with the ground; then move the wheel forward one complete revolution. The arc described by the marked point is a cycloidal curve. The formula for the period of a cycloidal pendulum is $T = 2\pi \sqrt{l/g}$—where l is the length of the pendulum, itself equal to twice the diameter of the generating circle, and g is the force of

gravity (cf. Westfall 1971, 165). Westfall points out that the principle of isochronous oscillation in a cycloid also enabled Huygens to establish a value for the force of gravity. Garry Wills (1979, 106–9) discusses Thomas Jefferson's interest in using an isochronous pendulum to establish a standard measure of length. Just as T will be the same for all pendulums where l and g are constant, so also will l be the same for all pendulums where T and g are constant.

15. Hooke writes: "Now the comparative Velocities of any body moved are in subduplicate proportion to the aggregates or sums of the powers by which it is moved, therefore the Velocities of the whole spaces returned are always in the same proportion with those spaces, they being both subduplicate to the powers and consequently all the times shall be equal" (1678b, 18). Westfall adds: "What [Hooke] had done was to apply Galileo's result—$v^2 \propto s$—derived for uniformly accelerated motion, to non-uniformly accelerated motion; and ignoring the complexities, he had drawn conclusions which were correct for reasons he did not understand" (1971, 212).

16. See also Gouk 1988, 116. Hooke expands upon the musical analogy in the 1678 lecture: "Suppose a number of musical strings, as A B C D E, *&c.* tuned to certain tones, and a like number of other strings, as *a,b,c,d,e*, &c. tuned to the same sounds respectively. A shall be receptive of the motion of *a*, but not of that of *b, c*, nor *d*; in like manner B shall be receptive of the motion of *b*, ... And so of the rest. ¶ Now as we find that musical strings will be moved by Unisons and Eighths, and other harmonious chords, though not in the same degree; so do I suppose that *the particles of matter* will be moved principally by such motions as are Unisons, as I may call them, ... and by other harmonious motions in less degree" (1678, 8–9).

17. The ratio is in fact somewhat less than 1 to 2. The wavelength of the extreme red is about 6,500 Å, of the extreme violet about 4,100 Å.

18. According to King, "his mature views, elaborated and clarified by commentators, came to dominate medical thought during the first half of the [eighteenth] century" (1978, 121); similarly, Cohen notes that "it would be extremely difficult to find any important scientist of the early and mid-eighteenth century who was not affected by his teaching, and more difficult still to find any scientific teacher more widely known or more influential than he was" (1956, 214). For a thorough discussion of Boerhaave's life and work, see Lindeboom 1968.

19. See also Boerhaave's definition of chemistry in his "Discourse of Chemistry Purging itself of its own Errors" (1983, 199–200), the inaugural oration he delivered when appointed Professor of Chemistry at Leiden in 1718.

20. This model also received influential support from Friedrich Hoffmann (1660–1742), the first professor of medicine at the University of Halle. In this model, it is the circulation of fluids, and particularly of blood and lymph, that constitutes the life of the organism (King 1978, 34–35).

21. Stahl was Professor of Medicine at the University of Halle. The "rational agent" to which Hartley refers Stahl termed the *anima*. See King 1964; for Stahl's chemical theory, see Duncan 1996, 52–56.

22. Readers familiar with George Cheyne's *Essay on Health* (1724) and *The English Malady* (1733) would have already encountered arguments in favor of the solidity of nerves (see note 4 above) and of the brain as the seat of the soul. Like the mechanists, Cheyne claims in the earlier work that "the *Soul* resides eminently in the *Brain,* where all the *Nervous* Fibres terminate inwardly" (1724, 144). Like the Stahlians, however, he also draws a sharp distinction between passive matter and active spirit: "As *Bodies* are purely *passive,* and are acted upon by other *Bodies,*... in *Spiritual* Beings... there is an *active, self-motive, self-determining Principle*" (1724, 147–48).

23. Hartley does not speculate how many orders of particles there are. His reference to "the molecules, the molecules of the molecules, etc." suggests that he envisions a series of aggregations. In addition, Hartley does not recognize that nerves have a cellular structure. Although single-celled organisms, sperm, "globules" in blood, and the cells in muscle fibers were observed under the microscope by Leeuwenhoeck and Hooke in the 1670s (cf. Hooke 1678a: "if you view the thred of a Ligament, you shall plainly see it to be made up of an infinite company of exceeding small threads smooth and round"), the biological function of cells was not understood. Similarly, in the imaginations of eighteenth-century scientists such as Hartley and Boerhaave, chemical reactions are modeled as microcosmic physical interactions. Given the absence of properly biological or chemical models, the description of biological or chemical processes presents, for Boerhaave and Hartley, a problem of physics, particularly in the physics of the very small.

24. According to Cheselden, each nerve fiber links one part of the body and one location in the brain: "The nerves seem, when examined with a microscope, to be bundles of strait fibres not communicating with one another: And I am inclined to think that every the minutest nerve, terminating in any part, is a distinct cord from its origin in the brain, or spinal marrow; or else I do not see how they would produce distinct sensations in every part" (1730, 235–36).

Chapter 4. Perception and Action

1. To us, examining the connections between Locke and Hartley seems inevitable; Locke is the first in the troika, Locke-Berkeley-Hume—a compound that every apprentice philosopher associates with *British empiricism*. How could one discuss Hartley without referring to Locke? In Hartley's case, the requirement is strengthened by the fact that he credits Locke for bringing the term *association* into use (*OM* 1.1.2.10). Indeed, it is often said of Hartley that he was attempting to wed Lockean psychology and Newtonian physics.

A note of caution is in order. The use of *empiricism* to describe "philosophy" in Britain in the eighteenth century is purely retrospective. In the medical circles of Hartley's day, *empiric* was a term of abuse. Joanna Stephens was an empiric—she had stumbled upon a medical treatment without having the slightest idea of how it worked. Hartley and Locke would have been offended had a critic called them *empirical*. More importantly, it is not clear that in the eyes of Hartley and his contemporaries Locke had the enormous stature that we accord him today. Akihito Suzuki makes the case that "there were very few, if any, medical writings in the earlier half of the century which explicitly embraced Locke's psychology" (1995, 337)—and, more strongly, that "medical psychology in England in the early eighteenth century was overtly *anti*-Lockean" (338). Viewed within the context of Suzuki's interpretation, Hartley's partial and qualified recommendation of Locke—whom he credits for providing a name for a phenomenon that "is so great and obvious, as scarcely to have escaped the notice of any writer," ancient or modern, "who has treated of these"(*OM* 1.1.2.10)—is hardly the obligatory nod toward the person acclaimed by all as the foremost British philosopher. It appears instead to be a challenge to then-ascendant psychological paradigms. To contemporary readers, Hartley's association with Locke may have suggested that he too held to the pernicious error that matter could think (see Suzuki 1995, 339–40). For more concerning the perception that Locke was "one of the most dangerous writers of the day," see Fox 1988, 8–9. For more on *empiricism* see Livingston 1998, 1–7.

2. Although Coleridge was a disciple of Hartley in the 1790s, he later became indebted to developments in German philosophy, particularly the idealism of Fichte and Schelling, which he saw as an alternative both to Hartleian "materialism" and to Cartesian dualism. His critique of Hartley in the *Biographia Literaria* shows his debt to German scholarship. As Engell and Bate point out in their edition of the *Biographia,* Coleridge, while writing the chapters on Hartley and associationism, drew heavily upon J. G. E. Maass's *Versuch über die Einbildungskraft* (1797).

3. Coleridge writes: "It is fashionable to smile at Hartley's vibrations and vibratiuncles; and his work has been re-edited by Priestley, with the omission of the *material* hypothesis. But Hartley was too great a man, too coherent a thinker, for this to have been done, either consistently or to any wise purpose. For all other parts of his system, . . . once removed from their mechanical basis, not only lose their main support, but the very motive which led to their adoption. Thus the principle of *contemporaneity,* which Aristotle had made the common *condition* of all the laws of association, Hartley was constrained to represent as being itself the sole *law*. For to what law can the action of *material* atoms be subject, but that of proximity in *place*? And to what law can their motions be subjected, but that of *time*?" (C 7:110). We should note here that Coleridge's objection is not limited specifically to Hartley's theory of vibrations; rather, his objection is to any theory that seeks to ground consciousness in neurophysiology.

4. The claim that, to Hartley, the mind is passive and ideas are atomistic appears with relative frequency in the secondary literature. For example, John Hayden writes: "Hartley negated reflection, found the mind *totally* passive, and made the association of ideas the *only* explanation of complex mental phenomena. The method of association, moreover, was limited by Hartley to contiguity in time, but his theory set out to explain *all* human experience" (1984, 96; see Hoeldtke 1967; Shelley 1983; Wells 1982, 270; Valentine 1989, 348; and also Coleridge in the preceding note). William James also states that "Hartley and James Mill improved upon Hume so far as to employ but a single principle of association, that of contiguity or habit. Hartley ignores resemblance" (1890, 2:600).

5. R. L. Gregory (1974) reports on the case of S.B., who gained his sight after receiving a corneal transplant at the age of fifty-two. Gregory states that the case is consistent with that of Cheselden's young patient, and that it tends to confirm the arguments advanced by Molyneux, Locke, and Berkeley. Gregory writes: "The principal theoretical interest of the case is that it gives strong evidence of cross-modal transfer, from touch to vision.... The ability to relate information across the senses is vital if objects are to attain symbolic meaning" (65). Further discussion of S.B. and of the Cheselden case appears in Oliver Sacks's study (1995, 108–52) concerning Virgil, another person who received his sight in adulthood. Virgil also experienced profound visual agnosia.

Susanna Millar (1994) proposes a model of "convergent active processing of interrelated networks" (CAPIN) to account for spatial coding—that is, the ability to relate sensory inputs to cues and frames of reference. Millar states that "the neurophysiological as well as the behavioural evidence suggests that spatial coding involves processing convergent inputs from different modalities" (83); however, "no sensory modality is necessary or sufficient, by itself, for spatial coding" (257). The abilities of children blind from birth to perform actions requiring an understanding of space support the notion that "there is more than one basis for recognizing information across modalities" (34).

6. Another discussion of the Molyneux problem and Cheselden's report appears in Robert Smith's massive *A Compleat System of Opticks* (1738, bk. 1, ch. 5, arts. 132-37, and the "Remarks" upon art. 132). Smith (1689–1768) was Plumian Professor of Astronomy from 1716–60, Master of Trinity College, Cambridge, and Master of Mechanics to the King. He collaborated in his optical researches with Hartley's colleague and fellow sufferer from the stone, James Jurin, whose *Essay upon Distinct and Indistinct Vision* is appended to Smith's *Opticks*. Although Smith appears not to have appreciated the full force of Cheselden's report, he does affirm the general point that it is to the correlation of different senses through association that we owe our capacities to perceive a coherent and ordered world (bk. 1, ch, 5, art. 132, §177). Hartley was one the subscribers who supported publication of Smith's *Opticks,* and in the section of the *Observations* in which he discusses our judgments concerning

the size and distance of objects, he refers "those who are disposed to examine the subjects . . . with accuracy" to the work of Smith and Jurin. He adds: "These gentlemen insist chiefly on optical considerations; but they every where admit the prevalence of association, though it is not always to their purpose to take express notice of it" (*OM* 1.2.4.58).

7. A similar point is made by Robert Greene in his *Essay on the Expansive and Contractive Forces* (1727): "Our Ideas Enter into the Mind, Complex and United, according to the Variety, with which our Senses are Capable of being Affected, or according to the Variety, with which one Sense is so" (609). Greene's *Essay* is a relentless, point-by-point refutation of Locke's. Although Greene, a fellow of Clare Hall, Cambridge, published his work at the university press in 1727—the year Hartley became a fellow of Jesus College—it does not seem likely that Hartley was influenced by him. Greene does not appear in the *Observations* or in the catalogue of Hartley's library. Greene's claim that Newton's discoveries only confirmed what he already knew would hardly endear him to fellows of the Royal Society. See Schofield 1970, 116–21.

8. James writes: "The baby, assailed by eyes, ears, nose, skin, and entrails at once, feels it all as one great blooming, buzzing confusion; and to the very end of life, our location of all things in one space is due to the fact that the original extents or bignesses of all the sensations which came to our notice at once, coalesced together into one and the same space" (1890, 1:488). Another testimony to the importance of joint impression.

9. It should be clear that Hartley was aware of the problem of focused attention. Coleridge raises as an objection to Hartley's theory an issue the theory seeks to address. Keep in mind that Coleridge opposes any and all physiological explanations of consciousness; to him, no explanation based on "the *material* hypothesis" can ever explain how people *choose* to direct their attention.

10. Coleridge, closely following Maass, objects to the idea that a could ever be associated with b in a way that would enable a to reproduce b—in his example, designated as m: "But the original impression from M was essentially different from the impression A: unless therefore different causes may produce the same effect, the vibration a could never produce the vibration m: and this therefore could never be the means, by which a and m are associated. . . . It is a mere delusion of the fancy to conceive the pre-existence of the ideas, in any chain of associations, as so many differently colored billiard-balls in contact, so that when an object, the billiard-stick, strikes the first or white ball, the same motion propagates itself through the red, green, blue, black, &c. and sets the whole in motion. No! we must suppose the very same force, which *constitutes* the white ball, to *constitute* the red or black . . . which is impossible" (C 7:108). It is indeed a "delusion of the fancy" to think that preexisting ideas are so many billiard balls—but the delusion is not Hartley's. His claim is that A and B, when experienced jointly, produce a and b as each is modified by the other, and also

the complex waveform *(a + b)*. The objection of Coleridge and Maass is based on the assumptions that each vibration correlates with one distinct idea, and that all ideas are separate entities. What is closer to the mark is the point that Coleridge declares "impossible": that the "same force" that "constitutes" the red ball also constitutes the black.

11. For all his criticism of the tradition of Locke and Hartley, James's own account of perception is close to Locke's. The "objects" we perceive "are nothing but clusters of qualities"; but the "simple ideas" out of which "complex ideas" are formed are, according to Locke, precisely qualities such as *wet* and *white*. Moreover, James's "simultaneous stimulation" is Hartley's "joint impression" by another name, and overall his account of the way in which "clusters of qualities" coalesce, and of the brain as "essentially a place of currents," is a restatement of Hartley's themes.

12. For an illuminating discussion of Hartley's statement that "we call the touch the reality, light the representative," see Douglas Lane Patey 1986, 143–44.

13. The example fails if the picture is two-dimensional: when rotated in three dimensions, a flat object will disappear when perpendicular to the viewer. But one could use a three-dimensional paper model. A person born blind in body would, according to the argument, be unable to predict whether the "knife" would cut the cheese.

14. Hartley also suggests that a person "destitute of feeling, and of the power of moving himself" could learn to anticipate the motions of objects provided that variations in sight impressions could be consistently correlated with verbal cues (*OM* 1.2.4.58). This seems inconsistent with his view that touch is "our first and principal key to the knowledge of the external world" (*OM* 1.2.1.30). Proposition 58 suggests that joint impression through any two sensory modalities is sufficient for perceptual categorization, while proposition 30 suggests that touch is fundamental.

15. Experimental confirmation of the differentiation of sensory and motor nerves awaited the work of Sir Charles Bell (1774–1842) and François Magendie (1783–1855). Robinson writes that the Bell-Magendie law "provided the structural foundation upon which reflex mechanisms had to be based. The contribution thus extended a line of inquiry initiated by Descartes, receiving important corroboration from the work of Stephen Hales and Robert Whytt, and theoretically rich amplification by David Hartley" (1995, 274).

16. Hartley conjectures that contraction is caused by "electrical" attraction (*OM* 1.1.3.16). Hartley's source may be Stephen Hales, who suggested in his *Hæmastatics* (1733) that electricity is responsible for muscular motion (see Allan and Schofield 1980, 54). Electricity was poorly understood in Hartley's day; the term generally refers to a force of attraction, of whatever kind. Although electrostatic generators had been available since the mid-seventeenth century, Leyden jars, which store electrical charges, were designed only in 1745.

Benjamin Franklin's *Experiments and Observations on Electricity* appeared in 1751, two years after Hartley's *Observations*.

17. In his comments on the reflex actions of the eye, Hartley refers the reader to the "ingenious theory" presented by James Jurin in his *Essay upon Distinct and Indistinct Vision* (see note 6 above). One of Jurin's concerns in his essay is to account for the eye's ability to focus upon objects at varying distances, and his work contains an extensive and detailed discussion of the manner in which the muscles of the eye modulate the shape of the cornea to achieve this purpose.

18. In the *Gentleman's Magazine,* "The Birks of Endermay" is given as the title of the tune—as it is in William Thompson's *Orpheus Caledonius* (1733). Arrangements of traditional tunes, often for three voices with an instrumental accompaniment, appear regularly in the monthly issues of the *Gentleman's Magazine;* Hartley, who played the violin, might have accompanied family and friends during one of their musical evenings, as they sang "The Birks of Endermay."

Chapter 5. Mindful Bodies, Embodied Minds

1. The standard account has its advocates today. Butler emphasized the compatibility of science and religion, the dualism of mind and body, the unity of consciousness, and the freedom of the will. The same themes are central to the thinking of Sir Karl Popper, Sir John Eccles, and Daniel N. Robinson. See Popper and Eccles 1977; Eccles 1979, 1980, and 1991; and Eccles and Robinson 1984.

2. John W. Yolton's *Thinking Matter* (1983) explores in great depth the responses to Locke's proposal that God could endow matter with the capacity of thought. See also Suzuki 1995, 339–40.

3. Those who take the passage at face value (e.g., Smith 1987) interpret Hartley as affirming a substance dualism in which "immaterial substance" is required for "the simplest sensation." I offer a different interpretation; see §5.7, 11.1, 11.2, and 11.3. See also Yolton 1983, 195–97.

4. As we noted at §4.2, Yolton cautions against taking these metaphors too literally. He writes that Arnauld and Locke both "insist that 'to be in the mind' just means 'to be understood' " (1984, 14, cf. 89). In a reading of Locke that avoids taking *white paper* and *presence-room* and *judgment* literally, as names of entities, to use such terms is simply to say, "a person forms ideas, which she understands." Moreover, if we should not take these terms and the phrase *in the mind* literally when reading Locke, then instead of saying that Hartley *extended* Locke's account of the "faculties" of judgment and will to the mind itself, it may be more accurate to say that Hartley *clarifies* an understanding of "mind" that is implicit in Locke's *Essay.*

5. Hartley's contemporaries would have been familiar with the distinction between popular and philosophical modes of speech, for the distinction was central to Isaac Newton's interpretation of the Bible: although Moses was in fact talking precisely about gravitation and the heliocentric system, he "accommodated his words to ye gross conceptions of ye vulgar" (quoted in Manuel 1963, 140). In this regard, Newton saw himself as restating in a properly philosophical mode of speech ancient truths known to Moses and both expressed and concealed by him.

6. According to Hartley, however, personal immortality was "taught all mankind by patriarchal revelations before and after the flood" (*OM* 2.4.3.86), and it is not clear that a future state is discoverable simply by the "light of nature." But then, the light of nature is not a constant; what people are able to discover and know is dependent upon what they have already discovered.

7. I do not know of a source from whence Hartley could have derived the concept of the elementary body in the form it is presented in the *Observations*. But see Robert Boyle (1744, 3:539), who attempts to work out how personal identity could maintain a material continuity from life through death to resurrection. See also Peter Sterry (1683, 436–41), who affirms that both the body and the soul of a "saint" survive death. Sterry states that "there is again in a Saint a holy, living, immortal Body, the seat of a holy, heavenly, and immortal Life, in as much as it is the Temple of the Holy Ghost" (1683, 436). This immortal body is not the body one normally perceives; it is rather a body that, like Adam's, is made out of the dust of the earth of Eden: "The Jewish Doctors teach us, that the dust, of which the Body of Man was made, was a fine and precious powder, in which all the excellencies of the whole Creation were exactly tempered, and mingled together in one Body. . . . The dust then of this ground, which composeth the Body of Man, was the manifold beauty, sweetness, virtue and life of Paradise, of the whole Paradisical state of things gathered together, contracting themselves into one, and shading themselves, like the beauties, sweetnesses, and virtues of a flower in its precious seed" (439). The body made of this, "the first Dust, the Dust before the Fall" (441), is present within a person's outward body, made of ordinary dust; at death the two bodies are separated, with the outward body returning to the ground and the immortal body to the "ground" of the "universal Darkness before the Light of the first day" (440).

8. For Hartley's further thoughts on the elementary body, see his letter of 25 Nov. 1751 to Edmund Law in Richard Warner 1830, 2:429. Of the elementary body, Priestley writes: "I see no reason why his scheme should be burdened with such an incumbrance as this" (Hartley 1775, xix). His own position was, he thought, more straightforward: assuming that "the whole man is of some *uniform composition*," it follows "that the whole man becomes extinct at death, and that we have no hope of surviving the grave but what is derived from the

scheme of revelation" (Hartley 1775, xx). Not everyone thought the hypothesis an encumbrance. Benjamin Rush discusses it, as one of four alternative ways of relating body and mind, in his "Lectures Upon the Mind" (Rush 1981, 413–16). Rush quotes a passage from William Paley's *Natural Theology* (1802) in which Paley also describes the concept. Although neither Rush nor Paley commit to it, both treat the elementary body as a live hypothesis.

Chapter 6. Languages

1. What Hartley says holds true of those deaf people who have remained without language. See Sacks 1989 for discussion of people who, after years of such languagelessness, experienced the explosive development of language, once they were introduced to a system of Sign.

2. Although a vegetarian, Hartley concludes that "abstinence from flesh meats seems left to each person's choice, and not necessary" (*OM* 2.3.2.52). But he adds that "taking away the lives of animals ... does great violence to the principles of benevolence and compassion." This violence is "most evident, in respect of the larger animals, and those with whom we have a familiar intercourse.... These creatures resemble us greatly in the make of the body ... [and] also in the formation of their intellects, memories, and passions, and in the signs of distress, pain, fear, and death."

3. Hartley adds that "the action of the hand is not an essential in this fourth method," for "composition by persons born blind has nearly the same effect." What method of composition would this be? My guess is that Nicholas Saunderson had perfected some system of "writing" that did not involve putting pen to paper. To teach geometry, Saunderson had invented a frame upon which he could string threads in order to create geometrical figures.

4. See *Dr. R. Grey's Memoria Technica* (1806): "The principle part of the method is briefly this: to remember anything in history, chronology, geography, &c. a word is formed, the beginning whereof being the first syllable or syllables of the thing sought, does, by frequent repetition, of course draw after it the latter part, which is so contrived as to give the answer. Thus, in history, the Deluge happened in the year before Christ two thousand three hundred forty-eight; this is signified by the word Del*etok*: Del standing for Deluge and *etok* for 2348." The "technical words" are formed according to a key, so that numbers can be expressed in syllables:

```
a   e   i   o   u   au  oi  ei  ou  y
1   2   3   4   5   6   7   8   9   0
b   d   t   f   l   s   p   k   n   z
```

5. Hartley's friend George Cheyne, in his *Philosophical Principles of Religion*, elevated analogy to the position of a fundamental principle of coherence in the universe. "All the *Integral* Parts of *Nature*," Cheyne writes, "have a beautiful *Resemblance, Similitude,* and *Analogy* to one another, and to the almighty *Original*, whose Images . . . they are" (1715, 1:5). Cheyne's concern is with the relationship between things as images and the reality to which they give expression. He uses the image of the cone of the earth's shadow to picture the relationship between the images and the original: "The *Supreme Creator* of all Things, and the whole *System* of Creatures, from the highest *Seraphim* down to *Brute Matter*, are here considered together as it were an *Infinite Cone* (like the *Shadow* of the dark side of the *Earth*, circumscribed by the Light of the *Sun* in the empty Spaces of our *System*) whose *Base* is the Supreme and Absolute Infinite, the Origin of the Being and Faculties of all created things; and its *Body*, is the whole *System* of Creatures" (2:A2). Within this cone, "there is a perpetual *Analogy*, (Physical not Mathematical) running on in a Chain, thro' the whole *System* of *Creatures*, up to their *Creator*" such that "the Visible are Images of the Invisible, the Sensible of the Insensible, the *Ectypical* of the *Architypical*, the *Creatures* of the *Creator*, at an absolutely infinite distance" (2:A3). Moreover, because all visible things are images of and emanations from the "absolute infinite," they also contain within themselves an innate disposition to return to their source: God, "when he made Creatures partaking of himself, Images, *Emanations, Effluxes* and Streams out of his own *Abyss of Being*, could not but impress upon their own most *intimate* Natures and Substances, a *Central* Tendency toward Himself, an Essential Principle of ReUnion with himself, which in him is a Principle of Attraction of them towards him, Analogous to this Principle [of gravitation] now mentioned in the Great Bodies of the Universe" (1:47). Although a reader might think Cheyne more a disciple of Plotinus than of Newton, he presented himself as a Newtonian who understood "this vast, if not infinite *Machin* of the *Universe*" to consist of "an infinite Number of lesser *Machines*, every one of which is adjusted by Weight and Measure" (1:2).

6. To intuition and demonstration Locke adds, as an afterthought, the "sensitive" apprehension of "the existence of particular external objects" (*HU* 4.2.14).

7. Hacking (1975, 33–35) notes that the concept of "internal evidence"—the evidence of a thing, as opposed to the "external evidence" of testimony—first appears in the Port Royal *Logic*.

8. Price's 1791 sermon on the anniversary of the storming of the Bastille became the occasion, and target, of Burke's *Reflections on the Revolution in France*.

9. In a critique of the notion that recognition memory involves a process of matching present impressions with stored ones, Reed writes: "Gibson and his students have argued that the perception of familiarity or 'sameness' is based on the attunement of a perceptual system to invariants amidst changing stimula-

tion" (1988, 236). Do Gibsonian invariance and Hartleian predictability of variation bear comparison? Although the sensory stimuli relating to a cat change, the "function" that is the idea *cat* predicts which changes are allowable, that is, consistent with my perception of a cat. And what the function does is point out certain invariances—ways in which certain types of sensory input predictably "vary with the varieties" of other types.

10. Like other searchers for the philosophical language, Hartley was curious about the age and purity of the languages of the world. See his letter to Edmund Law (6 November 1739), in Richard Warner (1830, 2:426), concerning the theory of David Malcolme, a Scots minister who proposed that "there was no confusion of tongues at Babel, . . . but that the one common language was first spoken according to different dialects, and as new words were introduced, became what are the different languages, which are therefore all related to each other, as mankind are themselves in their original; and that the Irish being the language of a corner . . . must be very simple, antique, and of great use in exploring the mutual relations of all." Hartley adds that "he is a man of learning, but somewhat desultory I think. Is there anything in his scheme?"

11. According to Jerome Christensen (1981, 54–57), Hartley's supposition that alphabetic writing is a gift of God is a key to understanding, as it were, the forces of attraction and repulsion at work in the writing of both Hartley and Coleridge. For discussion of the philosophical language in Hartley and Wordsworth, see Lamb 1982.

12. Leibniz, and later, Condorcet and Condillac also envisioned a philosophical language as a means to aid the progressive enlightenment of mankind. See Condorcet [1790] 1970, ch. 10; and concerning Condillac, Knowlson 1975, 171.

13. It would thus be a solution to what Foucault has called "the essential problem of Classical thought," which concerns "the relations between *name* and *order*: how to discover a *nomenclature* that would be a *taxonomy*, how to establish a system of signs that would be transparent to the continuity of being" (Foucault 1970, 208).

Chapter 7. The Emergence of Self

1. Compare John Stuart Mill's account of disinterested sympathy in his note 57 to chapter 23 of James Mill's *Analysis* (1869, 2: 302–26, esp. 305, 309).

Chapter 9. Annihilation of Self

1. The attainment of such love may also be viewed as a developmental potential that exists independently of its thematization within a religious tradition. Michael Washburn identifies "saintly compassion" as one of three "gifts"

that follow upon the completion of the project by which the ego separates from and then integrates with the "dynamic ground"—the "source of spiritual power" (1994, 314, see also 316). Washburn's theory is itself deeply indebted to the account of spiritual development articulated by St. John of the Cross; still, his position is that the great Spanish mystic speaks for all humanity: the dark nights of the senses and of the spirit which St. John describes are both culturally specific and universal. In Washburn's view, although saintly compassion may be a gift received by only a few exceptional persons, those persons may come from any land or culture.

2. Bernard McGinn cites the passage from Teresa quoted above near the beginning of *The Presence of the Word* (1991, xiii), his planned four-volume history of Western Christian mysticism. McGinn emphasizes (1991, xiv) that Teresa's identification of her "consciousness of the presence of God" with the term "mystical theology" points out the difficulty in taking *mysticism* to refer to a kind of *experience* that is separable from the contexts of its practice and interpretation. Rather than defining the term as referencing "a union of absorption or identity in which the individual personality is lost" (1991, xvi), McGinn suggests that mysticism be considered, first, "a part or element of religion," second, "a process or way of life," and third, "an attempt to express a direct consciousness of the presence of God" (1991, xv–xvi).

3. I use *Quietism* for the sake of convenience, without the pejorative intent of the original critics. We should keep in mind that it is not at all clear that the people called Quietists by their detractors thought of themselves as belonging to a separate movement, distinguishable from the many others who practiced the "inward life."

4. Hartley family papers, F55.

5. The writer also remarks that "the same Design appears clearly in the Writings of the *Apostles,* and in many books of the *Old Testament*: The pure Love of God, Union with him, Transformation into his Likeness, which presupposeth the Extirpation of *Self-love,* of the *Selfish* Principle, that we may love God with such a Love as he loves us" (Marsay 1749, 9).

6. See Walker 1964, 219–20 for more on Roach and Lee. For discussion of the Philadelphians see, in addition to Walker, E. P. Thompson 1993, 36–37, and Thune 1948. Roach and Lee were friends, both having been fellows of St. John's College, Oxford. Lee became Lead's secretary and son-in-law; Roach, while a leader of the Philadelphian Society, was from 1690 until 1730 the Rector at St. Augustine's church, Hackney.

7. In "A Letter concerning a Life truly Christian," Marsay (1749, 53) encourages his sister "to seek after that sacred Presence which hath already wrought this Desire in us to love him, and to abstain from that which is contrary to what this Love requires of us. Let us then labour after this Presence, and be persuaded that God is more present and nearer to us than we are to ourselves."

8. Fénelon is an advocate of what Charles Taylor in *Sources of the Self* calls an "ontic logos"—"the Platonic Idea" as "a self-manifesting reality.... in which the One turns into the Many, in which all possible niches are occupied." (1989, 160–61). According to Taylor, the "punctual self" of modernity "gains control through disengagement" (160); but such disengagement, whether turned outward as in theories of mechanism or inward as in the introspective psychologies of Descartes and Locke, alienates the subject from the ontic logos; finding a "logical" order becomes a matter of representation rather than of participation (168). The task, for such a self, is to manufacture a coherent picture of the world and of the self. On one level, Taylor's is a work of intellectual history: it tells the story of the "making of the modern identity." On another level, the work is a diagnosis of the sickness of modernity; it describes "what I think is wrong with the familiar and widely held perspectives" (502). And what is wrong is the loss of an ontic logos: "we are now in an age in which a publicly accessible cosmic order of meanings is an impossibility" (512).—However, the presence of the doctrine of an ontic logos in the thought of both Fénelon and Hartley suggests that the "making of the modern identity" is even more complicated than it appears in Taylor's account.

9. In a letter to his son David, written from Sodbury in August 1755, Hartley called mental prayer "the great secret of a pious and happy life. But I find it very difficult to attain to this great secret. I am persuaded, however, that it is attainable; and may be practised . . . to the unspeakable joy of all those who labour after it in earnest" (Warner 1817, 114).

10. We should also note here the similarity, and probable connections, between Hartley's theological position and Newton's. See Manuel 1963, 159.

Chapter 10. The Whole Body Fitly Joined Together

1. Of animals, Hartley writes: "if they should prove to be our brethren and sisters in this higher sense, in immortality as well as mortality, in the permanent principle of our minds, as well as the frail dust of our bodies; if they should be partakers of the same redemption as well as of our fall, and be members of the same mystical body, this would have a particular tendency to increase our tenderness for them" (*OM* 2.3.2.52).

2. The plurality of worlds was a popular topic of speculation in Hartley's day. For discussion see Michael J. Crowe 1986, Stephen J. Dick 1982, and Arthur O. Lovejoy 1960, 52, 125.

Chapter 11. Revolutionary Science

1. Benjamin Rush called Hartley "a saint of the first order" in a letter to John Adams (Rush 1951, 1035; see ch. 2, n. 45). Richard Warner, who knew

Hartley personally, wrote that his "countenance... beamed with all the lights of his luminous and virtuous mind" (quoted in Tagart 1855, 149). R. K. Webb (1998) cites the Cambridge radical Gilbert Wakefield, writing in 1804, who experienced this same luminosity when contemplating William Blake's engraving in the 1791 edition of the *Observations*: "Who can look at the delightful image of [Hartley's] person, prefixed to his work, without powerful emotions of love and admiration for the original? His 'human face divine' appears the residence of all that is good and great; it exhibits the intuition of genius, made venerable by a mixture of sweetness, modesty, gentleness, and complacency, beyond description." Edward Tagart also responded to "the angelic sweetness of his countenance" and asked: "Who can look at the engraving of it without feeling it an argument in favour of his religious and amiable philosophy, presenting as it does a singular combination of feminine purity and grace with manly intellectual power?" (1855, 144).

Along with Hartley's signficance as a moral exemplar, the *Observations* appears to have been part of the core curriculum in the dissenting academies. James Mill, John Stuart Mill, William B. Carpenter, and William Hazlitt all studied it as schoolboys. In addition, according to Christopher Wordsworth, "Hartley was considered a great light among philosophical minds at Cambridge" (1877, 123). Coleridge became a convert to Hartley's synthesis of physiology, metaphysics, and Christianity while a student there. For Hartley's influence on Priestley's ideas concerning education, see Watts 1983.

Kramnick emphasizes the "paradox... inherent in Hartley's 'optimistic materialism' and in that of his disciple Priestley": "as necessitarians they claimed mankind to be the passive product of circumstances"; but "as reformers they preached active intervention in controlling and changing circumstances, in educating, in order to produce progress, perfection, and paradise. It is this latter perspective that most characterizes Priestley and his fellow Hartleyian reformers. Other close friends of Priestley who were also taken with Hartley's associationist theories were busy reforming all of England's institutions" (1986, 16). Kramnick adds that "Warrington, Hackney, and the other dissenting academies were thus the great agencies of redemption" (17). For another evaluation of the academies, see Wykes 1996, 132–37.

Although many adopted the position articulated by Priestley, there were also many who sided with Reid. In America during the first half of the nineteenth century, the official mental and moral philosophy taught by the Unitarians who ran Harvard University was based on Reid and other advocates of Scottish common sense philosophy (see Howe 1988). The Priestleian alternative had few advocates in Cambridge, Mass.

2. Although sympathetic to Hartley's project, Lewes thought the theory of vibrations suffered from "a radical insufficiency": "What we want is to trace the mechanism of thought; the doctrine of vibration might help us, if from the known laws of vibratory bodies we could deduce explanations of mental

phenomena.... And I believe such deductions can be made; but not upon Hartley's vague theory.... To say that vibrations produce sensations throws little light. What is the specific velocity and sweep of each vibration? *That* would be valuable knowledge" (1880, 2:371).

3. The debate concerning this point is a main topic of John Yolton's *Thinking Matter* (1983). Yolton notes that the claim that the whole can possess only those properties that are inherent in the parts was made by Richard Bentley (quoted at 15) and Ralph Cudworth (quoted at 7). Yolton also notes that Anthony Collins, the deist and necessitarian, was one of the few who argued that organized matter could possess properties by virtue of its organization; Collins's debate with Samuel Clarke over this question was a main point of reference for later entrants into the controversy (42). Among those siding with Collins was Priestley ([1806] 1970, 76).

4. Priestley, *Experiments and Observations of Different Kinds of Air* (1774, xiv); quoted in Kramnick 1986, 12.

5. See also Benjamin Rush 1981, 184: "By the theory I have proposed, we render the existence and support of animal life the immediate act of a Supreme Being, by the instrumentality of causes which are constantly under his direction.... And hence it becomes as true in philosophy as it is in religion, that 'He is indeed the preserver of men,' and that 'In him we live and move and have our Being' " (Job 7.20, Acts 17.28).

6. The analogy may be continued: all the lines of pleasure terminate in God just as all lines of gravitational force terminate in a universal attractor at the center of the cosmos. Cheyne drew this analogy (see ch. 6, n. 5), as did Thomas Wright (1750, 79, and especially plates 24 and 25).

7. Godwin and Coleridge drew different conclusions from reading Hartley: the former emphasized the rational aspects of human nature, while the latter appears to have been most influenced by the emotional, developmental, and mystical aspects of Hartley's thought. See Coleridge's account of the "thinking and disinterested Patriots" in his "Moral and Political Lecture" of February 1795 (*C* 1.12) for a description that is saturated with the terms and concepts of Hartley's model of moral development. At the end of the description, Coleridge imagines the patriots looking forward "with gladdened heart to that glorious period when justice shall have established the universal fraternity of love." Echoing passages in Hartley and in Priestley, Coleridge then states that "these soul ennobling views bestow the virtues they anticipate"; when they attain them, the patriots will "dwell in the presence of the most high," and, "regarding every event as he that ordains it," see evil vanish; they perceive "the eternal form of universal beauty" (cf. *OM* 2.3.7.71; Priestley 1777b, xii–xiii, xiv; Coleridge, "Religious Musings," ll. 38–44.) See also §11.3; Allen 1996 and 1979.

Bibliography

Works by David Hartley

1733. *Some Reasons why the Practice of Inoculation ought to be Introduced into the Town of Bury at Present.* Bury St. Edmunds.

1738a. *Ten Cases of Persons who have taken Mrs. Stephens's Medicines for the Stone. With an Abstract of Some of the Experiments, Tending to Illustrate these Cases.* London: S. Harding.

1738b. *Proposal for Making Mrs. Stephens's Medicines Public.* London: S. Harding.

1738c. "An Account of the Contribution for making Mrs. Stephens's Medicines Public; with some Reasons for it, and Answers to the most remarkable Objections made against it." *History of the Works of the Learned.* June 1738, 443–56.

1738d. "To the Author of the History of the Works of the Learned" and "An Abstract of some Experiments, serving to illustrate the ten foregoing Cases." *History of the Works of the Learned.* August 1738, 126–35. The Abstract is reprinted from 1738a.

1739. *A View of the Present Evidence for and against Mrs. Stephens's Medicines, as a Solvent for the Stone. Containing a Hundred and Fifty-five Cases. With some Experiments and Observations.* London: S. Harding, J. Robinson, J. Roberts.

[1740]. Stephen Hales, *An Account of some Experiments and Observations on Mrs. Stephens's Medicine for dissolving the Stone: Wherein their Dissolving Power is inquir'd into, and shown.* To which is added, A Supplement to a Pamphlet, intitled, *A View of the present Evidence for and against Mrs. Stephen's Medicines,* &c. Being a Collection of some

Particulars relating to the Discovery of these Medicines, their Publication, Use and Efficacy. By David Hartley, M.A. F.R.S. London: T. Woodward, Printer to the Royal Society.

1740. *Recueil d'expériences et d'observations sur la pierre et en particulier sur les effets des remèdes de Mlle. Stephens.* Translated by M. Morand. Paris: chez Piget. [Another edition 1743, Paris: Durand.]

1741. And Francis Sandys. "Another Case of a Person bit by a Mad-Dog, drawn up by David Hartley, M.A. and Mr. Fr. Sandys, communicated to the Royal Society by Francis Wollaston, Esq., F.R.S.," *Philosophical Transactions* 40, no. 448 (June–July 1738), published 1741, 274–76. [The event occurred in 1732.]

1741. *De Lithontriptico a Joanna Stephens nuper invento dissertatio epistolaris.* Basel: J. Christ; Leiden: J. et H. Verbeek.

1746. *De Lithontriptico a Joanna Stephens nuper invento dissertatio epistolaris. Cui Adjicitur methodus exhibendi Lithontripticum sub formâ commodiore. Accedunt etiam Conjecturæ quædam de Sensu, Motu, & Idearum Generatione.* 2d. ed. Bath: J. Leake and G. Frederick, and London: C. Hitch and S. Austen.

1749. *Observations on Man, his Frame, his Duty, and his Expectations.* Bath and London: Samuel Richardson.

1752. "To Make the Lithontriptic Mass and Electuary." *Gentleman's Magazine* 22 (October 1752): 465–66.

1755. *Explication physique des sens, des idées, et des mouvements, tant volontaires qu'involuntaires.* Part 1 of the *Observations*, translated by Henri Jurain. Reims.

1772. *Betrachtungen über den Menschen.* Translated by Herman Andrew Pistorius. Rostock: Spieren Remarus.

1775. *Hartley's Theory of the Human Mind, on the Principle of the Association of Ideas; with Essays relating to the Subject of it.* An abridgement of the *Observations,* by Joseph Priestley. London: J. Johnson.

1791. *Observations on Man, his Frame, his Duty, and his Expectations.* To which are added notes and additions to the second part, translated from the German of Herman Andrew Pistorius. 2d ed. London: J. Johnson. (A third edition, in three volumes octavo, was published by Johnson the same year, and a fourth edition was reprinted by him in 1801.)

[1794?] N.d. *Conclusion of the Late Dr. Hartley's Observations on the Nature, Powers, and Expectations of Man; Strikingly Illustrated in the Events of the Present Times, with Notes and Illustrations, by the Editor.* London: J. Johnson.

1802. *De l'Homme, de ses facultés physiques et intellectuelles, des ses devoirs et de ses espérances.* Ouvrage traduit de l'anglais, avec des notes explicatives de Roch-Ambroise Sicard. Paris: Ducauroy.

1809. *Osservazioni sopra l'uomo, sua struttura, suoi doveri, ee sue speranze.* Volgarizzamento di Pietro Antoniutti. Venezia: Tip. Santini.
1810. *Prayers and Religious Meditations.* Bath: Richard Cruttwell. (Cruttwell also published a fifth edition of the *Observations* in this year, to which the *Prayers and Religious Meditations* were added.)
1834. *Observations on Man, his Frame, his Duty, and his Expectations.* 6th ed. London: Thomas Tegg and Son.
1959. *Various Conjectures on the Perception, Motion, and Generation of Ideas.* A translation of *Conjecturae quœdam de Sensu, Motu, & Idearum Generatione.* Translated by Robert E. A. Palmer, with Introduction and Notes by Martin Kallich. Augustan Reprint Society publication 77–78. Los Angeles: Williams Andrews Clark Memorial Library, University of California.

Primary Sources

Anon. 1723. *Lithotomus Castratu; or, Mr. Cheselden's Treatise on the High Operation for the Stone, Thoroughly Examin'd, and plainly found to be Lithotomia Douglassiana, &c. Under another Title: In a Letter to Dr. John Arbuthnot. With an Appendix, Wherein both Authors are fairly compar'd. To which is added, A Word of Advice to Surgeons.* London: T. Payne.

Anon. 1724. *Cystitomia Hypogastrica: or, The Method of the High Operation, in which the Stone is extracted out of the Bladder above the Os Pubis, in the Region of the Hypogastrium.* London: G. Strahan.

Anon. 1738a. "To Mr. David Hartley," *History of the Works of the Learned,* May 1738, 373–75.

Anon. 1738b. "To the Author of the History of the Works of the Learned," *History of the Works of the Learned,* July 1738, 56–62.

Anon. 1738c. "To the Author of the History of the Works of the Learned," *History of the Works of the Learned,* September 1738, 222–24.

Anon. 1739. Review of *A Treatise of Human Nature: Being an Attempt to Introduce the Experimental Method of Reasoning into Moral Subjects,* by David Hume. *History of the Works of the Learned,* November, 353–90, December, 391–404.

Anon. 1763. "Clutton's Analysis of Ward's Pills." *The Medical Museum: Or, A Repository of Cases, Experiments, Researches, and Discoveries, Collected at Home and Abroad.* Vol. 1: 79–81. London: W. Richardson and S. Clarke.

Anon. 1775–76. Review of *Hartley's Theory of the Human Mind,* edited by Joseph Priestley (1775). *Monthly Review* 53 (November 1775): 380–90 and 54 (January 1776): 41–47.

Anon. 1777. Review of *Letters on Materialism and Hartley's Theory of the Human Mind*, addressed to Dr. Priestley (1776). *Monthly Review* 56 (February 1777): 81–88.

Bayes, Thomas. 1731. *Divine Benevolence: Or, An Attempt to prove that the Principal End of the Divine Providence and Government is the Happiness of his Creatures.* Being an Answer to a Pamphlet, entitled, *Divine Rectitude: or, An Inquiry concerning the Moral Perfections of the Diety.* London: John Noon.

———. 1736. *An Introduction to the Doctrine of Fluxions, and Defense of the Mathematicians against the Objections of the Author of the* Analyst, *so far as they are designed to affect their general Methods of Reasoning.* London: John Noon.

Berington, Joseph. 1776. *Letters on Materialism and Hartley's Theory of the Human Mind.* London: Robinson.

Berkeley, George. [1709] 1948. *Essay towards a New Theory of Vision.* Edited by A. A. Luce. *Works,* vol. 1. London: Thomas Nelson & Sons.

———. [1710] 1949. *A Treatise Concerning the Principles of Human Knowledge.* Edited by A. A. Luce and T. E. Jessop. *Works,* vol. 2. London: Thomas Nelson & Sons.

Boerhaave, Hermann. 1713. *Institutiones Medicae in usus annuae Exercitationis Domesticus.* Leyden: Johannes vander Linden.

———. 1732. *Elementa Chemiae.* 2 vols. Leyden: Isaacum Severinum.

———. 1741. *A New Method of Chemistry; including the History, Theory, and Practice of the Art: Translated from the Original Latin of Dr. Boerhaave's Elementa Chemiœ, As Published by Himself. To which are added, Notes; and an Appendix, shewing the Necessity and Utility of Englarging the Bounds of Chemistry. With Sculptures.* 2d ed. 2 vols. Translated by Peter Shaw. London: T. Longman.

———. 1983. *Boerhaave's Orations.* Translated by E. Kegel-Brinkgreve and A. M. Luyekdijk-Elshout. Leiden: E. J. Brill and Leiden University Press.

Boyle, Robert. 1663. *Some Considerations touching the Usefulnesse of Experimental Naturall Philosophy.* Oxford: Henry Hall.

———. 1744. *Some Physico-Theological Considerations about the Possibility of the Resurrection.* In *The Works of the Honourable Robert Boyle,* 3: 357–405. London: A. Millar.

Bracken, Henry, M.D. 1739. *Lithiasis Anglicana: or, A Philosophical Enquiry into the Nature and Origin of the Stone and Gravel, in Human Bodies, &c. Wherein is considered, The Possibibility of dissolving such Animal Tartar or Calculous Concretion. In a Letter to David Hartley, M.D.* London: T. Cooper.

Brown, Thomas. 1798. *Observations on the Zoonomia of Erasmus Darwin, M.D.* Edinburgh: Mundell & Son.

Butler, Joseph. 1736. *The Analogy of Religion, Natural and Revealed, to the Constitution and Course of Nature*. London: John and Paul Knapton.

Byrom, John. 1767. *The Universal English Shorthand*. Manchester: Joseph Harrop.

———. 1854-57. *The Private Journal and Literary Remains of John Byrom*. Edited by Richard Parkinson. Publications of the Chetham Society, vols. 32, 34, 40, and 44. Manchester: The Chetham Society.

Campbell, Archibald. 1739. *The Necessity of Revelation: Or an Enquiry into the Extent of the Human Powers with Respect to Matters of Religion; Especially those two fundamental Articles, The Being of God and The Immortality of the Soul*. London: William Bowyer, At the Expence of the Society for the Encouragement of Learning.

Carpenter, Lant. 1842. *Memoirs of the Life of the Rev. Lant Carpenter, Ll.D., with Selections from his Correspondence*. Edited by Russell Lant Carpenter. Bristol: Philip and Evans, and London: Green.

Carpenter, William. 1874. *Principles of Mental Physiology, with their Applications to the Training and Discipline of the Mind, and the Study of its Morbid Conditions*. London: Henry S. King.

Charcot, Jean-Martin. 1887. *Leçons du Mardi á la Salpêtrière*. 2 vols. Paris: Bureaux du Progrès Médical.

Cheselden, William. 1728. "An Account of some Observations made by a young Gentleman, who was born blind, or lost his sight so early, that he had no Remembrance of ever having seen, and was couch'd between 13 and 14 Years of Age." *Philosphical Transactions* no. 402 (April, May, June 1728): 447-50. Reprinted in Cheselden 1730, 348–52.

———. 1730. *The Anatomy of the Human Body*. 4th ed. London: W. Bowyer.

Cheyne, George. 1715. *Philosophical Principles of Religion: Natural and Revealed, In Two Parts. Part I: Containing the Elements of Natural Philosophy, and the Proofs of Natural Religion arising from them. Part II: Containing the Nature and Kinds of Infinities, their Arithmetick and Uses: Together with the Philosophical Principles of Revealed Religion*. 2d. ed., 1st publication of part 2. London: George Strahan.

———. 1724. *An Essay on Health and Long Life*. London: George Strahan, and Bath: J. Leake.

———. 1733. *The English Malady: Or, a Treatise of Nervous Diseases of all Kinds, as Spleen, Vapours, Lowness of Spirits, hypochondriacal, and Hysterical Distempers, &c*. London: George Strahan, and Bath: J. Leake.

———. 1943. *The Letters of George Cheyne to Samuel Richardson (1733-43)*. Edited by Charles Mullett. Columbia, Mo.: University of Missouri Studies, vol. 18, no. 1.

Coleridge, Samuel Taylor. [1795] 1971. *Lectures 1795: On Politics and Religion*. Edited by Lewis Patton and Peter Mann. *The Collected Works of Samuel Taylor Coleridge,* vol. 1. Princeton: Princeton University Press.

———. [1817] 1983. *Biographia Literaria: or, Biographical Sketches of My Literary Life and Opinions.* Edited by James Engell and W. Jackson Bate. *The Collected Works of Samuel Taylor Coleridge,* vol. 7. Princeton: Princeton University Press.

Condorcet, Marie Jean Antoine Nicholas Caritat, Marquis de. [1790] 1970. *Esquisse d'un tableau historique des progrès de l'esprit humain.* Paris: J. Vrin.

Cordovero, Moses ben Jacob. [1588] 1960. *The Palm Tree of Deborah.* Translated by Louis Jacobs. London: Valentine, Mitchell.

Darwin, Erasmus. 1794, 1796. *Zoonomia: or, the Laws of Organic Life.* 2 vols. London: J. Johnson.

Descartes, Rene. 1985. *The Philosophical Writings of Descartes,* vol 1. Translated by John Cottingham, Robert Stoothoff, and Dugald Murdoch. Cambridge: Cambridge University Press.

Dostoyevsky, Fyodor. [1880] 1990. *The Brothers Karamazov.* Translated by Richard Pevear and Larissa Volokhonsky. San Francisco: North Point Press.

Douglas, James. 1726. *The History of the Lateral Operation: Or, An Account of the Method of Extracting a Stone, by making a Wound near the great Protuberance of the Os Ischium, through the Common Integuments and Levator Ani, into the Side of the Bladder, without touching the Urethra, Prostate Gland, Vesiculae Seminales, or any other of the Urinary or Seminal Vessels; first attempted by Frere Jacques in France, and afterwards successfully perform'd by Professor Rau in Holland.* London: G. Strahan.

Edwards, Jonathan. [1754] 1957. *The Freedom of the Will.* Edited by Paul Ramsey. *Works,* vol. 1. New Haven: Yale University Press.

Encyclopædia Britannica: or, A Dictionary of the Arts and Sciences, Compiled upon a New Plan. 1771. 1st ed. Edinburgh: A. Bell and C. Macfarquhar.

Fénelon, François de Salignac de la Mothe. 1735. *The Archbishop of Cambray's Dissertation on Pure Love, With an Account of the Life and Writings of the Lady, for whose sake the Archbishop was banish'd from Court. And the grievous Persecutions she suffer'd in* France *for her Religion.* London: Luke Hinde.

Francis de Sales, Saint. [1616] 1962. *The Love of God: A Treatise. (Traité de l'Amour de Dieu).* Translated by Vincent Kerns. Westminster, Maryland: The Newman Press; London: Burns and Oates.

'sGravesande, William James van. 1720. *Mathematical Elements of Natural Philosophy.* Translated by J. T. Desaguliers. London: J. Senex and W. Taylor.

Gay, John. [1731] 1739. "Preliminary Dissertation Concerning the Fundamental Principle of Virtue or Morality." In King 1739, xxvii–lv.

Greene, Robert. 1727. *The Principles of the Philosophy of the Expansive and Contractive Forces: or, An Inquiry into the Principles of Modern Philosophy, that is, into the Several Chief Rational Sciences, which are extant.* Cambridge: Cambridge University Press.

Gregory, David. 1702. *Astronomiæ Physicæ & Geometricæ Elementa.* Oxford: E Theatro Sheldoniano.

Godwin, William. [3d ed., 1798] 1976. *Enquiry Concerning Political Justice and its Influence on Morals and Happiness.* Edited by Isaac Kramnick. 1st ed., 1793. London: Penguin Books.

Guyon, Jeanne-Marie Bouvier de la Mothe. [1685] 1995. *Le Moyen court et autres récits: Une simplicité subversive.* Edited by Marie-Louise Gondal. Grenoble: Jérôme Millon.

Hales, Stephen. [1740]. *An Account of some Experiments and Observations on Mrs. Stephen's Medicine for dissolving the Stone: Wherein their Dissolving Power is inquir'd into, and shown.* (See Hartley [1740].)

———. 1769. *Statical Essays: containing Haemastatics; Or, An Account of some Hydraulic and Hydrostatical Experiments made on the Blood and Blood-Vessels of Animals.* 3d ed. 2 vols. London: Wilson and Nichol, Keith, Robinson and Roberts.

Hooke, Robert. 1665. *Micrographia: or, Some Physiological Descriptions of Minute Bodies Made by Magnifying Glasses with Observations and Inquiries Thereupon.* London: James Allestry.

———. 1678a. *Microscopium: or, Some new Discoveries made with and concerning Microscopes.* In *Lectures and Collections Made by Robert Hooke, Secretary of the Royal Society.* London: J. Martyn.

———. 1678b. *Lectures De Potentia Restituva, or of Spring, Explaining the Powers of Springing Bodies.* London: John Martyn. Collected in *Lectures Cutlerianae, or a Collection of Lectures: Physical, Mechanical, Geographical, & Astronomical.* London: John Martyn, for the Royal Society, 1679.

———. 1679. *A Description of Helioscopes and some other Instruments.* In *Lectures Cutlerianae, or a Collection of Lectures: Physical, Mechanical, Geographical, & Astronomical.* London: John Martyn, for the Royal Society.

Hutcheson, Francis. 1725. *An Inquiry into the Original of our Ideas of Beauty and Virtue.* London: J. Darby.

———. 1728. *An Essay on the Nature and Conduct of the Passions and Affections, with Illustrations on the Moral Sense.* London: J. Osborn and T. Longman.

James, William. 1890. *The Principles of Psychology.* 2 vols. New York: Henry Holt & Co.

———. [1896] 1992. "The Will to Believe." In *Writings 1878–1899.* New York: Library of America.

Jebb, John. 1787. *The Works: Theological, Medical, Political, and Miscellaneous.* Edited by John Disney. 3 vols. London: T. Cadell.

Jurin, James, M.D. 1738. *An Essay upon Distinct and Indistinct Vision.* Appended to Robert Smith 1738.

———. 1742. *An Account of the Effects of Soap-Lees taken internally, in the Case of James Jurin, M.D.* Printed with John Rutty, M.D., *An Account of Some New Experiments and Observations on Joanna Stephens's Medicine for the Stone: With some Hints for Reducing it from an Empirical to a Rational Use.* London: R. Manby.

King, William. 1739. *An Essay on the Origin of Evil.* Translated and corrected by Edmund Law. 3d ed. Cambridge: William Thurlbourn.

La Mettrie, Julien Offray de. [1748] 1996. *Machine Man and Other Writings.* Translated by Ann Thomson. Cambridge: Cambridge University Press.

Lead, Jane. 1681. *The Heavenly Cloud New Breaking.* London: for the author.

———. [1683] 1884. *The Revelation of Revelations, particularly as an Essay towards Unsealing, Opening, and Discovering the Seven Seals, the Seven Thunders, and the New-Jerusalem State.* London: A. Sowle. Autograph reprint, Glasgow: John Thomson.

———. 1694. *The Enochian Walks with God, Found out by a Spiritual-Traveller, Whose Face towards Mount Sion above was Set.* London: D. Edwards.

———. 1696–1700. *A Fountain of Gardens.* London: J. Bradford.

Lewes, George Henry. 1880. *The History of Philosophy, from Thales to Comte.* 2 vols. London: Longmans, Green, and Co.

Locke, John. [1690] 1975. *An Essay Concerning Human Understanding.* Edited by Peter H. Nidditch. Oxford: Clarendon Press.

Mackintosh, Sir James. 1836. *Dissertation on the Progress of Ethical Philosophy, chiefly during the 17th and 18th Centuries.* Edinburgh: Adam and Charles Black.

Maclaurin, Colin. 1748. *An Account of Sir Isaac Newton's Philosophical Discoveries.* London: Printed for the Author's Children.

Marsay, Charles-Hectore de Saint-George de. 1749. *Discourses On Subjects Relating to the Spiritual Life, Translated from the French. To which is prefixed, A Letter, giving some Account of the Author: with, Remarks on other Writers, commonly called Mystick or Spiritual.* Edinburgh: Tho. and Wal. Ruddimans.

Martineau, Harriet. 1877. *Harriet Martineau's Autobiography, with Memorials by Maria Weston Chapman.* 3 vol. 3d ed. London: Smith, Elder & Co.

Mede, Joseph. 1650. *The Key of Revelation, Searched and Demonstrated out of the Natural and Proper Character of the Visions.* Translated by Richard Moore. 2d ed. London: Phil. Stephens.

Mill, James. [1829] 1869. *Analysis of the Phenomena of the Human Mind.* A new edition with notes illustrative and critical by Alexander Bain, Andrew Findlater, and George Grote. Edited with additional notes by John Stuart Mill. 2 volumes. London: Longmans, Green, Reader, and Dyer.

Mill, John Stuart. 1859. Review of Alexander Bain, *The Senses and the Intellect* (1855) and *The Emotions and the Will* (1859). *The Edinburgh Review* 110, no. 224 (October 1859): 287–321.

———. [1873] 1924. *Autobiography*. With an Appendix of Hitherto Unpublished Speeches and a Preface by Harold J. Laski. London: Oxford University Press.

Moivre, Abraham de. [1718] 1756. *The Doctrine of Chances: A Method of Calculating the Probability of Events in Play*. 3d ed. London: A Millar.

Newton, Sir Isaac. 1729. *The Mathematical Principles of Natural Philosophy*. Translated by Andrew Motte. 2 vols. London: Benjamin Motte. Translation based on the second edition of the *Principia*, published in 1713.

———. 1730. *Opticks: or, A Treatise of the Reflections, Refractions, Inflections and Colours of Light*. 4th ed. London: William Innys.

———. 1733. *Observations on the Prophecies of Daniel, and the Apocalypse of St. John*. London: J. Darby and T. Browne.

Owen, Robert. [1813] 1970. *A New View of Society*. Edited by V. A. C. Gatrell. Harmondsworth: Penguin.

Parsons, James, M.D. 1742. *A Description of the Human Urinary Bladder, and Parts belonging to it: with Anatomical Figures Shewing its Make, Situation, &c. To which are added, Animadversions on Lithontriptic Medicines, Particularly those of Mrs. Stephens; and An Account of the Dissections of some Bodies of Persons who died after the Use of them*. London: J. Brindley.

Peacock, Thomas Love. [1818] 1924. *Nightmare Abbey*. Edited by H. F. B. Brett-Smith and C. E. Jones. *The Halliford Edition of the Works of Thomas Love Peacock*, vol. 3. London: Constable & Co.

Pemberton, Henry. 1728. *A View of Sir Isaac Newton's Philosophy*. London: S. Palmer.

Priestley, Joseph. 1774a. *An Examination of Dr. Reid's Inquiry into the Human Mind on the Principles of Common Sense, Dr. Beattie's Essay on the Nature and Immutability of Truth, and Dr. Oswald's Appeal to Common Sense in Behalf of Religion*. London: J. Johnson.

———. 1774b. *The Doctrine of Divine Influence on the Human Mind, Considered in a Sermon*. Bath: R. Cruttwell; London: J. Johnson.

———. 1777a. *Disquisitions Relating to Matter and Spirit. To which is added, The History of the Philosophical Doctrine concerning the Origin of the Soul, and the Nature of Matter; with its Influence on Christianity, especially with Respect to the Doctrine of the Pre-existence of Christ*. London: J. Johnson.

———. 1777b. *The Doctrine of Philosophical Necessity Illustrated: Being an Appendix to the Disquisitions Relating to Matter and Spirit. To which is added An Answer to the Letters on Materialism, and on Hartley's Theory of the Mind*. London: J. Johnson.

———. 1778. *A Free Discussion of the Doctrines of Materialism and Philosophical Necessity, in a Correspondence between Dr. Price and Dr. Priestley.* London: J. Johnson.

———. 1966. *A Scientific Autobiography of Joseph Priestley (1733–1804).* Selected Scientific Correspondence Edited with Commentary by Robert E. Schofield. Cambridge, Mass., and London: The M.I.T. Press.

———. [1806] 1970. *Autobiography of Joseph Priestley.* Contains *Memoirs of Dr. Joseph Priestley (written by himself).* Introduction by Jack Lindsay. Bath: Adams & Dart.

Reid, Thomas. [1764] 1785. *An Inquiry into the Human Mind, on the Principles of Common Sense.* 4th ed. London: T. Caddell; Edinburgh: J. Bell and W. Creech.

———. 1785. *Essays on the Intellectual Powers of Man.* Edinburgh: John Bell.

———. 1788. *Essays on the Active Powers of the Human Mind.* Edinburgh: John Bell.

Roach, Richard. 1725. *The Great Crisis.* London: N. Blandford.

———. 1727. *The Imperial Standard of the Messiah Triumphant; Coming Now in the Power and, Kingdom of his Father, To Reign with his Saints on Earth.* London: N. Blandford.

Robinson, Bryan. [1732] 1734. *A Treatise of the Animal Oeconomy.* 2d ed. Dublin: George Ewing and William Smith.

———. 1743. *A Dissertation of the Aether of Sir Isaac Newton.* Dublin: Geo. Ewing and Wil. Smith.

Rush, Benjamin. 1798. *Essays, Literary, Moral, and Philosophical.* Philadelphia: Thomas & Samuel.

———. 1948. *The Autobiography of Benjamin Rush.* Edited by George Corner. Princeton: Princeton University Press for the American Philosophical Society.

———. 1951. *The Letters of Benjamin Rush.* Edited by L. H. Butterfield. 2 vols. Princeton: Princeton University Press for the American Philosophical Society.

———. 1981. *Benjamin Rush's Lectures on the Mind.* Edited, annotated, and introduced by Eric T. Carlson, Jeffrey L. Wollock, and Patricia S. Noel. Philadelphia: American Philosophical Society.

Rutty, John, M.D. 1742. *An Account of Some New Experiments and Observations on Joanna Stephens's Medicine for the Stone: With some Hints for Reducing it from an Empirical to a Rational Use.* To which is subjoined: *An Account of the Effects of Soap-Lees taken internally, in the Case of James Jurin, M.D.* London: R. Manby.

Saunderson, Nicholas. 1740. *Elements of Algebra, in ten books.* Cambridge: Cambridge University Press.

Schimmelpenninck, Mary Anne Galton. 1860. *Life of Mary Anne Schimmelpenninck.* Edited by Christina C. Hankin. 4th ed. London: Longman.

Shaftesbury, Anthony Ashley Cooper, third Earl of. [1711] 1963. *Characteristics of Men, Manners, Opinions, Times, etc.* Edited by John M. Robinson. 1st ed., 1900; rpt., Gloucester, Mass.: P. Smith.

Shaw, Peter. 1728. *A New Practice of Physic.* 2 vols. London: J. Osborn and T. Longman.

Shelley, Mary Wollstonecraft. [1818] 1969. *Frankenstein: or, The Modern Prometheus.* Edited by M. K. Joseph. London: Oxford University Press.

Smith, Robert. 1738. *A Compleat System of Opticks: In Four Books, viz. A Popular, a Mathematical, a Mechanical, and a Philosophical Treatise.* Cambridge: Printed for the Author.

Sterry, Peter. 1675. *A Discourse of the Freedom of the Will.* London: John Starkey.

———. 1683. *The Rise, Race, and Royalty of the Kingdom of God in the Soul of Man. Opened in several Sermons upon Matthew 18.3. As also the Loveliness & Love of Christ Set forth in several other Sermons upon Psal. 45. v. 1, 2. Together with An Account of the State of a Saint's Soul and Body in Death.* London: Thomas Cockerill.

Tagart, Edward. 1855. *Locke's Writings and Philosophy Historically Considered, and Vindicated from the Charge of Contributing to the Scepticism of Hume.* London: Longman, Brown, Green, and Longmans.

Theresa of Avila, Saint. 1960. *The Life of Teresa of Jesus: The Autobiography of St. Teresa of Avila.* Translated by Alison Peers. Garden City, N.Y.: Doubleday.

Trigg, W. B. 1938. "The Correspondence of Dr. David Hartley and Rev. John Lister." *Transactions of the Halifax Antiquarian Society* 10: 230–78.

Walpole, Horace. 1751."An Account of the Right Honourable Horace Walpole Esq., drawn up by himself." *Philosophical Transactions* 48 (1751–52): 43–48.

———. 1752. "A Sequel of the Case of the Right Honourable Horace Walpole Esq.; relating to the stone, since his first Account in April 1750." *Philosophical Transactions* 48 (1751–52): 472–74.

Warner, Rebecca. 1817. *Original Letters, from Richard Baxter, Matthew Prior, Lord Bolingbroke, Alexander Pope, Dr. Cheyne, Dr. Hartley, Dr. Samuel Johnson, Mrs. Montague, Rev. William Gilpin, Rev. John Newton, George Lord Lyttleton, Rev. Claudius Buchanan, etc. etc.* Bath: Richard Cruttwell, and London: Longman, Hurst, Rees, Orme, and Brown.

Warner, Richard. 1830. *Literary Recollections.* 2 vols. London: Longman, Rees, Orme, Brown, and Green.

Whiston, William. 1709. *Sermons and Essays upon Several Subjects.* London: Benjamin Took.

———. 1738. *The Longitude Discovered by the Eclipses, Occultations, and Conjunctions of Jupiter's Planets.* London: John Whiston.

———. 1749. *Memoirs of the Life and Writings of Mr. William Whiston, containing Memoirs of Several of his Friends also.* London: Printed for the author.
White, Jeremiah. [1712] 1779. *The Restoration of All Things: Or, A Vindication of the Goodness and Grace of God, to be Manifested at Last, in the Recovery of His Whole Creation out of Their Fall.* 3d ed. London: John Denis & Son.
Wilkins, John. 1668. *An Essay Towards a Real Character, and a Philosophical Language.* London: The Royal Society.
Wright, Thomas. [1750] 1971. *An Original Theory or New Hypothesis of the Universe, Founded Upon the Laws of Nature, and Solving by Mathematical Principles the General Phœnomena of the Visible Creation; and Particularly the Via Lactea.* A facsimilie reprint of the first edition, London 1750. London: Macdonald, and New York: American Elsevier.

Secondary Sources

Allan, D. G. C., and R. E. Schofield. 1980. *Stephen Hales: Scientist and Philanthropist.* London: Scolar Press.
Allen, Richard C. 1979. The Habits of the Soul: Samuel Taylor Coleridge's Early Religious Thought and its Background, 1794-98. Ph.D. diss., University of Notre Dame.
———. 1991. "When Narrative Fails." *Journal of Religious Ethics* 21/1: 27–68.
———. 1996. "Charles Lloyd, Coleridge, and *Edmund Oliver.*" *Studies in Romanticism* 35, no. 2 (Summer): 245–94.
———. 1998. "A Philosophical Essay by Mark Akenside." *Notes & Queries* 243 (December 1998): 466–67.
Archibald, R. C. 1926. "A Rare Pamphlet of De Moivre and Some of His Discoveries," *Isis* 8: 671-84.
Auerbach, Erich. 1953. *Mimesis: The Representation of Reality in Western Literature.* Translated by Willard R. Trask. Princeton: Princeton University Press.
Bolzoni, Lina. 1991. "The Play of Images: The Art of Memory from its Origins to the Seventeenth Century." In *The Enchanted Loom: Chapters in the History of Neuroscience,* edited by Pietro Corsi, 16–65. Oxford and New York: Oxford University Press.
Brett, George Sidney. 1921. *A History of Psychology.* 3 vols. London: George Allen & Unwin.
Bruneau, Marie-Florine. 1998. *Women Mystics Confront the Modern World: Marie de l'Incarnation (1599–1672) and Madame Guyon (1648–1717).* Albany: State University of New York Press.

Buckley, Michael J. 1989. "Seventeenth-Century French Spirituality: Three Figures." In *Christian Spirituality: Post-Reformation and Modern*, edited by Louis Dupré and Don E. Saliers, 28–68. Volume 18 of *World Spirituality: An Encyclopedic Survey of the Religious Quest*. New York: Crossroad.

Chevallier, Marjolaine. 1994. *Pierre Poiret, 1646–1719: Du protestantisme à la mystique*. Histoire et Société, no. 26. Geneva: Labor et Fides.

Christensen, Jerome. 1981. *Coleridge's Blessed Machine of Language*. Ithaca: Cornell University Press.

Christie, W. H. 1993. "Francis Jeffrey's Associationist Aesthetics." *British Journal of Aesthetics* 33: 257-70.

Clark, Sir George. 1966. *A History of the Royal College of Physicians*. 2 vols. Oxford: Clarendon Press.

Clarke, Edwin. 1968. "The Doctrine of the Hollow Nerve in the Seventeenth and Eighteenth Centuries." In *Medicine, Science and Culture: Historical Essays in Honor of Owsei Temkin*, edited by Lloyd G. Stevenson and Robert P. Multhauf, 123–42. Baltimore: Johns Hopkins University Press.

Cohen, I. Bernard. 1956. *Franklin and Newton: An Inquiry into Speculative Newtonian Experimental Science and Franklin's Work on Electricity as an Example Thereof*. Memoirs of the American Philosophical Society, vol. 43. Philadelphia: The American Philosophical Society.

Crowe, Michael J. 1986. *The Extraterrestrial Life Debate, 1750–1900: The Idea of a Plurality of Worlds from Kant to Lowell*. Cambridge: Cambridge University Press.

Daston, Lorraine. 1988. *Classical Probability in the Enlightenment*. Princeton: Princeton University Press.

D'Elia, Donald. 1970. "Benjamin Rush, David Hartley, and the Revolutionary Uses of Psychology." *Proceedings of the American Philosophical Society* 114: 109–18.

Dennis, Del. 1995. "Humanistic Neuroscience, Mentality, and Spirituality." *Journal of Humanistic Psychology* 34, no. 2 (Spring): 34–72.

Duncan, Alastair. 1996. *Laws and Order in Eighteenth-Century Chemistry*. Oxford: Clarendon Press.

Dyson, Freeman. 1988. *Infinite in All Directions*. The Gifford Lectures for 1985. New York: Harper & Row.

Eccles, John C. 1979. *The Human Mystery*. Berlin, Heidelberg, and New York: Springer International.

———. 1980. *The Human Psyche*. Berlin, Heidelberg, and New York: Springer International.

———. 1991. *Evolution of the Brain: Creation of the Self*. London and New York: Routledge.

Eccles, John C., and Daniel N. Robinson. 1984. *The Wonder of Being Human: Our Brain and Our Mind.* New York: The Free Press, and London: Collier Macmillan.

Edelman, Gerald. 1987. *Neural Darwinism: The Theory of Neuronal Group Selection.* New York: Basic Books.

———. 1988. *Topobiology: An Introduction to Molecular Embryology.* New York: Basic Books.

———. 1989. *The Remembered Present: A Biological Theory of Consciousness.* New York: Basic Books.

———. 1992. *Bright Air, Brilliant Fire: On the Matter of the Mind.* New York: Basic Books.

Eliot, George. [1876] 1995. *Daniel Deronda.* Edited by Terence Cave. London and New York: Penguin Books.

Engler, Jack. 1986. "Therapeutic Aims in Psychotherapy and Meditation." In Wilber, Engler, and Brown, eds., 17–51.

Erikson, Erik. 1963. *Childhood and Society.* New York: Norton.

Estes, J. Worth. 1990. *Dictionary of Protopharmacology: Therapeutic Practices, 1700–1850.* Canton, Mass.: Science History Publications, U.S.A.

Farrell, Maureen, F.C.J. 1981. *The Life and Work of William Whiston.* New York: Arno Press. Reprint of Ph.D. diss., University of Manchester, 1973.

Fauvel, John, Raymond Flood, Michael Shortland, and Robin Wilson, eds. 1988. *Let Newton be!* Oxford: Oxford University Press.

Ferg, Stephen. 1981. "Two Early Works by David Hartley." *Journal of the History of Philosophy* 19: 173–89.

Force, James E. 1985. *William Whiston: Honest Newtonian.* Cambridge: Cambridge University Press.

Ford, Stephen. 1987. "*Coalescence:* David Hartley's 'Great *Apparatus.*' " In *Psychology and Literature in the Eighteenth Century,* edited by Christopher Fox, 199–224. New York: AMS Press.

Foucault, Michel. 1970. *The Order of Things: An Archaeology of the Human Sciences.* New York: Random House.

Fox, Christopher. 1988. *Locke and the Scriblerians: Identity and Consciousness in Early Eighteenth-Century Britain.* Berkeley and Los Angeles: University of California Press.

Frei, Hans. 1974. *The Eclipse of Biblical Narrative: A Study in Eighteenth and Nineteenth Century Hermeneutics.* New Haven and London: Yale University Press.

Fruchtman, Jack, Jr. 1992. "Late Latitudinarianism: The Case of David Hartley." *Enlightenment and Dissent* 11: 3–22.

Gay, Peter. 1969. *The Enlightenment: An Interpretation. The Science of Freedom.* New York: Alfred A. Knopf.

Gibson, James J. 1979. *The Ecological Approach to Visual Perception.* Boston: Houghton Mifflin.

Golinski, Jan. 1988. "The Secret Life of an Alchemist." In Fauvel et al., eds., 1988, 147–69.

Gondal, Marie-Louise. 1989. *Madame Guyon (1648–1717): Un Nouveau Visage.* Paris: Beauchesne.

Gregory, R. L. 1974. "Recovery from Blindness: A Case Study." In *Concepts and Mechanisms of Perception*, 65–130. London: Duckworth.

Haakonssen, Knud, ed. 1996. *Enlightenment and Religion: Rational Dissent in Eighteenth-Century Britain.* Cambridge: Cambridge University Press.

Hacking, Ian. 1975. *The Emergence of Probability: A Philosophical Study of Early Ideas about Probability, Induction, and Statistical Inference.* Cambridge: Cambridge University Press.

Hakfoort, Casper. 1988. "Newton's Optics: The Changing Spectrum of Science." In Fauvel et al., eds., 1988, 81–99.

Hall, David L., and Roger T. Ames. 1987. *Thinking Through Confucius.* SUNY Series in Systematic Philosophy. Albany: State University of New York Press.

Hancox, Joy. 1992. *The Byrom Collection.* London: Jonathan Cape.

———. 1994. *The Queen's Chameleon: The Life of John Byrom—A Study of Conflicting Loyalties.* London: Jonathan Cape.

Haven, Richard. 1959. "Coleridge, Hartley, and the Mystics." *Journal of the History of Ideas* 20: 477–89.

Hawking, Stephen. 1988. *A Brief History of Time: From the Big Bang to Black Holes.* New York: Bantam Books.

Hayden, John. 1984. "Wordsworth, Hartley, and the Revisionists." *Studies in Philology* 81: 94–118.

Henderson, George David. 1952. *Chevalier Ramsay.* London: Thomas Nelson and Sons.

Henry, John. 1988. "Newton, Matter, and Magic." In Fauvel et al., eds., 1988, 127–46.

Hesse, Mary. 1961. *Forces and Fields: The Concept of Action at a Distance in the History of Physics.* London and New York: Thomas Nelson and Sons.

Hillman, James. 1972. *The Myth of Analysis: Three Essays in Archetypal Psychology.* Evanston: Northwestern University Press.

Hoeldtke, Robert. 1967. "The History of Associationism and British Medical Psychology." *Medical History* 11, no. 1 (January): 46–65.

Hoffman, Edward. 1989. *The Way of Splendor: Jewish Mysticism and Modern Psychology.* Northvale, N.J., and London: Jason Aronson.

———, ed. 1995. *Opening the Inner Gates: New Paths in Kabbalah and Psychology.* Boston and London: Shambhala.

Howe, Daniel Walker. 1988 [1970]. *The Unitarian Conscience: Harvard Moral Philosophy, 1805–1861.* Middletown, Conn.: Wesleyan University Press.

Howse, Derek. 1980. *Greenwich Time and the Discovery of the Longitude.* Oxford: Oxford University Press.

Humphreys, A. L. 1932. *Bucklebury: A Berkshire Parish*. Reading: Published by the Author.
Hunt, Harry T. 1995. *On the Nature of Consciousness: Cognitive, Phenomenological, and Transpersonal Perspectives*. New Haven: Yale University Press.
Jackson, N. J. 1964. *Newark Magnus: The Story of a Gift*. Nottingham: J. & H. Bell.
Jacob, Margaret C. 1976. *The Newtonians and the English Revolution, 1689-1720*. Ithaca: Cornell University Press; Hassocks, Sussex: The Harvester Press.
Jung, C. G. 1960a. "On Psychic Energy." In *The Collected Works of C. G. Jung*, vol. 8, *The Structure and Dynamics of the Psyche*, edited by Sir Herbert Read, Michael Fordham, and Gerhard Adler, translated by R. F. C. Hull. New York: Pantheon Books.
———. 1960b. "A Review of the Complex Theory." In *The Collected Works of C. G. Jung*, vol. 8, *The Structure and Dynamics of the Psyche*, edited by Sir Herbert Read, Michael Fordham, and Gerhard Adler, translated by R. F. C. Hull. New York: Pantheon Books.
Kaku, Michio. 1995. *Hyperspace: A Scientific Odyssey through the 10th Dimension*. New York and London: Oxford University Press.
King, Lester S. 1964. "Stahl and Hoffman: A Study in Eighteenth-Century Animism." *Bulletin of the History of Medicine* 19: 118–30.
———. 1974. "George Cheyne, Mirror of Eighteenth-Century Medicine." *Bulletin of the History of Medicine* 48: 517–39.
———. 1978. *The Philosophy of Medicine: The Early Eighteenth Century*. Cambridge, Mass.: Harvard University Press.
Kohlberg, Lawrence. 1969. "Stage and Sequence: The Cognitive-Developmental Approach to Socialization." In *Handbook of Socialization Theory and Research*, edited by David A. Goslin. Chicago: Rand McNally.
Knowlson, James. 1975. *Universal Language Schemes in England and France, 1600-1780*. Toronto: University of Toronto Press.
Kramnick, Isaac. 1986. "Eighteenth-Century Science and Radical Social Theory: The Case of Joseph Priestley's Scientific Liberalism." *Journal of British Studies* 25, no. 1 (January): 1–30.
Kuhn, Thomas. 1970. *The Structure of Scientific Revolutions*. In *Foundations of the Unity of Science: Toward an International Encyclopedia*, edited by Otto Neurath, Rudolf Carnap, and Charles Morris, 53–272. Chicago: University of Chicago Press.
Lamb, Jonathan. 1982. "Hartley and Wordsworth: Philosophical Language and Figures of the Sublime." *MLN* 97: 1064–85.
Lane, Harlan. 1984a. *When the Mind Hears: A History of the Deaf*. New York: Random House.

———, ed. 1984b. *The Deaf Experience: Classics in Language and Education.* Translated by Franklin Philip. Cambridge, Mass.: Harvard University Press.

Leslie, Margaret. 1972. "Mysticism Misunderstood: David Hartley and the Idea of Progress." *Journal of the History of Ideas* 33: 625–32.

Lillywhite, Bryant. 1963. *London Coffee Houses: A Reference Book of Coffee Houses of the Seventeenth, Eighteenth, and Nineteenth Centuries.* London: George Allen and Unwin.

Lindbeck, George. 1984. *The Nature of Doctrine: Religion and Theology in a Postliberal Age.* Philadelphia: Westminster Press.

Lindeboom, G. A. 1968. *Herman Boerhaave: The Man and his Work.* London: Methuen & Co.

Livingston, Donald W. 1998. *Philosophical Melancholy and Delirium: Hume's Pathology of Philosophy.* Chicago and London: University of Chicago Press.

Manuel, Frank E. 1963. *Isaac Newton Historian.* Cambridge, Mass.: The Belknap Press of Harvard University Press.

Marsh, Robert. 1959a. "The Second Part of Hartley's System." *Journal of the History of Ideas* 20: 264–73.

———. 1959b. "Mechanism and Prescription in David Hartley's Theory of Poetry." *Journal of Aesthetics and Art Criticism* 17: 473–85.

———. 1965. *Four Dialectical Theories of Poetry: An Aspect of English Neoclassical Criticism.* Chicago: University of Chicago Press.

Maslow, Abraham. 1968. *Toward a Psychology of Being.* 2d ed. New York: Van Nostrand Reinhold Co.

———. 1970. *Motivation and Personality.* 2d ed. New York: Harper & Row.

Matt, Daniel C. 1996. *The Essential Kabbalah: The Heart of Jewish Mysticism.* San Francisco: Harper San Francisco.

McCalman, Iain. 1996. "New Jerusalems: Prophecy, Dissent, and Radical Culture in England, 1786–1830." In Haakonssen, ed., *Enlightenment and Religion,* 312–35.

McGinn, Bernard. 1991. *The Presence of God: A History of Western Christian Mysticism,* vol. 1: *The Foundations of Mysticism: Origins to the Fifth Century.* New York: Crossroad.

McKay, Alastair. 1995. "Faith, Hope, Gravity." An interview with Michio Kaku. *Scotland on Sunday.* 22 October 1995.

McMullin, Ernan. 1978. *Newton on Matter and Activity.* Notre Dame, Indiana: University of Notre Dame Press.

Millar, Susanna. 1994. *Understanding and Representing Space: Theory and Evidence from Studies with Blind and Sighted Children.* Oxford: Clarendon Press.

Millson, Cecilia. 1985. *The History of Donnington Hospital.* Newbury, Berks.: Countryside Books.

———. 1994. *Bucklebury's Heritage*. Donnington, Berks.: Privately published.
Murch, Jerome. 1893. *Biographical Sketches of Bath Celebrities, Ancient and Modern, with some Fragments of Local History*. London: Isaac Pitman & Sons, and Bath: William Lewis & Sons.
Oberg, Barbara Bowen. 1976. "David Hartley and the Association of Ideas." *Journal of the History of Ideas* 37: 441-54.
Page, Anthony. 1998. "The Englightenment and a 'Second Reformation': The Religion and Philosophy of John Jebb." *Enlightenment and Dissent*, no. 17.
Patey, Douglas Lane. 1986. "Johnson's Refutation of Berkeley: Kicking the Stone Again." *Journal of the History of Ideas* 47, no. 1: 139-45.
Pinto, Vivian De Sola. 1934. *Peter Sterry: Platonist and Puritan, 1613-1672*. Cambridge: Cambridge University Press.
Placher, William C. 1989. *Unapologetic Theology: A Christian Voice in Pluralist Conversation*. Louisville: Westminster John Knox Press.
———. 1996. *The Domestication of Transcendence: How Modern Thinking about God Went Wrong*. Louisville: Westminster John Knox Press.
Popper, Karl, and John C. Eccles. 1977. *The Self and its Brain*. Berlin, Heidelberg, and New York: Springer International.
Porter, Roy, ed. 1995. *Medicine in the Enlightenment*. Clio Medica 29: The Wellcome Institute Series in the History of Medicine. Amsterdam and Atlanta: Rodopi.
Powicke, Frederick J. 1926. *The Cambridge Platonists: A Study*. Cambridge, Mass.: Harvard University Press.
Radhakrishnan, Sarvepalli, and Charles A. Moore. 1957. *A Sourcebook in Indian Philosophy*. Princeton: Princeton University Press.
Rail, Tony, and Beryl Thomas. 1994. "Joseph Priestley's Journal while at Daventry Academy, 1754." *Enlightenment and Dissent*, no. 13, 49-113.
Raine, Kathleen. 1968. *Blake and Tradition*. 2 vols. The A. W. Mellon Lectures in the Fine Arts, 1962. Bollingen Series 35. Princeton: Princeton University Press.
Rattansi, Piyo. 1988. "Newton and the Wisdom of the Ancients." In Fauvel et al., eds., 1988, 185-201.
Reed, Edward S. 1988. *James J. Gibson and the Psychology of Perception*. New Haven and London: Yale University Press.
———. 1996a. *Encountering the World: Toward an Ecological Psychology*. New York and Oxford: Oxford University Press.
———. 1996b. *The Necessity of Experience*. New Haven and London: Yale University Press.
———. 1997. *From Soul to Mind: The Emergence of Psychology from Erasmus Darwin to William James*. New Haven: Yale University Press.
Ringrose, Ernest. 1939. Dr. David Hartley. Unpublished ms. Newark Library. Nottinghamshire County Council.

Bibliography

Robinson, Daniel N. 1985. *The Philosophy of Psychology.* New York: Columbia University Press.

―――. 1995. *An Intellectual History of Psychology.* 3d ed. Madison: University of Wisconsin Press and London: Arnold.

Roche, John. 1988. "Newton's *Principia.*" In Fauvel et al., eds., 1988, 43-61.

Rousseau, G. S. 1991a. *Enlightenment Borders: pre- and post-modern discourses: medical, scientific.* Manchester and New York: Manchester University Press.

―――. 1991b. *Enlightenment Crossings: pre- and post-modern discourses: anthropological.* Manchester and New York: Manchester University Press.

Rousseau, G. S., and Ray Porter, eds. 1980. *The Ferment of Knowledge: Studies in the Historiography of Eighteenth-Century Science.* Cambridge: Cambridge University Press.

Rudé, George. 1971. *Hanoverian London, 1714-1808.* London: Secker & Warburg.

Rusnock, Andrea A. 1995. "The Weight of Evidence and the Burden of Authority: Case Histories, Medical Statistics and Smallpox Inoculation." In Porter, ed., 1995, 289-315.

Sacks, Oliver. 1987. *The Man Who Mistook His Wife for a Hat and Other Clinical Tales.* New York: Harper & Row, Perennial Library.

―――. 1989. *Seeing Voices: A Journey into the World of the Deaf.* Berkeley and Los Angeles: University of California Press.

―――. 1995. *An Anthropologist on Mars: Seven Paradoxical Tales.* New York: Alfred A. Knopf.

Schaffer, Simon. 1980. "Natural Philosophy." In Rousseau and Porter, eds., 1980, 55-92.

Schofield, Robert E. 1961. "Boscovitch and Priestley's Theory of Matter." In *Roger Joseph Boscovitch: Studies in his Life and Work on the 250th Anniversary of his Birth,* edited by Lancelot Law Whyte, 108-72. London: G. Allen & Unwin.

―――. 1970. *Mechanism and Materialism: British Natural Philosophy in An Age of Reason.* Princeton: Princeton University Press.

―――. 1997. *The Enlightenment of Joseph Priestley: A Study of his Life and Work from 1733 to 1773.* University Park, Penn.: The Pennsylvania State University Press.

Selzer, Richard. 1974. "Stone." In *Mortal Lessons: Notes on the Art of Surgery,* 78-91. New York: Simon and Schuster.

Shapin, Steven. 1980. "Social Uses of Science." In Rousseau and Porter, eds., 1980, 93-142.

Shelley, Bryan Keith. 1983. "The Synthetic Imagination: Shelley and Associationism." *The Wordsworth Circle* 14, no. 1: 68-73.

Shuttleton, David E. 1995. "Methodism and Dr. George Cheyne's 'More Enlightening Principles.' " In Porter, ed., 1995, 316-35.

Smith, C. U. M. 1987. "David Hartley's Newtonian Neuropsychology." *Journal of the History of the Behavioral Sciences* 23: 123-36.

Sperry, Roger. 1983. *Science and Moral Priority: Merging Mind, Brain, and Human Values*. New York: Columbia University Press.

Stewart, Larry. 1986. "The Selling of Newton: Science and Technology in Early Eighteenth-Century England." *Journal of British Studies* 25 (April): 178–92.

Sturdy, David J. 1995. *Science and Social Status: The members of the Académie des Sciences, 1666–1750*. Woodbridge, Suffolk, and Rochester, New York: The Boydell Press.

Suzuki, Akihito. 1995. "Anti-Lockean Enlightenment? Mind and Body in Early Eighteenth-Century British Medicine." In Porter, ed., 1995, 336–59.

Tanner, Kathryn. 1988. *God and Creation in Christian Theology: Tyranny or Empowerment?* Oxford and New York: Basil Blackwell.

Thackray, Arnold. 1970. *Atoms and Powers: An Essay on Newtonian Matter-Theory and the Development of Chemistry*. Cambridge, Mass.: Harvard University Press.

Thompson, E. P. 1993. *Witness Against the Beast: William Blake and the Moral Law*. New York: The New Press, and Cambridge: Cambridge University Press.

Thompson, Richard F. 1993. *The Brain: A Neuroscience Primer*. 2d ed. New York: W. H. Freeman.

Thune, Nils. 1948. *The Behmenists and the Philadelphians: A Contribution to the Study of English Mysticism in the 17th and 18th Centuries*. Uppsala: Almqvist & Wiksells.

Uffenheimer, Rivka Schatz. 1993. *Hasidism as Mysticism: Quietistic Elements in Eighteenth Century Hasidic Thought*. Translated by Jonathan Chipman. Princeton: Princeton University Press, and Jerusalem: The Magnes Press.

Valentine, Elizabeth. 1989. "Neural Nets: From Hartley and Hebb to Hinton." *Journal of Mathematical Psychology* 33, no. 3: 348–57.

Verhave, Thom. 1973. "David Hartley: The Mind's Road to God." Introduction to David Hartley, *Hartley's Theory of the Human Mind*, a reprint of Hartley 1775.

Viseltear, Arthur J. 1967. "The Last Illness of Sir Robert Walpole, First Earl of Orford." *Bulletin of the History of Medicine* 41: 195–207.

———. 1968. "Joanna Stephens and the Eighteenth Century Lithontriptics: A Misplaced Chapter in the History of Therapeutics." *Bulletin of the History of Medicine* 42: 199–220.

Wade, Jenny. 1996. *Changes of Mind: A Holonomic Theory of the Evolution of Consciousness*. Albany: State University of New York Press.

Walker, D. P. 1964. *The Decline of Hell: Seventeenth-Century Discussions of Eternal Torment*. London: Routledge & Kegan Paul.

Warren, Howard C. 1921. *A History of the Association Psychology*. New York: Charles Scribner's Sons.

Washburn, Michael. 1988. *The Ego and the Dynamic Ground: A Transpersonal Theory of Human Development*. Albany: State University of New York Press.
———. 1994. *Transpersonal Psychology in Psychoanalytic Perspective*. Albany: State University of New York Press.
Watts, Ruth. 1983. "Joseph Priestley and Education." *Enlightenment and Dissent* 2: 83–100.
Webb, Martha Ellen. 1981. A Reexamination of the Inception, Development, and 'Newtonianism' of David Hartley's *Observations on Man* (1749). Ph.D. diss., University of Oklahoma.
———. 1988. "A New History of David Hartley's *Observations on Man*." *Journal of the History of the Behavioral Sciences* 24: 202–11.
———. 1989. "The Early Medical Studies and Practice of Dr. David Hartley." *Bulletin of the History of Medicine* 63: 618–36.
Webb, R. K. 1998. "Perspectives on David Hartley." *Enlightenment and Dissent*, no. 17.
Wells, Joan. 1982. "The Psychology of David Hartley and the Root Metaphor of Mechanism." *Journal of Mind and Behavior* 3, nos. 3–4: 259–74.
Westfall, Richard S. 1971. *Force in Newton's Physics: The Science of Dynamics in the Seventeenth Century*. London: Macdonald; New York: American Elsevier.
Wilber, Ken. 1983. *Eye to Eye: The Quest for a New Paradigm*. Garden City, N.Y.: Anchor Books.
Wilber, Ken, Jack Engler, and Daniel P. Brown. 1986. *Transformations of Consciousness: Conventional and Contemplative Perspectives on Development*. Boston: Shambhala.
Wills, Garry. 1979. *Inventing America: Jefferson's Declaration of Independence*. New York: Vintage Books.
Wordsworth, Christopher. 1877. *Scholae Academicae: Some Account of the Studies at the English Universities in the Eighteenth Century*. Cambridge: Cambridge University Press.
Wykes, David L. 1996. "The Contribution of the Dissenting Academy to the Emergence of Rational Dissent." In Haakonssen, ed., *Enlightenment and Religion*, 99–139.
Wylie, Ian. 1989. *Young Coleridge and the Philosophers of Nature*. Oxford: Clarendon.
Yates, Frances. 1966. *The Art of Memory*. Chicago: University of Chicago Press.
———. 1969. *The Theatre of the World*. Chicago: University of Chicago Press.
Yolton, John W. 1983. *Thinking Matter: Materialism in Eighteenth-Century Britain*. Minneapolis: University of Minnesota Press.
———. 1984. *Perceptual Acquaintance from Descartes to Reid*. Minneapolis: University of Minnesota Press.

Index

action, 6, 7, 116, 162–71, 308, 393; automatic, 163–64, 165, 212; complex, 162–63, 165, 170, 173, 399; decomplex, 162–63, 168–69, 170–71, 173, 199, 201, 211–12, 218, 399, 400; instinctual, 207, 209–10, 211, 347–48; and perception, 144, 158–59, 161, 399; secondarily automatic, 163, 165–68, 199, 212, 218, 399, 400; voluntary, 128, 163, 165–66, 168, 191, 192–93, 194, 195, 198–99, 218. *See also* agency, human; association; ideas; perception

aesthetic judgment, 299

aether, 83–84, 91–92, 94–95, 98, 99, 106–107, 111–12, 114, 383–84, 418–19

affection. *See* emotion

agency, human, 22–23, 179, 180, 186–201, 358, 360–61, 386–88, 394. *See also* action, voluntary; mechanism; necessity, philosophical; will

agnosia, visual, 151–52

Akenside, Mark, 413

algebra, comparison to geometry, 229–31, 232, 251, 253–54

Allen, Ralph, 413

ambition (class of intellectual pleasures and pains), 8, 74–75, 280, 282–84, 300–302, 306, 321–24; new modeled, 307, 395; as primary pursuit, 283, 291, 303, 401

analogy, 7, 104, 180, 204, 234–37, 255, 270, 373, 384–85, 430; leading to induction, 257–60, 262–63; in scientific reasoning, 244–45, 253–54

anger, D.H.'s analysis of, 17–22, 129, 275, 279, 311

animals: comparison to humans, 187–88, 205–11, 359, 360–61, 378, 390, 429, 433; instinctual behavior of, 207, 209–11, 347

annihilation of self, 6, 15, 44, 289, 291, 329, 331–33, 335, 337, 340, 346, 350, 352, 360–61, 373, 390, 393, 395, 397, 405, 432

Anselm, Saint, 40, 211

Aristotle, 4, 42, 85–86, 96, 195, 269, 283, 294, 423

arts of memory, 4, 232, 429
associated circumstances, 165–66, 170, 172–75, 191–201, 212–13, 387; and definition of words for emotions, 220, 223–24, 278, 358
association, theory of, 3, 4, 18–19, 21, 96, 117, 129, 133, 190, 206, 208, 210–11, 239, 267–69, 399, 423; and action, 164–68, 170–71; and analogical reasoning, 236–37, 247–48, 257–60; benevolence and happiness, leading to, 44–45, 81, 289–90, 293, 353–55, 365, 368–69; chemical analogy to, 3–4, 171–72, 297–98, 304–305, 365, 381; and language learning, 211–14, 225; and perception (joint impression), 136–38, 144, 146–53, 154–62, 171–72, 208, 222, 245–46, 393, 354, 361, 393, 399, 424, 425–26; and sense of self, 21. *See also* action; counterassociation; emotion; ideas, generation of; perception, theory of; self, sense of
association psychology, school of, 9–10, 16–17, 25. *See also* Mill, James; Mill, John Stuart
atonement, doctrine of, 40
attraction and repulsion, forces of, xii, 7, 88–89, 92, 93, 94, 110, 112–13, 119, 125–26, 182–83, 186, 297, 304, 363, 365, 381–82, 383–84. *See also* matter: Newtonian theory of active; Stephen Hales: chemical theory of
Auerbach, Erich, 38
Augustine, Saint, 8, 40, 344, 362

Baal Shem Tov, 334
Baer, Dov, 334, 343
Bain, Alexander, 3, 17
Bayes, Thomas, 243–44, 245

Bébian, Roch-Ambroise, 228
Bell-Magendie law, 426
Belsham, Thomas, 392
Belsham, William, 392
benevolence, 41–45, 272, 285, 289–90, 293, 307, 309, 310, 327–28, 333, 353–54, 355, 359
Bentley, Richard, 435
Berington, Joseph, 376–77, 380
Berkeley, George, 244, 376, 422–23; theory of vision, 140, 141, 143, 145, 147, 150, 152–53, 158, 162, 222, 424
Bernoulli, Jakob, 240, 242
Bible, 38–39, 44, 79, 178, 203, 204, 254, 342, 346, 348, 349, 350, 354, 428, 432; Berleberger, 340; defining boundaries of time, 31, 409–10; inspiration of writers, 210, 347–48; shape of narrative, 40, 395
Blake, William, xi, xiv, 15, 18, 23, 294, 324–25, 349–50, 355, 434
body, elementary. *See* resurrection of the body
body and mind: duality of, 11, 13–14, 179, 181, 186, 199, 201, 202–203, 204, 378–82, 398, 427; mechanism of, 137–39, 168, 182, 186–88, 191, 193, 198, 206, 387, 423, 430; unity of, 144–45, 166–67, 187, 189–90, 202, 377–82, 389, 404. *See also* identity, personal
Boehme, Jakob, 338, 339, 353
Boerhaave, Hermann, 62, 87, 104–106, 107, 108, 181, 421, 422
Boscovitch, Roger Joseph, 420
Bourignon, Antoinette, 336, 347
Boyle, Robert, 62, 83, 89, 428
Bracken, Henry, 414
brain, 106, 118, 132, 148, 151, 155–56, 158–60, 187, 202,

Index

206–208, 377, 379, 381–82, 389, 399, 426. *See also* body and mind; nerves, anatomy of; vibrations, theory of
Bruno, Giordano, 4
Butler, Joseph, 177–81, 188, 199, 201, 358, 360, 361, 380
Byrom, John, 16, 27–32, 35–41, 44–45, 72, 79–80, 177, 178, 300, 334, 336, 338, 341, 342, 347, 409, 411; Byrom's shorthand, 47–53, 231–32, 256

calculus, xii, 240, 244–46
Campbell, Archibald, 45, 410
Camus, Jean-Pierre, 335, 341
Caroline of Anspach, 56, 57, 177–78, 411
Carpenter, Lant, 2
Carpenter, William B., 3, 393, 434
causality, 155, 161, 170, 191. *See also* God, as only cause; mechanism
chances, doctrine of. *See* probability, theory of
Charcot, Jean-Martin, 3, 5, 205
chemical theory. *See* association: chemical analogy to; Hales, Stephen
Cheselden, William, 54–55, 63, 108–110, 115, 140–43, 145, 151, 177, 245, 246, 422, 424
Cheyne, George, 16, 28–29, 336–37, 338, 341, 342, 409, 419, 422, 430, 435
Clarke, Samuel, 79, 89, 420, 435
Coleridge, Samuel Taylor, 2, 23, 24, 392, 394, 431, 434, 435; criticism of mechanism of mind, 137–39, 168, 186, 188, 201, 423–24, 425–26; "Religious Musings," 2, 282, 285, 391, 393
Collins, Anthony, 435
Comenius, John Amos, 255
compassion. *See* sympathy
consciousness, 134, 154–55, 160–61, 172, 174, 186–87, 377–79, 425; unity of, 276, 358–59, 379–81, 389
Cornwallis, Charles, first earl, 53, 411–12
Cornwallis, Charles, second earl, 412
counterassociation, 24–25, 247–48, 304–305, 308, 321, 324, 326, 327. *See also* association
Cordovero, Moses ben Jacob, 8, 352
Cowper, William, 80
Cudworth, Ralph, 435
Cumberland, William Augustus, duke of, 177–78, 181, 411
cycloid. *See* isochronous motion

Darwin, Erasmus, 408
deafness, 3, 209, 226–28, 429
death, fear of, 286, 312, 316–19
Descartes, René, 87, 90–91, 105–106, 143, 185–86, 187–88, 206, 420, 426, 433
De Lithontriptico, 69, 413
development, D.H.'s model of, 6, 8, 9, 43–44, 161, 271, 280–82, 290–96, 321, 328–29, 332–33, 393, 397, 400–402, 404–405, 435; pathologies of, 8, 309–12, 319–20, 323–28; place of theopathy in, 15, 16–17, 397, 402-403. *See also* annihilation of self; imagination, ambition, self-interest, sympathy, theopathy, and moral sense; self, sense of
Diderot, Denis, 181–82
dissenting academies, 434
Ditton, Humphrey, 134
Donne, John, 96
Dostoyevsky, Fyodor, 373
dreams, 24, 204, 305
dress, significance of, 278–79, 300–301
Dyson, Freeman, 375

Edelman, Gerald, xiii, 116, 134, 148, 154–62, 163, 308, 399
Edwards, Jonathan, 195, 196, 334

ego, transcendence of. *See* annihilation of self
electricity, 85, 88, 94, 102, 103, 114, 163, 426
Eliot, George, 33, 283, 284, 285
emotion, 160, 194, 211; transference of, 21–22, 129, 266–80, 293–94, 297, 302, 306, 316, 322, 358, 393, 397; role of language in transference, 227, 270–71, 313. *See also* associated circumstances: definition of words for emotions; development, D.H.'s model of
Erickson, Erik, 400, 401
eternity: pure, 371–72; of punishment, 37–40, 318–19, 326, 351–53, 359, 391, 410; of universe, 6, 390
everlasting gospel, xii, 15, 79, 326, 340, 348, 367, 393, 395. *See also* universal salvation

Fénelon, François de Salignac de la Mothe, 16, 196, 335–36, 342–43, 344, 345, 347, 374, 385–86, 404, 433
Folkes, Martin, 50
force. *See* attraction and repulsion
Francis de Sales, Saint, 335, 341–42
Frankenstein. See Shelley, Mary
Franklin, Benjamin, 85, 427
free will. *See* action; agency, human; associated circumstances; body and mind: mechanism of; necessity, philosophical; will
Frei, Hans, 409–10
Freind, John, 65, 420
Freud, Sigmund, 400
future state (life after death), 179, 201–204, 317–18, 377, 368–69, 428–29. *See also* resurrection of the body

Garden, George, 336
Gassendi, Pierre, 106

Gay, John, 267–68, 270, 289, 310
Geoffroy, Claude-Joseph, 69, 70, 414, 415
George I, 411
George II, 49, 53, 57, 63, 71, 72, 177, 411
Gibson, James J., xiii, 193–94, 430–31
God, 40, 131, 182, 211, 238, 286, 290, 311, 312, 324, 349, 352–53, 359, 427; idea of, 314–16, 318, 365, 402; as infinitely benevolent, 43, 326, 367–68, 371–72, 389–90, 395; as moral governor, 178–79, 180; as only cause, 91–92, 196, 365, 383–86, 387–88, 435; pure love of, 332, 334, 335, 337, 342, 405, 432; union with, 342–43, 344–46, 355, 360–61, 363, 364–65; will of, 41–42, 288, 337, 364, 366–67, 388
Godwin, William, 23, 192, 196, 392, 393, 394, 435
grand unified theory (physics), 102–103, 385
gratification, denial of, 19, 322–24
'sGravesande, William, 84, 376
Greene, Robert, 425
Gregory, David, 420
Gregory, R. L., 424
Grey, Richard, 232, 429
Guyon, Jeanne-Marie Bouvier de la Mothe, 16, 335–36, 338, 345, 347–48, 386, 404

Hacking, Ian, 240, 430
Hales, Stephen, 31, 63, 84, 94, 105, 163, 236, 259, 365, 377, 381, 412, 416, 426; chemical theory of, 7, 64–67, 89, 108, 297, 304–305, 398, 414, 420; experiments on bladder stones, 59, 67–71
happiness: desire for, 267–69, 279, 289–90, 312–14; infinite, 361–

74; universal, 41–44, 81, 180, 181, 354–55, 359–60
harmony, musical, 96–100, 102–103, 104, 386, 421
Harrison, John, 36–37
Hartley, Alice (née Rowley), 75–76, 317, 367, 416–17
Hartley, David
  αιωνιος, interpretation of, 37–40, 342, 410. *See also* eternity; universal salvation
  appearance of, 28
  Bath, moves to, 77
  and John Byrom, 27–32, 35–41, 44–45, 347; acts on behalf of Byrom's shorthand, 47–53, 231–32, 411
  and Elizabeth Booth (sister), letters to, 29, 78
  benevolence, 41–45, 72, 74
  childhood of, 27, 78, 80
  death, fear of, 75, 317–18
  death of mother (Evereld Wadsworth), 76, 317
  education, 28
  evaluation of: by Lant Carpenter, 2; by Charcot, 3; by Coleridge, 2, 23; by Gilbert Wakefield, 434; by Benjamin Rush, 433; by Richard Warner, 433–34
  everlasting gospel, speaks of, 79
  and Stephen Hales, correspondence with, 416. *See also* Stephen Hales
  happiness, papers on, 44, 72, 289
  and John Lister, 39, 41–45, 46, 47, 80–81, 288, 289, 359–60, 391, 410, 418
  and Ch.-H. de Marsay, 337
  medical practice, 31, 284, 409, 412–13
  Elizabeth Packer, marriage to, 32–35, 410
  Packer brothers-in-law, relations with, 77–78
  prayers and meditations of, 29, 72–75, 317–18
  and Alice (née Rowley) Hartley, 75–76, 367, 416–17
  Saunderson, Nicholas, activities on behalf of, 45–47
  self-indulgence, regulation of, 29–30, 72
  smallpox, advocates variola inoculation for, 34, 53, 240, 413
  stone (bladder calculi), cure for, xii, 53–64, 68–71, 173, 376, 412–16. *See also* Stephen Hales, Joanna Stephens
  stone, suffers from, 30, 55, 74, 177, 292, 367
  universal salvation, belief in, 37–44, 78–79, 326, 359–60
  vegetarian, 29, 30, 429
  See also Elizabeth (née Packer) Hartley; Alice (née Rowley) Hartley; *Observations on Man*
Hartley, David, M.P., 35, 75, 77, 292, 408, 433
Hartley, Elizabeth (née Packer), 72, 177, 227, 317–18; illnesses of, 75, 76–77, 292, 367, 417; marriage to D.H., 32–35, 410
Hartley, Mary, 27, 33–34, 35, 53, 75, 76, 77, 292, 318, 408, 411, 412
Hartley, Winchcombe Henry, 77–78, 292, 417
Hawking, Stephen, 231
Hazlitt, William, 392, 434
heaven, 179, 315, 326
hell, 179, 326, 337, 348, 352, 360. *See also* eternity of punishment
Hillman, James, 403
Hoadley, Benjamin, M.D., 29, 409
Hobbes, Thomas, 86, 106, 178
Hoffmann, Friedrich, 421
Hooke, Robert, 37, 48, 94, 98, 99, 104, 230, 256, 361, 421, 422
human race, universality of. *See* universal man

Hume, David, 17, 137, 334, 422–23, 424
Hutcheson, Francis, 286–89, 310
Huygens, Christian, 37, 91, 94, 97–98, 102, 104, 240
hypotheses, in scientific inquiry, 246–53, 261–62

ideas, xi, 128, 129, 143–45, 164–65, 171–75, 190, 424; simple, 117, 134–36, 145, 171, 172, 189; complex, 136, 149, 162, 171, 172, 189, 190, 221–22, 426; decomplex, 171, 189, 190, 216–17, 269; generation of, 7, 133, 145–53, 246, 269, 399; hypercomplex, 188–90; motor, 165–66, 173; of reflection, 190, 222–24; and sensation, 117, 121, 133–38, 171; as "separate subjective entities," 137, 147, 153, 426; of touch, 152–53, 158, 426; visual, 139–43, 151–53, 169–70, 172, 222, 224, 426. *See also* action; association; emotion; perception; pleasure and pain
identity, personal, 144–45, 181, 201, 203, 379–82. *See also* body and mind; self, sense of
imagination (class of intellectual pleasures and pains), 8, 127, 280–84, 292–93, 294, 297–300, 302, 304–306, 321–24; new-modeled, 307, 362, 395; as primary pursuit, 303–304, 401
immortality, personal. *See* future state
inspiration, prophetic, 347–48
intuition, direct, 355, 373
Islam, Sufic, 334
isochronous motion, 37, 97–98, 101–102, 230, 253, 420–21

James, William, xiii, 5, 6, 17, 118, 145, 151–52, 155, 248, 265, 424, 425, 426; critique of psychological atomism, 137, 138, 147, 154, 161–62, 399
Jebb, John, 393
Jefferson, Thomas, 1, 407, 421
Jesus Christ, 2, 38, 40, 336, 342, 344–45, 346, 347, 348, 351, 352; mystical body of, 354, 355, 358, 388–89, 390–91, 393
John of the Cross, Saint, 336, 338, 403, 432
joint impression. *See* association, theory of: and perception
Judaism, 334, 352, 428. *See also* Kabbalah
Jung, C. G., 349–50, 400; theory of the complex, xiii, 274–76
Jurin, James, 53, 71, 411, 413, 424–25, 427
Justin Martyr, 345, 346–47

Kabbalah, 16, 334, 343, 349, 355, 403, 404
Kaku, Michio, 96, 231, 386
Keill, John and James, 65, 420
Kepler, Johannes, 97
King, William, 352
Kohlberg, Lawrence, 400, 401
Kramnick, Isaac, 2, 14, 376, 434

La Mettrie, Julien, 181–82
language: theory of, 6, 7, 144, 190, 194, 206, 209, 214, 224–28, 262–63, 393, 397; as "algebra," 7, 228–29, 233–34, 250–51, 373; learning, 211–18, 228, 234–35, 272, 277, 400; philosophical, 48, 197–99, 231–34, 253–56, 262, 354–55, 358, 366, 383, 390, 404, 428, 431; religious, 257, 348; and transference of emotion, 270–71, 273–79, 295
Laplace, Pierre Simon de, 191, 192
laughter, D.H.'s analysis of, 212, 271–73, 279, 298

Law, Edmund, 428, 431
Law, William, 28, 334, 336, 338
Lead, Jane, 16, 79, 339–40, 350, 355. *See also* Philadelphian Society
Leibniz, Gottfried Wilhelm, 52, 89, 179, 185, 187, 203, 379, 389, 419, 420, 431
Lewes, George Henry, 378, 399, 434–35
liberty, 196–201. *See* agency, human; necessity, philosophical
Lister, John, 39, 41, 43, 44–45, 46, 47, 72, 73, 80, 288, 289, 359–60, 391, 410, 418
lithotomy, 54, 71, 412. *See also* Hartley, David: cure for the stone
Lloyd, George, 32, 50, 177
Locke, John, xi, 4, 79, 107, 132, 150, 407, 422–23, 424, 425, 426, 433; association, irrationality of, 21, 24; ideas, 135–36, 138, 139–40, 142–43, 145–46, 153, 161–62 426; mind, 145, 188–89, 276; language, 7, 221–26, 228, 239, 256; knowledge, 237–38, 260–61, 430; thinking matter, 182, 423, 427; will, 144–45, 89, 193, 223, 358
longitude, determination of, 36–37
love, 24, 196–97, 286, 326, 332–33; child's learning to, 17–18, 281–82, 290. *See also* God, pure love of
Lull, Ramon, 4, 255
Luria, Isaac, 334

McGinn, Bernard, 432
Maclaurin, Colin, 84, 231, 376, 420
Mackintosh, James, 11, 14, 16, 378, 398, 407–408
Malebranche, Nicolas, 28, 144
Marsay, Charles-Hectore de Saint-George de, 331, 332, 336–38, 339, 340–41, 343, 344, 353, 355, 432
Martineau, Harriet, 3, 393
Maslow, Abraham, 400, 401
materialism, 186, 359, 379, 382–83. *See also* body and mind, unity of
matter: Cartesian theory of passive, 87, 89, 186, 187, 382; Lockean hypothesis of thinking, 182, 423, 427; Newtonian theory of active, 87–89, 186–87, 381–82, 383, 398, 420. *See also* attraction and repulsion, forces of; vibrations, theory of
mechanism, 13–14, 86–87, 89–91, 104–106, 107–108. *See also* agency, human; body and mind: mechanism of; necessity, philosophical
Mede, Joseph, 251
memory, 159–60, 188, 202, 203, 249, 270, 292, 298; false, 239, 271, 358; neurological basis of, 127–28, 148, 184; and present time, 369–70; and voluntary powers, 163, 175, 194, 195, 201, 308, 394, 405
Mencius, 402
Mersenne, Marin, 97, 98, 106
Mickleburgh, John, 414
Mill, James, 3, 4, 6, 10–11, 15, 16–17, 25, 393, 434
Mill, John Stuart, 3, 4–5, 6, 10, 171–72, 431, 434
mind, 118, 175, 224–26, 276, 358, 424. *See also* body and mind
Moivre, Abraham de, 43, 240, 242–43, 245, 254
Molyneux, William, 139–40, 150, 153, 162, 424
Molinos, Miguel de, 335
Monsey, Messenger, 412
Morand, Sauveur-François, 69, 415
moral sense (class of intellectual pleasures and pains), 282, 286–90, 307, 308, 311, 325, 327

motives, 194–96, 201, 387
movement, physical. *See* action
mystical theology, 335, 339, 341–42, 386, 432

necessity, philosophical, 23, 180, 181, 192, 195–201, 359, 379, 386–91. *See also* agency, human
nerves: anatomy of, 104–110; natural and induced states of, 106, 117–21, 125–27, 134, 135, 148, 208; reception and transmission of stimuli, 110–17, 133, 135–36, 183–84; sensory and motor, 163–64, 426. *See also* brain; vibrations, doctrine of
neurophysiology. *See* nerves; vibrations, doctrine of
Newcastle, Thomas Pelham-Holles, duke of, 53, 72, 76, 412, 413
Newton, Isaac, xii, 35, 37, 46, 79, 107, 108, 131–32, 178, 191, 230–31, 233, 247, 249, 251, 252, 404, 425, 430, 433; and musical harmony, 97, 98–100, 104; theory of history, 31, 39, 45, 428; theory of matter, 7, 65–66, 83–85, 87–92, 186–87, 381, 383–84, 418–19, 420

Observations on Man. *See also* Hartley, David
  composition of, 80–81, 290, 360, 418
  evaluation of, by: William James, 5; James Mackintosh, 11, 14, 378; Harriet Martineau, 3; John Stuart Mill, 3–5; Joseph Priestley, 2, 6, 11–13, 15, 408; Thomas Reid, 13–14, 379; Benjamin Rush, 1, 2, 417–18; Edward Tagart, 357, 393–94, 434; Howard C. Warren, 9–10. *See also* Hartley, David, evaluation of
  influence of, 1–6, 375–82, 391–94
  religious dimension of, 15–17, 81, 402–403
  translations of, 3, 376
Origen, 16
Owen, Robert, 192, 195, 196, 392, 394

Packer family, 32–35, 77–78, 417. *See also* Elizabeth (née Packer) Hartley
Paley, William, 429
paradisiacal state, return to, 255, 340, 350, 357, 368, 370
Peacocke, Thomas Love, 391–93
Pemberton, Henry, 84, 88, 163, 231, 376
perception, theory of, 6, 7, 115–16, 133–45, 146–54, 155–62, 171–72, 208, 245–46, 354, 361, 380–81, 393, 399, 426. *See also* action: and perception; association: and perception; ideas
Philadelphian Society for the Advancement of Piety and Divine Philosophy, 79, 339–41, 432. *See also* Jane Lead, Richard Roach
Pietism, 334. *See also* Quietism
Plato, 312, 344
pleasures and pains, physical, 212; limits of, 272–73, 303–304, 306, 327, 333; memory of, 18, 273, 370; neurophysiology of, 121–29, 184, 266; virtue and vice, correlation with, 41–44, 180–81. *See also* emotion
pleasures and pains, intellectual, 129, 266–67, 273–96; epigenetic, 281, 290–91; modeling and new-modeling other classes, 291–92, 294–95, 298, 307–308, 309, 321–22, 362, 394–95. *See also* development, Hartley's model of; emotion,

transference of; imagination, ambition, self-interest, sympathy, theopathy, moral sense; sense of self
Plotinus, 16, 403, 404, 430
Poiret, Pierre, 336
Pope, Alexander, 32, 131–32
prayer, mental, 345–46, 433
Price, Richard, 244, 379–80, 387, 389, 430
Priestley, Joseph, vii, 2, 5, 6, 11–14, 15, 88, 376–83, 386–91, 393, 408, 420, 434, 435; abridgment of the *Observations,* 10, 376, 423; on "uniform composition" of human person, 187, 202, 204, 377, 428–29
primary pursuits, classes of pleasure and pain as, 283–84, 291, 293, 303, 309, 311, 320–29, 333, 353–54, 358, 362, 364, 393, 397, 401, 405
probability, theory of, xii, 43, 180, 202, 238, 240–46. *See also* Thomas Bayes, Abraham De Moivre
propositions, assent to, 238–39, 240–41, 247
Pythagoras, 96, 97, 99, 420

Quietism, 335–38, 342–49, 432

Ramsay, Andrew Michael, 336, 340
Reid, Thomas, 12, 13–14, 16, 17, 179, 203, 377, 378, 379, 380, 386, 389, 398, 434
resurrection of the body, 201–204, 377
Richardson, Samuel, 1, 409
Roach, Richard, 16, 79, 339, 340, 432. *See also* Philadelphian Society
Robinson, Bryan, 419
Rowley, Alice. *See* Alice (née Rowley) Hartley

Royal Society, 28, 45, 48, 53, 68
Rumi, Jalal ad-Din, 334, 373
Rush, Benjamin, 1, 2, 6, 11, 15, 198, 388, 392, 405, 407, 417, 428, 435
Rutty, John, 70–71, 415

St. John, Henry, Viscount Bolingbroke, 32–33
salvation. *See* universal salvation
Śaṃkara, 343–44, 373
Saunderson, Nicholas, 45–47, 52, 72, 181–82, 226, 229, 231, 234, 376, 411, 429
savants, 210
Scotus Erigena, John, 16, 404
scientific inquiry, 300, 306
self, sense of, 8, 21, 24–25, 44, 194, 195–96, 265, 269, 273–98, 303–309, 321–22, 325–26, 333, 343, 361, 390, 393, 397, 400–401. *See also* annihilation of self; development, D.H.'s model of; primary pursuits; self-interest, abandonment of
self-deception, 270–71, 319–20
self-interest (class of intellectual pleasures and pains), 8, 211, 282, 284–85; abandonment of, 44, 289, 326–29, 332–34, 358, 366, 390, 393, 402, 432; gross, 284, 302–307, 323–24; refined, 285, 307–12, 324–25; rational, 285–86, 312–20, 325; as primary pursuit, 320–27. *See also* annihilation of self; self, sense of
sensation, 133, 145–46, 161; not a monad, 171, 361, 368–69. *See also* association, theory of: and perception; nerves; perception, theory of; vibrations, theory of
Shaftesbury, Earl of, 286–89, 310
Shaw, Peter, 50, 62–63, 105, 413
Shelley, Mary, 310
Shelley, Percy, 393, 407
shorthand. *See* John Byrom

Sicard, Roch-Ambroise, 3, 5, 227–28
Sloane, Hans, 53, 411, 413
smallpox, variola inoculation for, 34, 53, 240, 413
Smith, Robert, 50, 347, 376, 424–25
soap, 69–71, 414–15
Society for the Encouragement of Learning, 45, 50, 72, 410
Society for the Promotion of Christian Knowledge, 72, 416
solution of continuity. *See* pleasure and pain: limits of, and neurophysiology of
soul. *See* body and mind
spirit. *See* body and mind
Stahl, Georg Ernst, 62, 107–108, 188, 422
Stephens, Joanna, 51, 54–62, 68, 73, 79, 105, 173, 376, 412, 413, 414. *See also* Hartley, David: cure for the stone
Sterne, Laurence, 21
Sterry, Peter, 16, 79, 196–97, 200, 350–51, 353, 355, 357, 388, 404, 428
stone, the. *See* David Hartley: cure for the stone
Stukeley, William, 31, 45
Sydenham, Thomas, 62
sympathy (class of intellectual pleasures and pains), 8, 9, 281–82, 285, 292, 307–311, 321–22, 324, 325, 327–28, 332; new-models other classes, 309, 327, 395; as primary pursuit, 293–94, 311, 353–54, 397, 401, 405

Tagart, Edward, 357, 378, 393–94, 434
Tauler, Johannes, 336, 338
Taylor, Charles, 433
Teresa of Avila, Saint, 335, 432
theopathy (class of intellectual pleasures and pains), 8–9, 10, 281–82, 285, 307, 309, 321–22, 324, 325, 327–28, 332, 402; absence of, from psychology, 15, 16, 402–403; new-models other classes, 395; as primary pursuit, 311, 362, 364, 397, 401, 405
Thomas à Kempis, 335
time, measurement of, 37; scales of, 362–63, 366, 369, 371–72, 395. *See also* eternity; isochronous motion
Townshend, Charles "Turnip," 53, 411
transference. *See* emotion

Unitarians, Hartley's influence on, 2–3, 434
universal man, 349–55, 358. *See also* Jesus Christ, mystical body of
universal salvation, 2, 18, 37–44, 78, 79, 326, 338, 340, 359–60, 389. *See also* eternity of punishment; everlasting gospel; happiness, universal; universal humanity; Thomas Bayes; Ch.–H. de Marsay; Peter Sterry; Jeremiah White
universe: clockwork, 37; eternity of, 6, 390. *See also* worlds, plurality of
uroliths. *See* David Hartley: cure for the stone

Vedanta. *See* Śaṃkara
vibrations, theory of, 6, 7, 11, 106, 253, 378, 381–82, 385–86, 397, 398, 434–35; and association, 137–38, 146–47, 148–50, 165, 186, 202–203, 206, 210–11; effect on structure of nerves, 117–21, 134; physics of, 37, 93–104, 303; and pleasure and pain, 120, 121–28; and transmission of signals along nerves, 108–17, 163–64, 183–84

virtue and vice, 41–44, 180–81, 192. *See also* benevolence; moral sense
vision. *See* ideas, visual
Voltaire, 84, 419

Wakefield, Gilbert, 434
Walpole, Dorothy, 411
Walpole, Horace, 71
Walpole, Robert, 63, 71, 411
Ward, Joshua, 56, 57
Warner, Richard, 433–34
Warren, Howard C., 9–10, 15
Washburn, Michael, 403, 431–32
Wesley, John, 79, 334
Whiston, William, 35–37, 46, 66, 79, 91, 231, 254, 384, 410, 420
White, Jeremiah, 16, 79, 338, 340, 351–52, 355, 370, 388, 389, 404
Wilkins, John, 48, 232, 255–56, 258
will, 137, 144–45, 166, 167–69, 180, 189, 192–93, 196–201, 223, 276, 322–24, 337, 358, 364. *See also* action, voluntary; agency, human
Willis, Thomas, 107
Winchcombe family, 32, 227. *See also* Elizabeth (née Packer) Hartley
Wittgenstein, Ludwig, 166
words: clusters, of, and emotion, 273–79, 295, 314–16; definitions of, 214–16, 218–20, 221–22, 223, 250–51, 278. *See also* language
Wordsworth, Christopher, 434
Wordsworth, William, 2, 431
worlds, plurality of, 361–63, 366, 390, 433
Wright, Thomas, 435

Yolton, John, 143–44, 427, 435

Zinzendorf, Nicholas von, 334, 340–41